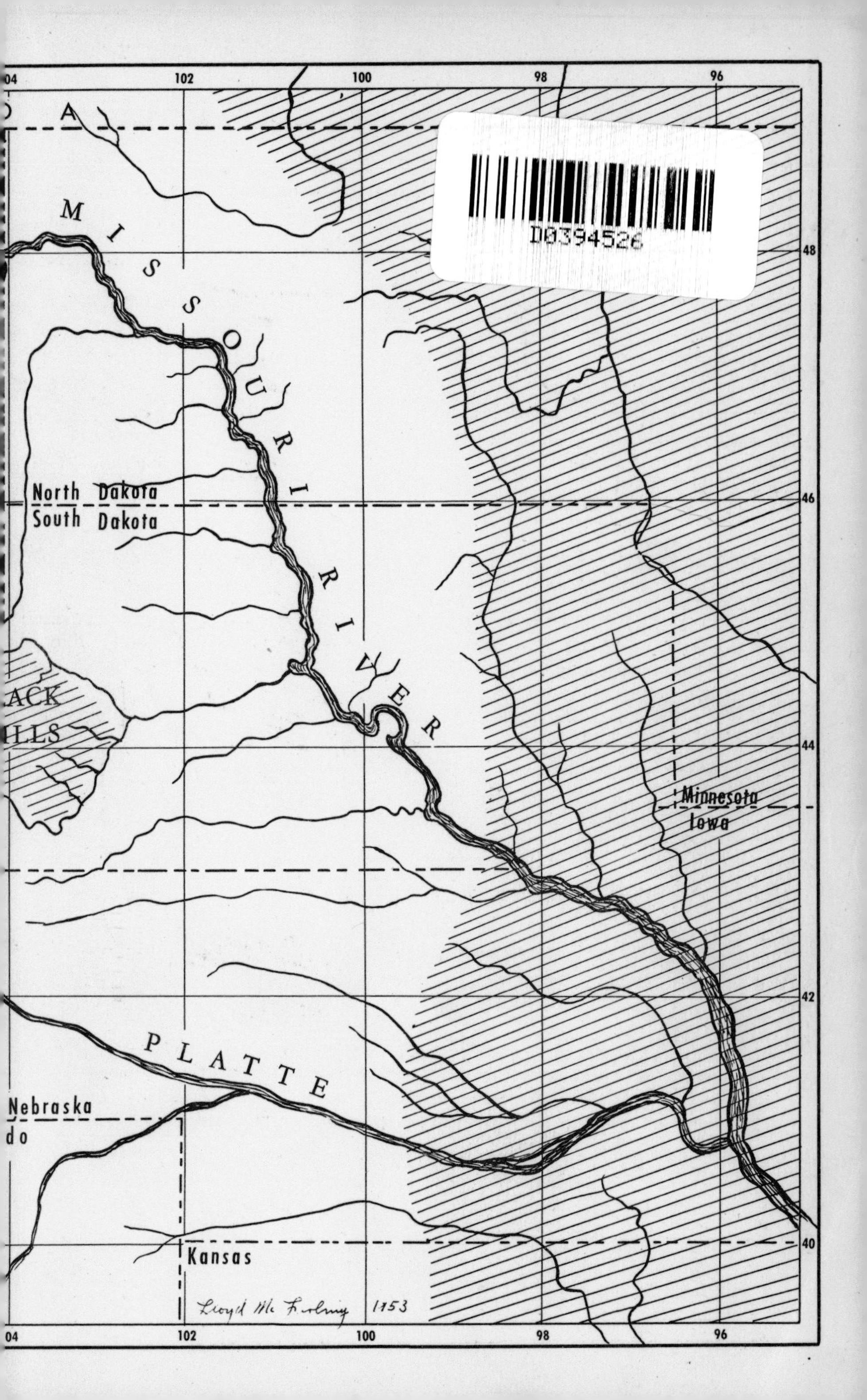

MISSOURI RIVER
PLATTE
North Dakota
South Dakota
Minnesota
Iowa
Nebraska
Kansas
102
100
98
96
48
46
44
42
40

EXPLORING
THE NORTHERN PLAINS

EXPLORING THE NORTHERN PLAINS 1804 - 1876

EDITED AND ILLUSTRATED BY

LLOYD McFARLING

THE CAXTON PRINTERS, LTD.
CALDWELL, IDAHO
1955

Library of Congress Catalog Number: 55-6753

Printed and bound in the United States of America by
THE CAXTON PRINTERS, LTD.
CALDWELL, IDAHO
77177

EDITOR'S INTRODUCTION

I

In this book history moves across geography in search of facts.

In 1804 the United States acquired the Northern Plains as a part of the Louisiana Purchase. The exploration of the area, begun long before by France and Spain, was pursued with a new vigor, a faster tempo, and a greater scope.

By 1876 the Plains Indians were essentially subjugated, the Black Hills gold rush was in full motion, and farmers were moving into the Northern Plains from the east and south. Exploration did not end in 1876 but it became relatively less important, and the era of settlement began.

II

The Great Plains is a physiographic province extending from Mexico well into Canada, bounded on the west by the Rocky Mountains and on the east by the Central Lowlands. For the purposes of this book the "Northern Plains"—northern with respect to the United States—extend from the Canadian border to the valley of the Platte River.

On the west the Northern Plains end where the Rocky Mountains begin. On the east there is no border that can be easily defined. The slope of the land, rising toward the west, is gradual; the change in climate, more nearly arid toward the west, is gradual; the vegetation changes with the climate and the elevation, and there is no perceptible line of demarkation between the tall grasses of the lowlands and the short grasses of the plains. Historians and geographers and meteorologists have tried to fix a definite border between the two physiographic provinces, based on meridian lines, or contour lines, or rainfall lines, but with no certain agreement. The purposes of this book do not require a precise border. Our explorations will reach eastward to the valley of the James River in North and South Dakota, and to the Missouri in Nebraska. Most of our travels will be within the area bounded by the valleys of three important rivers—the Yellowstone, the Missouri, and the Platte. This area includes in a general way the eastern half of Montana and Wyoming, the western half of North Dakota and South Dakota, and the northern half of Nebraska, but we shall not often refer to state lines, because most of the explorations we deal with antedated the creation of the states.

III

This province was once thought to be a part of that mythical domain known as the Great American Desert. Of course there are small areas of land within the Northern Plains where conditions of soil and vegetation approach those of the desert; but the region is not a desert, it is a grassland.

Grasslands are geographic facts of major importance. Wherever they occur, on the steppes of Siberia, the veldts of Africa, the pampas of South America, or our own Great Plains, a primitive nomadic culture arises. Animals move from place to place in search of grass; man follows the animals. A limited, mobile, and vigorous population develops.

The wild grass plant is an efficient factory. It converts raw materials drawn from the soil and air and sunshine into a finished product, dried and stored on the stem. It is also a very good soil conservation service, holding the soil in place, protecting it from wind and water erosion, and enriching it with humus.

To convert the product of the grass plant into food suitable for man, another factory is required. Any herbivorous mammal will do, but under primitive conditions the Great Plains was particularly fortunate in being the home of the buffalo or bison. The buffalo converted the grass into food, clothing, shelter, and sport for the American Indian of the plains.

During the first three quarters of the nineteenth century the Indian and the buffalo aroused the continuous interest of the plains traveler, but grass—the most important botanical fact of the plains—received little attention. Away from the navigable rivers the necessity of finding grass for horses and mules and oxen was a conditioning factor of all travel, but the presence of grass was so nearly universal that its importance was generally ignored. Even the specialist in botany gave his attention almost entirely to more noticeable plants of much lesser importance.

Grass requires moisture, of course—not too much and not too little—but with a wide range of tolerance. If rainfall is plentiful varieties of grass plants develop that grow tall and are closely spaced; if rainfall is meager the plants are shorter and farther apart, or in bunches. The traveler who comes out of the Central Lowlands and goes westward across the Northern Plains somewhere crosses an imaginary line where the average annual rainfall is twenty inches. As he goes westward the average rainfall becomes less until it reaches perhaps not more than ten inches near the western border of the plains. The grass becomes shorter and less plentiful, but—notwithstanding certain propaganda that we read and heard in the 1930's—there is no place where a jack rabbit needs to carry a lunch or a canteen.

IV

Many early travelers looked upon the Northern Plains as a barrier to get across as soon as possible. Many historians seem to have the same opinion. Yet the region was important in the development of the fur trade; it furnished two routes for the westward movement; within it occurred a major gold rush; and it was the place where the Plains Indian wars reached their climax.

The proverbial wildness of the West was as plentiful on the Great Plains as it was anywhere. During the era of exploration danger was always potential and sometimes present, and the geographer's gun was more important than his compass or sextant. But in this book we do not deal primarily with the more spectacular and dramatic aspects of history.

We deal with facts. We want to find out things . . . the course of a river . . . the temperature of a spring . . . the height of a hill . . . the number of wagon-miles from Fort Pierre to Fort Laramie . . . the range of the grizzly bear . . . the odor of sagebrush . . . the flavor of boiled dog . . . the habitat of *Psoralea esculenta* . . . the navigability of the Platte . . . the location of the Sioux-Crow frontier . . . the way a bullboat is built . . . the number of buffalo hides required to make a tepee . . . how six mules are guided by one line. . . .

Mostly they are small facts, but if we get enough of them, and if we add them up correctly, we will get a reasonably accurate concept of the Northern Plains during the era of exploration.

If you put a fact into the mind of any man and leave it there for any great length of time, it will change. It may dwindle to invisibility or grow to enormous proportions. So in this book we pick each fact as fresh as we can find it. We go to the man who saw, heard, felt, tasted, or smelled the fact; and who wrote about it while the image in his mind still had sharp edges.

V

In this book an explorer is anyone who goes and sees and comes back and tells. He may command a formal exploring expedition, or he may merely go up the river for the ride. He may be a soldier, a scientist, a journalist, a priest, or a prince.

He must be intelligent. He must be able to write with tolerable clarity. He may or may not have literary ability, but he must have integrity. The ideal may be expressed in Thomas Jefferson's description of Meriwether Lewis: ". . . honest, disinterested, liberal, of sound understanding, and a fidelity to truth so scrupulous that whatever he should repeat would be as certain as if seen by ourselves. . . ."

VI

Man frequently falls short of the ideal. Romanticism was rampant in the first three quarters of the nineteenth century, and its influence may have led a few of our writers to depart a little from that strict objectivity which we like to find in the report of an explorer. Perhaps the desire to be literary influenced others. All of them depended to some extent on information received from other men, always a potential source of error. And while the bulk of the material herein presented is factual, there cannot be avoided some resort to opinion, conjecture, and belief.

Then, too, a book of this kind necessarily has its own inherent defects. It cannot cover the subject completely. Compared to the total bulk of available writings, it can only present a group of samples of what a man might read if he had the time and the library facilities to cover the field thoroughly.

I have tried to choose writings that are representative of the conditions affecting exploration in all parts of the Northern Plains from 1804 to 1876. To this basic material I have added maps, notes, a chronology, and a bibliography for the purpose of filling some of the gaps, correcting occasional mistakes, and clarifying geographical and historical relationships.

TABLE OF CONTENTS

PART ONE: ALONG THE MISSOURI RIVER

PART TWO: ON THE GREAT MEDICINE ROAD

PART THREE: ACROSS THE PLAINS AND BADLANDS

PART FOUR: TO AND THROUGH THE BLACK HILLS

LIST OF MAPS

PART ONE

ALONG THE MISSOURI RIVER

Chapter 1

1804

COUNCIL WITH THE TETON SIOUX,

by Captain William Clark

In 1770 William Clark was born into a prominent family of Virginia planters. The family moved to Louisville, Kentucky, in 1785, and built a house which William inherited in 1799 and where he lived, when not otherwise engaged, until 1804.

One of William's older brothers was General George Rogers Clark and it is possible that he may have accompanied the general in an expedition against the Indians on the Wabash River when he was only sixteen years old. In 1792 he was commissioned a lieutenant of infantry and spent the next four years in garrison duty and Indian warfare along the Ohio and the Wabash and as far west as the Mississippi. Under General Anthony Wayne he participated in the campaign that included the battle of Fallen Timbers. He resigned from the army in 1796.

In 1803 he was invited by Captain Meriwether Lewis to share the command of an exploring expedition which President Jefferson proposed to send up the Missouri River and across the mountains to the Pacific coast. He was promised rank equal to that of Lewis. The War Department disregarded the promise and sent him a lieutenant's commission. Lewis immediately overruled the War Department and promoted him to captain, and the rank has been confirmed by all historians.

The Lewis and Clark expedition was organized during the summer and fall and winter of 1803 and on May 14, 1804, it set out from Camp Dubois, on the Mississippi River near St. Louis. That fall the party reached the villages of the Mandan Indians, wintered there, and in 1805 went on to the mouth of the Columbia River. In 1806 the expedition returned, reaching St. Louis September 23.

The captains and several subordinates kept extensive notes which were rewritten into journals at the end of the trip. From these journals Philadelphia publisher Nicholas Biddle, with the help of journalist Paul Allen, prepared a narrative of the expedition which was first published in 1814. The *Original Journals . . .* were edited by Reuben Gold Thwaites and first published in seven volumes and an atlas in 1904 and 1905.

From the Thwaites text of the original journals I am reprinting Captain Clark's account of the travels from September 21 through September 28, 1804. This narrative tells something of the difficulties of the upstream struggle, and it also tells the story of the first diplomatic contact between the United States of America and the Teton division of the Sioux Nation.

After the great adventure William Clark lived at St. Louis, where he became brigadier general of militia, governor of Missouri Territory, and Superintendent of Indian Affairs. He died in 1838.

William Clark was a big redheaded man, blunt, practical, honest, tough, resourceful, and vigorous. By birth he was a country gentleman, by training a frontiersman, and by any standards a man to ride the river with. He had little formal schooling. He took language by frontal assault, and had little taste for the strategy and tactics of grammar. His writings continually remind us of the statement attributed to President Jackson to the effect that a man doesn't have much originality unless he can spell a word in more than one way. His journals are sometimes difficult to read, but always worth the effort.

21st. *of September Friday* 1804—

at half past one o'clock this morning the Sand bar on which we Camped began to under mind and give way which allarmed the Serjeant on Guard, the motion of the boat awakened me; I got up & by the light of the moon observed that the Sand had given away both above and below our Camp & was falling in fast. I ordered all hands on as quick as possible & pushed off, we had pushed off but a few minits before the bank under which the Boat & perogus lay give way, which would Certainly have Sunk both Perogues,[1] by the time we made the opsd. Shore our Camp fell in, we made a 2d. Camp for the remainder of the night. & at Daylight proceeded on to the Gouge of this Great bend and Brackfast, we Sent a man to Measure (step off)[2] the Distance across the gouge, he made it 2,000 yds., The distance arround is 30 Mls. The hills extend thro: the Gouge and is about 200 foot above the water. in the bend as also the opposit Sides both above and below the bend is a butifull inclined Plain, in which there is great numbers of Buffalow, Elk & Goats in view feeding & scipping on those Plains Grouse, Larks & the Prarie bird is Common in those Plains.

We proceeded on passed a (1)[3] Willow Island below the mouth of a Small river called Tylors R about 35 Yds. wide which Coms in on the L. S.[4] 6 Miles above the Gouge of the bend, at the Mouth of this river the two hunters a head left a Deer & its Skin also the Skin of a White wolf. We observe an emence number of Plover of Different kind collecting and takeing their flight Southerly, also Brants, which appear to move in the Same Direction. The Cat fish is Small and not so plenty as below.

(2) The Shore on each Side is lined with hard rough Gulley Stone of different Sises, which has roled from the hills & out of Small brooks, Ceder is Common here, This day is warm, the wind which is not hard blows from the S. E., we Camped at the lower point of the Mock Island on the S. S. this now

Connected with the main land, it has the appearance of once being an Island detached from the main land Covered with tall Cotton Wood. We Saw Some Camps and tracks of the Seaux which appears to be old, three or four weeks ago, one frenchman I fear has got an abscess on his they [thigh—ED.], he Complains verry much we are makeing every exertion to reliev him

The Praries in this quarter Contains great q^ts. of Prickley Pear.

22nd. of September Satturday 1804—

a thick fog this morning detained us untill 7 oClock passed a butifull inclined Prarie on both Sides in which we See great numbers of Buffalow feeding. (1) took the Meridean altitude of the Suns Upper Limb 92°. 50′ 00″. [with] the Sextent the Lat^d. produced from this Obsevation is 44° 11′ 33″ 3/10 North.

(2) passed a Small Island on the L. S. imediately above passed a Island Situated nearest the L. S. ab^t. 3 Miles long, behind this Is^d. on the L. S. a Creek Comes in about 15 yards wide, this Creek and Island are Called the 3 Sisters, a butifull Plain on both Sides of the river.

(3) passed a Island Situated nearest the S. S. imediately above the last Called Ceder Island this Island is about 1½ miles long & nearly as wide Covered with Ceder, on the South Side of this Island Mr. Louiselle a trader from S^t. Louis built a fort of Ceder & a good house to trade with the Seaux & Wintered last winter;[5] about this fort I observed a number of Indian Camps in a Conecal form. they fed their horses on Cotton limbs as appears. here our hunters us joined haveing killed 2 Deer & a Beaver, they Complain much of the Mineral Substances in the barren hills over which they passed Distroying their mockessons.

(4) we proceeded on and Camp^d. late on the S. Side below a Small Island in the bend S. S. Called Goat Island, The large Stones which lay on the Sides of the banks in Several places lay some distance in the river, under the water and is dangerous, &c.

I walked out this evening and killed a fine Deer the Musquiters is verry troublesom in the bottoms.

23rd. of September Sunday 1804—

Set out under a gentle breeze from the S. E. (1) passed a Small Island Situated in a bend to the L. S. Called Goat Island, a Short distance above the upper point a Creek of 12 yards wide Coms in on the S. S. we observed a great Smoke to the S. W. I walked on Shore & observed Buffalow in great Herds at a distance

(2) passed two Small Willow Islands with large Sand bars makeing out from them, passed (2) Elk Island about 2½ Miles long & ¾ Mile Wide Situated near the L. S. Covered with Cotton Wood and read Currents Called by the french Gres de Beuff. & grapes &c. &c.

the river is nearly Streight for a great distance wide and Shoal (4) passed a Creek on the S. S. 16 yards wide we Call Reuben Creek,[6] as R. Fields found it. Camped on the S. S. below the mouth of a Creek on the L. S. three Souex boys Came to us Swam the river and inform$^{d.}$ that the Band of Seauex called the *Tetongues (Tetons)* of 80 Lodges were Camped at the next Creek above, & 60 Lodges more a Short distance above, we gave those boys two Carrots of Tobacco to Carry to their Chiefs, with directions to tell them that we would Speek to them tomorrow

Cap$^{t.}$ Lewis walked on Shore this evening, R. F. Killed a Doe Goat,

24$^{th.}$ *September Monday* 1804—

Set out early a fair day the wind from the E. pass the mouth of Creek on the L. S. Called Creek on high Water, (*High Water*) passed (1) a large Island on the L. S. about 2 Miles & ½ long on which Colter had Camped & Killed 4 Elk, the wind fair from the S. E. we prepared Some Clothes and a fiew Meadels for the Chiefs of the Teton's bands of Seoux which we expect to See to day at the next river, observe a great Deel of Stone on the Sides of the hills on the S. S. we Saw one Hare, to day, prepared all things for Action in Case of necessity, our Perogus went to the Island for the Meet, Soon after the man on Shore run up the bank and reported that the Indians had Stolen the horse We Soon after Met 5 Ind$^{s.}$ and ankered out Som distance & Spoke to them informed them we were friends, & Wished to Continue So but were not afraid of any Indians, Some of their young men had taken the horse Sent by their Great father for their Cheif and we would not Speek to them untill the horse was returned to us again.

passed (2) a Island on the S. S. on which we Saw Several Elk, about 1½ Miles long Called Good humered [*humoured*] Isl$^{d.}$ Came to about 1½ Miles above off the Mouth of a Small river about 70 yards wide Called by Mr. Evens[7] the Little Mississou [*Missouri*] River, The Tribes of the Seauex Called the Teton,[8] is Camped about 2 Miles up on the N. W. Side, and we Shall Call the River after that Nation, *Teton*[9] This river is 70 yards wide at the mouth of Water, and has a considerable Current we anchored off the mouth

the french Perogue Come up early in the day, the other did not Get up untill in the evening Soon after we had Come too. I went & Smoked with the Chiefs who came to See us here all well, we prepare to Speek with the Indians tomorrow at which time we are informed the Indians will be here, the French Man who had for Some time been Sick, began to blead which allarmed him 2/3 of our party Camped on board the remainder with the Guard on Shore.

25[th.] *Sept.*—

A FAIR Morning the Wind from the S. E. all well, raised a Flag Staff & made a orning or Shade on a Sand bar in the mouth of Teton River, for the purpose of Speeking with the Indians under, the Boat Crew on board at 70 yards Distance from the bar The 5 Indians which we met last night Continued, about 11 OClock the 1[t.] & 2[d.] Chief Came we gave them Some of our Provisions to eat, they gave us Quantitis of Meet Some of which was Spoiled we feel much at a loss for the want of an interpeter the one we have can Speek but little.

Met in Council at 12 oClock and after Smokeing, agreeable to the useal Custom, Cap. Lewis proceeded to Deliver a Speech which we [were—ED.] oblige[d] to Curtail for want of a good interpeter all our party paraded. gave a Medal to the Grand Chief Call[d.] in Indian *Un ton gar Sar bar* in French *Beeffe nure* [Beuffle noir] Black Buffalow. Said to be a good Man, 2nd Chief *Torto hon gar* or the *Parti sin* or Partizan *bad* the 3[rd.] is the Beffe De Medison [Beuffe de Medecine] his name is *Tar ton gar Wa ker* 1[st.] Considerable Man *War zing go.* 2[nd.] Considerable Man *Second Bear—Mato co que par.*

Envited those Cheifs on board to Show them our boat and such Curiossities as was Strange to them, we gave them 1/4 a glass of whiskey which they appeared to be verry fond of, Sucked the bottle after it was out & Soon began to be troublesom, one the 2[d.] Cheif assumeing Drunkness, as a Cloake for his rascally intentions I went with those Cheifs (*in one of the Perogues with 5 men—3 & 2 Ind[s.]*) (which left the boat with great reluctiance) to Shore with a view of reconsileing those men to us, as Soon as I landed the Perogue three of their young Men Seased the Cable of the Perogue, (*in which we had pressents &c*) the Chiefs Sold$^{r.}$ [*each Chief has a soldier*] Huged the mast, and the 2$^{d.}$ Chief was verry insolent both in words & justures (*pretended Drunkenness & staggered up against me*) declareing I should not go on, Stateing he had not receved presents sufficent from us, his justures were of Such a personal nature I felt My self Compeled to Draw my Sword (*and Made a Signal to the boat to prepare for action*) at this Motion Cap$^{t.}$ Lewis ordered all under arms in the boat, those with me also Showed a Disposition to Defend themselves and me, the grand Chief then took hold of the roap & ordered the young Warrers away, I felt My Self warm & Spoke in verry positive terms.

Most of the Warriers appeared to have ther Bows strung and took out their arrows from the quiver. as I (*being surrounded*) was not permited (*by them*) to return, I Sent all the men except 2 Inp$^{s.}$ [Interpreters] to the boat, the perogue Soon returned with about 12 of our determined men ready for any event. this movement caused a no: of the Indians to withdraw at a distance, (*leaving their chiefs & soldiers alone with me*). Their treatment to me was verry rough & I think justified roughness on my part, they all lift my Perogue, and Council$^{d.}$ with themselves the result I could not lern and nearly all went off after remaining in this Situation Some time I offered my hand to the 1. & 2. Chiefs who refus$^{d.}$ to receve it. I turned off & went with my men on board the perogue, I had not pros$^{d.}$ more the [than] 10 paces before the 1$^{st.}$ Cheif 3$^{rd.}$ & 2 Brave Men Waded in after me. I took them in & went on board

We proceeded on about 1 Mile & anchored out off a Willow Island placed a guard on Shore to protect the Cooks & a guard in the boat, fastened the Perogues to the boat, I call this Island bad humered Island as we were in a bad humer.

26$^{th.}$ *of September Wednesday* 1804—

Set out early proceeded on and Came to by the Wish of the Chiefs for to let their Squars [squaws] & boys see the Boat and Suffer them to treat us well great numbers of men womin & children on the banks viewing us, these people Shew great anxiety, they appear Spritely, Generally ill looking & not well made their legs [*& arms*] Small generally, [*high cheek bones, prominent eyes*] they Grese & Black [*paint*] themselves [*with coal*] when they dress [*the disting$^{d.}$ men*] make use of a hawks

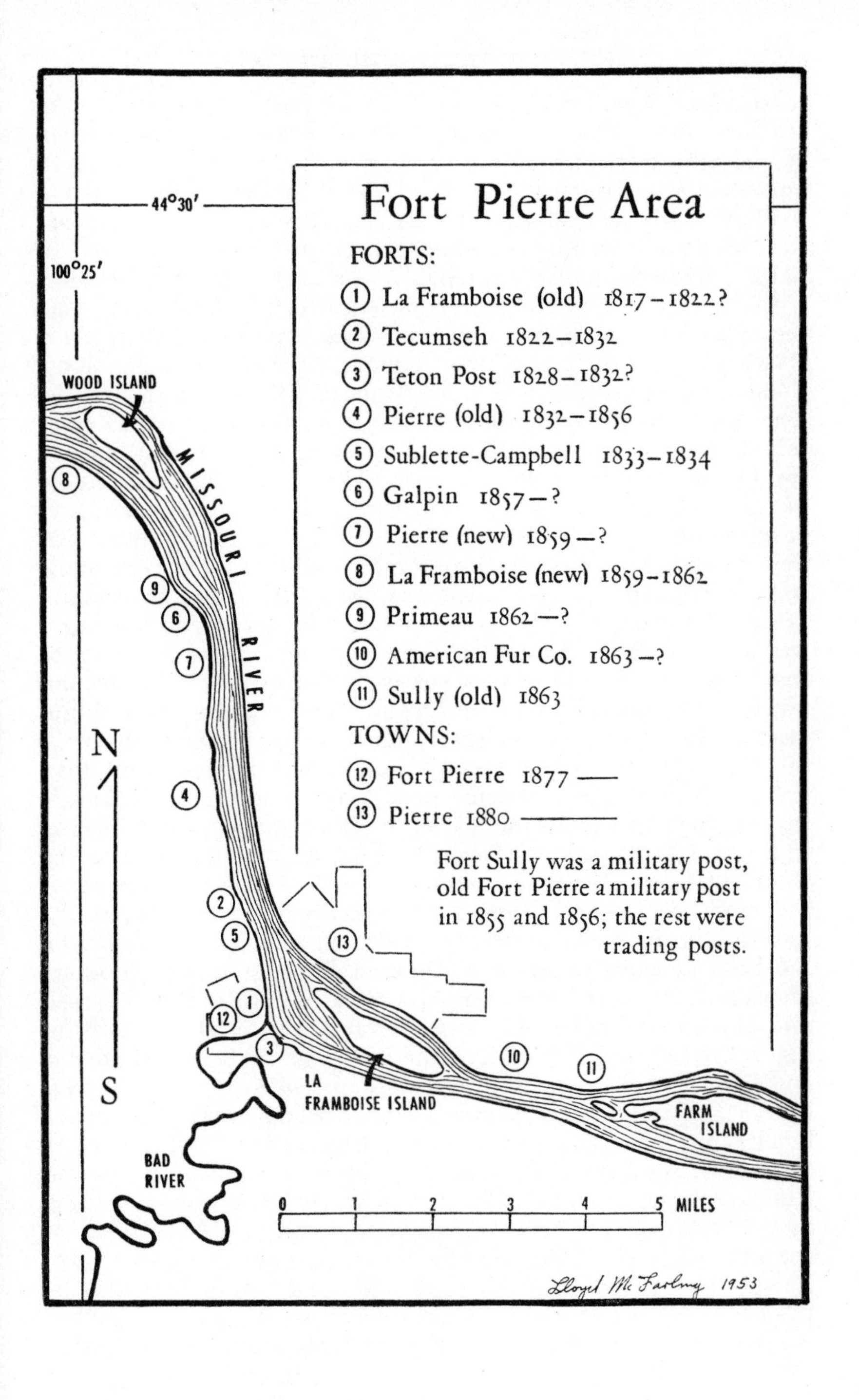
Fort Pierre Area
FORTS:
1 La Framboise (old) 1817–1822?
2 Tecumseh 1822–1832
3 Teton Post 1828–1832?
4 Pierre (old) 1832–1856
5 Sublette-Campbell 1833–1834
6 Galpin 1857–?
7 Pierre (new) 1859–?
8 La Framboise (new) 1859–1862
9 Primeau 1862–?
10 American Fur Co. 1863–?
11 Sully (old) 1863
TOWNS:
12 Fort Pierre 1877 —
13 Pierre 1880 —
Fort Sully was a military post, old Fort Pierre a military post in 1855 and 1856; the rest were trading posts.
44°30′
100°25′
WOOD ISLAND
MISSOURI RIVER
N
S
LA FRAMBOISE ISLAND
FARM ISLAND
BAD RIVER
0 1 2 3 4 5 MILES
Lloyd McFarling 1953

feathers [*Calumet feather adorned with porcupine quills & fastened to the top of the head & falls backwards*] about their heads. the men [wear] a robe & each a polecats Skin, for to hold ther *Bawe roley* [*Bois roule*] for Smoking, fond of Dress & Show badly armed with fusees, &c. The Squaws are Chearfull fine look'g womin not handsom, High Cheeks Dressed in Skins a Peticoat and roab which foldes back over ther Sholder, with long wool, do all their laborious work & I may Say perfect Slaves to the Men, as all Squars of Nations much at War, or where the Womin are more noumerous than the men. after Comeing too Capt. Lewis & 5 men went on Shore with the Cheifs, who appeared disposed to make up & be friendly, after Captain Lewis had been on Shore about 3 hours I became uneasy for fear of Deception & Sent a Serjeant to See him and know his treatment which he reported was friendly, & they were prepareing for a Dance this evening The[y] made frequent Selicitiations for us to remain one night only and let them Show their good disposition towards us, we deturmined to remain, after the return of Capt. Lewis, I went on Shore on landing I was receved on a elegent painted B.[uffalo] Robe & taken to the Village by 6 Men & was not permited to touch the ground untill I was put down in the grand Concill house on a White dressed Robe. I saw Several Maha[10] Prissners and Spoke to the Chiefs [telling them that—ED.] it was necessary to give those prisoners up & become good friends with the Mahas if they wished to follow the advice of their great father I was in Several Lodges neetly formed as before mentioned as to the Baureily (*Bois Brulé*—Yankton)[11] Tribe. I was met (*on landing from the boat*) by about 10 Well Dressd. young Men who took me up in a roabe Highly adecrated and Set me Down by the Side of their Chief on a Dressed Robe in a large Council House, this house formed a 3/4 Circle of Skins Well Dressed and Sown together under this Shelter about 70 Men Set forming a Circle in front of the Cheifs a plac of 6 feet Diameter was Clear and the pipe of peace raised on (*forked*) Sticks (*about 6 or 8 inches from the ground*) under which there was swans down scattered, on each Side of this Circle two Pipes, the (*two*) flags of Spain 2 & the Flag we gave them in front of the Grand Chief a large fire was near in which provisions were Cooking, in the Center about 400lbs. of excellent Buffalo Beef as a present for us. Soon after they Set me Down, the Men went for Capt. Lewis brought him in the same way and placed him also by the Chief in a fiew minits an old man rose & Spoke aproveing what we had done & informing us of their situation requesting us to take pity on them & which was answered. The great Chief then rose with great State [speaking—ED.] to the Same purpote as far as we Could learn & then with Great Solemnity took up the pipe of Peace & after pointing it to the heavins the 4 quarters of the Globe & the earth, he made Some disertation, (*then made a Speech*) lit it and presented the Stem to us to Smoke, when the Principal Chief Spoke with the Pipe of Peace he took in one hand some of the most Delicate parts of the Dog which was prepared for the fiest & made a Sacrefise to the flag. [this sentence misplaced in MS., but properly placed by us.—ED.] after A Smoke had taken place, & a Short Harange to his people, we were requested to take the Meal (*& then put before us the dog which they had been cooking & Pemitigon & ground potatoe*[12] *in Several platters Pem*ⁿ· *is Buff*ᵃ *meat dried or jerked pounded & mixed with grease raw. Dog Sioux think great dish used on festivals eat little of dog—pem*ⁿ· *& pot*ᵉ *good.*) We Smoked for an hour (*till*) Dark & all was Cleared away a large fire made in the Center, about 10 Musitions playing on tambereens (*made of hoops & Skins stretched*), long Sticks with Deer & Goats Hoofs tied so as to make a gingling noise, and many others of a Similer Kind, those Men began to Sing, & Beet on the Tamboren, the Women Came forward highly Deckerated in their Way, with the Scalps and Tropies of War of their fathers Husbands Brothers or near Connections & proceeded to Dance the War Dance (*Women only dance jump up & down—five or six young men selected accompanied with songs the tamborin making the song extempore words & music every now & then one of the com*ʸ *come out & repeat some exploit in a sort of song—this taken up by the young men and the women dance to it*) which they done with great Chearfullness untill about 12 oClock when we informed the Cheifs that they were [*must be*] fatigued [*amusing us*] &c. they then retired & we Accompᵈ· by 4 Cheifs returned to our boat, they Stayed with us all night. Those people have Some brave men which they make use of as Soldiers those men attend to the police of the Village Correct all errors I saw one of them to day whip 2 Squars, who appeared to have fallen out, when he approachᵈ· all about appeared to flee with great turrow [terror]. at night they keep two 3, 4 5 men at different Distances walking around Camp Singing the accurrunces of the night

All the Men on board 100 paces from Shore Wind from the S. E. moderate one man verry sick on board with a Dangerass Abscess on his Hip, All in Spirits this evening.

In this Tribe I saw 25 Squars and Boys taken 13 days ago in

a battle with the Mahars in this battle they Destroy^d 40 Lodges, Killed 75 Men, & som boys & Children, & took 48 Prisoners Womin & boys which they promis both Capt. Lewis and my self Shall be Delivered up to Mr. Durion[13] at the Bous rulie (*Bois brulé*) Tribe, those are a retched and Dejected looking people the Squars appear low & Corse but this is an unfavourable time to judge of them

We gave our Mahar intep^tr. some fiew articles to give those Squars in his name Such as Alls, needles &c. &c.

I saw & eat Pemitigon the Dog, Grou^d. potatoe made into a Kind of homney, which I thought but little inferior. I also Saw a Spoon Made of a horn of an Animell of the Sheep Kind[14] (*the mountain ram of Argalia*) the Spoon will hold 2 quarts.

27th. *of Sept. Thursday* 1804—

I rose early after a bad nights Sleep found the Chief[s] all up, and the bank as useal lined with Spectators we gave the 2 great Cheifs a Blanket a peace, or rether they took off agreeable to their Custom the one they lay on and each one Peck of corn. after Brackfast Capt. Lewis & the Cheifs went on Shore, as a verry large part of their nation was comeing in, the Disposition of whome I did not know one of us being sufficent on Shore, I wrote a letter to Mr. P. Durion & prepared a meadel & Some Coms^ns. (*Certificates*) & Sent to Cap Lewis at 2 oClock Capt. Lewis Returned with 4 Chiefs & a Brave Man (Conside^e Man) named *War cha pa* or on his Guard when the friends of those people [*the Scioux*] die they run arrows through their flesh above and below their elbows as a testimony of their Greaf.

after Staying about half an hour, I went with them on Shore, Those men left the boat with reluctience, I went first to the 2^d. Cheifs Lodge, where a croud came around after Speeking on various Subjects I went to a principal mans lodge from them to the grand Chiefs lodge, after a fiew minits he invited me to a Lodge within the Circle in which I Stayed with all their principal Men untill the Dance began, which was Similer to the one of last night performed by their women with poles (*in their hands*) on which Scalps of their enemies were hung, Some with the Guns Spears & War empliments of (*taken by*) their husbands [&c.] in their hands.

Capt. Lewis Came on Shore and we Continued untill we were Sleepy & returned to our boat, the 2nd. Chief & one principal Man accompanied us, Those two Indians accompanied me on board in the Small Perogue; Capt. Lewis with a guard Still on

Shore the man who Steered not being much acustomed to Steer, passed the bow of the boat & the peroge Came broad Side against the Cable & broke it which obliged me to order in a loud voice all hands up & at their ores, my preemptry order to the men and the bustle of their getting to their ores allarmd. the Cheifs, together with the appearance of the Men on Shore, as the boat turnd. The Cheif hallowaed & allarmed the Camp or Town informing them that the Mahars was about attacking us (*them*). In about 10 minits the bank was lined with men armed the 1st. Cheif at their head, about 200 men appeared and after about ½ hour returned all but about 60 men who continued on the bank all night, the Cheifs Contd. all night with us. This allarm I as well as Capt. Lewis Considered as the Signal of their intentions (which was to Stop our proceeding on our journey and if Possible rob us) we were on our Guard all night, the misfortune of the loss of our Anchor obliged us to Lay under a falling bank much exposd. to the accomplishment of their hostile intentions. P. C. our Bowman who cd. Speek Mahar informed us in the night that the Maha Prisoners informed him we were to be Stoped. we Shew as little Sighns of a Knowledge of their intentions as possible all prepared on board for any thing which might hapen, we kept a Strong guard all night in the boat, no Sleep

28th. *of September* 1804 *Friday*—

Made many attemps in different ways to find our anchor, but Could not, the Sand had Covered it, from the Misfortune of last night our boat was laying at Shore in a verry unfavourable Situation, after finding that the anchor Could not be found we determined to proceed on, with great difficuelty got the Chiefs out of our boat, and when we was about Setting out the Class Called the Soldiers took possession of the Cable the 1st. Cheif which was Still on board, & intended to go a Short distance up with us. I told him the men of his nation Set on the Cable, he went out & told Capt. Lewis who was at the bow the men Who Set on the roap was Soldiers, and wanted Tobacco Capt. L [*said*] would not agree to be forced into any thing, the 2d. Chief Demanded a flag & Tobacco which we refusd. to Give Stateing proper reasons to them for it after much Dificuelty—which had nearly reduced us to necessity to hostilities I threw a Carrot of Tobacco to 1st. Chief took the port fire from the gunner. Spoke so as to touch his pride The Chief gave the Tobacco to his Soldiers & he jurked the rope from them and handed it to the bowsman we then Set out under a Breeze from the S. E. about 2 miles up we observed the 3rd. Chief on Shore beckining to us we took him on board he informed us the roap was held by the order of the 2d. Chief who was a Double Spoken man, Soon after we Saw a man Comeing full Speed, thro: the plains left his horse & proceeded across a Sand bar near the Shore we took him on board & observed that he was the Son of the Chief we had on board we Sent by him a talk to the nation Stateint [stating] the cause of our hoisting the red flag undr. the white, if they were for peace Stay at home & do as we had Directed them, if the[y] were for war or were Deturmined to stop us we were ready to defend our Selves, we halted one houre & ½ on the S. S. & made a Substitute of Stones for a ancher, refreshed our men and proceeded on about 2 Miles higher up & Came to a verry Small Sand bar in the middle of the river & Stayed all night, I am verry unwell for want of Sleep Deturmined to Sleep to night if possible, the Men Cooked & we rested well.[15]

NOTES TO CHAPTER 1

1. The pirogues were canoes made from hollowed-out logs. From Camp Dubois to the Mandan villages the expedition also used a keelboat fifty-five feet long.

2. When Reuben Gold Thwaites began editing the manuscripts of the Original Journals he found interlineations made by William Clark, and by previous editors. He published most of these interlineations, and some emendations of his own, indicating the various sources as follows: corrections presumably by Nicholas Biddle were printed in italics enclosed by parentheses; additions by Clark, by Elliott Coues, and by "an unknown hand" were printed in italics enclosed by brackets; and signed or unsigned emendations by Thwaites were indicated by roman type, enclosed in brackets. Italics not enclosed in parentheses or brackets indicated words underlined by Clark or Lewis. Parentheses enclosing roman type were published as found in the original manuscript. Thwaites, ed., *Original Journals*, I, p. 11, note 1.

3. Figures in parentheses refer to compass courses, distances, and similar information published by Thwaites, but omitted from the present reprinting.

4. Lewis and Clark used the terms "larboard side" (left) and "starboard side" (right) to designate the sides of the stream. Usually the terms were abbreviated, L. S. and S. S.

5. An account of this trading expedition is contained in *Tabeau's Narrative of Loisel's Expedition to the Upper Missouri*, edited by Annie Heloise Abel.

6. Later called East Medicine Knoll Creek, and East Medicine River (cf. Nicollet, chap. 16). The Geological Survey map of the Canning, South Dakota, Quadrangle (edition of 1937) shows the name as Medicine Creek.

7. John Evans ascended the Missouri River from St. Louis to the Mandan villages in 1795 and is supposed to have made a map of the river. About 1915 a map of the Missouri River was found in the files of the Federal

Bureau of Indian Affairs, with markings indicating that it had been in the possession of Lewis and Clark. A reproduction of this map was published in the *Geographical Review*, May, 1916, with an article "A New Lewis and Clark Map," by Annie Heloise Abel. Probably this was a copy of the "Evans Map."

8. The Teton division of the Sioux Nation consisted of seven tribes; the Brulés, Sans Arcs, Blackfeet Sioux, Minneconjou, Two Kettles, Oglala, and Uncpapa. The band that Lewis and Clark met at this place was a part of the Brulé tribe. George E. Hyde, *Red Cloud's Folk*, p. 29.

9. This stream is now called the Bad River, a translation of the original Sioux name. It enters the Missouri River at the town of Fort Pierre, South Dakota. The region around the mouth of Bad River became one of the most important fur-trading areas on the Missouri River. Several trading posts were established in the vicinity, the most prominent being Fort Pierre, built by the American Fur Company in 1832 about three miles above the mouth of Bad River, on the right (west) bank of the Missouri. It was sold to the government in 1855 and became a military fort, which was abandoned in 1857. The town of Fort Pierre began to be built about 1876 and became a terminal of one of the four principal trails to the Black Hills during the gold rush. On a hilltop within the limits of Fort Pierre, on February 17, 1913, a group of school children found a lead plate buried on March 30, 1743, by the Chevalier de la Verendrye and companions, who were probably the first white people to enter the present states of North and South Dakota.

10. By Maha (or Mahar) Clark meant the Omaha Indians, traditional enemies of the Sioux, living west of the Missouri and north of the Platte in what is now northeastern Nebraska.

11. Lewis and Clark had met a band of Yankton Sioux, which Clark incorrectly called Bois Brulé, near the mouth of the James River. Clark wrote on August 29: "the Scioues Camps are handsom of a Conic form Covered with Buffalow Roabs Painted different colours and all compact & handsomly arranged, Covered all round an open part in the Centre for the fire, with Buffalow roabs, each Lodg has a place for Cooking detached, the lodges contain from 10 to 15 persons." Thwaites, ed., *Original Journals*, I, pp. 128-29.

12. "Pemitigon" was pemmican, usually made of dried buffalo meat, pounded to a powder and mixed with buffalo fat, but sometimes containing fruit or nuts. The "potatoe" was probably *Psoralea esculenta*, or wild turnip, called *pomme blanche* by the Canadian French.

13. Pierre Dorion was descending the Missouri with some companions on two rafts loaded with furs and tallow when he met Lewis and Clark on June 12. He had lived with the Yankton Sioux for about twenty years. Lewis and Clark employed him as interpreter and he went up the river with them, until they reached the Yankton Indians. Here the explorers left him, with instructions to attempt to make peace among the various tribes and to take some of the principal chiefs to Washington to visit the President.

14. The Rocky Mountain sheep.

15. As the party proceeded the Sioux made friendly overtures, but the explorers were careful to avoid further entanglements while in Sioux territory. The Sioux chief left the boat September 30. On October 12 Clark wrote: "a curious custom with the Souix as well as the rickeres is to give handsom squars to those whome they wish to Show some acknowledgements to. The Seauex we got clare of without taking their squars, they followed us with Squars two days. . . ." Thwaites, ed., *Original Journals*, I, p. 189.

Chapter 2

1806

FROM THE MUSSELSHELL TO THE LITTLE MISSOURI,

by Captain Meriwether Lewis

Meriwether Lewis was born August 18, 1774, in Albemarle County, Virginia. When he was ten years old his family moved to Georgia, but he returned to Virginia at thirteen to study Latin, mathematics, and science for five years.

At twenty he joined the militia engaged in suppressing the Whisky Rebellion. In 1795 he entered the regular army with the rank of ensign. He was made a lieutenant in 1796 and a captain in 1797. He served under General Anthony Wayne in campaigns against the Indians in the old Northwest Territory, and for a while was paymaster of his regiment.

In 1801 Captain Lewis was appointed private secretary to President Thomas Jefferson. Retaining his army rank, he spent the next two years in this position, and in 1803 was selected by the President to lead the proposed expedition to the Pacific coast. He asked and received permission to share the leadership with William Clark, spent a short time studying the sciences at Philadelphia, and was soon on his way down the Ohio River, recruiting volunteers and organizing the "Corps for Northwestern Discovery."

The Lewis and Clark expedition left Camp Dubois, near St. Louis, in May, 1804, and returned to St. Louis in September, 1806. Soon after his return Lewis was commissioned brigadier general and appointed governor of Louisiana Territory. While traveling by horseback through Tennessee on a journey to Washington he died of a gunshot wound during the night of October 11, 1809. It was reported that he had killed himself, but many historians believe that he was murdered for the small amount of money that was in his possession.

Thomas Jefferson described Lewis in these words: "Of courage undaunted; possessing a firmness and perseverance of purpose which nothing but impossibilities could divert from its direction; careful as a father of those committed to his charge, yet steady in the maintenance of order and discipline; intimate with the Indian character, customs, and principles; habituated to the hunting life; guarded, by exact observation of the vegetables and animals of his own country, against losing time in the description of objects already possessed; honest, disinterested, liberal, of sound understanding, and a fidelity to truth so scrupulous, that whatever he should report would be as certain as if seen by ourselves; . . ."

The narration that follows is reprinted from the Thwaites edition of the *Original Journals* and covers the period from August 1 to August 12, 1806. At this time the party was divided—Clark was descending the Yellowstone and Lewis was moving down the Missouri.

Friday August 1st. 1806.

The rain still continuing I set out early as usual and proceeded on at a good rate. at 9. A. M. we saw a large brown bear swimming from an island to the main shore we pursued him and as he landed Drewyer and myself shot and killed him; we took him on board the perogue and continued our rout. at 11. A. M. we passed the entrance of Mussel shell river. at 1 in the evening we arrived at a bottom on S. W. side where there were several spacious Indian lodges built of sticks and an excellent landing. as the rain still continued with but little intermission and appearances seemed unfavorable to it's becomeing fair shortly, I determined to halt at this place at least for this evening and indeavour to dry my skins of the bighorn which had every appearance of spoiling, an event which I would not should happen on any consideration as we have now passed the country in which they are found and I therefore could not supply the deficiency were I to loose these I have. I halted at this place being about 15 ms. below Missel shell river, had fires built in the lodges and my skins exposed to dry. shortly after we landed the rain ceased tho' it still continued cloudy all the evening. a white bear[1] came within 50 paces of our camp before we perceived it; it stood erect on it's hinder feet and looked at us with much apparent unconsern, we seized our guns which are always by us and several of us fired at it and killed it. it was a female in fine order, we fleesed it and extracted several gallons of oil. this speceis of bear are nearly as poor at this season of the year as the common black bear nor are they ever as fat as the black bear is found in winter; as they feed principally on flesh, like the wolf, they are most fatt when they can procure a sufficiency of food without rispect to the season of the year. the oil of this bear is much harder than that of the black bear being nearly as much so as the lard of a hog. the flesh is by no means as agreeable as that of the black bear, or Yahkah or partycoloured bear of the West side of the rocky mountains. on our way to-day we killed a buck Elk in fine order the skins and a part of the flesh of which we preserved. after encamping this evening the hunters killed 4 deer and a beaver. The Elk are now in fine order particularly the males. their horns have obtained their full growth but have not yet shed the velvet or skin which covers them. the does are found in large herds with their young and a few young bucks with them. the old bucks yet herd together in parties of two to 7 or 8.

Saturday August $2^{ed.}$ 1806.

The morning proved fair and I determined to remain all day and dry the baggage and give the men an opportunity to dry and air their skins and furr. had the powder parched meal and every article which wanted drying exposed to the sun. the day proved warm fair and favourable for our purpose. I permitted the Fieldses to go on a few miles to hunt. by evening we had dryed our baggage and repacked it in readiness to load and set out early in the morning. the river fell 18 inches since yesterday evening. the hunters killed several deer in the course of the day. nothing remarkable took place today. we are all extreemly anxious to reach the entrance of the Yellowstone river where we expect to join Cap$^{t.}$ Clark and party.

Sunday August $3^{rd.}$ 1806.

I arrose early this morning and had the perogue and canoes loaded and set out at half after 6 A. M. we soon passed the canoe of Colter and Collins who were on shore hunting, the men hailed them but received no answer we proceeded, and shortly after overtook J. and R. Fields who had killed 25 deer since they left us yesterday; deer are very abundant in the timbered bottoms of the river and extreemly gentle. we did not halt today to cook and dine as usual having directed that in future the party should cook as much meat in the evening after encamping as would be sufficient to serve them the next day; by this means we forward our journey at least 12 or 15 miles P$^{r.}$ day. we saw but few buffaloe in the course of this day, tho' a great number of Elk, deer, wolves, some bear, beaver, geese a few ducks, the party coloured co[r]vus [magpie], one Callamet Eagle, a number of bald Eagles, red headed woodpeckers &c. we encamped this evening on N. E. side of the river 2m$^{s.}$ above our encampment of the 12$^{th.}$ of May, 1805. soon after we encamp[ed] Drewyer killed a fat doe. the Fieldses arrived at dark with the flesh of two fine bucks, besides which they had killed two does since we passed them making in all 29 deer since yesterday morning. Collins and Colter did not overtake us this evening.

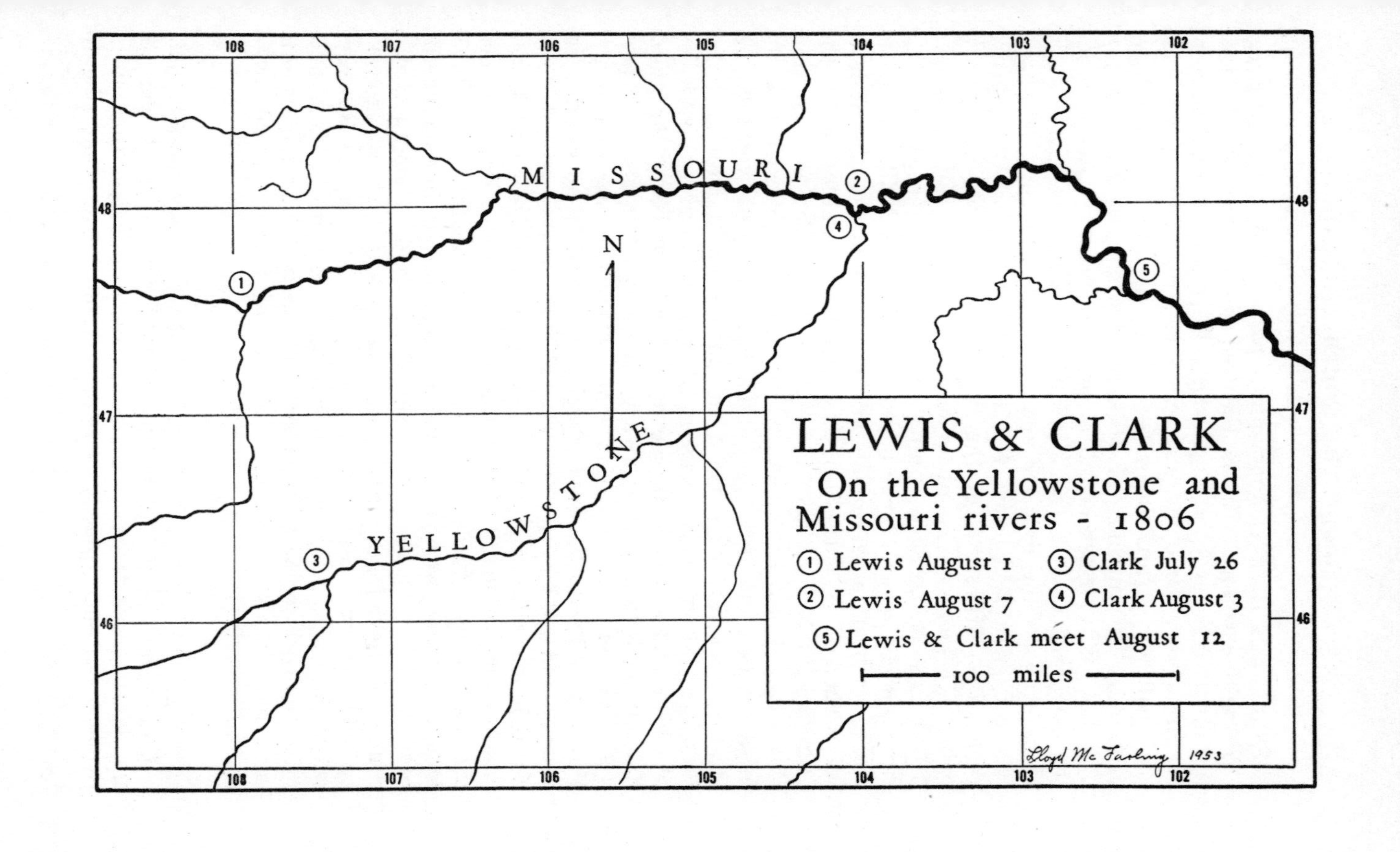
LEWIS & CLARK
On the Yellowstone and Missouri rivers - 1806
① Lewis August 1
② Lewis August 7
③ Clark July 26
④ Clark August 3
⑤ Lewis & Clark meet August 12
100 miles
MISSOURI
YELLOWSTONE
N
108
107
106
105
104
103
102
48
47
46
Lloyd McFarling 1953

Monday August 4th. 1806.

Set out at 4 A. M. this morning. permited Willard and Sergt. Ordway to exchange with the Fieldses and take their small canoe to hunt today. at ½ after eleven O'Ck. passed the entrance of big dry river; found the water in this river about 60 yds. wide tho' shallow. it runs with a boald even current. at 3 P. M. we arrived at the entrance of Milk river where we halted a few minutes. this stream is full at present and it's water is much the colour of that of the Missouri; it affords as much water at present as Maria's river and I have no doubt extends itself to a considerable distance North. during our halt we killed a very large rattlesnake of the speceis common to our country. it had 176 scutæ on the abdomen and 25 on the tail, it's length 5 feet. the scutæ on the tail fully formed. after passing this river we saw several large herds of buffaloe and Elk we killed one of each of these animals and took as much of the flesh as we wished. we encamped this evening two miles below the gulph on the N. E. side of the river. Tonight for the first time this season I heard the small whippoorwill or goatsucker of the Missouri cry. Colter and Collins have not yet overtaken us. Ordway and Willard delayed so much time in hunting today that they did not overtake us untill about midnight. they killed one bear and 2 deer. in passing a bend just below the gulph it being dark they were drawn by the currant in among a parsel of sawyers,[2] under one of which the canoe was driven and throwed Willard who was steering overboard; he caught the sawyer and held by it; Ordway with the canoe drifted down about half a mile among the sawyers under a falling bank, the canoe struck frequently but did not overset; he at length gained the shore and returned by land to learn the fate of Willard whom he found was yet on the sawyer; it was impossible for him to take the canoe to his relief. Willard at length tied a couple of sticks together which had lodged against the sawyers on which he was and set himself adrift among the sawyers which he fortunately escaped and was taken up about a mile below by Ordway with the canoe; they sustained no loss on this occasion. it was fortunate for Willard that he could swim tolerably well.

Tuesday August 5th. 1806.

Colter and Collins not having arrived induced me to remain this morning for them. the hunters killed four deer this morning near our encampment. I remained untill noon when I again reimbarked and set out concluding that as Colter and Collins had not arrived by that time that they had passed us after dark the night of the 3rd. inst. as Sergt. Ordway informed me he should have done last evening had not the centinel hailed him. we continued our rout untill late in the evening when I came too and encamped on the South side about 10 miles below little dry river. on our way we killed a fat cow and took as much of the flesh as was necessary for us. The Fieldses killed 2 large bear this evening one of them measured nine feet from the extremity of the nose to that of his tail, this is the largest bear except one that I have seen. we saw several bear today as we passed but did not kill any of them. we also saw on our way immence herds of buffaloe & Elk, many deer Antelopes, wolves, geese Eagles &c. but few ducks or prarie hens. the geese cannot fly at present; I saw a solitary Pillacon [pelican] the other day in the same situation. this happens from their sheding or casting the f[e]athers of the wings at this season.

Wednesday August 6th. 1806.

A little after dark last evening a violent storm arrose to the N. E. and shortly after came on attended with violent Thunder lightning and some hail; the rain fell in a mere torrant and the wind blew so violently that it was with difficulty I could have the small canoes unloaded before they filled with water; they sustained no injury. our situation was open and exposed to the storm. in attending to the canoes I got wet to the skin and having no shelter on land I betook myself to the orning of the perogue which I had, formed of Elkskin, here I obtained a few hours of broken rest; the wind and rain continued almost all night and the air became very cold. we set out early this morning and decended the river about 10 miles below Porcupine river when the wind became so violent that I laid by untill 4 P. M. the wind then abaiting in some measure we again resumed our voyage, and decended the river about 5 miles below our encampment of the 1st. of May 1805 where we halted for the night on the S. W. side of the river. after halting we killed three fat cows and a buck. we had previously killed today 4 deer a buck Elk and a fat cow. in short game is so abundant and gentle that we kill it when we please. the Fieldses went on ahead this evening and we did not overtake them. we saw several bear in the course of the day.

Thursday August 7th. 1806.

It began to rain about midnight and continued with but little intermission until 10 A. M. today. the air was cold and extreemly unpleasant. we set out early resolving if possible to reach the Yelowstone river today which was at the distance of 83 ms. from our encampment of the last evening; the currant favoured our progress being more rapid than yesterday, the men plyed their oars faithfully and we went at a good rate. at 8 A. M. we passed the entrance of Marthy's river which has changed it's entrance since we passed it last year, falling in at preasent about a quarter of a mile lower down. at or just below the entrance of this river we meet with the first appearance of Coal birnt hills and pumicestone, these appearances seem to be coextensive. here it is also that we find the first Elm and dwarf cedar on the bluffs, the ash first appears in the instance of one solletary tree at the Ash rapid, about the Elk rapid and from thence down we occasionally meet with it scattered through the bottoms but it is generally small. from Marthy's river to Milk river on the N. E. side there is a most beautifull level plain country; the soil is much more fertile here than above. we overtook the Fieldses at noon. they had killed 2 bear and seen 6 others, we saw and fired on two from our perogue but killed neither of them. these bear resort the river where they lie in wate at the crossing places of the game for the Elk and weak cattle; when they procure a subject of either they lie by the carcase and keep the wolves off untill they devour it. the bear appear to be very abundant on this part of the river. we saw a number of buffaloe Elk &c. as we passed but did not detain to kill any of them. we also saw an unusual flight of white gulls about the size of a pigeon with the top of their heads black. at 4 P. M. we arrived at the entrance of the Yellowstone river. I landed at the point and found that Capt. Clark had been encamped at this place and from appearances had left it about 7 or 8 days. I found a paper on a pole at the point which mearly contained my name in the hand wrighting of Capt. C. we also found the remnant of a note which had been attatched to a peace of Elk'shorns in the camp; from this fragment I learned that game was scarce at the point and musquetos troublesome which were the reasons given for his going on; I also learnt that he intended halting a few miles below where he intended waiting my arrival. I now wrote a note directed to Colter and Collins provided they were behind, ordering them to come on without loss of time;

this note I wraped in leather and attatched to the same pole which Capt. C had planted at the point; this being done I instantly reimbarked and decended the river in the hope of reaching Capt. C's camp before night about 7 miles below the point on the S. W. shore I saw some meat that had been lately fleased and hung on a pole; I directed Sergt. Ordway to go on shore [and] examine the place; on his return he reported that he saw the tracks of two men which appeared so resent that he beleived they had been there today, the fire he found at the plce was blaizing and appeared to have been mended up afresh or within the course of an hour past. he found at this place a part of a Chinnook hat which my men recognized as the hat of Gibson; from these circumstances we concluded that Capt. C's camp could not be distant and pursued our rout untill dark with the hope of reaching his camp in this however we were disappointed and night coming on compelled us to encamp on the N. E. shore in the next bottom above our encampment of the 23rd. and 24th. of April 1805. as we came too a herd of buffaloe assembled on the shore of which we killed a fat cow.

Friday August 8th. 1806.

Beleiving from the recent appearances about the fire which we past last evening that Capt. Clark could be at no great distance below I set out early; the wind heard [hard] from the N. E. but by the force of the oars and currant we traveled at a good rate untill 10 A. M. by which time we reached the center of the beaver bends about 8 ms. by water and 3 by land above the entrance of White earth river. not finding Capt. Clark I knew not what calculation to make with rispect to his halting and therefore determined to proceed as tho' he was not before me and leave the rest to the chapter of accedents. at this place I found a good beach for the purpose of drawing out the perogue and one of the canoes which wanted corking and reparing. the men with me have not had leasure since we left the West side of the Rocky mountains to dress any skins or make themselves cloaths and most of them are therefore extreemly bare. I therefore determined to halt at this place untill the perog[u]e and canoe could be repared and the men dress skins and make themselves the necessary cloathing. we encamped on the N. E. side of the river; we found the Musquetoes extreemly troublesome but in this rispect there is but little choise of camps from hence down to St. Louis. from this place to the little Missouri there is an abundance of game I shall therefore when I leave this place travel at my leasure and avail myself of every opportunity to collect and dry meat untill I provide a sufficient quantity for our voyage not knowing what provision Capt. C. has made in this rispect. I formed a camp unloaded the canoes and perogue, had the latter and one of the canoes drawn out to dry, fleased what meat we had collected and hung it on poles in the sun, after which the men busied themselves in dressing skins and making themselves cloaths. Drewyer killed 2 Elk and a deer this evening. the air is cold yet the Musquetoes continue to be troublesome.

Saturday August 9th. 1806.

The day proved fair and favourable for our purposes. the men were all engaged dressing skins and making themselves cloathes except R. & J. Fields whom I sent this morning over the river with orders to proceed to the entrance of the White earth river in surch of Capt. C. and to hunt and kill Elk or buffaloe should they find any convenient to the river. in the evening these men returned and informed me that they saw no appearance of Capt. Clark or party. they found no game nor was there a buffaloe to be seen in the plains as far as the eye could reach. nothing remarkable took place in the course of the day. Colter and Collins have not yet overtaken us I fear some missfortune has happened them for their previous fidelity and orderly deportment induces me to believe that they would not thus intentionally delay. the Perogue is not yet sufficiently dry for reparing. we have no pitch and will therfore be compelled to use coal and tallow.

Sunday August 10th. 1806.

The morning was somewhat cloudy I therefore apprehended rain however it shortly after became fair. I hastened the repairs which were necessary to the perogue and canoe which were compleated by 2 P. M. those not engaged about this business employed themselves as yesterday. at 4 in the evening it clouded up and began to rain which puting a stop to the opperation of skindressing we had nothing further to detain us, I therefore directed the vessels to be loaded and at 5 P. M. got under way the wind has blown very hard all day but did not prove so much so this evening as absolutely to detain us. we decended this evening as low nearly as the entrance of white-Earth river and encamped on the S.W. side. the musquetoes more than usually troublesome this evening.

Monday August 11th. 1806.

We set out very early this morning. it being my wish to arrive at the birnt hills by noon in order to take the latitude of that place as it is the most northern point of the Missouri, I enformed the party of my design and requested that they would exert themselves to reach the place in time as it would save us the delay of nearly one day; being as anxious to get forward as I was they plyed their oars faithfully and we proceeded rapidly. I had instructed the small [c]anoes that if they saw any game on the river to halt and kill it and follow on; however we saw but little game untill about 9 A.M. when we came up with a buffaloe swimming the river which I shot and killed; leaving the small canoes to dress it and bring on the meat I proceeded. we had gone but little way before I saw a very large grizzly bear and put too in order to kill it, but it took wind of us and ran off. the small canoes overtook us and informed that the flesh of the buffaloe was unfit for uce and that they had therefore left it. half after 11 A.M. we saw a large herd of Elk on the N. E. shore and I directed the men in the small canoes to halt and kill some of them and continued on in the perogue to the birnt hills; when I arrived here it was about 20 minutes after noon and of course the observation for the °'s meridian Altitude was lost. jus[t] opposite to the birnt hills there happened to be a herd of Elk on a thick willow bar and finding that my observation was lost for the present I determined to land and kill some of them accordingly we put too and I went out with Cruzatte only. we fired on the Elk I killed one and he wounded another, we reloaded our guns and took different routs through the thick willows in pursuit of the Elk; I was in the act of firing on the Elk a second time when a ball struck my left thye about an inch below my hip joint, missing the bone it passed through the left thye and cut the thickness of the bullet across the hinder part of the right thye; the stroke was very severe; I instantly supposed that Cruzatte had shot me in mistake for an Elk as I was dressed in brown leather and he cannot see very well; under this impression I called out to him damn you, you have shot me, and looked towards the place from whence the ball had come, seeing nothing I called Cruzatte several times as loud as I could but received no answer; I was now preswaded that it was an indian that had shot me as the report of the gun did not appear to be more than 40 paces from me and Cruzatte appeared to be out of hearing of me; in this situation not knowing how many indians there might be concealed in the bushes I thought best to make good my retreat to the perogue, calling out as I ran for the first hundred paces as loud as I could to Cruzatte to retreat that there were indians hoping to allarm him in time to make his escape also; I still retained the charge in my gun which I was about to discharge at the moment the ball struck me. when I arrived in sight of the perogue I called the men to their arms to which they flew in an instant, I told them that I was wounded but I hoped not mortally, by an indian I believed and directed them to follow me that I would return & give them battle and releive Cruzatte if possible who I feared had fallen into their hands; the men followed me as they were bid and I returned about a hundred paces when my wounds became so painfull and my thye so stiff that I could scarcely get on; in short I was compelled to halt and ordered the men to proceed and if they found themselves overpowered by numbers to retreat in order keeping up a fire. I now got back to the perogue as well as I could and prepared my self with a pistol my rifle and air-gun being determined as a retreat was impracticable to sell my life as deerly as possible. in this state of anxiety and suspense I remained about 20 minutes when the party returned with Cruzatte and reported that there were no indians nor the appearance of any; Cruzatte seemed much allarmed and declared if he had shot me it was not his intention, that he had shot an Elk in the willows after he left or seperated from me. I asked him whether he did not hear me when I called to him so frequently which he absolutely denied. I do not beleive that the fellow did it intentionally but after finding that he had shot me was anxious to conceal his knowledge of having done so. the ball had lodged in my breeches which I knew to be the ball of the short rifles such as that he had, and there being no person out with me but him and no indians that we could discover I have no doubt in my own mind of his having shot me. with the assistance of Sergt. Gass I took off my cloaths and dressed my wounds myself as well as I could, introducing tents of patent lint into the ball holes, the wounds blead considerably but I was hapy to find that it had touched neither bone nor artery. I sent the men to dress the two Elk which Cruzatte and myself had killed which they did in a few minutes and brought the meat to the river. the small canoes came up shortly after with the flesh of one Elk. my wounds being so situated that I could not without infinite pain make an observation I determined to relinquish it and proceeded on. we came within eight miles of our encampment of the 15th. of April 1805 and encamped on N. E. side. as it was painfull to me to be removed I slept on board the perogue; the pain I experienced excited a high fever and I had a very uncomfortable night. at 4 P. M. we passed an encampment which had been evacuated this morning by Capt. Clark, here I found a note from Capt. C. informing me that he had left a letter for me at the entrance of the Yelow stone river, but that Sergt. Pryor who had passed that place since he left it had taken the letter; that Sergt. Pryor having been robed of all his horses had decended the Yelowstone river in skin canoes and had overtaken him at this encampment. this I fear puts an end to our prospects of obtaining the Sioux Cheifs to accompany us as we have not now leasure to send and engage Mr. Heney on this service, or at least he would not have time to engage them to go as early as it is absolutely necessary we should decend the river.[3]

Tuesday August 12th. 1806.

Being anxious to overtake Capt. Clark who from the appearance of his camps could be at no great distance before me, we set out early and proceeded with all possible expedition at 8 A.M. the bowsman informed me that there was a canoe and a camp he believed of whitemen on the N.E. shore. I directed the perogue and canoes to come too at this place and found it to be the camp of two hunters from the Illinois by name Joseph Dickson and Forest Hancock.[4] these men informed me that Capt. C. had passed them about noon the day before. they also informed me that they had left the Illinois in the summer [of] 1804 since which time they had been ascended the Missouri, hunting and traping beaver; that they had been robed by the indians and the former wounded last winter by the Tetons of the birnt woods; that they had hitherto been unsuccessfull in their voyage having as yet caught but little beaver, but were still determined to proceed. I gave them a short discription of the Missouri, a list of distances to the most conspicuous streams and remarkable places on the river above and pointed out to them the places where the beaver most abounded. I also gave them a file and a couple of pounds of powder with some lead. these were articles which they assured me they were in great want of. I remained with these men an hour and a half when I took leave of them and proceeded. while I halted with these men Colter and Collins who seperated from us on the 3rd. i[n]st rejoined us. they were well no accedent having happened. they informed me that after proceeding the first day and not overtaking us that they had concluded that we were behind and had delayed several days in waiting for us and had thus been unable to join us untill the present mome[n]t. my wounds felt very stiff and soar this morning but gave me no considerable pain. there was much less inflamation than I had reason to apprehend there would be. I had last evening applyed a poltice of peruvian barks. at 1 P. M. I overtook Capt. Clark and party and had the pleasure of finding them all well. as wrighting in my present situation is extreemly painfull to me I shall desist until I recover and leave to my fri[e]nd Capt. C. the continuation of our journal. . . .

NOTES TO CHAPTER 2

1. The bear sometimes called white, and sometimes yellow, by early explorers was the grizzly bear (*Ursus horribilis*). Lewis first saw the grizzly bear a few miles below the mouth of the Yellowstone on the upriver journey, April 29, 1805. He wrote: ". . . I walked on shore with one man. about 8. A.M. we fell in with two brown or yellow [*white*] bear; both of which we wounded; one of them made his escape, the other after my firing on him pursued me seventy or eighty yards, but fortunately had been so badly wounded that he was unable to pursue so closely as to prevent my charging my gun; we again repeated our fir[e] and killed him." Thwaites, ed., *Original Journals*, I, p. 350.

2. A sawyer was a tree that had been torn from the bank and had become fixed in the river, usually with the branches extending downstream.

3. Hugh Henney was a trader employed by the Hudson's Bay Company. Lewis and Clark met him at the Mandan villages during the winter of 1804-5. On July 24, while descending the Yellowstone, Clark dispatched Sergeant Pryor and Privates Hall, Shannon, and Windsor with horses on a trip to the Mandan Indians, with a letter to Henney requesting him to persuade some of the Sioux chiefs to accompany the expedition back to Washington. Two days later the horses were stolen by Indians. The men returned to the Yellowstone, killed some buffaloes, made two bullboats from the hides, and followed Clark's party down the Yellowstone and the Missouri, rejoining him on August 8.

4. These hunters were the first white men the explorers had seen since leaving the Mandan villages April 7, 1805.

Chapter 3

1811

THE ARIKARA VILLAGES,

by Henry Marie Brackenridge

Henry Marie Brackenridge, lawyer, author, diplomat, and jurist, was born in Pittsburgh in 1786 and died in the same city in 1871.

In 1811 he ascended the Missouri River to the Arikara and Mandan villages, traveling with a trading expedition led by Manuel Lisa.

At the same time another expedition, led by Wilson Price Hunt, was traveling up the river, en route for Fort Astoria at the mouth of the Columbia. A race developed between the two expeditions. Hunt, ahead, feared Lisa's influence might turn the Indians against him, if Lisa got to the Indians first. Lisa, behind, wished to catch up with the Astorians in order that the two parties might pass through the dangerous Sioux country together. The competitors met at the Great Bend of the Missouri, a quarrel developed, and a duel between the leaders was narrowly averted. Amicable relations were restored at a council with the Arikara Indians on June 12, 1811.

Brackenridge returned to St. Louis in the fall of 1811, and in 1814 published his Journal as part of the book *Views of Louisiana.* In 1816 he published a revised edition of the *Journal of a Voyage up the River Missouri.* In 1904 this was reprinted in *Early Western Travels,* edited by Reuben Gold Thwaites.

From the edition of 1814 I am reprinting Brackenridge's description of the Arikara villages.

Thursday 13*th.* This morning, found ourselves completely drenched by heavy rains, which continued the whole night. The chief has not given his answer as to the conditions of the trade. It is for him, usually to fix the price, on a consultation with his subordinate chiefs, to this the whole village must conform. The Indian women and girls, were occupied all this morning in carrying earth in baskets, to replace that which the rain had washed off their lodges. Rambled through the village, which I found excessively filthy, the 'villainous smells,' which every where assailed me, compelled me at length, to seek refuge in the open plain. The lovers of Indian manners, and mode of living, should contemplate them at a distance. The rains had rendered their village little better than a hog pen; the police appeared to me, in *some particulars,* extremely negligent. Some of the ancient cities of the old world, were probably like this village, inattentive to that cleanliness so necessary to health, where a great mass of beings are collected in one place; and we need not be surprised at the frequency of desolating plagues and pestilence. The village is swarming with dogs and children. I rank these together, for they are inseparable companions. Wherever I went, the children ran away, screaming and frightened at my outré and savage appearance. Let us not flatter ourselves with the belief, that the effect of our civilization and refinement, is to render us agreeable and lovely to the eyes of those whom we exclusively denominate savages! The dogs, of which each family has thirty or forty, pretended to make a show of fierceness, but on the least threat, ran off. They are of different sizes and colors. A number are fattened on purpose to eat, others are used for drawing their baggage. It is nothing more than the domesticated wolf. In wandering through the prairies, I have often mistaken wolves for Indian dogs. The larger kind has long curly hair, and resembles the shepherd dog. There is the same diversity amongst the wolves of this country. They may be more properly said to howl, than bark.

The lodges are constructed in the following manner: Four large forks of about fifteen feet in height, are placed in the ground, usually about twenty feet from each other, with hewn logs or beams across; from these beams other pieces of wood are placed slanting; smaller pieces are placed above, leaving an aperture at the top to admit the light, and to give vent to the smoke. These upright pieces are interwoven with osiers, after which, the whole is covered with earth, though not sodded. An opening is left at one side, for a door, which is secured by a kind of projection of ten or twelve feet, enclosed on all sides, and forming a narrow entrance, which might be easily defended. A buffaloe robe suspended at the entrance, answers as a door. The fire is made in a hole in the ground, directly under the aperture at the top. Their beds elevated a few feet, are placed around the lodge, and enclosed with curtains of dressed elk skins. At the upper end of the lodge, there is a kind of trophy erected; two buffaloe heads, fantastically painted, are placed on a little elevation; over them are placed a variety of consecrated things, such as shields, skins of a rare or valuable kind, and quivers of arrows. The lodges seem placed at random, without any regularity or design, and are so much alike, that it was for some time before I could learn to return to the same one.

The village is surrounded by a palisade of cedar poles, but in a very bad state. Around the village there are little plats enclosed by stakes, intwined with osiers, in which they cultivate maize, tobacco, and beans; but their principal field is at the distance of a mile from the village, to which, such of the females, whose duty it is to attend to their culture, go and return morning and evening. Around the village they have buffaloe robes stuck on high poles. I saw one so arranged as to bear a resemblance to the human figure, the hip bone of the buffaloe represented the head, the sockets of the thigh bones looked like eyes.

Friday 14*th*. It rained again last night, which prevented the trade from commencing until some time in the day. Mr. Lisa sent a quantity of goods to the lodge of the principal chief before mentioned, called le Gauchée, and Hunt to the one who accompanied him to meet us, *le Gros,* the principal war chief. The price of a horse was commonly ten dollars worth of goods at first cost. Hunt had resolved to purchase horses at this place, and proceed by land to the Columbia, being assured by some hunters, who met him before his arrival here, that this would be his best route.[1]

Mr. Bradbury[2] and I, took a walk into the upper village, which is separated from the lower by a stream about twenty yards wide—Entered several lodges, the people of which received us with kindness, placed mats and skins for us to sit on, and after smoking the pipe, offered us something to eat; this consisted of fresh buffaloe meat served in a wooden dish. They had a variety of earthen vessels, in which they prepared their food, or kept water. After the meat, they offered us homony made of corn dried in the milk, mixed with beans, which was prepared with buffaloe marrow, and tasted extremely well; also pounded and made into gruel. The prairie turnip,[3] is a root very common in the prairies, with something of the taste of the turnip, but more dry; this they eat dried and pounded, made into gruel. Their most common food is homony and dried buffaloe meat. In one of the lodges which we visited, we found the doctor, who was preparing some medicine for a sick lad. He was cooling with a spoon a decoction of some roots, which had a strong taste and smell, not unlike jalap. He showed us a variety of simples which he used. The most of them were common plants with some medical properties, but rather harmless than otherwise. The boy had a slight pleurisy. The chief remedy for their diseases, which they conceive to be owing to a disorder of the bowels, is rubbing the belly and sides of the patient, sometimes with such violence, as to cause fainting. When they become dangerous, they resort to charms and incantations, such as singing, dancing, blowing on the sick, &c. They are very successful in the treatment of wounds. When the wound becomes very obstinate, they commonly burn it, after which it heals more easily.

Saturday 15*th.* Fine weather—Took a walk with Mr. Bradbury through the country, which is entirely open, and somewhat hilly. Large masses of granite were usually found on the highest knobs. We saw a great variety of plants, and some new ones—One or two of the vallies are beautiful, with scarcely any shrubs but dwarf trees, scattered along a rivulet.

On our return in the evening, an alarm prevailed in the village, which appeared to be all in commotion. We were informed that the Sioux, their enemies, were near. This was probably all preconcerted. I was shewn, at the distance of about two miles, four horsemen on the top of a hill, at full gallop, passing and re-passing each other; this I understand is the signal given by the scouts, some of whom are constantly on the alert, of the approach of an enemy. To give intelligence of the appearance of a herd of buffaloe, instead of crossing each other, they gallop backward and forward abreast. Presently the warriors issued from the village with great noise and tumult, some on foot, others on horse-back, and pursued the direction in which the signals were made, down the river, and past an encampment. They observed no regular march, but ran helter skelter, like persons in one of our towns to extinguish a fire—and keeping up a continual halooing to encourage each other. Some of them were dressed in their most splendid manner. The tops of the lodges were crowded with women and children, and with the old men who could give no assistance, but by their lungs, which were kept busily employed: yet there were several who sallied forth, almost half bent with the weight of years. I counted upwards of five hundred in all. They soon after returned; whether they had chased away the enemy, or the alarm had turned out false, I never learned.

Sunday 16*th.* In the course of the day several parties arrived from different directions. According to custom they were met by warriors and conducted to the council lodge, where they gave an account of what had occurred, which was afterwards announced to the village by heralds. These contribute to enliven the village; though independent, they continually present a busy and animated scene. Great numbers of men are engaged in the different games of address and agility, others judging, or looking on, and many employed in a variety of other ways. There are a great number of women constantly at work in dressing buffaloe robes, which are placed on frames before the lodges. One of the parties which arrived today, came from the Snake nation, where they had stolen horses. This arrested their employments for a moment, the immediate friends and relatives of such as returned, spent the evening in rejoicing, while several females who had lost a relation, retired to the hills behind the village, where they continued to cry the whole afternoon.

In the evening they usually collect on the tops of the lodges, where they sit and converse: every now and then the attention of all was attracted by some old man who rose up and declaimed aloud, so as to be heard over the whole village. There was something in this like a quaker meeting. Adair labors to prove the Indian tribes to be descended from the Jews,[4] I might here adduce this as an argument in favor of these people being a colony of quakers.

Monday 17*th*. This day arrived a deputation from the Chienne nation,[5] to announce that those people were on their march to this village, and would be here in fifteen days. I sometimes amused myself with the idea of forming a gazette of the daily occurrences. We here see an independent nation, with all the interests and anxieties of the largest; how little would its history differ from that of one of the Grecian states! A war, a treaty, deputations sent and received, warlike excursions, national mourning or rejoicing, and a thousand other particulars, which constitute the chronicle of the most celebrated people.

In the evening, about sundown, the women cease from their labors, and collect into little knots, and amuse themselves with a game something like jack-stones; five pebbles are tossed up in a small basket, with which they endeavor to catch them again as they fall.

Tuesday 18*th*. Confidence had been somewhat restored between the leaders of the two parties since the council in the village. Mr. Hunt having resolved to start from this village, a bargain was made with Mr. Lisa, for the sale of Hunt's boats and some merchandise; in consequence of which, we crossed the river in order to make the exchange, after which we returned and encamped. We are to set off to-morrow morning to the Mandan villages.

Before I bid adieu to Arikara, I must note some general matters relating to their character and manners.

The men are large and well proportioned, complexion somewhat fairer than Indians commonly are. Generally go naked: the dress they sometimes put on seems more for ornament than any advantage it is to them; this consists of a sort of cassoc or shirt, made of the dressed skin of the antelope, and ornamented with porcupine quills, died a variety of colors; a pair of leggings, which are ornamented in the same way. A buffaloe hide dressed with the hair on, is then thrown over the right shoulder, the quiver being hung on the other, if he be armed with a bow. They generally permit their hair to grow long; I have, in one or two instances, seen it reach to their heels; they sometimes increase it by artificial means, commonly with horse hair. It is divided into a number of locks matted at intervals, with a braid of white earth, a substance resembling putty. Sometimes it is rolled up in a ball, and fixed on the top of the head. They always have a quantity of feathers about them; those of the black eagle are most esteemed. They have a kind of crown made of feathers, such as we see represented in the usual paintings of Indians, which is very beautiful. The swan is in most estimation for this purpose. Some ornament the neck with necklace made of the claws of the white bear. To their heels they sometimes fasten foxes' tails, and on their leggings suspend deers' hoofs, so as to make a rattling noise as they move along. On seeing a warrier dressed in all his finery, walking with his wife, who was comparatively plain in her dress or ornaments, I could not but think this was following the order of nature, as in the peacock, the stag, and almost all animals, the male is lavishly decorated, while the female is plain and unadorned. I intend this as a hint to some of our petit maitres. The dress of the female consists of a long robe made of the dressed skins of the elk, the antelope, or the agolia,[6] and ornamented with blue beads, and strips of ermine, or in its place, of some white skin. The robe is girded round the waist with a broad zone, highly ornamented with porcupine quills, and beads. They are no better off than were the Greeks and Romans, in what we deem at present so essential, but like them they bathe themselves regularly, twice a day. The women are much fairer than the men; some might be considered handsome any where —they are much more numerous than the men, the consequence of the wars in which the nation is constantly engaged. Polygamy is general, they have often four or five wives. Their courtship and marriage resemble that of most of the Indian nations; if the parties are mutually agreeable to each other, there is a consultation of the family; if this be also favourable, the father of the girl, or whoever gives her in marraige, makes a return for the present he had previously received from the lover—the match is then concluded.

They display considerable ingenuity of taste in their works of art: this observation applies to all the American nations, from the Mexicans to the most savage. Their arms, household utensils, and their dresses, are admirably made. I saw a gun which had been completely stocked by an Indian. A curious instance of native ingenuity which came under my notice, ought not to be omitted. I was told one day, of an old Indian who was making a blanket; I immediately went to see him. To my surprise, I found an old man, perfectly blind, seated on a stool before a kind of frame, over which were drawn coarse threads, or rather twists of buffaloe wool, mixed with wolf's hair; he had already made about a quarter of a yard of very coarse rough cloth. He told me that it was the first he had attempted, and that it was in consequence of a dream, in which he thought he had made a blanket like those of the white people. Here are the rudiments of weaving. They make beautiful jugs or baskets with osier, so close as to hold water.

I observed some very old men amongst them—the country is so extremely healthy, that they arrive to a very great age. About twenty years ago, the small pox destroyed a great number of them.[7] One day, in passing through the village, I saw something brought out of a lodge in a buffaloe robe, and exposed to the sun; on approaching, I discovered it to be a human being, but so shrivelled up, that it had nearly lost the human physiognomy: almost the only sign of life discernible, was a continual sucking its hands. On inquiring of the chief, he told me that he had seen it so ever since he was a boy. He appeared to be at least forty-five. It is almost impossible to ascertain the age of an Indian when he is above sixty; I made inquiries of several, who appeared to me little short of an hundred, but could form no satisfactory conjecture. Blindness is very common, arising probably from the glare of the snow, during a greater part of the year. I observed the goitre, or swelled neck, in a few instances.

Their government is oligarchical, but great respect is paid to popular opinion. It is utterly impossible to be a great man amongst them, without being a distinguished warrior, though respect is paid to birth, but this must be accompanied by other merit, to procure much influence. They are divided into different bands or classes; that of the pheasant, which is composed of the oldest men; that of the bear, the buffaloe, the elk, the dog, &c. Each of these has its leader who generally takes the name of the class, exclusively. Initiation into these classes, on arriving at the proper age, and after having given proofs of being worthy of it; is attended with great ceremony. The band of dogs, is considered the most brave and effective in war, being composed of young men under thirty. War parties are usually proposed by some individual warrior, and according to the confidence placed in him, his followers are numerous or otherwise. In these excursions they wander to a great distance, seldom venturing to return home without a scalp, or stolen horses. Frequently when unsuccessful they "cast their robes," as they express it, and vow to kill the first person they meet, provided he be not of their own nation. In crossing the river, they use canoes made of the buffaloe hide, or a few pieces of wood fastened together. They usually leave some token, as a stake, which is marked so as to convey some idea of their numbers, the direction which they have taken, &c. To avoid surprise, they always encamp at the edge of a wood; and when the party is small, they construct a kind of fortress, with wonderful expedition, of billets of wood, apparently piled up in a careless manner, but so arranged as to be very strong, and are able to withstand an assault from a much superior force. They are excellent horsemen—they will shoot an arrow at full speed, and again pick it up from the ground without stopping: sometimes they will lean entirely upon one leg, throwing their bodies to that side, so as to present nothing but the leg and thigh, on the other. In pursuit of the buffaloe, they will gallop down steep hills, broken almost into precipices. Some of their horses are very fine, and run swiftly, but are soon worn out, from the difficulty of procuring food for them in winter, the smaller branches of the cotton wood tree being almost the only fodder which they give them. Their hunting is regulated by the warriors chosen for the occasion, who urge on such as are tardy, and repress often with blows, those who would rush on too soon. When a herd of buffaloe is discovered, they approach in proper order, within half a mile, they then separate and dispose themselves, so as, in some measure, to surround them, when at the word, they rush upon them at full speed, and continue as long as their horses can stand it: a hunter usually shoots two arrows into a buffaloe, and then goes in pursuit of another; if he kills more than two in the hunt, he is considered as having acquitted himself well. The tongue is the prize of the person who has slain the animal; and he that has the greater number, is considered the best hunter of the day. Their weapons consist of guns, war clubs, spears, bows, and lances. They have two kinds of arrows, one for the purpose of the chase, and the other for war; the latter differs in this particular, that the barb or point is fastened so slightly, that when it enters the body, it remains in, and cannot be drawn out with the wood; therefore, when it is not in a vital part, the arrow is pushed entirely through. They do not poison them. Their bows are generally very small; an elk's horn, or two ribs of a buffaloe, often constitute the materials of which they are made. Those of wood are of willow, the back covered with sinews. Their daily sports, in which, when the weather is favorable, they are engaged from morning till night, are principally of two kinds. A level piece of ground appropriated for the purpose, and beaten by frequent use, is the place where they are carried on. The first is played by two persons, each armed with a long pole; one of them rolls a hoop, which, after having reached about two-thirds of the distance, is followed at half speed, and as they perceive it about to fall, they cast their poles under it; the pole on which the hoop falls, so as to be nearest to certain corresponding marks on the hoop and pole, gains for that time. This game excites great interest, and produces a gentle, but animated exercise. The other differs from it in this, that instead of poles, they have short pieces of wood, with barbs at one end, and a cross piece at the other, held in the middle with one hand; but instead of the hoop before mentioned, they throw a small ring, and endeavor to put the point of the barb through it. This is a much more violent exercise than the other.

With respect to their religion, it is extremely difficult, particularly from the slight acquaintance I had with them, to form any just idea. They have some notion of a Supreme Being, whom they call the "Master of Life," but they offer him no rational worship, and have but indistinct ideas of a future state. Their devotion manifests itself in a thousand curious tricks, of slight of hand, which they call magic, and which the vulgar amongst them believe to be something supernatural. They are very superstitious. Besides their public resident lodge, in which they have a great collection of magic, or sacred things, every one has his private magic in his lodge [or] about his person.[8] Any thing curious is immediately made an amulet, or a talisman; and is considered as devoted or consecrated, so as to deprive them of the power of disposing of it. The principal war chief lately took advantage of this, ingeniously enough. He obtained a very fine horse, which he was desirous of keeping, but fearing that some one might ask him as a gift, and as to refuse would be considered as evincing a narrowness of mind unbecoming a great man, who ought not to set his heart upon a matter of so little importance, he announced that he had given him to his magic. Some parts of their religious exercises are the most barbarous that can be imagined. I observed a great number whose bodies were scarred and cut in the most shocking manner; I was informed that this was done in their devotion; that to shew their zeal, they sometimes suspend themselves by the arms or legs, or the sides, by hooks. I was shewn a boy, who had drawn two buffaloe heads by cords drawn through the fleshy part of his sides, nearly a quarter of a mile. I might enumerate a variety of other particulars, in which this strange self punishment is carried to the greatest lengths. They have frequent holy days, when the greater part of the village appears to desist from labor, and dress out unusually fine. On these occasions, each one suspends his private magic on a high pole before his door; the painted shields, quivers of a variety of colors, scarlet cloth, and highly ornamented buffaloe robes, which compose these trophies, produce a very lively effect. I several times observed articles of some value suspended in the woods. I was told they often leave their property in this manner, without being under any apprehension that any of the same tribe will touch it, provided that there be the least sign to shew that it is not lost. A kind of superstition similar to that of the Druids, which protected their offerings hung up in the woods.

Since the affair of lieut. Prior, who commanded the party despatched by the United States, to take home the Mandan chief, these people have been friendly to the whites. They speak of the occurrence with regret, and declare that it was done by bad people whom they could not restrain.[9]

To give an account of the vices of these people would be to enumerate some of the more gross, prevalent amongst us. The savage state, like the rude uncultivated waste, is contemplated to most advantage at a distance. They have their rich and their poor, their envious, their proud, overbearing, their mean and grovelling, and the reverse of these. In some respects they appear extremely dissolute and corrupt—whether the result of refinement, or vice,[10] or the simplicity of nature, I am not able to say. . . .

Seeing the chief one day in a thoughtful mood, I asked him what was the matter—"I was wondering" said he "whether you white people have any women amongst you." I assured him in the affirmative. "Then" said he, "why is it that your people are so fond of our women, one might suppose they had never seen any before?"[11]

NOTES TO CHAPTER 3

1. From 1806 to about 1840 the exploration of the Northern Plains was left largely to fur traders and to travelers who accompanied their expeditions. One of the most important expeditions was that led by Wilson Price Hunt, a partner in John Jacob Astor's American Fur Company. In 1811 Hunt led a party of about sixty traders and trappers up the Missouri to the Arikara villages. From the Arikara and Cheyenne Indians he obtained horses and continued his journey overland, across northern South Dakota and central Wyoming. After many hardships Hunt arrived at Astoria, near the mouth of the Columbia River. In 1812 Robert Stuart, with a small party, started back across the continent. Robbed of their horses by Indians, the little band crossed the divide at or near South Pass, wintered on the Platte near the Nebraska-Wyoming border, and reached St. Louis in 1813. The story of these travels is told in Washington Irving's *Astoria.* Among the sources used by Irving were the journals of Brackenridge and Bradbury (cf. chap. 4, *post.*). A more critical recent study of the two overland trips is found in *The Discovery of the Oregon Trail,* edited by Philip Ashton Rollins.

2. John Bradbury was a British botanist who came up the river with Hunt. An excerpt from his journal is reprinted in chap. 4, *post.*

3. *Psoralea esculenta.*

4. The supposed descent of the American Indian from the lost tribes of Israel is not taken seriously by modern scholars. It is generally thought that the ancestors of the Indian came to America from Siberia by way of Alaska in late Pleistocene times.

5. In 1811 the Cheyenne Indians occupied the valley of the Cheyenne River, near the Black Hills.

6. Spelled "agalia" in Thwaites' reprinting of the second edition. The argali is an Asiatic wild sheep similar in appearance to the American Rocky Mountain sheep, or bighorn, which was probably the animal Brackenridge was thinking of.

7. A severe smallpox epidemic had occurred among the Plains Indians about 1786, another began in 1837.

8. "Or" is omitted from the first edition, but appears in the Thwaites' reprinting of the second edition.

9. Sheheke (Big White), a Mandan chief, accompanied Lewis and Clark down the Missouri in 1806 and was taken to Washington. Nathaniel Prior, or Pryor, was a sergeant under Lewis and Clark. In 1807, with the rank of ensign, he commanded a small military expedition organized for the purpose of returning Sheheke to the Mandan villages. The military party was accompanied by a trading expedition led by Pierre Chouteau. The Arikara and Mandan Indians were at war, and the presence of Sheheke among the white men led to an attack by the Arikaras. Three of Pryor's men were wounded; three of Chouteau's men were killed and seven were wounded. The white men retreated down the river, and Pryor took Sheheke

back to St. Louis. In 1809 Sheheke was returned to his people by the St. Louis Missouri Fur Company.

10. In Thwaites' reprinting of the second edition this appears as "refinement in vice."

11. In the original printing of the 1814 edition, where sentences came to a close near the end of the line, dashes were used to fill out the line. If such dashes were used in the present reprinting they would not necessarily appear at the ends of lines. For this reason they are omitted.

Chapter 4

1811

FROM THE ARIKARA VILLAGES TO THE NIOBRARA RIVER,

by John Bradbury

John Bradbury, a Scotchman living in England, was employed by the Liverpool Botanical Society to visit the United States and study and collect the native plants. Thomas Jefferson advised him to go to St. Louis, and gave him a letter of introduction which described him as "a botanist of the first order, . . . a man of entire worth and correct conduct. . . ."

He arrived at St. Louis in 1810, spent the winter there, and in 1811 ascended the Missouri River to the Arikara and Mandan villages with the expedition led by Wilson Price Hunt.

In July he returned to St. Louis in one of Manuel Lisa's boats, accompanied by Henry Marie Brackenridge. On December 5 he left St. Louis for New Orleans in charge of a boatload of lead belonging to a friend. On this trip the normal hazards of navigation were complicated by the severest earthquake that has occurred in North America in historic times.

Bradbury remained in the United States until the end of the war of 1812-15, but before the war broke out he sent some of his collections of plants to England. When he got to England he was greatly irked to find that some of the plants had been inspected and named by "a person of the name of Pursh."

Bradbury published his *Travels in the Interior of America* . . . in Liverpool in 1817. It was reprinted in *Early Western Travels*, edited by Reuben Gold Thwaites, in 1904. It is one of the most interesting and readable of the travel books of the period, and has considerable historical value. The narrative that follows, describing Bradbury's descent of the Missouri, from July 17 to 21, 1811, is from the original edition.

On the 17th I took leave of my worthy friends, Messrs. Hunt, Crooks, and M'Kenzie, whose kindness and attention to me had been such as to render the parting painful; and I am happy in having this opportunity of testifying my gratitude and respect for them: throughout the whole voyage, every indulgence was given me, that was consistent with their duty, and the general safety. Mr. Lisa[1] had loaded two boats with skins and furs, in each of which were six men. Mr. Brackenridge, Amos Richardson, and myself were passengers. On passing our camp, Mr.

Hunt caused the men to draw up in a line, and give three cheers, which we returned; and we soon lost sight of them, as we moved at the rate of about nine miles per hour. I now found, to my great surprise, that Mr. Lisa had instructed Mr. Brackenridge not, on any account, to stop in the day, but if possible, to go night and day. As this measure would deprive me of all hopes of adding to my collection any of the plants lower down the river, and was directly contrary to our agreement, I was greatly mortified and chagrined; and although I found that Mr. Brackenridge felt sensibly for my disappointment, yet I could not expect that he would act contrary to the directions given by Lisa, and had in consequence the mortification during the day, of passing a number of plants that may probably remain unknown for ages.

Our descent was very rapid, and the day remarkably fine; we had an opportunity, therefore, of considering the river more in its *tout ensemble* than in our ascent, and the changes of scenery came upon us with a succession so quick, as to keep the eye and the mind continually employed. We soon came in sight of the bluffs which border the Chayenne river, stretching as far as the eye could reach, and visible only through the low intervals in those bordering the Missouri. Before night we passed the Chayenne, and during a few moments had a view of its stream, for two or three miles above its junction with the Missouri. It is one of the largest rivers that falls into it, being at least 400 yards wide at its mouth, and navigable to a great distance.[2] The banks appear to be more steep than those of the Missouri, and are clothed with trees to the water's edge. On both sides of the river we saw numberless herds of buffaloe, grazing in tranquillity, some of them not a quarter of a mile from us when we passed them. We continued under way until late in the evening, and encamped on an island; a measure we determined to pursue when practicable, as we knew that to fall into the hands of the Sioux would be certain death.

18th.—We set out early, and continued under way during the whole of the day without interruption, and encamped on Great Cedar Island, where a French trader, named L'Oiselle, formerly had a post or trading house. This island is about two miles in length, and mostly covered with very fine cedar, and some rose and currant bushes, considerably overrun with vines, on which some of the grapes were already changing colour.

19th.—In the early part of the day we arrived at the upper part of the Great Bend, and continued to see innumerable herds of buffaloes on both sides of the river. I now found that although

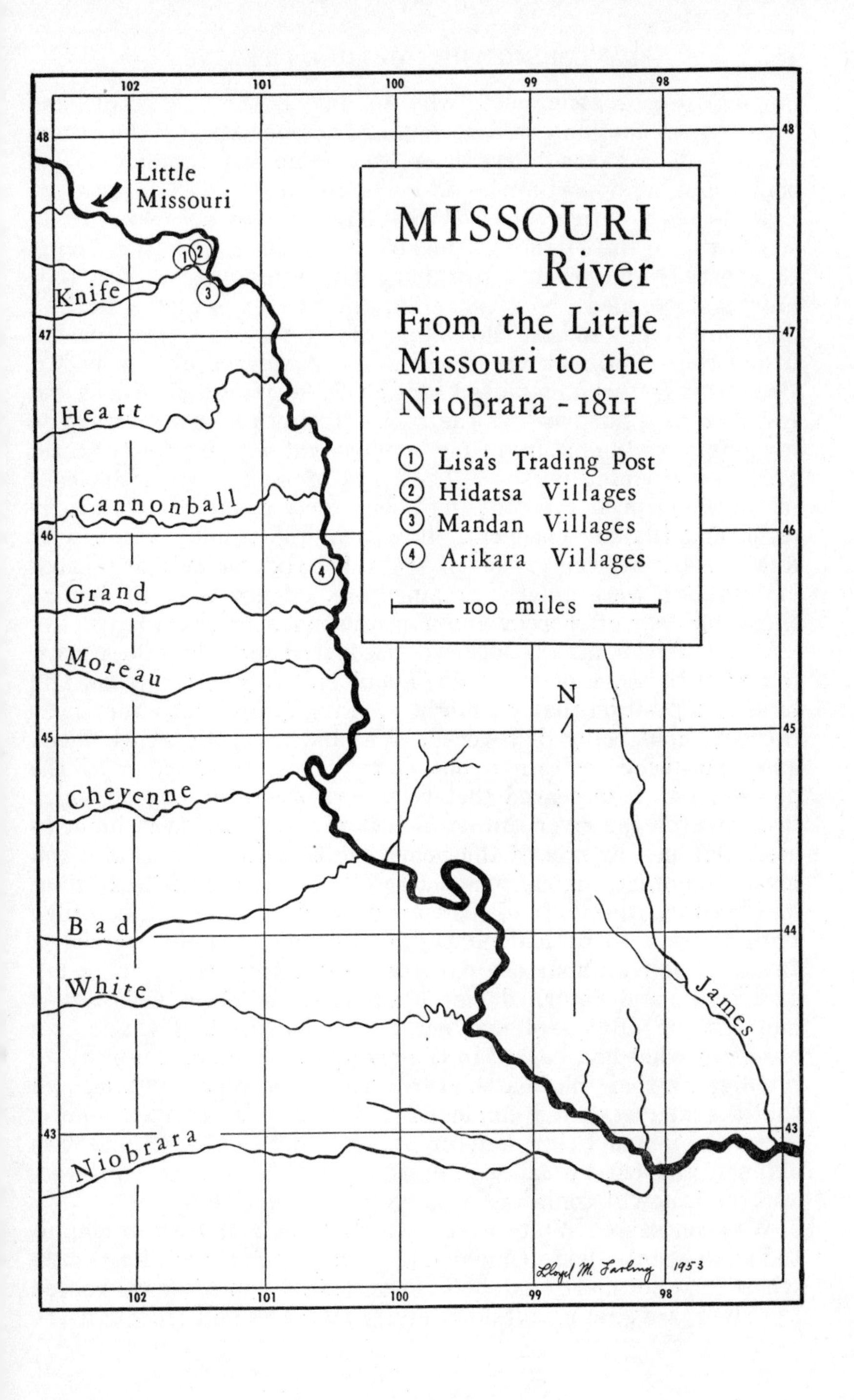
MISSOURI River
From the Little Missouri to the Niobrara - 1811
1 Lisa's Trading Post
2 Hidatsa Villages
3 Mandan Villages
4 Arikara Villages
100 miles
Little Missouri
Knife
Heart
Cannonball
Grand
Moreau
Cheyenne
Bad
White
Niobrara
James
N
102
101
100
99
98
48
47
46
45
44
43
Lloyd M. Farling 1953

our *patron*, or steersman, who conducted the first boat, and directed our motions, was determined to obey strictly the orders of Lisa as regarded expedition, yet from his timidity I had some hope of opportunities to collect.

Before we entirely passed the Great Bend a breeze arose, which ruffled the surface of the river: He put ashore, not daring to proceed, and we lay to during the remainder of the day, having descended about 280 miles in two days and a half. I determined not to lose this opportunity to add a few species to my collection, and was accompanied in my excursion by Mr. Brackenridge, who employed himself in keeping a good look out for fear of a surprise by the Sioux, a precaution necessary to my safety, as the nature of my employment kept me for the most part in a stooping posture. The track of land which is inclosed in the Bend probably contains about forty square miles, nearly level, and the soil excellent. It was at this time covered with fine grass, scattered groves of trees, betwixt which many herds of buffaloes were quietly grazing: we did not wish to disturb them, for fear of thereby enabling the Sioux to discover us.

20th.—About nine o'clock we discovered some buffaloes grazing near the edge of the river, about half a mile below us, and in such a position that we might apparently approach very near them without being discovered. We landed a little above them, and approached within about sixty yards, when four of the party fired. It appeared that two were wounded, one of which fled towards the river, into which it plunged, and was immediately pursued by one of the boats, whilst the party ashore followed the other, among whom I ran, but I was much less intent on obtaining the buffalo, than on procuring some plants which I knew were to be had on the bluffs, and actually succeeded. In about half an hour the party gave up the pursuit, being unsuccessful, and returned discouraged to the place where they had left me. But as I had not gone over the bluffs, and had observed what had passed in the river, I gave them the pleasing intelligence that the boat had overtaken the other buffalo, and that the men were now employed in dragging the carcass ashore. We soon joined them, and in a few minutes the animal was skinned and cut up. It was by much the fattest we had seen, and the tallow it contained was very considerable.

We soon passed White River, which is inferior both in magnitude and beauty to the Chienne, if we may judge from its mouth, where it is not more than 300 yards wide. Soon after we passed the river, we saw a buffalo running over the bluff towards the

Missouri, which put us on our guard, as we considered it a certain indication of Indians being near. Immediately below the river the vast vein of iron ore commences which has been before mentioned.[3] I again noticed its exact conformity on both sides of the river, in point of elevation and thickness of the vein.

As the evening approached we noticed a succession of flashes of lightning, just appearing over the bluffs, on the opposite side of the river. This did not for some time excite much attention, as it was by no means an uncommon occurrence; but we soon began to apprehend impending danger, as we perceived that the storm advanced with great rapidity accompanied with appearances truly terrific. The cloud was of a pitchy blackness, and so dense as to resemble a solid body, out of which, at short intervals, the lightning poured in a stream of one or two seconds in duration. It was too late to cross the river, and, unfortunately for us, the side on which we were was entirely bounded by rocks. We looked most anxiously for some little harbour, or jutting point, behind which we might shelter ourselves; but not one appeared, and darkness came on with a rapidity I never before witnessed. It was not long that any choice was left us. We plainly heard the storm coming. We stopped and fastened our boats to some shrubs, (*Amorpha fruticosa*) which grew in abundance out of the clefts of these rocks, and prepared to save ourselves and our little barks if possible. At each end of the boats there was a small deck: under these we stowed our provisions, &c.: next to the decks were piled the packs of skins, secured by ropes, and in the middle a space of about twelve feet long was left for the oarsmen. Fortunately for us, we had some broad boards in each boat, designed as a defense against arrows, in case of an attack by the Sioux. These boards we placed on the gunwale of the boats, and crammed our blankets into such parts as the lightning enabled us at intervals to see did not fit closely. Before we had time to lash our boards the gale commenced, and in a few minutes the swell was tremendous. For nearly an hour it required the utmost exertion of our strength to hold the boards to their places, and before the storm abated we were nearly exhausted, as also were those who were occupied in baling. As the river is in this place nearly a mile in breadth, and being on the lee shore, the waves were of considerable magnitude, and frequently broke over the boats. Had our fastenings given way, we must inevitably have perished. When the wind abated the rain increased, and continued for the greater part of the night, during which my friend Brackenridge and myself lay on the deck, rolled up in our wet blankets, congratulating ourselves on our escapes. For myself I felt but little: two years in a great measure spent in the wilds, had inured me to hardships and inclemencies; but I felt much for my friend Brackenridge. *Poor young man,* his youth, and the delicacy of his frame, ill suited him for such hardships, which, nevertheless, he supported cheerfully.[4]

In the morning the sun rose unobscured, which was to us extremely welcome, as its heat soon rendered us comparatively comfortable. We passed the river L'Eau qui Court,[5] and shortly afterward the place where we met the Poncar Indians, and as the wind began to blow fresh, we stopped five or six miles lower down, nearly at the place where I met the three Indians on the 24th of May. This enabled me to procure roots of the new species of currant, although with much pain and difficulty, having four miles at least to wade through water and mud, as the river had recently overflowed its banks. On my return to the boats, as the wind had in some degree abated, we proceeded, and had not gone more than five or six miles before we were surprised by a dull hollow sound, the cause of which we could not possibly imagine. It seemed to be one or two miles below us; but as our descent was very rapid, it increased every moment in loudness, and before we had proceeded far, our ears were able to catch some distinct tones, like the bellowing of buffaloes. When opposite to the place from whence it proceeded, we landed, ascended the bank, and entered a small skirting of trees and shrubs, that separated the river from an extensive plain. On gaining a view of it, such a scene opened to us as will fall to the lot of few travellers to witness. This plain was literally covered with buffaloes as far as we could see, and we soon discovered that it consisted in part of females. The males were fighting in every direction, with a fury which I have never seen paralleled, each having singled out his antagonist. We judged that the number must have amounted to some thousands, and that there were many hundreds of these battles going on at the same time, some not eighty yards from us. It will be recollected that at this season the females would naturally admit the society of the males. From attentively observing some of the combats nearest to us, I am persuaded that our domestic bull would almost invariably be worsted in a contest with this animal, as he is inferior to him both in strength and ferocity. A shot was fired amongst them, which they did not seem to notice. Mr. Brackenridge joined me in preventing a volley being fired, as it would have been useless, and therefore wanton; for if we had killed one I am certain the weight of his carcass in gold would not have bribed us to fetch him. I shall only observe farther, that the noise occasioned by the trampling and bellowing was far beyond description. In the evening, before we encamped, another immense herd made its appearance, running along the bluffs at full speed, and although at least a mile from us, we could distinctly hear the sound of their feet, which resembled distant thunder.

NOTES TO CHAPTER 4

1. Manuel Lisa, born of Spanish parents in New Orleans at an unknown date, came to St. Louis about 1790 and became a prominent fur trader. He led an expedition up the Missouri and Yellowstone rivers in 1807 and established a trading post at the mouth of the Bighorn River. He was one of the organizers and partners of the St. Louis Missouri Fur Company and became its ablest leader of trading and trapping expeditions. After the company dissolved in January, 1814, he was a partner in the Missouri Fur Company (1814-17) and president of the second Missouri Fur Company, organized in 1819. From 1814 to 1817 he was subagent for the Indians on the Missouri above the Kansas, and by a judicious combination of trade and diplomacy succeeded in keeping these Indians from joining the British during the War of 1812-15. He died in 1820. Lisa was sagacious and energetic, and was accused of being unscrupulous, but Hiram Martin Chittenden says (*American Fur Trade of the Far West,* chap. 5): ". . . in every instance there is present the animus of jealousy on the part of rival traders, and such evidence must be taken with much allowance. . . . His code was the code of the wilderness. He practiced it with unflinching severity, and his superior skill was chiefly what roused the ire of his less expert rivals."

2. At the mouth of the Cheyenne River on October 1, 1804, Lewis and Clark met Jean Valle, a fur trader from St. Louis who ". . . wintered last winter 300 Leagues up the Chien River under the Black mountains, he informs us that this river is verry rapid and difficuelt even for Perogues (Canoos) to assend and when riseing the Swels is verry high. . . ." Thwaites, ed., *Original Journals,* I, p. 176. There was never any steamboat traffic on the Cheyenne.

3. On June 28 and 29 Bradbury observed in the banks of the Missouri a substance he thought was hematite. He considered it an ". . . enormous body of ore, without doubt sufficient to supply the whole of North America with iron for thousands of years; . . ." Bradbury, *Travels. . . ,* pp. 80-82. At the time he was near the site of the present city of Chamberlain, South Dakota. No iron has ever been mined there, but a large deposit of low-grade manganese ore is known to be in the vicinity.

4. Of this incident Brackenridge wrote: "For myself, I was accustomed to these things; but I felt for my friend Bradbury. Poor old man, the exposure was much greater than one of his years could well support. His amiable ardor in the pursuit of knowledge did not permit him for a moment to think of his advanced age; . . ." Thwaites, ed., *Early Western Travels,* VI, p. 149. There is no indication in Bradbury's journals that he was especially old. Ewan, in *Rocky Mountain Naturalists,* says Bradbury was born in 1768, which would make him forty-three in 1811—this may have seemed old to Brackenridge, who was twenty-five.

5. The Niobrara River.

Chapter 5

1832

FIRST STEAMBOAT TO FORT UNION,

by George Catlin

The first steamboat to go above Council Bluffs on the Missouri River was the *Yellowstone*, operated by the American Fur Company. In 1831 it reached Fort Tecumseh, near the mouth of Bad River. In 1832, on its second voyage, it reached Fort Union, near the mouth of the Yellowstone River. Among the passengers was George Catlin (1796-1872), artist and student of the American Indian.

Catlin was not very proficient in art or anthropology but he attained a considerable reputation because of the intensity of his enthusiasm and the novelty of his subject matter.

He spent several years among the Indians, made hundreds of drawings and paintings, and collected great quantities of Indian artifacts. He exhibited these widely in the United States and Europe.

In 1841 Catlin published his *North America Indians, Being Letters and Notes on Their Manners, Customs, and Conditions, Written During Eight Years' Travel Amongst the Wildest Tribes of Indians in North America, 1832-1839.* Several editions have since been published, some having slightly different titles. The following narrative of Catlin's journey from St. Louis to Fort Union in the spring of 1832 is reprinted from an edition published in London in 1851.

Since the date of my former Letter, I have been so much engaged in the amusements of the country, and the use of my brush, that I have scarcely been able to drop you a line until the present moment.

Before I let you into the amusements and customs of this delightful country however, (and which, as yet, are secrets to most of the world), I must hastily travel with you over the tedious journey of 2000 miles, from St. Louis to this place; over which distance one is obliged to pass, before he can reach this wild and lovely spot.

The Missouri is, perhaps, different in appearance and character from all other rivers in the world; there is a terror in its manner which is sensibly felt, the moment we enter its muddy waters from the Mississippi. From the mouth of the Yellow

Stone River, which is the place from which I am now writing, to its junction with the Mississippi, a distance of 2000 miles, the Missouri, with its boiling, turbid waters, sweeps off, in one unceasing current; and in the whole distance there is scarcely an eddy or resting-place for a canoe. Owing to the continual falling in of its rich alluvial banks, its water is always turbid and opaque; having at all seasons of the year, the colour of a cup of chocolate or coffee, with sugar and cream stirred into it. To give a better definition of its density and opacity, I have tried a number of simple experiments with it at this place, and at other points below, at the results of which I was exceedingly surprised. By placing a piece of silver (and afterwards a piece of shell, which is a much whiter substance) in a tumbler of this water, and looking through the side of the glass, I ascertained that those substances could not be seen through the eighth part of an inch; this, however, is in the spring of the year, when the freshet is upon the river, rendering the water, undoubtedly, much more turbid than it would be at other seasons; though it is always muddy and yellow, and from its boiling and wild character and uncommon colour, a stranger would think, even in its lowest state, there there was a freshet upon it.

For the distance of 1000 miles above St. Louis, the shores of this river (and, in many places, the whole bed of the stream) are filled with snags and raft, formed of trees of the largest size, which have been undermined by the falling banks and cast into the stream; their roots becoming fastened in the bottom of the river, with their tops floating on the surface of the water, and pointing down the stream, forming the most frightful and discouraging prospect for the adventurous voyageur.

Almost every island and sand-bar is covered with huge piles of these floating trees, and when the river is flooded, its surface is almost literally covered with floating raft and drift wood; which bids positive defiance to keel-boats and steamers, on their way up the river.

With what propriety this "Hell of waters" might be denominated the "River Styx," I will not undertake to decide; but nothing could be more appropriate or innocent than to call it the River *of Sticks*.

The scene is not, however, all so dreary; there is a redeeming beauty in the green and carpeted shores, which hem in this huge and terrible deformity of waters. There is much of the way though, where the mighty forests of stately cotton wood stand, and frown in horrid dark and coolness over the filthy abyss below; into which they are ready to plunge headlong, when the mud and soil in which they were germed and reared has been washed out from underneath them, and with the rolling current are mixed, and on their way to the ocean.

The greater part of the shores of this river, however, are without timber, where the eye is delightfully relieved by wandering over the beautiful prairies; most of the way gracefully sloping down to the water's edge, carpeted with the deepest green, and, in distance, softening into velvet of the richest hues, entirely beyond the reach of the artist's pencil. Such is the character of the upper part of the river especially; and as one advances towards its source, and through its upper half, it becomes more pleasing to the eye, for snags and raft are no longer to be seen, yet the current holds its stiff and onward, turbid character.

It has been, heretofore, very erroneously represented to the world, that the scenery on this river was monotonous, and wanting in picturesque beauty. This intelligence is surely incorrect, and that because it has been brought perhaps, by men who are not the best judges in the world of Nature's beautiful works; and if they were, they always pass them by, in pain or desperate distress, in toil and trembling fear for the safety of their furs and peltries, or for their lives, which are at the mercy of the yelling savages who inhabit this delightful country.

One thousand miles or more, of the upper part of the river, was, to my eye, like fairy-land; and during our transit through that part of our voyage, I was most of the time rivetted to the deck of the boat, indulging my eyes in the boundless and tireless pleasure of roaming over the thousand hills, and bluffs, and dales, and ravines; where the astonished herds of buffaloes, of elks, and antelopes, and sneaking wolves, and mountain-goats, were to be seen bounding up and down over the green fields; each one and each tribe, band, and gang, taking their own way, and using their own means to the greatest advantage possible, to leave the sight and sound of the puffing of our boat; which was, for the first time, saluting the green and wild shores of the Missouri with the din of mighty steam.

From St. Louis to the falls of the Missouri, a distance of 2600 miles, is one continued prairie; with the exception of a few of the bottoms formed along the bank of the river, and the streams which are falling into it, which are often covered with the most luxuriant growth of forest timber.

The summit level of the great prairies stretching off to the west and the east from the river, to an almost boundless extent, is from two to three hundred feet above the level of the river; which has formed a bed or valley for its course, varying in width from two to twenty miles. This channel or valley has been evidently produced by the force of the current, which has gradually excavated, in its floods and gorges, this immense space, and sent its débris into the ocean. By the continual overflowing of the river, its deposits have been lodged and left with a horizontal surface, spreading the deepest and richest alluvion over the surface of its meadows on either side; through which the river winds its serpentine course, alternately running from one bluff to the other; which present themselves to its shores in all the most picturesque and beautiful shapes and colours imaginable—some with their green sides gracefully slope down in the most lovely groups to the water's edge; whilst others, divested of their verdure, present themselves in immense masses of clay of different colours, which arrest the eye of the traveller, with the most curious views in the world.

These strange and picturesque appearances have been produced by the rains and frosts, which are continually changing the dimensions, and varying the thousand shapes of these denuded hills, by washing down their sides and carrying them into the river.

Amongst these groups may be seen tens and hundreds of thousands of different forms and figures, of the sublime and the picturesque; in many places for miles together, as the boat glides along, there is one continued appearance, before and behind us, of some ancient and boundless city in ruins—ramparts, terraces, domes, towers, citadels and castles may be seen,—cupolas, and magnificent porticoes, and here and there a solitary column and crumbling pedestal, and even spires of clay which stand alone—and glistening in distance, as the sun's rays are refracted back by the thousands of crystals of gypsum which are embedded in the clay of which they are formed. Over and through these groups of domes and battlements (as one is compelled to imagine them), the sun sends his long and gilding rays, at morn or in the evening; giving life and light, by aid of shadows cast, to the different glowing colours of these clay-built ruins; shedding a glory over the solitude of this wild and pictured country, which no one can realise unless he travels here and looks upon it.

It is amidst these wild and quiet haunts that the mountain-sheep, and the fleet-bounding antelope sport and live in herds, secure from their enemies, to whom the sides and slopes of these bluffs (around which they fearlessly bound) are nearly inaccessible.

The grizzly bear also has chosen these places for his abode; he sullenly sneaks through the gulphs and chasms, and ravines, and frowns away the lurking Indian; whilst the mountain-sheep and antelope are bounding over and around the hill tops, safe and free from harm of man and beast.

Such is a hasty sketch of the river scenes and scenery for 2000 miles, over which we tugged, and puffed, and blowed, and toiled for three months, before we reached this place. Since we arrived here, the steamer has returned, and left me here to explore the country and visit the tribes in this vicinity, and then descend the river from this place to St. Louis; which Tour, if I live through it, will furnish material for many a story and curious incident, which I may give you in detail in future epistles, and when I have more leisure than I have at the present moment. I will then undertake to tell how we astonished the natives, in many an instance, which I can in this Letter but just hint at and say adieu. If anything did ever literally and completely "astonish (and astound) the natives," it was the appearance of our steamer, puffing and blowing, and paddling and rushing by their villages which were on the banks of the river.

These poor and ignorant people, for the distance of 2000 miles, had never before seen or heard of a steam-boat, and in some places they seemed at a loss to know what to do, or how to act; they could not, as the Dutch did at Newburgh, on the Hudson River, take it to be a *"floating saw-mill"*—and they had no name for it—so it was, like everything else (with them), which is mysterious and unaccountable, called *medicine* (mystery). We had on board one twelve-pound cannon and three or four eight-pound swivels, which we were taking up to arm the Fur Company's Fort at the mouth of Yellow Stone; and at the approach of every village they were all discharged several times in rapid succession, which threw the inhabitants into utter confusion and amazement—some of them laid their faces to the ground, and cried to the Great Spirit—some shot their horses and dogs, and sacrificed them to appease the Great Spirit, whom they conceived was offended—some deserted their villages, and ran to the tops of the bluffs some miles distant; and others, in some places, as the boat landed in front of their villages, came with great caution, and peeped over the bank of the river to see the fate of their chiefs, whose duty it was (from the nature of their office) to approach us, whether friends or foes, and to go on board. Sometimes, in this plight, they were instantly thrown "neck and heels" over each other's heads and shoulders—men, women and children, and dogs—sage, sachem, old and young—all in a mass, at the frightful discharge of the steam from the escape-pipe, which the captain of the boat let loose upon them for his own fun and amusement.

There were many curious conjectures amongst their wise men, with regard to the nature and powers of the steam-boat. Amongst the Mandans, some called it the "big thunder canoe"; for, when in distance below the village, they saw the lightning flash from its sides, and heard the thunder come from it; others called it the "big medicine canoe with eyes"; it was *medicine* (mystery) because they could not understand it; and it must have eyes, for said they, "it sees its own way, and takes the deep water in the middle of the channel."

They had no idea of the boat being steered by the man at the wheel, and well they might have been astonished at its taking the deepest water. I may (if I do not forget it) hereafter give you an account of some other curious incidents of this kind, which we met with in this voyage; for we met many, and some of them were really laughable.

The Fort in which I am now residing was built by Mr. M'Kenzie, who now occupies it. It is the largest and best-built establishment of the kind on the river, being the great or principal head-quarters and depôt of the Fur Company's business in this region. A vast stock of goods is kept on hand at this place; and at certain times of the year the numerous out-posts concentrate here with the returns of their season's trade, and refit out with a fresh supply of goods to trade with the Indians.

The site for the Fort is well selected, being a beautiful prairie on the bank near the junction of the Missouri with the Yellow Stone rivers; and its inmates and its stores well protected from Indian assaults.

Mr. M'Kenzie is a kind-hearted and high-minded Scotchman; and seems to have charge of all the Fur Company's business in this region, and from this to the Rocky Mountains. He lives in good and comfortable style, inside of the Fort, which contains some eight or ten log-houses and stores, and has generally forty or fifty men, and one hundred and fifty horses about him.[1]

He has, with the same spirit of liberality and politeness with which Mons. Pierre Chouteau treated me on my passage up the river, pronounced me welcome at his table, which groans under the luxuries of the country; with buffalo meat and tongues, with beavers' tails and marrow-fat; but *sans* coffee, *sans* bread and butter. Good cheer and good living we get at it however, and good wine also; for a bottle of Madeira and one of excellent Port are set in a pail of ice every day, and exhausted at dinner.

At the hospitable board of this gentleman I found also another, who forms a happy companion for *mine host;* and whose intellectual and polished society has added not a little to *my* pleasure and amusement since I arrived here.

The gentleman of whom I am speaking is an Englishman, by the name of Hamilton,[2] of the most pleasing and entertaining conversation, whose mind seems to be a complete store-house of ancient and modern literature and art; and whose free and familiar acquaintance with the manners and men of his country give him the stamp of a gentleman; who has had the curiosity to bring the embellishments of the enlightened world, to contrast with the rude and the wild of these remote regions.

We three *bons vivants* form the group about the dinner-table, of which I have before spoken, and crack our jokes and fun over the bottles of Port and Madeira, which I have named; and a considerable part of which, this gentleman has brought with great and precious care from his own country.

This post is the general rendezvous of a great number of Indian tribes in these regions, who are continually concentrating here for the purpose of trade; sometimes coming, the whole tribe together, in a mass. There are now here, and encamped about the Fort, a great many, and I am continually at work with my brush; we have around us at this time the Knisteneaux, Crows, Assinneboins and Blackfeet, and in a few days are to have large accessions.[3]

The finest specimen of Indians on the Continent are in these regions; and before I leave these parts, I shall make excursions into their respective countries, to their own native fire-sides; and there study their looks and peculiar customs; enabling me to drop you now and then an interesting Letter. The tribes which I shall be enabled to see and study by my visit to this region, are the Ojibbeways, the Assinneboins, Knisteneaux, Blackfeet, Crows, Shiennes, Grosventres, Mandans, and others; of whom and their customs, their history, tradition, costumes, etc., I shall in due season, give you further and minute accounts.

NOTES TO CHAPTER 5

1. Fort Union, at first called Fort Floyd, was begun in the fall of 1828 and remained in operation until about 1867. It was located about six miles above the mouth of the Yellowstone on the left (north) bank of the Missouri. It was the largest and best-equipped of all the American Fur Company trading posts. The buildings were enclosed by a twenty-foot stockade, 220 by 240 feet, with stone bastions 24 feet square and 30 feet high at the southwest and northeast corners. A detailed description of the fort as it was in 1843 is contained in *Audubon and His Journals*, edited by Maria R. Audubon, II, 180-88. Prince Maximilian visited the fort twice in 1833 and described his experiences in Chapters 16 and 22 of his *Travels in the Interior of North America*, reprinted in Volume XXIII of *Early Western Travels*, edited by Reuben Gold Thwaites. Charles Larpenteur, long a clerk at the fort, narrated his experiences in *Forty Years a Fur Trader on the Upper Missouri*, edited by Elliott Coues. Fort Union was general headquarters for other forts farther up the Missouri and on the Yellowstone under the supervision of Kenneth McKenzie, who was in charge of the American Fur Company's affairs in this territory from 1828 to about 1834.

2. James Archbold Hamilton, an Englishman of good education and aristocratic manners, was McKenzie's principal assistant.

3. "Around us" is not very definite. It is not likely that all these tribes were at Fort Union at one time in 1832, for the Blackfeet were traditional enemies of both the Assiniboins and the Crows. The Assiniboins and Knistineaus (Crees) usually traded at Fort Union, the Blackfeet at Fort McKenzie at the mouth of Marias River, and the Crows at one of several posts operated at various times on the Yellowstone River. Maximilian saw Assiniboin, Ojibway, and Cree Indians at Fort Union in 1833. At Fort McKenzie Maximilian witnessed a battle between bands of Assiniboins and Blackfeet, August 28 and 29, 1833. Maximilian, *Early Western Travels*, XXIII, chaps. 16, 20, and 22.

Chapter 6

1833

FROM FORT UNION TO FORT CLARK,

by Prince Maximilian

Alexander Philip Maximilian, Prince of Wied, was born in 1782. At an early age he became interested in the study of the natural sciences. These pursuits were interrupted by war; he became a major general in the Prussian army and was awarded the Iron Cross. When Napoleon was defeated Maximilian turned his attention to the affairs of science.

In 1815 he went to South America for two years' study of the flora and fauna and the native races. The collections and writings that resulted from the trip established his reputation as an exploring naturalist of the first rank.

In 1832 Maximilian came to the United States. In 1833 he ascended the Missouri River by steamboat to Fort Union, and went on by keelboat to Fort McKenzie. At this fort he had the pleasure of observing a typical battle between the Blackfeet and Assiniboin Indians. He nearly obtained a fresh Assiniboin head for scientific study, but the Blackfeet got to it first, and when they went on, it had no scientific value. The prince was irked by this loss to science, but he wrote an excellent account of the Indians and the battle, collected a good deal of flora and fauna, including two live bears, and descended the river in mackinaw boats by way of Fort Union to Fort Clark. He spent the winter of 1833-34 at Fort Clark, observing the natural history of the region and studying the Hidatsa and Mandan Indians. In the spring he returned to St. Louis and in July left the United States.

Maximilian was fifty-one years old in 1833, but appeared older. Alexander Culbertson, years later, remembered him as a man of nearly seventy, but well preserved, of medium height, slender, without teeth, fond of his pipe, speaking broken English, unostentatious, but somewhat irascible in his treatment of his assistants. He usually wore a white slouch hat, a rusty black velvet coat, and "probably the greasiest pair of trousers that ever encased princely legs."

His assistants were his servant, Driedoppel, and Charles Bodmer.

Bodmer was a Swiss artist of considerable ability; a fair colorist, a good designer, and an excellent draftsman. In later years he attained a respectable position in European art, but in this country he is known chiefly for the anthropological accuracy of the drawings and paintings of the Indians of the Missouri River that were used to illustrate Maximilian's account of his journey.

Maximilian's *Travels in the Interior of North America* was first published in German. It was translated by H. Evans Lloyd and published in

England in 1843. In 1905-6 the English translation was reprinted as Volumes XXII to XXIV of *Early Western Travels*, edited by Reuben Gold Thwaites.

Hiram Martin Chittenden called Maximilian's *Travels* "the most complete and elaborate work ever prepared upon this region. . . . The work covers a great variety of subjects—narrative, anecdote, history, ethnology, geology, natural history—and omitting a few errors, it is exceedingly accurate, discriminating, and judicious in all its scope."

From Chapter 23 of the English edition of 1843 I am reprinting Maximilian's account of his journey from Fort Union to Fort Clark, October 30 to November 8, 1833.[1]

On the 30th of October, the weather being fine, we left Fort Union, and stopped for a moment at Fort William,[2] opposite the mouth of the Yellow Stone, to take leave of Mr. Campbell. The thicket of willows on the steep bank of the river had been cut down, in order to open a view to the yet unfinished fort, which is about 300 paces from the bank. Mr. Campbell presented me with some specimens of natural history, and furnished me with cigars, of which we had long been deprived; they really are a great comfort on a long voyage. We took charge of his letters, and having taken leave, proceeded on our voyage. As the provisions for my people consisted of bad old bacon, and my own stock was limited to a ham which had been obligingly left to me, from the very scanty stock of provisions at Fort Union, with some coffee, sugar, and ship biscuit, we were very desirous of obtaining some game, and went on shore on a tongue of land, on the south bank, where we soon saw several wolves, and a troop of seven deer, but could not get near enough to fire at them. Great clouds of smoke rose from several parts of the prairie, doubtless caused by the wood-cutters of Fort William, the hunters of which we likewise perceived at a distance. The thickets were quite stripped of their foliage; the buffalo berry bushes alone yet bore some sere yellow leaves. Prairie hens, magpies, and the coal titmouse, the latter sitting among the willow bushes, were the only specimens of the feathered tribe which we observed. Numerous tracks of animals were visible on the beach, and among them the small delicate footprint of two different kinds of mice. We proceeded till eight o'clock in the evening, when we lay to, as it grew too dark to venture farther. Afterwards, however, the moon rose in great splendour, and towards morning we had a sharp frost.

Very early on the 31st we saw numerous flights of prairie hens crossing the river in companies of thirty or forty, and heard the whistling of the elk stag, which, at times, like that of our European stags, is heard at a late hour. When we lay to for breakfast, we were in a thick forest, with the same underwood as we have before mentioned, especially buffalo berries, in great abundance. They were of a beautiful bright red colour, and very palatable, for, like our sloes, they require a touch of the frost before they are good eating, yet they were still astrigent and acid; mixed with sugar, however, they were not unpleasant. With this fruit we refreshed our bears and my little fox, to which they afforded an agreeable variety in their food, but we did not fare so well ourselves, having hitherto tried, whenever it was possible, to obtain game, but in vain. Everywhere we found traces of beavers, gnawed trunks of trees, abattis and paths trodden smooth. The willow thickets were frequented by the coal mouse and magpie. As our firing had been ineffectual upon a flock of white swans and some wild geese, we again lay to near the Rivière Bourbeuse (White Earth River of Lewis and Clark),[3] and some of our hunters traversed the country, while the boat remained fastened under the steep bank. Flakes of ice already floated down the Missouri, and broke, with much noise, against the snags in the water. This ice comes from the tributary rivers; in this place it came from the Rivière Bourbeuse, and the noise occasioned by it is increased by that of the banks falling in, the dashing of the waves, and the high wind. My live animals, which would not eat pork, were half famished, and the bears especially made an incessant growling, which was in every respect highly disagreeable. Our hopes were disappointed; the hunters had missed two head of game; and, at four in the afternoon, I continued the voyage, though very slowly, because my people complained of fatigue. If the Canadians are not always well fed, there is no depending upon their perseverance. We lay to early for the evening, and the people dispersed in the forest to hunt. At the spot where we now were, we saw many traces of all kinds of game. Beyond a close thicket of young poplars (cotton wood), were sand hills covered with yellow grass, and yet further distant, a forest of lofty poplars, beneath which the ground was clothed with a dark red undergrowth of cornus, rose, and buffalo berry bushes, entwined round their stems with clematis and vine; a few grapes were still hanging on the branches, but they were very small and indifferent, and did not suit the taste of even my little fox. The hunters were again unsuccessful: they had seen nothing but the usual species of birds; and as for me, I found only a small flock of *Fringilla linaria,* which were so tame that they almost settled upon our fowling-pieces. Our supper was extremely frugal; but on the morning of the following day, the 1st of November, when we lay to at a scattered forest, Morrin was so fortunate as to kill a large elk, which quite revived our sunken spirits. In this forest there were deeply trodden paths of wild animals, and great numbers of prairie hens, which, however, were extremely shy; when they were roused they uttered a note almost like that of our snipes, not, however, fainter toward the close, but louder and stronger. The ground was so dry, and the withered leaves rustled so beneath our feet as we trod upon them, that we could not get near them. The small striped squirrel was pretty frequent here. Another elk was afterwards shot, so that we were well provided for several days, and the lamentations of my hungry animals were put a stop to. As we proceeded on our voyage we frequently saw game, and the prairie hens, like all birds of that kind, flew about us with the swiftness of an arrow.

The singular red, burnt, conical summits of the hills attracted our attention, till we lay to, at a little before four o'clock, near an extensive forest on the south bank, to dress our dinner. The poplar wood was thin, near the bank, but had a thick undergrowth of roses, in which were a greater number of traces of wild animals than we had yet seen, a sight which instantly set our hunters in motion. I found the pretty little four-striped squirrel (*Tamias quadrivittatus*),[4] in great numbers, which ran quickly along the ground, and up the trees, with the fruit of the rose in its mouth. My people caught one of these delicate creatures alive, which, to my great regret, afterwards made its escape. On account of the dry leaves we could not closely approach large game, though we heard the noise of considerable herds of them; and all our hunters returned before dark, except Mr. Bodmer, whom we looked for in vain. Night came on, we called, fired our pieces, but could obtain no intelligence of our fellow-traveller. We waited until eight o'clock, in no small anxiety, till at length we heard a shot higher up the river, which we immediately answered. Dreidoppel and Hugron instantly proceeded in that direction, and at length happily returned with our lost companion. In pursuing a stag, Mr. Bodmer had often changed his direction, and at last got quite bewildered; he had walked eight or ten miles, had been entangled in terrible thorny thickets, and got into a morass. At length he reached the prairie, where he perceived a troop of about twenty Indians, and hastened back into the forest; then, notwithstanding the Indians were so near, he fired six shots as signals of distress, and at length had the pleasure of descrying, from a hill, the shining surface of the river; thitherward he worked his way, directly through the thickets. As soon as he had been refreshed with some food, we loosened from the bank, where our presence had been betrayed by so many shots. We, however, lay to at a sand bank a little further down on the opposite side, and there passed a cold night, without fire or covering, in a high wind.

Next day, the 2nd November, was cold and bleak, and the tempestuous wind so unfavourable that we could only pass one tongue of land, and were compelled to stop nearly the whole day. A boat, laden with maize, belonging to Mr. Campbell, here passed us; it had left the Mandan villages a fortnight before. We had made our fire in a close thicket of poplars, under a high steep bank, sheltered from the wind. Our hunters dispersed in different directions, and I soon heard a shot not far distant, on which I advanced. Dreidoppel had roused two Virginian deer, and wounded one of them. We followed the trace of this animal, which we killed, and I succeeded in shooting the other deer, which would not abandon its companion. This success afforded us some fresh game, and my people employed themselves in cooking all the remainder of the day, nor would anything induce them to stir from the spot. We found, in the forest, traces of large bears, saw the prairie fox come out of its burrow, and found no other animals, except the small striped squirrel and one species of birds, the coal mouse, which defies the severe winter in these parts. In the afternoon we hoped to shoot wolves or foxes that might be attracted by the entrails of the deer we had killed, and, therefore, concealed ourselves; but only crows, ravens, and magpies, were lured by the bait. At six in the evening it grew dark; we increased our fire for the night, about which we sat till nine o'clock, while my *engagés* lay snoring on the ground. The surrounding wood was pitch dark; the wolves howled incessantly on both sides of the river, till the moon rose, and the wind abated, so that we were able to proceed before daybreak on the 3rd of November.

We again observed the black strata of the bituminous coal, and found fine fragments, which had fallen down, together with the pieces of the grey sand-stone of the adjoining strata. I increased my collections with the most interesting series of the rocks of the Upper Missouri, which, I regret to say, have not reached Europe, as they were irrecoverably lost.[5] On this voyage down the river I had better opportunities of examining the singular red, burnt, and conical tops of the summits of the bank, and they afforded me much interest. The rocky walls, and the red hills, covered with fragments burnt red, exactly resembled the refuse of our brick kilns, and they emitted, when struck, a clear sound, like that of the best Dutch clinkers. Under those red cones we generally saw a stratum of the bituminous coal; both often appeared together. I observed several slight hollows, resembling craters, surrounded by pyramids of the red rock. Caverns and holes, too, frequently appeared in this clay and sand-stone; and the remarkable light grey rocks, marked with darker transverse stripes, and with bright red tops, which now were pink, or different shades of crimson, as the faint rays of the sun here and there tinged them, and gave them a highly picturesque appearance. The swallows' nests fixed against the perpendicular walls, of which the Prince de Musignano made a drawing, were now completely deserted by their tenants. At noon we lay to at a prairie, which we explored while my people were cooking their dinner; but we found only ravens, crows, magpies, and prairie hens. The ground between the yellow, sere grass, was so dry that the dust rose at every step; it was, in some places, overgrown with rose bushes, from two to four feet high, symphoria, and groups of poplars. We did not encounter any buffaloes till we reached Fort Clarke; they appeared to have retired from the river; very frequently, however, we saw the paths and traces of other animals. Flocks of prairie hens, forty or more together, seemed particularly to choose, as their resort, the drift-wood on the banks of the river. A magpie was so tame that it settled on the rudder of the boat, while Morrin was at the helm. Towards evening we lay to, on the steep bank, where the kingfisher, the magpie, and the wren (doubtless, *Troglodytes hyemalis*), had taken up their abode, the latter among the dry drift-wood. Here we kindled our fire, in a tall poplar forest, where stems two feet thick nearly formed a circle. As we had passed the territory of the most dangerous Indians, and the nights became more and more cold, we constantly kept up a fire at our bivouac, and on this evening began our night-watches, because we were approaching a very numerous Indian tribe near the Missouri. Mr. Bodmer amused himself with taking a sketch of our bivouac in the forest, where we leaned against the trees, sat around the fire and smoked our pipes, amidst the concert of the howling wolves and the screeching owls. . . .

On the 4th of November, we passed, at noon, the mouth of

White Earth River (*Rivière Blanche*), or Goat Penn River of Lewis and Clarke. At this spot there was, formerly, a fort, which was abandoned in 1829, when Fort Union was built.[6] A little below the mouth of this river, the high wind obliged us to lay to; woods and thickets, with high dry grass, and prairies, either bare or covered with artemisia,[7] formed an extensive wilderness, traversed by the paths of stags and buffaloes, where we found many deer's horns and other remains of these animals, as well as tracks of enormous bears (*Ursus ferox*). We did not, however, see any large game, but only prairie hens, and a few stray blackbirds and flocks of the small finches (*Fringilla linaria*), which were picking up the seeds of the plants among the grass. It appeared that this wilderness had been visited by Indians a short time before. After a considerable halt we proceeded at two o'clock, passed the Butte Carrée, and lay to, in the evening, near a narrow strip of wood on the steep southern bank, behind which extended the prairie. The night was clear, the wind cold, and the moon rose at twelve o'clock.

The morning of the 5th of November was bleak and chilly, and the wind numbed the fasting travelers, till we lay to, at eight o'clock, at a prairie overgrown with thick bushes, where we prepared our breakfast, and where the number of prairie hens immediately induced our hunters to bestir themselves. I had unluckily loaded my piece with small shot, for a Virginian deer ran close by me from out of a thicket, which I might otherwise have very easily shot. We saw a troop of elks, and our little friend, the striped squirrel, which, however, is not yet found so low down the river as the Mandan villages. At eleven o'clock we proceeded on our voyage, in which we were protected by the high banks from the bleak wind, and enlivened and cheered by the sun. A herd of antelopes crossed the Missouri before us, and we in vain attempted to intercept them. These pretty animals generally leave the Missouri at this time, and hasten, on the approach of winter, to the Black Hills. A magpie alighted on the rudder, uttering its note, "twit, twit," which is quite different from that of the European magpie. We saw but few ducks and other water fowl, which had before afforded us so much amusement; doubtless, because they found more subsistence on the lakes, which were not yet frozen. We lay to, for the night, on the southern bank, where the forest was completely laid waste by the beavers. They had felled a number of large trees, chips of which were scattered about on the ground. Most of the trees were half gnawed through, broken down, or dead, and in this manner a bare place was formed in the forest. Not far off we saw in the river a beaver den, or, as the Americans call it; a beaver lodge, to which there was a very well trodden and smooth path, which we availed ourselves of, to go to and from our boat. Nature appears to have peculiarly adapted these remarkable animals to the large thickets of poplar and willow of the interior of North America, where the Whites, on their first arrival, found them in immense numbers, and soon hastened to sacrifice these harmless creatures to their love of gain. Numerous tracks of animals of all kinds, especially elks, bears, and wolves, were observed; the wolves prowled around us at no great distance, and at ten o'clock, when I had the watch, they came between our bright fire and the boat, which was only forty paces distant, being attracted by the smell of the meat.

On the next day, the 6th, we likewise met with many gnawed trees, which proved that the number of the beavers was still pretty considerable. Morrin had shot in the morning a fat fawn, which was gladly welcomed by us. We had traversed a forest admirably suited to the chase, when we met with a great deal of game, but, on account of the dry leaves, could not get near enough. Besides the animals which I have often mentioned, we saw some new species of birds, of which, however, I was quite unable to obtain a specimen.

At noon we passed the Little Missouri, at the mouth of which there were now extensive sand banks; we stopped a little below it, and found a spot very favourable for the chase, in a forest alternating with morass, high grass, and various plants, where we followed some fresh traces of large elks, without, however, being able to overtake them. We proceeded on our voyage till late in the night, and slept at a spot in the forest which was so dense, that we were compelled to hew down the bushes to make a space for our fire and resting-place. The night was dark, and the loud howling of the wolves was our never-ceasing music. Towards the morning there was a sharp frost, and the sky was partially clouded with the west wind. Our good genius had made us set out unusually early on the 7th November, for we had scarcely left the bank in the morning twilight, when we heard several shot, and soon after, at the very place where we had halted and slept, the loud voices of the Indians calling us to return. They were, probably, a hunting party of Manitaries,[8] who had been attracted in the early morning by the light of our fire. Being very happy at having, weak as we were, escaped visitors so little to be trusted, our *engagés* rowed with all their might, and there was soon a good distance between us. Our breakfast was prepared at nine o'clock, when we lay to on the north bank, in a narrow strip of forest, where we found some old Indian hunting lodges, built, in a conical form, of dry timber. They had, doubtless, been left by the Manitaries, who had come thus far on their hunting excursions. The lower part of the huts, or lodges, was covered with the bark of trees; the entrance was square, and bones were scattered in all directions. We proceeded with a bleak, high wind, saw the singular tops of the hills, and, in the forest, the stages made of poles, where the Indian hunters dry the flesh of the animals they have taken in the chase. About twelve o'clock we came to the spot where some stakes indicated the former site of a Mandan village. Manoel Lisa, the Spanish fur dealer, had formerly a trading post at this place.[9] Rather further on, after we had turned a point of land, we saw a white horse on the bank, and soon after a group of Indians, with their horses, which they had brought to the river to water. In the wood, close by them, was a winter village of the Manitaries, or Gros Ventres, to which they had removed only two days previous, from their summer dwellings, and whose present chief was Itsichaicha, which the Canadians translate, Monkey-face. They hailed us, but I would not stop, and, the current being strong, we rapidly passed them. An Indian woman, with a handsome brown hound, probably of the European race, stood on the bank, and formed a very interesting object in the wild winter scene. We were now in the centre of the territory of the Manitaries, and were in momentary expectation of meeting with these Indians; in fact, we soon saw several of them on foot and on horseback. We had just doubled a point of land, and were looking for a sheltered spot for landing, when we observed some huts in a lofty wood of poplars, and were immediately called to by some Whites and Indians. We recognized old Charbonneau,[10] and landed at once. It appeared that Messrs. Soublette and Campbell had founded a trading post in the Manitari villages, and that their people, together with these Indians, had arrived but yesterday at the winter village, situated at no great distance. The clerk, who had the management of the business here, was Mr. Dougherty, brother to the Indian agent, who had likewise accompanied Major Long in his expedition to the Rocky Mountains, and who had, at present, old Charbonneau as interpreter. The latter had lately quitted the American Fur Company, but subsequently returned into their service. The Indians, under their principal chief, Lachpitzi-Sihrish (the yellow bear), had arrived, as I have said, but yesterday, in the winter village; and Dougherty, with Charbonneau and several *engagés,* lived in some huts hastily erected on the bank of the river, while a better and more substantial house was building in the Indian village. Mr. Dougherty, to whom we delivered letters from Mr. Campbell, would not suffer us to proceed, and entertained us with much hospitality. It gave us much pleasure to be again in human society, after having been so long deprived of it. While we were chatting and smoking our cigars, we perceived, near where we were sitting, a row of large casks, and learned that they were all filled with gunpowder, which, considering the high wind that blew directly into the hut, was a great want of prudence. Many interesting Indians came successively, among whom was the old chief, who was particularly struck with our long beards, from which these people have a kind of aversion. The night was stormy and very dark: some of us slept in the boat; Dreidoppel and our *engagés* in the huts on shore.

The morning of the 8th November was bleak, cold, and frosty. I left the place early, accompanied by Charbonneau, and, after proceeding four miles, landed on the southern bank, to look for a petrified trunk of a tree, which Charbonneau had mentioned to me. While my people were taking their breakfast in a poplar wood, we proceeded alternately through thickets and open plains, towards the neighbouring hills, to the Fontaine Rouge, which was now a marsh covered with ice: not far from this was the tree, which is supposed to be part of an old cedar (*juniperus*); it is the lower part of a hollow trunk, with a portion of the roots; and, though this mass still perfectly shows the formation of the wood, it is now converted into a sounding stone. As the whole of this interesting specimen was much too ponderous to be removed; I carried off a good many fragments, without, however, disfiguring the tree, which will, doubtless, some day, find a place in some museum in the United States. This kind of petrified wood is not, by any means, unfrequent on the Missouri. Of the many interesting specimens of this kind which I had collected, very few have found their way to Europe.

After breakfast we continued our voyage, at eleven o'clock, and came to the spot where Mr. Pilcher's residence formerly stood, about eleven miles from Fort Clarke.[11] At twelve o'clock we were opposite the first Manitari summer village, and saw, on the other side, many Indians, who hallooed to Charbonneau. They had some smooth-haired hounds, spotted brown and white, with hanging ears, which were, doubtless, of European race. The invitations to land became more vociferous and numerous, and Charbonneau advised us to comply with them, which we did: we were immediately conducted, by a distinguished man, Ita-Widahki-Hisha (the red shield), to his tent, which stood apart on the prairie, on the summit of the bank. The white leather tent was new, spacious, and handsomely ornamented with tufts of hair of various colours, and at each side of the entrance finished with a stripe and rosettes of dyed porcupine quills, very neatly executed. It had been well warmed by a good fire, a most refreshing sight to us. We took our seats around it, with the numerous family, the brother and uncle of the chief, young men, women, and children. The chief had rather a long beard, like the Punca chief, Shudegacheh, and his right breast was tattooed with black stripes. The old uncle had a very ugly countenance; he was fat, and his dress negligent and slovenly. The wife of the chief held a child in her lap, with a thick hare lip. A large dish of boiled maize and beans was immediately set before us; it was very tender and well dressed, and three of us eat out of the dish with spoons made of the horn of buffalo, or bighorn; after which the red Dacota pipe went round. Our people had likewise obtained refreshments, and presented the Indians, in return, with some tobacco and gunpowder. After we had conversed half an hour, through Charbonneau, with these friendly people, and given them an account of our battle with the Assiniboins, their enemies, we took leave and proceeded on our voyage. The Indians accompanied us to the river-side, and on our way thither we saw the skin of a large white wolf hung on a tree, doubtless, by way of medicine, or offering. We left at one o'clock, and at two reached the Manitari village, Awachawi, which lay close to the bank; a couple of women, in their round leather boats, set us across the river; they had hung some wood to their vessel, and rowed with great rapidity; some others were proceeding towards the river, with their boats hanging on their heads and down their backs. I shall describe these boats in the sequel. At three o'clock we reached the Mandan village of Ruhptare, where a number of Indians came to the bank to greet their friends; Charbonneau hid himself, that they might not recognize him and invite him ashore. He had five names among these Indians—the chief of the little village; the man who possesses many gourds; the great horse from abroad; the forest bear; and a fifth, which, as often happens among these Indians, is not very refined. After we had passed the bend in the river, we saw the second Mandan village, Mih-Tutta-Hang-Kush, and, at no great distance beyond it, Fort Clarke,[12] which we reached at four o'clock, and were welcomed on the shore by Mr. Kipp, the director and clerk of the Fur Company, who led us to his house.

NOTES TO CHAPTER 6

1. My information about the life of Maximilian is derived mainly from Thwaites' Preface to the *Travels*. The description of the prince as remembered by Alexander Culbertson is from Bradley's "Affairs at Fort Benton." The quotation from Chittenden is from *The American Fur Trade of the Far West*. Discussions of Bodmer's Indian paintings (and of Catlin's) appear in DeVoto's *Across the Wide Missouri*, and Ewers' *Plains Indian Painting*.

2. Fort William was established in 1833 on the left bank of the Missouri below the mouth of the Yellowstone, by William Sublette and Robert Campbell, who sold it to the American Fur Company in 1834. At this time Maximilian's party consisted of himself, Driedoppel, Bodmer, Henry Morrin, and four French-Canadian *engages*. He had with him a collection of natural history specimens including two live bears and a live fox, in cages.

3. Now called Muddy River.

4. Grinnell, chap. 28, *post*, calls this animal the Missouri ground squirrel.

5. Most of Maximilian's collections were destroyed when the American Fur Company steamboat *Assiniboin* was wrecked and burned near the mouth of Heart River June 1, 1835.

6. This fort was built by James Kipp for the Columbia Fur Company in the winter of 1825-26. The property and personnel of the Columbia Fur Company on the Upper Missouri was taken over by the American Fur Company in 1827.

7. Several species of artemisia, commonly called sage, are found on approximately the western two thirds of the Northern Plains.

8. The Hidatsa Indians of the modern ethnologist were sometimes called Minitaree and sometimes Gros Ventres of the Missouri. They belonged to the Siouan linguistic family, but were more closely related to the Crows than they were to the tribes that are called Sioux, or Dakota. Maximilian found their language differed greatly from that of the Mandans, another Siouan tribe, but in most respects the culture of the Hidatsa and the Mandans was similar. Their villages were close together and they were usually allied in war. The smallpox epidemic of 1837 nearly destroyed both tribes; the survivors began to live together in one village for mutual protection against their enemies.

9. Brackenridge and Bradbury visited this fort in 1811. It was about twelve miles above Knife River, on the Missouri, and at that time was managed by Reuben Lewis, a brother of Meriwether Lewis. "The Fort consisted of a square block-house, the lower part of which was a room for furs: the upper part was inhabited by Mr. Lewis and some of the hunters belonging to the establishment. There were some small outhouses, and the whole was surrounded by a pallisade, or piquet, about fifteen feet high. I found attached to it a very pretty garden, in which were peas, beans, sallad, radishes, and other vegetables, under the care of a gardener, an Irishman, who shewed it to me with much self-importance." Bradbury, *Travels*, p. 143.

10. Toussaint Charbonneau and his wife, Sacajawea, had accompanied

Lewis and Clark from the Mandan villages to the mouth of the Columbia and back in 1805 and 1806. He told Maximilian in 1833 that he had lived with the Minitarees for thirty-seven years. He was employed by various fur companies and by the government as an interpreter, and sometimes as trader or hunter. There seems to be no record of him after 1839.

11. This was Joshua Pilcher, author of chap. 7, *post*.

12. Fort Clark was the most important American Fur Company trading post between Fort Pierre and Fort Union. It was built in 1831 and named after William Clark. It was located about eight miles below the mouth of Knife River, on the right bank of the Missouri, near where Lewis and Clark spent the winter of 1804-5.

Chapter 7

1838

THE INDIAN TRIBES OF THE UPPER MISSOURI,

by Joshua Pilcher

Joshua Pilcher was born in Virginia in 1790, arrived in St. Louis about 1815, and soon became prominent in the fur trade. He was a partner in the second Missouri Fur Company when it was organized in 1819, and became president after the death of Manuel Lisa in 1820. When the company dissolved about 1830 he became associated with the American Fur Company.

Pilcher was an able manager of trading posts and expeditions. He worked the Missouri River to the Mandan villages and the Platte to the Rocky Mountains.

In 1823 Pilcher was managing a post on the Missouri below the Great Bend when the second Ashley-Henry expedition was attacked by the Arikara Indians. Colonel Henry Leavenworth, commanding Fort Atkinson, organized a punitive expeditionary force and moved up the river with six companies of infantry, about 220 men. Pilcher joined the expedition with about 60 fur traders and 700 Sioux warriors. The Ashley-Henry expeditions furnished another 50 men and the combined forces, under the supreme command of Colonel Leavenworth, moved against the enemy.

Two of Leavenworth's keelboats sank with some loss of men and equipment but in each case he was able to report that the whisky was saved. With a thousand fighting men and an unknown quantity of whisky, Leavenworth arrived before the Arikara villages August 9, 1823. During the next three days there was a good deal of military and diplomatic maneuvering and a little cautious fighting. Then the Arikaras withdrew from their villages, at night. They were not much punished. The Sioux were not much impressed by the army's fighting ability. The fur traders were hopping mad. Leavenworth returned to Fort Atkinson and reported a successful campaign. The ultimate disposition of the whiskey is a historical mystery.

In 1835 Pilcher was appointed subagent on the Upper Missouri River. In 1839 he became Superintendent of Indian Affairs at St. Louis, and served until 1841. He died in 1843.

The memory of the Leavenworth campaign still rankled when Pilcher wrote the following essay, which appeared in the *Report of the Secretary of War* for 1838 under the title: "Extract from the Report of Joshua Pilcher."

The tribes originally assigned to the agent for the Upper Missouri, were the several bands of Sioux of that river, the Puncas and Cheyennes; since which time, all the Indians formerly embraced within the Mandan sub-agency have been assigned to him. They consist of Mandans, Minitarees, Crows, Assineboins, Crees, Blackfeet &c., and extend over the country west of the Mahas of the Missouri River, to the Rocky mountains; and from Arkansas river to the mouth of the Yellowstone.

It must be obvious to any one acquainted with the extent of the country and the habits of the Indians, that a general personal intercourse on the part of the agent is impracticable, and that his interviews with many of the tribes must result from casualty or accident.

The Puncas are a small band of the Maha tribe, and inhabit the country north of *L'Eau qui Coure* river, live a wandering life, and live almost exclusively by the chase, and trade chiefly at the mouth of *L'Eau qui Coure.*[1] They maintain friendly relations with the different bands of Sioux, and unite with them in resisting the assaults of the Pawnees of the River Platte.

The Sioux of the Upper Missouri are divided into the following bands; all speak the same language and range over the whole extent of country from the Mandan villages to the head of the rivers Platte and Arkansas: the Houkpapas, Sawons, Ogablallas, Tetons, and Yanktons.[2] These are the five principal bands, which are subdivided into a number of smaller bands, each deriving a name, either from the chief or partisan that heads it, or from some other trivial circumstance. They all lead a wandering life, and rely on the chase for subsistence. A very extensive trade has been carried on with them for many years, and no Indians ever manifested a greater degree of friendship for the whites in general, or more respect for our Government, than the Sioux. One of the bands above alluded to (the Yanktons) receive an annuity from the Government, having been one of the bands included in the treaty of Prairie du Chien in 1830. Some efforts have been made to induce this band to adopt a system of cultivation similar to that pursued by the Pawnees, Mahas, and some other tribes of the Upper Missouri; but a total indisposition to any other labor or exertion than such as appertain to the chase, has convinced the agent that any further attempt to improve their condition in that respect will be useless untill the means of subsistence from other sources shall have so essentially failed as to *drive* them to some other pursuit.

In addition to the several bands of Sioux before alluded to,

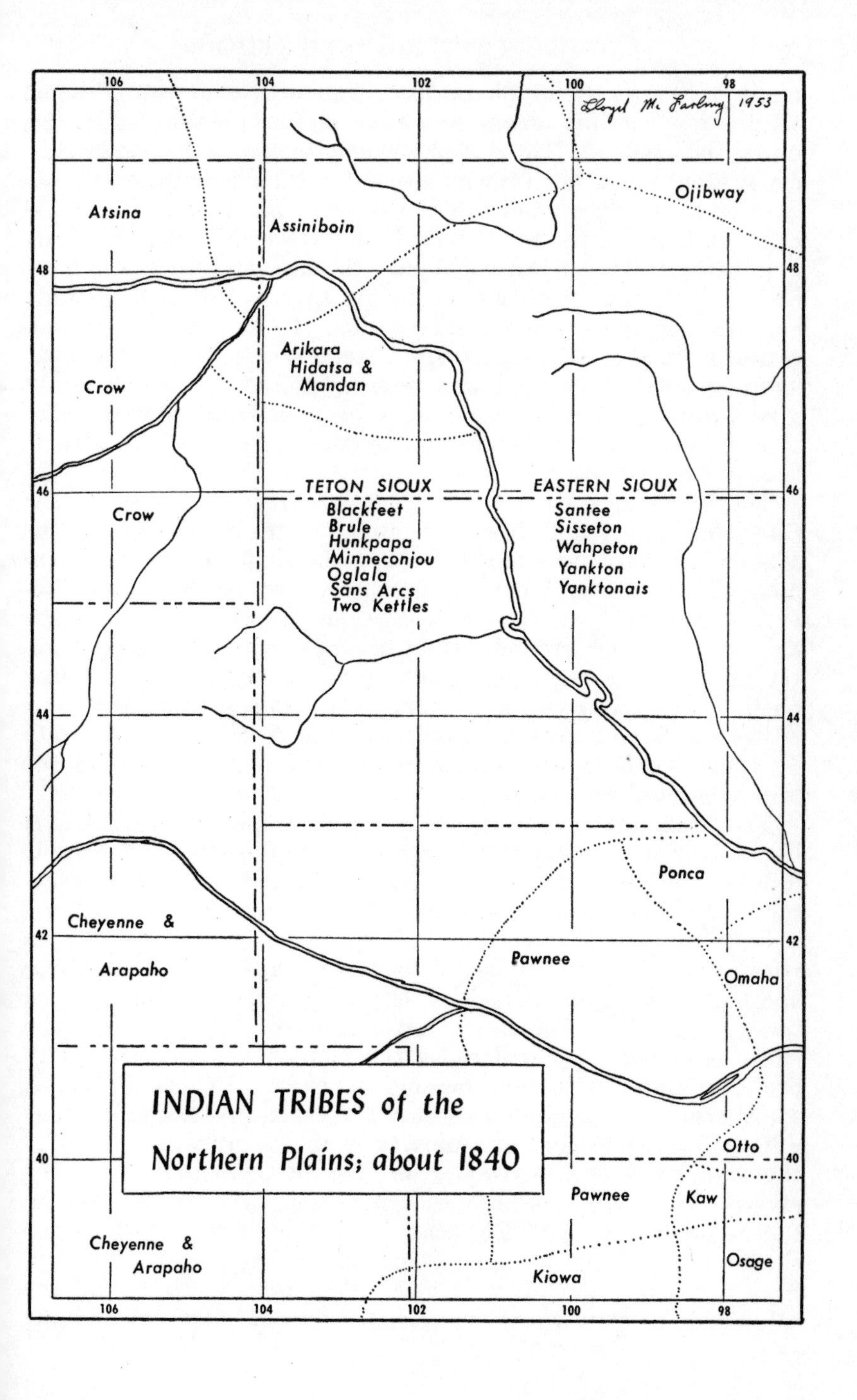
106
104
102
100
98
Lloyd McFarling 1953
Atsina
Assiniboin
Ojibway
48
Arikara
Hidatsa &
Mandan
Crow
46
TETON SIOUX
Blackfeet
Brule
Hunkpapa
Minneconjou
Oglala
Sans Arcs
Two Kettles
EASTERN SIOUX
Santee
Sisseton
Wahpeton
Yankton
Yanktonais
Crow
44
Ponca
Cheyenne &
Arapaho
42
Pawnee
Omaha
INDIAN TRIBES of the
Northern Plains; about 1840
40
Otto
Pawnee
Kaw
Cheyenne &
Arapaho
Kiowa
Osage

many of the *St. Peter* Sioux[3] have wandered over the Missouri within the last five years and may be considered, I suppose, under the agent for that region. Among them are the Yanktonas, a powerful band, not famous either for their general good conduct or their attachment to our Government. It is to these and other Indians on the St. Peters, that we are indebted for many acts of hostility committed during the late war with England, and the feeling engendered during that period will readily account for their present disposition. In the first communication I made to the department after my appointment as subagent in 1835, this band was referred to, as one which might give future trouble. Since then I have had occasion to refer to some depredations committed by them, and shall be glad if they are not followed by others.

The Cheyennes are a small tribe, who formerly lived on the Cheyenne river, and being in amity with the Sioux of the Missouri, ranged over and hunted in the same country, in common with the Sioux; but in consequence of jealousy and difficulties inseparable from Indians when different tribes occupy the same hunting grounds, the Cheyennes abandoned the country of the Sioux some years ago, and are now generally found on the Arkansas river, and carry on a trade with some of our citizens at a post on that river, near the crossing of the *Santa Fe road.* Their habits are, in all respects, such as those of the tribes heretofore mentioned.[4]

The Mandans and Minitarees are a couple of small tribes living in the permanent villages on the Missouri, about 1,600 miles above St. Louis, and cultivate corn and some other vegetables, making frequent excursions into the prairies for a supply of buffalo meat and robes, in which they have frequent rencontres with other tribes, but heretofore have sustained themselves against all assaults. During the last year, however, one of these tribes (the Mandans) have been so diminished by the small pox that they will cease to exist as a nation, and will probably unite with and become dependent on the Riccaras, (formerly their neighbors,) who have taken possession of their villages, and will continue to occupy them, probably, much to the annoyance of the traders as they pass up and down the river, and of those whose establishments are located among the Sioux below. The Riccaras[5] have long been notorious for their treachery and barbarity, and, within my own recollection, have murdered and pillaged more of our citizens than all the other tribes between the western borders of Missouri and the heads of the Columbia river. Since the earliest intercourse of the whites with the tribes on the Upper Missouri, until about eight years since, they had a village similar to that of the Mandans, about 170 miles below, and their habits, in all respects, were the same; and, though traders occasionally went among them, they committed frequent acts of hostility upon single individuals and small parties in different sections of the country; and in 1823 they committed such an outrage upon a party of our citizens[6] as to cause the officer then in command at Council Bluffs to fit out an expedition against them, in which he was joined by a number of volunteers; and having been an actor in the scene myself, I was so unfortunate as to differ with some others, and regard the result as a total failure; believing, as I did, that a *mistaken lenity* would only tend to exasperate the offenders, and lead to future acts of hostility of a character more aggravated than those previously committed. How far I may have been correct will be shown by subsequent events. The expedition alluded to led to one of a different character shortly after. In 1825 commissioners were sent up the Missouri as high as the Yellowstone, accompanied by a competent military force, though their objects were altogether pacific.[7] Treaties were entered into with all the tribes along the line of Missouri, as high as the Yellowstone, including the Riccaras of course. The efforts of our citizens to extend their trade into those remote regions commenced soon after, and by the application of additional means, and a more judicious organization of their business than had existed previous to that time, a very profitable and peaceable trade was opened with most of the tribes on the Missouri for a distance of more than 2,000 miles. In prosecuting their business, however, it was found that none of our operations with the Riccaras had changed their disposition, or was likely to result in any thing but increased abuses, as the extension of their business presented additional opportunities for pillage and exaction. All boats ascending the river, and parties passing over land, were laid under heavy contribution, and they were frequently beat and abused, and sometimes wantonly murdered, by wandering war parties, at a time when the tribe were gratified by having traders in their village. About the year 1831, the persons interested in the business, unwilling to submit longer to such outrages, determined to resort to the only means of punishment within their reach, and with this view withdrew the trade, and deprived them of supplies which habit had rendered almost indispensable. Thus situated, they were harrassed by their old enemies, the Sioux of St. Peters, until compelled to abandon their location on the Missouri and resort to the chase alone for the means of living. From that time until 1836, they continued to lead a wandering life, ranging through the country south of the Yellowstone to the head of the river Platte; down that river to the Pawnee villages; from thence across to the Arkansas; up that river to its source; and in these excursions have killed about seven and thirty of our citizens. Several of these outrages have been committed since Governor Dodge's council with them in 1835.[8] In 1836 they crossed the country from the river Platte and joined the Mandans, or rather took possession of their villages, being the stronger party; and as the Mandans have been literally annihilated, by causes heretofore alluded to, it may be considered a position which the Riccaras will occupy in future; and, if I mistake not, much to the annoyance of those who have been so imprudent as to invite them thither and encourage their continuance.

I have deemed it advisable to enter somewhat into details respecting these Indians, not by way of recommending any measures to be taken against them at present, but merely to develope their character and habits, and in the anticipation of *complaints;* none of which, unless of a character altogether different from such as I am led to expect, should receive the shadow of attention.

The same power that *drove* them from the banks of the Missouri, has been used to induce them to return, merely for the sake of a few packs of buffalo robes, and if heavy contributions upon all expeditions passing into the country above, and the exposure of all the establishments below, should be the consequence, the persons interested must attribute it to their own imprudence and folly. The Indian trade, when judiciously conducted, is its own best protection, and, moreover, the Government has quite enough on our immediate frontier to occupy its forces, without wandering into those remote regions to protect the trade. If let alone, it will protect itself.

The Assinaboins are a band of Sioux,[9] and their number heretofore has been imperfectly known; they range over the country on the Assinaboin, a branch of North Red river, and west in the direction of the Rocky mountains, between the Missouri and Sats-katch u-an rivers. Until a few years past, their intercourse has been confined to the British companies on the Assinaboin and Sats-katch u-an rivers, but, since our own traders have extended the line of establishments up the Missouri to the

Great Falls, a distance of 2,500 miles, most of the Assinaboin trade has been drawn to that river, and is carried on at Fort Union, near the mouth of the Yellowstone.

The Blackfeet are a tribe of Indians very numerous, and consist of five principal or distinct bands, viz: the Blackfeet, Blood Indians, Searcies, Peagans, and *Gros Ventres.*[10] These several bands inhabit the mountains and range over all that region of country, from the head waters of the Sats katch-u-an and Athabaska rivers, to the Arkansas and river Platte. Though they are called indiscriminately *Blackfeet,* I believe some of the bands speak different languages. They are frequently found along the foot of the mountains on the waters of the Yellowstone, and at other times on the different tributaries of the Columbia, and Colorado of the west. The aggregate number of these several bands is imperfectly known, and has been variously stated: believing my own means of information to be as likely to lead to as correct a conclusion as any other, I have heretofore estimated them at 60,000 souls, but cannot undertake to assume that as the *correct* number. Until a few years past our citizens have had no friendly intercourse with these Indians. Soon after the exploration of the Missouri and Columbia rivers, by Lewis and Clarke, many of them engaged in a system of trapping and hunting in the mountains, which has continued ever since. Some of their expeditions have been very successful, but they have uniformly encountered the hostility of the different bands of Blackfeet and many bloody rencontres have been the consequence. About six years ago, a large trading post was erected for the Blackfeet, by some of our citizens near the falls of Missouri,[11] 2,500 miles above St. Louis. Previous to that time most of their trade had been carried on at one of the Hudson's Bay Company posts on the Sats-kach-u-an river. The establishment on the Missouri, however, has drawn most of the trade in that direction, like that of the Assinaboins. The reasons are very obvious. Their chief articles for barter are buffalo robes, an article which the British companies never purchase; which, together with the liberal prices allowed by our own traders, has drawn most of the Indians to the posts along the lines of the Missouri.

The Crees are a very numerous tribe of Indians, inhabiting the country north of the Sats-katch-u-an river, from the foot of the mountains down to the lakes, and extend over all the region north as far as Hudson's bay. A band of that tribe have been drawn over to the Missouri, and trade at Fort Union, near the mouth of the Yellowstone.

The Crows are a band of wandering Indians, inhabiting the country on the Yellowstone river; there is nothing essentially different in their character and habits from the other tribes embraced in this report. They have generally maintained a friendly understanding with all the whites that have passed through their country, and a profitable trade is carried on with them at the mouth of *Rosebud* river, a branch of the Yellowstone.[12] No peace has ever been known to exist between them and the Blackfeet, and as they frequently roam over the same region of country, many bloody conflicts ensue between the parties.

With all the Indians embraced in this report, our citizens carry on an extensive trade, and the whole region of country alluded to is traversed with carts, wagons, and pack-horses, as circumstances require in the prosecution of their business; nor do the mountains present any obstruction to wheel carriages, in crossing to the region of the Columbia. The intercourse with that country is practicable, easy, and constantly increasing.

It will be perceived that all the Indians embraced in this report are much the same in their general character and habits of life, except the two small tribes of Mandans and Minitarees; all rely exclusively on the chase for a living, and wander over immense regions in quest of game, and in these excursions the different tribes occasionally meet and part on friendly terms, but such relations are seldom of long duration. War parties from one tribe against another are almost incessantly in motion; and, owing to the great number of whites that are now in the habit of traversing this great northwestern region for various purposes, it is a matter of no surprise when one of them falls a victim to his own wanderings, and a trait of character inseparable from wild savages.

The tribes herein mentioned, with the exception of some of the Sioux, are so remote as to render it very certain that our frontier will never be troubled by them; nor have the emigrating Indians any thing to fear, so long as they confine themselves to the limits prescribed to them. In regard to the number of each tribe, I will just remark, that it is impossible to ascertain it with precision; and as the department has been lately furnished with ample estimates on that subject, which will be found among the published reports of the last and preceding years, I will refer to those reports as data, with the single exception of the Mandans and Minitarees, each having been estimated at 15,000 souls, when 2,500 Minitarees and 1,600 Mandans was, in my opinion, the extent of their numbers.

NOTES TO CHAPTER 7

1. In modern terms these were the Ponca and Omaha Indians. The "L'Eau qui Coure" was sometimes called Running Water, and is now the Niobrara River.

2. In the *Seventh Annual Report of the Bureau of American Ethnology, 1885-1886*, the Dakota, or Sioux, tribes are classified in the following manner:

A. Santee
B. Sisseton
C. Wahpeton
D. Yankton
E. Yanktonais
F. Teton
  (a) Brulé
  (b) Sans Arcs
  (c) Blackfeet
  (d) Minneconjou
  (e) Two Kettles
  (f) Ogalalla
  (g) Uncpapa

The term Sawon or Saone has been variously and loosely used. Hyde says (*Red Cloud's Folk*, p. 12) that S. R. Riggs was told at Fort Pierre in 1840 that it was a nickname that the Oglalas and Brulés had applied to the other five Teton tribes, but (p. 13) that the name was also given to groups of Sioux who lived on the upper Minnesota River early in the eighteenth century.

3. The Minnesota River was called the St. Peter, or St. Pierre, River in 1838.

4. The Cheyennes migrated westward out of present Minnesota near the end of the eighteenth century, lived for a while on the Sheyenne River in what is now eastern North Dakota, then moved to the Cheyenne River west of the Missouri in present South Dakota. They remained here about thirty years, then moved farther west and south, dividing into two main groups called the Northern and Southern Cheyennes. They were very closely allied to the Arapahoes, and after about 1830 with the Teton Sioux.

5. The Arikaras, sometimes called Rees, belonged to the Caddo linguistic family and were related to the Pawnees. They were culturally similar to the Mandans and Hidatsas, with whom they were alternately at peace and at war.

6. The second Ashley-Henry expedition, led by William Henry Ashley, while trading for horses at the Arikara villages, was attacked by the Arikaras on June 2, 1823. Twelve whites were killed, two more soon died from wounds, and nine others were wounded. This affair led to the Leavenworth campaign against the Arikaras.

7. The expedition of 1825 was under the command of General Henry Atkinson, who was accompanied by Indian Agent Benjamin O'Fallon. Treaties were made in which the Indians acknowledged the supremacy of the United States and were promised its friendship and protection. There were also provisions relating to trade and the punishment of both

Indians and whites for offenses committed against each other. A brief "Journal of the Atkinson-O'Fallon Expedition," edited by Russell Reid and Clell G. Gannon, appeared in the *North Dakota Historical Quarterly*, October, 1929, pp. 5-56.

8. In 1835 Colonel Henry Dodge, with three companies of the First Regiment of Dragoons, about 120 men, journeyed up the Platte to the Rocky Mountains, went south to the Arkansas River, then along the Arkansas Valley to his starting point, Fort Leavenworth. On the Platte River, near the forks, he met the Arikara and held a friendly council with them.

9. The Assiniboins belonged to the Siouan linguistic family but were traditional enemies of the tribes usually called Sioux.

10. The Blackfeet were ". . . the South Piegan, North Piegan, Blood and North Blackfeet. Under their protection were the Gros Ventre (Atsina), a division of Arapaho. and a small tribe of foreigners, the Sarsi of the Déné family. . . ." Wissler, *Indians of the United States*, p. 86. The Blackfeet should not be confused with the Blackfeet Sioux, a Teton tribe. The Atsinas were sometimes called Gros Ventres of the Prairie, while the Hidatsas were called Gros Ventres of the Missouri. To make things more difficult for the historian and the reader the term Gros Ventre was often used by early writers without qualification, and once in a while it was applied to the Crow tribe. The term probably was derived from the ability of the Indians to put away great quantities of food.

11. Fort McKenzie, at the mouth of Marias River, about sixty miles below the Great Falls of the Missouri.

12. This is an allusion to Fort Van Buren, built in 1835, and abandoned and burned by the owners in 1842. For other "Crow Posts" on the Yellowstone, see note 7, chap. 18, *post*.

PART TWO

ON THE GREAT MEDICINE ROAD

Chapter 8

1820

FROM COUNCIL BLUFFS TO THE PLATTE FORKS,

by Dr. Edwin James

In the spring of 1819 the United States Army began a military operation that was at first called the Yellowstone expedition. An impressive armed force left St. Louis in four steamboats with the intention of ascending the Missouri River to the mouth of the Yellowstone. One steamboat sank, two stopped for the winter near present Atchison, Kansas, and one reached Council Bluffs, on the west bank of the Missouri about sixteen miles above the present city of Omaha. Here the army established Engineer Cantonment, sometimes called Camp Missouri, and spent the winter. In the spring the original plans were changed and no attempt was made to go farther up the Missouri. The Cantonment was moved to the top of the bluffs and became Fort Atkinson.

From Council Bluffs, in 1820, Major S. H. Long led a small exploring expedition up the valleys of the Platte and South Platte to the Rocky Mountains, thence south along the mountains, and back to near St. Louis by way of the Red, Canadian, and Arkansas rivers.

Among the explorers was Edwin James, botanist, geologist, and surgeon, who wrote *An Account of an Expedition from Pittsburgh to the Rocky Mountains, Performed in the Years 1819 and '20.* This report was published in Philadelphia and London in 1822 and 1823, and reprinted in *Early Western Travels* in 1905. From the Philadelphia edition I am reprinting the narrative of travel from Council Bluffs to the Forks of the Platte, June 6 to 18, 1820, omitting a description of the Pawnee villages.

Edwin James was born in Vermont in 1797, where he studied botany and geology and medicine. After the Long expedition he was an Assistant Surgeon in the United States Army from 1823 to 1833. He became interested in Indian languages and in 1833 published a translation of the New Testament into Ojibway. In 1837 and 1838 he was subagent for the Potawatomi Indians. He spent the final years of his life on a farm near Burlington, Iowa, where he operated a station of the Underground Railroad. He died in 1861.

James was a competent botanist. His knowledge of geology was limited by the undeveloped state of that science in 1820. His *Account* was based in part on notes taken and collections made by Assistant Naturalist T. R. Peale, and by Thomas Say, who was destined to become one of America's best-known zoologists. From the standpoint of scientific study this was the best equipped expedition to traverse the Great Plains for many years, and the *Account* contributed greatly to scientific knowledge, as well as being an interesting narrative of travel.

But the *Account* had one grave defect. James thought that white men would never be able to inhabit the Great Plains, and some of his statements contributed to, if they did not originate, the myth of the Great American Desert. But we should not blame James too much, for nearly every traveler who wrote about the Great Plains prior to the Civil War came to the same erroneous conclusion. For more than half a century there was something in the mind of the traveler that kept him from seeing the wealth of the grasslands.

The party, as now arranged, consisted of the following persons:

S. H. Long, Maj., U.S. Topographical Engineers, commanding the expedition.

J. R. Bell, Captain Lt. Artillery, to act as Journalist.

W. H. Swift, assistant Topographer, commanding guard.

Thos. Say, Zoologist, &c.

E. James, Botanist, Geologist, and Surgeon.

T. R. Peale, assistant Naturalist.

Saml. Seymour, Landscape Painter.

Stephen Julien, Interpreter, French and Indian.

H. Dougherty, Hunter.

D. Adams, Spanish Interpreter.

Z. Wilson, Baggage Master.

Oakley and Duncan, Engagees.

Corporal Parish, and six privates of the U. S. army.

To these we expected an addition, on our arrival at the Pawnee villages, of two Frenchmen, to serve as guides and interpreters, one of them having already been engaged.

Twenty-eight horses and mules had been provided, one for each individual of the party, and eight for carrying packs. Of these, six were the property of the United States, being furnished by the commanding officer at Camp Missouri; the remaining sixteen were supplied by Maj. Long, and others of the party. Our saddles and other articles of equipage, were of the rudest kind, being, with a few exceptions, such as we had purchased from the Indians, or constructed ourselves.

Our outfit comprised the following articles, of provisions, Indian goods, &c.; viz. 150lb. of pork, 500lb. of biscuit, 3 bushels of parched corn meal, 5 gallons of whiskey, 25lb. coffee, 30lb. sugar, and a small quantity of salt, 5lb. vermilion, 2lb. beads, 2 gross of knives, 1 gross of combs, 3 doz. fire steels, 300 flints, 1 doz. gun worms, 2 gross of hawk's bells, 2 doz. mockasin awls,

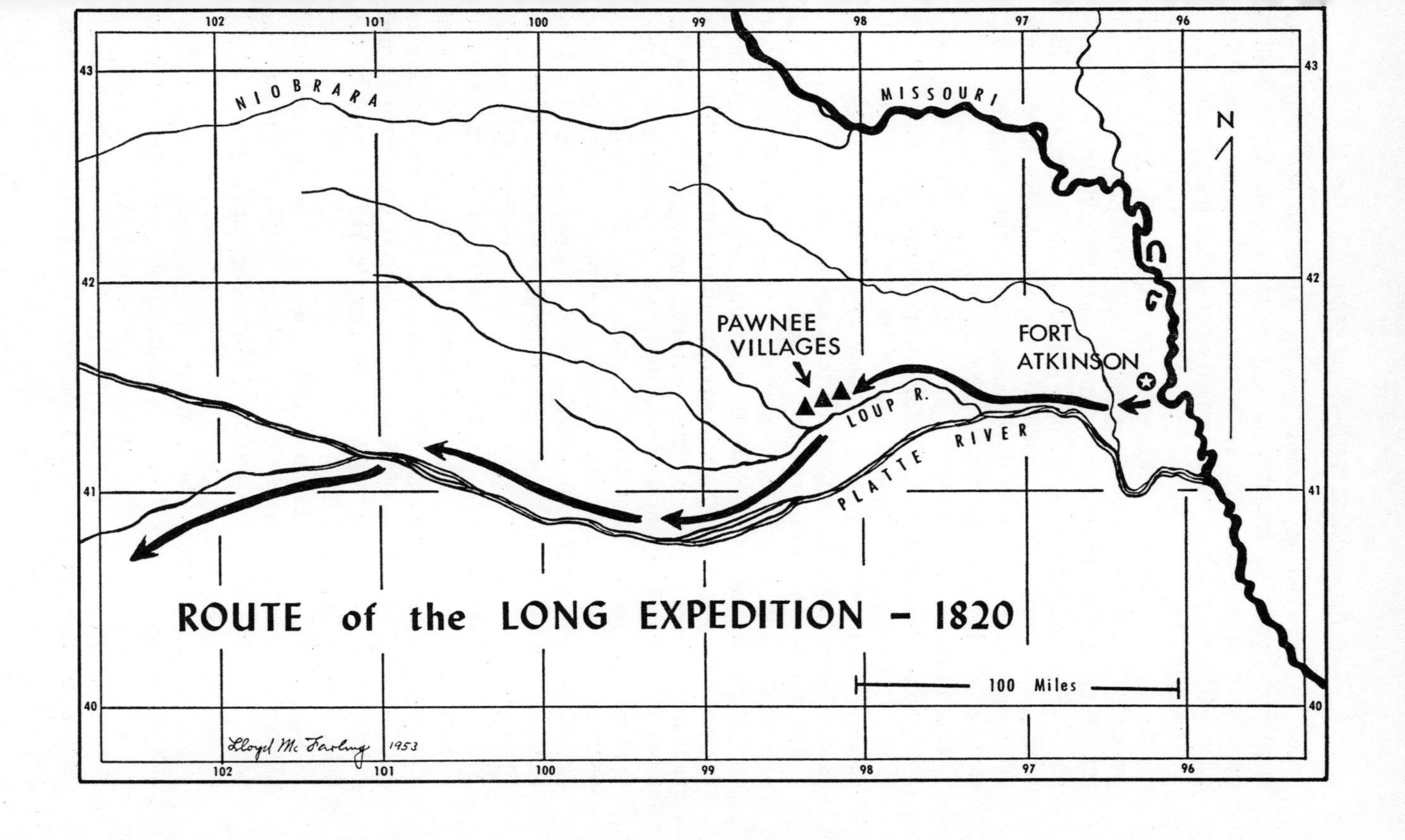
NIOBRARA
MISSOURI
N
PAWNEE VILLAGES
FORT ATKINSON
LOUP R.
PLATTE RIVER
ROUTE of the LONG EXPEDITION - 1820
100 Miles
Lloyd Mc Farling 1953
102
101
100
99
98
97
96
43
42
41
40

1 doz. scissors, 6 doz. looking glasses, 30lb. tobacco, and a few trinkets, 2 axes, several hatchets, forage-bags, canteens, bullet-pouches, powder-horns, tin canisters, skin canoes, packing-skins, pack cords, and some small packing-boxes for insects, &c.

The gentlemen of the party were supplied with such instruments as were deemed indispensably requisite in their several pursuits. The instruments for topographical purposes were, three travelling, and several pocket compasses; one sextant, with radius of five inches; one snuff-box sextant; one portable horizon with glass frame and mercurial trough; one and a half pounds of mercury, in a case of box-wood; two small thermometers; several blank books, portfolios, &c.

The hunters, interpreters, and attendants were furnished with rifles or muskets; the soldiers were armed exclusively with rifles, and suitably equipped. Our stock of ammunition amounted in all to about 30 pounds of powder, 20 of balls, and 40 of lead, with a plentiful supply of flints, and some small shot.

Several of the Indians about Council Bluff, to whom our proposed route had been explained, and who had witnessed our preparations, affected to laugh at our temerity, in attempting what they said we should never be able to accomplish. They represented some part of the country, through which we intended to travel, as so entirely destitute of water and grass, that neither ourselves nor our horses could be subsisted while passing it. Barony Vasquez, who accompanied Captain Pike, in his expedition to the sources of the Arkansa, assured us there was no probability we could avoid the attacks of hostile Indians, who infested every part of the country. The assault which had been recently made by a party of the Sauks and Foxes, upon a trading boat belonging to Messrs. Pratte and Vasquez, on the Missouri, above Council Bluff, in which one man was killed, and several wounded, had at this time spread considerable terror among those in any degree exposed to the hostilities of the Indians.

With these prospects, and with the very inadequate outfit above described, which was the utmost our united means enabled us to furnish, we departed from Engineer Cantonment, at 11 o'clock, on the 6th of June.

The path leading to the Pawnee villages runs in a direction a little south of west from the cantonment, and lies across a tract of high and barren prairie for the first ten miles. At this distance it crosses the Papillon, or Butterfly creek, a small stream discharging into the Missouri three miles above the confluence of the Platte. Lieutenant Graham and Mr. J. Dougherty accompanied us about five miles on our way; we were also met by Lieutenant Talcott from Camp Missouri, who crossed the bluffs on foot, to take leave of us. Much delay was occasioned, as we passed along, by the derangement of the packs, the obstinacy of the mules, and the want of dexterity and experience of our engagees; we however arrived early in the afternoon at the Papillon, where we encamped.

The Papillon, although it traverses a considerable extent of country, was at this time but a trifling stream. Its channel is narrow, the banks steep, and like many other streams which have their whole course in these arid plains, it is nearly destitute of water, except in rainy seasons.

During the night some rain fell, but as we were furnished with three tents, sufficiently large to shelter all our party, we experienced little inconvenience from the storm. Our baggage was also effectually protected, being laid in heaps, and covered with bear-skins; which were also spread over it when placed upon the pack-horses, during our march by day.

We had each two small blankets, which were carried upon our horses, one being placed under the saddle, and the other upon it. These, with the addition, in some instances, of a great coat, or a blanket-capot, and a valise or a pair of holsters, to supply the place of a pillow, were our only articles of bedding.

On morning of the 7th, a new disposition was made, in relation to the pack-horses, a man being appointed to attend particularly to each. We breakfasted, and recommenced our journey at an early hour, and moving forward at an easy pace, arrived about ten o'clock at the Elk-horn, a considerable river, tributary to the Platte. On the preceding evening, we had been joined at our camp by a party of four Frenchmen, on their way to a hunting camp of the Omawhaws to trade. We purchased of them two small brass kettles, to complete our supply of camp furniture. One of these men had been of Pratte and Vasquez's party, at the time of the late attack, and had received, in that affair, a wound in the back from a rifle ball, which was yet unhealed. In the morning they accompanied us to the Elk-horn, where the wounded Frenchman was one of the first to strip and plunge into the river. Surprising accounts are given of the hardihood, and patience under suffering, manifested by the Indians; but we have rarely seen one of them exhibit a more striking instance of insensibility to pain, than this Frenchman.

The Elk-horn, called *Wa-ta-tung-ya* by the Otoes, is, where we crossed it, about thirty yards wide, and during a great part of the year, too deep and rapid to admit of being forded. At this time our horses were barely able to keep their feet, in crossing the deepest part of the channel. Our heavy baggage was ferried across in a portable canoe, consisting of a single bison hide, which we carried constantly with us. Its construction is extremely simple; the margin of the hide being pierced with several small holes, admits a cord, by which it is drawn into the form of shallow basin.[1] This is placed upon the water, and is kept sufficiently distended by the baggage which it receives; it is then towed or pushed across. A canoe of this kind will carry from four to five hundred pounds. The squaws, who are exceedingly expert in this sort of navigation, transport not only their baggage, but their children, and sometimes adults, across large rivers, in these canoes, and with the most perfect safety. They place their children on the baggage, and convey the whole across the stream, by swimming themselves, and urging their charge before them to the opposite shore. It is rare that any unpleasant accident occurs in this primitive mode of ferrying. The Elk-horn enters the Platte about fifty miles above the confluence of that river and the Missouri. Its whole course is through a country nearly destitute of timber. The low plains which extend along its bank have a fertile soil; but the want of timber opposes a serious obstacle to their settlement.

The soil and climate here are so entirely similar to those of the country about Grand river and the Little Platte, already described, that no change in the vegetable productions could be expected. A species of onion, with a root about as large as an ounce ball, and bearing a conspicuous umbel of purple flowers, is very abundant about the streams, and furnished a valuable addition to our bill of fare.

Soon after crossing the Elk-horn we entered the valley of the Platte, which presented the view of an unvaried plain, from three to eight miles in width, and extending more than one hundred miles along that river, being a vast expanse of prairie, or natural meadow, without a hill or other inequality of surface, and with scarce a tree or a shrub to be seen upon it. The woodlands, occupying the islands in the Platte, bound it on one side; the river-hills, low and gently sloped, terminate it on the other.

At about three o'clock, P. M., a party of ten Indians were seen crossing the plain, towards the Platte, at a great distance before us. Soon after we arrived at a small creek, where was some scattered timber; here we determind to halt for the night, being informed by our guide that we would meet with no wood for twenty miles beyond.

As Indians had been seen in the afternoon, and we were aware of their being still in our neighborhood, it was thought proper to stake the horses as near as possible to the camp, and to station two sentinels, who were to be relieved during the night.

In our encampment we observed the following order. The three tents were pitched in a right line, all fronting in the same direction. In advance of these, at the distance of four feet, our baggage was arranged in six heaps, one at the right, and one at the left of the entrance to each tent, and protected from the weather by bear-skins thrown over them. This disposition was made, not only for the convenience of the party, but that our baggage, in case of an attack of the Indians, might serve as a kind of breast-work, behind which we might be, in some measure, sheltered from danger. At any rate, having our baggage thus arranged, we should know where to find it, and where to rally, in any emergency by day or night.

On the ensuing morning, (8th,) we continued our journey along the north side of the valley of the Platte, at the distance of four or five miles from the river, the direction of our course south, 85° west, which we followed near twenty miles.

In all our marches we observed the following order. Capt. Bell, mounted on a horse whose gait was regular and uniform, and well calculated for the estimation of distances, preceded the party, attended by our guide.—The soldiers and attendants, formed into two squads, for the better management of the pack-horses, followed in single file.—The scientific gentlemen occupied any part of the line that best suited their convenience.—Major Long followed in the rear, for the purpose of superintending the re-adjustment of deranged packs, and urging any disposed to linger, to the observance of a close order of march, a duty attended with no inconsiderable trouble and perplexity.

Though our route lay at the distance of several miles from the Platte, we could distinctly see the narrow and interrupted line of timber which grows along its course, and occasionally we had a transient view of the river itself, spreading like an expansive lake, and embosoming innumerable islands. About eighteen miles from our encampment, our course led us into the valley of a small river, called La petite Coquille or Muscle-shell creek, which we ascended six miles, not deviating from the course we had taken. In the middle of the day we encountered a violent thunder-storm without dismounting from our horses. The plain about us, for a great distance, was destitute of timber, and so level that our party formed the most prominent object in an extent of several miles. It is not surprising that, in this situation, we were a little startled at seeing the lightning strike upon the ground at the distance of two hundred yards from us. We could not have been deceived, in relation to this appearance, as we distinctly saw the water and mud thrown several feet into the air by the shock. The storm was so violent that, notwithstanding all our care, we could not prevent our baggage from being wet. We crossed the Coquille six miles above the place where it enters the valley of the Platte. This we effected with some difficulty, the banks being steep and muddy, and immediately afterwards encamped to dry our baggage.

The Coquille is about eight yards across; its bed muddy and the current moderate. Its course is circuitous, traversing some inconsiderable tracts of fertile and well wooded bottom land: in one of these our camp was placed. The night was warm and the mosquitoes swarming in inconceivable multitudes.

Our baggage had been wet on the preceding day, and again by a heavy shower in the night: as the morning was cloudy, we remained in camp for some time, and attempted to dry our clothes and blankets by a large fire. After breakfasting we again got upon our horses, and travelling nearly south-west, arrived in the afternoon at the valley of the Wolf river, or Loup fork of the Platte.[2] This river is called by the Indians the Little Missouri, on account of its resemblance, in the velocity of its current, the turbidness of its waters, and other respects, to that river.

Its sources are in the country of the Poncaras, opposite those of the Quicurre.[3] Like the Platte, its immediate valley is a broad and woodless plain, almost without any perceptible unevenness of surface, and bounded on each side by parallel ranges of low and barren hills.

During our ride, as we were approaching the Loup fork, we met two Pawnee Indians, handsomely mounted, and, as they informed us, on their way to dance the calumet dance with the Omawhaws. We gave them a small quantity of tobacco, and they departed, appearing highly pleased. In the fertile grounds, along the valley of the Loup fork, we observed several plants which we had not before seen: among these was one belonging to the family of the *Malvaceae,* with a large tuberous root which is soft and edible, being by no means ungrateful to the taste. We observed also the downy spike of the rabbit's-foot plantain (Plantago *Lagopus,* Ph.) intermixed with the short grasses of the prairie. The long-flowered Puccoon, (Batschia *longiflora,* N.) a larger and more beautiful plant than the B. *canescens* is here frequent. As we proceed westward, some changes are observed in the character of the soil and the aspect of vegetation, The Larkspurs and Lichnedias, (species of Phlox and Delphinium,) so common and beautiful in all the country between St. Louis and Council Bluff, are succeeded by several species of Milk vetch, some Vicias, and the superb Sweet pea (Lathyrus *polymorphus*). Every step of our progress to the west brought us upon a less fertile soil. We had as yet seen no game except a few antelopes, too wild and watchful to be taken without much trouble. In the low prairies we saw several curlews and marbled godwits, with their young; Bartram's sand-piper was also very frequent.

A little before sun-set we crossed Grape creek, a small and rapid stream of clear water, and soon after arrived at the Loup fork, where we encamped. The banks of this river are of a fine white sand, and are elevated no more than about eight feet above the surface of the stream, at a time of low water. It does not however appear that the low plains, contiguous to the Loup fork, are at any season inundated, the channel being sufficiently wide, and the current rapid enough to discharge all the water, which may at any time be brought down from above.

In the evening, and on the following morning, observations were taken to ascertain the magnetic variation, which was found to be 13½° east.

On the morning of the 10th, we crossed Beaver creek, six miles southwest of our encampment. Here we were compelled to carry across our baggage by hand, the creek being too deep and muddy to admit risking it on the pack-horses.

In fording this difficult stream, we had the misfortune to lose an important part of the lock of an air-gun, and as there were no means of replacing the lost article, it was determined to send back the gun from the Pawnee villages by one of the traders, who was soon to return to the Missouri.[4]

* * * * *

On the morning of the 14th, we left our encampment, opposite the village of the Pawnee Loups, and proceeded on our journey, taking the most direct course towards the Platte. Our party had here received an addition of two men, one named Bijeau, engaged as guide and interpreter, the other, Ledoux, to serve as hunter, farrier, &c. Both were Frenchmen, residing permanently among the Pawnees, and had been repeatedly on the head waters of the Platte and Arkansa, for the purpose of hunting and trapping beaver. Bijeau was partially acquainted with several Indian languages; in particular, that of the Crow nation, which is extensively understood by the western tribes, and, by frequent intercourse with the savages he had gained a complete knowledge of the language of signs, universally current among them. The great number, and the wide dissimilarity of the dialects of the aborigines render this method of communication necessary to them, and it is not surprising it should have arrived at considerable perfection among tribes who, from their situation and manner of life, must often find occasion to make use of it.

Besides these two men, a young Spaniard, a refuge from some of the settlements of New Mexico, joined our party, intending to accompany us as far as his fear of his own countrymen would permit. He had probably been guilty of some misdemeanor, which made it necessary to avoid his former acquaintances, and, on this account, he could not be induced to accompany us into the neighborhood of the Spanish settlements. The Frenchmen brought with them three horses and a mule, so that our party, which was now supposed to be made up for the journey, consisted, exclusive of the Spaniard, of twenty-two men, thirty-four horses and mules, and two dogs.

We were well armed and equipped, each man carrying a yauger or rifle gun, with the exception of two or three who had muskets; most of us had pistols, all tomahawks and long knives, which we carried suspended at our belts. We believed ourselves about to enter on a district of country inhabited by lawless and predatory bands of savages, where we should have occasion to make use, not only of our arms, but of whatever share of courage and hardihood we might chance to possess.

The country which we passed on the 14th, lying between the Loup fork and the Platte, has an undulating surface, except that portion of it which comprises the bottom lands of the two rivers. The ridges are of little elevation, destitute of stone of any kind, and irregular in direction; the soil is sandy and infertile. The high and barren parts of this tract are occupied by numerous communities of the Prairie dog or Louisiana marmot.

On arriving near the Platte we observed a species of prickly pear (Cactus *ferox. N.*) to become very numerous. It resembles the common prickly pear of New Jersey, (C. *opuntia.*) but is larger, and protected by a more formidable armature of thorns. Our Indian horses were so well acquainted with this plant, and its properties, that they used the utmost care to avoid stepping near it. The flowers are of a sulphur yellow, and when fully expanded are nearly as large as those of the garden pæony, and crowded together upon the summits of the terminal articulations of which the plant consists. These articulations, (or segments contained between the joints) are oblong and flattened, being longer and thicker than a man's hand. A second species, the *C. mamillaris, N.* occurs on the dry sandy ridges between the Pawnee villages and the Platte. The beautiful Cristaria *coccinea. Ph.* (Malva *coccinea. N.*) is very frequent in the low plains along the Platte. Its flowers have nearly the aspect of those of the common wild rose, except that they are more deeply coloured.

We arrived at the Platte, a little before sun-set, the distance from the Pawnees being, according to our computation, twenty-five miles. After entering the valley of the river, we travelled several miles across an unvaried plain, and at length passing down by a gradual descent of a few feet, we came upon a second level tract, extending to the river.

The soil of the first of these portions is a bed of sand, intermixed with small water-worn pebbles and gravel; that of the latter is more fertile, and produces a luxuriant vegetation.

Our guide informed us that the Platte, opposite the point where we entered its valley, contains an island which is more than one day's journey across, and about thirty miles in length.[5]

At no great distance from our camp, which was placed immediately on the brink of the river, we found the body of a horse lying dead in the edge of the water. The animal had, in all probability, been recently lost by a war party of Indians.

15th. Soon after leaving our camp we crossed a small stream, tributary to the Platte, from the north. It is called Great Wood river, and has some timber along its banks.

Our provisions being nearly exhausted two of the hunters were sent forward in search of game, but after some time they rejoined the party, having killed nothing.

Shortly afterwards a single bison was discovered some miles ahead of the party, and travelling apparently in the same direction. Four of our hunters, having disencumbered their horses of all their baggage, spurred forward in the pursuit, but none of them were able to overtake the animal, except the young Spaniard, who came near enough to wound it with an arrow; but his horse being exhausted he was compelled to desist from the pursuit, and suffer the bison to escape.

Having ascended the Platte about sixteen miles, we halted to make such a dinner as the condition of our stores would allow; and here the Spaniard took his leave of us to return to the Pawnees.

In the scenery of the Platte there is the utmost uniformity; a broad plain, unvaried by any object on which the eye can rest, lies extended before us; on our right are the low and distant hills which bound the valley; and on our left the broad Platte, studded with numerous small but verdant islands. On these islands is usually a little timber, which is not met with in other situations. We were fortunate in finding, towards evening, an old Indian encampment, where were poles, stakes, &c. which had been brought from the islands, and here we placed our camp. Some antelopes were seen during the day, but so wild and vigilant that all our efforts to take them proved unsuccessful. Our supper, therefore, was not of the choicest kind, and, what was infinitely more vexatious to us, was limited in quantity.

On the following day we passed a number of prairie dog villages, some of them extending from two to three miles along the river. Though much in want of game, most of our exertions to take these animals were without success. A number were killed, but we were able to possess ourselves of no more than two of them. These we found to be in good condition and well flavoured.[6] Their flesh nearly resembles that of the ground hog, or woodchuck (Arctomys *Marylandica*).

In some small ponds near the Platte we saw the common species of pond weed (Potamogeton *natans* and P. *fluitans*. Ph.) also the Utricularia longirostris? of Leconte, and an interesting species of Myriophillum.

By observations at morning and evening the magnetic variation was found thirteen and a half degrees east. In the middle of the day the heat was excessive, and we were under the necessity of halting at a place where no shade could be found to shelter us from the scorching rays of the sun, except what was afforded by our tents, which were set up for this purpose. Here we remained until 4 P. M. when we resumed our journey. We crossed towards evening a small creek, three miles beyond which we arrived at an old Indian camp where we halted for the night. We had not been long here before a tremendous storm of wind assailed our tents with such violence, that it was only by stationing ourselves outside, and holding the margin to the ground, that we were able to keep them standing.

Two of the hunters who had been sent out during the afternoon, returned to camp late in the evening, bringing in a buck antelope, a highly acceptable acquisition to us, as we had been for some time restricted to short commons. The flesh we found palatable, being very similar in every respect to that of the common deer.

We had proceeded but a few miles from our camp, on the following morning, when we perceived a number of antelopes at a little distance in the prairie. Being on the windward side of the party, they were not able, by their sense of smelling, to inform themselves of the nature of the danger which was approaching. One of them, "the Patriarch of the flock," leaving his companions came so near our line as to be within the reach of a rifle ball, and was killed by Lieutenant Swift.

The antelope possesses an unconquerable inquisitiveness, of which the hunters often take advantage to compass the destruction of the animal. The attempt to approach immediately towards them in the open plain, where they are always found, rarely proves successful. Instead of this the hunter getting as near the animal as is practicable without exciting alarm, conceals himself by lying down, then fixing a handkerchief, or cap, upon the end of his ramrod continues to wave it, still remaining concealed. The animal, after a long contest between curiosity and fear, at length approaches near enough to become a sacrifice to the former.

In the afternoon a single bison was seen at the distance of several miles, being the second since we had left the Pawnee villages, which were now about a hundred miles distant, and we were beginning to fear that the representations of the Indians, in relation to the difficulty of procuring game to subsist so large a party as ours, would prove true. We found, however, that every part of the country, which we had recently passed, had, at no distant period, been occupied by innumerable herds of bisons. Their tracks, and dung, were still to be seen in vast numbers, and the surface of the ground was strewed with skulls, and skeletons, which were yet undecayed.

At 4 o'clock P. M. we arrived at an old Indian encampment, opposite an island, on which was some wood, and perceiving that none would be met with for many miles ahead, we determined to halt here for the night.

The 18th, being Sunday, we remained in camp. . . . The plain about our encampment was strewed with the bones of the bison, and other animals; and among the rest we distinguished some of men. We picked up a number of human skulls, one of which we thought it no sacrilege to compliment with a place upon one of our pack-horses. Our guides could give us no satisfactory information of the time and manner in which the several persons, to whom these bones formerly belonged, had been compelled to lay them down in this place; it is certain, however, that at no very distant period a battle had been fought, or a massacre committed, on this spot.

We had now arrived at a point about two hundred miles distant from the confluence of the Platte and Missouri, yet the character of the former river was but little changed. It was still from one to three miles in breadth, containing numerous islands, covered with a scanty growth of cotton wood willows, the Amorpha fruticosa, and other shrubs.

NOTES TO CHAPTER 8

1. This was a variety of bullboat, apparently distended only by the baggage that was placed in it. Usually the bullboat was built over a framework of small trees or tree branches.

2. Now called Loup River.

3. A variation of L'Eau qui Court. Now called the Niobrara. The sources of the Loup are in the sand-hill country of northwestern Nebraska. The source of the Niobrara is farther west and a little north, in eastern Wyoming.

4. Omitted here is a description of a visit to the Pawnee villages. The Pawnees belonged to the Caddo linguistic group, and were related to the Arikaras. In 1820 there were probably about ten thousand Pawnees living in four villages in the Loup Valley. Like the Arikaras, Mandans, and Hidatsas, they lived in earth-covered lodges and did some farming, but ranged far into the plains to hunt buffaloes. They were probably the only Plains Indians to make human sacrifices, a practice that was discontinued early in the nineteenth century. Their numbers were greatly reduced by smallpox in 1837-38 and by cholera in 1849-50. They were traditional enemies of the Sioux, and usually friendly to whites, but committed some depredations against fur traders and travelers. Their history and culture is narrated and described in George E. Hyde's *Pawnee Indians*, 1951.

5. This was Grand Island—actually a series of islands divided by the channels of the Platte—important to pioneer travelers as a landmark

and source of fuel. Near its western end, on the right (south) bank of the Platte, Fort Kearney was established in 1848 to protect emigrants on the Oregon Trail. The Oregon Trail, coming from the southeast, first reached the Platte near Fort Kearney.

6. It was difficult to secure the prairie dog because it usually managed to get in its den, even when shot. It was not usually eaten for this reason, and perhaps, also, because it was called a dog. Actually it was not a dog but a rodent, allied to the marmots. Lewis and Clark called it "the barking squirrel."

Chapter 9

1839

FROM THE PLATTE FORKS TO FORT LARAMIE,

by Dr. F. A. Wislizenus

Frederick Adolph Wislizenus was born in Germany in 1810. In 1833 he joined an unsuccessful student uprising at Frankfort, and was forced to flee to Switzerland, where he continued his scientific and medical studies, taking his M.D. degree at Zurich. After some work in the hospitals of Paris he came to the United States in 1835 and in 1836 began practicing medicine at Mascoutah, Illinois, not far from St. Louis.

In 1839 Wislizenus "felt the need of mental and physical recreation" and decided he would make a journey to the wilder parts of the West. He went up the Missouri River to Westport, bought a horse and a mule and some baggage, and joined a caravan bound for the fur traders' rendezvous in the Rocky Mountains.

There were twenty-seven persons in the caravan. Nine of them were in the service of Pierre Chouteau, Jr., and Company, three were missionaries, two were wives of missionaries, and the rest were going to the mountains, to Oregon, or to California for various reasons. The fur company had four two-wheeled carts, each drawn by two mules and loaded with eight hundred to nine hundred pounds of trade goods. There were fifty to sixty pack horses and mules to carry the rest of the baggage. The caravan leader was ". . . Mr. Harris, a mountaineer without special education, but with five sound senses, that he well knew how to use."

They followed the trace that was soon to become known as the Oregon Trail, northwest to the Platte near Grand Island, west along the south bank of the Platte to the Forks, across the South Platte, along the North Platte past Fort Laramie to near Red Buttes, across the North Platte, up the Sweetwater River to South Pass, and across the pass to the rendezvous on Green River. With a smaller party Wislizenus traveled on to Fort Hall. With three companions he returned by a route which took him across the Laramie Plains, south near the edge of the Front Range of the Rocky Mountains, and back to Missouri over the Sante Fe Trail.

In 1840 Wislizenus published an account of his journey, in German. The narrative was translated into English by the doctor's son, and republished by the Missouri Historical Society in 1912 under the title *A Journey to the Rocky Mountains in the Year 1839*. From this edition I am reprinting Chapters 7 and 8 describing the travel from near the Forks of the Platte to Fort Laramie, about May 30 to June 14, 1839.

Except for trips to Mexico and Europe, Wislizenus spent the rest of his life in St. Louis, where he practiced medicine for many years. He became blind a few years before his death in 1889.

Our hunting party consisted of only three men. We had ridden but a few miles, when we saw Indians in the distance, who had probably seen us long before. One of them galloped toward us. He had no clothing except an apron about the loins; and no arms except bow and arrows. We halted. The Indian gave his hand in sign of friendship, and let us understand that a great Indian encampment was in the vicinity. Though the news was unwelcome, especially as we did not know to what tribe these Indians belonged, we continued our hunt. We soon saw buffalo, but they had been put into such turmoil by the Indians, who were hunting them, that it was a long time before we got a shot. From a hill I could survey the hunting of the Indians, and admire their skill as riders and as marksmen. Most of them were armed only with bow and arrow, though a few had guns. After we had ridden perhaps ten miles, we were lucky enough to kill three head. The last one was a cow. For a while she looked on as we flayed a bull, but forfeited her life by her curiosity. She had a calf with her that took to flight. The cow's udder was full of milk. We sucked out the milk, and found it refreshing and palatable. Laden with the hides, we returned at evening to the camp, where in our absence the Indians had also arrived. We now learned that there were on the other side of the river about five miles up stream a camp or village of several tribes of Sioux (Shiennes, Brulés, Tetons, and Arapahoes) and of the Ogallallas.[1] The Ogallallas and Sioux had formerly been at war; but had made peace shortly before this, and had united. The Indians who visited our camp had received small presents, especially tobacco; and, as the fur company still had some flour, had been regaled with sweetened mush, which was so much to their taste that, after satiating themselves to the full, they had taken the remainder with them. They also requested powder and whiskey, which was refused them on the pretext that we had no superfluity of the former, and nothing at all of the latter. Our leader, Harris, thoroughly realized that these unwelcome guests would further trouble us, and that just now was a most inadvisable time for crossing the river. So at night, after all the Indians had left, he caused the few barrels of spirits which he had with him to be buried, and enjoined on all of us the greatest vigilance. The night passed quietly. The next morning about sixty Indians on horseback appeared on a little rise in the neighborhood of our camp. They rode in a line up to our camp, giving a salute in our honor out of as many guns as they could muster, and sat down with us in a semi-circle. All appeared in gala attire, decked as far as possible with ornaments and bright rags, and with their faces freshly painted. One of them wore a red English uniform, on which he prided himself not a little. They had three leaders with them. One of them delivered an address, which may have been very eloquent, but of which none of us understood a word. To judge by his gestures, however, he had taken the pale faces to his heart, and expected in return evidences of our appreciation thereof. The pipe of peace was of course not forgotten, but went around the circle several times. The Indians received tobacco, which was divided out among the warriors by these leaders, and were again regaled with sweetened mush. In the afternoon, a second party of Indians arrived a-foot, with two divers colored flags, on one of which a star was embroidered, and on the other a cock. The Indian who bore the former was painted red in the face; he who bore the other, wholly black. Speeches and smoking, presents and feeding were repeated. Toward evening our guests left us, seemingly satisfied with their reception. While this was going on in our camp the rest of the Indians had broken up their own camp, and had established themselves across the river just opposite to us. The whole shore became alive. The tents were erected in several rows for about a mile along the river, and formed an interesting, though hardly agreeable, sight. The high, conical, leather tents with the projecting tent poles looked from a distance not unlike a sea-port. By our estimate there might be seven or eight hundred tents; later on, we heard there were about a thousand. As each of them contained at least one family, we estimated the whole number at five to six thousand. Our situation was critical. Separated from such a crowd, eager for robbing and plundering, and so superior to us in numbers, merely by a river, whose passage offered no special difficulties, there remained for us, should it come to hostilities, nothing but quietly to allow ourselves to be robbed, perhaps even scalped, or else to defend ourselves to the utmost without any hope for success. True, the Indians who had visited our camp today had behaved pretty decently; but every Indian has sufficient self-control to conceal his real plans. Besides, the Sioux have repeatedly shown themselves treacherous. All we could do for the time was to shun all cause for hostilities, and quietly delay the crossing of the river until the Indians should leave us. For they had given out that they were going the next day from here to the North Fork.

Morning appeared, but the Indian camp had not budged. On the other hand, we received abundant visits in ours. The river was about a quarter of a mile broad; quite rapid to be sure, but generally not very deep, so that one could cross a-foot or on horseback without much swimming. Besides, the Indians had made a little canoe out of buffalo hides, on which they crossed. Many squaws paid us their respects today. As none of us understood the Indian language, we had to communicate by signs, wherein the Indians have great skill. We obtained by barter with them several articles, such as tanned skins, mocassins, buffalo hides and the like. For a piece of chewing tobacco as big as a hand one could get a fine buffalo hide. Some Indians would sell everything they had on. But all showed immense curiosity.

They were continuously about us in our tents; all objects that were new to them they stared at and handled, not failing to appropriate some when unobserved. The two wives of the Missionaries were special objects of their curiosity. Among the guests who visited us today there was a leader of the Ogallallas, Bullbear by name.[2] He is rather aged and of squat, thick figure. He had one of his seven wives with him. Our leader knew him from former days as a friend of the whites, and so invited him to stay with his wife over night. Bullbear gave us to understand that he could answer for his tribe, but not for the others; and readily accepted. The other Indians toward evening went back over the river.

Mrs. Bullbear is not ugly, and knows how to accept the presents made to her with much grace. Her leather shirt is richly adorned with beads and embroidery. All night through matters were lively in the Indian camp. Dreadfully piercing notes came to us over the water; and then a chorus of some thousand dogs howled such night music as I have never yet heard. The next morning we saw with pleasure how the Indians struck their tents, packed their horses and dogs, and gradually set themselves in motion toward the North Fork. We watched the march with our spy-glasses. The North Fork was only about three miles from us. The Indians crossed it, and set up their camp on the further shore. They also seemed to watch us, for they directed little mirrors toward us. Glad to be rid of our guests, we set in earnest about finishing the canoe at which we had hitherto worked but slowly. These canoes are made in the following manner: Small trunks of some wood that bends easily are split; out of these a boat-shaped frame-work is made with some cross-pieces inside; this is firmly bound with thongs of buffalo leather and willow bark, and all gaps are stopped with withes; and buffalo hides, sewed together, with the hair inside, are stretched as taut as can be over the whole. Then it is dried in the air, and the outside daubed over with a mixture of buffalo tallow and ashes. Our canoe was covered with three buffalo hides, and was about fifteen feet long by a width in the middle of five to six feet.[3] It was finished toward evening, but we still spent the night here, to dig up the buried barrels of spirits. The next morning our canoe was put into the water. Though everything seemed quiet in the Indian camp, our leader preferred to cross the river somewhat further up. He detailed four men to draw up the canoe along the shore. The rest of us marched about ten miles and camped again on the river. The canoe arrived too late for crossing that same day; but on the next day we finally accomplished our passage. The river was rather broad and swift, but deep in only a few places. As far as walking was possible, the four men pulled the boat through the water; then paddles and poles were used, during which time we were often carried far down stream. Each passage to and fro took over an hour. First, all the baggage and the empty carts were carried over in the canoe; then the passengers; finally the horses and mules were driven through the water. Apart from some few mishaps, arousing more laughter than sympathy, all went well. In addition, we made ten miles that day, going up the stream, and camping on it. [End of Chapter 7.]

The left bank of the southern Platte, which we are now ascending, is very sandy; the vegetation is scant. The bluffs close at hand are also of sandstone. A tower-like column of pure river sand rises in noticeable prominence. For some days we went up the river. We observed very many bitter herbs, especially wormwood[4]; also *Pomme Blanche* (*Psoralea esculenta*), whose knobby root contains much starch, has a pleasant taste, and is gathered by the Indians. Long garlands of blooming wild roses frequently extended along the river. We saw no buffalo, but our hunters shot on the bluffs several antelope, so that we suffered no want. On the third day (June 6th) we left the river, going across a plateau in a northwesterly direction toward the North Fork. On this plateau we saw for the first time wild horses. They were very skittish. Their sense of smell is said to be very keen. We also got sight of the European rabbit, which is not found in the eastern part of the United States. The day was very sultry. We covered eighteen miles before we found some water in a puddle. In the afternoon, while we were again on the march, we were overtaken by a terrible hailstorm. Some of the hailstones were as big as pigeon eggs. The horses on which we rode could hardly be held in check; but the pack animals ran away as if under the lash. The hailstorm lasted, with short interruptions, about half an hour. We then gathered up our pack animals, which had run miles in the meantime, and camped near Ash Creek, which empties into the North Fork. The next morning we reached the North Fork, but it was noon before we could find a passage for our carts. The North Fork with its surroundings is just like the South Fork—much sand, little wood, no buffalo. We are now to go up the right side of the river about one hundred and sixty miles to Fort Laramie. The next day we saw four Indians on the further bank. They swam over. They were Shiennes. They gave us to understand that their tribe had parted from the Sioux and would be here in a few days to go up the river with us. They urged us, therefore, to wait. Our leader acted as if he did not understand them, gave them some tobacco, and went on. The next day we received a second embassy, but with no better result. The bluffs of our side, on which I now saw for the first time some cedars, gradually diminished until they were lost in the prairie. But behind them reddish cliffs arose, steeper and more imposing than we had yet seen. The sand formation prevails in them also. Several such rows of cliffs are crowded together *en echelon,* with a grassy embankment in front of each, flattening down at the end of the chain. Each chain consists of more or less broken down (weather worn) rocks, often presenting the strangest of shapes. So the first cliff in the first chain, perhaps eight miles from the river, presented quite the appearance of an old castle or citadel. More remarkable still is the last cliff of the same chain. Its tower-like top is seen from a distance of thirty or forty miles, for which reason it has been called the chimney. It is only a mile from the river. The cone-shaped base constitutes about three-fourths of its height, the pyramidal top one-quarter of it. The foundation is limestone; above it is crumbling sandstone. The height of the whole is given as 525 feet; that of the top part as 125 feet.[5]

Heavy down-pourings of rain often interrupted our journey. Almost daily we had thunderstorms, for which the Platte is notorious. One time we had to stay in camp almost all day on account of the rain; but by way of compensation we found a quantity of pine wood and cedar wood, washed down from the rocks on which it grows sparsely; and beside the blazing fire we laughed at the weather and forgot all discomfort. The next day the sky cleared. We traveled somewhat away from the river, toward the left, and enjoyed a picturesque landscape. All about were rocks piled up by Nature in merry mood, giving full scope to fancy in the variety of their shapes. Some were perfect cones; others flat round tops; others, owing to their crenulated projections, resemble fortresses; others old castles, porticos, etc. Most of them were sparsely covered with pine and cedar. The scenery has obvious resemblance to several places in Saxon Switzerland.

At noon we halted in a little valley where rocks from either side confronted each other at a distance of half a mile. A fresh spring meanders through the valley. We encamped on the hill from which the spring flows. The place had something romantic about it. All around grew pine and cedars, wild roses, gooseberries and currants; from the top of the hill one enjoyed a wide prospect. On the one side the Chimney and the whole chain of rocks we had passed showed themselves; on the other side, fresh hills. Before us lay the Platte. The magnificent surroundings, the clear sky and fresh antelope meat put us all in good humor. But increasing sultriness reminded us soon that we had not yet received our daily allowance of thunder showers. We traveled twelve miles in the rain that afternoon, and camped by the stream, at whose spring we had our noon rest. It was so swollen by the rains that we had to postpone crossing till the next day. The next morning we crossed it, as well as Horse Creek, only a few hundred steps further on, and then turned, over a long uninteresting hill, again toward the river. From the top of the hill we saw in the western distance the Black Hills,[6] a chain of mountains we must cross later on.

Near the Platte I saw on this occasion for the first time a so-called prairie-dog village. Single dwellings of this strange animal we had already observed on the South Fork; but here we had a whole colony before us, and also got a look at some of the shy inhabitants. The prairie dog (prairie marmot, *Arctomys*

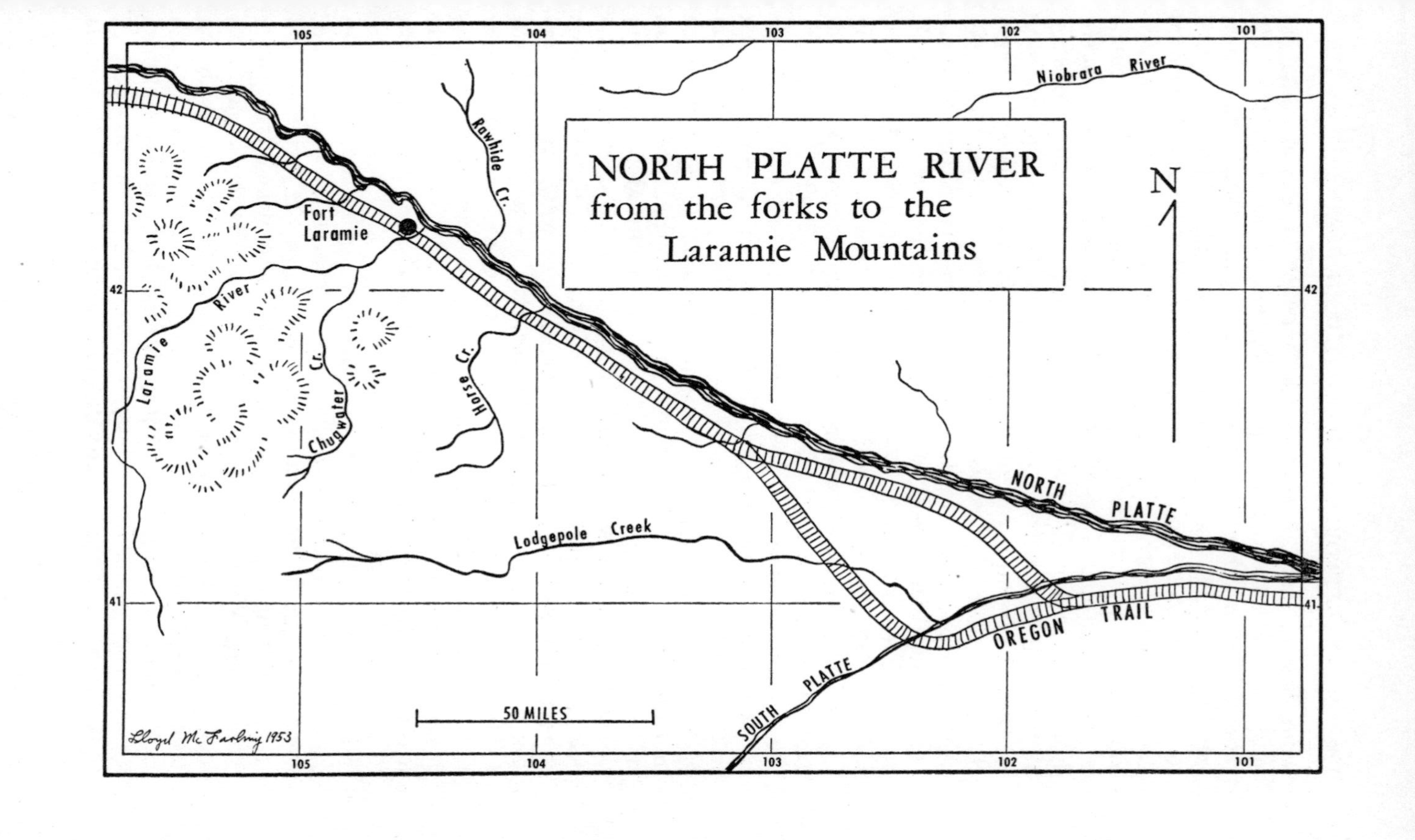
NORTH PLATTE RIVER
from the forks to the
Laramie Mountains
N
Niobrara River
Rawhide Cr.
Fort Laramie
Laramie River
Chugwater Cr.
Horse Cr.
Lodgepole Creek
NORTH PLATTE
SOUTH PLATTE
OREGON TRAIL
50 MILES
105
104
103
102
101
42
41
Lloyd McFarling 1953

ludovicianus, Ord), resembles the hamster of Europe, and belongs to the same genus. He is sixteen inches long; the hair yellowish-brownish-reddish; the head broad; the ears short; the body stout, the hairy tail about two inches long. The five toes on each foot are of very unequal length. This animal digs itself holes underground. The earth thrown out forms toward the exterior a firm round wall. The funnel-shaped entrance is one or two hands broad. For a foot it runs perpendicularly down; then obliquely inward and downward. Such dwellings, at moderate space from each other, can be seen spread over an area of several acres, or even miles. That is called a village. Hundreds, even thousands of these animals live in this way neighborly together. In fair weather they come out of their holes to sun themselves; squat quaintly on their hind legs, and utter a sharp, twittering sound. At man's approach they raise a fiercer cry, wagging their short tails withal, as if prepared for serious combat. If one comes nearer, however, they withdraw into their holes, at most peeping out. Even if one shoots them, they fall back into their holes and are not easily got out. In each hole several live together. Often six or eight can be seen retiring into one hole. The prairie dog lives on the seeds of several kinds of grass; but his dwelling is usually found in sandy regions, where grass grows scantily. He is found rather plentifully on either side of the Rocky Mountains. He sleeps through the winter, and so stuffs up the opening of his hole in the fall with grass. One often sees different animals creep into these holes, especially rattlesnakes, which are numberless in these regions, lizards, turtles, and a small kind of owl (*Stryx hypogaea,* Bonap). This *quodlibet* of animals cannot possibly constitute a friendly family; but Pike assures us that he has repeatedly seen a prairie dog, a horned frog and a turtle withdraw into the same hole. The owls and rattlesnakes seem to do most damage to the prairie dogs.

The North Platte, which we were now ascending, was here better supplied with wood than below, especially with cottonwood. We spent the night on its banks, in the neighborhood of an old winter camp. A number of cottonwood trees were lying about, which had been used partly for fencing, partly as fodder for the horses. (In winter the horses are fed with the bark of the tree.)

The next morning (June 14th), we left camp in good humor, for the crochety master of human crochets, I mean the weather, smiled on us; and the vicinity of Fort Laramie, but sixteen miles distant, promised us a speedy meeting with human beings. Before we reached the fort, we encountered the first "pale faces" we had seen since our departure from Missouri. They were French Canadians, clad half Indian fashion in leather, and scurrying along on their ponies, bedight with bells and gay ribbons, as if intent to storm some battery. Old acquaintances greeted each other, question piled on question; and each briefly told, in Canadian patois, the adventures he had been through. Meanwhile we came in view of the fort.

At a distance it resembles a great blockhouse; and lies in a narrow valley, enclosed by grassy hills, near by the left bank of the Laramie, which empties into the North Platte about a mile below. Toward the west a fine background is formed by the Black Hills, a dark chain of mountains covered with evergreen trees. We crossed the Laramie toward noon, and encamped outside the fort. The fort itself first attracted my attention. It lies on a slight elevation, and is built in a rectangle of about eighty by a hundred feet. The outside is made of cottonwood logs, about fifteen feet high, hewed off, and wedged closely together. On three sides there are little towers on the wall that seem designed for watch and defense. In the middle a strong gate, built of blocks, constitutes the entrance. Within, little buildings with flat roofs are plastered all around against the wall, like swallows' nests. One is the store house; another the smithy; the others are dwellings not unlike monks' cells. A special portion of the court yard is occupied by the so-called horse-pen, in which the horses are confined at night. The middle space is free, with a tall tree in it, on which the flag is raised on occasions of state. The whole garrison of the fort consists of only five men; four Frenchmen and a German. Some of them were married to Indian women, whose cleanliness and neat attire formed an agreeable contrast to the daughters of the wilderness whom we had hitherto seen. In this connection, let me call attention to a mistaken idea often entertained as to these forts. They are often thought of as military forts, occupied by regular troops, and under military rule, whereas they are mere trading forts, built by single trading companies, and occupied by a handful of hired men to have a safe point for storing their goods, from which barter may be carried on with the Indians. Such forts exist on both sides of the Rocky Mountains, established by American and English companies; but nowhere is there a military fort erected by the government of either country. The simple construction, as above described, protects them adequately against any attack on the part of the Indians. Out of abundant caution some of them have a little cannon on the wall. As far as I know, there is no fort on the North Platte save Fort Laramie; but several American trading companies have built forts along the South Platte, the Arkansas, the Green River, and the Missouri. Beyond the Rocky Mountains are only English forts. Fort Laramie was built in 1835[7] by Robert Campbell, and was then called Fort William. Later, it passed into other control, and was re-christened Fort Laramie after one Laramie, who was killed here by the Indians. The custom of perpetuating the memory of departed friends by transferring their names to the place where they fell, is so habitual in the Rocky Mountains, and the occasions giving rise to it are unfortunately so frequent, that at least half the names owe their origin to such events. The fort is at present in possession of Piggit, Papin and Jaudron. In many respects it has a very favorable location. There is sufficient wood in the vicinity and good pasture. A few days' journey further there is abundance of buffalo and other game, and the Platte from this point is navigable for small boats; at least Campbell has already gone down from here to the Missouri in buffalo boats. Then, too, it is a very suitable center for trade with important Indian tribes, especially the Sioux and Crows. The last named Indians had recently levied a small contribution from the fort, in that they had driven off sixteen horses grazing in the vicinity in full daylight and in view of two guards. Luckily the fort had a superfluity of horses, so that the loss was not serious. In addition to horses, the fort owns property that is of very great value in this region; that is, several cows. No attention is paid to agriculture, although the ground seems suitable for it. Hunting is the sole reliance for food. All we found in stock at that time was dried buffalo meat, of which we took a supply with us. As we stayed there the rest of the day, several races took place between our horses and those of the fort; and of course there was betting and swapping of horses. I swapped my horse, which was somewhat run down by the journey and thin, for a swift, well fed Indian horse trained to hunt buffalo. The Indian horses are said to have come originally from Mexico. They are of a small breed, and seldom can be called handsome; but they are very swift and hardy, and as they know no food save grass, are much more suitable for such a journey than American horses, which usually grow lean on mere grass. Still American horses, because they are larger and handsomer, are much sought after by whites and Indians, and, when once they are acclimated, are superior.

The distance from the boundary of Missouri to Fort Laramie, according to our daily reckoning, amounts to 755 miles, and was made by us in six weeks. All distances here can of course only be approximated. For this purpose we repeatedly counted the steps made in a given time, and found our average rate to be three miles an hour.

NOTES TO CHAPTER 9

1. The tribal names are badly garbled. Brulés and Oglalas belonged to the Teton division of the Sioux Nation—Cheyennes and Arapahoes were non-Sioux tribes. The next sentence will be correct if we substitute "Cheyennes" for "Ogallallas."

2. Bull Bear (*Mato Tatanyka*) was at this time the principal chief of the Oglalas. A chief of unusual ability, he was opposed by a faction of the tribe led by Smoke. In the fall of 1841 Bull Bear was killed in an intratribal squabble, and his faction came under the leadership of Whirlwind. Francis Parkman (cf. chap. 12, *post*) lived in Whirlwind's village for a time in 1846 and became acquainted with young Bull Bear, one of the thirty sons of the former chief.

3. This is an excellent description of the manner of constructing a bullboat.

4. Wormwood was another name for artemisia or sage. On page 72 of the *Journey*, Wislizenus describes ". . . wild sage or wild wormwood (*Artemisia columbiensis*). This Artemisia is found on both sides of the Rocky Mountains, in sandy soil, where the grass grows sparsely or not at all. It is of varying size. Sometimes it is stunted, and scarce a foot or two high, but at times it attains the height of a man, and then its stem is as thick as an arm. The wood consists, . . . of many twisted fibres, is of no use to the carpenter, but makes a good fire and holds its glow very long. The foliage is characterized by its bitterness. If any gets into our food, it is scarcely eatable."

5. Chimney Rock, a well-known landmark.

6. The Laramie Mountains of modern terminology.

7. The first trading post on the Laramie River near its confluence with the Platte was built in 1834. By some historians the construction is credited to William L. Sublette and by others to Robert Campbell. Sublette and Campbell were partners at the time, and Sublette was in command of the fur traders who began building the fort, about June 1, 1834. It was named Fort William, and afterward Fort John, but soon became generally known as Fort Laramie. In 1837 Alfred Jacob Miller painted two pictures of the fort, which are reproduced in DeVoto's *Across the Wide Missouri*. This was the fort that existed in 1839. Before Fremont's first trip west in 1842—probably in 1841—the fort was rebuilt a little farther up the Laramie. This second Fort Laramie was sold to the United States in 1849 and became the famous army post of that name. The history of the trading post and military post is told in *Fort Laramie and the Pageant of the West, 1834-1890*, by Hafen and Young.

Chapter 10

1842

FROM FORT LARAMIE TO THE RED BUTTES,

by Lieutenant John C. Fremont

John Charles Fremont was born in 1813 and died in 1890. His adventures as explorer, soldier, politician, and promoter have caused much historical controversy. He has been called "The Pathfinder," "The West's Greatest Adventurer," and things less complimentary.

In his youth Fremont was a brilliant and lazy student. He was expelled from college, when near graduation, for neglecting his studies. He became a teacher of mathematics in the United States Navy, but resigned after one cruise. In 1837 he worked as surveyor in a party exploring a proposed railroad route from Charleston to Cincinnati.

In 1839 Fremont assisted J. N. Nicollet in his exploration of the upper Mississippi Valley. The expedition was an advanced course in theoretical and practical geography under a master teacher, and the student did not neglect his studies.

In 1841 Fremont eloped with Jessie Benton, daughter of Senator Thomas Hart Benton, of Missouri, an influential advocate of western expansion. Fremont was a poor and unknown lieutenant in the Topographical Corps of the United States Army. The senator was not pleased, but he soon became reconciled to his son-in-law, and put his political power, which was great, behind the young explorer.

On June 10, 1842, Lieutenant John Charles Fremont left Cyprian Chouteau's trading post near the mouth of the Kansas River with his first independent command, about twenty-five men, with Charles Preuss, topographer, as assistant, and Kit Carson, mountain man, as guide. The expedition followed the Oregon Trail to the Forks of the Platte. Fremont, with a few men, went up the South Platte to Fort St. Vrain, then north to Fort Laramie. Preuss, with the rest of the party, went on along the trail to Fort Laramie. On his way he met a party of trappers, led by Jim Bridger, who told him the Indians were "scouring the upper country in war parties of great force."

At Fort Laramie Fremont was advised to turn back. He offered to release any of his party who "were disposed to cowardice," and one man asked to be released. Fremont hired an Indian guide and an interpreter, Carson made his will, and the expedition moved on.

The chapter which follows is from Fremont's "Report of the Exploring Expedition to the Rocky Mountains in the Year 1842, . . ." dated March 1, 1843, at Washington, D.C., as published by Gales and Seaton in 1845. It describes the travel from Fort Laramie to Red Buttes, from about July 16 to July 29, 1842.

I walked up to visit our friends at the fort, which is a quadrangular structure, built of clay, after the fashion of the Mexicans, who are generally employed in building them. The walls are about fifteen feet high, surmounted with a wooden palisade, and form a portion of ranges of houses, which entirely surround a yard of about one hundred and thirty feet square. Every apartment has its door and window—all, of course, opening on the inside. There are two entrances, opposite each other, and midway the wall, one of which is a large and public entrance; the other smaller and more private—a sort of postern gate. Over the great entrance is a square tower with loopholes, and, like the rest of the work, built of earth. At two of the angles, and diagonally opposite each other, are large square bastions, so arranged as to sweep the four faces of the walls.[1]

This post belongs to the American Fur Company,[2] and, at the time of our visit, was in charge of Mr. Boudeau.[3] Two of the company's clerks, Messrs. Galpin and Kellogg, were with him, and he had in the fort about sixteen men. As usual, these had found wives among the Indian squaws; and, with the usual accompaniment of children, the place had quite a populous appearance. It is hardly necessary to say, that the object of the establishment is trade with the neighboring tribes, who, in the course of the year, generally make two or three visits to the fort. In addition to this, traders, with a small outfit, are constantly kept amongst them. The articles of trade consist, on the one side, almost entirely of buffalo robes; and, on the other, of blankets, calicoes, guns, powder, and lead, with such cheap ornaments as glass beads, looking-glasses, rings, vermillion for painting, tobacco, and principally, and in spite of the prohibition, of spirits, brought into the country in the form of alcohol, and diluted with water before sold. While mentioning this fact, it is but justice to the American Fur Company to state, that, throughout the country, I have always found them strenuously opposed to the introduction of spirituous liquors. But, in the present state of things, when the country is supplied with alcohol—when a keg of it will purchase from an Indian every thing he possesses—his furs, his lodge, his horses, and even his wife and children—and when any vagabond who has money enough to purchase a mule can go into a village and trade against them successfully, without withdrawing entirely from the trade, it is impossible for them to discontinue its use. In their opposition to this practice, the company is sustained, not only by their obligation to the laws of the country and the welfare of the Indians, but clearly, also, on grounds of policy; for, with heavy and expensive outfits, they contend at manifestly great disadvantage against the numerous independent and unlicensed traders, who enter the country from various avenues, from the United States and from Mexico, having no other stock in trade than some kegs of liquor, which they sell at the modest price of thirty-six dollars per gallon. The difference between the regular trader and the *coureur des bois,* (as the French call the itinerant or peddling traders,) with respect to the sale of spirits, is here, as it has always been, fixed and permanent, and growing out of the nature of their trade. The regular trader looks ahead, and has an interest in the preservation of the Indians, and in the regular pursuit of their business, and the preservation of their arms, horses, and every thing necessary to their future and permanent success in hunting: the *coureur des bois* has no permanent interest, and gets what he can, and for what he can, from every Indian he meets, even at the risk of disabling him from doing any thing more at hunting.

The fort had a very cool and clean appearance. The great entrance, in which I found the gentlemen assembled, and which was floored, and about fifteen feet long, made a pleasant, shaded seat, through which the breeze swept constantly; for this country is famous for high winds. . . .

The road led over an interesting plateau between the North fork of the Platte on the right, and Laramie river on the left. At the distance of ten miles from the fort, we entered the sandy bed of a creek, a kind of defile, shaded by precipitous rocks, down which we wound our way for several hundred yards, to a place where, on the left bank, a very large spring gushes with considerable noise and force out of the limestone rock. It is called the "Warm Spring," and furnishes to the hitherto dry bed of the creek a considerable rivulet. On the opposite side, a little below the spring, is a lofty limestone escarpment, partially shaded by a grove of large trees, whose green foliage, in contrast with the whiteness of the rock, renders this a picturesque locality. The rock is fossiliferous, and, so far as I was able to determine the character of the fossils, belongs to the carboniferous limestone of the Missouri river, and is probably the western limit of that formation. Beyond this point I met with no fossils of any description.

I was desirous to visit the Platte near the point where it leaves the Black hills, and therefore followed this stream, for two or three miles, to its mouth; where I encamped on a spot which afforded good grass and *prêle* (*equisetum*) for our animals. Our tents having been found too thin to protect ourselves and the instruments from the rains, which in this elevated country are attended with cold and unpleasant weather, I had procured from the Indians at Laramie a tolerably large lodge, about eighteen feet in diameter, and twenty feet in height. Such a lodge, when properly pitched, is, from its conical form, almost perfectly secure against the violent winds which are frequent in this region, and, with a fire in the centre, is a dry and warm shelter in bad weather. By raising the lower part, so as to permit the breeze to pass freely, it is converted into a pleasant summer residence, with the extraordinary advantage of being entirely free from mosquitoes, one of which I have never seen in an Indian lodge. While we were engaged very unskilfully in erecting this, the interpreter, Mr. Bissonette,[4] arrived, accompanied by the Indian and his wife. She laughed at our awkwardness, and offered her assistance, of which we were frequently afterward obliged to avail ourselves, before the men acquired sufficient expertness to pitch it without difficulty. From this place we had a fine view of the gorge where the Platte issues from the Black hills, changing its character abruptly from a mountain stream into a river of the plains. Immediately around us the valley of the stream was tolerably open; and at the distance of a few miles, where the river had cut its way through the hills, was the narrow cleft, on one side of which a lofty precipice of bright red rock rose vertically above the low hills which lay between us.

July 22.—In the morning, while breakfast was being prepared, I visited this place with my favorite man, Basil Lajeunesse. Entering so far as there was footing for the mules, we dismounted, and, tying our animals, continued our way on foot. Like the whole country, the scenery of the river had undergone an entire change, and was in this place the most beautiful I have ever seen. The breadth of the stream, generally near that of its valley, was from two to three hundred feet, with a swift current, occasionally broken by rapids, and the water perfectly clear. On either side rose the red precipices, vertical, and sometimes overhanging, two and four hundred feet in height, crowned with green summits, on which were scattered a few pines. At the foot of the rocks was the usual detritus, formed of masses fallen from above. Among the pines that grew here, and on the occasional banks, were the cherry, (*cerasus virginiana,*) currants, and grains de boeuf (*shepherdia argentea.*). Viewed in the sunshine of a pleasant morning, the scenery was of a most striking and romantic beauty, which arose from the picturesque disposition of the objects, and the vivid contrast of colors. I thought with much pleasure of our approaching descent in the canoe through such interesting places; and, in the expectation of being able at that time to give to them a full examination, did not now dwell so much as might have been desirable upon the geological formations along the line of the river, where they are developed with great clearness. The upper portion of the red strata consists of very compact clay, in which are occasionally seen imbedded large pebbles. Below was a stratum of compact red sandstone, changing a little above the river into a very hard siliceous limestone. There is a small but handsome open prairie immediately below this place, on the left bank of the river, which would be a good locality for a military post. There are some open groves of cottonwood on the Platte. The small stream which comes in at this place is well timbered with pine, and good building rock is abundant.

If it is in contemplation to keep open the communication with Oregon territory, a show of military force in this country is absolutely necessary; and a combination of advantages renders the neighborhood of Fort Laramie the most suitable place, on the line of the Platte, for the establishment of a military post. It is connected with the mouth of the Platte and the Upper Missouri by excellent roads,[5] which are in frequent use, and would not in any way interfere with the range of the buffalo, on which the neighboring Indians mainly depend for support. It would render any posts on the Lower Platte unnecessary; the ordinary communication between it and the Missouri being sufficient to control the intermediate Indians. It would operate effectually to prevent any such coalitions as are now formed amongst the Gros Ventres, Sioux, Cheyennes, and other Indians, and would keep the Oregon road through the valley of the Sweet Water and the South Pass of the mountains constantly open. . . .

To the south, along our line of march to-day, the main chain of the Black or Laramie hills rises precipitously. . . . An inverted cone of black cloud (cumulus) rested during all the forenoon on the lofty peak of Laramie mountain, which I estimated to be about two thousand feet above the fort, or six thousand five hundred above the sea.[6] We halted to noon on the *Fourche Amère,* so called from being timbered principally

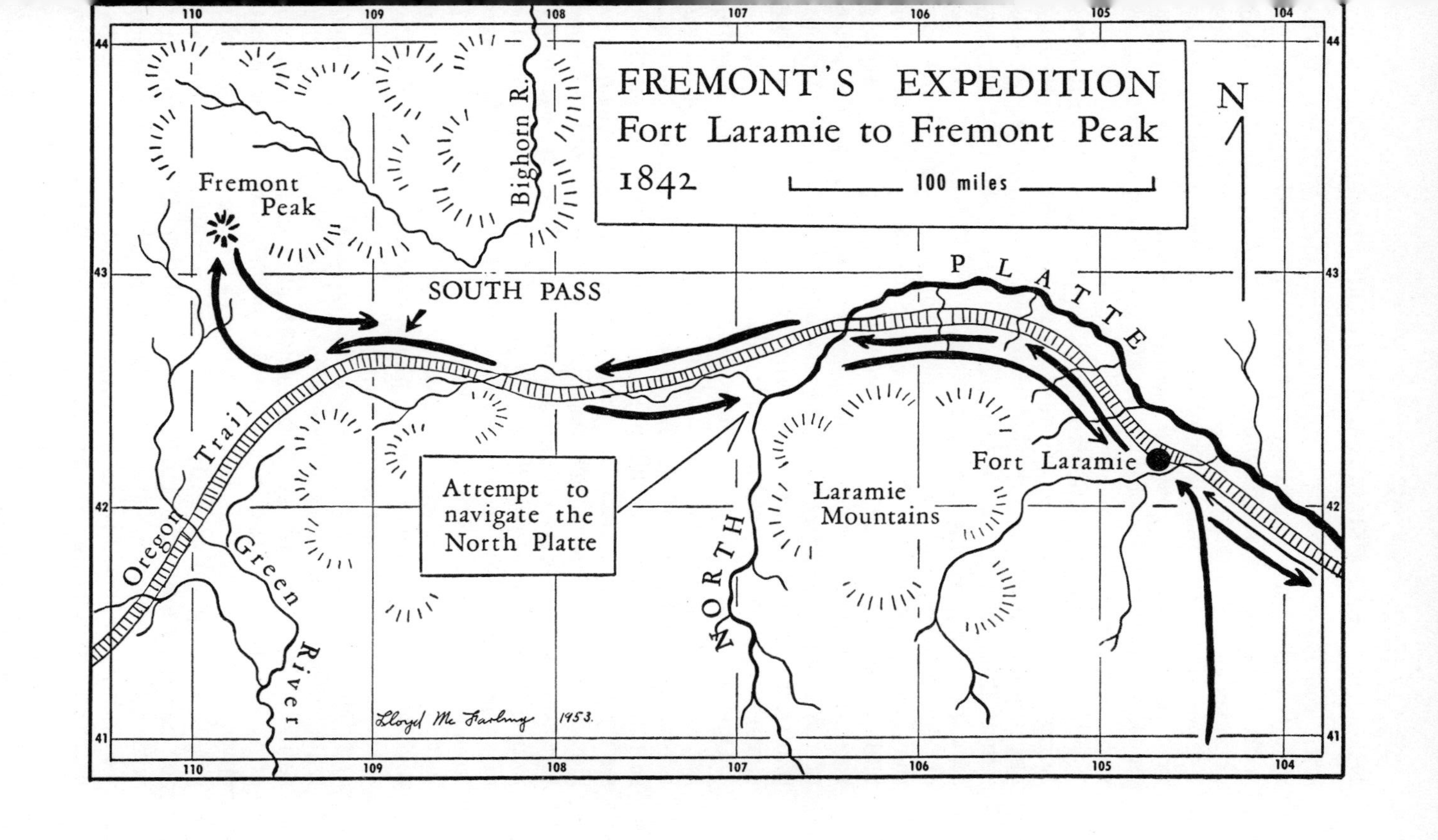

FREMONT'S EXPEDITION
Fort Laramie to Fremont Peak
1842
100 miles
N
Fremont Peak
Bighorn R.
SOUTH PASS
PLATTE
NORTH
Fort Laramie
Laramie Mountains
Attempt to navigate the North Platte
Oregon Trail
Green River
Lloyd Mc Farling 1953.
110
109
108
107
106
105
104
44
43
42
41

with the *liard amère,* (a species of poplar) with which the valley of the little stream is tolerably well wooded, and which, with large expansive summits, grows to the height of sixty or seventy feet.

The bed of the creek is sand and gravel, the water dispersed over the broad bed in several shallow streams. We found here, on the right bank, in the shade of the trees, a fine spring of very cold water....

With the change in the geological formation on leaving Fort Laramie, the whole face of the country has entirely altered its appearance. Eastward of that meridian, the principal objects which strike the eye of a traveler are the absence of timber, and the immense expanse of prairie, covered with the verdure of rich grasses, and highly adapted for pasturage. Wherever they are not disturbed by the vicinity of man, large herds of buffalo give animation to this country. Westward of Laramie river, the region is sandy, and apparently sterile; and the place of the grass is usurped by the *artemisia* and other odoriferous plants, to whose growth, the sandy soil and dry air of this elevated region seem highly favorable.

One of the prominent characteristics in the face of the country is the extraordinary abundance of the *artemisias.* They grow every where—on the hills, and over the river bottoms, in tough, twisted, wiry clumps; and, wherever the beaten track was left, they rendered the progress of the carts rough and slow. As the country increased in elevation on our advance to the west, they increased in size; and the whole air is strongly impregnated and saturated with the odor of camphor and spirits of turpentine which belong to this plant. This climate has been found very favorable to the restoration of health, particularly in cases of consumption; and possibly the respiration of air so highly impregnated by aromatic plants may have some influence.

Our dried meat had given out, and we began to be in want of food; but one of the hunters killed an antelope this evening, which afforded some relief, although it did not go far among so many hungry men. At eight o'clock at night, after a march of twenty-seven miles, we reached our proposed encampment on the *Fer-à-Cheval,* or Horse-shoe creek. Here we found good grass, with a great quantity of *prêle,* which furnished good food for our tired animals. This creek is well timbered, principally with *liard amère,* and, with the exception of Deer creek, which we had not yet reached, is the largest affluent of the right bank between Laramie and the mouth of the Sweet Water.

July 23.—The present year had been one of unparalleled drought, and throughout the country the water had been almost dried up. By availing themselves of the annual rise, the traders had invariably succeeded in carrying their furs to the Missouri; but this season, as has already been mentioned, on both forks of the Platte they had entirely failed. The greater number of the springs, and many of the streams, which made halting places for the *voyageurs,* had been dried up. Every where the soil looked parched and burnt; the scanty yellow grass crisped under the foot, and even the hardiest plants were destroyed by want of moisture. I think it necessary to mention this fact, because to the rapid evaporation in such an elevated region, nearly five thousand feet above the sea, almost wholly unprotected by timber, should be attributed much of the sterile appearance of the country, in the destruction of vegetation, and the numerous saline efflorescences which covered the ground. Such I afterward found to be the case.

I was informed that the roving villages of Indians and travellers had never met with difficulty in finding an abundance of grass for their horses; and now it was after great search that we were able to find a scanty patch of grass, sufficient to keep them from sinking; and in the course of a day or two they begin to suffer very much. We found none to-day at noon; and, in the course of our search on the Platte, came to a grove of cottonwood, where some Indian village had recently encamped. Boughs of the cottonwood yet green covered the ground, which the Indians had cut down to feed their horses upon. It is only in the winter that recourse is had to this means of sustaining them; and their resort to it at this time was a striking evidence of the state of the country. We followed their example, and turned our horses into a grove of young poplars. This began to present itself as a very serious evil, for on our animals depended altogether the further prosecution of our journey.

Shortly after we had left this place, the scouts came galloping in with the alarm of Indians. We turned in immediately toward the river, which here had a steep high bank, where we formed with the carts a very close barricade, resting on the river, within which the animals were strongly hobbled and picketed. The guns were discharged and reloaded, and men thrown forward, under cover of the bank, in the direction by which the Indians were expected. Our interpreter, who, with the Indian, had gone to meet them, came in, in about ten minutes, accompanied by two Sioux. They looked sulky, and we could obtain from them only some confused information. We learned that they belonged to the party which had been on the trail of the emigrants, whom they had overtaken at Rock Independence, on the Sweet Water. Here the party had disagreed, and came nigh fighting among themselves. One portion were desirous of attacking the whites, but the others were opposed to it; and finally they had broken up into small bands, and dispersed over the country. The greater portion of them had gone over into the territory of the Crows, and intended to return by way of the Wind river valley, in the hope of being able to fall upon some small parties of Crow Indians. The remainder were returning down the Platte, in scattered parties of ten and twenty; and those whom we had encountered belonged to those who had advocated an attack on the emigrants. Several of the men suggested shooting them on the spot; but I promptly discountenanced any such proceeding. They further informed me that buffalo were very scarce, and little or no grass to be found. There had been no rain, and innumerable quantities of grasshoppers had destroyed the grass. This insect had been so numerous since leaving Fort Laramie, that the ground seemed alive with them; and in walking, a little moving cloud preceded our footsteps. This was bad news. No grass, no buffalo—food for neither horse nor man. I gave them some plugs of tobacco, and they went off, apparently well satisfied to be clear of us; for my men did not look upon them very lovingly, and they glanced suspiciously at our warlike preparations, and the little ring of rifles which surrounded them. They were evidently in a bad humor, and shot one of their horses when they had left us a short distance.

We continued our march, and, after a journey of about twenty-one miles, encamped on the Platte. During the day, I had occasionally remarked among the hills the *psoralea esculenta,* the bread root of the Indians. The Sioux use this root very extensively, and I have frequently met with it among them, cut into thins slices and dried. In the course of the evening we were visited by six Indians, who told us that a larger party was encamped a few miles above. Astronomical observations placed us in longitude 104° 59′ 59″, and latitude 42° 39′ 25″.

We made the next day twenty-two miles, and encamped on the right bank of the Platte, where a handsome meadow afforded tolerably good grass. There were the remains of an old fort here, thrown up in some sudden emergency, and on the opposite side was a picturesque bluff of ferruginous sandstone. There was a handsome grove a little above, and scattered groups of trees bordered the river. Buffalo made their appearance this afternoon, and the hunters came in, shortly after we had encamped, with three fine cows. The night was fine, and observations gave for the latitude of the camp, 42° 47′ 40″.

July 25.—We made but thirteen miles this day, and encamped about noon in a pleasant grove on the right bank. Low scaffolds were erected, upon which the meat was laid, cut up into thin strips, and small fires kindled below. Our object was to profit by the vicinity of the buffalo, to lay in a stock of provisions for ten or fifteen days. In the course of the afternoon the hunters brought in five or six cows, and all hands were kept busily employed in preparing the meat, to the drying of which the guard attended during the night. . . .

July 26.—Early this morning we were again in motion. We had a stock of provisions for fifteen days carefully stored away in the carts, and this I resolved should only be encroached upon when our rifles should fail to procure us present support. . . . In six miles from our encampment . . . we crossed a handsome stream, called *La Fourche Boisée.*[7] It is well timbered, and, among the flowers in bloom on its banks, I remarked several *asters.*

Five miles further, we made our noon halt, on the banks of the Platte, in the shade of some cottonwoods. There were here, as generally now along the river, thickets of *hippophae,* the *grains de boeuf*[8] of the country. . . .

. . . . Eight miles further we reached the mouth of Deer creek, where we encamped. . . . It is the largest tributary of the Platte, between the mouth of the Sweet Water and the Laramie. . . .

July 27.—Nothing worthy of mention occured on this day; we travelled later than usual, having spent some time searching for grass, crossing and recrossing the river before we could find a sufficient quantity for our animals. . . . We had travelled this day twenty-seven miles. . . .

July 28.—In two miles from our encampment, we reached the place where the regular road crosses the Platte. There was two hundred feet breadth of water at this time in the bed, which has a variable width of eight to fifteen hundred feet. The channels were generally three feet deep, and there were large angular rocks on the bottom, which made the ford in some places a little difficult. Even at its low stages, this river cannot be crossed at random, and this has always been used as the best ford. The low stage of the waters the present year had made it fordable in almost any part of its course, where access could be had to its bed. . . .

We continued our way, and four miles beyond the ford Indians were discovered again; and I halted while a party were sent forward to ascertain who they were. In a short time they returned, accompanied by a number of Indians of the Oglallah band of Sioux. From them we received some interesting information. They had formed part of the great village, which they informed us had broken up, and was on its way home. The greater part of the village, including the Arapahoes, Cheyennes, and Oglallahs, had crossed the Platte eight or ten miles below the mouth of the Sweet Water, and were now behind the mountains to the south of us, intending to regain the Platte by way of Deer creek. They had taken this unusual route in search of grass and game. They gave us a very discouraging picture of the country. The great drought, and the plague of grasshoppers, had swept it so that scarce a blade of grass was to be seen, and there was not a buffalo to be found in the whole region. Their people, they further said, had been nearly starved to death, and we would find their road marked by lodges which they had thrown away in order to move more rapidly, and by the carcasses of the horses which they had eaten, or which had perished by starvation. Such was the prospect before us.

When he had finished the interpretation of these things, Mr. Bissonette immediately rode up to me, and urgently advised that I should entirely abandon the further prosecution of my exploration. *"Le meilleure avis que je pourrais vous donner c'est de virer de suite."* "The best advice I can give you, is to turn back at once." It was his own intention to return, as we had now reached the point to which he had engaged to attend me. In reply, I called up my men, and communicated to them fully the information I had just received. I then expressed to them my fixed determination to proceed to the end of the enterprise on which I had been sent; but as the situation of the country gave me some reason to apprehend that it might be attended with an unfortunate result to some of us, I would leave it optional with them to continue with me or to return.

Among them were some five or six who I knew would remain. We had still ten days' provisions; and, should no game be found, when this stock was expended, we had our horses and mules, which we could eat when other means of subsistence failed. But not a man flinched from the undertaking. "We'll eat the mules," said Basil Lajeunesse; and thereupon we shook hands with our interpreter and his Indians, and parted. With them I sent back one of my men, Dumés, whom the effects of an old wound in the leg rendered incapable of continuing the journey on foot, and his horse seemed on the point of giving out. Having resolved to disencumber ourselves immediately of every thing not absolutely necessary to our future operations, I turned directly in toward the river, and encamped on the left bank, a little above the place where our council had been held, and where a thick grove of willows offered a suitable spot for the object I had in view.

The carts having been discharged, the covers and wheels were taken off, and, with the frames, carried into some low places among the willows, and concealed in the dense foliage in such a manner that the glitter of the iron work might not attract the observation of some straggling Indian. In the sand, which had been blown up into waves among the willows, a large hole was then dug, ten feet square, and six feet deep. In the meantime, all our effects had been spread out upon the ground, and whatever was designed to be carried along with us separated and laid aside, and the remaining part carried to the hole and carefully covered up. As much as possible, all traces of our proceeding were obliterated, and it wanted but a rain to render our *cache* safe beyond discovery. All the men were now set at work to arrange the pack saddles and make up the packs. . . .

July 29.—All our arrangements having been completed, we left the encampment at 7 o'clock this morning. In this vicinity the ordinary road leaves the Platte, and crosses over to the Sweet Water, which it strikes near Rock Independence. Instead of following this road, I had determined to keep the immediate valley of the Platte so far as the mouth of the Sweet Water, in the expectation of finding better grass. To this I was further prompted by the nature of my instructions. To Mr. Carson was assigned the office of guide, as we had now reached a part of the country with which, or a great part of which, long residence had made him familiar. In a few miles we reached the Red Buttes, a famous landmark in this country, whose geological composition is red sandstone, limestone, and calcareous sandstone and pudding-stone.

NOTES TO CHAPTER 10

1. This was not the trading post described by Wislizenus (*ante*, chap. 9) but a later structure, probably built in 1841. The first Fort Laramie was built of wood; this of adobe brick made of sun-dried clay.

2. In 1834 the American Fur Company sold its western branch, with headquarters at St. Louis, to Pratte, Chouteau and Company. In 1838 the name was changed to Pierre Chouteau, Jr., and Company. The original name remained in use on the plains for many years.

3. James Bordeau, whose name was spelled in many ways by many travelers, was a trader in the Fort Laramie region for many years.

4. Joseph Bissonette, another trader.

5. There was a trail from Fort Laramie to Fort Pierre, on the Missouri, used after about 1834 to transport supplies to Fort Laramie and furs to Fort Pierre. I am not familiar with any record of a road from the mouth of the Platte at this time, but the route was feasible. North of Fort Laramie there were Indian trails leading to the Yellowstone. South, a trade route led along the edge of the Front Range of the Rocky Mountains to the Spanish settlements at Taos and Santa Fe. In later years Fort Laramie was to be on the Bozeman Trail to Montana Territory and the Cheyenne and Black Hills Trail during the Black Hills gold rush.

6. Fort Laramie was 4,263 feet above sea level, and Laramie Peak 10,274. Fremont's barometric observations at the fort were nearly right, but his estimate of the height of the peak was much too low.

7. This stream is now called Boxelder Creek.

8. Buffalo berries.

Chapter 11

1842

THE CANYONS OF THE UPPER PLATTE,

by Lieutenant John C. Fremont

In the last chapter we left Lieutenant Fremont at the Red Buttes on the Oregon Trail, traveling westward with about twenty-five men, guided by Kit Carson. He went up the valley of the Sweetwater River to South Pass and turned northwest into the Wind River Mountains. Here he climbed what he supposed to be the highest mountain in the range. It was probably the Fremont Peak of today, but may have been the slightly higher Gannett Peak.

Fremont then went back to South Pass and turned eastward. The following chapter describes his attempt to navigate the Sweetwater and the Platte, during the period August 19 to 24, 1842. It is from the "Report" of the 1842 expedition.

Fremont returned to Missouri along the Oregon Trail. In 1843, en route to Oregon and California, he journeyed again over South Pass, after entering present Wyoming a little west of Cheyenne and crossing the Laramie Plains. In 1846 and 1847 he made a third trip west, took part in the War with Mexico, and became involved in a jurisdictional dispute between the Army and Navy. He was ordered to Washington under arrest, tried by court-martial for mutiny and other military offenses, and found guilty. The President set aside the verdict but Fremont resigned from the Army.

Fremont conducted two private expeditions to California after this, was a senator from that state for twenty-one days, was an unsuccessful candidate for President in 1856, and in the Civil War served briefly with no credit to himself as a major general. After the war he became involved in some questionable railway promotions and for a time was governor of Arizona Territory.

Fremont was at his best as an explorer. He never claimed the name of Pathfinder, and it was no fault of his that the paths he followed for twenty thousand miles had already been found, for the most part, by Indians and mountain men and fur traders. His greatest talents were in the fields of topography and description and narration. His observations were accurate and his descriptions eloquent. His narrations make exploration seem like high adventure—which it often is. His reports were widely read and contributed greatly to what Senator Benton liked to call the Manifest Destiny of the American people. Cities sprang from the ashes of his campfires.[1]

August 19.—We left our camp on Little Sandy river about seven in the morning, and traversed the same sandy, undulating country. The air was filled with the turpentine scent of the various *artemisias,* which are now in bloom, and, numerous as they are, give much gayety to the landscape of the plains. At ten o'clock, we stood exactly on the divide in the pass,[2] where the wagon-road crosses, and, descending immediately upon the Sweet Water, halted to take a meridian observation of the sun. The latitude was 42° 24′ 32″.

In the course of the afternoon we saw buffalo again, and at our evening halt on the Sweet Water the roasted ribs again made their appearance around the fires; and, with them, good humor, and laughter, and song, were restored to the camp. Our coffee had been expended, but we now made a kind of tea from the roots of the wild-cherry tree.

August 23.—Yesterday evening we reached our encampment at Rock Independence,[3] where I took some astronomical observations. Here, not unmindful of the custom of early travellers and explorers in our country, I engraved on this rock of the Far West a symbol of the Christian faith. Among the thickly inscribed names, I made on the hard granite the impression of a large cross, which I covered with a black preparation of India-rubber, well calculated to resist the influence of wind and rain. It stands amidst the names of many who have long since found their way to the grave, and for whom the huge rock is a giant gravestone.

* * * * *

In obedience to my instructions to survey the river Platte, if possible, I had determined to make an attempt at this place. The India-rubber boat was filled with air, placed in the water, and loaded with what was necessary for our operations; and I embarked with Mr. Preuss and a party of men. When we had dragged our boat for a mile or two over the sands, I abandoned the impossible undertaking, and waited for the arrival of the party, when we packed up our boat and equipage, and at 9 o'clock were again moving along on our land journey. We continued along the valley on the right bank of the Sweet Water, where the formation, as already described, consists of a grayish micaceous sandstone, and fine-grained conglomerate, and marl. We passed over a ridge which borders or constitutes the river hills of the Platte, consisting of huge blocks, sixty or eighty feet cube, of decomposing granite. The cement which united them was probably of easier decomposition, and has disappeared and left them isolate, and separated by small spaces. Numerous horns of the mountain-goat were lying among the rocks; and in the ravines were cedars, whose trunks were of extraordinary size. From this ridge we descended to a small open plain, at the mouth of the Sweet Water, which rushed with a rapid current into the Platte, here flowing along in a broad tranquil, and apparently deep stream, which seemed, from its turbid appearance, to be considerably swollen. I obtained here some astronomical observations, and the afternoon was spent in getting our boat ready for navigation the next day.

August 24.—We started before sunrise, intending to breakfast at Goat Island. I had directed the land party, in charge of Bernier, to proceed to this place, where they were to remain, should they find no note to apprize them of our having passed. In the event of receiving this information, they were to continue their route, passing by certain places which had been designated. Mr. Preuss accompanied me, and with us were five of my best men, viz. C. Lambert, Basil Lajeunesse, Honore Ayot, Benoist, and Descoteaux. Here appeared no scarcity of water, and we took on board, with various instruments and baggage, provisions for ten or twelve days. We paddled down the river rapidly, for our little craft was light as a duck on the water; and the sun had been some time risen, when we heard before us a hollow roar, which we supposed to be that of a fall, of which we had heard a vague rumor, but whose exact locality no one had been able to describe to us. We were approaching a ridge, through which the river passes by a place called "cañon," (pronounced *Kanyon,*)—a Spanish word, signifying a piece of artillery, the barrel of a gun, or any kind of a tube; and which, in this country, has been adopted to describe the passage of a river between perpendicular rocks of great height, which frequently approach each other so closely overhead as to form a kind of tunnel over the stream, which foams along below, half choked up by fallen fragments. Between the mouth of the Sweet Water and Goat Island, there is probably a fall of three hundred feet, and that was principally made in the cañons before us; as, without them, the water was comparatively smooth. As we neared the ridge, the river made a sudden turn, and swept squarely down against one of the walls of the cañon with a great velocity, and so steep a descent, that it had, to the eye, the appearance of an inclined plane. When we launched into this, the men jumped overboard, to check the velocity of the boat, but were soon in water up to their necks, and our boat ran on; but we succeeded in bringing her to a small point of rocks on the right, at the mouth of the cañon. Here was a kind of elevated sand-beach, not many yards square, backed by the rocks, and around the point the river swept at a right angle. Trunks of trees deposited on jutting points twenty or thirty feet above, and other marks, showed that the water here frequently rose to a considerable height. The ridge was of the same decomposing granite already mentioned, and the water had worked the surface, in many places, into a wavy surface of ridges and holes. We ascended the rocks to reconnoitre the ground, and from the summit the passage appeared to be a continued cataract foaming over many obstructions, and broken by a number of small falls. We saw nowhere a fall answering to that which had been described to us as having twenty or twenty-five feet; but still concluded this to be the place in question, as, in the season of floods, the rush of the river against the wall would produce a great rise; and the waters, reflected squarely off, would descend through the passage in a sheet of foam, having every appearance of a large fall. Eighteen years previous to this time, as I have subsequently learned from himself, Mr. Fitzpatrick,[4] somewhere above on this river, had embarked with a valuable cargo of beaver. Unacquainted with the stream, which he believed would conduct him safely to the Missouri, he came unexpectedly into this cañon, where he was wrecked, with the total loss of his furs. It would have been a work of great time and labor to pack our baggage across the ridge, and I determined to run the cañon. We all again embarked, and at first attempted to check the way of the boat; but the water swept through with so much violence that we narrowly escaped being swamped, and were obliged to let her go in the full force of the current, and trust to the skill of the boatmen. The dangerous places in this cañon were where huge rocks had fallen from above, and hemmed in the already narrow pass of the river to an open space of three or four and five feet. These obstructions raised the water considerably above, which was sometimes precipitated over in a fall; and at other places, where this dam was too high, rushed through the contracted opening with tremendous violence. Had our boat been made of wood, in passing the narrows she would have been staved; but her elasticity preserved her unhurt from every shock, and she seemed fairly to leap over the falls.

In this way we passed three cataracts in succession, where, perhaps 100 feet of smooth water intervened; and, finally, with a shout of pleasure at our success, issued from our tunnel into the open day beyond. We were so delighted with the performance of our boat, and so confident in her powers, that we would not have hesitated to leap a fall of ten feet with her. We put to shore for breakfast at some willows on the right bank, immediately below the mouth of the cañon; for it was now 8 o'clock, and we had been working since daylight, and were all wet, fatigued and hungry. While the men were preparing breakfast, I went out to reconnoitre. The view was very limited. The course of the river was smooth, so far as I could see; on both sides were broken hills; and but a mile or two below was another high ridge. The rock at the mouth of the cañon was still the decomposing granite, with great quantities of mica, which made a very glittering sand.

We re-embarked at nine o'clock, and in about twenty minutes reached the next cañon. Landing on a rocky shore at its commencement, we ascended the ridge to reconnoitre. Portage was out of the question. So far as we could see, the jagged rocks pointed out the course of the cañon, on a winding line of seven or eight miles. It was simply a narrow, dark chasm in the rock; and here the perpendicular faces were much higher than in the previous pass, being at this end two to three hundred, and further down, as we afterwards ascertained, five hundred feet in vertical height. Our previous success had made us bold, and we determined again to run the cañon. Everything was secured as firmly as possible; and having divested ourselves of the greater part of our clothing, we pushed into the stream. To save our chronometer from accident, Mr. Preuss took it, and attempted to proceed along the shore on the masses of rock, which in places were piled up on either side; but, after he had walked about five minutes, everything like shore disappeared, and the vertical wall came squarely down into the water. He therefore waited until we came up. An ugly pass lay before us. We had made fast to the stern of the boat a strong rope about fifty feet long; and three of the men clambered along among the rocks, and with this rope let her down slowly through the pass. In several places high rocks lay scattered about in the channel; and in the narrows it required all our strength and skill to avoid staving the boat on the sharp points. In one of these, the boat proved a little too broad, and stuck fast for an instant, while the water flew over us; fortunately, it was but for an instant, as our united strength forced her immediately through. The water swept overboard only a sextant and a pair of saddlebags. I caught the sextant as it passed by me; but the saddlebags became the prey of the whirlpools. We reached the place where Mr. Preuss was standing, took him on board, and, with the aid of the boat, put the men with the rope on the succeeding pile of rocks. We found this passage much worse than the previous one, and our position was rather a bad one. To go back was impossible; before us, the cataract was a sheet of foam; and shut up in the chasm by the rocks, which, in some places, seemed almost to meet overhead, the roar of the water was deafening. We pushed off again; but, after making a little distance, the force of the current became too great for the men on shore, and two of them let go the rope. Lajeunesse, the third man, hung on, and was jerked headforemost into the river from a rock about twelve feet high; and down the boat shot like an arrow, Basil following us in the rapid current, and exerting all his strength to keep in mid channel—his head only seen occasionally like a black spot in the white foam. How far we went, I do not exactly know; but we succeeded in turning the boat into an eddy below. "*'Cré Dieu,*" said Basil Lajeunesse, as he arrived immediately after us, "*Je crois bien que j'ai nagé un demi mile.*" He had owed his life to his skill as a swimmer, and I determined to take him and the two others on board, and trust to skill and fortune to reach the other end in safety. We placed ourselves on our knees, with the short paddles in our hands, the most skilful boatman being at the bow; and again we commenced our rapid descent. We cleared rock after rock, and shot past fall after fall, our little boat seeming to play with the cataract. We became flushed with success, and familiar with the danger; and, yielding to the excitement of the occasion, broke forth together into a Canadian boat-song. Singing, or rather shouting, we dashed along; and were, I believe, in the midst of the chorus, when the boat struck a concealed rock immediately at the foot of a fall, which whirled her over in an instant. Three of my men could not swim, and my first feeling was to assist them, and save some of our effects; but a sharp concussion or two convinced me that I had not yet saved myself. A few strokes brought me into an eddy, and I landed on a pile of rocks on the left side. Looking around, I saw that Mr. Preuss had gained the shore on the same side, about twenty yards below; and a little climbing and swimming soon brought him to my side. On the opposite side, against the wall, lay the boat bottom up; and Lambert was in the act of saving Descoteaux, whom he had grasped by the hair, and who could not swim; "*Lâche pas,*" said he, as I afterward learned, "*lâche pas, cher frère.*" "*Crains pas,*" was the reply, "*Je m'en vais mourir avant que de te lâcher.*" Such was the reply of courage and generosity in this danger. For a hundred yards below, the current was covered with floating books and boxes, bales and blankets, and scattered articles of clothing; and so strong and boiling was the stream, that even our heavy instruments, which were all in cases, kept on the surface, and the sextant, circle, and the long black box of the telescope, were in view at once. For a moment, I felt somewhat disheartened. All our books—almost every record of the journey—our journals and registers of astronomical and barometrical observations—had been lost in a moment. But it was no time to indulge in regrets; and I immediately set about endeavoring to save something from the wreck. Making ourselves understood as well as possible by signs, (for nothing could be heard in the roar of the waters,) we commenced our operations. Of every thing on board, the only article that had been saved was my double barrelled gun, which Descoteaux had caught, and clung to with drowning tenacity. The men continued down the river on the left bank. Mr. Preuss and myself descended on the side we were on; and Lajeunesse, with a paddle in his hand, jumped on the boat alone, and continued down the cañon. She was now light, and cleared every bad place with much less difficulty. In a short time, he was joined by Lambert; and the search was continued for about a mile and a half, which was as far as the boat could proceed in the pass.

Here the walls were about five hundred feet high, and the fragments of rocks from above had choked the river into a hollow pass, but one or two feet above the surface. Through this and the interstices of the rock, the water found its way. Favored beyond our expectations, all of our registers had been recovered, with the exception of one of my journals, which contained the notes and incidents of travel, and topographical descriptions, a number of scattered astronomical observations, principally meridian altitudes of the sun, and our barometrical register west of Laramie. Fortunately, our other journals contained duplicates of the most important barometrical observations which had been taken in the mountains. These, with a few scattered notes, were all that had been preserved of our meteorological observations. In addition to these we saved the circle; and these, with a few blankets, constituted every thing that had been rescued from the waters.

The day was running rapidly away, and it was necessary to reach Goat island, whither the party had preceded us, before night. In this uncertain country, the traveller is so much in the power of chance, that we became somewhat uneasy in regard to them. Should anything have occurred, in the brief interval of our separation, to prevent our rejoining them, our situation would be rather a desperate one. We had not a morsel of provisions—our arms and ammunition were gone—and we were entirely at the mercy of any straggling party of savages, and not a little in danger of starvation. We therefore set out at once in two parties, Mr. Preuss and myself on the left, and the men on the opposite side of the river. Climbing out of the cañon, we found ourselves in a very broken country, where we were not yet able to recognize any locality. In the course of our descent through the cañon, the rock, which at the upper end was of the decomposing granite, changed into a varied sandstone formation. The hills and points of the ridges were covered with fragments of a yellow sandstone, of which the strata were sometimes displayed in the broken ravines which interrupted our course, and made our walk extremely fatiguing. At one point of the cañon the red argillaceous sandstone rose in a wall of five hundred feet, surmounted by a stratum of white sandstone; and in an opposite ravine a column of red sandstone rose, in form like a steeple, about one hundred and fifty feet high. The scenery was extremely picturesque, and, notwithstanding our forlorn condition, we were frequently obliged to stop and admire it. Our progress was not very rapid. We had emerged from the water half naked, and, on arriving at the top of the precipice, I found myself with only one moccasin. The fragments of rock made walking painful, and I was frequently obliged to stop and pull out the thorns of the *cactus*, here the prevailing plant, and with which a few minutes' walk covered the bottoms of my feet. From this ridge the river emerged into a smiling prairie, and, descending to the bank for water, we were joined by Benoist. The rest of the party were out of sight, having taken a more inland route. We crossed the river repeatedly—sometimes able to ford it, and sometimes swimming—climbed over the ridges of two more cañons, and towards evening reached the cut, which we here named the Hot Spring gate. On our previous visit in July, we had not entered this pass, reserving it for our descent in the boat; and when we entered it this evening, Mr. Preuss was a few hundred feet in advance. Heated with the long march, he came suddenly upon a fine bold spring gushing from the rock, about ten feet above the river. Eager to enjoy the crystal water, he threw himself down for a hasty draught, and took a mouthful of water almost boiling hot. He said nothing to Benoist, who laid himself down to drink; but the steam from the water arrested his eagerness, and he escaped the hot draught. We had no thermometer to ascertain the temperature, but I could hold my hand in the water just long enough to count two seconds. There are eight or ten of these springs, discharging themselves by streams large enough to be called runs. A loud hollow noise was heard from the rock, which I supposed to be produced by the fall of water. The strata immediately where they issue is a fine white and calcareous sandstone, covered with an incrustation of common salt. Leaving this Thermopylae of the west, in a short walk we reached the red ridge which has been described as lying just above Goat Island. Ascending this, we found some fresh tracks and a button, which showed that the other men had already arrived. A shout from the man who first reached the top of the ridge, responded to from below, informed us that our friends were all on the island; and we were soon among them. We found some pieces of buffalo standing around the fire for us, and managed to get some dry clothes among the people. A sudden storm of rain drove us into the best shelter we could find, where we slept soundly, after one of the most fatiguing days I have ever experienced.[5]

NOTES TO CHAPTER 11

1. The last sentence paraphrases one by Jessie Benton Fremont, quoted in *Rocky Mountain Naturalists*, p. 33, by Joseph Ewan. Perhaps the best book on the explorer's life is *John Charles Fremont, an Explanation of His Career*, by Goodwin. *Fremont and '49*, by Dellenbaugh, deals mainly with the explorations. *Fremont, the West's Greatest Adventurer*, two volumes, by Nevins, is too laudatory. *The Year of Decision, 1846*, by DeVoto, is extremely critical of Fremont's California adventures. The latter book is not a biography but gives considerable space to Fremont.

2. South Pass, where the Oregon Trail crossed the continental divide, was the most important central pass across the Rocky Mountains. It was a nearly level plateau about twenty-five miles wide and about 7,550 feet above sea level. It may have been crossed by Robert Stuart in 1812, but the evidence indicates that the Stuart route was a little south of the main pass. It may have been crossed by Etienne Provost in 1823. It was certainly crossed by Thomas Fitzpatrick with a party of Ashley-Henry trappers in the spring of 1824, and most historians consider this the "effective" discovery. Over South Pass went the Oregon and California

trails, the Mormon Trail, and nearly all the central travel to the Far West until the Union Pacific Railroad was completed in 1869.

3. Independence Rock was one of the landmarks of the Oregon Trail and it is still visited by tourists traveling over Highway 220 between Casper and Muddy Gap, Wyoming. It is a granite rock 1,950 feet long, 850 feet wide, and 193 feet high. Perhaps 50,000 names have been carved, scratched, or written on the rock, but many have been weathered away. The cross that Fremont carved is no longer visible. Federal Writers' Project, American Guide Series, *Wyoming* . . . pp. 386-87.

4. Thomas Fitzpatrick, called "Broken Hand" by the Indians, was mountain man, trapper, trader, guide, and first agent for the Indian tribes of the Great Plains from the Platte to the Arkansas. He led the party that "effectively" discovered South Pass. His biography has been published under the title *Broken Hand* . . . by Hafen and Ghent.

5. The confluence of the Sweetwater and North Platte rivers, where Fremont launched his boat, is now covered by the waters of Pathfinder Reservoir. A short distance down the Platte is Alcova Reservoir. A few miles below Alcova Reservoir is Fremont's Island, where the Wyoming Guide says Fremont camped in 1842. Probably this is the Goat Island of the "Report."

Chapter 12

1846

THE OGLALA SIOUX,

by Francis Parkman

A great historian must combine the abilities of a scientist, a philosopher, and an artist. Francis Parkman (1823-93) was equally able in investigating, organizing, and expressing historical phenomena. Among historians his reputation rests upon the high quality of his several books dealing with the long struggle between the French and English for the possession of colonial North America; but his most popular book was his first, *The Oregon Trail*. It was the narrative of a trip which he made to the Black Hills of his day and the Laramie Mountains of ours, in the summer of 1846. His purpose was the study "of the manners and characters of the Indians in their primitive state." It was a part of his rigorous self-training as a historian.

Accompanied by his cousin, Quincy Adams Shaw; his guide and hunter, Henry Chatillon; and a Canadian-French muletier, Delorier, Parkman left Westport May 9, 1846. The four men traveled sometimes with a party of English tourists, sometimes with emigrants, and sometimes alone. They went over the Oregon Trail to the Laramie Mountains where Parkman camped, wandered, and hunted with the Oglala Indians from June 15 to August 3. Then they went south along the Front Range of the Rocky Mountains to the Arkansas River and returned to Westport over the Santa Fe Trail.

During much of the time he spent in the Laramie Mountains Parkman was ill. When he wrote *The Oregon Trail* he was suffering from the first of his many attacks of near-blindness. His notes were read to him by Shaw and others, and he dictated the book. It was published serially in the *Knickerbocker Magazine* from February, 1847, to February, 1849, and first printed in book form in March, 1849. It has been republished in many editions.

The following excerpt is taken from Chapter 11 of the Fourth Edition, revised by the author and published in 1872. At the opening of the chapter Parkman was in camp on Laramie River, near the mouth of Chugwater Creek, about eighteen miles southwest of Fort Laramie. At the fort his party had been augmented by one Raymond, "a long-haired Canadian, with a face like an owl's," and "a vagrant Indian trader named Reynal," plus the latter's squaw and two Indian nephews. They were awaiting the arrival of the wandering Oglala village led by Whirlwind.[1]

Reynal heard guns fired one day, at the distance of a mile or two from the camp. He grew nervous instantly. Visions of

Crow war-parties began to haunt his imagination; and when we returned (for we were all absent), he renewed his complaints about being left alone with the Canadians and the squaw. The day after, the cause of the alarm appeared. Four trappers, called Morin, Saraphin, Rouleau, and Gingras, came to our camp and joined us. They it was who fired the guns and disturbed the dreams of our confederate Reynal. They soon encamped by our side. Their rifles, dingy and battered with hard service, rested with ours against the old tree; their strong rude saddles, their buffalo-robes, their traps, and the few rough and simple articles of their traveling equipment were piled near our tent. Their mountain-horses were turned to graze in the meadow among our own; and the men themselves, no less rough and hardy, used to lie half the day in the shade of our tree, lolling on the grass, lazily smoking, and telling stories of their adventures; and I defy the annals of chivalry to furnish the record of a life more wild and perilous than that of a Rocky Mountain trapper.

With this efficient reinforcement the agitation of Reynal's nerves subsided. We began to conceive a sort of attachment to our old camping ground; yet it was time to change our quarters, since remaining too long on one spot must lead to unpleasant results, not to be borne unless in case of dire necessity. The grass no longer presented a smooth surface of turf; it was trampled into mud and clay. So we removed to another old tree, larger yet, that grew by the side of the river a furlong distant. Its trunk was full six feet in diameter; on one side it was marked by a party of Indians with various inexplicable hieroglyphics, commemorating some warlike enterprise, and aloft among the branches were the remains of a scaffold, where dead bodies had once been deposited, after the Indian manner.

"There comes Bull-Bear," said Henry Chatillon, as we sat on the grass at dinner. Looking up, we saw several horsemen coming over the neighboring hill, and in a moment four stately young men rode up and dismounted. One of them was Bull-Bear, or Mahto-Tatonka, a compound name which he inherited from his father, the principal chief in the Ogillallah band.[2] One of his brothers and two other young men accompanied him. We shook hands with the visitors, and when we had finished our meal—for this is the approved manner of entertaining Indians, even the best of them—we handed to each a tin cup of coffee and a biscuit, at which they ejaculated from the bottom of their throats, "How! how!" a monosyllable by which

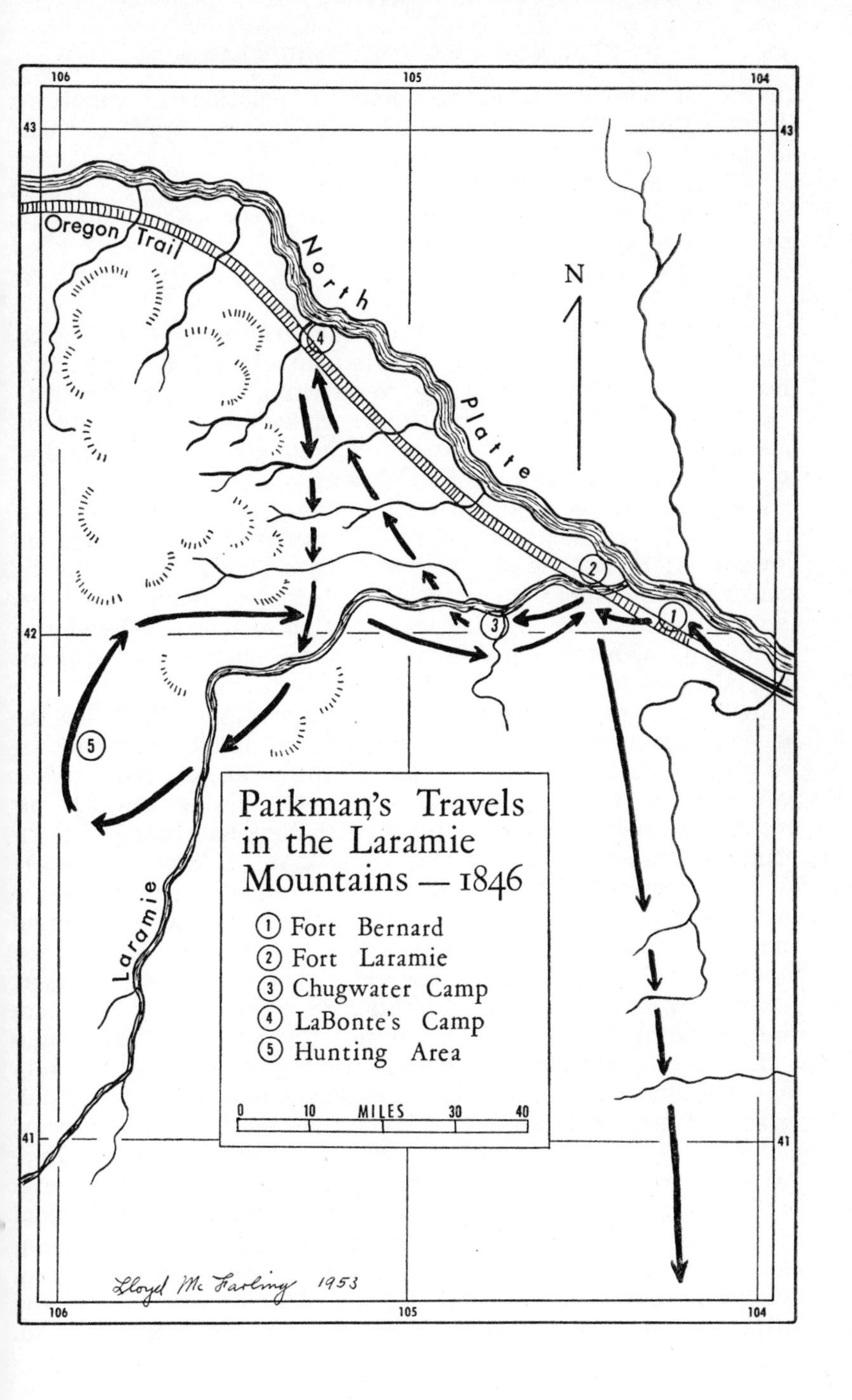
106
105
104
43
42
41
Oregon Trail
North Platte
Laramie
N
Parkman's Travels in the Laramie Mountains — 1846
1 Fort Bernard
2 Fort Laramie
3 Chugwater Camp
4 LaBonte's Camp
5 Hunting Area
0 10 MILES 30 40
Lloyd McFarling 1953

an Indian contrives to express half the emotions of which he is susceptible. Then we lighted the pipe, and passed it to them as they squatted on the ground.

"Where is the village?"

"There," said Mahto-Tatonka, pointing southward; "it will come in two days."

"Will they go to war?"

"Yes."

No man is a philanthropist on the prairie. We welcomed this news cordially, and congratulated ourselves that Bordeaux's interested efforts to divert The Whirlwind from his congenial vocation of bloodshed had failed of success, and that no further obstacles would interpose between us, and our plan of repairing to the rendezvous at La Bonté's camp.[3]

For that and several succeeding days, Mahto-Tatonka and his friends remained our guests. They devoured the relics of our meals; they filled the pipe for us, and also helped us to smoke it. Sometimes they stretched themselves side by side in the shade, indulging in railery and equivocal jokes, ill becoming the dignity of brave and aspiring warriors, such as two of them in reality were.

Two days dragged away, and on the morning of the third we hoped confidently to see the Indian village. It did not come; so we rode out to look for it. In place of the eight hundred Indians we expected, we met one solitary savage riding towards us over the prairie, who told us that the Indians had changed their plan, and would not come within three days. Taking along with us this messenger of evil tidings, we retraced our footsteps to the camp, amusing ourselves by the way with execrating Indian inconstancy. When we came in sight of our little white tent under the big tree, we saw that it no longer stood alone. A huge old lodge was erected by its side, discolored by rain and storms, rotten with age, with the uncouth figures of horses and men and outstretched hands that were painted upon it, well nigh obliterated. The long poles which supported this squalid habitation thrust themselves rakishly out from its pointed top, and over its entrance were suspended a "medicine-pipe" and various other implements of the magic art. While we were yet at a distance, we observed a greatly increased population of various colors and dimensions, swarming about our quiet encampment. Morin, the trapper, having been absent for a day or two, had returned, it seemed, bringing all his family with him. He had taken to himself a wife, for whom he had paid the established price of one horse. This looks cheap at first sight, but in truth the purchase of a squaw is a transaction which no man should enter into without mature deliberation, since it involves not only the payment of the price, but the burden of feeding and supporting a rapacious horde of the bride's relatives, who hold themselves entitled to feed upon the indiscreet white man. They gather about him like leeches, and drain him of all he has.

Morin had not made an aristocratic match. His bride's relatives occupied but a contemptible position in Ogillallah society; for among these democrats of the prairie, as among others more civilized, there are virtual distinctions of rank and place. Morin's partner was not the most beautiful of her sex, and he had the bad taste to array her in an old calico gown, bought from an emigrant woman, instead of the neat tunic of whitened deerskin usually worn by the squaws. The moving spirit of the establishment was an old hag of eighty. Human imagination never conceived hobgoblin or witch more ugly than she. You could count all her ribs through the wrinkles of her leathery skin. Her withered face more resembled an old skull than the countenance of a living being, even to the hollow, darkened sockets, at the bottom of which glittered her little black eyes. Her arms had dwindled into nothing but whip-cord and wire. Her hair, half black, half gray, hung in total neglect nearly to the ground, and her sole garment consisted of the remnant of a discarded buffalo-robe tied round her waist with a string of hide. Yet the old squaw's meagre anatomy was wonderfully strong. She pitched the lodge, packed the horses, and did the hardest labor of the camp. From morning till night she bustled about the lodge, screaming like a screech-owl when anything displeased her. Her brother, a "medicine-man," or magician, was equally gaunt and sinewy with herself. His mouth spread from ear to ear, and his appetite, as we had occasion to learn, was ravenous in proportion. The other inmates of the lodge were a young bride and bride groom, the latter one of those idle, good-for-nothing fellows who infest an Indian village as well as more civilized communities. He was fit neither for hunting nor war, as one might see from the stolid unmeaning expression of his face. The happy pair had just entered upon the honeymoon. They would stretch a buffalo-robe upon poles, to protect them from the rays of the sun, and spreading under it a couch of furs, would sit affectionately side by side for half the day, though I could not discover that much conversation passed between them. Probably they had nothing to say; for an Indian's supply of topics for conversation is far from being copious. There were half a dozen children, too, playing and whooping about the camp, shooting birds with little bows and arrows, or making miniature lodges of sticks, as children of a different complexion build houses of blocks.

A day passed, and Indians began rapidly to come in. Parties of two, three, or more would ride up and silently seat themselves on the grass. The fourth day came at last, when about noon horsemen appeared in view on the summit of the neighboring ridge. Behind followed a wild procession, hurrying in haste and disorder down the hill and over the plain below; horses, mules, and dogs; heavily burdened *traineaux*,[4] mounted warriors, squaws walking amid the throng, and a host of children. For a full half-hour they continued to pour down; and keeping directly to the bend of the stream, within a furlong of us, they soon assembled there, a dark and confused throng, until, as if by magic, a hundred and fifty tall lodges sprang up. The lonely plain was transformed into the site of a swarming encampment. Countless horses were soon grazing over the meadows around us, and the prairie was animated by restless figures careering on horseback, or sedately stalking in their long white robes. The Whirlwind was come at last.[5] One question yet remained to be answered: "Will he go to the war in order that we, with so respectable an escort, may pass over to the somewhat perilous rendezvous at La Bonté's camp?"

This still remained in doubt. Characteristic indecision perplexed their councils. Indians cannot act in large bodies. Though their object be of the highest importance, they cannot combine to attain it by a series of connected efforts. King Philip, Pontiac, and Tecumseh, all felt this to their cost. The Ogillallah once had a war-chief who could control them; but he was dead, and now they were left to the sway of their own unsteady impulses.

As this Indian village and its inhabitants will hold a prominent place in the rest of the story, perhaps it may not be amiss to glance for an instant at the savage people of which they form a part. The Dahcotah or Sioux range over a vast territory, from the river St. Peter to the Rocky Mountains. They are divided into several independent bands, united under no central government, and acknowledging no common head. The same language, usages, and superstitions form the sole bond between them. They do not unite even in their wars. The bands of the east fight the Objibwas on the Upper Lakes; those of the west make incessant war upon the Snake Indians in the Rocky Mountains. As the whole people is divided into bands, so each band is divided into villages. Each village has a chief, who is honored and obeyed only so far as his personal qualities may command respect and fear. Sometimes he is a mere nominal chief; sometimes his authority is little short of absolute, and his fame and influence reach beyond his own village, so that the whole band to which he belongs is ready to acknowledge him as their head. This was, a few years since, the case with the Ogillallah. Courage, address, and enterprise may raise any warrior to the highest honor, especially if he be the son of a former chief, or a member of a numerous family, to support him and avenge his quarrels; but when he has reached the dignity of chief, and the old men and warriors, by a peculiar ceremony, have formally installed him, let it not be imagined that he assumes any of the outward signs of rank and honor. He knows too well on how frail a tenure he holds his station. He must conciliate his uncertain subjects. Many a man in the village lives better, owns more squaws and more horses, and goes better clad than he. Like the Teutonic chiefs of old, he ingratiates himself with his young men by making them presents, thereby often impoverishing himself. If he fails to gain their favor, they will set his authority at naught, and may desert him at any moment; for the usages of his people have provided no means of enforcing his authority. Very seldom does it happen, at least among these western bands, that a chief attains to much power, unless he is the head of a numerous family. Frequently the village is principally made up of his relatives and descendants, and the wandering community assumes much of the patriarchal character.

The western Dahcotah have no fixed habitations. Hunting and fighting, they wander incessantly, through summer and winter. Some follow the herds of buffalo over the waste of prairie; others traverse the Black Hills, thronging, on horseback and on foot, through the dark gulfs and sombre gorges, and emerging at last upon the "Parks," those beautiful but most perilous hunting-grounds. The buffalo supplies them with the necessaries of life; with habitations, food, clothing, beds and fuel; strings for their bows, glue, thread, cordage, trail-ropes for their horses, coverings for their saddles, vessels to hold water, boats to cross streams, and the means of purchasing all that they want from the traders. When the buffalo are extinct, they too must dwindle away.

War is the breath of their nostrils. Against most of the neighboring tribes they cherish a rancorous hatred, transmitted from father to son, and inflamed by constant aggression and retaliation. Many times a year, in every village, the Great Spirit is called upon, fasts are made, the war-parade is celebrated, and the warriors go out by handfuls at a time against the enemy. This fierce spirit awakens their most eager aspirations, and calls forth their greatest energies. It is chiefly this that saves them from lethargy and utter abasement. Without its powerful stimulus they would be like the unwarlike tribes beyond the mountains, scattered among the caves and rocks like beasts, and living on roots and reptiles. These latter have little of humanity except the form; but the proud and ambitious Dahcotah warrior can sometimes boast heroic virtues. It is seldom that distinction and influence are attained among them by any other course than that of arms. Their superstition, however, sometimes gives great power to those among them who pretend to the character of magicians; and their orators, such as they are, have their share of honor.

But to return. Look into our tent, or enter, if you can bear the stifling smoke and the close air. There, wedged close together, you will see a circle of stout warriors, passing the pipe around, joking, telling stories, and making themselves merry after their fashion. We were also infested by little copper-colored naked boys and snake-eyed girls. They would come up to us, muttering certain words, which being interpreted conveyed the concise invitation, "Come and eat." Then we would rise, cursing the pertinacity of Dahcotah hospitality, which allowed scarcely an hour of rest between sun and sun, and to which we were bound to do honor, unless we would offend our entertainers. This necessity was particularly burdensome to me, as I was scarcely able to walk, from the effects of illness, and was poorly qualified to dispose of twenty meals a day. So bounteous an entertainment looks like an outgushing of good-will; but, doubtless, half at least of our kind hosts, had they met us alone and unarmed on the prairie, would have robbed us of our horses, and perhaps have bestowed an arrow upon us besides.

* * * * *

. . . Mahto-Tatonka . . . left behind him a goodly army of descendants, to perpetuate his renown and avenge his fate. Besides daughters, he had thirty sons, a number which need not stagger the credulity of those acquainted with Indian usages and practices. We saw many of them, all marked by the same dark complexion, and the same peculiar cast of features. Of these, our visitor, young Mahto-Tatonka, was the eldest, and some reported him as likely to succeed to his father's honors. Though he appeared not more than twenty-one years old, he had oftener struck the enemy, and stolen more horses and more squaws, than any young man in the village. Horse-stealing is well known as an avenue to distinction on the prairies, and the other kind of depredation is esteemed equally meritorious. Not that the act can confer fame from its own intrinsic merits. Any one can steal a squaw, and if he chooses afterwards to make an adequate present to her rightful proprietor, the easy husband for the most part rests content, his vengeance falls asleep, and all danger from that quarter is averted. Yet this is regarded as a pitiful and mean-spirited transaction. The danger is averted, but the glory of the achievement also is lost. Mahto-Tatonka proceeded after a more dashing fashion. Out of several dozen squaws whom he had stolen, he could boast that he had never paid for one, but snapping his fingers in the face of the injured husband, had defied the extremity of his indignation, and no one yet had dared to lay the finger of violence upon him. He was following close in the footsteps of his father. The young men and the young squaws, each in their way, admired him. The former would always follow him to war, and he was esteemed to have unrivalled charm in the eyes of the latter. Perhaps his impunity may excite some wonder. An arrow shot from a ravine, or a stab given in the dark, require no great valor, and are especially suited to the Indian genius; but Mahto-Tatonka had a strong protection. It was not alone his courage and audacious will that enabled him to career so dashingly among his compeers. His enemies did not forget that he was one of thirty warlike brethren, all growing up to manhood. Should they wreak their anger upon him, many keen eyes would be ever upon them, and many fierce hearts thirst for their blood. The avenger would dog their footsteps everywhere. To kill Mahto-Tatonka would be an act of suicide.

Though he found such favor in the eyes of the fair, he was no dandy. He was indifferent to the gaudy trappings and ornaments of his companions, and was content to rest his chances of success upon his own warlike merits. He never arrayed himself in gaudy blanket and glittering necklaces, but left his statue-like form, limbed like an Apollo of bronze, to win its way to favor. His voice was singularly deep and strong, and sounded from his chest like the deep notes of an organ. Yet after all, he was but an Indian. See him as he lies there in the sun before our tent, kicking his heels in the air and cracking jokes with his brother. Does he look like a hero? See him now in the hour of his glory, when at sunset the whole village empties itself to behold him, for to-morrow their favorite young partisan goes out against the enemy. His head-dress is adorned with a crest of the war-eagle's feathers, rising in a waving ridge above his brow, and sweeping far behind him. His round white shield hangs at his breast, with feathers radiating from the centre like a star. His quiver is at his back; his tall lance in his hand, the iron point flashing against the declining sun, while the long scalp-locks of his enemies flutter from the shaft. Thus, gorgeous as a champion in panoply, he rides round and round within the great circle of lodges, balancing with a graceful buoyancy to the free movements of his war-horse, while with a sedate brow he sings his song to the Great Spirit. Young rival warriors look askance at him; vermilion-cheeked girls gaze in admiration; boys whoop and scream in a thrill of delight, and old women yell forth his name and proclaim his praises from lodge to lodge.

Mahto-Tatonka was the best of all our Indian friends. Hour after hour, and day after day, when swarms of savages of every age, sex, and degree beset our camp, he would lie in our tent, his lynx-eye ever open to guard our property from pillage.

The Whirlwind invited us one day to his lodge. The feast was finished and the pipe began to circulate. It was a remarkably large and fine one, and I expressed admiration of it.

"If the Meneaska likes the pipe," asked The Whirlwind, "why does he not keep it?"

Such a pipe among the Ogillallah is valued at the price of a horse. The gift seemed worthy of a chieftain and a warrior; but The Whirlwind's generosity rose to no such pitch. He gave me the pipe, confidently expecting that I in return would make him a present of equal or superior value. This is the implied condition of every gift among the Indians, and should it not be complied with, the present is usually reclaimed. So I arranged upon a gaudy calico handkerchief an assortment of vermillion, tobacco, knives, and gunpowder, and summoning the chief to camp, assured him of my friendship, and begged his acceptance of a slight token of it. Ejaculating, *How! how!* he folded up the offerings and withdrew to his lodge.

* * * * *

When the sun was yet an hour high, it was a gay scene in the village. The warriors stalked sedately among the lodges, or along the margin of the stream, or walked out to visit the bands of horses that were feeding over the prairie. Half the population deserted the close and heated lodges and betook themselves to the water; and here you might see boys and girls, and young squaws, splashing, swimming, and diving, beneath the afternoon sun, with merry screams and laughter. But when the sun was resting above the broken peaks, and the purple mountains threw their shadows for miles over the prairie; when our old tree basked peacefully in the horizontal rays, and the swelling plains and scattered groves were softened into a tranquil beauty,—then the scene around our tent was worthy of a Salvator. Savage figures, with quivers at their backs, and guns, lances, or tomahawks in their hands, sat on horseback, motionless as statues, their arms crossed on their breasts and their eyes fixed in a steady unwavering gaze upon us. Others stood erect, wrapped from head to foot in their long white robes of buffalo-hide. Others sat together on the grass, holding their shaggy horses by a rope, with their dark busts exposed to view as they suffered their robes to fall from their shoulders. Others again stood carelessly among the throng, with nothing to conceal the matchless symmetry of their forms. There was one in particular, a ferocious fellow, named The Mad Wolf, who, with the bow in his hand and the quiver at his back, might have seemed, but for his face, the Pythian Apollo himself. Such a figure rose before the imagination of West, when on first seeing the Belvedere in the Vatican, he exclaimed, "By God, a Mohawk!"

When the prairie grew dark, the horses were driven in and secured near the camp, and the crowd began to melt away. Fires gleamed around, duskily revealing the rough trappers and the graceful Indians. One of the families near us was always gathered about a bright fire that lighted up the interior of their lodge. Withered, witch-like hags flitted around the blaze; and here for hour after hour sat a circle of children and young girls, laughing and talking, their round merry faces glowing in the ruddy light. We could hear the monotonous notes of the drum from the Indian camp, with the chant of the war-song, deadened in the distance, and the long chorus of quavering yells, where the war-dance was going on in the largest lodge. For several nights, too, we heard wild and mournful cries, rising and dying away like the melancholy voice of a wolf. They came from the sisters and female relatives of Mahto-Tatonka, who were gashing their limbs with knives, and bewailing the death of Henry Chatillon's squaw.[6] The hour would grow late before all went to rest in our camp. Then, while the embers of the fires glowed dimly, the men lay stretched in their blankets on the ground, and nothing could be heard but the restless motions of the crowded horses.

NOTES TO CHAPTER 12

1. The best biography of Francis Parkman is Mason Wade's *Francis Parkman, Heroic Historian.* Wade has also edited *The Journals of Francis Parkman,* in two volumes. Volume II contains the journals Parkman kept on his Oregon Trail trip.

2. This Bull Bear was a son of the Oglala Chief Bull Bear that Wislizenus met on the Platte River below Fort Laramie in 1839. (cf. chap. 9, *ante,* also note 2.) The spelling of the Indian name, as given by Hyde (*Red Cloud's Folk,* p. 40), is "Mato Tatanyka."

3. James Bordeau was in charge of Fort Laramie at this time, during the absence of the regular *bourgeois,* or manager, Pierre Papin. Parkman had met Papin taking a fleet of fur-laden boats down the Platte a few days earlier. At this time the Indians were trying to organize a large war party for an expedition against the Shoshoni tribe, and Parkman anticipated joining the party to study the art of Indian warfare at first hand. Bordeau, on the contrary, was trying to divert the attention of the Indians to hunting, in the interest of trade. For several reasons, chiefly the inconstancy of the Indian mind, the war plans came to nothing.

4. Usually spelled *traveau.* Two or more poles were tied to a pony's shoulders, the other ends of the poles dragged on the ground, with cross-pieces behind the horse to carry burdens. Smaller *traveaux* were used on dogs. Probably the use of the dog *traveau* antedated the introduction of the horse to North America by Spanish explorers in the sixteenth century.

5. Whirlwind was now chief of the Oglala band formerly led by Bull Bear the elder, but had fewer followers and less influence than his predecessor.

6. Henry Chatillon's Indian wife, Bear Robe, sister of young Bull Bear, had recently died in Whirlwind's village.

Chapter 13

1849

FOLLOWING THE EMIGRANT TRAIL,

by Captain Howard Stansbury

In a good year with good luck and much labor a fur trader might float a few small boatloads of furs down the Platte. Otherwise it was not navigable. Yet its valley became the greatest avenue of overland travel across the Great Plains. The Platte was in the right place, and its flood plain made a smooth, well-grassed, gently sloping road to the mountains. It was the best wagon route to the West, and Manifest Destiny rode on wagons.

In 1827 William Henry Ashley, on a trading trip, took a small wheeled cannon to Great Salt Lake. It was the first wheeled vehicle to go over South Pass.

In 1830 Smith, Jackson, and Sublette hauled their trade goods to the rendezvous on Wind River in ten wagons drawn by five mules each, and two smaller vehicles, called dearborns, pulled by one mule each. This caravan turned north from the trail a little east of South Pass. Two years later Captain Bonneville took the first wagons through the pass. Wheels reached Fort Hall in 1836, the Columbia in 1840, and the mouth of the Willamette in 1843.

In 1843, 900 people took 120 wagons and 2,000 cattle to the Willamette Valley. It was called "the great migration." The next year there were 1,200 emigrants, in 1845 there were 3,000, and in 1846 the number dropped to about 1,600. It jumped in 1847, with some 4,500 people going to Oregon, perhaps 1,000 to California, and about 4,000 to Utah. In 1848 the travel dropped. On January 24, 1848, James W. Marshall picked a few small nuggets of gold out of the millrace of Sutter's mill, but the news of this discovery moved slowly eastward and had little or no effect on the emigration until 1849.

In 1849 about 75,000 people entered California. About 42,000 went overland, and more than half of the overland travel was along the central route, which was beginning to be called the Oregon and California Trail. The travel probably increased in 1850. On June 17 a correspondent for the *Daily Missouri Republican* reported from Fort Laramie that 30,954 men, 439 women, 508 children, 7,113 wagons, 19,386 horses, 6,471 mules, and 18,238 oxen had passed the fort.

To the Indians all this was great medicine, and the trail was the Great Medicine Road. They begged a great deal, stole a few horses, and occasionally took a white scalp in a casual way, but for the most part they were friendly. Then cholera broke out among them, thousands died, and the hearts of the living began to get bad. The destruction of grass and game along the trail made matters worse. After the treaty of Fort Laramie in 1851, the government began to pay annuities to the Indian tribes, and in part these annuities were for the use of the Oregon and California Trail. But this did not wholly correct the conditions which made conflict between the whites and the reds inevitable. In 1854 the Grattan Massacre occurred, in 1855 the Harney expedition invaded the Indian country, and for more than twenty years there was intermittent warfare on the Northern Plains.

Howard Stansbury (1806-63) was a captain in the Topographical Corps of the United States Army who was sent to Utah on an exploring expedition in 1849, returning in 1850. The following chapter is a series of excerpts from his report: *Exploration and Survey of the Valley of the Great Salt Lake of Utah,* printed in 1852 by order of the Senate of the United States.

Before leaving Fort Leavenworth, we were joined by a small party of emigrants for California, who desired to travel in our company for the sake of protection, and who continued with us as far as Salt Lake City. . . .

The cholera had for a considerable time been raging on the Missouri; and as we passed up, fearful rumours of its prevalence and fatality among the emigrants on the route daily reached us from the plains. On the day we left Fort Leavenworth, one member of our little party was carried to the hospital in a state of collapse, where he died in twenty-four hours. The only officer attached to my command had been ill for several weeks, with severe attacks of intermittent fever, which now merged into chronic dysentery, and he was, in consequence, unable to sit on his horse, or to do duty of any kind. These were rather discouraging circumstances for an outset; but, at length, on the 31st day of May, our preparations being completed, we commenced our journey, my own party consisting in all of eighteen men, five wagons, and forty-six horses and mules; while that of Mr. Sackett, our fellow-traveller, contained six persons, one wagon, one travelling carriage, and fifteen animals. Lieutenant Gunnison, being too ill to travel in any other manner, was carried on his bed, in a large spring wagon, which had been procured for the transportation of the instruments. . . . My party consisted principally of experienced *voyageurs,* who had spent the best part of their lives among the wilds of the Rocky Mountains, and to whom this manner of life had become endeared by old associations. We followed the "emigration road," (already broad and well beaten as any turnpike in our country,) over a rolling prairie, fringed on the south with trees. . . .

Although the route taken by the party has been travelled

by thousands of people, both before and since we passed over it, I have thought that some brief extracts from the daily journals of the expedition might not be without interest; for, although nothing very new may perhaps be elicited, still it is not improbable that they will convey, to such as peruse them, a more correct idea of what the thousands have had to encounter who have braved this long journey in search either of a new home in Oregon, or of that more alluring object—the glittering treasure of California.

* * * * *

Monday, June 18.—

* * * * *

After travelling up the Blue for about twelve miles, we left it and crossed the ridge dividing its waters from those of the Nebraska or Platte River. The character of this ridge is that of an extensive level plateau, or table, with slight undulations: the soil is composed of sand and clay, having occasionally water standing on it in pools, which, however, are dry most of the summer. On arriving at the western edge of the plateau, the country became more elevated, and presented a range of small hills of a sandy reddish clay, with a sharp outline toward the river, forming the "coast of the Nebraska," and also constituting the bluff bounding the river valley on the south. From this elevated position the valley presented a lovely appearance. The bottom was as level as a floor, covered with short fresh grass of the richest green, without a shrub or bush to interrupt the view. Beyond this verdant carpet of two miles in breadth, flowed the river of which we had heard so much, while a dense growth of large timber, covering Grand Island, which lay immediately before us, formed a fit framework for this lovely picture of calm and quiet beauty.

Archambault, our guide, told me that the last time he had passed this spot, the whole of the immense plain, as far as the eye could reach, was black with herds of buffalo. Now, not so much as one is to be seen; they have fled before the advancing tide of emigration. Driven from their ancient and long-loved haunts, these aboriginal herds, confined within still narrowing bounds, seem destined to final extirpation at the hand of man. The prairie bottom of the Platte is here elevated but a very few feet above the river in its present stage, which, however, is higher than usual. The appearance of the water is precisely that of the Mississippi and Missouri, of a muddy white, and its current is, like theirs, constantly boiling and eddying in restless turbulence. It is quite shallow, as its name, both in Indian and French, indicates, so that I found no difficulty in riding my mule over to the island, at the head of which we encamped for the night, after a march of thirty-two miles.

* * * * *

Tuesday, June 19.—Ther. at 5 o'clock, 70°. Men and animals much fatigued by the journey of yesterday. We travelled up the Platte fifteen miles, and encamped within two miles of Fort Kearny, on the bank of the river, for the sake of water and grass. Wood for cooking could be procured only by wading the river, and bringing it from the opposite side on the shoulders of the men. After encamping, rode up to the fort, and called upon the commanding officer, Colonel Bonneville, whose adventures among the Rocky Mountains are so well known to the world.[1] He received us very courteously, offering us every facility in his power in furtherance of our progress. We remained at this post until the afternoon of the 21st, to recruit the mules, get many of them shod, and to procure such necessary supplies as could be obtained. The post at present consists of a number of long low buildings, constructed principally of adobe, or sun-dried bricks with nearly flat roofs; a large hospital-tent; two or three workshops, enclosed by canvas walls; store-houses constructed in the same manner; one or two long adobe stables, with roofs of brush; and tents for the accommodation of the officers and men. There are stationed here two companies of infantry and one of dragoons. I was told that the hailstorms had been very frequent this season and quite destructive, cutting down the weeds and stripping the trees of their foliage.

Lieutenant Gunnison being still quite feeble, and unable to ride on horseback, I purchased for his use a little spring-carriage, which had been left here by a party of emigrants. Such abandonments are very common; most of these sanguine and adventurous companies, by the time they get thus far, beginning to find out that they have started on their journey with more than they can contrive to carry. In order to lighten their load, most of them dispose of every thing they can possibly spare, and at almost any price. Flour and bacon, for example, had been sold as low as one cent per pound; and many, being unable to sell even at that price, had used their meat for fuel. The pack company from Boston, which had passed us on the route, and which we found encamped here on our arrival, left before our departure. As they had been entirely unaccustomed to the operation of packing, their mules, as was to be expected, were in a most horrible condition, with galled backs and sides that made one shudder to behold. The proper mode of arranging the load of these suffering animals is an art taught only by experience. These people, though belonging to a race famous for foresight and calculation, had, like others from less thrifty and managing portions of the Union, been selling and giving away all they could dispense with. While encamped here we have had several severe thunder storms, accompanied with heavy rains and violent winds.

* * * * *

Monday, July 2.—Ther. at sunrise, 68°; Bar. 26.63. After travelling up the river for fourteen miles, it was determined to make the crossing of the South Fork by fording. In preparation for this movement, one of the wagons, as an experimental pioneer, was partially unloaded, by removing all articles liable to injury from water, and then driven into the stream; but it stuck fast, and the ordinary team of six mules being found insufficient to haul it through the water, four more were quickly attached, and the crossing was made with perfect safety, and without wetting any thing. In the same manner were all the remaining wagons crossed, one by one, by doubling the teams, and employing the force of nearly the whole party wading alongside to incite and guide the mules, lest, from some sudden eccentricity, to which those animals are so constantly prone, a wagon might be capsized or precipitated into a hole. The water was perfectly opake with thick yellow mud, and it required all our care to avoid the quicksands with which the bottom is covered. The labor was excessive, on both men and animals, as the river was nearly half a mile wide, and the current from recent rains ran with great rapidity and force. Wading such a stream breast-deep four or five times, with such treacherous footing, was very exhausting, and we were glad to encamp, immediately after crossing, upon the left bank. Both man and beast suffered more from this day's exertion than from any day's march we have yet made. About one and a-half miles above the crossing a new Indian lodge was seen standing entirely alone. A fact so unusual excited our curiosity: upon going to the place, it was found to contain the body of an Indian (probably a chief) raised upon a low platform or bier, surrounded by all the implements believed by these simple children of the forest to be necessary for his use in the spirit-land. The lodge was carefully and securely fastened down at the bottom, to protect its charge from the wolves. . . . We are now, by our measurements, four hundred and seventy-nine miles from Fort Leavenworth, and one hundred and eighty from Fort Kearny.

Tuesday, July 3.—Morning cool and delightful; Ther. at sunrise, 71°; Bar. 26.59; Wind S. W., fresh and bracing. Today we crossed the ridge between the North and South Forks of the Platte, a distance of eighteen and a-half miles. As we expected to find no water for the whole of this distance, the India-rubber bags were filled with a small supply. The road struck directly up the bluff, rising quite rapidly at first, then very gradually for twelve miles, when we reached the summit, and a most magnificent view saluted the eye. Below and before us was the North Fork of the Nebraska, winding its way through broken hills and green meadows; behind us the undulating prairie rising gently from the South Fork, over which we had just passed; on our right, the gradual convergence of the two valleys was distinctly perceptible; while immediately at our feet were the heads of Ash Creek, which fell off suddenly into deep precipitous chasms on either side, leaving only a high narrow ridge, or backbone, which gradually descended, until, toward its western termination, it fell off precipitately into the bottom of the creek. Here we were obliged, from the steepness of the road, to let the wagons down by ropes, but the labor of a dozen men for a few days would make the descent easy and safe. The bottom of Ash Creek is tolerably well wooded, principally with ash and some dwarf cedars. The bed of the stream was entirely dry, but toward the mouth several springs of delightfully cold and refreshing water were found, altogether the best that has been met with since leaving the Missouri. We encamped at the mouth of the valley, here called Ash Hollow. The traces of the great tide of emigration that had preceded us were plainly visible in remains of camp-fires, in blazed trees covered with innumerable names carved and written on them; but, more than all, in the total absence of all herbage. It was only by driving our animals to a ravine some distance from the camp, that a sufficiency for their subsistence could be obtained.

* * * * *

Wednesday, July 4.—At 9 A.M., Bar. 26.76; Ther. 68°. This being a national festival, I determined to spend the day here and celebrate it as well as our limited means would permit. A salute was fired morning and evening, and a moderate allowance of grog served out to the men, which, with a whole day's rest and plenty of buffalo-meat, rendered them quite happy. We had observed yesterday, on the opposite side of the river, a number of Indian lodges, pitched on the bank; but the total absence of any living or moving thing about them induced us from curiosity to pay them a visit. In order to do this it was necessary to cross the river, here nearly a mile in width, with a strong, rapid current. I was afraid to risk any of the animals, as the bottom was known to be very treacherous and full of quicksands; so it was determined we should wade it. Having stripped to our drawers, we tied our shirts and moccasins around our necks to keep them dry, and, accompanied by five or six of the men, commenced the passage. The water was up to our middle, and the strong and constant pressure of the current rendered our efforts to bear up against it very fatiguing. We struggled on, but very slowly, from the yielding nature of the sandy and marly bottom, which was immediately washed from beneath the foot every time it was placed on the ground. If we stood still in the same spot, even for a short time, the bottom would be so rapidly excavated from beneath us, that a hole of sufficient depth would be formed to render swimming necessary. After continuing these tedious and laborious efforts until we had nearly reached the opposite shore, on advancing a single step we found ourselves in water beyond our depth, (the channel of the river running close to the bank,) and the shirts we had so carefully endeavored to keep dry were in a moment thoroughly soaked. We made out, however, to scramble ashore.

I put on my moccasins, and, displaying my wet shirt, like a flag, to the wind, we proceeded to the lodges which had attracted our curiosity. There were five of them, pitched upon the open prairie, and in them we found the bodies of nine Sioux, laid out upon the ground, wrapped in their robes of buffalo-skin, with their saddles, spears, camp-kettles, and all their accoutrements, piled up around them. Some lodges contained three, others only one body, all of which were more or less in a state of decomposition. A short distance apart from these was one lodge which, though small, seemed of rather superior pretensions, and was evidently pitched with great care. It contained the body of a young Indian girl of sixteen or eighteen years, with a countenance presenting quite an agreeable expression: she was richly dressed in leggings of fine scarlet cloth, elaborately ornamented; a new pair of moccasins, beautifully embroidered with porcupine quills, was on her feet, and her body was wrapped in two superb buffalo-robes, worked in like manner. She had evidently been dead but a day or two; and to our surprise a portion of the upper part of her person was bare, exposing the face and a part of the breast, as if the robes in which she was wrapped had by some means been disarranged, whereas all the other bodies were closely covered up. It was, at the time, the opinion of our mountaineers that these Indians must have fallen in an encounter with a party of Crows; but I subsequently learned that they had all died of the cholera, and that this young girl, being considered past recovery, had been arrayed by her friends in the habiliments of the dead, enclosed in the lodge alive, and abandoned to her fate—so fearfully alarmed were the Indians by this, to them, novel and terrible disease. But the melancholy tale of this poor forsaken girl, does not end here. Her abandonment by her people, though with inevitable death before her eyes, may perhaps be excused from the extremity of their terror; but what will be thought of the conduct of men enlightened by Christianity, and under no such excess of fear, who, by their own confession, approached and looked into this lodge while the forsaken being was yet alive, and able partially to raise herself up and look at them, but who, with a heartlessness that disgraces human nature, turned away, and, without an effort for her relief, left her alone to die! Which company deserved the epithet of savages, the terrified and flying red men, or the strong-hearted whites who thus consummated their cruel deed?

* * * * *

Thursday, July 5th.—Bar. 26.67. Ther. 56°. We commenced our journey to-day up the North Fork of the Platte. . . . Encamped on the bank of the river, after a tedious march of twenty-three miles. Just above us, was a village of Sioux, consisting of ten lodges. They were accompanied by Mr. Badeau,[3] a trader; and, having been driven from the South Fork by the cholera, had fled to the emigrant-road, in the hope of obtaining medical aid from the whites. As soon as it was dark, the chief and a dozen of the braves of the village came and sat down in a semicircle around the front of my tent, and, by means of an interpreter, informed me that they would be very glad of a little coffee, sugar, or biscuit. I gave them what we could spare. They told us there was another and larger band encamped about two miles above, many of whom were very sick with the cholera: they themselves had been afflicted with it, but had in a great measure recovered, although they were in great dread of its return. As soon as they were told I had a doctor, or "medicine-man," with me, and received assurances that some medicines should be prepared for them, and left with the trader, (who had married among them,) they expressed much delight, and returned to their village, where, soon after, the sound of the drum and the song, expressive of the revival of hope, which had almost departed, resounded from the "medicine lodge," and continued until a late hour of the night. In the meantime, I directed a quantity of medicine to be prepared, with the necessary directions for using it. The following morning we paid a visit in passing, to the upper village, which contained about two hundred and fifty souls. They were in the act of breaking up their encampment, being obliged to move farther up the river to obtain fresh grass for their animals. A more curious, animated, and novel scene I never witnessed. Squaws, papooses, dogs, puppies, mules, and ponies, all in busy motion, while the lordly, lazy men lounged about with an air of listless indifference, too proud to render the slightest aid to their faithful drudges. Before the lodge of each brave was erected a tripod of thin slender poles about ten feet in length, upon which was suspended his round white shield, with some device painted upon it, his spear, and a buckskin sack containing his "medicine" bag. It reminded me forcibly of the scenes of Ivanhoe and the Crusaders, and impressed me with the singularity of the coincidence in the customs of what were then the most refined nations of the world, with those of these wild and untutored savages. The cholera had been quite bad among them, and was still raging. I visited nearly every lodge, in company with the doctor and Mr. Bissonette[3] the trader, and medicine was administered to all who required it. It was touching to witness the moral effect produced by the mere presence of a "medicine-man" upon these poor wretches. They swallowed the medicine with great avidity, and an absolute faith in its efficacy, which, I have little doubt, saved many a life that would otherwise have been lost. I shall never forget one poor fellow, a tall, fine-looking young man of about twenty-five. He had been sick three days, and we found him sitting on the ground, his blanket drawn closely around him, and his chin resting upon his knees, the image of despair,—very quiet, but the expression of his countenance showing that he had made up his mind that he must die. To add to his despondence, a young man from the next lodge had just been carried out and buried. The doctor examined him closely, and then requested the interpreter to tell him that the worst was passed, and that, with care and attention, he would soon entirely recover. Never did I behold any thing like the change which, in an instant, came over the expressive countenance of this poor savage. His face flushed, the fire came into his eyes, and a radiant smile of confidence and hope, which was beautiful to behold, broke through the previous gloom. He raised his eyes, till now sternly fixed upon the ground, gently smote his hands together, turned his head toward his squaw, who was standing behind him, and in a low and silvery tone communicated to her the joyful news. It was to him a perfect resurrection from the dead; for he seemed now to entertain no doubt of his recovery, but received the assurance of the doctor as if it had been the fiat of fate. It was a moving sight, and although we could not understand a single word that passed, the whole scene was perfectly intelligible. After administering to all who stood in need, a quantity of medicine was left with Mr. Bissonette, with the necessary directions.

* * * * *

Monday, July 9.—

. . . Three miles from the Chimney Rock, the road gradually leaves the river for the purpose of passing behind Scott's Bluff, a point where a spur from the main ridge comes so close to the river as to leave no room for the passage of teams. There was no water between these two points, a distance of more than twenty miles, and we were consequently obliged to go on until nine o'clock, when we encamped at the bluff, on a small run near a delicious spring, after having been in the saddle sixteen hours without food, and travelled thirty-one and a-half miles. The march was a severe one upon the animals, as they were in harness, after the noon halt, for seven successive hours, without water. The afternoon was oppressively hot, and the gnats and musquitoes almost insufferable. There is a temporary blacksmith's shop here, established for the benefit of the emigrants, but especially for that of the owner, who lives in an Indian lodge, and had erected a log shanty by the roadside, in one end of which was the blacksmith's forge, and in the other a grog-shop and sort of grocery.[4] The stock of this establishment consisted principally of such articles as the owner had purchased from the emigrants at a great sacrifice and sold to others at as great a profit. Among other things, an excellent double wagon was pointed out to me, which he had purchased for seventy-five cents. The blacksmith's shop was an equally profitable concern; as, when the smith was indisposed to work himself he rented the use of shop and tools for the modest price of seventy-five cents an hour, and it was not until after waiting for several hours, that I could get the privilege of shoeing two of the horses, even at that price, the forge having been in constant use by the emigrants. Scott's Bluff, according to our measurement, is five hundred and ninety-six miles from Fort Leavenworth; two hundred and eighty-five from Fort Kearney, and fifty-one from Fort Laramie.

Thursday, July 12.—Bar. 26.13; Ther. at sunrise, 53°. We arrived today at Fort Laramie, and encamped a short distance above, on Laramie's Fork, a fine, rapid stream, about fifty yards wide. Here we remained until the 18th, recruiting our animals, getting them shod, repairing our wagons, and making the necessary arrangements for continuing our journey. I here unpacked one of the barometers which I had taken charge of for the Smithsonian Institution, to be left at this post. It had stood the journey admirably, was in perfect order, and was gladly received by Lieutenant Woodbury, of the corps of Engineers. Observations also were made for the latitude of the post, which placed it in lat. 42° .12′ 38.″ 2, long. 104° 31′ 26″.

Fort Laramie, formerly known as Fort John, was one of the posts established by the American Fur Company for the protection of their trade. Its walls are built in the usual style of such structures, of adobe or unburnt brick. The company sold it to the United States Government; and their people, when we arrived, were temporarily encamped near the ford of the creek, having recently surrendered the possession of the post to the troops, whom we found engaged in preparing for its extension and in the erection of additional quarters, under the superintendence of Lieutenant Woodbury. It is garrisoned at present by two companies of Infantry and one of Mounted Rifles, under command of Major Sanderson, of the latter corps, by whom we were received with the greatest courtesy, and promptly furnished with such supplies as were within the resources of his command. I procured here fifteen additional mules, and our stock now consisted of fifty-six mules, five horses, four steers for beef, and two milch-cows, one of which we had found on the prairie, abandoned or lost by her owners.

The country has risen considerably since leaving Scott's Bluff, and the general flora indicates a much drier atmosphere: the grasses especially are brown and burned up wherever the earth is not directly moistened by proximity to some stream. The soil around Fort Laramie appears to be sterile, owing no doubt to the extreme dryness of the air and the almost total absence of dews. The great quantity of coarse conglomerate, too, which, by its disintegration, leaves the surface covered with gravel, must operate as a great impediment to cultivation. The rocks, however, contain the elements of fertility, being composed of limestone, clay, and sand; and I have no doubt that, with the aid of irrigation, the bottom lands of Laramie Creek might be made to produce most abundant crops. Hay is cut about eight miles up the stream in quantity sufficient for the wants of the garrison.

NOTES TO CHAPTER 13

1. Benjamin L. E. Bonneville was a captain in 1832. On leave from the army, he led a fur-trading and trapping expedition to the Rocky Mountains. From 1832 to 1835 he explored a large part of the territory from the Yellowstone to the Columbia and as far south as Salt Lake. A group of his trappers, led by Joseph R. Walker, made a side trip to California. The story of the exploration is told in *The Adventures of Captain Bonneville,* by Washington Irving.

2. This was James Bordeau, temporarily in charge of Fort Laramie when Parkman visited it in 1846.

3. Joseph Bissonette. He was interpreter for Fremont in 1842.

4. The owner's name was Robidoux. The history of the establishment is given in "Robidoux's Trading Post at 'Scott's Bluffs,' and the California Gold Rush," by Merrill J. Mattes, in *Nebraska History,* XXX (June, 1949), 95-138.

PART THREE

ACROSS THE PLAINS AND BADLANDS

Chapter 14

1823

FROM NIOBRARA RIVER TO PONCA CREEK,

by Prince Paul of Wurttemberg

Friederich Paul Wilhelm, Prince of Wurttemberg, was born in 1797 and died in 1860. He served in the armies of Wurttemberg and Prussia, but laid aside the uniform at the age of twenty to devote himself to the study of the natural sciences and to exploration. He made three trips to the United States, in 1822-24, 1829-31, and 1849-51.

During his first trip Prince Paul ascended the Missouri River to Fort Atkinson, traveling with fur traders in a keelboat. He left the river there and traveled overland, visited the Omaha and Ponca Indians, crossed the valleys of Niobrara River, Ponca Creek, and White River, and returned to the Missouri a few miles above the mouth of the White.

On his second trip Prince Paul again ascended the Missouri River, probably to or near the Rocky Mountains. On his third trip he visited Mexico, California, and Panama, and in 1851 traveled over the Oregon Trail through South Pass and visited Salt Lake City.

Prince Paul kept a careful journal of his first trip and rewrote it in the form of a narrative which was published in Germany in 1835. It was translated from the German by Dr. William G. Bek and published in 1941 in Volume XIX of the *South Dakota Historical Collections*, under the title: "First Journey to North America in the Years 1822 to 1824." In this work the author's title is shown as "Duke of Wurtemberg," but a letter he wrote to William Clark was signed "Prince of Wurtemberg," and he is usually referred to by that title. He sometimes traveled under the name of "Baron of Braunsberg."

The narrative shows internal evidence of having been written, or rewritten, after 1831, for there are many references to information obtained on the second trip.

The following chapter covers Prince Paul's travels in the valleys of Niobrara River and Ponca Creek, from August 15 to 19, 1823. The prince had brought with him from Germany as servant and hunter a man named J. G. Schlape, who became seriously ill on August 12. He was also accompanied at this time by "a certain Rodger, commonly called Bell," and "a halfbreed, named Monbrun, also called *La Malice*, an experienced hunter, a sinister fellow of genuine Indian nature, but courageous and faithful." The party had two or three horses and three mules.

On the 15th of August the way led toward the northwest, thru an interminable desert. I found no water, not even in the deep creek-bed, which I reached at the approach of night. Not until it had become quite dark did Monbrun succeed in discovering some water in a creek, whose banks were surrounded by high and almost barren hills. Here I ordered a halt to be made. The horses had made a distance of 30 English miles, and therefore were extremely tired and thirsty. The heat had risen to 28° R.[1] Our discomfort was increased by a rather strong wind from the southwest. In the North American prairies this wind takes the place of the sirocco. My hunter had been transported to this place by my men and the Indians. As long as he was in a conscious state, he could not make up his mind to stay behind with the Omahas. Now his condition had become so serious that I expected his death any moment. I was therefore placed in a great predicament, for it was impossible to make a longer stay here because of the lack of provisions. Many antelopes appeared on the ridge of the neighboring hills or came to the stream to drink, but because they were extremely shy we made futile chase after them.

On the morning of August 16, after a very difficult ride of six hours over high elevations and thru deep ravines we reached the eau qui courre,[2] near its influx into the Missouri. This stream is bordered by steep hills. These hills, however, run out a short distance from the mouth of the stream, where low lands border both sides of it. The southern bank near the mouth of the stream expands into a beautiful prairie region with tall grass. The northern bank is covered with tall timber. A wooded plain, which joins upon a row of hills, forms a triangular wooded point. The mouth is about 42° 57′ northern latitude and 98° 8′ western longitude from Greenwich.[3]

When we reached the river, I saw two Indians on horseback, hastening from an elevation on the opposite bank. These good people had seen my expedition coming, and had come to show us a good place to ford the stream. The water flowed swiftly and in places contained much quicksand. Eau qui courre was discovered in early times by French furtraders. If I am not mistaken, the brothers Chouteau were the first white men to tread its banks.[4] It was more accurately determined by the Lewis and Clark expedition, who reached it on September 4, 1804. They called it Rapid Water River. The engineers of that expedition found it to be 76 yards wide at its mouth.[5] This was, however, a survey made at the lowest stand of the water. When crossed the same river seven years later, in the middle of the winter, it was unusually swift, broad and deep, and caused us a great deal of delay and difficulty because of the large amount of drifting ice. This time it was not deep, but so swift that in places three or four feet deep, the horses had the greatest difficulty in wading thru. At the same time the bed of the stream is very uneven, full of sandbars and muddy places, which are caused by deposits of clay, and are extremely slippery. These banks, as also those of the Missouri are formed of yellow ochre, an observation which did not escape Lewis and Clark.

On the whole the region north of 42° 30′ northern latitude takes on a character strikingly different from that of the lower Missouri. Great masses of volcanic rocks[6] take the place of the sandstone and limestone formations which prevail farther down the stream. The pleasing green of the prairie is replaced by bare, lava-covered hills. The prevailing vegetation is cactus and yucca. These cover great stretches of land and transfix the traveler into a tropical clime. Strikingly peculiar and manifestly unique is the geographic distribution of plants which show the greatest analogy to the temperate volcanic plateaus of Mexico and Peru, and which seem to have been transferred, as if by magic, from the regions of the Andes into the midst of the prairie country of the central part of the United States. The splendid bartonia which seems strangely out of place here, is confined to a very limited space, and covers the banks of the rivers with its beautiful flowers. This plant belongs to the cacti and has been very excellently illustrated by Barton.

The yucca which I mentioned earlier seems also to be new. It sends out a flowering stalk with large white blossoms, which resemble yucca aloefolia. The plant itself scarcely becomes more than two or three feet high. The seeds germinated perfectly in my garden, and the plant does well under the climatic conditions of southern Germany. One of the cacti is the opuntia missouriensis. The other, not yet definitely determined, is a small mamillaria, with splendid red blossoms, which I should like to call septentrionalis. (This mamillaria has been confused with mamillaria simplex.)

When I entered the bed of the river large flocks of ducks and geese took wing, and several wolves (canis nubilus, S.) fled from their hiding places into willow-thickets. Here I saw for the first time the northern hare, probably different from lepus variabilis.[7] In the winter this hare is snowwhite down to the toes and lower part of the paws, which are yellowish. The tips of the ears are dark black, shading into a light brown color This is a very large hare. In the summer it is light brown except the belly, which is entirely white.

The two Indians reported that the chief of the Poncas Chu-ge-ga-chae, the Great Smoke, or la Boucanne was in that region. Since I could not help the condition of my German servant, I resolved to surrender the unfortunate man to the mercy of the Indian chief, and decided to have this ruler of the wilderness, who was generally regarded as a good man, called. Contrary to the advice of my companions I caused a halt to be made. Camp was therefore made on a small elevation near the bank of the river. I requested the Indians to represent to their chief the deplorable condition of the sick man, and to appeal to his sympathy. The Indians galloped away and soon disappeared beyond the hills.

I utilized the remainder of the day in examining the surrounding country, and by adding a few good plants to my herbarium. Strikingly pretty legumes were entwined in the short grass, and the cassia chaemachrista with its beautiful yellow flowers and its mimosa-like, feathery leaves covered the low places on the bank of the river. A galega and a desmodium (hedysarum, glutinosum, Wild.?) were found. The sticky hulls of the latter had become ripe, and clung so tightly to our clothing that they could not be loosened even with the aid of a knife. However, desmodium is a very pretty flowering perennial plant whose rose red blossoms stay in bloom for several months. On the higher prairie an abundance of dalea and astragalus grew, moreover, a very luxuriant melilotus, which ought to furnish an excellent fodder. Of the trees I saw the American cedar (juniperus oxycedrus). This tree extends a considerable distance up the Missouri, as far as 45° of latitude. It furnishes a very fine and useful timber. Tetrao Phasianellus was found here and there. Its habits are the same as those of tetrao cupido. A large pretty grossbeak, brown with yellow belly and white dots lives either singly or in small flocks in these parts, and seems to frequent the wild cherry trees in the prairie. These cherries, which produce dark red fruit in grape-like clusters have a pleasing and cooling taste. A variety of plum with rather large, red fruit is seen frequently in these prairies, but does not form such large clumps as farther north. In the northern regions the cherries cover large tracts of land and constitute a real source of food for the Indians in the summer.

At daybreak Chu-ge-ga-chae arrived with a crowd of Indians.

With him was his son Ka-hi-ge-schin-ga. In the language of the Indians this name means a little chief. They had ridden the whole night and their horses were very tired. Chu-ge-ga-chae was a man of fifty, tall and very stout. An extremely large nose disfigured his face. Unfortunately this Indian chief, known for his bravery and goodness of heart died a few years ago. He lies buried near the place where we had our meeting. A large heap of stones marks the place where his remains rest. He was a man whose excellent character deserved a better fate than that of only being a chief in the prairie. His generous deeds refute the fabulous and absurd accounts which some travelers employ to defame a people, whose customs and usages they are not able to judge.

At his arrival he manifested his sincere distress over the sad condition of my servant, and promised me solemnly to give him all the aid that was in his power to give. Among the Poncas who had come along was a creole who had lived among the Sioux as an interpreter. He looked even wilder than the Indians. He seemed, however, to be a good man. He praised Chu-ge-ga-chae very much and assured me without reservation that I might be without concern regarding the care the sick man would receive. He stated that the chief entertained every hope for his recovery, and that the patient, once having arrived at the Indian camp, would receive the best of care. All these promises were indeed fulfilled punctually and unselfishly. The sick man's health was restored completely, and a few months later he was brought back to Fort Atkinson.

After I had spoken with Chu-ge-ga-chae for a short while concerning his affairs, and his relations with the Sioux, I gave orders to start on our journey. The son of the chief together with some of the warriors accompanied us over the adjoining hills to a height from which one could see the procession of the Poncas. (In their own language they call themselves Puncaras.) The whole horde had followed their chief during the night. They were apparently only a few miles away. They advanced in the same order as had the Omahas, only they maintained a strong and well-armed rear guard as a protection against a probable attack on the part of the Dakotahs or Sioux. Ka-hi-ge-schin-ga gave me the advice to follow the trail of the Puncaras up the Ponca River, in order to avoid the scarcity of water. From the source of this river, I was told, I was to hasten in a northerly direction, and cross the stony desert which separates the Ponca from the White River. He at the same time admonished me to supply my caravan with sufficient water, since we could not find any water over a distance of fifty English miles.

About ten o'clock in the morning we reached the Ponca, at a place from which one could look down on the Missouri. Tall cottonwoods shaded this little stream. Its charming banks broke the monotony of that region most agreeably. Not far from this place is a most remarkable fortification,[8] which belonged to a nation long extinct, of whose history we know nothing. On a conical elevation are breastworks in the form of a circle. This circle is more than 100 paces in diameter. In its entire circuit it had stood up well during all these centuries. This fortress was a part of a system of warfare that was entirely different from that practiced by the Indians of today. The selection of the site itself proves that the fortification was designed for a considerable stay. It is remarkable how little the Indians of the lower Missouri region know of the art of protecting themselves against a sudden attack, by means of well worked out devices of defense. The Indians of the farther north country, on the other hand, are much more skillful in this respect. They know how to secure themselves on their expedition by barricades of tree trunks against a sudden attack. They also attempt to protect their villages by strong palisades. Near the Rocky Mountains I found four-sided fortifications made of tree trunks. They belonged to the Blackfeet and Assiniboins. Sometimes such fortifications were found six or eight in a series, at some distance from one another.

While crossing the Ponca I shot a deer of that variety which the creoles call chevreuil a queue noire, which Mr. Say has very correctly classified as cervus macrotys. This variety of deer Mr. Say has correctly analyzed as cervus macrotys.[9] This species belongs to cervus dama without palmated antlers. It attains the size of the European deer. It appears to constitute a transition between the smaller deer and the elk. The antlers of this deer are forked, and usually grow longer than those of cervus virginianus. The extraordinarily large ears of this deer produce a striking effect, as does also the black spot on the short tail. Further north this deer becomes more numerous, while the Virginia deer becomes more rare. The color of the adult blacktail deer is red shading into yellow, somewhat lighter than the Virginia deer. In their mode of living they are alike.

The Ponca extends almost in a straight direction to the northwest, running parallel to the Eau qui courre. Here and there it is shaded by fine oaks and cottonwoods. In places high hills force it into a narrow channel, and then again it spreads out, its banks touching upon extensive prairie lands. The summits of the hills are covered with short curly grass, among which the Missouri cactus grows. The bed of the river is sandy, and the banks are steep and high. In the afternoon a cold northwest wind began to blow, which reduced the temperature of the air from 18° to 8° R., and forced me to get out my warmer clothing, since I had become quite unaccustomed to such changes in temperature. That night I spent among some willow bushes and cottonwoods on the bank. The cold during the night may have hurt the wolves, for they howled pitiably, so that I could not sleep. At midnight the sky became clear and the thermometer registered 1.4° above zero. On the morning of August 18 a thick hoarfrost covered the land, and the whole vegetation mourned because of the sudden change in heat condition. The thermometer had registered a few lines above zero. The Ponca is scarcely 1800 Rhenish feet above sea level, so that we have here added proof as how strongly the northwest wind acts upon the thermometer even at this latitude.

High hills compelled me to leave the Ponca a few miles to one side, in order to reach the plateau which lies between the Ponca and the Eau qui courre. This plateau is called Pan-haesch-na-bae by the natives and Buttes de medecine by the creoles. This remarkable hill formation rises out of the plain and appears as a four sided rock, 400 to 500 feet high, with abrupt sides. On the flat summit boulders lie scattered. This striking rock, as also an isolated high hill, almost two degrees to the north, in the neighborhood of Grand detour, called Man-haesch-na-bae, la Grande butte de medecine, are most noteworthy points for the geographer. Their longitude and latitude ought to be accurately determined. Since my way took me close to this formation, I regretted exceedingly the loss of my instruments, which made it impossible to undertake observations of this kind.

* * * * *

To the east, that is toward the Missouri great clouds of smoke were seen rising. It was a prairie fire, which even in this season began to consume the prairie grass. These fires gradually extend over the entire boundless prairie country, and sweep away the season's growth of grass in a sea of flames.

At noon I reached the Ponca, fifty miles from its mouth. A new surprise awaited me here. All the hills on the other side were covered with great herds of bison. These were the first animals of this kind which I had seen in the wild state. We made preparations at once for the hunt, and crossed the stream. We tried to hide behind a ridge to the leeward of the animals. Horses and mules were fettered and bound together as quickly as possible, with strong thongs of bison leather, such as the Indians make use of. In our haste, however, we forgot to take my mantle and the water container from the back of the mule. This I later regretted very much. The halfbreed Monbrun picked out the fittest of our horses, saddled and bridled it in Indian fashion, and then galloped away, selecting a round-about way, behind the hills and thru ravines, observing the wind so cleverly that he was on a full run among the herd before the animals were aware of it. Suddenly one could see countless bisons running about in an extraordinary confusion. The whole prairie, far and wide, was one confusion of excited animals. Without knowing which way to go, they ran to and fro. It seemed as if the herd would turn to the northwest. Suddenly, however, they changed their course and rushed with extreme speed between the Ponca and the hill where my pack animals were. The region where Monbrun had come upon the herd was now pretty well cleared of the creatures. There I saw the man sitting on his horse and resting after he had killed three of the bison.

I found protection from the approaching herd behind a boulder. Here I observed how the vanguard of the animals, frightened at the sight of our horses and mules, rushed in a straight line toward the river. Now the enormous creatures passed close by me. For more than an hour I had the opportunity of seeing the animals at close range. The unaccustomed sight amazed me. Only after a considerable time one becomes accustomed to the sight of such huge animals. In time they become a familiar sight to the traveler. The hunters pass indifferently among them, killing only those animals that they need for food. It is a shame that from sheer wantonness a countless number of these harmless creatures are uselessly sacrificed. It is extremely easy to hunt the bison with firearms after one has once learned this method of hunting.

A most disagreeable accident might have caused me the greatest embarrassment. In spite of the precaution and care with which my men had fettered and tied the pack animals, misfortune willed it that the herd of bison should run just in the direction where the horses had been left. The latter became

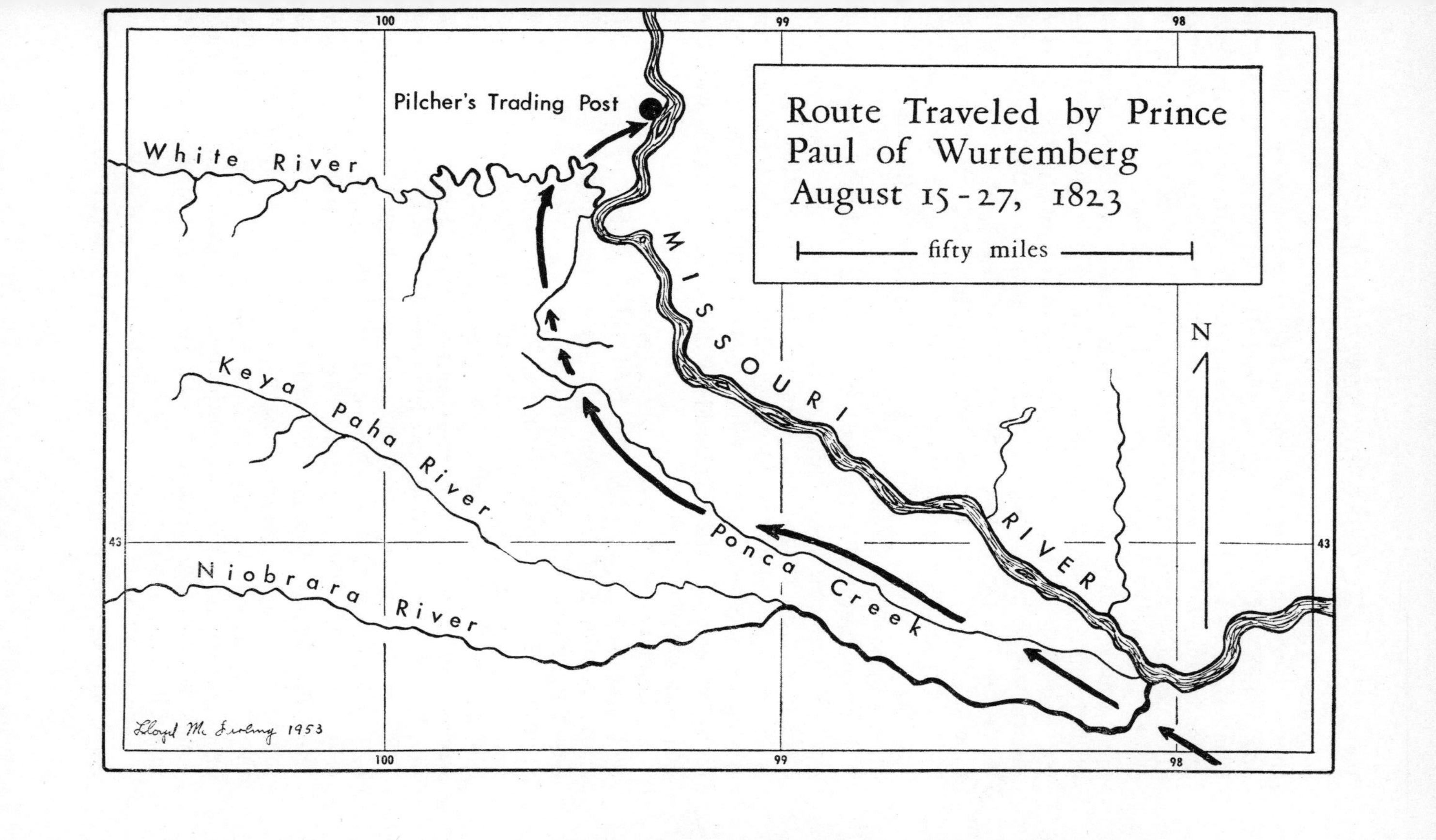
Route Traveled by Prince
Paul of Wurtemberg
August 15-27, 1823
fifty miles
N
Pilcher's Trading Post
White River
MISSOURI RIVER
Keya Paha River
Ponca Creek
Niobrara River
100
99
98
43
Lloyd M. Irving 1953

so much frightened, that they broke away, freed themselves of their fetters and fled. A mule which had not been unloaded, and which carried my mantle and the water container also escaped. The whole evening was spent in hunting for the lost animals, but they were not found till the following morning, all except the mule, which could not be found again. Probably frightened by the pack, which had become loosened, he must have followed the buffalo. This loss was very distressing, especially since it involved the loss of the water container. This was especially regrettable as I was about to traverse the already mentioned desert region, and necessity demanded that we should be supplied with drinkable water. My men sought to make good this loss by drying the bladders of the bisons Monbrun had killed. These they blew up and later filled them with water. This water, however, took on such a repulsive taste that it was almost impossible to make use of it.

In the night a heavy shower with thunder and lightning passed over us. The ceaseless rolling of the thunder, the sharp electric discharges and the bellowing of the bison gave this night the true character of the wilderness. The bison that had run in such great numbers to the Ponca were badly frightened. Their restlessness was still increased by the fact that this was the breeding season.

I missed my mantle very much, since I had nothing to protect myself with against the cold rain. About midnight the storm passed and the moon illumined the gloomy landscape. Great numbers of bison passed close to our camp. A few bulls approached fearlessly to within a few feet. Since a scant fire had to be maintained, it seemed to me that these animals were blinded by the blaze and at the same time attracted by it. I have often observed that wild animals like to come close to a fire, indeed often so close that they can be killed.

Early the next morning Rodger brought back the horses that had run away. As I still hoped to find the mule, I decided to roam over the plain till noon. This plain separates the Ponca from the Eau qui courre. I made use of the time to observe the bison at as close range as possible, and to shoot some of them. Of the bulls only the tongue can be eaten during the breeding season. They disseminate a pungent odor of musk, which is even more pungent than that of the stag during the breeding season.

During the morning I was surprised in a peculiar manner. As I was behind a steep height, I saw several human heads protruding over the ridge. I recognized them at once as those of Indians. I made signs of friendship and soon saw an Indian warrior climb to the summit of the hill and beckon with a blanket. Since I recognized this as a sign of peace, intended for me, I waved my handkerchief. The Indians withdrew and disappeared toward the west, all except the one who had given me the sign. He approached me unarmed and gave me his hand. He was a tall handsome man of about thirty, whose face and body, however, were made ugly by a layer of white chalky earth. He directed my attention to the bison I had killed. Then he pointed in the direction of the Eau qui courre and repeatedly pronounced the word Poncara. He also pointed to the north and several times pronounced the word Wa-schi, which means white people. I now understood the Indian who meant to say that he belonged to a war party that had gone out after the Poncaras and that many Americans and creoles were coming from the north. By this he meant the expedition of General Leavenworth against the Arikaras.[10] A large body of Sioux had gone with this officer as auxiliary troops. The Indian warrior now began dressing the bison which I had killed, and we parted as friends.

I must remark that the Indians, even if they are in a region that abounds in game, avoid killing any animal, when they are on an expedition of war, in order that they may not be betrayed to their enemies by the remains. Therefore they sometimes suffer the greatest hunger, especially if they spend a long time in a hiding place.

Later I learned that I really had not been mistaken in regard to the Indians. They were Sioux of the Teton tribe. These Indians are called Si-schan-ko, or burnt posteriors, cu brule, not bois brule or burnt wood, as they are often called incorrectly. The group which I saw comprized only twenty men, the whole party numbered perhaps more than a hundred. During my stay among the Pawnees this war party disturbed the latter near the Platte River. The invaders lost their chief in an engagement with the Wolf-Pawnees.

NOTES TO CHAPTER 14

1. To convert the Reaumur scale to the Fahrenheit scale, multiply by 2.25 and add 32. 28° R. equals 95° F.

2. The Niobrara River.

3. Note by Prince Paul: "Unfortunately I could not make accurate measurements, since all my instruments had either been lost or had become

utterly useless. On my second journey the sky was invisible because of a bad snowstorm."

4. Prince Paul had been entertained by Pierre Chouteau, Sr. (1758-1849) and Auguste Chouteau (1749-1829) at St. Louis. Perhaps they told him of some visit to the Niobrara but it is not probable they were the first white visitors. The Mallet brothers probably reached it in 1739, on a trip from St. Louis to Santa Fe. Federal Writers' Project, American Guide Series, *Nebraska*, p. 47. Henri Folmer, "The Mallet Expedition of 1739. . . ." *The Colorado Magazine*, September, 1939, pp. 161-73.

5. Clark wrote in his journal September 4, 1804: "this River is 152 yards Wide at the Mouth & 4 feet Deep. . . ." Thwaites, ed., *Original Journals*, I, 138-39.

6. The science of geology was young in Prince Paul's day, which may partially account for his errors in that field. He wrote of volcanoes, lava, and volcanic rock while traveling in a region where the rock is sedimentary. Perhaps he mistook eroded sandstone and limestone, colored with iron or other minerals, for lava. Moreover, at the time he traveled, there was a prevailing belief that there were volcanoes in this region, a belief caused by the appearance of smoke rising from the tops of conical hills. In 1839 Nicollet called these hills pseudovolcanoes, and thought the smoke was due to the decomposition of minerals reached by percolating waters. Nicollet, "Report Intended to Illustrate a Map. . . ." pp. 39-40.

7. Probably *Lepus campestris*, one of the varieties of hare commonly called the jack rabbit.

8. Not far from this place, on the bank of the Missouri, on September 2, 1804, William Clark examined and mapped what he thought was an ancient fortification. It is now known to be a natural geologic formation. Perhaps Prince Paul was deceived in the same manner.

9. The curious repetition appears in the translated text. The mule deer was called *Cervus macrotys* (or *macrotis*) in Prince Paul's day; it is now known as *Odocoileus hemonius*. *Cervus virginianus* has been renamed *Odocoileus virginianus*.

10. Cf. chapter 7, *ante*. Prince Paul was ascending the Missouri at the time of the Leavenworth campaign and picked up information from several sources. On June 27, near Fort Osage, he met a boatman who had participated in the fight between the Ashley forces and the Arikaras. On August 23 he reached Fort Recovery where he was entertained by Joshua Pilcher. Here he found that "all the Sioux were very much excited because of the result of the expedition against the Arikaras. It also seemed to me that the members of the Fur Company were not pleased with the result of the war." Later the Prince met Colonel Leavenworth at Fort Atkinson. On a trip to the Missouri in 1829 he visited the battleground. Contrary to most historians, he approved Leavenworth's conduct of the expedition. He thought Leavenworth's regular forces were too weak for a successful attack on the Arikara village, that Leavenworth could not have relied upon the allied Indians and fur traders, and that ". . . it would have been an act of madness on the part of the commandant to have risked the lives of soldiers against a horde of Indians living so far from every settlement, especially in a terrain so disadvantageous."

Chapter 15

1823

FROM PONCA CREEK TO WHITE RIVER,

by Prince Paul of Wurttemberg

In this chapter we follow Prince Paul's travels from August 19 to August 23, 1823. He went north from the valley of Ponca Creek to White River and northeast to the nearest trading post on the Missouri, near the present city of Chamberlain, South Dakota.

This trading post was operated by Joshua Pilcher of the Missouri Fur Company. It was probably the post that was sometimes called Fort Recovery, established in 1822. Here Prince Paul met Joshua Pilcher and some of the Sioux Indians who had recently returned from the Leavenworth campaign against the Arikaras.

He also met Toussaint Charbonneau, who invited him to visit another post "20 miles upstream," which must have been Fort Kiowa. The post was almost bare of provisions, the Indians were hungry and mourning ceaselessly for relatives lost while fighting the Arikaras. Prince Paul stayed overnight and returned to Pilcher's post.

It was not his first contact with the Charbonneau family. On June 21, 1823, near the mouth of the Kansas River, he met Baptiste Charbonneau. When he returned to Europe he took Baptiste with him. This son of Toussaint Charbonneau and Sacajawea was born early in 1805 at the Mandan villages, and with his parents accompanied Lewis and Clark to the Pacific coast and back. Baptiste spent several years in Europe as a protégé of the prince, acquired a European education of sorts, and returned to the plains and mountains of the United States to become a guide, interpreter, and fur trader.

On the twenty-ninth of August Prince Paul left Pilcher's post, in a small boat provided by Joshua Pilcher, for his journey to Fort Atkinson. In the boat were Mr. Leclerc of the fur company, two Americans, an Irishman, two half-breeds, and a Negro. And Friedrich Paul Wilhelm, Prince of Wurttemberg. The Missouri was a cosmopolitan river in 1823.

At noon my men joined me. They, too, had observed the Indians, and were much concerned, because they had recognized them as Sioux, and were afraid of them. The Sioux are, however, dangerous only as enemies. As such they are cruel and bloodthirsty. As friends they are just as loyal and very grateful. In the course of my journey, I had, by chance, the good fortune to render a favor to a Sioux of high rank. On my second journey, in the midst of winter, under the most trying climatic conditions the son of this warrior rescued me and my companions from a very critical situation. This he did at great personal sacrifice.

Tho very tired from walking thru the tall grass and fatigued by the great heat, I continued my journey. Near evening we crossed the Ponca and stopped there several hours to let our exhausted horses rest. I had ridden thru countless herds of buffalo. Since the wind was favorable they allowed us to come close to them. The old bulls even remained lying in the river and eyed us calmly. These large, frightful monsters, relying on their enormous strength, seem to defy almost any enemy. The cows on the other hand, are very shy, and it requires great caution on the part of the hunter to slip up on them. The great herds maintain a peculiar order on their march, and thus make broad trails, sometimes several feet wide, which are tramped out deep. Frequently several such trails run one beside the other, forming regular roads. The creoles and the Canadians call them chemins de boeufs. Since we were obliged to ride in such trails, freshly made by the herds, we had to exercise the greatest caution in the selection of camp sites. Unless the wind apprises these creatures of the proximity of the camp, they walk right thru it, stampeding the horses and often endangering the men and the baggage. These animals, usually old bulls and old cows, follow the trail stubbornly. If the vanguard has once passed over an object, the others do not allow themselves to be deterred by anything.

The evening was very beautiful. Near ten o'clock, however, a strong wind arose which was followed by a thunderstorm, equally as severe as the one on yesterday. Lightning struck some nearby trees. Frightened herds of bison fled in the greatest confusion, seeking the ravines among the hills or the wooded banks of the river. Amid the flashes of lightning I saw them often near our camp. The rising sun dispelled the clouds. The wind turned to the southeast and from August twenty to September three we had no more rainfall. The heat of the day was very oppressive, but the nights began to be cool. In this region of the Ponca the ground rises more and more, and takes on a volcanic character....

The Ponca is forced into a narrow bed. The sides are for the most part wall-like, abrupt cliffs. Only here and there the banks are shaded by low trees. Deep bison trails cut up the narrow valley. At intervals of 200 and 300 paces the stream had to be crossed. The narrow valley affords no other way out. A large number of bison grazed in this gorge. At our approach they fled over the hills. On this day we killed several of these animals. The cows are extremely fat and their meat is excellent. It excels the best beef in quality. The cows are a third smaller than the full grown bulls. The calves which were born in March are already fairly large. They were reluctant to leave their mothers that had been killed, and even attacked the hunters courageously, when they attempted to approach the bodies of the dead cows. The wounded animals fled and offered fight only when severely pressed. Loaded with meat we went to a convenient place to stop for dinner. While my companions prepared the meal, I made use of the time to study the surrounding country. From an elevation I could see the Eau qui courre and the Ponca distinctly. These two streams run almost always parallel to each other. The region is hilly, overgrown with short grass and permeated with deep hollows, up and down which one must climb with much effort. The Eau qui courre seemed broad and swollen, a result of the heavy rain of the previous night.

A lot of antelopes, in groups of three and four, grazed on the prairie, and as far as the eye could reach I saw bisons. My men thought I was lost and were just ready to start on a search for me. In spite of the great heat I ordered to break camp and to continue the march. Progress was especially difficult as the bed of the Ponca was so muddy that the pack animals sank down to their bellies. We had to cross the stream five times. The bisons had tramped out the banks of the stream so deep in places, that it was hard to travel. They had also made deep wallows in the bed itself. Some of our mules fell into some of these holes and our baggage got soaked. In some places, especially toward the region where the Ponca divides into two branches the water was shallow. There the banks were overgrown with a dense growth of willows and American dogwood.

We spent the night on an island in the stream. The hungry wolves of this region, who had scented fresh meat, ventured to come so close to camp that we had to kill several of them to rid ourselves of the tormentors. . . .

During the night of August 24 the thermometer sank to 8° above zero. The mosquitoes became less numerous. My men had spent the night on guard. All sorts of signs had caused them to fear the presence of a party of hostile Indians.

Rodger suffered great pain from a peculiar injury to his

hand. This wound he had gotten while attempting to capture a porcupine. The quills of these animals, hystrix dorsata (erethizon dorsata, Fr. Cuvier) produce ugly wounds which heal poorly if the quill breaks off in the wound. Instead of coming out by festering it penetrates deeper into the flesh. This may even result in the loss of a member.

In the morning a strong wind blew from the east. The heat was much reduced. At noon the thermometer registered 13.5°. I had to cross the Ponca frequently. It became more and more swampy. The herds of buffalo did not decrease in number. At noon the entire plain was covered with them. In the afternoon it began to rain. The wind turned to the northeast. Toward evening the sky became clear, and the air was painfully cold. The tributary of the Ponca which I followed divided into two branches. It contained less and less water and finally became entirely dry.

I computed the length of the Ponca from the junction of the two branches to the confluence with the Missouri at about 140 English miles. This is counting all the bends, of course. Without these the distance may amount to a little more than 100 English miles. I calculated the latitude of my night's camp of the 20th to the 21st as 42° 40′.[1]

The region southwest of the tributaries is a rather level prairie. It extends thus as far as the Eau qui courre. To the north and east, however, an extremely wild region sets in. . . .

The journey was now continued directly to the north, in an attempt to cross a chain of rocky hills. These hills rise to a considerable height above the plains. After a march of three hours we reached the first row of these hills. They form truncated cones or cylinders with bare summits, strewn with cubical boulders, or columns. I rode past some hills of dazzling whiteness. One of these resembled a large tower, and was marked by broad black bands. These rocks reminded me of the towerlike formations in the region Pirna in Saxony. From here a twenty-mile plain extends, interrupted only by small elevations. The spaces intervening represent the beds of driedup creeks. The land is desolate and uninhabited. Here and there one saw a lone bison, hunting its scant food on adjoining heights. Antelopes ran a short distance ahead of the horses, stopping frequently to observe us more closely and then again taking flight. Great numbers of wolves followed us at a slight distance and uttered their terrible howls from time to time. These waste regions were swept by a cold northeast wind which was very painful, and against which I could hardly protect myself. We made 40 English miles on this day, and found not a drop of water anywhere. On the next evening man and beast had to go thirsty. The cold increased, so that the short, curly grass was covered with hoarfrost, and the thermometer fell to 2.4° R. below zero.

Early the next morning we started, altho I was quite stiff from the cold. We continued our journey northward thru the wasteland. By noon we reached the hills which border the plain to the northeast. Along the base of these hills winds a stream, whose banks are sparsely wooded. On the older charts this stream is called Shannon's River.[2] I was greatly disappointed to find its bed dry. Thus we were doomed to endure painful thirst for some time yet. The wind subsided toward the morning, and at once the temperature rose to a degree that was alarming to men already famished. I ordered the horses to be unsaddled, and camped in the shade of a few linden trees and oaks.

I was very much surprised to find doves and song birds here, and concluded from this that there ought to be some pools of water near. However, in spite of every effort, no water could be found. After an hour's rest, I ordered that we should start again, in order to leave this desolate region as soon as possible, a region which may justly have some similarity with one's conception of hades. High, conical, sharp-pointed, rocky hills are separated from one another by deep, steep-walled ravines. The floors of these ravines are strewn with great boulders, or broken by deep holes. Wide-mouthed caves open into the sides of the walls. They contain lava and cinders. Craters of extinct volcanoes, now filled with ashes and other volcanic matter, testify by their funnel shaped depressions of their former extent and location. After a dangerous ride of two hours I passed over this ridge, the picture of which will remain deeply impressed on my mind, . . .

Soon I entered another such high plain, which was bounded on the north by high hills. It extends perfectly level for seven miles. Here, too, nature seemed to have died out. Neither birds nor mammals were to be seen. My companions were of the opinion that the White River was beyond the above named ridge. According to my calculation, however, this stream was yet 20 miles away. The most tormenting thirst compelled us to ride as rapidly as possible. Since the ridge opened to the northeast, we rode thru deep ravines and found, as I had surmised, a wilderness surrounded by high hills, but no drinking water. For fear of famishing we continued our way far into the night. The bright light of the moon illuminated the desolate region. The hope of finding water made us forget our weariness, however, the rough ground, being full of holes, and the many prickly cacti presented too many hinderances to allow further advance by night. Without food, tormented by the keenest thirst, we had to stop for the night. After midnight dense clouds rose along the horizon. However, it did not rain, and the cold became painful.

Early on the 23d my men and horses, exhausted by thirst, had to start again. I estimated the distance to the White River at fifteen English miles. The country continued to present the same aspect, always desolate, full of boulders, bearing the imprint of subterranean fires. Beyond an elevation some Indians were making signals with a small mirror, on which they caught the rays of the sun. These reflections can be seen at a great distance. The sight of human beings filled me with joy. It filled my men with terror, because they always suspected enemies. Surmising that the Indians might be Cheyennes or Sahones,[8] who are the terror of travelers, my men refused to move on. I insisted on my purpose of advancing without delay, thinking that it would be better to face a fight with the Indians than die of thirst. Moreover, the lay of the land was such that we could reach the White River without getting into an ambush. I was of the opinion, furthermore, that the Cheyennes might be encamped near the Rocky Mountains, and that there might be no danger from the Sahones, since they likely were engaged with their archenemies, the Arikaras. Finally, at about ten o'clock I saw the White River, in a narrow tree-covered valley, surrounded by high hills. The creoles call this river Riviere blanche. We reached it after descending a steep hill, which was overgrown with opuntia and was almost impassable, being strewn with boulders and broken lava.

The White River flows over a bed of white clay. Its water is so empregnated with the latter, that it, at low water resembles a thin gray paste. The river is not deep but contains great stretches of quicksand and beds of clay. The latter dries up quickly after the recession of the water. The deeper layers remain soft and slimy, so that one sinks into it deeper and deeper at every step. The horses sank so deep into the soft ground that finally we had to wade thru on foot. Tho I was extremely thirsty, I could scarcely make myself drink of the water in the river. The slimy stuff was so repulsive. My companions, however, drank immoderately of it, and at once felt colic-like pains. We tried in vain to cook something. The water remained thick and would not settle any earthy particles. In this respect it differed greatly from the water of the Missouri.[4]

I stopped for an hour, which time the men spent in great anxiety. Soon after starting three Indians came toward us. My men at once jumped from their horses and prepared to fight. I called their attention to the fact that there were two men and a woman who were approaching, and that three persons coming in broad daylight could have no evil intentions. The new arrivals were an elderly man, a youth and a young woman. The latter carried a basket full of something. They belong to the tribe of Yanktons, a member of the Sioux or Dakota nation, which live in peace with the Americans. The man told much regarding the expedition which the Americans had made against the Arikaras. This expedition had failed of its purpose. He described most accurately the way to the nearest American factory, which was perhaps twenty miles away. The woman gave me a basket of wild plums, which in this region are of excellent quality. They are of a variety not hitherto described. I sought to compensate them for the gift by giving them some tobacco, powder, and some flint stone, for the man had a gun, but the youth had only a lance. The Indian also reported that the people whom we had seen on the hill were likewise Sioux of his tribe, who accompanied some hunters of the Missouri Fur Company, whose business it was to supply the post with game.

The way we now took was a most difficult one. We had to wade thru the shallow river nine times, for it winds around and around in the narrow valley which it waters. Plum trees and hypophaea canadensis, called graine de boeuf grew on the banks of the river. The berries of the latter are somewhat sour. They grow in great numbers on the upper Missouri. Soon I saw several young Indians who were hunting. I asked them to guide me to the factory which was ten miles away. As we left White River we had to climb hills that rose 1000 feet above the bed of the Missouri. Hereupon came a high plateau, from whose northeastern slope the Missouri and the house of the factory could be seen. About two miles from the Missouri the hills descend abruptly. The slopes are composed of weathered lava, sparsely covered with cacti and grass. The wind blew violently from the northeast and the thermometer rose to 25° in the shade,—an unbearable heat. . . . Extremely tired and exhausted

I reached the foot of the hills and rode across the level prairie which separates the Missouri from the hills. Here I saw one of the colonies or towns of barking marmots, arctomys ludoviciana,[5] called chiene de prairie by the creoles. There was a countless number of them. They undermine great stretches of land and inhabit gregariously extensive dens and tunnels. This small, handsome animal, about the size of the European squirrel, has a tail a few inches long. The skin of the prairie dog is yellow. It usually sits so that the upper part of its body protrudes from the opening of its burrow. The bark of this remarkable rodent resembles that of a small dog. At the approach of danger they continue barking till they slip into their burrow. They disappear so quickly that one can scarcely capture them by shooting.

About 800 paces from the Missouri tall cottonwoods and oaks stand. A small brook enters the river near the point where at that time the factory was. Since then the post has become completely dilapidated. Mr. Joshua Pilcher, at that time the superintendent of the Missouri Fur Company, received me at the factory in the friendliest manner. I soon felt compensated for the many privations I had endured.

NOTES TO CHAPTER 15

1. Prince Paul's astronomical instruments had been either broken or made useless by moisture. The only instrument in tolerable condition at this time was a sextant which he later found "did not meet the requirements" he expected of it. He was farther north than he thought, probably about 43° 12′.

2. Probably Bull Creek on modern maps.

3. Cf. note 2, chap. 7, *ante*. Probably Prince Paul meant some of the Teton tribes.

4. "The water of White River is very peculiar, containing a large quantity of calcareous and aluminous matter held in suspension, so that it has much the appearance of milk. When allowed to stand for a short time, or whenever it is found in pools, a thick scum may be seen on the surface very much of the appearance and consistency of rich cream; removing this, and the thinner portion is of a much lighter color, like milk. It is very astringent to the taste, and its medical effect is quite the reverse of the water previously used." Hayden, Appendix E to Warren, "Explorations in the Dacota Country in the Year 1855."

5. The black-tailed prairie dog has been renamed *Cynomys ludovianus.*

Chapter 16

1839

FROM FORT PIERRE TO DEVILS LAKE,

by Joseph Nicolas Nicollet

Joseph Nicolas Nicollet was born in France in 1786, of poor parents. Noticing his unusual intelligence, a priest taught him to read and write and obtained for him a college scholarship. He became a teacher of mathematics, an astronomer, and a geographer.

In 1832 Nicollet came to the United States and in 1836 he began his greatest geographical work—the exploration of the Upper Mississippi Valley. He spent the winter of 1836-37 at Fort Snelling, at the mouth of the Minnesota River. In 1837 he was invited by the Secretary of War to visit Washington, and was authorized to continue his explorations at government expense.

After some more work on the Mississippi in 1838, Nicollet ascended the Missouri to Fort Pierre in 1839. At Fort Pierre he reorganized his party for land travel and went overland through the valley of the James River to Devils Lake, thence southeast into present Minnesota, where he continued his explorations during the summer, returning to St. Louis and to Washington that fall. In Washington he prepared the most accurate map yet made of the Upper Mississippi Valley, and wrote a report of his travels. While writing the brief introduction to the report, Nicollet died in 1843.

The chapter that follows describes Nicollet's trip from Fort Pierre to Devils Lake, July 1 to July 29, 1839.[1]

I supplied myself at Fort Pierre with all I could desire in the way of horses, vehicles, munitions, and provisions; but, in respect to men, the post was at that time itself in want, so that it could spare me only six. I had brought up with me from St. Louis only five men, who, for my purposes, were certainly worth ten. Four among them had proved themselves by numerous journeys across the prairies, as well as voyages over the Rocky mountains. One of them was Etienne Provost,[2] known as *l 'homme des montagnes*—the man of the mountains. I may remark here, that these western voyageurs are distinguished from the same set of men who do service on the northern lakes, by their never singing, and, although apparently sullen and discontented, are most faithful, cautious, and courageous in the midst of all dangers. The fifth man was Louis Zindel, who had belonged to the Prussian artillery, and, though totally inexperienced as a traveller in the Indian country, possessed otherwise many qualifications that rendered him most useful to me. He was a capital maker of rockets and fire-works, which proved very servicable to me both for defense and for signal.

Being at Fort Pierre, I met with a Mr. May, of Kentucky, and a young man from Pembina, who expressed a desire to join my party, as they were on their way to the British colony situated on Red river of the North. The accession of their company, and the great acquaintance possessed by the former with all things relating to the west, made me rather anxious than otherwise to have them among us. I had previously engaged William Dixon as a guide and interpreter, when we stopped at the Huppan-Kutey prairie. I now thought it advisable to engage, in the same capacity, Louison Fréniere, and the son of Baptiste Dorion, the interpreter at the post. Both Dixon and Fréniere had the reputation throughout the country of being the most adventurous and successful hunters, as well as the most experienced guides.[3]

On the 1st of July, Provost, whom I had promoted to the rank of headman, came to announce that all our equipment was in readiness; at the same time Louis Zindel reported that he had prepared his rockets and other defensive missiles; which being duly inspected I gave orders to have the whole transported to the left bank of the Missouri. The roll being called, it was found that, including Mr. Fremont, Mr. Geyer, and myself, we mustered in all a force of nineteen strong.[4] It was but a small one; but, relying on the pyrotechnics of Louis Zindel, the expectation of meeting with our reinforcement from Lac-qui-parle,[5] our own good arms, and an abundance of ammunition, we shouted our huzza of departure, and got under way; not, however, without encountering some difficulties during two days, that I will now relate.

For the previous two weeks the waters of the Missouri had considerably swollen, so that the breadth of the river, at the place where we were to cross it, was a mile and a half: the current was very strong, and our passage could not be effected, notwithstanding all the activity and experience of my men, in less than a day and a half,—the afternoon of the 1st. and the whole of the 2d. of July. Mr. Fremont, Mr. Geyer, and myself, took advantage of this delay to close our scientific labors on the spot, and to post up our journals and field-books.

* * * * *

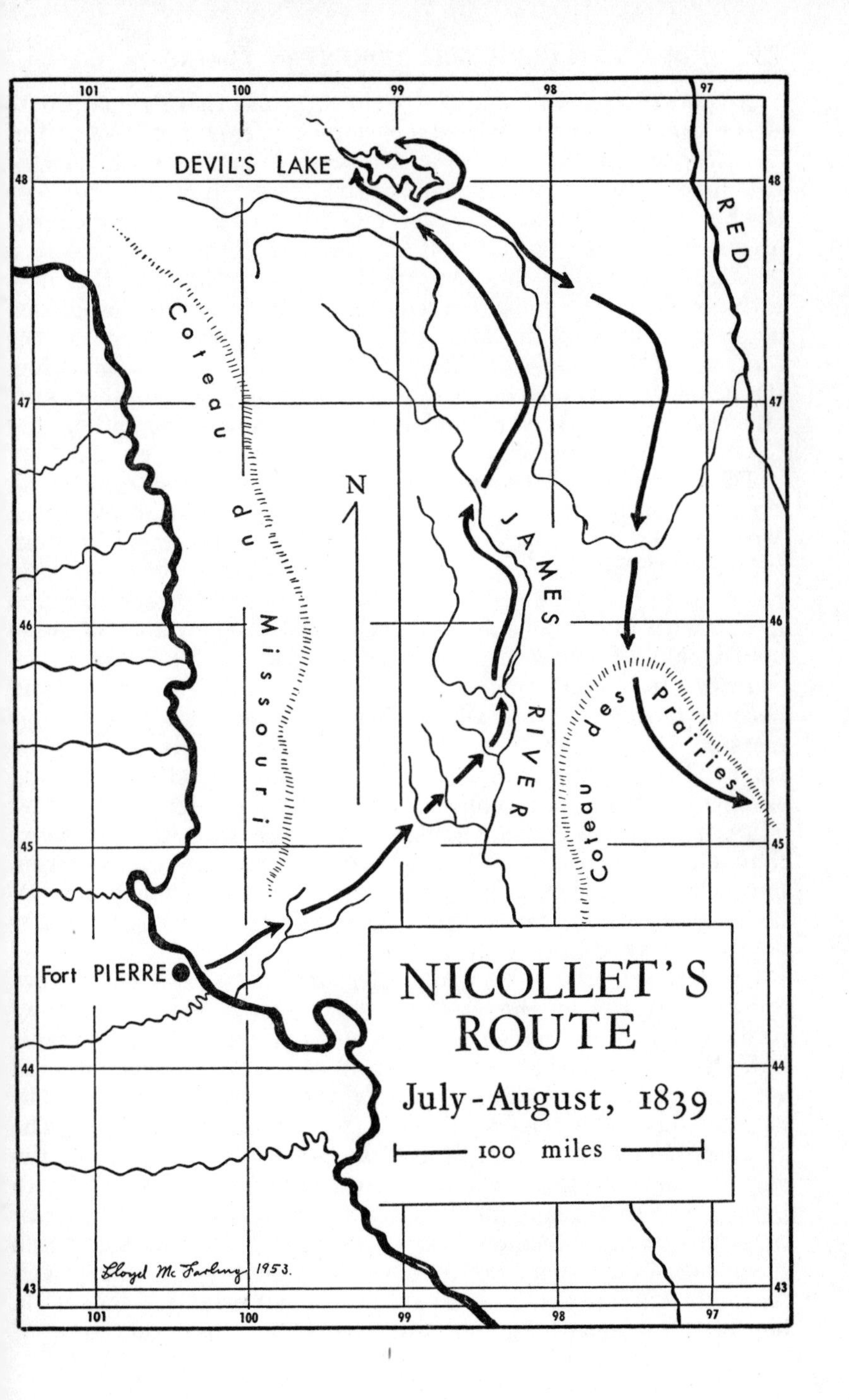

DEVIL'S LAKE
RED
Coteau du Missouri
N
JAMES RIVER
Coteau des Prairies
Fort PIERRE
NICOLLET'S ROUTE
July-August, 1839
100 miles
101
100
99
98
97
48
47
46
45
44
43
Lloyd McFarling 1953.

On the 2d day of July, at 4 o'clock, p. m., there remained to effect the passage of seventeen horses across the river. But the bark which had been procured was too small and too feeble to support more than the men. It became necessary to urge the horses to swim across—each man of the party taking charge of one horse. It may be well supposed that there was no lack of confusion during this truly perilous ferry; and, to this day, I thank God that men, horses, and baggage were not buried under the slime of the Missouri. The night was passed at the foot of the hills opposite Fort Pierre; and the next morning, the whole caravan (consisting of nineteen persons, ten cars,[6] and thirty horses) were under way, ascending the hill to the Coteau du Missouri above.

The plateau that crowns the hills just referred to, has an elevation of not more than 500 feet above the waters of the Missouri; but its slope on the river side is very steep; so that, referring to the map along its whole length from the *Ni-obrarah* river, it will be seen to drain nothing but short creeks. Hence it was with great difficulty, and not until after a lapse of three hours, that we succeeded in reaching the open and unbroken country. In the meanwhile, the scouters had fallen upon a small herd of buffaloes, from which they obtained a very acceptable mess of fresh meat, of which we had been deprived for some time. This circumstance, together with the necessity of making sundry repairs to our vehicles, induced me to order a halt, after a less number of hours than is usual; for we were not more than eight miles to the NE. of Fort Pierre. It will be seen, however, that, from this spot, our journeys assumed a regularity that will dispense with the necessity of my giving any detailed accounts of them.

On reaching the Coteau du Missouri,[7] there are no further apparent traces of the cretaceous formation. It is a rolling prairie, the soil of which is a mixture of fine sand and gravel; but still, it is partly covered by a short, sweet-scented, and grateful verdure. An inspection of the gullies shows that the basis of this soil is the erratic deposite previously described. The silicious particles of the soil are blackened by the smoke of the vernal and autumnal fires of the prairies; and as the growth is too scant to prevent the dust from being raised by the almost incessant winds that blow over them, the traveler is very much inconvenienced. There are no springs to quench the thirst; and it is only at wide distances apart that small pools are met with, bordered by aquatic plants towards which the experience of his guide is necessary to bring him to his bivouac, where he must needs have recourse to the dried dung of the buffalo for fuel. It was in the hope of extricating ourselves from difficulties of this kind that we made an examination of the forks of the East Medicine river, which empties into the Missouri about fifteen miles below Fort Pierre.

This last-mentioned river derives its name from a beautiful hill on its right bank, called by the Sioux *Pahah wakan*—translated by the voyageurs "Butte de Medicine," and in English, Medicine Hillock, or knoll. It is to be remarked, in fact, of the prairies of this region, that they present such low insulated hillocks, to which the Sioux apply the somewhat generic name of *ré* or *pahah*, according as they are more or less elevated above the surrounding plain. The affix *wakan* indicates that the locality is to them peculiarly remarkable, or even sacred, and a spot which they select in preference for some of their ceremonies.

We ascended to the top of the *Pahah-wakan* to enjoy the view over the vast prairie before us, where we could discern herds of buffalo as far as the eye could reach. This was, to say the least of it, a very consoling prospect.

Before quitting the forks of East Medicine river, we had made an ample supply of water and wood; a necessary precaution, for soon every appearance of running water disappeared. The green plains regain their uniformity, bounded only by the horizon, and presenting a smooth surface, without one sprig of grass higher than another. The deep furrows made by the buffaloes in their migrating excursions from north to south, and south to north, are the only irregularities of the surface. However, as the direction of our route is towards the eastern border of the plateau we could not help remarking, that there the undulations of the prairie are shorter, their intervals deeper, and, finally swell into hills of 80 to 100 feet in elevation. We had then reached the dividing ridge between the waters that empty into the Missouri, and those that flow into the river Jacques.[8] The mean elevation of this ridge above the sea is 2,100 feet, and goes to 2,200 feet, if the mean height of the hillocks formed of the erratic deposite be taken into the estimate. One of the points of this ridge is indicated upon the map as my astronomical station of the 6th of July, on the route taken by us over these regions; which route is also laid down. Five or six miles from this station we reached the extreme verge of the eastern limits of the Coteau du Missouri, whence a most magnificent spectacle presents itself, extending over the immense hydrographical basin of the *Tchan-sansan,* or river Jacques.

Dixon, in truth, had been managing a surprise for us; he had been leading me through ravines and over hills, until we gained the spot upon which he wished to place me. Noticing my admiration, he characteristically exclaimed "well, come now, you want geography: look! there's geography for you."

Soon after we commenced to descend the eastern slope of the plateau, and came upon an encampment of Yanktons whom we had previously met on the *Huppan-kutey* prairie,[9] and to whom we had communicated the plan of our itinerary. They were friends or connections of Dixon and Fréniere, whom we were glad to overtake. The encampment consisted of eleven lodges, containing about one hundred and ten persons; and as they were abundantly supplied with provisions, they were enjoying themselves in the fullness of their heart.

We pitched our own tents upon the same prairie, and I had an opportunity to enter into a long conversation with the chief of the party, (the Eagle,)[10] one of the most intelligent and brave Indians with whom I ever became acquainted. He gave me some very important information in reference to the conduct of our expedition across the prairies, so as to avoid any unpleasant rencounter with the warlike parties that meet here during the hunting season. Perceiving that I had but a few men with me, he kindly offered an additional escort of his men; which offer I thought proper to decline, for two reasons: first, because I was unwilling to deprive his party of an assistance and protection that it might itself want on some emergency; and next, for the more prudential consideration of preserving an absolute neutrality. For, in case of meeting with any hostile parties, an attack might be commenced, the baggage robbed, and the horses stolen, before having time to reconcile matters by a friendly intercourse.

Early the next morning, having distributed our presents to the Yanktons, we continued our descent of the Coteau du Missouri along the *Wamdushka,* or Snake River, that takes its rise on the plateau, which we had just left, to empty itself into the *Tchan sansan.* Thence we proceeded to lake *Tchan-ra-ra-chedan,* or lake of the "scattered small wood," the aspect of which is grateful to the traveller, but, from the impurity of its water, affords him but little relief; and then, fifteen to eighteen miles farther, we reached the river Jacques, at a very celebrated spot, called by the Sioux *Otuhu-oju*—meaning, literally, the place "where the oaks spring up," but which I have designated on my map as the "Oakwood Settlement."

Otuhu oju (or, as the French call it, *Talle de Chênes*) was the place of rendesvous which I had assigned to the reinforcement that was to meet me from Lac qui-parle. It had been for the 8th to the 12th of July, and we reached it on the 10th —with laudable exhilaration, it may be believed, after one year's appointment, made in defiance of all unforseeable accidents. The estimate which I have made of the distance between this place and Fort Pierre is about 110 miles; its actual elevation above the sea is about 1,340 feet, and the descent from the Coteau du Missouri to the river Jacques not less than 750 feet. The last 50 miles, by our route, belong to the east slope of the Coteau du Missouri; but, as we were obliged to select our ground, allowing for this, the whole direct distance is probably 40 miles. In a similar way, estimating the distance to the head of the Coteau des Prairies, which is 30 miles to the east: the basin of the river Jacques between the two coteaux, and in the latitude of *Otuhu Oju,* may be laid down as having a breadth of 80 miles, sloping gradually down from an elevation of 700 to 750 feet. These dimensions, of course, vary in the different parts of the valley; but what I have said will convey some idea of the immense prairie watered by the *Tchan-sansan,* which has been deemed by all travellers to those distant regions perhaps the most beautiful within the territory of the United States.

I hazard, in conclusion of my remarks on the physical geography of the valley just described, the suggestion that it has been scooped out by some powerful denuding cause, and that its original geological character was such as is now observed in the Coteau du Missouri and the Coteau des Prairies, by which it is bounded.[11]

It is only necessary to cast a glance over the map, to form an idea of the importance of *Tchan-sansan* river. It takes its rise on the Plateau of the Missouri, beyond the parallel of 47° N.; and after pursuing nearly a north-and-south course, empties into the Missouri river below 43°. It is deemed navigable with small hunting canoes for between 500 and 600 miles; but, below *Otuhu oju,* it will float much larger boats, and there are no other obstacles in its navigation than a few rafts. When we turned away from the river in latitude 47° 27′, its breadth was from 80 to 100 feet; and we could discover by the water marks on its banks, that, in the season of freshets, it widens out here to 100 yards, and south of *Otuhu Oju* to 200 yards. The shores of the river are generally tolerably well wooded, though only at intervals; the trees consisting principally of elm, ash, bar oak,[12] poplar, and willows. Along these portions where it widens into lakes, very eligible situations for farms would be found; and if the Indian traders have hitherto selected positions south of the Otuhu oju, it was doubtless in consequence of its more easy navigation into the Missouri.

The most important tributary to the *Tchan-sansan*, coming into it from its right shore, is the *Pey-watpa* of the Sioux, the riviere aux Ormes of the French—Elm river; which Mr. Featherstonhaugh, relying too implicitly on the well meant information given to him by his good old guide, puts down on his map as emptying into the Missouri.[13]

Elm river might not deserve any especial mention as a navigable stream, but is very well worthy of notice on account of the timber growing on its own banks and those of its forks. Hence it is that the Indian hunting parties, proceeding upon their winter chase across the Coteau des Prairies to the Coteau du Missouri, always take this route; not only, perhaps, for the supply of wood, but also in the expectation of meeting with game. The trading-post of Fort Pierre, occasionally sends an agent to barter with these migratory Indians. It was in this capacity of agent that Louison Fréniere spent among them the winter of 1836-'37, during which he encountered some trying difficulties.[14] The buffaloes did not make their appearance that winter, and the small-pox spread itself among all the tribes that frequent this region, to their extermination. He was left without provisions, and with no other resource than that afforded by the roots of plants which he managed to dig up from beneath the snow. The men attached to his own service died of hunger; and when the spring came, his house was surrounded by dead bodies, alone, amidst this ravage of cold, hunger, and disease.

Ascending the shores of the *Tchan-sansan*, the bordering plains are observed to rise gradually up to the level of the Plateau du Missouri on one side, and that of the *Shayen-oju*[15] on the other; so that the bed of this long river lies more and more deep. We left it at the spot called by the voyageurs *Butte-aux-Os*, (or bone hillock, bone hill,) in consequence of a large heap of bones of animals that the Indians have gathered up and arranged in a certain order. A few miles further we had reached the plateau of the *Shayen oju*. This table land may be considered as a continuation of the Coteau des Prairies; the head of which having yielded, to make way for the passage of the *Shayen-oju*, rises again to form the dividing ridge between the head waters of the *Tchan-sansan* and those of the Red river of the North.[16] This extension of the Coteau des Prairies goes on blending itself with the ascending plains that rise toward the Rocky Mountains, and that divide the waters of the Missouri from those of the long river *Saskatchawan,* that empties into the great Winipik lake.

The *Shayen oju* derives its name from having been formerly occupied by a nation called the Shayens, who were driven from it and pursued beyond the Missouri, where they are still to be found. It is a river of some importance, being navigable by canoes, and its banks well wooded. The extent of its navigation is from near the *Mini-wakan,* or Devil's lake, to its confluence with the Red river of the North. Its valley possesses a fertile soil, and offers many inducements to its settlement; being, moreover, reputed as frequented by animals yielding the finest peltry, to the extent that its exploration is really dangerous, because of the rival and contending parties of Indians that one is exposed to meet with.

On reaching the plateau of the *Shayen-oju,* we were at once surprised and saddened at the sight of still interminable plains extending before us; for we had hoped that, after crossing the river, some variety would present itself, to relieve the monotony of the scenery, and the listlessness consequent upon it, which seemed to be gaining upon our party. The Indians and buffaloes, that give animation to the prairies, had not made their appearance for many days; the heat was excessive; the thermometer three times had reached 93°, and we were scare of water; our horses were harassed by flies, and, worse than all, the whole party appeared to be, and were, dissatisfied. I could not but feel the responsibility of my situation, and made an effort to secure the successful result of our expedition, which for a while seemed to be endangered. A trifling incident brought about the change.

I had brought along with me in my medicine chest some *tartaric acid* and *bi-carbonate of soda,* with which I composed an effervescent draught, that was freely distributed among the party. They thus found themselves unexpectedly relieved; and, regaining new energy, we proceeded on our journey. The spirits of the party were further enlivened by falling in with a herd of buffaloes a few hours after. It was an immense herd, whose migration to the southwest obstructed our onward progress, for three days and nights. But it was necessary, for safety's sake, to get out of their path; and, besides, they might be fleeing before some hostile party of Indians; so that we preferred to take a safer position on a branch of the *Shayen oju,* laid down on my map as the *Tampah,* or Birch creek.

On the second day after reaching the latter position, Dixon and Fréniere announced some Indians, of whom three were brought into our camp, who gave information that, about eight miles off, there was an encampment of three hundred lodges, consisting of Yanktons, Sissitons, and Yanktonnans, preparing for a "*surround,*" with which it would be very dangerous to interfere. It was deemed, therefore, advisable, before advancing, to have some previous conversation with the chief of the party. Accordingly, after some necessary precautions, on the afternoon of the third day, having forced our way through the buffaloes, we met two chiefs, *Wahanantan* and *Manka-indlah,* who were advancing to meet us and invited us into their camp, where we had a most animating reception. I caused many presents to be distributed among them, which brought about talks, feasts, dances, songs, and the whole series of their usual ceremonies. This lasted twenty-four hours; after which we resumed our line of march, parting on terms of perfect amity from our new acquaintances.

Having explored the plains of the right side of *Shayen oju,* we crossed the river, and directed our route towards the *Miniwakan,* or Devil's lake. As we advance, the wooded borders of Devil's lake gradually came into view, the rounded summits of the hills looming above the horizon. There is one of these hills in particular which the Sioux call the *Mini wakan-chante*—literally meaning "the heart of the enchanted water," and translated by the voyageurs "the heart of Devil's lake." We could see its summit at a distance of more than 30 miles, though it is not more than 300 feet above the waters of the lake. Still, I was reminded, by its appearance, of some of the dome-shaped summits of the Jura, as seen from the plain of Burgundy. Its name is derived from its shape; when seen in a certain direction, being that of a heart; expressed, in the Sioux language by the word *chante,* and its vicinity to the lake called by them *Miniwakan,*—enchanted water.

The sultriness of the day, and a lack of water, compelled us to come to a halt sooner than we had expected, at a distance of thirteen or fourteen miles beyond the Shayen, and four or five miles from Devil's lake. This lake is supplied by three or four smaller lakes, which we were happy to fall upon, as they afforded us good water and wood. The Metis of the Red river had, we perceived, formed a camp, not far from the spot selected by us, which they had vacated but a few days before, on their return home, as we judged from the deep cuts of their loaded wagons. This was rather a disappointment to me, as I particularly wished to become acquainted with this people, among whom, it is said, are to be found the best hunters, the most expert horsemen, and the bravest warriors of the prairies. The information I have of them is this: They are called the Metis, or half-breeds, being descendents of Canadians, English, and Scotch, crossed with Chippeways, Kristinaux, Assiniboins, Sioux, &c., &c. They represent the remains of Lord Selkirk's colony and of the Hudson Bay Company. As for many years they were only in small numbers, their incursions within the limits of the United States were attended with danger to themselves, in consequence of outrages committed upon them by the full breeds, the Sioux, the Rikaras, the Mandans, the Minitarees, &c. But they have since greatly increased; they number from 600 to 800 people, and have become so formidable as to compel those tribes to seek an alliance with them, and thus to maintain peace. The Metis call themselves "free people," (*gens libres;*) but by their neighbors they are designated as *"Metis of the Red river," "the Red-river People," "the People of the North."*

It is their usage to come twice a year upon the territory of the United States where the buffalo abounds: each family has its cart or wagon drawn by oxen; each hunter has his horse, which is remarkably fleet. They are accompanied by missionaries, who regulate both their temporal and spiritual concerns. Their first campaign is made at the setting in of summer; their second in the fall of the year; and they remain about two months. Sometimes they divide themselves into two bands; directing themselves in this respect according to the distribution which they have previously ascertained of the buffalo herds over these immense plains. One half of the hunters alternately watch over the camp, and the other half are in active pursuit of the game; and the slaughter of the buffaloes is kept up, according to settled usage, until each wagon is loaded with the spoils of ten of these animals.

The next day (being the 29th of July), we took up our line of march, and by mid-day reached the borders of *Mini-wakan* lake. We selected, for the spot of our first encampment, the head of a small bay, sheltered by a copse; and we remained nine days on the borders of the lake; during which, we occupied three distinct stations, as well under the necessity of securing ourselves against the invasion of warlike parties, as to supply ourselves with fresh water from adjoining pools and small lakes.

It is not easy, however, to delineate the figure of the lake. Its first appearance did not realize the anticipations we had been led to form of it from popular account. The lake is on the plateau of the *Shayen-oju,* and is surrounded by swells and hills varying in height from 20 to 250 feet that so project into it as not to permit the whole expanse to be seen but from one spot, which I shall presently describe.

The prominent hill-top, previously alluded to by the name of *Mini-wakan-chante,* is the only beacon to traveller leading to the lake; but even from its summits no idea can be formed of this beautiful sheet of water. He must go to a smaller eminence, known as the *Butte du Milieu* by the French voyageurs, whence alone the eye can take in the principal contours of the lake.

The greatest extension of Devil's lake is at least 40 miles—but may be more, as we did not, and could not, ascertain the end of the northwest bay, which I left undefined on the map. It is bordered by hills that are pretty well wooded on one side, but furrowed by ravines and coulees, that are taken advantage of by warlike parties, both for attack and defense, according to circumstances. The lake itself is so filled up with islands and promontories, that, in travelling along its shores, it is only occasionally that one gets a glimpse of its expanse. This description belongs only to its wooded side; for, on the opposite side, the shores, though still bounded by hills, are destitute of trees, so as to exhibit an embankment to the east from 10 to 12 miles long, upon an average breadth of three-quarters of a mile. The average breadth of the lake may be laid down at 15 miles. Its waters appear to be the drainings of the surrounding hills. We discovered no outlets in the whole extent of about three quarters of its contour we could explore. At all events, if there be any; they do not empty into the Red river of the North, since the lake is shut up in that direction, and since we found its true geographical position to be much more to the north than it is ordinarily laid down upon maps. A single depression at its lower end would intimate that, in times of high water, some discharge might possibly take place; but then it would be into the *Shayen-oju.*

As to the natural history of the waters of the *Mini-wakan,* it is shortly told. They are too brackish to be drunk, excepting by horses, who swallow them with avidity; they have a deeper green color than those of the neighboring lakes that are not salt. I had no means of ascertaining the density of the waters of this lake; but having caused several gallons of it to be evaporated by distillation, I subsequently made an analysis of the residuum, which proved to be a mixture of sulphates and hydrochlorates of soda and magnesia.

As we were not provided with nets, we could not ascertain what species of fish inhabit it. My guides assured me that there were several, and some of a large size; and this was afterwards confirmed to me by some Indians with whom I conversed on the subject. It is a fact, that my men, after a thunder-gust, found on the beach a number of red fish, and a pike which we judged would weigh several pounds. Strawberry vines were found in abundance on the sunny side of the lake.

Finally, and in conclusion of my description of the region about this lake, I may add that the soil is found, in dry weather, to be covered with a saline efflorescence, which sufficiently accounts for its being a great resort of the buffaloes. It also produces a variety of new and interesting plants, some of which will be found in the catalogue of plants under appendix B. This region, by its natural reasons, would admit of numerous settlements. Accordingly, some have been attempted by the traders, but were abandoned in consequence of the hostile spirit of the Indians, who know, by experience, that the buffaloes abandon their usual licks so soon as settlements are made upon them.[17]

NOTES TO CHAPTER 16

1. The "Report Intended to Illustrate a Map of the Hydrographical Basin of the Upper Mississippi River" shows the author's name as I. N. Nicollet. The *I* is evidently a misprint. The geographer's first name is usually given as "Jean," but the biography by Louise Phelps Kellogg in the *Dictionary of American Biography* says it should be "Joseph."

2. Etienne Provost, French-Canadian hunter, trapper, and guide, was born about 1782 and died in 1850. He worked for various fur companies and as a free trapper, ranging from the Missouri to the Rocky Mountains. In 1823 he crossed the continental divide to the sources of the Colorado River, and may have traveled through South Pass at that time. Probably he was the first white man to visit Great Salt Lake.

3. The "Mr. May" may have been William May, at the time an employee of Pierre Chouteau, Jr., and Company. In 1846 Parkman met a "May" at Fort Laramie. He was killed by Arapahoe Indians that summer.

Not much is known about Fréniere. In 1847 he was employed as interpreter by G. C. Mallock, Indian agent, Upper Missouri Agency, who described him as "a half-breed Sioux . . . a good man, as well as a good interpreter . . . a native of the country. . . ." *Report of Secretary of War, 1847*, p. 853.

William Dixon was the half-breed son of Robert Dixon (usually spelled Dickson), a prominent British fur trader and Indian agent. William

Dixon was born probably about 1801; he entered the fur trade at an early age, came to the Missouri as early as 1832, and was employed in various capacities by the American Fur Company and its successors. He was in charge of Dickson's Post, also called Vermilion Post, on the Missouri between the James and the Vermilion, and, later, of another Vermilion post below the Vermilion River, where Nicollet met him. In 1837 he was a guide for Count Francesco Arese, who wrote that he was "a fine mixture of the good points of the two races." Evans, ed., *A Trip to the Prairies. . . .* Nicollet named a bluff on the Missouri "Dixon's Bluff."

4. Fremont was Lieutenant John Charles Fremont. Charles Geyer was a botanist attached to the expedition.

5. A lake on the Minnesota River. The expected reinforcements did not join Nicollet's party.

6. The word is so spelled in the printed report. Undoubtedly it should be "carts."

7. The Coteau du Missouri marks the edge of the physiographic area sometimes called the Missouri Plateau, and is considered by Fenneman (*Physiography of Western United States*) to be the eastern border of the Great Plains at this point. The coteau is a glacial moraine deposited at the border of a pre-existing plateau, and marks the western extent of continental glaciation in this area.

8. The Jacques or *Tchan-sansan* River has also been called the Dakota, but appears on modern maps as the James, and is locally called the Jim.

9. The *Huppan-kutey* prairie extended eastward from Fort Vermilion.

10. In 1837 Arese had as guide from the mouth of the Vermilion River to the Minnesota River a Sioux named Eagle. This Eagle was apparently not a chief at the time but was an Indian of superior ability and may have become a chief by 1839. In the Vermilion area a little later there was a chief known to the whites as War Eagle. It is possible, but not certain, that Arese's Eagle, Nicollet's Eagle, and War Eagle were the same.

11. The "powerful denuding cause" was glaciation. About 1841 Agassiz began to develop his theories of continental glaciation. It is apparent that Nicollet was not acquainted with the theory, when he wrote his report, yet his reasoning, so far as it went, was correct.

12. Probably "burr oak" is intended.

13. G. W. Featherstonhaugh, a geologist employed by the Bureau of Topographical Engineers, wrote a "Report of a Geological Reconnoissance Made in 1835, From the Seat of Government, By Way of Green Bay and the Western Territory, to the Coteau de Prairie, An Elevated Ridge, Dividing the Missouri from the St. Peter's River" (24th. Cong., 1 Sess., *Senate Doc. 333*, 1836).

14. The date appears to be incorrect. All authorities agree that the smallpox appeared among the Indians of the Upper Missouri in the summer of 1837, being introduced to the trading posts by the steamboat *St. Peter's*.

15. The Sheyenne River (spelled with an *S*) flows eastward across southeastern North Dakota and empties into Red River. The Cheyennes lived on its banks for a few years about the end of the eighteenth century, then moved southwest across the Missouri to the Cheyenne (spelled with a *C*) of Wyoming and South Dakota.

16. The Coteau des Prairies, another glacial moraine, borders the valley of the James on the east.

17. Fort Totten, a military post, was established on the shore of Devils Lake in 1867. In 1883 steamboat service was begun, between the town of Devils Lake and the fort, and to other points. Steamboat service was discontinued in 1909. At that time, due to the lowering of the water level, the shore of the lake had receded four miles from the town. Federal Writers' Project, American Guide Series, *North Dakota*.

Chapter 17

1843

BUFFALO HUNTING AT FORT UNION,

by John James Audubon

John James Audubon was born in Santo Domingo in 1785. His prosperous French father took him to France at an early age, and there he received his education. When about fifteen years old he became interested in drawing mammals and birds. Later he studied drawing briefly under Jacques Louis David.

Audubon came to America in 1803 for two years, returned to France for a year, then came again to the United States. For several years, with various partners, he was engaged in various business enterprises. All of them failed. In 1819 he was jailed for debt and released as a bankrupt.

During this time he had been studying and painting birds and mammals. He had married in 1808 and for several years most of the burden of supporting the Audubon family was assumed by his wife. Audubon explored the Ohio and lower Mississippi Valley, painted birds, and earned what he could by painting portraits and street signs and by working as a taxidermist. By 1824 he was seeking a publisher. The search took him to Philadelphia, to Edinburgh, and to London. The elephant folio edition of *The Birds of America* began to appear in 1827 and was published serially for eleven years, while Audubon solicited subscriptions in England, France, and the United States.

The Birds of America brought Audubon so much fame that his paintings of mammals have received little attention. Yet Audubon was a lifelong student and painter of mammals, and when the birds were taken care of he turned his attention to the task of painting and publishing *The Viviparous Quadrupeds of North America*, assisted by his sons John and Victor, also artists. To complete his study of mammals in the field he made a trip up the Missouri River to Fort Union in 1843. A large part of the journal of the trip was lost from the fall of 1843 to 1896, when one of his granddaughters found it in the back of an old secretary. It was published in 1897 in *Audubon and His Journals*, edited by Maria R. Audubon, with zoological and other notes by Elliott Coues. From this edition I am reprinting Audubon's account of his experiences while hunting buffalo at Fort Union, July 26 to August 11, 1843.

On his Missouri River journey Audubon was accompanied by John G. Bell, taxidermist; Isaac Sprague, artist-naturalist; Lewis Squires, general assistant; and "his old friend," Edward Harris. Audubon was fifty-eight years old and he complained a little because he could "no longer draw twelve or fourteen hours without a pause or thought of weariness." But his eyesight was "far keener than that of many a younger man."

The folios of the *Quadrupeds* were published from 1845 to 1848. Audubon died in 1851.

July 26, Wednesday. We were all on foot before daybreak and had our breakfast by an early hour, and left on our trip for Buffalo cows. The wagon was sent across by hauling it through the east channel, which is now quite low, and across the sand-bars, which now reach seven-eighths of the distance across the river. We crossed in the skiff, and walked to the ferry-boat—I barefooted, as well as Mr. Culbertson;[1] others wore boots or moccasins, but my feet have been tender of late, and this is the best cure. Whilst looking about for sticks to support our mosquito bars, I saw a Rabbit standing before me, within a few steps, but I was loaded with balls, and should have torn the poor thing so badly that it would have been useless as a specimen, so let it live. We left the ferry before six, and went on as usual. We saw two Antelopes on entering the bottom prairie, but they had the wind of us, and scampered off to the hills. We saw two Grouse, one of which Bell killed, and we found it very good this evening for our supper. Twelve bulls were seen, but we paid no attention to them. We saw a fine large Hawk, apparently the size of a Red-tailed Hawk, but with the whole head white. It had alighted on a clay hill or bank, but, on being approached, flew off to another, was pursued and again flew away, so that we could not procure it, but I have no doubt that it is a species not yet described. We now crossed Blackfoot River, and saw great numbers of Antelopes. Their play and tricks are curious; I watched many of the groups a long time, and will not soon forget them. At last, seeing we should have no meat for supper, and being a party of nine, it was determined that the first animal seen should be run down and killed. We soon saw a bull, and all agreed to give every chance possible to Squires. Mr. C., Owen,[2] and Squires started, and Harris[3] followed without a gun, to see the chase. The bull was wounded twice by Squires, but no blood came from the mouth, and now all three shot at it, but the bull was not apparently hurt seriously; he became more and more furious, and began charging upon them. Unfortunately, Squires ran between the bull and a ravine quite close to the animal, and it suddenly turned on him; his horse became frightened and jumped into the ravine, the bull followed, and now Squires lost his balance; however, he threw his gun down, and fortunately clung to the mane of his horse and recovered his seat. The horse got away and saved his life, for, from what Mr. C. told me, had he fallen, the bull would have killed him in a few minutes, and no assistance could be afforded him, as Mr. C. and Owen had, at that moment, empty guns. Squires told us all; he had never been so bewildered and terrified before. The bull kept on running, and was shot at perhaps twenty times, for when he fell he had *twelve balls* in his side, and had been shot twice in the head. Another bull was now seen close by us, and Owen killed it after four shots. Whilst we were cutting up this one, La Fleur and some one else went to the other, which was found to be very poor, and, at this season smelling very rank and disagreeable. A few of the best pieces were cut away, and, as usual, the hunters ate the liver and fat quite raw, like Wolves, and we were now on the move again. Presently we saw seven animals coming towards us, and with the glass discovered there were six bulls and one cow. The hunters mounted in quick time, and away after the cow, which Owen killed very soon. To my surprise the bulls did not leave her, but stood about one hundred yards from the hunters, who were cutting her in pieces; the best parts were taken for dried meat. Had we not been so many, the bulls would, in all probability, have charged upon the butchers, but after a time they went off at a slow canter. At this moment Harris and I were going towards the party thus engaged, when a Swift Fox started from a hole under the feet of Harris' horse. I was loaded with balls, and he also; he gave chase and gained upon the beautiful animal with remarkable quickness. Bell saw this, and joined Harris, whilst I walked towards the butchering party. The Fox was overtaken by Harris, who took aim at it several times, but could not get sight on him, and the little fellow doubled and cut about in such a manner that it escaped into a ravine, and was seen no more. Now who will tell me that no animal can compete with this Fox in speed, when Harris, mounted on an Indian horse, overtook it in a few minutes? We were now in sight of a large band of cows and bulls, but the sun was low, and we left them to make our way to the camping-place, which we reached just before the setting of the sun. We found plenty of water, and a delightful spot, where we were all soon at work unsaddling our horses and mules, bringing wood for fires, and picking service-berries, which we found in great quantities and very good. We were thirty miles from Fort Union, close to the three Mamelles, but must have travelled near fifty, searching for and running down the game. All slept well, some outside and others inside the tent, after our good supper. We had a clear, bright day, with the wind from the westward.

July 27, Thursday. This morning was beautiful, the birds

singing all around us, and after our early breakfast, Harris, with La Fleur and Mr. Culbertson, walked to the top of the highest of the three Mamelles; Bell went to skinning the birds shot yesterday, among which was a large Titmouse of the Eastern States, while I walked off a short distance, and made a sketch of the camp and the three Mamelles. I hope to see a fair picture from this, painted by Victor, this next winter, God willing.[4] During the night the bulls were heard bellowing, and the Wolves howling, all around us. Bell had seen evidences of Grizzly Bears close by, but we saw none of the animals. An Antelope was heard snorting early this morning, and seen for a while, but La Fleur could not get it. The snorting of the Antelope is more like a whistling, sneezing sound, than like the long, clear snorting of our common Deer, and it is also very frequently repeated, say every few minutes, when in sight of an object of which the animal does yet not know the nature; for the moment it is assured of danger, it bounds three or four times like a sheep, and then either trots off or gallops like a horse. On the return of the gentlemen from the eminence, from which they had seen nothing but a Hawk, and heard the notes of the Rock Wren, the horses were gathered, and preparations made to go in search of cows. I took my gun and walked off ahead, and on ascending the first hill saw an Antelope, which, at first sight, I thought was an Indian. It stood still, gazing at me about five hundred yards off; I never stirred, and presently it walked towards me; I lay down and lowered my rifle; the animal could not now see my body; I showed it my feet a few times, at intervals. Presently I saw it coming full trot towards me; I cocked my gun, loaded with buck-shot in one barrel and ball in the other. He came within thirty yards of me and stopped suddenly, then turned broadside towards me. I could see his very eyes, his beautiful form, and his fine horns, for it was a buck. I pulled one trigger—it snapped, the animal moved not; I pulled the other, snapped again, and away the Antelope bounded, and ran swiftly from me. I put on fresh caps, and saw it stop after going a few hundred yards, and presently it came towards me again, but not within one hundred and fifty yards, when seeing that it would not come nearer I pulled the trigger with the ball; off it went, and so did the Antelope, which this time went quite out of my sight. I returned to camp and found all ready for a move. Owen went up a hill to reconnoitre for Antelopes and cows; seeing one of the former he crept after it. Bell followed, and at this moment a Hare leaped from the path before us, and stopped within twenty paces. Harris was not loaded with shot, and I only with buck-shot; however, I fired and killed it; it proved to be a large female, and after measuring, we skinned it, and I put on a label "Townsend's Hare, killed a few miles from the three Mamelles, July 27, 1843."[5] After travelling for a good while, Owen, who kept ahead of us, made signs from the top of a high hill that Buffaloes were in sight. This signal is made by walking the rider's horse backwards and forwards several times. We hurried on towards him, and when we reached the place, he pointed to the spot where he had seen them, and said they were travelling fast, being a band of both cows and bulls. The hunters were mounted at once, and on account of Squires' soreness I begged him not to run; so he drove me in the wagon as fast as possible over hills, through plains and ravines of all descriptions, at a pace beyond belief. From time to time we saw the hunters, and once or twice the Buffaloes, which were going towards the fort. At last we reached an eminence from which we saw both the game and the hunters approaching the cattle, preparatory to beginning the chase. It seems there is no etiquette among Buffalo hunters, and this proved a great disappointment to friend Harris, who was as anxious to kill a cow, as he had been to kill a bull. Off went the whole group, but the country was not as advantageous to the pursuers, as to the pursued. The cows separated from the bulls, the latter making their way towards us, and six of them passed within one hundred yards of where I stood; we let them pass, knowing well how savage they are at these times, and turned our eyes again to the hunters. I saw Mr. C. pursuing one cow, Owen another, and Bell a third. Owen shot one and mortally wounded it; it walked up on a hill and stood there for some minutes before falling. Owen killed a second close by the one Mr. C. had now killed, Bell's dropped dead in quite another direction, nearly one mile off. Two bulls we saw coming directly towards us, so La Fleur and I went under cover of the hill to await their approach, and they came within sixty yards of us. I gave La Fleur the choice of shooting first, as he had a rifle; he shot and missed; they turned and ran in an opposite direction, so that I, who had gone some little distance beyond La Fleur, had no chance, and I was sorry enough for my politeness. Owen had shot a third cow, which went part way up a hill, fell, and kicked violently; she, however, rose and again fell, and kept kicking with all her legs in the air. Squires now drove to her, and I walked, followed by Moncrevier, a hunter; seeing Mr. C.

and Harris on the bottom below we made signs for them to come up, and they fortunately did, and by galloping to Squires probably saved that young man from more danger; for though I cried to him at the top of my voice, the wind prevented him from hearing me; he now stopped, however, not far from a badly broken piece of ground over which had he driven at his usual speed, which I doubt not he would have attempted, some accident must have befallen him. Harris and Mr. C. rode up to the cow, which expired at that moment. The cow Mr. C. had killed was much the largest, and we left a cart and two men to cut up this, and the first two Owen had killed, and went to the place where the first lay, to have it skinned for me. Bell joined us soon, bringing a tongue with him, and he immediately began operations on the cow, which proved a fine one, and I have the measurements as follows: "Buffalo Cow, Killed by Mr. Alexander Culbertson, July 27, 1843. Nose to root of tail, 96 inches. Height at shoulder, 60; at rump, 55½. Length of tail vertebrae, 13, to end of hair, 25; from brisket to bottom of feet, 21½; nose to anterior canthus, 10½; between horns at root, 11⅜; between tops of ditto, 17⅛; between nostrils, 2¼; length of ditto, 2½; height of nose, 3⅛; nose to opening of ear, 20; ear from opening to tip, 5; longest hair on head, 14 inches; from angle of mouth to end of under lip, 3½." Whilst we were at this, Owen and Pike were hacking at their cow. After awhile all was ready for departure, and we made for the "coupe"[6] at two o'clock, and expected to have found water to enable us to water our horses, for we had yet some gallons of the Missouri water for our own use. We found the road to the "coupe," which was seen for many, many miles. The same general appearance of country shows throughout the whole of these dreary prairies; up one hill and down on the other side, then across a plain with ravines of more or less depth. About two miles west of the "coupe," Owen and others went in search of water, but in vain; and we have had to cross the "coupe" and travel fully two miles east of it, when we came to a mere puddle, sufficient however, for the night, and we stopped. The carts with the meat, and our effects, arrived after a while; the meat was spread on the grass, the horses and mules hoppled and let go, to drink and feed. All hands collected Buffalo dung for fuel, for not a bush was in sight, and we soon had a large fire. In the winter season this prairie fuel is too wet to burn, and oftentimes the hunters have to eat their meat raw, or go without their supper. Ours was cooked however; I made mine chiefly from the liver, as did Harris; others ate boiled or roasted meat as they preferred. The tent was pitched, and I made a bed for Mr. C. and myself, and guns, etc., were all under cover; the evening was cool, the wind fresh, and no mosquitoes. We had seen plenty of Antelopes; I shot at one twenty yards from the wagon with small shot. Harris killed a Wolf, but we have seen very few, and now I will wish you all good-night; God bless you!

July 28, Friday. This morning was cold enough for a frost, but we all slept soundly until daylight, and about half-past three we were called for breakfast. The horses had all gone but four, and, as usual, Owen was despatched for them. The horses were brought back, our coffee swallowed, and we were off, Mr. C. and I, in the wagon. We saw few Antelopes, no Buffalo, and reached the ferry opposite the fort at half-past seven. . . . A half-breed well known to Provost[7] has been here to make a bargain with me about Bighorns, Grizzly Bear, etc., and will see what he and his two sons can do; but I have little or no confidence in these gentry. I was told this afternoon that at Mouse River, about two hundred miles north of this, there are eight hundred carts in one gang, and four hundred in another, with an adequate number of half-breeds and Indians, killing Buffalo and drying their meat for winter provisions, and that the animals are there in millions.[8] When Buffalo bulls are shot from a distance of sixty or seventy yards, they rarely charge on the hunter, and Mr. Culbertson has killed as many as nine bulls from the same spot, when unseen by these terrible beasts. . . .

August 5, Saturday. . . . Provost tells me that Buffaloes become so very poor during hard winters, when the snows cover the ground to the depth of two or three feet, that they lose their hair, become covered with scabs on which the Magpies feed, and the poor beasts die by hundreds. One can hardly conceive how it happens, notwithstanding these many deaths and the immense numbers that are murdered almost daily on these boundless wastes called prairies, besides the hosts that are drowned in the freshets, and the hundreds of young calves who die in early spring, so many are yet to be found. Daily we see so many that we hardly notice them more than the cattle in our pastures about our homes. But this cannot last; even now there is a perceptible difference in the size of the herds, and before many years the Buffalo, like the Great Auk, will have disappeared; surely this should not be permitted. . . .

August 10, Thursday. . . . Although I have said much about

Buffalo running, and butchering in general, I have not given the particular manner in which the latter is performed by the hunters of this country,—I mean the white hunters,—and I will now try to do so. The moment that the Buffalo is dead, three or four hunters, their faces and hands often covered with gunpowder, and with pipes lighted, place the animal on its belly, and by drawing out each fore and hind leg, fix the body so that it cannot fall down again; an incision is made near the root of the tail, immediately above the root in fact, and the skin cut to the neck, and taken off in the roughest manner imaginable, downwards and on both sides at the same time. The knives are going in all directions, and many wounds occur to the hands and fingers, but are rarely attended to at this time. The pipe of one man has perhaps given out, and with his bloody hands he takes the one of his nearest companion, who has his own hands equally bloody. Now one breaks in the skull of the bull, and with bloody fingers draws out the hot brains and swallows them with peculiar zest; another has now reached the liver, and is gobbling down enormous pieces of it; whilst, perhaps, a third, who has come to the paunch, is feeding luxuriously on some—to me—disgusting-looking offal. But the main business proceeds. The flesh is taken off from the sides of the boss, or hump bones, from where these bones begin to the very neck, and the hump itself is thus destroyed. The hunters give the name of "hump" to the mere bones when slightly covered by flesh; and it is cooked, and very good when fat, young, and well broiled. The pieces of flesh taken from the sides of these bones are called *filets,* and are the best portion of the animal when properly cooked. The fore-quarters, or shoulders, are taken off, as well as the hind ones, and the sides, covered by a thin portion of flesh called the *depouille*, are taken out. Then the ribs are broken off at the vertebrae, as well as the boss bones. The marrow-bones, which are those of the fore and hind legs only, are cut out last. The feet usually remain attached to these; the paunch is stripped of its covering of layers of fat, the head and the backbone are left to the Wolves, the pipes are all emptied, the hands, faces, and clothes all bloody, and now a glass of grog is often enjoyed, as the stripping off the skins and flesh of three or four animals is truly very hard work. In some cases when no water was near, our supper was cooked without our being washed, and it was not until we had travelled several miles the next morning that we had any opportunity of cleaning ourselves; and yet, despite everything, we are all hungry, eat heartily, and sleep soundly. When the wind is high and the Buffaloes run toward it, the hunter's guns very often snap, and it is during their exertions to replenish their pans, that the powder flies and sticks to the moisture every moment accumulating on their faces; but nothing stops these daring and usually powerful men, who the moment the chase is ended, leap from their horses, let them graze, and begin their butcher-like work.

August 11, Friday. The weather has been cold and windy, and the day has passed in comparative idleness with me. . . . The activities of Buffaloes is almost beyond belief; they can climb the steep defiles of the Mauvaises Terres in hundreds of places where men cannot follow them, and it is a fine sight to see a large gang of them proceeding along these defiles four or five hundred feet above the level of the bottoms, and from which pathway if one of the number makes a mis-step or accidentally slips, he goes down rolling over and over, and breaks his neck ere the level ground is reached. Bell and Owen saw a bull about three years old that leaped a ravine filled with mud and water, at least twenty feet wide; it reached the middle at the first bound, and at the second was mounted on the opposite bank, from which it kept on bounding, till it gained the top of quite a high hill. Mr. Culbertson tells me that these animals can endure hunger in a most extraordinary manner. He says that a large bull was seen on a spot half way down a precipice, where it had slid, and from which it could not climb upwards, and either could not or would not descend; at any rate, it did not leave the position in which it found itself. The party who saw it returned to the fort, and, on their way back on the *twenty-fifth* day after, they passed the hill, and saw the bull standing there. The thing that troubles them most is crossing rivers on the ice; their hoofs slip from side to side, they become frightened, and stretch their four legs apart to support the body, and in such situations the Indians and white hunters easily approach, and stab them to the heart, or cut the hamstrings, when they become an easy prey. When in large gangs those in the centre are supported by those on the outposts, and if the stream is not large, reach the shore and readily escape. Indians of different tribes hunt the Buffalo in different ways; some hunt on horseback, and use arrows altogether; they are rarely expert in reloading the gun in the close race. Others hunt on foot, using guns, arrows, or both. Others follow with patient perseverance, and kill them also. But I will give you the manner pursued by the Mandans. Twenty to fifty men start, as the occasion suits, each provided with two horses, one of which is a pack-horse, the other fit for the chase. They have quivers with from twenty to fifty arrows, according to the wealth of the hunter. They ride the pack horse bare-back, and travel on, till they see the game, when they leave the pack-horse, and leap on the hunter, and start at full speed and soon find themselves amid the Buffaloes, on the flanks of the herd, and on both sides. When within a few yards the arrow is sent, they shoot at a Buffalo somewhat ahead of them, and send the arrow in an oblique manner, so as to pass through the lights. If the blood rushes out the nose and mouth the animal is fatally wounded, and they shoot at it no more; if not, a second, and perhaps a third arrow, is sent before this happens. The Buffaloes on starting carry the tail close in between the legs, but when wounded they switch it about, especially if they wish to fight, and then the hunter's horse shies off and lets the mad animal breathe awhile. If shot through the heart, they occasionally fall dead on the instant; sometimes, if not hit in the right place, a dozen arrows will not stop them. When wounded and mad they turn suddenly round upon the hunter, and rush upon him in such a quick and furious manner that if horse and rider are not both on the alert, the former is overtaken, hooked and overthrown, the hunter pitched off, trampled and gored to death. Although the Buffalo is such a large animal, and to all appearances a clumsy one, it can turn with the quickness of thought, and when once enraged, will rarely give up the chase until avenged for the wound it has received. If, however, the hunter is expert, and the horse fleet, they outrun the bull, and it returns to the herd. Usually the greater number of the gang is killed, but it very rarely happens that some of them do not escape. This however is not the case when the animal is pounded, especially by the Gros Ventres, Black Feet, and Assiniboins. These pounds are called "parks," and the Buffaloes are made to enter them in the following manner: the park is sometimes round and sometimes square, this depending much on the ground where it is put up; at the end of the park is what is called a *precipice* of some fifteen feet or less, as may be found. It is approached by a funnel-shaped passage, which like the park itself is strongly built of logs, brushwood, and pickets, and when all is ready a young man, very swift of foot, starts at daylight covered over with a Buffalo robe and wearing a Buffalo head-dress. The moment he sees the herd to be taken, he bellows like a young calf,

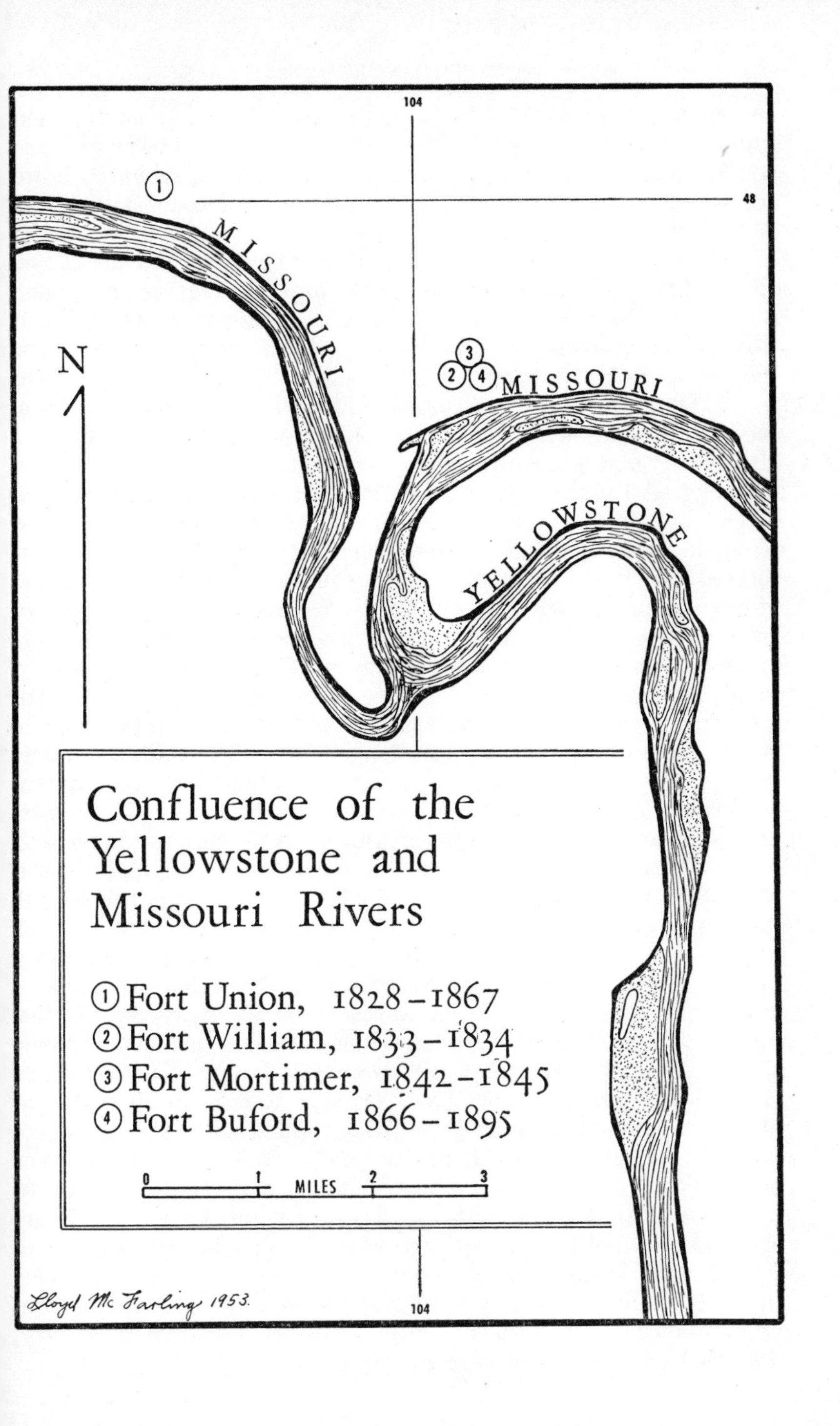
104
48
MISSOURI
N
MISSOURI
YELLOWSTONE
Confluence of the Yellowstone and Missouri Rivers
① Fort Union, 1828–1867
② Fort William, 1833–1834
③ Fort Mortimer, 1842–1845
④ Fort Buford, 1866–1895
0 1 MILES 2 3
Lloyd McFarling 1953.
104

and makes his way slowly towards the contracted part of the funnel, imitating the cry of the calf, at frequent intervals. The Buffaloes advance after the decoy; about a dozen mounted hunters are yelling and galloping behind them, and along both flanks of the herd, forcing them by these means to enter the mouth of the funnel. Women and children are placed behind the fences of the funnel to frighten the cattle, and as soon as the young man who acts as decoy feels assured that the game is in a fair way to follow to the bank or "precipice," he runs or leaps down the bank, over the barricade, and either rests, or joins in the fray. The poor Buffaloes, usually headed by a large bull, proceed, leap down the bank in haste and confusion, the Indians all yelling and pursuing till every bull, cow, and calf is impounded. Although this is done at all seasons, it is more general in October or November, when the hides are good and salable. Now the warriors are all assembled by the pen, calumets are lighted, and the chief smokes to the Great Spirit, the four points of the compass, and lastly to the Buffaloes. The pipe is passed from mouth to mouth in succession, and as soon as this ceremony is ended, the destruction commences. Guns shoot, arrows fly in all directions, and the hunters being on the outside of the enclosure, destroy the whole gang, before they jump over to clean and skin the murdered herd. Even the children shoot small, short arrows to assist in the destruction. It happens sometimes however, that the leader of the herd will be restless at the sight of the precipices, and if the fence is weak will break through it, and all his fellows follow him, and escape. The same thing sometimes takes place in the pen, for so full does this become occasionally that the animals touch each other, and as they cannot move, the very weight against the fence of the pen is quite enough to break it through; the smallest aperture is sufficient, for in a few minutes it becomes wide, and all the beasts are seen scampering over the prairies, leaving the poor Indians starving and discomfited. Mr. Kipp[9] told me that while travelling from Lake Travers to the Mandans, in the month of August, he rode in a heavily laden cart for six successive days through masses of Buffaloes, which divided for the cart, allowing it to pass without opposition. He has seen the immense prairie back of Fort Clark look black to the tops of the hills, though the ground was covered with snow, so crowded was it with these animals; and the masses probably extended much further. In fact it is *impossible to describe or even conceive* the vast multitude of these animals that exist even now, and feed on these ocean-like prairies.

NOTES TO CHAPTER 17

1. Alexander Culbertson was an important figure in the fur trade of the Upper Missouri from 1833 to his retirement about 1861. For several years he was in charge of Fort McKenzie, where Prince Maximilian met him in 1833. Later he became superintendent of the trading posts under the jurisdiction of Fort Union. He married Na-ta-wis-ta-cha, a Blackfoot woman, about 1840. He served the government as special agent and interpreter at various times and was sometimes called "major," an honorary title given to all Indian agents.

2. "Mr. C" was Alexander Culbertson. "Owen" was Owen McKenzie, half-breed son of Kenneth McKenzie.

3. This was Edward Harris. His journal of the trip was edited by John Francis McDermott and published in 1951 under the title, *Up the River with Audubon, the Journal of Edward Harris.*

4. A reproduction of a picture, "Camp at the Three Mamelles," appears opposite page 118, Volume II, of *Audubon and His Journals.* These hills are now called Three Buttes. They are near Sidney, Montana.

5. A painting of two prairie hares, or white-tailed jack rabbits, (*Lepus townsendii*), is reproduced on page 136 of *Audubon's Animals,* edited by Alice Ford. *Audubon's Animals* reproduces many paintings of animals by John James Audubon and John Woodhouse Audubon, including several animals studied on the Missouri River trip.

6. This "coupe" was a gap in the hills, according to the journal of Edward Harris.

7. Etienne Provost. Cf. chap. 16, *ante.*

8. These hunters were the Metis or half-breeds described by Nicollet in chap. 16, *ante.*

9. James Kipp was a Canadian who came to the Upper Missouri in 1822 as an employee of the Columbia Fur Company. He was in charge of several posts, as different times, for the American Fur Company and its successors.

Chapter 18

1851

FROM FORT UNION TO FORT ALEXANDER,

by Father Pierre Jean De Smet

Pierre Jean De Smet was born in Belgium in 1801. He came to the United States in 1821, and to Missouri in 1823. In 1827 he was ordained a priest of the Society of Jesus, and in 1838 began his distinguished labors as a missionary to the Indians. His first mission was among the Potawatomi at the site of the present city of Council Bluffs.

In 1840 Father De Smet was sent to Oregon Territory to survey the possibilities for Catholic missions in that region. With this journey he initiated a series of travels to the mountains and plains of western United States that was to continue for thirty years, interspersed with trips to eastern cities and to Europe to raise funds for missionary work.

During his travels Father De Smet wrote much about the history, natural history, geography, and anthropology of the plains and mountains. His writings were in the form of letters but in content they were really informal essays, and intended for publication. Many of them actually were published, chiefly in Catholic church publications; they were widely read in the United States and in Europe, and contributed a great deal of authentic information to the slowly growing knowledge of the West.

Among Father De Smet's writings published in the United States were three valuable books: *Letters and Sketches: with a Narrative of a Year's Residence among the Indian Tribes of the Rocky Mountains* (1843); *Oregon Missions and Travels over the Rocky Mountains in 1845-46* (1847); and *Western Missions and Missionaries, a Series of Letters* (1863). These writings and others were collected and published by Hiram Martin Chittenden and Alfred Talbot Richardson in four volumes in 1905 under the title *Life, Letters and Travels of Father Pierre-Jean de Smet, 1801-1873.*

In this chapter and the following I am reprinting Father De Smet's account of his trip from Fort Union to Fort Laramie, July 31 to about September 10, 1851, from an 1881 edition of *Western Missions and Missionaries.*

Through the summer of 1851 the government was preparing for the council with the Indians of the plains and eastern Rocky Mountains which culminated in the treaty of 1851, usually called the treaty of Fort Laramie. Because of his great influence among the Indians Father De Smet had been sent to Fort Union to persuade the northern Indians to attend the council. From Fort Union, with Alexander Culbertson and a number of Indians, he went southwest and south to the Oregon trail near Red Buttes, and eastward along the Oregon Trail to Fort Laramie. Over most of the route the trip was the first journey made by wheeled vehicles.

The whole forenoon of the 31st of July, the day on which the Church celebrates the Feast of St. Ignatius, founder of the Society of Jesus, was employed in making preparations for our journey into the interior of the country. Mr. Culbertson,[1] superintendent of the forts on the Mississippi[2] and the Yellowstone rivers, is a distinguished man, endowed with a mild, benevolent and charitable temper, though, if need be, intrepid and courageous. He has always given me marks of kindness and friendship, but most particularly in this last tour. Being at the head of our troop, he was able to aid me in my project.

We numbered thirty-two persons; the greater part were Assiniboins, Minataries, and Crows, who were repairing to the great Indian council to be held in the vicinity of Fort Laramie, and by the same route that we had chosen, which was scarcely less than 800 miles in length. Two four-wheeled wagons and two carts, for transporting our provisions and our baggage, composed our whole convoy. The four vehicles were in all probability the first that had ever crossed this unoccupied waste. There is not the slightest perceptible vestige of a beaten track between Fort Union and the Red Buttes, which are on the route to Oregon, and 161 miles west of Fort Laramie.

Having dined, we crossed the river with our baggage. Following the course of one of the little tributaries of the Yellowstone, we advanced about six miles. We had with us a skillful hunter of the Blackfeet tribe, and he made a happy commencement by bringing us two fine deer as the first fruits of his ability. The mosquitoes attacked us on all sides, leaving us no repose. We were forced to combat them continually with branches, handkerchiefs, and smoke. The last is the most efficacious weapon for dissipating these sanguinary insects, but it is at the same time the most difficult for the traveller to support. Night came on, and brought with it a terrible storm. The thunder rolled above our heads and the clouds discharged torrents of water.

On the 1st of August, at six o'clock in the morning, we resumed our route. We took all possible precaution to avoid meeting any hostile band. The Indians who accompanied us kept their eyes on the earth to discover any recent tracks of an enemy. An extraordinary experience gives them an admirable tact in detecting trails which are imperceptible to others. The foes that our travelling companions dreaded most in the section we were about to traverse, were the Blackfeet and the Sioux. After breakfasting in the neighborhood of the source of the

Fox river, we journeyed from morning till night over hilly and undulating plains, bounded by ranges of hills which stretch from the Yellowstone to the Missouri. From time to time we descried promontories in the distance, which serve as guides to the traveller. At the close of the day we pitched our camp at the base of the Tetons of the Yellowstone. These Tetons derive their name from a group of lofty hills situated in one of those delightful valleys which are numerous in these parts, and which, being surrounded by trees and shrubbery of various kinds, form a most agreeable contrast to the plains that we had just left behind, so destitute of wood and water. Wild fruit, such as plums, cherries, gooseberries, sorbs, buffalo-berries, or *Shepherdia angelica,* abound. Among the vegetables and roots we noticed the *Psoralea esculenta,* or Breadroot; its white apple, and its charming white, oval blossom, nearly three inches in circumference, is universally found in this uncultivated solitude, and would deserve a place in a garden of choice plants; the savages value it highly. The wild onion and the sweet onion bear handsome flowers; these plants would undoubtedly improve with culture. The roots of the water-arrow (*Sagittaria rigida*), and those of the wild Lily of the Valley (*Convallaria borealis*), are equally prized by the Indians, who call them *Swan potatoes.* Peanuts are also a delicious and nourishing root, found commonly in low and alluvial lands. The above-named roots form a considerable portion of the sustenance of these Indians during winter. They seek them in the places where the mice and other little animals, in particular the ground-squirrel, have piled them in heaps.[3]

The mosquitoes tormented us greatly during the day. They especially worried our horses and mules, which were literally covered with them. For us, we had taken measures against their attacks by covering our heads with sacks formed of coarse gauze.

The distance between the Tetons and Fort Union is about eighty miles.[4] We saw very few deer, from time to time an antelope or buck was roused from repose and fled at our approach. Traces of several kinds of bear, especially the grizzly bear, are very common; the latter are found in the woody places and along the streams and rivulets. We succeeded in killing three, not without great effort and danger. Our hunter brought us two fine, fat antelopes, which were soon dressed and served up for our supper. One of the Indians killed a skunk (*Mephitis Americana*). The strong odor of this animal is intolerable to

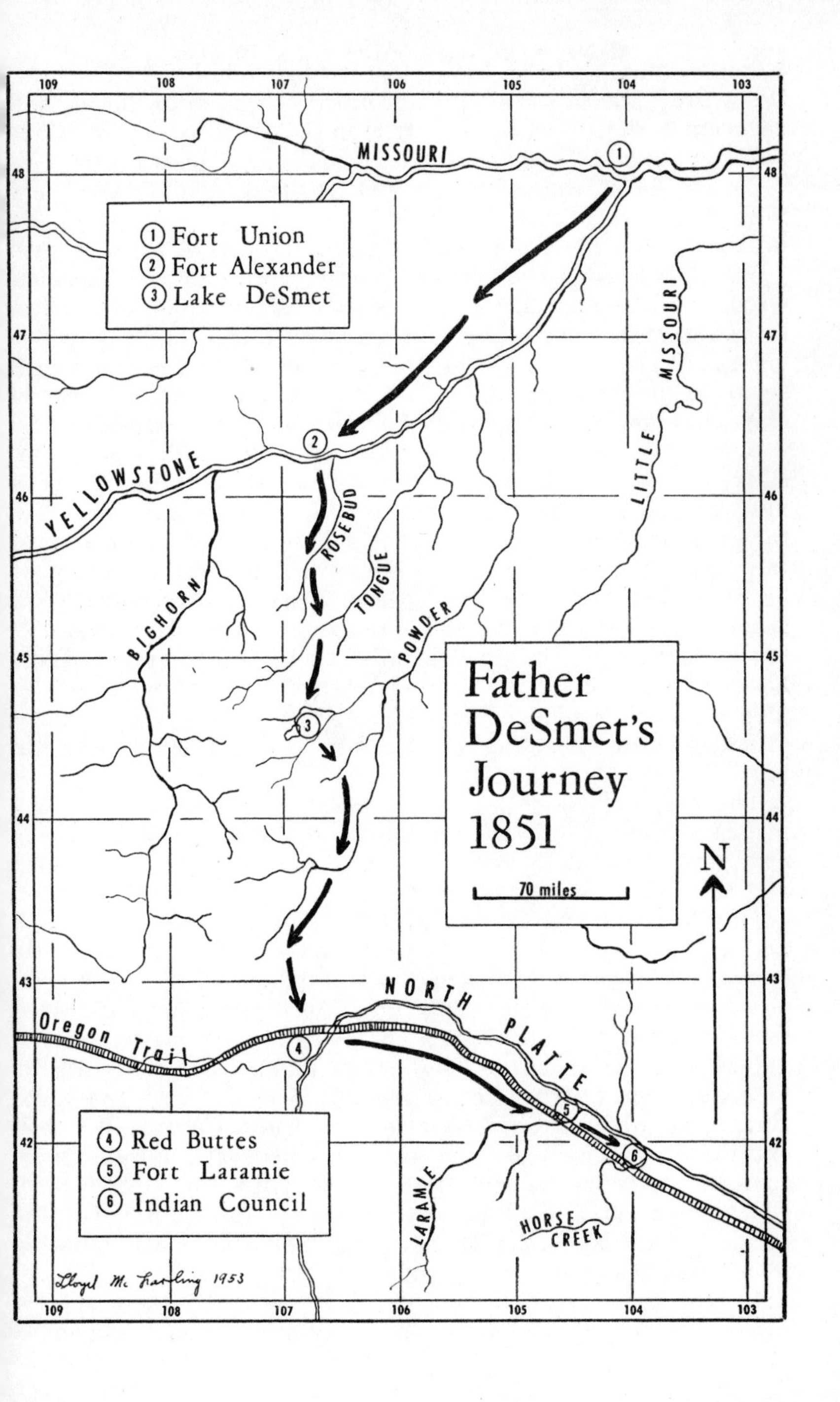
MISSOURI
1 Fort Union
2 Fort Alexander
3 Lake DeSmet
MISSOURI
LITTLE
YELLOWSTONE
ROSEBUD
TONGUE
POWDER
BIGHORN
Father DeSmet's Journey 1851
70 miles
N
NORTH PLATTE
Oregon Trail
4 Red Buttes
5 Fort Laramie
6 Indian Council
LARAMIE
HORSE CREEK
Lloyd McFarling 1953

the whites; the savages, on the contrary, appear to like it, and deem its flesh exquisite. How true is the proverb: *De gustibus non disputandum!*—there is no accounting for tastes.

On the 2d of August we set out at break of day, and were fanned by a refreshing breeze. The country through which we progressed was full of interest: the valleys were covered with a luxuriant verdure, intermingled with flowers of various hues. Groves of cotton-wood, elm, and ash, as well as groups of service-trees and cherry-trees, offered themselves along the beds of dry rivers and streamlets. We ascended, step by step, the hills which separate the waters of the Missouri from those of the Yellowstone, like so many insuperable barriers furrowed with profound ravines. We triumphed over these obstacles with great difficulty, and at length attained the summit of the hills. There a most magnificent spectacle unrolled itself before our eyes. Nature has accumulated in this spot a great variety of her most fantastical caprices. On one side is displayed a succession of beautiful prairies, here and there interrupted with groves of stunted trees and shrubs, and terminating in verdant hills dotted with groups of cedar and pine; on the other are shapeless heaps of red and white clay and piles of stones, which, viewed at a distance, resemble brick-kilns, from their peculiar color: although thrown together without any apparent order, they add much interest to the landscape.

The region through which we passed for several days furnished evident proofs that it has been strongly volcanic, even at a very recent date, for the surface is still covered with lava and scoriae. I counted as many as seventy conical hills, from twenty to a hundred feet in height, grouped in one single plain and in the space of from four to five miles: they had evidently gone through the ordeal of fire. Some of these hills were composed of cinders that the earth in her fiery convulsions appeared to have vomited from her center.[5] Several times, after having gained some miles on the heights, we found ourselves suddenly facing an almost perpendicular descent, formed of rock and white clay, down which we had to let our vehicles by hand. We then entered into a chain of valleys and fertile prairies watered by springs and rivulets, and embellished with the cotton-wood, elm, ash, cedar, and pine; in other places the summits of the hills are remarkable for their beauty, and the rich undulating plains for their abundant verdure.

On the fourth day of our march we descried thousands of bison; the whole space between the Missouri and the Yellowstone was covered as far as the eye could reach. Hitherto the mosquitoes had greatly tormented us, but now they entirely vanished. We sought the cause of this phenomenon. The Indians told us that the absence of our winged enemies was owing to the prodigious number of buffaloes which were grazing in the neighboring plains, and which attracted these insects. In fact, we saw these noble animals throwing the earth on their bodies by means of their horns and feet, or rolling themselves in the sand and dust, and thus filling the air with clouds, in the endeavor to rid themselves of their vexatious followers. The lot of these animals appeared bad enough, for they were pursued day and night. During a whole week we heard their bellowings like the noise of distant thunder, or like the murmurs of the ocean waves beating against the shore. It may be said that it is the country in which the buffalo and herds of deer are generally found in the greatest abundance. A good hunter might easily kill here, in the course of a day, several cows, deer, a mountain-goat, a red-tailed and a black-tailed buck, an antelope, hares, and rabbits. He might fire twice upon a grizzly bear, and perhaps meet a gray and a silver fox. To this list of animals we may add the beaver, otter, badger, prairie-dog, and several kinds of wild fowl, principally pheasants and grouse. It is easy to see that our hunters possess the power of selecting a repast. In truth, we regaled ourselves with what was most delicate, and left a great quantity of flesh in the plains for the benefit of the vultures and wolves, whose howlings and rejoicings already resounded on every side.

An Assiniboin gave us a singular proof of his dexterity in the chase; I cannot forbear mentioning it. Alone and on foot, he stealthily approached a large herd of buffalo cows. As soon as he was near enough to them to allow of their hearing him, he began to imitate the cry of a young calf. At once the cows ran toward the place of concealment of the ingenious hunter, and he killed one of them. The troop, alarmed, withdrew hastily and in great disorder. He reloaded his rifle and renewed his cry; the cows stopped, returned as if by enchantment, and he killed a second. The Assiniboin assured us that he could easily have taken more by the same strategem, but thinking two cows were enough for us, he suffered the rest to go.

Travellers in these upper regions enjoy an excellent appetite. I have been more than once astonished at the enormous quantity of meat that a man is capable of consuming without injury to his health; it would hardly be credited in Europe. One and even two buffalo tongues, a side of venison or other meat, and some additional trifles, are not considered a large portion for one meal.

On the 7th of August we crossed lands intersected with numerous ravines and dried streams. The soil was much lighter than that we last trod; it was covered with a species of wild artemisia, or wormwood—an infallible mark of sterility. The aspect of all the ravines, shores and beds of rivers and streams, as well as that of every eminence, proves that there are numerous veins of mineral coal in this section. The observation that I made on the quality of the soil induces me to believe that these deposits of coal extend as far as the numerous coal mines which exist in the territories watered by the Saskatchewan and Athabasca lake, of which I have already spoken, in my letters in 1845 and 1846, after travelling over those places.

Evident tokens convince the traveller that the immense plains that he is crossing, and on which not even a shrub grows, have not always been destitute of wood. Petrified trunks and entire trees frequently meet the eye. Astonishment and admiration seize the mind, and excite conjectures concerning the manner in which these changes have been wrought. But what answer offer to the question, "Why are not these lands wooded as they must have been in former times?" The steppes of Asia, the pampas of South America and the western prairies of this hemisphere, seem to possess a common and uniform character; generally speaking, they have neither trees nor shrubs on them. Some observers attribute it to the action of frequent fires which have passed over these localities; others to the change undergone in the climate, or to the natural sterility of the soil; and, in fine, there are some who pretend that some operation or convulsion of nature has destroyed the forests which formerly existed here, and reduced them to their present condition. I have examined different localities; and the enormous heaps of shells of the testaceous kind and of the genus muscula, of which I found some feet distant from the summits of the loftiest hills, and which were incorporated in alluvial earth, and mingled with sand and water-worn pebbles, convinced me that this portion of land has undergone changes as great as they are amazing.

On the same day we traversed a mountainous elevation which stretches as far as the Owl-head Buttes. These buttes or mounds, in this ocean-like prairie, serve as guides to the warrior, the traveller, and the hunter, who can perceive them thirty miles off. From the summit of this extensive eminence we contemplated, with pleasing wonder, the "White Earth country," or clay plains of the Yellowstone. From south to north they measure from thirty to forty miles. When on this height, the imagination discovers the ruins of ancient villages, and one seems to see confused rows of broken columns, forts with their turrets and bastions, towers, domes, walls in decay, castles and edifices of every sort. Some of these pillars of red and white hardened clay rise to an elevation of from 50 to 100 feet. It would have gratified me much to have passed one or two days in an attentive examination of these volcanic productions.[6] I presume that the soil is not unlike that near the White Earth river, a tributary of the Missouri, and that it contains the same species of interesting fossils. . . .

From the Owl Buttes, where we encamped on the 7th of August, to the source of the Immel, a distance of nearly thirty miles, we travelled on the highlands. The surface was rugged, cut by deep ravines, and excessively difficult to pass with our vehicles. At every step we met volcanic remains. For two days our route offered on the right and left burnt hills, some of which were covered with lava and scoriae and had evidently been craters, whence volcanic matter had been ejected into the neighboring plain.

At the decline of the same day we were witnesses of a singularly beautiful phenomenon. The moon was surrounded by four circles; the first was of a beautiful azure, the second a rich purple, and the third white, while the fourth was obscure or black. In the midst of all these circles the queen of night shone brilliantly. The savages augured from this sign that some hostile band was near, and passed the whole night under arms, watching.

On the 10th we quitted the highlands and advanced about twenty miles, over a barren, rugged space, excavated by rains. A kind of salamander, vulgarly called "horned frog," lizards and rattlesnakes, were most abundant. . . .

On the 11th we arrived at the upper portion of a gently sloping plain. Having crossed it, we found ourselves at Fort Alexander,[7] situated on the banks of the Yellowstone, and at a short distance from the little river Rosebud. Fort Alexander is one hundred miles[8] distant from Fort Union. The winter, it is said, is extremely severe in these regions, commencing in November, and only terminating in the month of April.

NOTES TO CHAPTER 18

1. Alexander Culbertson was in charge of Fort Union at this time. Cf. note 1, chap. 17, *ante*.

2. The word should be "Missouri."

3. "The groundnut, or *Apios tuberosa*, is very useful to the Indian. It grows very abundantly along the river bottoms, and is gathered in large quantities by a kind of wood-mouse for his winter store. The squaws make a business, during the months of October and November, of robbing these little animals, and I have often seen several bushels of the tubers in a single lodge. They are boiled with dried buffalo meat, and make a rich and palatable dish." Hayden, Appendix E to Warren, "Explorations in the Dacota Country. . . ."

4. The Chittenden and Richardson text gives the mileage at thirty, which is a reasonable estimate if, as seems likely, these hills were the "Three Mamelles" of Audubon's journal, or the "Three Buttes" of today.

5. Like Prince Paul (cf. note 6, chap. 14, *ante*), Father De Smet thought he saw evidences of volcanic action where there were no volcanoes. The "ordeal by fire" may have been the burning of lignite coal, which existed in this region, and which is mentioned later in the chapter.

6. These hills were not volcanic, but were typical badland-type formations caused by the erosion of sedimentary deposits.

7. The American Fur Company and its successors built at least four trading posts, at different times, on the Yellowstone River, for the Crow Indian trade. They are sometimes called "the Crow Posts." Fort Cass was built in 1832, about three miles below the mouth of the Bighorn River. It was abandoned in 1835. Fort Van Buren was built in 1835 near the mouth of Rosebud Creek. It was abandoned and burned by the owners in 1842. In the same year Fort Alexander was built about twenty miles by land (or forty miles by water) above the mouth of Rosebud Creek, at a place called Adam's Prairie, on the left bank of the Yellowstone.

The evidence is conflicting regarding the abandonment of Fort Alexander and the building of Fort Sarpy. It is probable that the two names were applied to the same fort at different times, and it is possible that there were two successive forts named Sarpy. Father De Smet, traveling with Alexander Culbertson, was in a very good position to know the correct name of the fort he visited in 1851—he called it Fort Alexander.

At some date before 1859 the fur company built Fort Sarpy on the right bank of the Yellowstone about twenty-five miles below the mouth of Bighorn River. Captain Raynolds visited it in 1859 (cf. chaps. 22-23, *post*). It had been abandoned when Lieutenant Maynadier, of the Raynolds expedition, returned to the same place in the summer of 1860.

Besides the American Fur Company posts, other trading posts were built on the Yellowstone; such as Manuel's Fort (1807-11); Fort Benton (which should not be confused with the more important Fort Benton of a later date on the Missouri), built by the Missouri Fur Company (1822-23); and a post built by Ashley and Henry in 1823, which was probably abandoned in 1824. These posts were near the mouth of the Bighorn River. On the Bighorn, near the mouth of the Little Bighorn; Fox, Livingston and Company built a post, probably in 1843, that was soon abandoned.

8. The Chittenden and Richardson text gives the distance as "about 200 miles," which is more nearly correct.

Chapter 19

1851

FROM FORT ALEXANDER TO FORT LARAMIE,

by Father Pierre Jean De Smet

This chapter is a continuation of Father De Smet's description of his travels from Fort Union to Fort Laramie, reprinted from the 1881 edition of *Western Missions and Missionaries, A Series of Letters.*

The route ran south and a little west of Fort Alexander, near the mouth of the Rosebud on Yellowstone River, to the Oregon Trail at Red Buttes, thence eastward to Fort Laramie, and about thirty-five miles farther down the Platte to the place where the Indian treaty of 1851 was signed, at the mouth of Horse Creek on the North Platte River.

Between Fort Alexander and the Red Buttes, Father De Smet came close to the battle grounds of two Indian wars—the Red Cloud War of 1866-68, and the final struggle with the northern tribes in 1876-77. These regions will be more fully explored in the later chapters of this book. I believe Father De Smet's account of his trip in 1851 was the first published description of this interesting country.

After remaining six days at Fort Alexander, allowing our animals time to repose, and also awaiting the arrival of a barge belonging to the American Fur Company, which was freighted with some of our effects, we passed over the Yellowstone on the 17th of August, at about two o'clock. We passed over a high and very level plain; for a distance of five miles the soil is light, sandy, and entirely covered with green toads, as the *voyageurs* call different kinds of cactus—plants that are noted for the splendor of their flowers and for their grotesque and varied shapes. The round and the oval, about the size of a hen's egg, abound in this plain, and are set with long thorns, hard, and as fine and sharp as needles. When trampled by the horses' feet, these thorns spring up and adhere to the legs and belly of the animals, and thus render them furious and unmanageable. We soon arrived in Rosebud Valley, and continuing our route until sunset we encamped on the borders of a little river bearing the same name, and quite near a beautiful pond, over which a new dam had been constructed by the beavers.

This section of the country offered us frequent occasions of admiring the labors and ingenious industry of these intelligent animals. They are more numerous here than in any other district I have visited, and I am told that their preservation is chiefly attributable to the continual excursions of war-parties, either Sioux, Assiniboins, or Blackfeet, all implacable enemies of the Crows, and these prevent the huntsman and the savages from hazarding a chase in these parts. At present, the fur of the beaver is of so little value that their search is almost abandoned. In ancient times the Crows held the beaver in the highest veneration because this nation imagined that they became beavers after death. This article of their creed entailed the loss of his scalp to many a bold huntsman among the whites, for every Crow Indian considered himself bound to protect, defend and avenge, even with death, the spirits of *his near relations*, in their second state of existence. During late years this dogma of faith has been erased from their religious code, to the great detriment certainly of the poor beavers. Such superstitions will never wholly disappear until the Catholic faith enlightens these wilds, over which the darkness of paganism still hangs.

For four days we continued ascending the valley of the Rosebud, about one hundred miles, as high as the sources of the river. There again we found the soil light and sandy; it was covered with wild rose-bushes, cactus, and artemisia of several varieties, and intersected with ravines which were exceedingly difficult to be crossed with baggage-wagons. The shores of this river relieve the eye with an occasional group of cotton wood, intermingled with plum, cherry, and service trees, which thrive here in undisturbed plenty.

The Little Wolf Mountains, whose rivulets give rise to the Rosebud River, have in general a charming appearance in their hills and acclivities—and in their combined aspect as a whole chain. The absence of water, especially of spring-water, is a painful privation to travellers in this season of the year. We found, indeed, some holes of stagnant water, in the dry beds of the rivers, but the taste is almost insupportable. The buffalo-herds are less numerous here than in the lands lying further north, owing no doubt to bands of warriors that roam over the space. Yet we perceived at every moment large troops of stags, and a great many deer and mountain-sheep. We remarked recent traces of enemies—such as the slain carcasses of very dangerous wild animals, the impress of human feet in the sand, concealed encampments, and half-quenched fires. Consequently we redoubled our vigilance, in order to avoid a perilous surprise. A beautiful chief's-coat, of scarlet cloth, and trimmed with gold lace, suspended from the branch of a tree, was perceived waving in the air like a floating banner. There was a race to win the prize; an Assiniboin having carried it off, it was most carefully scrutinized. The conclusion was, that it had been offered only the day before by some Blackfoot chief. These Indians, when on the warpath, frequently make such offerings either to the sun or to the moon, hoping thus to render them propitious, so that through their intervention they may obtain many scalps and horses. The most precious objects which they possess and which they esteem most, are often thus sacrificed. The Mandans, the Arickaras, and their neighbors, go still further: they cut off fingers, and make deep incisions in the fleshy parts of the body before starting for war, in order to obtain the same favors of their false gods.

On my last visit to the Riccaries, Minataries and Mandans, I could not discern a single man at all advanced in years whose body was not mutilated, or who possessed his full number of fingers. How profound their ignorance! How fearful the idolatry in which these unhappy tribes are plunged! To this sombre picture we may add a passionate love of gaming, which consumes the hours which should be devoted to necessary repose; a sloth which nothing but hunger can arouse; an innate inclination to dissimulation, gluttony, and to whatever can flatter sensuality. And still, amid this ocean of miseries, they feel an indescribable need of invoking a power superior to man: they listen attentively to any instruction which reveals to them the means of procuring his favor, and give them information of his attributes. They love the missionary, and ever listen to him with delight; and in his quality of priest receive him with friendship and respect. To judge by the respect and friendship shown me as a priest, on all occasions and circumstances, by the Indians on the Upper Missouri, I am satisfied that if a few zealous priests were stationed here, they would soon become generous Christians, full of zeal and ardor for the glory of our God and his holy law. "They would know their Father who is in heaven, and Him whom he has sent on earth;" they would become faithful disciples of the Redeemer, who so ardently desires the salvation of all, and who did not disdain to shed his blood for them on the cross.

On the 22d of August we quitted the head of the Rosebud and crossed the mountainous train which separates it from Tongue River. The crest of this chain presents a continuation of sandstone cliffs, under a multitude of varied and fantastical shapes. The sides are almost perpendicular, and consequently very difficult to ascend with our wagons. The aid of every arm was necessary to sustain the teams. For several days we had had to camp by ponds filled with disgusting water. How agreeable the contrast to find ourselves on the borders of this beautiful river, the waters of which are pure as crystal! How eagerly did we allay our burning thirst! The horses and mules appeared to rejoice, neighing and rearing with impatience; as soon as their bridles were loosened, they plunged into the waves and indulged in long draughts. When the whole caravan had assuaged their thirst, we continued our route. We traversed an undulating plain; and perceiving in the distance a prominent point of land which appeared sparkling with crystals, we named it Diamond Hill. It was covered with large pieces of mica. For the first time since we left Fort Alexander we breakfasted beside beautiful springs of fresh water, the most remarkable in the country.

After advancing about twenty-three miles that day, we camped on the banks of Tongue River. There we had new occasion to recall and arrange our recollections of the land we had seen. Coal also appears as abundant south of the Yellowstone as above it; we met it everywhere. The slopes of the hills are well wooded with larch and pines of every variety up to the very summit, throughout the whole extent of the Little Wolf chain. This we left for that of the Great Wolf, which we reach before arriving at the Black Hills. These mountains form spurs of the Rocky Mountains; the principal summits are over 13,000 feet high.[1] On the 23d we left Tongue River. For ten hours we marched over mountain and valley, following the course of one of its tributaries, making, however, only about *twenty-five miles*. On the day following we crossed a chain of lofty mountains to attain the Lower Piney Fork, nearly twenty miles distant. We arrived quite unexpectedly on the borders of a lovely little lake about six miles long, and my travelling companions gave it *my name*.[2] There our hunters killed several wild ducks. On quitting the lake, we discovered another elevated portion of land on which red mounds and scoriae, volcanic remains, are scattered in all directions, as far as the Upper Piney Fork; and there petrified trees are met with at every step.

Toward evening we encamped at the base of a mountain, after advancing about twenty-five miles, and thought ourselves favored in finding a pool of water. The next twenty-four miles were taken in the direction of Sandy River, through undulating plains and mountainous hills.

On the 27th of August we reached Powder River, one of the principal tributaries of the Yellowstone. Our wagoners will not soon forget the difficulty of conducting their teams through this last route, for it was a very miserable, elevated, sterile plain, covered with wormwood and intersected with countless ravines, and they vowed they would never be caught driving a wagon there again.

The valley of the Powder River, in the neighborhood of the Buttes aux Callebasses,[3] which are in sight, is three or four miles wide. Although the soil was light, the verdure was fine and the grazing abundant. The part where I crossed the valley is well wooded, and they told me that wood, especially cotton wood and fruit trees, is abundant all along the river. This valley forms a beautiful contrast with the high plains of these parts, which are the very picture of aridity and desolation, with naught but weeds, rocks and deep ravines.

Here we happened to meet with three young Indians of the Crow tribe. They had been on the lookout for a Sioux camp, intending to steal horses, but had not succeeded. These young men advised us to pursue the vale of a little river which they pointed out to us, assuring us that by taking that direction we should soon arrive at Fort Laramie. I was surprised at this counsel, for the course of the valley was southwest; however, we followed the route indicated by the Crows. This proved the most rugged and difficult part of our journey, hence we styled it "the valley of a thousand miseries." A name could not have been better chosen. Imagine a river with perpendicular banks, winding in a serpentine course through a narrow valley, so that in a distance of three miles we were obliged to cross it ten or twelve times, with carts and wagons, at the imminent risk of killing our horses and mules and destroying our vehicles. The soil, too, was sterile, and as we journeyed on water became scarce—on the fifth day it failed completely, and it did again on the last. The night that ensued was a hard trial, for after so long a march we had not a drop of water to quench our burning thirst.

On the 1st of September, having traversed three chains of hills, we gradually attained the summit of the Black Hills. We had one cart less, and one heavy wagon so broken that it had to be tied together with strips of raw buffalo-hide. From the summit we were so happy as to perceive a distant lake. We eagerly hastened in that direction, for we were consumed with thirst, and had serious fears for our beasts of burden, which were slackening their weary pace. To our astonishment, we directly perceived that we were still at a great distance from Fort Laramie. Instead of being near that fort, in accordance with the assurances of the three Crows, we discovered ourselves in sight of the Red Buttes, twenty-five miles off. This is a well-known spot on the "Great Oregon Route" and is one hundred and sixty miles from Fort Laramie. On the top of the Black Hills I left a little souvenir of my passage,—on a very high rock of a remarkable form, I carved a large and handsome cross. Ah! may the Indian tribes scattered throughout the wild solitude soon learn the great truths which this holy emblem announces! May they soon leave the bondage in which error has chained them during innumerable ages!

The whole region over which we passed, south of the Yellowstone, offers only feeble hopes to civilization. The soil is light, wood scarce, and water wanting during a large portion of the year. It is a country favorable solely to hunters and wandering tribes. All the animals common in the wilderness abound, and during long years to come they will rest undisturbed in their possessions. When all the fertile tracts, yet vacant in the immense Indian territory, will be occupied, then only will the lands below the Yellowstone attract attention; then alone will necessitous and persevering industry succeed in drawing any considerable portion of this region from its present barrenness.

In the neighborhood and along the base of the Black Hills there lies a very extensive tract of fertile and tillable land. The verdure is rich and abounds in all the valleys, and these valleys penetrate the mountains like so many veins, where millions of domestic animals might be raised; for the springs and rivulets so seldom occurring in the central section between the Yellowstone and the Black Hills, are very numerous in the interior and at the base of these mountains. There are also a great many sites favorable to the erection of mills. The climate is reputed delightful, and the noble forests of cedar and pine would abundantly supply the necessities of a population. Mines of lead and iron are very numerous.[4]

The 2d day of September, we found ourselves on the "Great Route to Oregon," over which, like successive ocean surges, the caravans, composed of thousands of emigrants from every country and clime, have passed during these latter years to reach the rich gold mines of California, or to take possession of the new lands in the fertile plains and valleys of Utah and Oregon. These intrepid pioneers of civilization have formed the broadest, longest, and most beautiful road in the whole world— from the United States to the Pacific Ocean. On the skirts of this magnificent highway there is an abundance of grass for supplying the cattle and animals appertaining to the caravans which are incessantly travelling on it, from early spring to autumn, every succeeding year.

Our Indian companions who had never seen but the narrow hunting-paths by which they transport themselves and their lodges, were filled with admiration on seeing this noble highway, which is as smooth as a barn-floor swept by the winds, and not a blade of grass can shoot on it on account of the continual passing. They conceived a high idea of the countless *White Nation*, as they express it. They fancied that all had gone over that road, and that an immense void must exist in the land of the rising sun. Their countenances testified evident incredulity when I told them that their exit was in nowise perceived in the *lands of the whites*. They styled the route the *Great Medicine Road of the Whites*. The term medicine is applied by them to whatever they find grand, religious, mysterious or incomprehensible. They visited and examined in detail all the forsaken camping-grounds on the way; they brought a great variety of objects to me to have their use and signification explained; they filled their pouches with knives, forks, spoons, basins, coffee-pots, and other cooking articles, axes, hammers, etc. With the bits of earthenware which bore any figure or inscription, they fabricated some ornament for their necks and ears. How wonderful will be the accounts given of the *Great Medicine Road* by our unsophisticated Indians when they go back to their villages, and sit in the midst of an admiring circle of relatives!

But these relics collected by our savage friends were not the sole vestiges of the great multitude of emigrants who, in search of gold, had crossed this vast plain with a rare courage and unheard-of fatigues and difficulties. The bleached bones of domestic animals disseminated profusely along the route; the rising mound hastily made over the grave of a parent or friend deceased during the long journey, and the tribute offered to memory in a coarse and rudely-carved inscription on a narrow strip of board or on a stone, with other graves which offered no such testimonial of affection, furnish ample and melancholy proofs that death had considerably thinned their ranks. By such disasters thousands of emigrants have found themselves suddenly arrested, and been mocked in the flattering hope of wealth and pleasure.

The countless fragments of conveyances, the heaps of provisions, tools of every kind, and other objects with which the emigrants must have provided themselves at great expense, but which the most impatient, eager to outstrip others in the Western Eldorado, had forsaken and cast aside, testify to that bold recklessness with which they hazard everything in this enterprise which had proved fatal to thousands. The picture traced by Thornton in his Journal of 1848, is the most shocking that can be contemplated. Arrived in the arid lands of California, the famine had at first reduced them to eating their horses and mules; soon they had recourse to dead bodies; then the dying were not spared, and at last they actually devoured each other![5] What a salutary proof of the uncertainty that accompanies the grandest perspectives in the life of man, and of the deceptions that unveil to him his native weakness!

We followed the great road south of the Platte to the foot of the Great Black Hills.[6] On this road we found ourselves relieved from those obstacles which had so often endangered our vehicles and our animals. After eight days' journey along the Platte, we arrived at Fort Laramie without the least trouble or accident. The commander of the fort informed us that the Great Council was to take place at the mouth of Horse River,[7] in a vast plain situated nearly thirty-five miles lower down on the Platte. The next day I accepted the polite invitation of the respected Col. Campbell,[8] and took a seat in his carriage. We arrived at the plain of the intended council about sunset. There the superintendent, Col. M. Mitchell,[9] received me with warm friendship and cordiality, and insisting that I should become his guest during the whole time of the council. All the others showed me great respect.

In the immense plain above-mentioned, we found about a thousand lodges, that is to say, ten thousand Indians, representing Sioux, Cheyennes and Rapahoes, with several deputations from the Crows, Snakes or Soshonies, Arickaras, Assiniboines, and Minataries. . . .[10]

NOTES TO CHAPTER 19

1. As used in this letter the term "Black Hills" has three different meanings. At this point Father De Smet refers to the Big Horn Mountains.

Later he applies the term to some hills between Powder River and the Red Buttes. Near the end of the letter he uses the term, as it was normally used in his day, to denote the range that we now call the Laramie Mountains.

2. The body of water is still called Lake De Smet. It is about ten miles north of Buffalo, Wyoming.

3. Pumpkin Buttes, prominent landmarks in southwestern Campbell County, Wyoming.

4. This paragraph describes the region along the east side of the Big Horn Mountains. There has never been any lead or iron mining in this area.

5. This is a reference to the Donner party, which became snowbound in the Sierra Nevada Mountains in the winter of 1846-47.

6. The Laramie Mountains of today.

7. Usually called Horse Creek.

8. Robert Campbell (1804-79) was a prominent fur trader and St. Louis businessman. He was a partner of William L. Sublette for about ten years, beginning in 1832. Sublette and Campbell built Fort William on the Missouri a few miles below Fort Union in 1833, but sold it to the American Fur Company in 1834. Also, in 1834, the firm built the Fort William which was the precursor of Fort Laramie, on Laramie River near its junction with the Platte. Cf. note 7, chap. 9, *ante.*

9. David D. Mitchell (1806-61) was one of the ablest men in the fur trade. In 1832 he built Fort McKenzie, at the mouth of Marias River, for the American Fur Company. He was a lieutenant colonel of volunteers in the Mexican War. In 1851 he was Superintendent of Indian Affairs at St. Louis, and in this capacity was one of the negotiators of the Indian treaty of that year.

10. The preamble to the treaty of 1851 listed the following participating tribes: the Sioux or Dakotas, Cheyennes, Arapahoes, Crows, Assiniboins, Gros Ventres, Mandans, and Arikaras. The treaty was an attempt to establish peace among the Indian tribes, and between the Indians and the whites. The Indians agreed to recognize the right of the government to establish roads and military and other posts in their territories, and they were promised annuities amounting to the value of $50,000 a year for fifty years. When the Senate confirmed the treaty it reduced the term of years to fifteen. The Indians agreed "to abstain in future from all hostilities against each other," then went home and began fighting as usual.

Chapter 20

1855

EXPLORATIONS IN THE DAKOTA COUNTRY,

by Lieutenant Gouverneur K. Warren

Gouverneur Kemble Warren was born in 1830. He graduated from West Point Military Academy in 1850 and received the commission of brevet second lieutenant in the Corps of Topographical Engineers. He spent the next four years in engineering work on the Mississippi and Ohio rivers, and in compiling maps and reports resulting from the exploration of proposed railroad routes to the Pacific Coast. In 1854 he was promoted to the rank of second lieutenant and in 1855 was appointed Topographical Engineer of the expedition against the Sioux Indians under the command of Brevet Brigadier General William S. Harney.

This expedition was an attempt on the part of the government to punish the Indians for the so-called Grattan Massacre of August 19, 1854, in which Lieutenant John L. Grattan, twenty-nine enlisted men, and one civilian interpreter were killed near Fort Laramie.

Harney organized his expedition at Fort Leavenworth in the summer of 1855 and proceeded over the Oregon Trail to Fort Laramie. En route he attacked a probably peaceful camp of Sioux Indians on Blue Water Creek, across the Platte from Ash Hollow, and gave them a severe beating. After counciling with several bands of Indians at Fort Laramie, Harney led the Sioux expedition northeast over the trail to Fort Pierre. That trading post had been purchased by the army and was now a military fort. Harney established his winter headquarters at Fort Pierre and in the spring made a temporary peace with the Indians.

Lieutenant Warren's travels in 1855 as Topographical Engineer of the expedition, but not always with the troops, are described in this and the following chapter, reprinted from his official report on "Explorations in the Dacota Country, in the Year 1855."

Published with the report were two maps of the Northern Plains. These maps were made from information collected by Warren during his topographical surveys, plus data accumulated by Nicollet, Fremont, Stansbury, and other explorers. They were the first reasonably accurate maps ever made of this area. The maps and the report together constitute a geographical achievement of great importance.

My duties in connexion with the "Sioux Expedition" required me to go up the Missouri River to Fort Pierre, lay out a military reserve for that post, and examine the river as high up as the mouth of the Shyenne.

Having accomplished this, and rendered a report thereon,[1] I proceeded across the country direct from Fort Pierre to Fort Kearny. From this point I accompanied the army to Fort Laramie, and thence to Fort Pierre. From Fort Pierre I returned to the settlements at the mouth of the Big Sioux, by the direct route through Minnesota.[2]

Over the routes traversed, sketches and notes were taken, and collateral information was sought from every available source....

The routes traversed lead over the great plains between the Missouri, the Platte and the Shyenne, and nowhere entered the mountains. Of the geology of this interesting section . . . much new information has been gained by Dr. F. V. Hayden, who is at present preparing his results. . . .[3]

The country north of White river is clayey; south of this stream it is sandy. This difference has an important bearing on roads through the two sections, as the former is almost everywhere impracticable in the wet seasons, while the latter is not materially injured by rain, and in some parts is improved by it. The water in the former is generally not constant, and wherever it stands in pools is frequently salt. The streams rise and fall suddenly, and their bottoms are more or less muddy and difficult to ford.

In the sandy region the rain that falls sinks into the surface and does not run off suddenly nor evaporate; pure water in small lakes, springs, and clear running streams are the consequence, but they are not numerous. The streams and lakes have sandy bottoms and are easy to ford.

The grass in the clay region, is, as a general thing, superior to that in the other, being finer and more nutritive; but along the banks of the streams, where the clay and sand in either region are mixed, there is not much difference. Wood generally exists along the banks of all the streams where it has not been destroyed by fire, or by the Indians for forage and fuel. Pine timber is found on l'Eau qui Court, on the southern branches of White river, and in the Black Hills. From my observation, I think that continuous settlements cannot be made in Nebraska, west of the 97th meridian, both on account of the unfavorable climate and want of fertility in the soil.[4]

Grasshoppers occasionally devastate the country, stripping it in places of almost every green thing.

The *Black Hills* of Nebraska are believed to be composed of primitive rocks, and are the eastern portions of the great mountain belt.[5] They are in somewhat detached ridges, ranging NW to SE and probably have their continuation in Snowy, Bears Paw, and Little Missouri, mountains of the upper Missouri and the Cyprus mountains, &c. in the British possessions.

Bear Peak,[6] between the forks of the Shyenne, as well as *Raw Hide Peak,* a little west of north from Fort Laramie, is a detached portion of this range, and both believed to be of primitive rock. All the other hills, peaks, or buttes to the east of these are stratified rocks, the remains of vast denudation. The rocky precipices and ridges on White river, between it and l'Eau qui Court, and on the Platte, are generally soft calcareous stone or marl, occasionally capped with hard grit.

The Bad Lands, (les Mauvaises Terres,) as generally understood, lie between the Shyenne and White rivers, and extend east along the latter stream as far as the forks. They belong to the tertiary period. Dr. Hayden thinks that the Bijou Hills are a part of the same formation; and I should think, from their appearance, the Dog's Ears and Turtle Hills also form a part of it. They lie in an extended ridge, coming from the direction of the Bad Lands of White river, and have similar lithological character. I did not, however, make sufficent examination to detect any fossil remains. Where the road passes through the Mauvaises Terres from White river to the head of Bad River, the surface is, in many places, covered with chalcedony, and is hard; in others it is clay, and in wet weather very soft. Through this section some of the streams have clayey beds, some of them sandy. The precipitous ridges of the Mauvaises Terres are about two hundred feet high, and are very striking in appearance. Black tailed deer and big horn are to be found here.

The Sand Hills, (les Buttes de Sable) present their most characteristic appearance just north of Calamus river, spread out in every direction to the extreme verge of the horizon. The sand is nearly white, or lightish yellow, and is about three fourths covered with coarse grass and other plants, their roots penetrating so deep that it is almost impossible to pull them out.

The sand is formed into limited basins, over the rims of which you are constantly passing up one side and down the other, the feet of the animals frequently sinking so as to make the progress excessively laborious.

The scenery is exceedingly solitary, silent, and desolate, and depressing to one's spirits.[7] Antelope, and at some times buffalo are numerous. This is the common war ground for the Dacotas, Crows, Omahas, Poncas, and Pawnees. The character of the country is well calculated to cover a stealthy approach or retreat, and if one keeps as much as possible to the hollows he may even fire his rifle within a quarter of a mile of any enemy's camp without the faintest sound reaching it. Two parties may pass close without being aware of each other's presence, and I consider it hopeless to attempt to capture any who had sought refuge in the Sand Hills. Further west, these hills, I am told, increase in height, and are impassable for horses. Their east and west limits are not well known, but they undoubtedly occupy all the country between Loup Fork and l'Eau qui Court, and form a lasting barrier to any direct economical wheel communication between them. Their width where we crossed is sixty miles. . . .[8]

RIVERS.

The *Missouri* is the most important river as regards our dealings with the Dacotas. Flowing through the middle of their country, it furnishes us with a base from which, with short lines of march, we can reach almost any portion of their lands and many of them have their permanent home upon its banks. My remarks upon it will be confined wholly to that portion below the mouth of the Shyenne, and which came under my own observation.

The bottom lands and some of the larger islands are from fifteen to twenty feet above low water, and rarely overflowed, though during the melting of the snows this sometimes happens. The wood on these bottom lands, from being large and dense, as in the state of Missouri; gradually becomes thinner as we ascend to the mouth of the Vermillion, and above this it generally is only a narrow belt, varying from a single tree to groves half a mile in width, alternating on either side or occupying a few of the larger islands; sometimes these, as Farm Island, below Fort Pierre, and the large island below the mouth of the Shyenne, contain prairies in their interior. I believe, however, that timber sufficient for the wants of a military post exists everywhere within reasonable distance on the Missouri; as high up as the Big Shyenne,[9] and above this the timber is said to improve.

. . . . On both sides of l'Eau qui Court,[10] at its mouth, is a little of very beautiful country, and the Poncas raise considerable corn in this neighborhood, and winter here; it would furnish a handsome site for a military post. The same is true of the right bank of the Missouri, from White river to the Great Bend, at the former situation of old Fort Aux Cedres and Fort Lookout. Another eligible site is on the point ten to fifteen miles below the Shyenne. It is my opinion that no point above the Vermillion could be relied upon for many years to come to raise corn for the support of a cavalry post; above this it must be transported.

The crossing of the Missouri at low water is very difficult by any means. It cannot easily be forded, and shoals would prevent a boat from floating across, except she be of very light draft and small dimensions. I am convinced, however, from what I have seen during a season of unparalleled difficulties to navigation, that, with suitable preparation, the Missouri can always be relied upon as a channel to convey any necessary amount of supplies. The removal of some of the snags and boulders would greatly improve it, but even as it is, with a better knowledge of the channel on the part of those navigating it, and more suitably constructed boats, this stream would lose much of its terror to them.

* * * * *

The wood used by steamboats above the mouth of the Big Sioux is cut by their crews as they proceed. . . . There is . . . wood enough for steam navigation for many years. . . .

My trip was made in the steamboat Clara, drawing 5½ feet of water. She had to be lightened at the mouth of l'Eau qui Court, and again at the bar above the mouth of White river, and at the foot of the Great Bend. She was 39 days from St. Louis to Fort Pierre.

The Clara was so hard to handle when the wind blew strong, that she frequently could not be kept in the channel. The requisites of a good steamboat for Missouri navigation are, a strong bottom, a boiler that burns the minimum amount of wood, as little as possible of top hamper, wheels well forward, and considerable breadth of beam, so as to give as much control over her motions as possible. The Clara was the reverse of all this, but Captain Cheever, her commander, was a most skillful river man, and his untiring efforts overcame all difficulties.

The main rise on the Missouri occurs between April 20, and June 1.

The Platte river is the most important tributary of the Missouri in the region under consideration; its broad and grass-covered valley leading to the west, furnishes one of the best wagon roads of its length in America. From its mouth to the forks, the bluffs are from two to five miles from the water, making an intermediate bottom valley of from four to eight miles wide. From the forks to Fort Laramie, the bluffs occasionally come down to the water's edge, and the road has to cross the points of the ridges. From Ash Hollow[11] to Fort Laramie, the road is sometimes heavy with sand. Fine cotton wood grows along the banks, and on the islands, from the mouth to Fort Kearny; from here up it is scarce, and of small size. Cedar is found in the ravines of the bluffs, in the neighborhood of the forks, and above. The river is about a mile wide, and flows over a sandy bottom; when the banks are full, it is about six feet deep throughout, having a remarkably level bed; but it is of no use for navigation, as the bed is so broad that the water seldom attains sufficient depth, and then the rise is of short duration.

The water is somtimes so low, as was the case last season, that it can be crossed anywhere without difficulty, the only care requisite being to avoid quicksands.

The manner in which this stream spreads out over its entire bed in low water, is one of its most striking features, and it is peculiar to the rivers of the sandy region. A short distance above Fort Laramie, the Platte comes out from among the gorges and cañons, and its character there is that of a mountain stream.

Loup River, a large branch of the Platte, some 200 yards wide, is, where I saw it, in every respect similar to the latter below the forks, and a fine road could, without doubt, be made along its valley, which is about two miles wide. Its banks are low, like those of the Platte, but are much better wooded. The Pawnees lived in numbers on this stream, till the hostility of the Dacotas drove them from their homes. . . .

L'Eau qui Court or *Rapid river* has its source just west of Rawhide Peak, about twenty-five miles north of Fort Laramie, and flows for the most part through a sterile country. Where I crossed it, August 15th, it was about 200 yards wide, the banks are one hundred and forty feet high, and the river difficult to approach. High precipices of soft, calcerous sandstone stood in places at the water's edge. The valley was very narrow, and it was impossible to course along it without frequently taking to the ridges. The water was clear and flowed swiftly over a sandy bed. In the side ravines, which are all filled with pine or scrubly oak, are numerous springs. The stream might answer for rafting in the floods, but would furnish no navigation.

White river rises about 35 miles east of the source of Rapid river, and in about the same latitude. Its course for the first 15 or 20 miles is through a narrow gorge, thence it emerges into a broad, open valley, through which it flows for 90 miles, and then enters the high, precipitous cliffs of the Bad Lands; it winds through these to the South Fork, and thence to its mouth it has a beautifully wooded and grassy valley of about one mile wide. Below the Bad Lands, its valley cannot be followed without frequently taking to the high prairie bluffs. At the forks, the river is about 140 yards wide; a short distance above the mouth, about 200 yards. The south fork has large pines upon it and so have most of the southern branches above this stream, and they are much resorted to by the Indians. The water from these streams is clear, and similar to Rapid river.

The Bad river, Wahpa Shicha, or *Little Missouri river* is about 90 miles long, rising just east of the Bad Lands. The same difficulty is experienced as with the lower part of White river, if you attempt to follow along its valley. The valley is from one half to one mile wide, well grassed and wooded. The bed of the stream is soft and miry, and generally not fordable. The approach to the valley is not difficult for wagons in dry weather. Cottonwood exists in considerable quantities mixed with willow, and in some places ash and oak. Wild plums are abundant. A portion of this valley is adapted to raising Indian corn. When flooded, the river is from 25 to 40 yards wide, and cannot then be crossed without a good bridge or ferry. I am not informed of the extent to which it overflows its immediate banks which are about 10 feet high. This stream flows through a section abounding in salt springs, and salt incrustations are almost everywhere visible, but the water is generally palatable.

Big Shyenne, Washté Wahpa or *Good river* rises west of the Black Hills. The north fork, it is said, breaks through, as in the case of Laramie river. The forks are about 100 miles from the mouth. The south fork rises not far from the source of l'Eau qui Court. After leaving the Black Hills this stream flows between high clay bluffs, winding about in its valley, and is in many respects similar to White river and Bad river, being difficult to pursue with wagons. The stream near its mouth is about 200 yards wide, the bottom is generally muddy, and not easily crossed. Fine cotton wood exists along its banks, and pine on its sources in the Black Hills. The stream could be used for rafting.

* * * * *

Routes, Transportation, &c.

From Fort Leavenworth to Fort Kearny there is a good prairie road, with a ferry on the Blue river. The road from Fort Kearny along the south side of the Platte to the crossing of the south fork, is perfectly level and well broken; the ground, a few inches below the surface, is gravel or sand, and ordinary rains do not seriously affect it. In crossing the divide from the south fork to the north, we gain the summit by easy slopes, but the descent is very sudden into Ash Hollow on the north fork, and it would be almost impractible to take a loaded wagon up this steep. Ash hollow is bounded on all sides by rocky escarpments from 50 to 100 feet high, and much labor would be required to make a permanently good road for getting down to it. The route this far is the one usually followed by the emigration which leaves the western part of Missouri for Oregon and California, and it continues usually along the south side of the north fork to Laramie river, which is crossed by a good bridge.

We crossed the north fork at Ash Hollow, and passed up on the north side, which is probably preferable when the river is low enough to be easily crossed. The Mormon emigration, and that which leaves the vicinity of Kanesville, Iowa, I am informed, strikes across the country to the Platte, follows this to the mouth of Wood river, then up this stream to near its source and crosses to the Platte again in the vicinity of Big Cottonwood Spring, and continues on the north side all the way to Fort Laramie. This route has to cross the Elk Horn, a stream about 30 yards wide, and Loup Fork, 200 yards wide, which, when flooded, must be ferried over, and perhaps might not be passable for many days at a time. This route, I am informed, is quite heavy and difficult during wet seasons. If it should be used to supply Fort Laramie the stores would have to be crossed over the north fork of the Platte, but at a point so near the Fort they might be left on the north side in charge of a detachment from the garrison. The route along the south side of the Platte has at least to cross the south fork, which, in the time of melting snows and spring floods, would occasion serious delay. I am not, therefore, prepared to say whether Fort Laramie could be best supplied from Fort Leavenworth, or from the points of starting of the Mormon emigration near Florence, above the mouth of the Platte; the distance of land transportation is in favor of the latter. The scarcity of wood along the Platte is a serious objection to winter travel. The bottom, along which the road lies, is very seldom overflowed. I think it altogether probable that a good route could be found leading up Loup Fork toward its source, and then crossing over to the Platte—it should be examined.

It was thought that the route from Fort Pierre to Fort Laramie might be used to supply the latter post, the stores being transported by steamboats up the Missouri. I believe the steamboat transportation perfectly practicable up to Fort Pierre for any requisite amount of provisions and stores, yet they could not be relied upon to reach there before the 15th of July, and the cost would be considerable. The land transportation would then be 323 miles. But the road, even in good seasons, is rough and contains numerous hills, requiring heavy hauling, and in wet seasons would be almost impassable, as it lies throughout in a clay region. For 12 miles on the head of White river, the road is in the last degree bad at all times; there is reason, however, to think that this portion could be avoided. But when we consider that the train for transportation from Fort Pierre to Fort Laramie must be procured from the States at a distance of 500 to 600 miles, it is doubtful if at any time economy would select this route as a channel through which to supply Fort Laramie.

Very much in the same light must we view the project of supplying Fort Laramie from the mouth of Rapid river, supposing a post established at that point, viz: the distance one hundred to four hundred miles, from which the means of land transportation must be obtained and the probable difficulties of the route itself. This proposed road would have to keep on the divide north or south of Rapid river, and most probably to the north, or if it entered the valley would be forced to cross the stream frequently, or take again to the bluffs. Unlike the Platte, or the main portion of White river now followed by the Pierre and Laramie road, the Rapid river has no continuous broad valley on either side, and could not be followed by wagons at the points at which I have visited it. A better route would no doubt be found along the valley of Turtle Hill creek, a branch of l'Eau qui Court, to near its head; it must then take

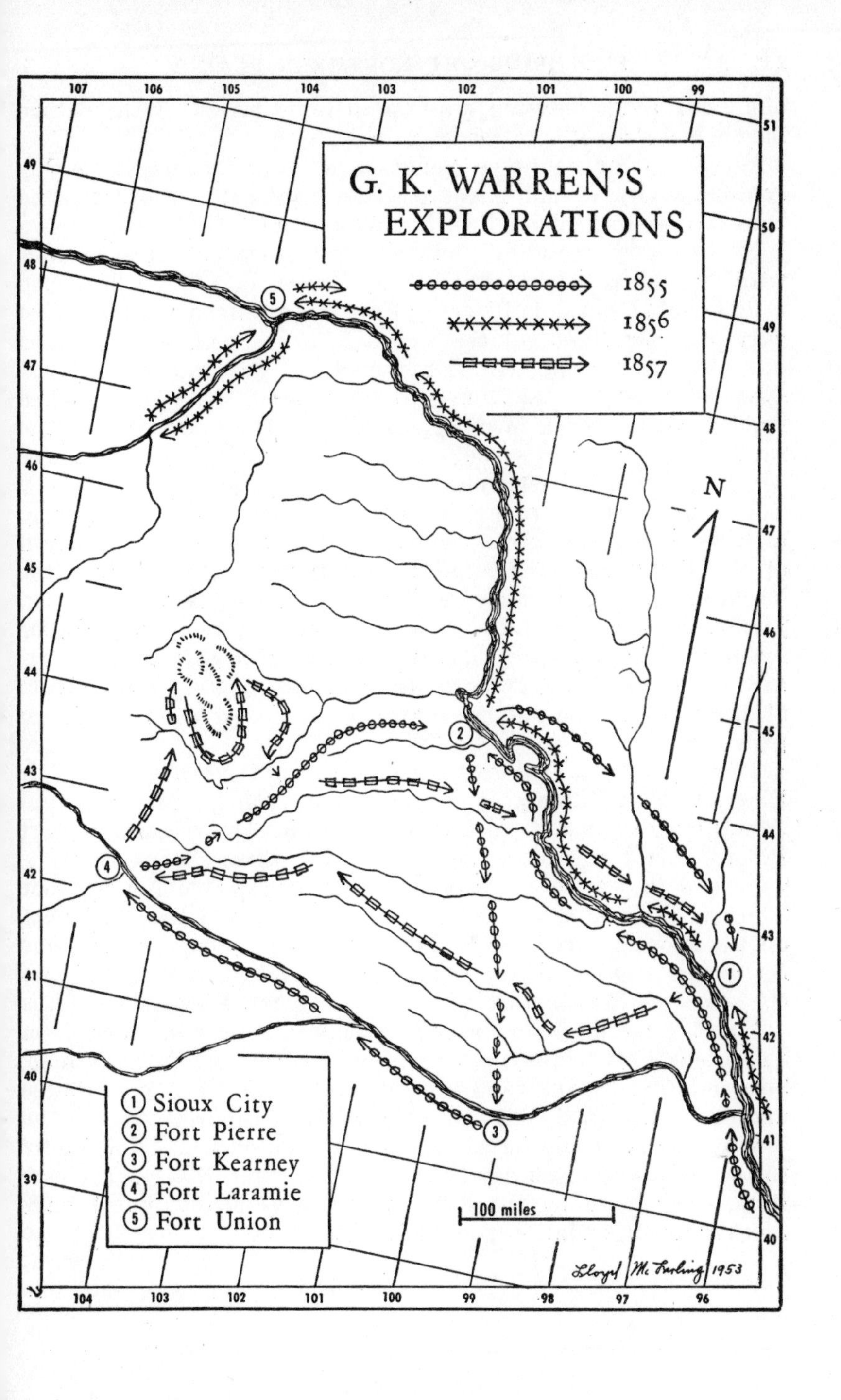

G. K. WARREN'S EXPLORATIONS
1855
1856
1857
N
100 miles
① Sioux City
② Fort Pierre
③ Fort Kearney
④ Fort Laramie
⑤ Fort Union
Lloyd McFarling 1953

along the divide between White and Rapid rivers, of the nature of which I am not informed.

Wood will no doubt be found on all the streams along this route, but we should have to make frequent detours to find camps if we are confined to the divide.

The country is sandy and the road would be good in wet weather; there is undoubtedly good grass.

The route from Fort Pierre to Fort Kearny in summer answers very well for light vehicles or pack trains, and wood, water, and grass are sufficient for travelling purposes; the large streams, however, that have to be crossed, and which, when flooded, would occasion delay, as well as the difficulties of the sand hills, render this route unfit for more than the ordinary communication between posts.

The direct route from Sioux City to Fort Pierre, by the way of Fire Steel creek, is very good; there is a ferry at the mouth of the Big Sioux, and a good ford in low stages across the Vermillion and James rivers. Scarcity of fuel is a serious objection to winter travel. A better route in cold weather, or when the streams are flooded, though somewhat longer, lies nearer the Missouri, crossing the Vermillion and James rivers at their mouths and at these two places ferry boats should be provided.

I have no special information concerning the route from Fort Pierre to Fort Ridgely; it is probably good and very direct, but James river cannot be forded if it is high. The road from Fort Pierre, direct to the mouth of Shyenne river, forty miles, is very bad in wet weather, and almost impassable for wagons. The road leading to the American Fur Company's trading house, on the Moreau, crosses the Shyenne about twenty miles from its mouth and is bad in wet weather, though not so hilly as the other, as it avoids the side ravines of the Missouri.

Detail directions for travelling on the routes between Fort Pierre and Fort Kearny, between Fort Kearny and Fort Laramie, between Fort Laramie and Fort Pierre and between Fort Pierre and Sioux City will be found at the end of this report.

A good road could be had from near the mouth of the Platte to the mouth of l'Eau qui Court, following the Elk Horn river; it has been used by the American Fur Company, but I have no definite information concerning it.

NOTES TO CHAPTER 20

1. Warren's report was in the form of a letter dated August 7, 1855, to the Assistant Adjutant General of the Sioux expedition. It was published in *South Dakota Historical Collections*, I, 390-94.

2. Warren's explorations in 1855 were within the present states of South Dakota, Nebraska, and Wyoming. His report included a day-to-day journal of his travels (except while on the Missouri River), in addition to the more generalized conclusions which are partially reprinted here.

3. A brief report by Dr. Hayden was published as an appendix to the Warren report.

4. Once more—the myth of the Great American Desert.

5. By "primitive" rocks Warren probably meant igneous, but perhaps he meant both igneous and metamorphic rocks. By the "Black Hills of Nebraska" he meant the Black Hills of modern terminology, which are chiefly in South Dakota but extend into Wyoming. In 1855 Nebraska Territory reached from the Missouri to the Rockies, and from the fortieth parallel to Canada.

6. Usually called Bear Butte. During the 1855 explorations Hayden made a side trip to this butte and climbed it.

7. "Every time that I have traveled over these plains, I have found myself amid a painful void. . . . It would be impossible for me to describe the sombre silence that reigns in this vast desert. You may pass weeks there, on the march, without meeting a living soul. And yet we become habituated to it—like it. Solitude seems to give scope to man's intellectual faculties; the mind seems more vigorous, the thought clearer. . . ." De Smet, *Life, Letters and Travels* (Chittenden and Richardson, eds.), II, 647-48. Father De Smet used the word "desert" to denote an uninhabited area, without regard to climate or vegetation.

8. The Nebraska sand hills occupy about 24,000 square miles between the Platte and Niobrara rivers, chiefly between the 99th and 103d meridians of longitude. The topography is dunelike, the soil is very sandy, but with some exceptions the region is well grassed.

9. Now called the Cheyenne.

10. The Niobrara.

11. Ash Hollow is mentioned later by Warren, and described by Stansbury in Chapter 13, *ante*. It was at the mouth of Ash Creek, an intermittent stream that was usually dry. Blue Water Creek, called Blue Creek on modern maps, entered the Platte on the north side a little higher up. On this stream the battle of Blue Water was fought, September 3, 1855, between Harney's forces and a band of Brulé Sioux led by Little Thunder. Harney reported 86 Indians killed, 5 wounded, and about 70 women and children captured; while the white casualties amounted to 4 killed, 4 severely wounded, 3 slightly wounded, and one missing. *Report of the Secretary of War*, 1955.

Chapter 21

1855

INDIANS AND MILITARY POSTS,

by Lieutenant Gouverneur K. Warren

In this chapter I am reprinting another excerpt from Lieutenant Warren's report on "Explorations in the Dacota Country, in the Year 1855." The last chapter was mainly a discussion of geographical matters, including existing and possible routes of communication and supply in the southern part of the Northern Plains. The present chapter deals more particularly with the Indians, and especially the Teton group of Sioux Indian tribes; and with military posts. Both chapters show that the young lieutenant was intelligently interested in the relationships between geography and military science. His knowledge of strategy and tactics was demonstrated in the Civil War, where he became a corps commander, attained the rank of major general of volunteers, and received four brevets for gallant and meritorious service.

In 1856 Lieutenant Warren, with Dr. Hayden and other assistants, ascended the Missouri to Fort Union, and then went about 130 miles up the Yellowstone. He traveled by steamboat, wagon, pack train, bullboat and Mackinaw boat. The principal object of the trip was the mapping of the Missouri and Yellowstone rivers. Steamboat Captain Joseph La Barge ". . . remembered him well, as he was in the pilot house nearly all the time. He was very active, and kept his men vigorously employed gathering information. At night he went on shore and took observations. . . . He was, . . . a handsome man, with a fine head and clear eye, at that time rather slender, but well built and erect. He was always pleasant, and was liked by his men, but was nevertheless a strict disciplinarian. . . ."[1]

INDIANS AND MILITARY POSTS.

The *Dacotas* occupy most of the country we have been considering, and are scattered over an immense territory, extending from the Mississippi on the east to the Black Hills on the west, and from the forks of the Platte on the south to Devil's Lake on the north. They say their name means leagued or allied, and they sometimes speak of themselves as the "Ocheti Shaowni" or "Seven Council Fires." These are the seven principal bands which compose the nation, viz:

"1. *The Mde-wakan-tonwans,* meaning village of the Spirit Lake."

"2. *Wahpekutes,* meaning leaf shooters."

"3. *Wahpe-tonwans,* meaning village in the leaves."

"4. *Sisi-tonwans,* meaning village of the marsh."

These four constitute the Mississippi and Minesota Dacotas, and are called by those on the Missouri *"Isanties."* They are estimated at 6,200 souls. Some of these are said to give much trouble to the settlers in northwestern Iowa and in Nebraska and are charged with outrages during the past season. Fort Ridgely is in their country.

5. *The Ihanktonwans,* village at the end, (Yanktons,) sometimes called Wichiyela or "First Nation."

They are found at the mouth of the Big Sioux, and between it and James river, and on the opposite bank of the Missouri. They are supposed to number 360 lodges. Contact with the whites has considerably degenerated them, and their distance from the present buffalo ranges renders them comparatively poor.

6. *The Ihanktonwannas,* one of the "end village" bands (Yanktonais) range between James river and the Missouri as high north as Devil's Lake. They number 800 lodges, and are spirited and warlike. They fought against the United States in the war of 1812, and their chief went on a visit to England. "From the Wazikute branch of this band the Assinniboins, or Hohe of the Dacotas, are said to have sprung."

7. *"The Titonwans, village of the prairie,* are supposed to constitute more than one-half of the whole Dacota nation." They live on the western side of the Missouri, and take within their range the Black Hills from between the forks of the Platte to the Yellowstone river. They are allied by marriage with the Shyennes and Aricarees, but are mortal enemies of the Pawnees.[2]

The Titonwans, except a few of the Brules on White river, and some of the families connected with the whites by marriage, have never planted corn. They are divided into seven bands, viz:

1. *Unkpapas, they who camp by themselves.* They live on the Missouri near the mouth of the Moreau, and roam from the Big Shyenne up to the Yellowstone and west to the Black Hills. They formerly intermarried extensively with the Shyennes. They number about 365 lodges.

2. *Sihasapas, Blackfeet.* Haunts and homes same as the Unkpapas; number 165 lodges. These two bands have very little respect for the power of the whites.

3. *Oo-he-non-pas, two boilings or two kettle band.* These are now very much scattered among other bands. They number about 100 lodges.

4. *Sichangus, burnt thighs, Brulés,* claim the country along White river and contiguous to it. They number 480 lodges. They include the Wazazhas, to which belonged Matoiya, (the Scattering Bear,)[3] made chief of all the Dacotas by the government and who was killed by Lieutenant Grattan.

5. *Ogalalas, they who live in the mountains,* live between the forks of the Platte and number 360 lodges.

6. *Minikanyes, they who plant by the water,* live on and between the forks of the Shyenne and in the Black Hills; number 200 lodges.

7. *Itahzipchois, Bowpith, Sans Arc,* claim in common with the Minikanyes, and number 170 lodges. These last two bands have been exceedingly troublesome to the emigration.[4]

The Dacotas, on and west of the Missouri, which includes all but the Isanties, are the only ones I have heard estimated. I should think that eight inmates to a lodge, and one fifth of them warriors, an ample allowance. We would then have:

	Lodges	*Inmates*	*Warriors*
Ihanktonwans, (Yanktons)	360	2,880	572
Ihanktonwannas, (Yanktonais)	800	6,400	1,240
Unkpapas	365	2,920	584
Sihasapas, (Blackfeet)	165	1,280	256
Oohenonpas, (Two Kettle)	100	800	160
Sichangus, (Brulé)	480	3,840	748
Ogalalas	360	2,880	576
Minikanyes	200	1,600	320
Itazipchois, (Sans Arc)	170	1,360	272
Total[5]	3,000	24,000	4,800

These Dacotas formerly all lived around the headwaters of the Mississippi and Red river of the north, and in their migration to the southwest have pushed the Shyennes (with whom they are on friendly terms) in advance, leaving their name to the Shyenne of Red river, to the Big Shyenne of the Missouri, and to the section of country they now occupy between the Platte and the Arkansas.

In the summer the Dacotas follow the buffaloes in their ranges over the prairie, and in the winter fix their lodges in the clusters or fringes of wood along the banks of the lakes and streams. The bark of the cottonwood, which furnishes food for their horses during the winter snows, have led to immense destruction of this timber, and many streams have been thinned, or entirely stripped of their former beautiful groves.

Their horses are obtained by traffic with the Indians further south who have stolen them in New Mexico, or are caught wild on the plains towards the Rocky mountains. The nation is one of the most skilful and warlike and most numerous in our Territory; and could they be made to feel a due confidence in their own powers, would be most formidable warriors. In single combat on horseback they have no superiors—a skill acquired by constant practice with their bows and arrows and long lances, with which they succeed in killing their game at full speed. The rapidity with which they shoot their arrows, and the accuracy of their aim, rivals that of a practiced hand with the famed revolver.

Notwithstanding the destruction of their numbers by small pox and cholera, it is the opinion of some that they are increasing in numbers rather than diminishing, except where they mingle with the settlements on the frontier. It has been well said that theft is an Indian virtue.

The love of renown and desire of plunder leads them far from their homes, and many of the depredations along the Platte are committed by the Unkpapas and Sihasapas, whose homes are further from it than those of any of the Titonwans. The Isanties or Dacotas of the St. Peter's also carry their ravages into Nebraska, and are there the most dreaded of all the savages.

When any redress or reparation is sought, or punishment threatened for these offenses, the same excuse is always made: "The old men opposed it, but the young men could not be restrained." So long as the smiles of the females, the admiration of his comrades, and ultimate influences with his tribe continue to be the reward of daring exploits, these, to say nothing of the Indian's often absolute necessities, will prove too strong in the breast of the youthful warrior for the counsels and frowns of age, or for the peaceful policy of the Indian Bureau.

Military occupation is essential to the safety of the whites, and the military posts should be in such positions, and occupied by such numbers, as effectually to overawe the ambitious and turbulent, and sustain the counsel of the old and prudent.

They should be placed well in the country whence the marauders come, as well as on the frontier and lines of communication they are designed to protect. In making this occupation we should look to the future. Agricultural settlements have now nearly reached their western limits on our great plains; the tracts beyond must ever be occupied by a pastoral people, whether civilized or savage. If the Indian is not doomed to speedy extirpation, if he is to have a permanent home, here is where it must be located, and the military posts should contemplate a permanency which they have not heretofore possessed.[6]

Posts situated near the Indians' homes, designed to restrain, might be garrisoned by infantry, and they should be large from the outset, to command immediate respect. Those situated near the settlements for protection should be cavalry, both on account of the facility with which they can move to threatened points, or pursue the offenders, and for the comparative ease with which the horses could be maintained during the winter, and be ready for early and efficient service in the spring.

With good commanders, and forces sufficient to sustain them in the measures they may take for chastising or restraining the Indians and protecting them from the injustice of the whites, peace can be maintained without exterminating the red man, whose manliness has much to admire, and whose fate deserves our sympathy.

Upon the principles I have mentioned, I should recommend that an infantry post be maintained in the neighborhood of Fort Pierre. Of all the points yet occupied in the Dacota country, this is the most central. Good prairie roads lead from it in every direction, and the experienced guides and traders of the American Fur Company have explored them all. Formerly, it was no uncommon thing to see six hundred lodges camped around this fort at one time. A spot to which so many could assemble must be no unimportant one from which to pursue them to their homes. A navigable river leads direct to the place, and the post can be supplied with certainty, if proper preparations are made. I have the opinions of the most successful steamboat captains to this effect.[7]

A permanent establishment here, with the occasional movement of troops between it and Fort Laramie, must entirely drive the disaffected and dangerous Dacotas from all the country south of this route.

Another post of, say four companies, should be kept up at the mouth of l'Eau qui Court to restrain the Poncas.

A cavalry post should be established in the neighborhood of the mouth of Big Sioux river,[8] as protection to the settlements in Iowa and Nebraska from the Ihanktonwans and Isanties, and co-operate with the troops at Fort Pierre. Forage could be economically procured at this point, and it is probably the most western in this latitude, or north of it, that horses could reasonably be maintained so as to be prepared for an early spring campaign.

Future necessity may require the establishment of a post near the Moreau river, among the Unkpapas, or on the left bank in the country of the Ihanktonwannas.

On the line of the Platte, Fort Kearny must, for a long time, be beyond the frontier settlements, and is a necessary post for the protection of emigrants.

Fort Laramie will always be in the Indian country as long as there is one, and makes a most valuable point for protection to travel. West of Fort Laramie temporary protection should be afforded, when necessary, by patrols and escorts and also between Forts Laramie and Kearny.

Not less than one regiment, four companies, at Fort Kearny, and six at Fort Laramie should be kept on this line.

A winter campaign could not often be made with success in the Dacota country, and all that should be attempted is to preserve the men and animals for early spring operations, when the emaciated condition of the Indian horses would prevent them escaping and insure their easy capture.

The present war should not be abandoned until the Unkpapas, Minikanyes, and Ihanktonwannas have felt or acknowledged the power of the general government, and be made to entertain for our citizens a feeling of respect, in which they have heretofore been sadly wanting. If active operations are to be carried on during the coming season in the Dacota country, it is against them the forces should be directed, from both Fort Laramie and Fort Pierre.

The punishment inflicted on the Brules and Ogalales at Blue Water has taught them a useful lesson, which they will not soon forget.

The Pawnees, about eight hundred warriors, with whom the Dacotas are at war, and the Poncas, three hundred warriors, with whom they are friendly, occupy the southeastern part of Nebraska; to the southwest are the Shyennes, one thousand, between whom and the Ogalala Dacotas the most friendly relations exist. The Crows, a powerful and warlike tribe, occupy the country between the Black Hills and Wind River mountains, about the sources of the Yellowstone. They made a treaty of peace with the Dacotas at Horse Creek, in 1849 but they are enemies at heart.[9] The small bands of Mandans, Aricarees, and Minnitares, and the powerful one of the Assinniboins, are on the north.

CONCLUSION.

Very little is known as to the accurate geography and topography of the Crow Country and Black Hills, and, in fact, of any portion of Nebraska west of the Missouri, and the road from Fort Pierre to Fort Laramie.

The same causes that brought on the war with the Sioux will, no doubt, continue to operate, and the time is not distant when we shall have a similar necessity for chastising the Crows and northern Missouri Dacotas, who have, as yet, seen nothing of the power of the United States, nor feel any respect for it. It seems to me, therefore, in a purely military point of view, of the greatest importance to gain a knowledge of that region, while the peaceful disposition of these tribes may permit, and before they become maddened by the encroachments of the white man. It is therefore, respectfully requested that a recommendation be made to Congress, through the proper channel, for an appropriation of $50,000, for military and geographical explorations in the territory of Nebraska.

A reconnaissance, which could be made at small expense on the Fur Company's steamboat, should be made of the Missouri river from Fort Pierre to the mouth of the Yellowstone; one should also be made of Loup Fork of the Platte, and of the country between White river and l'Eau qui Court, for the purpose of seeking good communication between Fort Laramie and the Missouri river.[10] Routes from Fort Laramie to the Yellowstone, and of the country around and between the forks of the Shyenne, deserve examination.[11] The future necessities of Indian warfare will undoubtedly render information in this territory of the last degree valuable.

Accompanying this report is a map of a portion of the Dacota country, on a scale of 1 to 600,000. It embraces all the explorations within the limits compassed by it, including those of Major Long, J. N. Nicollet, Captain Fremont and Captain Stansbury. The sketches by Lieutenant Curtis of the route from Fort Pierre to the mouth of White river, and of Mr. P. Carrey, from Fort St. Vrain to Fort Laramie, were made with a pocket compass, and estimated distances—those made by myself, are with prismatic compass and odometer measurements of distance. Barometer observations were taken on the route from Fort Pierre to Fort Kearny, and thence to Fort Laramie; the observations and results are appended to this report. A barometric profile of the route from Fort Pierre to Fort Kearny is also given. From not getting my instruments in time, I was unable to make any astronomical observations. The latitude of Fort Pierre is taken from Nicollet, that of Fort Kearny, and the latitude and longitude of Fort Laramie, are taken from Captain Stansbury. The longitude of Fort Pierre and Fort Kearny are taken from the general map, which I compiled in the office of the Pacific Railroad Exploration, and are the result of comparison of several determinations.

The longitude of no point on this map, distant from the boundary of the States, can be considered certain within 5 to 10 miles.[12] The surveys with the compass and odometer were very carefully made.

I also present another map on a scale of 1 to 300,000 giving the location of the different bands of Indians, and such other information as I was enabled to obtain from the hunters and trappers. Though it is not reliable where surveys have not been made, still it is the best that our present knowledge will permit. . . .

For information about portions of the country I have not visited, I had the benefit of frequent consultation with Colon Campbell, Michael Desomet, Jean Lefebre, James Boldeaux, Joseph Jewett, James Baker, Dr. Hayden, Mr. Galpin, Henry Goulet, Alexander Culbertstone, and others, whose statements I have endeavored to combine.[13]

* * * * *

It is perhaps, proper to allude here to the journey performed from Fort Pierre to Fort Kearny, since nearly all the knowledge I have gained, and whatever service I may have rendered, resulted immediately from it.

When I was preparing for the undertaking, and had secured a party of six persons, exclusive of Mr. Carrey and myself, I was counselled most earnestly by my brother officers not to make it, and the commanding officer at Fort Pierre thought seriously of interposing his authority as my military superior to prevent so "rash" an attempt, which presented to him nothing but a prospect of my certain destruction. The route was known to lead through the country of the Brulés (supposed to be our worst enemies,) and nothing was known as to their position or intention. We would, also, it was said, meet the Poncas and Pawnees, and neither would hesitate to rob, or even "wipe out" a party as small as mine, well knowing the offense would be charged upon the Brulés. Moreover, much of the route was wholly unknown and untraveled, and there was no estimating the obstacles and delays we might encounter. My intention, however, had not been formed without due consideration of these things, and careful conversation with the men of the country. The weather was as yet too warm, it being the first of August, for the war parties to have formed, and it was the season for making "sweet corn," so that the Indians would likely be thus engaged. The party was made up of the most experienced prairie men, four of them being half-breed Dacotas, and we were well armed; we were determined to be constantly on our guard, and to travel in the night if we came in the vicinity of an enemy; no fire was to be lighted at night, nor tent pitched. Mr. Galpin of the Fur Company assured me he did not believe I would meet an Indian, and the result verified his predictions. We saw fresh trails of the Poncas on l'Eau qui Court, and of the Brulés in the Sand Hills, and some deserted Pawnee camps on Loup Fork, but no Indians. We performed the journey in fifteen days.

I was thus enabled to carry out the instructions under which I had gone to Fort Pierre to participate in the campaign under General Harney, and perform the duties required of me as topographical engineer of the expedition.

I hope the explanation will free me from any charge of having acted with rashness or imprudence.

The general conclusions which I have drawn from my own observations and studies (though I may not have fully demonstrated them) are, that the portion of Nebraska (which I have visited) lying north of White river is mostly of a clay formation, and that south of it is mainly of sand; that but a small portion of it is susceptible of cultivation west of the 97th meridian; that the Territory is occupied by powerful tribes of roving savages, and is only adapted to a mode of life such as theirs; that it must long remain an Indian country; that the Indians should be made to feel the power of the United States; that the military posts in consequence, should contemplate permanency; that Forts Laramie and Pierre are the most important positions yet occupied; that the latter can always be supplied by steamboats on the Missouri; that the former must be supplied by way of the valley of the Platte; that a great deal yet remains to be learned of this vast territory; and that it is of the utmost importance to acquire a thorough knowledge of it without delay.

NOTES TO CHAPTER 21

1. The quotation is from *History of Early Steamboat Navigation on the Missouri River, Life and Adventures of Joseph La Barge. . . .* by Chittenden. The 1856 and 1857 explorations were reported by Warren in "Explorations in Nebraska. Preliminary Report. . . ." in the *Report of the Secretary of War*, 1858. Chapter 25, *post*, describes Warren's travels at the border of the Black Hills in 1857.

2. The Sioux and the Arikaras were usually enemies. There were short intervals of peace and perhaps some intermarrying, but not enough to maintain a permanent alliance.

3. This Indian, called Brave Bear by George E. Hyde, was designated chief of the Teton Sioux tribes by the white negotiators at the treaty of 1851; but to most of the Indians the title had no meaning. Actually he was merely the leading chief of the Brulé tribe. He was mortally wounded in the Grattan Fight, August 19, 1854, and Little Thunder succeeded him as head chief of the Brulés.

4. For a more modern classification of the Sioux tribes see note 2, chap. 7, *ante*.

5. Pre-reservation estimates of Indian populations are not very reliable. The total number of Sioux was estimated by the Office of Indian Affairs as 27,500 in 1836, 21,600 in 1837, 19,660 in 1847, and 27,423 in 1855.

6. Coupled with the myth of the Great American Desert was the idea of a permanent Indian frontier. This idea dominated the thinking of officials dealing with the Indians from about 1830 to about 1860. Notwithstanding the constant movement of the American people westward, the delusion persisted that the movement was about finished; and that the Indians would be left in possession of the rest of the country, which was not considered good enough for white people anyway. This persistent delusion caused much of the mistreatment of the Indian.

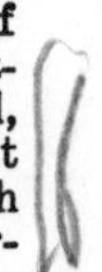

7. The army purchased Fort Pierre from Pierre Chouteau, Jr., and Company in 1855 and converted the trading post into a military post. The strategic location was good, but the immediate surroundings had been damaged by overgrazing and overhunting. The post was old, dilapidated, and almost worthless for military purposes. Harney arrived after the purchase was made, and was thorougly dissatisfied with the post. In the summer of 1856 he moved part of his command down the Missouri to a place on the right bank about thirty miles above the mouth of the Niobrara and began to build Fort Randall. In 1857 the remaining troops were transferred to the new post and Fort Pierre was abandoned. In 1863 (old) Fort Sully was established a few miles below Fort Pierre, on the opposite side of the river. In 1866 this post was abandoned and (new) Fort Sully was built on the left bank of the Missouri about thirty miles above Fort Pierre. The second Fort Sully was occupied by troops until 1894. Thus Warren's recommendation for a post in the neighborhood of Fort Pierre was followed, except for the period 1857 to 1863, while his further recommendation for a post at the mouth of the Niobrara was substantially adopted when Fort Randall was built. Fort Randall was abandoned in 1884. See also note 9, chap. 1, *ante*.

8. This was not done, but a portion of Harney's force was stationed in a temporary camp on the Big Sioux in 1856.

9. The date should be 1851.

10. These reconnaissances were made by Warren in 1856 and 1857.

11. This was done, in part, by Captain Raynolds in 1859 and 1860. Cf. chaps. 22 and 23, *post*.

12. Nicollet's longitude for Fort Pierre (100° 12′ 30″) was about ten miles too far east; his latitude (44° 23′ 28″) was about right.

13. Colon Campbell was perhaps "Colonel" Robert Campbell. James Boldeaux was James Bordeau, trader in the Fort Laramie area, mentioned by Fremont, Parkman, and other travelers. James Baker was a well-known mountain man. Dr. Hayden was the distinguished exploring geologist, author of Chapter 24, *post*. Mr. Galpin was C. E. Galpin, sometimes called Gilpin, a trader for many years on the Platte and Missouri. Alexander Culbertstone was Alexander Culbertson, mentioned by Audubon and De Smet. I have no knowledge of the other men mentioned in this paragraph.

Chapter 22

1859

POWDER RIVER VALLEY,

by Captain William F. Raynolds

In 1859 Lieutenant Warren was assigned to the Military Academy at West Point as an instructor in mathematics. The further explorations of the Northern Plains that he had recommended were continued by William Franklin Raynolds, a West Point graduate of 1843, now a captain in the Corps of Topographical Engineers.

The Raynolds expedition left Fort Pierre in July, 1859; moved westward through the valley of the Cheyenne and along the northern edge of the Black Hills to Powder River; followed Powder River Valley nearly to the Yellowstone; turned south along the Yellowstone and the eastern border of the Big Horn Mountains; then moved south and a little east to the Platte River, where it went into winter quarters on Deer Creek. It left Deer Creek in the spring of 1860; traveled by a route south of the Big Horns to the area drained by the Three Forks of the Missouri; and explored areas along the middle Yellowstone, and along the Missouri above the Yellowstone.

Raynolds was escorted by a small detail of infantry and assisted by Lieutenant H. E. Maynadier of the Topographical Engineers; J. D. Hutton, Topographer and Assistant Artist; J. H. Snowden, Topographer; H. E. Fillebrown, Meteorologist and Artist; Dr. Ferdinand Vandiveer Hayden, Naturalist and Surgeon; Dr. M. C. Hines, Surgeon and Assistant Naturalist; George Wallace, Timekeeper and Computer; and seven men employed on verbal orders of the Secretary of War "without special duties." Although Hayden was employed as naturalist and surgeon, and was qualified in both those categories, he functioned mainly as a geologist.

The expedition produced two important reports and two valuable maps. Unfortunately the preparation and publication of the reports and maps was delayed by the Civil War, in which Hayden served as surgeon, and Raynolds became a brevet brigadier general.

Raynolds' "Report of the Exploration of the Yellowstone and Missouri Rivers in 1859-60" was completed in 1867 and published by the government in 1868. Included was a map of the area from the Platte to the Missouri and west to the Three Forks. The map contained some data collected between the end of the field trip in 1860 and the publication of the report.

Hayden's *Geological Report of the Exploration of the Yellowstone and Missouri Rivers, 1859-60* was separately published by the government in pamphlet form in 1869. The attached geological map was the Raynolds base map, colored to symbolize the various geological areas.

The following chapter is made up of excerpts from Captain Raynolds' report of his travels in the Powder River Valley from July 20 to August 15, 1859.

Wednesday, July 20.—

* * * * *

About an hour after the train was in motion, our Indian guide was missing and has not been since seen. . . . Mr. Hutton reports having seen signal fires near Bear Lodge, and the probability is that he has gone to join his tribe. I cannot believe that he meditates mischief, but that he is afraid to remain with us longer, as we are now nearly out of the Sioux country, and will soon be among the Crows. He has spoken repeatedly along the route of accompanying us through the entire trip, but his courage has probably failed with the prospect of meeting the hereditary enemies of his tribe.

His services have been of the greatest value; his minute knowledge of the country having excellently qualified him for his important duties, while his invariable good humor and honest face had made him a universal favorite with all the party, and had given foundation for the hope that he was an exception to the usual rule as to Indian honesty. He has, however, testified to his thorough training as a savage, by taking with him the mule, saddle and bridle, that I had furnished him. The important nature of the assistance he has rendered us will far more than compensate for the value of the stolen property; but his method of collecting his pay was peculiarly Indian, and hardly to be justified by civilized law or the code of natural honesty.[1]

* * * * *

Thursday, July 21.— . . . Our route lay up the fork of the Little Missouri, some little distance from the stream, that we might avoid the numberless gullies and the inevitable sage, whose perpetual recurrence rendered our line of march very devious.

We crossed several tributaries of the Little Missouri, now dry, one being distinguished by a little timber upon its banks. Barren sage and cactus plains and naked hills describe the country through which we have passed to-day, the latter having been apparently once covered with grass, since eaten off by the buffaloes, which have been today seen in large numbers upon all sides. Some of these animals came very boldly up to the train, and, in one or two instances, with very ludicrous results.

Three large bulls charged down upon us at one point in the march, to the great alarm of one of the escort, who dropped his gun, and, raising his hands, exclaimed, in all the accents of mortal terror, "Elephants! elephants! my God! I did not know that there were elephants in this country!" On another occasion, as a band was passing close by the train, one of the teams started in full pursuit, and was with great difficulty checked. It was probably the first buffalo chase on record with a six-mule team.

* * * * *

We are now within a mile or two of the drainage of Powder river, and as soon as we shall have passed the crest before us we will be out of the Sioux or Dakota country.[2] The fires still continue in the distance; but no Indians have made their appearance, and their promise to permit us to pass through unmolested has been unbroken. Except for purposes of communication with our Indian Guide the interpreter has been useless. My American guide, Bridger,[3] is now on familiar ground and appears to be entirely at home in this country. I therefore anticipate no difficulty in dispensing with the services of our fugitive Indian.

* * * * *

Friday, July 22.—Our route this morning was nearly west and directly up the valley in which we were encamped. Numerous ravines entered it upon both sides, all being more or less wooded. Taking advantage of a convenient spur, we ascended to the summit of the ridge by a long and gradual slope of about two and a half miles from camp, and from the point thus reached looked down upon the valley of Powder river.

The view unfolded before us was grand, though uninviting from the appearance of desolation and the hardships threatened in our future marches. Rugged, chalk-like hills stretched off to the distant horizon, barren and forbidding, the surface of the interlying valleys being variegated with clumps of trees, denoting occasional presence of water-courses, hardly worthy to be dignified with the name of streams. The gorges of the ridge upon which we stood, however, were filled with pines, many over two feet in diameter, that would excellently answer for building purposes and the other uses of lumber. The ridge at the point of our crossing is 4,288 feet above the sea level, while the elevation on each side is considerably higher. This seems to be a continuation of the Black Hills and of the great outlier of the Rocky Mountains, which further south forms the eastern boundary of "the parks." No evidence of upheaval can be observed however, nor are there any reasons for calling this elevation a mountain, yet it forms one of the great topographical features of the country, and upon many of the old maps it appears as the Black Mountains.

Our route, after running along this spur for a mile or two, turned down an abrupt winding hill to a lower spur, between two of the small branches of Little Powder river. We followed this crest over an exceedingly bad road, which, in many places, was not of sufficient width to permit the passage of a single wagon for about six miles, when we were compelled to abandon it and descend to the valley on our left. There we expected to find water, but the bed of the stream was perfectly dry, and an attempt to supply the deficiency by digging also failed. We were commencing to contemplate the pleasant prospect of passing the night thirsty, when word was brought that some of the party had found water upon the north side of the ridge. There being no certainty of its presence ahead, and the guide confessing his ignorance as to where any could be found, I concluded to retrace our steps something over a mile across the ridge to a point at which it was known to exist.

The spur, along the summit of which we had been travelling and which we now crossed, is as perfect a specimen of "bad lands" as can be found in the country. It is almost wholly devoid of vegetation. Its sides have been washed into deep and impassable ravines by fierce rains, and with the numerous spurs of similar characteristics that radiate from it upon all sides it presents a phase of desolation peculiar to this region.

The entire district is totally unfit for the home of the white man, and indeed it seems to have been deserted by the Indians. Animal life has not entirely forsaken it, however; for, among the scattered pines in the heads of the ravines, several grizzly bears have been started by the party, and scattered bands of buffalo have been seen roaming among the barren hills in the distance, as if in search of food.

We encamped about 3 p. m., having marched 15 miles. The water is salt, and so impregnated with buffalo urine as to be scarcely usable. Grass is very scarce, but there is a fair supply of fuel.

Saturday, July 23.—Our route today was directly down the branches of Little Powder river upon which we had been encamped. Our guide Bridger favored following the bank of the stream, but it was ascertained to be impracticable, as we found ourselves to be in a perfect labyrinth of gullies, whose crossings would necessitate an immense amount of labor with the pick and shovel, attended, of course, with serious delay.

We, therefore, again ascended the ridge. . . . We followed this till, coming to a valley that was apparently practicable, we descended it, only to find it was wholly impassable. We then crossed the ridge, between the valley of our camp fork and the Little Powder, and with great trouble descended into the valley of the latter, where a ride of half a mile across the bottom brought us to the stream itself. It is now small and insignificant, being not over five feet wide and two or three inches in depth; but its bed, 100 yards in width, with banks 15 or 20 feet in height, shows that, at times, it is a large river, while the drift-wood above its banks proves its occasional great depth.

The valley is from half a mile to two miles in width, and a fringe of cottonwood trees gives it an appearance more inviting than a closer examination justifies.

* * * * *

Tuesday, July 26.—I this morning gave directions for the command to continue its march down the stream, while I, with two companions, ascended the high grounds upon the left of the route, to obtain a more extended view of the surrounding country, and if possible see the valley of the main Powder river. The hills were rugged and bare, rising to the height of about 500 feet above the level of the stream. From their summit the Powder was in plain sight, at a distance not exceeding four miles.

The landscape before us was wide in extent, but characterized by forbidding desolation. The valleys of the Powder and its branch were marked by narrow and sinuous belts of green, but these, with here and there a solitary pine of stunted growth, constituted all the verdure that relieved the monotony of barrenness. Naked brown hills rose upon all sides, broken into irregular peaks, and with their sides torn into deep and impassable gullies by the mountain torrents—a petrified representation of an angry sea in all the fury of a storm.

* * * * *

During the afternoon several frightened buffaloes charged through camp and were shot by the party. The river at this point is about 80 yards wide, and about two feet deep. The bed is a quicksand, making it necessary to be very cautious in crossing, and both above and below our camp the stream is divided by islands and bars into several channels.

Wednesday, July 27.—The river banks having been sufficiently cut down to enable our teams to reach the water, we were ready to resume our forward movement at 5½ o'clock this morning. Before starting we thought the river had fallen considerably, but on entering the stream it was found that the bed had been deepened by the shifting of the sandbanks in the current, and it was thus deeper than when first reached last night. The work of cutting down the banks thus proved almost useless, for by the time half of the teams had crossed it became necessary to seek another ford, which was ultimately found about half a mile above. By 7 o'clock we were all safely on the left bank. Our route lay down the valley of Powder river, which was covered with large sage bushes, through which we were compelled to break a road. After travelling thus about six miles we reached a point at which the stream flowed against a cut bank, and a deep gully rendered it necessary that we should either cross the stream, or abandon it and ascend the hills. The river bed being a mere quicksand, and it having been demonstrated by trial that it could not be crossed even on horseback, we were compelled to accept the latter alternative. After a long and hard pull over lands washed and badly cut up by rains, we reached a fine open plain, sloping almost imperceptibly to a stream, distant some six or eight miles. We passed easily and rapidly along the crest separating this stream from Powder river, the hills between our course and the river valley being so abrupt as to prevent our descending into the latter again, until we had marched nearly eight miles. When we did finally regain the valley it was found to be filled with buffalo and although the party was greatly fatigued with the arduous labors of the day, a general chase commenced, resulting in the increase of our stock of provisions by a bountiful supply of fresh meat. One large band charged directly upon the train and were only turned by a well-directed volley. The grass, on the river, surpassed our expectations in its quality, thus indicating that the buffalo have been in the valley but a short time. Their lowing is heard all about our camp this evening.

* * * * *

Thursday, July 28.—

* * * * *

The buffaloes are very poor and their meat tough and unpalatable, but the supply is abundant, and their chase affords capital sport for the party. Antelope in bands of from five to ten are seen almost every hour, and my great surprise is that the game succeeds in finding in this desert sufficient food to sustain life. The presence of these animals in such large numbers in this barren region is explained by the fact that this valley is a species of neutral ground between the Sioux and the Crows and other bands nearer the mountains, or, more correctly speaking, the common war ground visited only by war parties, who never disturb the game, as they would thereby give notice to their enemies of their presence. For this reason the buffalo remain here undisturbed, and indeed would seem to make the valley a place of refuge.

* * * * *

Monday, August 1.—Our route today was still down the valley of Powder river. . . .

After reaching camp, Bridger started in search of a route across the hills towards Tongue river. We are now within 40 or 50 miles of the mouth of the Powder, and the character of the stream cannot change materially in that distance, and its further exploration is comparatively useless. It is, moreover, absolutely essential that we should, as soon as possible, enter a region better provided with grass for the benefit of our animals, and I hope to do so by crossing the hills.

We know that the valley of Mizpah creek, the head of which we saw on the 27th, is not far to the west of us, and our first object will be to reach and pass it. As matters now stand, we shall, be compelled either to abbreviate our marches very materially or our animals will soon be entirely broken down. Bridger returned late at night after a six-hours' ride and makes a rather discouraging report, but thinks we will be able to succeed in at least crossing the Mizpah. . . .

* * * * *

Friday, August 5.—The stream upon which we are encamped is called by Bridger Pumpkin creek, taking its name from a species of wild gourd that is said to be found upon its banks.

Its bed is some 30 or 40 yards wide, and in the wet season would be impassable. The stream is not of great length, but empties into the Tongue river some six or eight miles below this point. Our route this morning lay down its valley crossing the creek every few hundred yards, as its course is very crooked, and the nature of the country prevents our leaving its banks. The soil is sandy and the strength of our mules has consequently been much overtasked.

After a march of this character for six miles, we passed over a low ridge to Tongue river, which at first resembled a mere tributary of Pumpkin creek. Its valley is no wider, and at this point there is but little timber, and, as the water was wholly invisible, the creek apparently was the larger. Upon a closer approach, however, Tongue river was found to be a fine rapid stream, from 70 to 100 yards in width and 13 inches deep, flowing over a gravelly bottom. Its water is clear and for the season very cold.

Upon reaching its banks, we looked in vain for grass for our animals. The little that was found proved totally insufficient, and we therefore encamped in a grove of young cottonwoods and supplied the deficiency in pasturage by our previous expedient of lopping off and feeding to the mules and horses the young and succulent boughs.

The point of junction of Tongue river and the Yellowstone was pointed out by Bridger to-day as we passed along, and, as it is not more than 12 or 15 miles distant, the Yellowstone cannot be correctly located upon our maps by about 15 miles. Bridger now advised that we travel up Tongue river some distance, before crossing to the west, for the purpose of avoiding the bluffs on the Yellowstone. This is not in accordance with my pre-conceived plan, but I shall accept his advice out of deference to his remarkable knowledge of the country.

After encamping, some of the party succeeded in catching several very fine cat-fish over 18 inches long, furnishing an agreeable variety in our monotonous bill of fare.

* * * * *

Tuesday, August 9.—We this morning left Tongue river and started across the hills to the westward. . . .

. . . The ravines upon each side of us were impassable, and the selection of the road proved Bridger's excellence as a guide. To the right of our course lay a range of beautifully rose-tinted

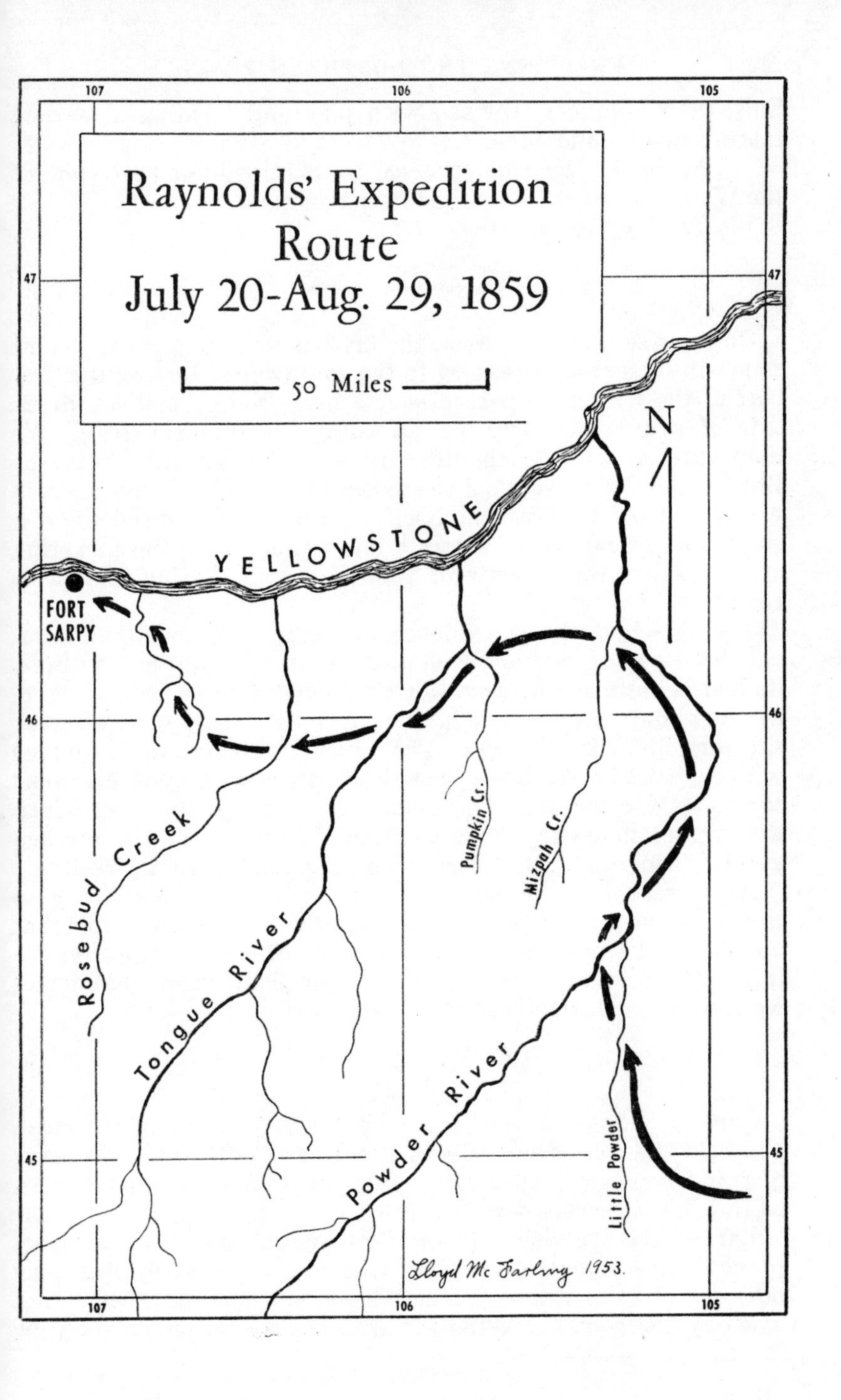

Raynolds' Expedition
Route
July 20-Aug. 29, 1859
50 Miles
107
106
105
47
46
45
N
YELLOWSTONE
FORT
SARPY
Rosebud Creek
Tongue River
Powder River
Pumpkin Cr.
Mizpah Cr.
Little Powder
Lloyd Mc Farling 1953.

hills, their summits crowned with pine and forming a marked feature in the landscape.

. . . From the last ridge crossed we obtained our first view of the Wolf or Chetish mountains in the distance.

Wednesday, August 10.—

* * * * *

Our course lay to the west, the broken country upon the right rendering a detour necessary to the southward. During the first half of the march we passed over a high, rolling plateau, destitute of grass or water, but affording an excellent road. We then entered with much difficulty a ravine draining into the Rosebud, and thus reached the valley of a dry fork, down which we passed to the Rosebud itself, where we encamped upon a small spot of salt grass scarcely large enough for the picketing of our mules; the scarcity of pasturage still continuing in this region.

The Rosebud shows evidence of being occasionally an important stream, but now contains no running water whatever, its bed being a mere succession of stagnant pools, which, from the fact that the water is several feet below the general level, are very difficult of access. The entire river bottom is covered with sage, and a scattered growth of cottonwood upon its banks completes the picture. The distant hills in the south in which the stream finds its source are plainly visible, and a marked gap in them apparently denotes an easy road in that direction.

After reaching the camp Bridger examined the country to the west for several miles, and reports a good road for that distance, but seems uncertain as to its continuance. If our vague information relative to the position of Fort Sarpy is correct we should reach that post this week.

* * * * *

Sunday, August 14.—We passed the day in camp as usual, and held the customary religious services. With these two days of rest I hope we shall have no further trouble with our beasts, as they have recruited wonderfully.

Large fires are visible in the Wolf mountains this afternoon, probably the signals of Indians who are undoubtedly watching our movements, although they have not showed themselves. The day has been exceedingly warm, the thermometer standing at 108° Fahr. . . . Last night, however, I was cold under two blankets. . . .

Monday, August 15.—We left camp at 6½ o'clock, our course bearing down the valley of Emmel's fork. . . .

After a march in this fashion down the valley about half way to the Yellowstone, the bed of the creek became so miry that its further crossing was impossible, and we therefore climbed with much difficulty the spur of hills upon our left and, crossing it, descended thence to the valley of the Yellowstone. . . .

From the summit of the hill we obtained our first view of the Yellowstone valley itself, of which over 50 square miles was visible, literally black with buffalo, grazing in an enormous herd whose numbers defy computation, but must be estimated by hundreds of thousands. . . .

A short and abrupt descent of a few feet leads from the terrace, upon which we are encamped, to the water's edge. The bank is covered with a rich growth of weeds and salt grass, which, fortunately for us, the buffalo do not relish but our mules devour with avidity. Large cottonwood trees also border the stream, so that we can say, what we have not been able to say for a long time, wood, water and grass are abundant. The distance travelled today is 16.4 miles, and the total, since leaving Fort Pierre, 546 miles.

NOTES TO CHAPTER 22

1. The Sioux Indian guide, whose name is not given, had been employed at Fort Pierre. More than a year later Raynolds met the Indian again at Fort Pierre and wrote in his journal for September 8, 1860: "I had the pleasure of meeting here my Sioux guide, who piloted us through the Shayene country last year, and deserted us near Powder river, taking with him a valuable mule. He greeted me very cordially, and appeared to regard his knavery as highly amusing. The stolen mule, however, was nowhere visible, and retaliatory measures were, of course, out of the question. It is also worth mentioning that this Indian described to me the entire route of the expedition as far as the Yellowstone, proving that we had been carefully watched."

2. The frontier between the Sioux and the Crow Indians was moving westward. The treaty of 1851 made an attempt to establish territories for the various bands of Indians. The eastern edge of the Crow territory was stated to be "up Powder River to its source; thence along the main range of the Black Hills. . . ." This was the theoretical frontier recognized by Raynolds in 1859, but the pressure of the Sioux had been continuous during the years 1851 to 1859 and the actual frontier in 1859 was farther west. As Raynolds says later, they were separated by a sort of no-man's-land, which was raided by both tribes, but not regularly occupied by either. Warren found Sioux in force west of the Black Hills in 1857. Raynolds, in 1859, did not meet the Crows until he was much farther west.

3. This was James Bridger (1804-81), plainsman, mountain man, trapper, fur trader, scout, and guide. He came into the Northern Plains with

the first Ashley-Henry expedition in 1822, and remained in the Northern Plains and Rocky Mountains almost continuously until a few years before his death. He founded Fort Bridger in 1843 and with his partner, Louis Vasques, operated it for several years. At one time he was a partner in the Rocky Mountain Fur Company. His later years of active life were spent mainly as a guide to private and government expeditions. He was in the Powder River country in 1855 as guide to Sir St. George Gore, a wealthy Irish sportsman. Probably Bridger could neither read nor write, but he had an extensive and accurate knowledge of the geography, fur trade, and Indian life of the Northern Plains and northern Rocky Mountains. In his professional duties as guide and scout he was highly dependable—off duty he was an amateur liar of high rank. He invented a unique method of measuring the height of a mountain—climb to the top, dig a hole to salt water, and measure the hole! Book-length biographies of Bridger have been written by J. Cecil Alter and Stanley Vestal.

Chapter 23

1859

THE CROW INDIANS,

by Captain William F. Raynolds

In this chapter Captain Raynolds tells of his activities during the period August 17 to August 30, 1859. It was necessary to wait until supplies were brought up the Yellowstone River in the Mackinaw boats of the fur company. The explorers brought their notebooks up to date and held a council with the Crow Indians.

The Crow, or Absaroka, Indians were a part of the Siouan linguistic group, related to the Hidatsas. According to their traditions, the Crows separated from the Hidatsas during a quarrel over the stomach of a buffalo. This occurred on the Missouri near the mouth of Heart River at about the end of the seventeenth century. The Crows moved south and west and occupied the country surrounding the Black Hills, ranging west to the Yellowstone and the Big Horns. Pressure from their inveterate enemies, the Cheyennes and Arapahoes and Sioux, forced them farther west until they were in the Yellowstone Valley in 1859. From 1832 to 1859 the American Fur Company and its successors maintained trading posts on the Yellowstone for the Crow trade. A few years later the lower Yellowstone came under the control of the Sioux and the Crows were forced back farther up the river and into the Big Horn Mountains.

Wednesday, August 17.—We remained in camp awaiting the return of the exploring parties and busily plotting, computing, copying notes, repacking supplies, &c, &c.

Two Crow Indians came into camp about 3 p. m. being the first human beings outside of the party seen for 50 days. They report having passed Lieutenant Maynadier and his party this morning, and state that the boat with our supplies was at the mouth of Tongue river 15 days since, in which case it should have reached this point by this time. Their village of 100 lodges is two days' march behind them, and they have come down to receive their annuities.

These Indians are of much lighter color than the Sioux, and have a less savage and repulsive expression. They are well formed and of medium height. In their costume the most striking feature is a cap made of *par fleche,* or prepared buffalo hide, consisting of a large visor shading the eyes, with the addition of a band of the same material encircling the head, the upper edge of which is cut into points, imparting a decidedly regal appearance. It is entirely crownless, however, and thus affords no protection whatever to the head. They are well mounted, and armed with both gun and bow and arrows. They do not present a very formidable appearance, but have the reputation of being as good warriors as any tribe in this region.

Thursday, August 18.—We are still in camp and employed as yesterday. Lieutenant Maynadier and party returned about noon. They reported that Fort Sarpy is only about nine miles above camp and in this bottom. The party ascended the river some 20 miles above the trading-house, and reached a bluff impassable even on horseback, at which point it will be necessary either to cross the stream or leave it and make a detour through the hills. Lieutenant Maynadier reports that it is useless to attempt to reach the mouth of the Big Horn by the valley upon this side. As it is possible that Mr. Snowden's party may have passed the boats without seeing them, I have engaged the Indians, who are yet with us, to go down the river, and carry a letter to Mr. Meldrum, the agent of the American Fur Company, who is expected up in them.

Our hunter finds no difficulty in abundantly supplying us with meat, and in a short time to-day killed seven buffaloes. Men with carts were sent out to bring in the choice pieces.

Friday, August 19.—The Indians left camp early this morning for the boat. About 10 a. m. a band of 30 or 40 savages were seen coming up the river and proved to be Crows, headed by "Two Face," a sub-chief, who rode into camp in full court costume, announcing his name by the expressive procedure of touching his face and holding up two fingers. He calmly took temporary possession of the largest tent, making himself completely at home. He had supposed that it was my quarters, judging from its size that it belonged to the commander, a mistake that I was in no haste to correct. He soon discovered his error, however, and transferred his hospitality (the only term for his general appropriation of things) to my tent. From him I learned that his band had left the boat the day previous and that Mr. Snowden and his party were close at hand.

The latter arrived about noon bringing with him Major Schoonover, the Indian agent.[1] Mr. Snowden met the boats 41 miles below, (by land,) and reported that it would require five or six days for them to reach our camp. He also brought a request from Mr. Meldrum that I would send him the assistance of a number of men and animals, a request I shall gladly comply with, as I am very anxious to shorten my stay here as greatly as possible.

Major Schoonover reports that during the journey up a small war party of Sioux obtained possession of the horses belonging to the boats and were induced to return them only with great difficulty and under circumstances that were at one time seriously threatening. This outrage was the more aggravated from the fact that Major Schoonover is also the agent for the Sioux, and thus they were robbing their own agent.

The reputation of this tribe for principle is poor, even among savages, and they will plunder friend or foe alike if immunity is certain. The Sioux also informed Major Schoonover that a band of 350 picked warriors had started to intercept and attack my expedition. If the story is true, their courage failed, for their distant signal fires have been the only evidences of their neighborhood.

Our party, however, is formidable in numbers and excellently armed, and the latter fact I impressed upon the Sioux Chiefs at Fort Pierre by affording them ocular demonstration of the improved quality of our fire-arms. While I do not overrate our own strength in frontier warfare, I entertain no apprehension of Indian hostilities, for the savages are too cowardly to attack where there is a prospect of a resistance so determined and so effective. The story told Major Schoonover was probably a mere piece of Indian bravado.

* * * * *

Monday, August 22.—The Crows are encamped in large numbers a mile or so up the river and in close vicinity to camp, and are becoming very troublesome. Like all Indians, they are importunate beggars, and about camp they take constant and the most disagreeable liberties, thronging into our tents, rolling their filthy bodies up in our blankets, and prying into everything accessible. Their personal uncleanliness is disgusting, and their bodies are covered with vermin. They have no ideas of chastity, and greater general degradation could be with difficulty imagined. The men take pride in appearing in all the tawdry finery they can obtain. The common dress is woolen clothing such as pantaloons, shirts, and hats, purchased from the traders, blankets (which are plenty) and buffalo skins forming the outer covering.

The full state dress used by the chiefs and great warriors on extraordinary occasions, is quite imposing, consisting of moccasins ornamented with beads, leggings of skins, embroidered also with beads and porcupine quills dyed the most brilliant colors, and a large outer covering somewhat resembling the Mexican *serapa,* but made of skin and richly decorated. Ermine skins are highly prized by them, and almost invariably the *serapa* is fringed with them. Vermillion is freely used as a war paint, and it is not uncommon to see the entire face as brilliant as the best Chinese pigment can make it.

The chief of the lower band, Two Bears, wore moccasins consisting of the paws of a grizzly bear, with the claws and horny portion of the foot preserved.

Eagle feathers are used to ornament the head, and a Crow glories in his long hair, which is worn straight down the back, frequently reaching to the knees. This is filled with gum, forming a compact mass, and is generally dotted over with white spots of paint.

Only in cases of extreme grief—mourning for friends &c.—is the hair ever cut. A more senseless display of grief, common among them, is to gash the forehead and allow the blood to flow over the face, remaining there until worn off by time or obliterated by dirt.

As among all savages, the women are the mere slaves of the men, doing all the menial service. A case in point caused considerable amusement in our party. A young Indian, almost a mere lad, with a stout and fine looking squaw wife, has pitched his lodge a short distance from camp, upon the opposite side of a small branch of the river. In all their visits to camp the wife carries her liege-lord upon her shoulders through the water with the most obsequious devotion.

The Crows are fairer than the Sioux, many of the mountain band being sallow and hardly a shade darker than whites who undergo similar exposure. This fact was so marked that the first seen were supposed to be half-breeds, but we were assured that they were of pure Indian descent.

Tuesday, August 23.—Soon after dinner today Lieutenant Maynadier returned to camp, and with him came Mr. Robert Meldrum, the agent of the Fur Company, who is in charge of the long-expected boats, which are still some 20 miles below. It has been found almost impossible to navigate the Yellowstone, the water being too low, although the vessels, which are batteaux,[2] draw only 18 inches. At Mr. Meldrum's suggestion I shall send down a number of the wagons to-morrow to receive part of the freight and thus lighten the load.

The afternoon and evening was spent in conversation with Mr. Meldrum, obtaining information from him with reference to the most feasible routes before us and the peculiarities of life among the Indians. He is undoubtedly the best living authority in regard to the Crows, outside of the tribe, having spent over 30 years in their country, during that time visiting the regions of civilization but once, and on that occasion spending only 19 days in St. Louis. He has long lived among these Indians, assuming their dress and habits, and by his skill and success in leading their war parties has acquired distinction, rising to the second post of authority in the tribe. He of course speaks their language perfectly, and says that it has become more natural to him than his mother tongue. I noted the alacrity with which he ceased speaking English whenever an opportunity offered.[3]

The Indians were so troublesome about camp today that I posted a double guard at night for the purpose of freeing us from the annoyance of their visits.

Wednesday, August 24.—Six wagons started this morning for the boats under the wagon master, accompanied by a guard, with Mr. Meldrum acting as guide.

The Crows are still swarming about camp, although they have not been quite as troublesome as for a few days past. The men do not seem dishonest, and Mr. Meldrum says that we need not distrust them, but added that the women and children would steal everything possible, and it has therefore been found necessary to keep a rather strict watch upon all portable articles.

Our mules and the beasts of the Indians have thoroughly consumed the grass in this vicinity, and it will be soon necessary to find new pasturage. Our animals are immensely improved in condition by the rest and nourishing food obtained during our halt.

Thursday, August 25.—The wagons that were sent to meet the boats returned this evening with full loads, and there are now hopes that we shall be able to resume our march from this point in a few days. The day was chiefly spent writing and computing. The Indians, save two or three lodges, all left to day and ascended the river to Fort Sarpy, where they will await the arrival of the boats with their annuities.

Friday, August 26.—The long expected boats came up this evening, but our supplies are so confused with those of the

Fur Company and of the Indian agent, that it will be necessary to unload the cargoes entirely, and I have therefore concluded to have them push directly on to the fort where we will join them on Monday.

* * * * *

Monday, August 29.—We struck our tents and resumed our march early in the morning. An accident to one of the escort teamsters, who was thrown from his horse and struck by one of the wagon wheels in the head, receiving a severe scalp wound, delayed us some time, as, after his injuries had received proper attention from Dr. Hines, we were compelled to empty one of the spring wagons carrying the instruments, and thus extemporize an ambulance. For this reason we did not reach Fort Sarpy until after 10 o'clock, having traversed during our 10-mile march the wide open valley of the Yellowstone, differing in no essential respect from that in which we have been encamped for the past two weeks.

We found the trading-house situated in the timber on what during high water would be an island, a channel, now dry, passing to the south of it. The "fort" is an enclosure about 100 feet square, of upright cottonwood logs 15 feet high, the outer wall also forming the exterior of a row of log cabins which are occupied as dwelling houses, store-houses, shops, and stables. The roofs of these structures are nearly flat, and formed of timber covered to the depth of about a foot with dirt, thus making an excellent parapet for purposes of defense, the preparations for resistance to possible attacks being further perfected by loopholes in the upper part of the outer row of logs. The entrance is through a heavy gate which is always carefully closed at night. No flanking arrangements whatever exist, and the "fort" is thus a decidedly primitive affair. It is amply sufficient, however, to protect its inmates against the schemes and the martial science of the Indians.[4]

We found that the boats had but just arrived, and everything was still in confusion, while the agent of the Fur Company had promptly commenced traffic with the savages, considerately allowing our matters to take care of themselves. I found assembled at this point the largest of the three bands into which the Crows are divided, and I therefore determined to improve the opportunity by holding a council to-morrow and explaining to them the purposes of my visit to their country. The necessary notifications have been accordingly sent to the various chiefs.

Tuesday, August 30.—The entire morning was consumed in endeavoring to bring to a focus our arrangements for the Indian council. An annoying delay, however, resulted from a cause that would be hardly admissable in ordinary diplomatic conferences. The horse of the head chief was missing, supposed to have been stolen by the Blackfeet, and the entire energies of the tribe were devoted to the recovery of the animal or discovery of the robbers, to the exclusion of all other business, however important. Search ultimately discovered the animal in a neighboring wood, whither he had strayed, and at 1 o'clock the council convened for the discussion of such secondary questions as the relations of the Crows and the President.

I told them I had come among them by order of the President, not to do harm, but that I might ascertain their condition, and return and report. I was not a trader, nor did I come among them as their agent. Many years had passed since any one had been through their country in the way that I was then going, for no other object but to see them and the country. The President was in the habit of sending out persons to visit all parts of his country, both among the whites and the Indians, and this was my entire errand.

I should do no harm, would endeavor not to drive off the buffalo, and would only kill what was absolutely necessary for my party to eat. I also expressed my gratification at the fact that, although I had been among them for some days, property had not been molested, and added that I hoped we would continue constantly friends. I then invited them to reply, and volunteered to take their messages, if they desired to send any, to the President.

Red Bear, the head chief, was sitting upon one side of the circle, and did not seem inclined to answer at first. I subsequently ascertained that his reluctance was occasioned by the fact that he had come down from the mountains without his court dress, and disliked to appear save in his paraphernalia. The urging of Two Bears, the chief of the lower band, and second chief of the tribe, prevailed at last, however, and he came forward, dressed in semi-civilized style, with pants, shirt, and hat, and said, with a quiet and dignified air:

BROTHER, we are glad to see you. We are glad to hear from the Great Father. The Absaroukas (the true or Indian name of the Crows) have always been the friend of the whites, and have always treated them well; we have never killed a white man. We are perfectly willing you should pass through our country. You can do so without being molested. Should you, however, wish to stop in the country and build houses, we should object to your doing so. We are a small tribe. You see here the most of us. We have enemies on all sides, the Sioux on the east, the Blackfeet on the west, and they are making war on us all the time. We want to be let alone, and we want our Great Father to protect us.

I replied that I would tell the President their wishes, but they must make peace and not always be at war. They are, indeed, a small band compared with their neighbors, but are famous warriors, and, according to common report, seldom fail to hold their own with any of the tribes unless greatly outnumbered. Their numerical inferiority will, however, undoubtedly result in their ultimate extermination in the interminable war among the hostile tribes in this region.

I was very favorably impressed by the dignified, quiet manner of this chief. His whole deportment was so in contrast with the blustering of the Sioux orators we met at Fort Pierre that it was remarked by all. The Sioux were loud and rapid talkers, gesticulating most vehemently. Red Bear, on the contrary, stood quietly within three or four feet of me, with his hands clasped in front of him, and looking me steadily in the eye, spoke as calmly as quietly as was possible. Mr. Meldrum acted as interpreter, and there was an additional advantage in his being able to express the chief's ideas in better English than was possible by the half-breed interpreters at Fort Pierre. Indeed, Red Bear, the chief of the Crows, and the Frog, sub-chief of the Brulé band of Sioux, were the only Indians I met who inspired me with the slightest admiration, or who in any degree came up to imaginary standards of Indian character we are apt to get from reading popular romances of Indian life.

The "talk" ended by the distribution of a few presents from my limited stock, and the setting forth of the usual "feast," consisting of coffee and hard bread, which proved highly satisfactory.

After the close of the "talk" I succeeded in procuring, through the traders, (who shrewdly prevent the Indians from dealing directly with us, and thus realize large profits for themselves from both parties,) seven ordinary horses— an addition to my stock of animals greatly needed. The balance of the day was consumed in perfecting arrangements for the resumption of the march.

NOTES TO CHAPTER 23

1. Schoonover was agent for the Sioux and Crow Indians. If he made any report in 1859 it was not printed in the *Report of the Secretary of the Interior* for that year. The Commissioner of Indian Affairs reported that nothing of importance happened among the Indians of the Upper Missouri during the year.

2. Probably this was the boat usually called a Mackinaw. These boats were constructed at the trading posts and were usually used only for downstream traffic. They had flat or nearly flat bottoms, were ten to twelve feet wide and forty to sixty feet long, carried about fifteen tons of freight, and with a crew of five made about 75 to 150 miles per day, downstream, on the Missouri.

3. Robert Meldrum (1801-65) was chief trader for Pierre Chouteau, Jr., and Company at the Crow posts for several years, and had charge of forts Alexander and Sarpy at different times. He is mentioned by Larpenteur as being in the employ of the fur company as early as 1835, but had probably lived among the Crows before that date. The Indians called him "Round Iron."

4. Apparently Fort Sarpy did not have bastions at two opposite corners, as did most of the trading posts. For the history of the post see note 7, chap. 18, *ante*.

Chapter 24

1866

THE WHITE RIVER BADLANDS,

by Dr. Ferdinand V. Hayden

Ferdinand Vandeveer Hayden was born in 1829, graduated from Oberlin College in 1850, and received his M.D. from Albany Medical College in 1853. In the same year he made a fossil-collecting trip into the region we now call the White River Badlands, in South Dakota. In 1854 he visited the Upper Missouri, and during the next three summers was an assistant to Lieutenant Warren. In 1858 he explored part of Kansas and in 1859-60 he was a member of Captain Raynolds' scientific staff.

During the Civil War Dr. Hayden was a surgeon in the Union Army, attaining the rank of brevet lieutenant colonel.

In the fall of 1865 Dr. Hayden became professor of geology at the University of Pennsylvania. He remained in this position until 1872, but continued his explorations and in 1866 made another trip to the White River Badlands. He described this journey in his *Geological Report of the Exploration of the Yellowstone and Missouri Rivers, 1859-60*, published in 1869, from which I am reprinting the following chapter.

Dr. Hayden resigned his position at the University of Pennsylvania in 1872 to devote his full time to geological explorations. His work covered much of the region now included in the states of Kansas, Nebraska, South Dakota, North Dakota, Montana, Wyoming, Idaho, Utah, and Colorado. Out of it grew the United States Geological Survey. Ill health forced his retirement in 1886 and he died in 1887.

During the summer of 1866 I made a tour to the Bad Lands of Dakota, under the auspices of the Academy of Natural Sciences of Philadelphia, for the purpose of clearing up some uncertain or doubtful points in the geology of that most interesting region. With a letter of introduction from Professor Joseph Henry to General Grant, stating the object of my mission to that country, I procured from the general an official order requiring all commanding officers in the Departments of the Missouri and the Platte to furnish all the facilities for carrying out my scientific explorations in their power not inconsistent with the public service. I also received great courtesy and aid from General P. St. G. Cooke at Omaha City, and General Myers, chief quartermaster of that department, from Major H. Dyer, in command at Fort Randall, who furnished me with my entire outfit, that being my starting point from the Missouri. From all the United States army officers that I met I received every possible kindness and facility that could be afforded. It has always been the policy of the army to advance the interests of science, especially in these far western regions, and I think it may safely be affirmed that they have done more for the natural history and geography of the far west than any other class of professional men.

I left Fort Randall[1] August 3, 1866, with a six-mule team, five soldiers, a guide, Indian hunter, and my faithful assistant, James Stevenson, who has been with me for years, traveling over various portions of the west. Our wagon was the largest of the army type, covered, and loaded with rations for our entire party for sixty days. We passed up the valley of Garden creek, which flows by the fort. There is a fringe of trees on each side of the creek, for the most part elm—a few cottonwoods. Like all the country bordering on streams, this portion is filled with ravines, rendering traveling laborious. . . . This creek is called Garden creek from the fact that for many years the officers and soldiers of Fort Randall have cultivated vegetables at different points on its bottom lands, and with few exceptions they have been quite successful. . . .

At the mouth of Turtle creek, we have the Forked Buttes,[2] two hills which form prominent land marks. Their summits are capped with from 30 to 40 feet of porus, gritty limestone, which has been worn away much by atmospheric agencies. Below is a bed of yellowish sandy marl, in which I found a few fragments of a turtle and some horse teeth, enough to determine the geological position. The buttes are about 200 feet in height above the level prairie, or about 600 feet above the bed of the Niobrara. . . .

As we proceeded up the valley of the Niobrara, on the north side, even for 50 or 60 miles, the river cuts down into the cretaceous rocks, but gradually the tertiary beds begin to appear and to cover the upland country. There is also evidence of considerable thickness of a recent deposit made up of the transported materials of older tertiary beds. These beds also contain fragments of turtles, doubtless *Testudo niobrarensis,* which is found very abundantly on the Loup Fork and Niobrara river. The surface of the country is covered more or less with waterworn pebbles. About midway between the mouth of Turtle creek and that of Rapid river, the recent or pliocene beds take possession of the country. At the summit there is a bed of hard, light gray sandstone, which gives the abrupt character to the numerous ravines; beneath it is a bed of light gray sand, which contains many fossil remains. At another locality is found from two to four feet of chalky limestone, breaking into thin laminae, filled with small fresh-water shells. Beneath this are six or eight feet of gray friable sandstone, filled with fragments of bones; below, light yellow marl, with sandy layers of harder rock, 100 to 300 feet thick, containing many kinds of bones in a more or less fragmentary condition. This last locality is about 25 miles below the mouth of Rapid river. These deep ravines, which are very numerous, and from their geological structure having more the form of cañons, render traveling quite impossible with wagons, and very difficult with pack mules, except by passing around the heads of them all, at a distance of from five to eight miles from the Niobrara river. Much has been said of the pine timber along this stream and its branches. I would simply say that it is of very poor quality, not much of it, and quite inaccessible.

For a considerable distance before reaching Rapid river the sand hills are very conspicuous on the south side of the Niobrara. Indications have been seen several times on the north side, but no well-defined hills. Rapid river really forms the eastern border of the sand hills on the north side of the Niobrara. These hills form a remarkable feature of the surface of the country in this region. They cover an area of about 20,000 square miles; the surface composed of loose moving sand, which is blown by the winds into round or conical hills, and these hills in turn are wrought upon by the winds and are scooped out and moved farther eastward. They occupy much of the country on both sides of the Niobrara, rendering traveling almost impossible. Our wagon wheels sank into the soft sand one to two feet. The vegetation is very scarce, a few plants clinging with a sort of hopeless tenacity to the sides of the hills, and in some cases protecting them from the winds. The yucca, or "Spanish needles," seems to grow even more luxuriantly in this almost soilless region.[3]

Near Rapid river the denuded tertiary hills contain a great many fragments of bones and teeth, several species of horses, and more particularly the bones of an elephant and mastodon. The articulations are of enormous size; and so abundant were they that we might have loaded our wagon in a single day. The evidence is clear that a considerable variety of species and vast numbers of individuals were entombed in these sandy beds. . . .

Rapid river joins the Niobrara in about longitude 100° 23′, and is named Mini-chá-du-ra-wák-pa by the Dakota Indians. At its mouth it is about eight yards wide, with a valley from one-fourth to one-half a mile wide, fringed for a few miles up the stream with trees, but soon becoming entirely destitute of trees. It is the most beautiful creek we have seen since leaving the Missouri; the soil is fertile, and the whole valley is clothed with the finest grass. No region could be better adapted for grazing purposes. I am certain that toward the head of this stream I saw many acres of grass that would furnish two to three tons of hay each. Leaving Rapid river we passed over the hills gently sloping towards the source of Little White river. After coming to the divide between Niobrara and Little White river, we descended eight miles to the river bottom. The country all around Little White river is exceedingly rugged, reminding one of the Bad Lands proper. No human being has ever explored this portion of the country before.[4] There is a bed of hard rock that caps the high hills which aids in protecting their summits; but many of them are entirely denuded, and look quite white in the distance. It is easy here to ascertain the source of the material of the sand hills. Along the river are from 400 to 600 feet of pliocene sand, much of it loosely aggregated together. The beds are made up of thin layers, with sometimes a bed of fine chalky material, but exhibiting all the irregularities of deposition seen along our river banks. All these beds, becoming so easily decomposed, are incoherent. Sand is the result, which at once becomes subject to the winds. The harder layers project out, adding much to the ruggedness of these mural fronts. I can see no marked dip in any direction, but the beds appear to be horizontal everywhere, so that we must have seen already from 800 to 1,000 feet of the pliocene beds. There are some very excellent fossils, as teeth and jaws of horses, fragments of turtles.

This portion of Little White river is too rugged for settlements, but an excellent region for Indians. The stream varies from 12 to 15 yards in width, runs swiftly, averaging about one foot in depth, bottom mostly quicksands. Leaving this portion of Little White river we passed over the rugged hills west and southwestward, and again struck the same stream near its head, where it is entirely destitute of trees. It is here, however, a fine clear running stream, 9 or 10 yards wide. The surface of the country, and especially the highest hills, are covered with water-worn pebbles of all kinds. We here saw for the first time the peculiar flesh-colored beds which characterize the White River territory, and in searching among the denuded spots I found a few fragments of *Oreodon culbertsonii.* This formation is so peculiar that although description may not fully show the difference between it and the pliocene beds, yet the eye can detect it anywhere. There is a small thickness of what may be called a drift deposit here, containing great quantities of water-worn teeth and bones. I detected those of the horse and mastodon. From this point to White Earth creek, a tributary of White river, the little streams flow between steep banks, which caused us some trouble, inasmuch as we were obliged to bridge them all. The pliocene beds have disappeared, and the miocene beds of White river occupy the entire country. Our course was nearly westward, along the heads of the little streams that flow into White river. Eagle Nest Butte is a very prominent landmark, and aids us much in determining approximately the thickness of these tertiary beds originally. It is a long square hill, from about 500 feet above the prairie around, and is capped with some of the pliocene beds. In 1855 I passed near the base of this hill, and spent some time in examining it. Upon the summit I found several species of the remains of mammals characterizing the pliocene beds. We have here a presentation of about 600 feet of tertiary rocks. From the remains already gathered from this region we see how abundant these animals must have been in ancient times, and yet one-fiftieth part can never meet the eye of man. Countless numbers of them must have been destroyed by erosion, and only a small portion, now and then, by special favor of aqueous agencies, is disentombed.

Our traveling has been very difficult along this divide. Never before did a wagon pass along this route. We have made up our minds that no portion of the country is wholly impassable for wagons, which is an important matter in a military point of view. We can see, far to the northward, the long ranges of peaks and domes which are usually called the "Bad Lands." The basis rocks all along our route are the cream-colored indurated marls, denuded in a few places. There is also a much more indurated bed which caps the hills, which I have called the red grit bed in my former explorations. Above this there is, in many localities, a layer of limestone. The tops of these hills must be from 1,000 to 1,200 feet above the bed of White river.

* * * * *

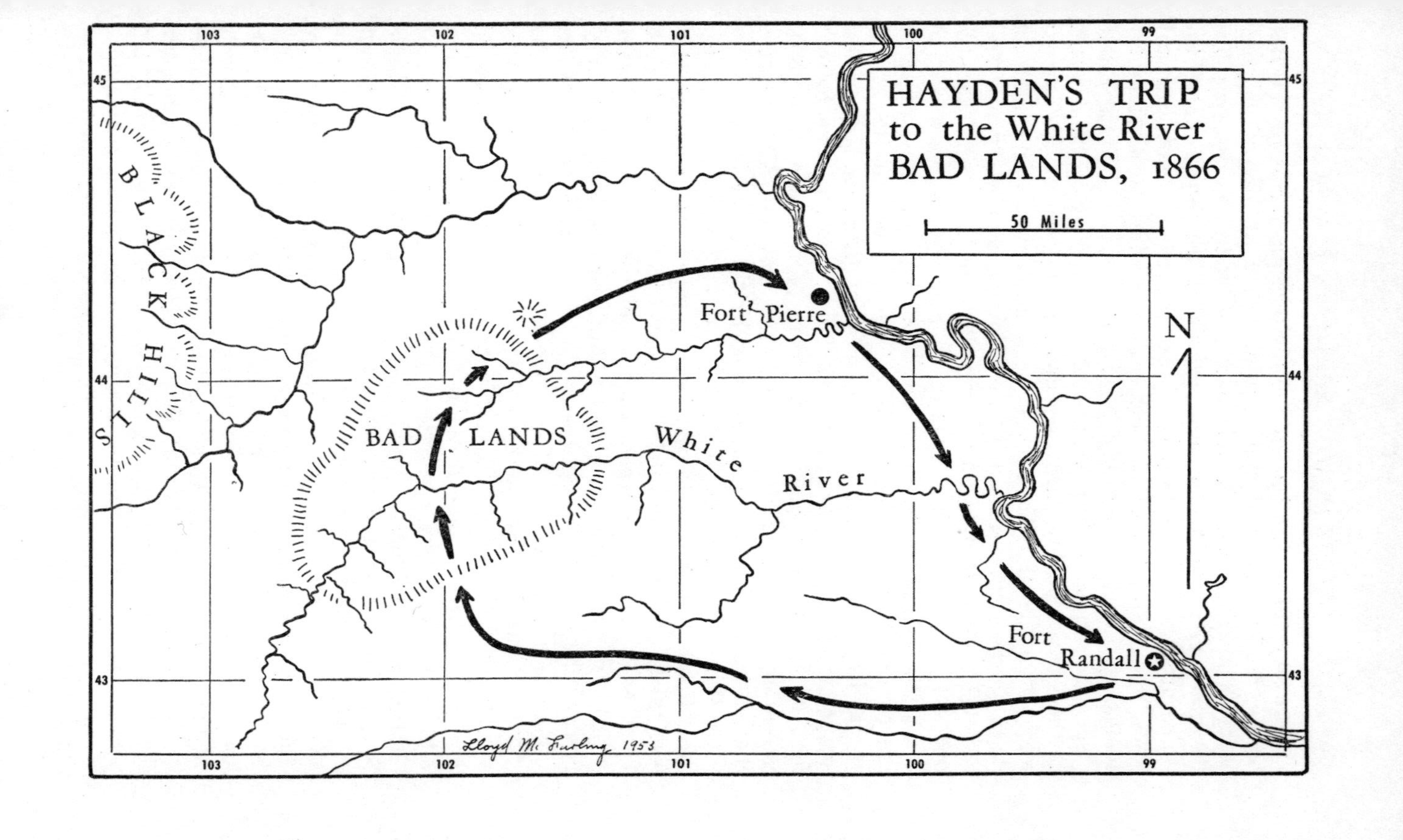
HAYDEN'S TRIP
to the White River
BAD LANDS, 1866
50 Miles
N
Fort Pierre
Fort Randall
White River
BAD LANDS
BLACK HILLS
103
102
101
100
99
45
44
43
Lloyd McFarling 1953

On every side arose the unique picturesque forms of the Bad Lands, more wonderful and fantastic than at any other point before visited by me. Some portions look in the distance like cream-colored basaltic columns, others an amphitheater or the shape of arcs of a circle with a vast number of seats in many rows, one above the other; others resembling gothic temples, domes, towers, and fortresses. The west side of White Earth creek has much the appearance of a huge French palace, and as the early morning sun rests upon it every nook and corner seems lighted up with a strange wild beauty. The sides of these washed hills are worn into furrows, and every few feet there is a layer two to four feet in thickness, harder than the rest, which projects out, forming in many instances a sort of verandah. All these beds are full of calcareous and aluminous concretions which break in pieces on exposure to the atmosphere. Running through the beds in every direction, but vertical to the stratifications, are seams varying from one inch to four feet, of fine clay or silex in the form of chalcedony. This is caused by the filling up of cracks or fissures. This feature characterizes all of the area occupied by the miocene beds.

On White Earth creek, and on White river at this point, the titanotherium bed, the lowest bed of this great basin, is 120 feet thick, and the oreodon bed above from 150 to 200 feet. This bed is of a deep cream color, composed of mud or marl, with bands varying from a dull reddish brown to a light gray. Toward the summit the light gray bands increase, and there are numerous but thin layers of rusty-colored sand-stone. The sides of the washed hills are here very nearly perpendicular, looking like immense mud walls. Mixed with the debris at the base of the hills are great quantities of rocks, sometimes thinly laminated sandstone clay concretions with irregular fracture, or small masses of limestone and some layers of flint. The titanotherium bed contains more silex than any other bed in this group. In many places the rounded summits of the hills, composed of the materials of this bed, are literally paved with the sharp fragments, and the vertical seams run in every direction across the surface from one and one-fourth to one inch in thickness. There are also numerous globular masses of chalcedony scattered through the bed, some of which are very beautiful as cabinet specimens. . . . The lower portion of titanotherium bed is composed mostly of a greenish gray clay with pinkish bands, but toward the summits are numerous lighter bands, which give it the banded appearance in the distance. Although the two beds, titanotherium and oreodon, are quite distinct, and the practiced eye can detect them anywhere, yet the line of separation between them is difficult to define, so imperceptibly does the one graduate into the other. In the dry season the traveling is most excellent, but even a small shower will render the materials of these beds a most tenacious, slippery mud, rendering traveling next to impossible. The oreodon bed in a dry time is indurated almost like solid rock, so that a mule in traveling over it scarcely makes an impression.

There is some chalcedony and at different points evidently local ledges of sandstone. . . . In the White River valley, at this point, the country is more marked in its ruggedness than in any portion of what is known as the Bad Lands. There is no sinking away of the surface, as some have supposed, but a simple washing out of the country into innumerable gullies or cañons, and in some instances removing 400 or 500 feet of the entire mass for many square miles in extent, leaving only isolated pyramids, peaks, and columns as witnesses. Indeed, one may travel for miles over a level plateau clothed with grass, when suddenly we come to an abrupt descent from 400 to 600 feet to a plateau below,[5] upon which are set as it were these pyramids, long ridges, denuded columns, &c.; but the strata are all horizontal, and as we pass from point to point each bed corresponds in each separate ridge, column, or pyramid, so that we know that the beds once extended in unbroken continuity all over this country, and we also see that there has been no dislocation of the strata. We can, however, in many localities follow the outer rim of this great lake basin, and in some localities this shore-line indicates a depression of 60 or 80 feet. The best illustration is seen along the north side of the great basin from Bear creek, a tributary of the Shyenne, to Pinan's spring, the source of Teton river. The shore-line resembles much that of any of our northern lakes: a gradual slope, while the little streams, which have cut their way through to flow into the Shyenne, reveal with perfect clearness the relations of the tertiary beds to those of the cretaceous beneath.

* * * * *

As this is our point of departure for home, after our labors in the Bad Lands, we will look back for a moment to dwell upon a few points. It is supposed by many that this miocene formation, occupying an area at least 100 miles long and 60 to 80 broad, will furnish to the world an almost limitless supply of specimens of fossil remains. Already over 40 species of extinct vertebrata have been discovered and disentombed, which will be mentioned more in detail in a subsequent portion of this report. I would reply to that supposition that the supply of good specimens is already very nearly exhausted, and that the labor required to collect will prevent in the future the possibility of large collections being obtained.

There seems to have been a belt or zone on both sides of the divide between White river and the Shyenne, about eight miles wide and 10 to 20 long, where these remains were exposed by erosion in great quantities. Formerly it was not a difficult matter to collect a ton of these rare and valuable fossils in a few days, now it requires as many months. Since the discovery of this basin two large collections have been made by Dr. Evans, one by Mr. Culbertson, and three by the writer, besides some smaller collections by numerous individuals whose names are not known to me. Among these specimens Dr. Leidy has already recognized more than 700 individuals of a single species, *Oreodon culbertsonii,* a sort of ruminant pig, combining some of the characters of a camel, deer and hog. I[t] had canine teeth for tearing flesh, ruminant teeth like those of a deer and evidently chewed its cud. Now this area over which these remains seemed so abundantly distributed, has been most carefully searched and every specimen that could possibly meet the eye has been gathered.

If we pass beyond the limits of this belt we find a few remains, it is true, but they are very scarce, and usually in an extremely fragmentary condition.

I have hunted all day among the most rugged of the washed hills on White river and did not obtain 50 pounds weight of fossils—not a good head or turtle among them. At various times I have traversed nearly all this great basin, and I think I speak with a degree of confidence when I say that not more than one more large collection will ever be brought from that country, and that will be gathered with the greatest amount of labor.[6]

There is another point which I will refer to here. Many scientific men have said to me, "in a few years these remains will be exposed by the washing of storms as abundantly as ever." I would say that during the past summer I examined with great care the ground so carefully searched over by Mr. Meek and myself in 1853, just 13 years ago, and that passed over by myself and assistant in 1855, 11 years ago, and in that time I doubt whether a single specimen has been exposed by the rains. I looked diligently for the slightest evidence in that direction and could find none. Even the debris around a turtle or head which we had gathered at that time seemed to remain undisturbed. It is to be recollected that atmospheric influences do not operate here as in regions east of the Mississippi. It is safe to say that not more than 10 or 15 inches of rain falls here during the year.[7]

After securing our wagon-load of the fossil remains of mammals and turtles, we started for the Missouri river by way of what is called the Old Fort Pierre Road.[8] I do not think that wagons had passed over it since 1855, and in consequence the trail had in many cases almost or entirely disappeared. After leaving Bear creek we ascend a very steep hill, and then travel eastward for 50 miles, or with a broad level plateau covered with fine grass and almost as level as the quiet sea on our left hand, while on our right are the tall domes and spires of the Bad Lands. We travel as it were along the northern rim of this great tertiary lake. We travel, however, over the cretaceous beds. Bear and Sage creeks have long been noted places for cretaceous fossils. They are found here in large quantities in fine dark-bluish calcareous concretions, nearly globular in form, from 3 inches to 10 feet in diameter, and immediately on exposure to the atmosphere they have a tendency to crack into pieces, so that with a moderate sized hammer one may knock them in pieces and work out the beautiful shells like bullets from a mold. . . .

. . . Grindstone Hills . . . are long square hills on each side of the road, 50 miles distant from the Bad Lands, and like Bijoux Hills and Medicine Butte, form distant outliers of the great pliocene lake. There is here 150 or 200 feet of sandstone, some portions a fine conglomerate or pudding stone made up of water-worn pebbles, and among the rocks are found some fragments of teeth and bones much water-worn. These hills, scattered over the country, seem to act as witnesses or monuments to show the vast extent of erosion in this country. With the exception of these isolated hills, our entire road from Bear creek near the base of the Black Hills, by way of Fort Pierre to Fort Randall on the Missouri, was over cretaceous beds. In the neighborhood of Medicine Hills there were a large number of long ridges and hills, which were plainly remnants of pliocene beds. We arrived at Fort Randall after an absence from that point of 52 days, and having made the circuit of 650 miles with a six-mule team and a wagon weighing 1,775 pounds, one of the largest size.

Our conclusion was, that any portion of this rugged country, with care and patience, may be traversed with any number of wagons for military purposes.

NOTES TO CHAPTER 24

1. Fort Randall was established in 1856 on the right bank of the Missouri, at about Latitude 43° 12′. For many years it was the principal military post in this region. It was abandoned in 1884.

2. Hayden's "Turtle Creek" was called Keha Paha River by Warren and so appears on modern maps. The "Forked Buttes" are not shown on any of my maps. Perhaps these hills were the *Buttes de Medicine* described by Prince Paul in Chapter 14.

3. Cf. note 8, chap. 20, *ante,* for another description of the sand hills.

4. It is quite likely that the region had been explored by Indians and perhaps by white trappers and traders. Warren went completely around it in 1855. In 1857 he explored the valley of the Niobrara, not far south. In 1859 four companies of the Fourth Artillery, with twenty-three wagons, passed through the Niobrara Valley from Fort Laramie to Fort Randall. Lieutenant Anderson, "Report of a March. . . . ," in *Report of the Secretary of War,* 1859. In 1865 an expedition led by James A. Sawyer, with a military escort, explored a proposed wagon road from Sioux City to Virginia City, Montana, along the Niobrara and south of the Black Hills. The route was not well chosen and the proposed road became unnecessary when the Union Pacific-Central Pacific railroad was completed in 1869. Reminiscences of a member of the Sawyer party are found in *Pioneering in the Northwest,* by Holman and Marks.

5. Probably this refers to what is now known as the Pine Ridge Escarpment, a prominent physiographic feature that divides the northern edge of the High Plains from the southern edge of the Missouri Plateau. This scarp forms an irregular line running roughly east to west from near the Missouri River into Wyoming. It has a maximum height of about one thousand feet. The High Plains extend from this escarpment south nearly to the Rio Grande River, are more level and less dissected by streams than the lower plains to the east or the Piedmont area along the Front Ranges of the Rocky Mountains to the west. North of the Pine Ridge Escarpment the area called the Missouri Plateau extends west to the Rocky Mountains, north into Canada, and east to the Missouri Coteau. Along the line of the escarpment the Missouri Plateau is lower than the High Plains, due to the erosion of great quantities of the former surface of the earth. This erosion is continuing and the Pine Ridge Escarpment is migrating southward, enlarging the area of the Missouri Plateau and diminishing the area of the High Plains. The migration of the scarp line is slow in terms of historic time, rapid in terms of geological time.

6. Hayden was unduly pessimistic about the quantity of fossils remaining. After a hundred years of collecting the White River Badlands region is still a happy hunting ground for the paleontologist. Considerable excavation work is now required, but fossils are still being obtained.

7. Probably Hayden's estimate of annual rainfall was correct, but we cannot now accept the inference that there was little erosion. Discussing the same badlands in *Physiography of Western United States,* p. 68,

Fenneman has pointed out that aridity is one of the factors favorable to the formation of badlands "partly because it is adverse to vegetation and partly because rain in arid climates is more concentrated into quick torrential showers which erode much more than do the slower rains of humid climates. . . ."

8. This was the road from Fort Laramie to Fort Pierre, mapped by Warren in 1855. It was not used much after it was mapped, due to the decline of the fur trade and the failure of the army to maintain Fort Pierre. Later, during the Black Hills gold rush, the eastern part of the road was the approximate location of the trail from the town of Fort Pierre to Rapid City; while portions of the road near Fort Laramie were apparently used for travel to Red Cloud and Spotted Tail agencies after they were established in 1873 and 1870.

PART FOUR

TO AND THROUGH THE BLACK HILLS

Chapter 25

1857

THE BORDER OF THE BLACK HILLS,

by Lieutenant Gouverneur K. Warren

In 1857 Lieutenant Warren organized a small expedition at Sioux City, and traveled southwest to the Loup River, where a rendezvous had been arranged with other members of his party. He then explored the valley of the Loup nearly to its head, crossed the sand hills to the Niobrara, followed the Niobrara nearly to its source, and went to Fort Laramie to obtain more supplies and reorganize his party.

From Fort Laramie Warren traveled north by pack train to explore the Black Hills. The following account of the expedition is reprinted from Warren's report: "Explorations in Nebraska" in the *Report of the Secretary of War*, 1858.

On this trip Warren did not penetrate the interior of the Black Hills, but skirted nearly two thirds of their border, from Inyan Kara on the west around the southern edge and north to Bear Butte on the northeast. Two years later Captain Raynolds approached the Black Hills from the east at Bear Butte, and continued along their northern edge to the valley of the Little Missouri. The Warren and Raynolds expeditions nearly encircled the Black Hills, leaving their interior unexplored for another fifteen years.

The party, on leaving Fort Laramie, was divided into two parts, as, owing to the lateness of the seasons, it was impossible to accomplish all the objects of the expedition by keeping together. Though in doing this I subjected each portion to the possibility of being defeated by the Indians, I deemed the case to justify the risk. The wagons were, half of them, turned in to the quartermaster, and the remainder, with the escort under Lieutenant McMillan, were to proceed down the Niobrara, and await me in longitude 101° 30′. Mr. J. H. Snowden went with this party to make the topographical reconnaissances; Dr. Moffit also accompanied it. My own party consisted of Dr. Hayden, Mr. Carrington, and Mr. Engel, and we had with us 17 men as packers, &c., and Mr. Morin as a guide and interpreter. Our supplies were packed on mules.

Setting out from Fort Laramie on the 4th of September, we

proceeded direct for the Black Hills *via* Raw Hide butte, Old Woman creek, the South Fork of the Shyenne, and Beaver Creek; up a branch of this last we entered the Black Hills. We continued north to the vicinity of the Inyan Kara, (or the peak which makes the mountain,) a remarkable high basaltic peak, one of the highest of these mountains, and so far to the north that we had a full view of the prairie beyond.

Here we were met by a large force of the Dakotas, who made such earnest remonstrances and threats against our proceeding into their country that I did not think it prudent for us, as a scientific expedition, to venture further in this direction. Some of them were for attacking us immediately, as their numbers would have insured success; but the lesson taught them by General Harney, in 1855, made them fear they would meet with retribution, and this I endeavored to impress upon them. We were at the time almost in sight of the place where these Indians had plundered Sir George Gore in 1855, for endeavoring to proceed through their country, and one of them was actually mounted on one of his best horses taken at that time.[1] Sir George Gore's party was only about half as numerous as mine;[2] but there were a number of my party which I had picked up at Fort Laramie on whom we placed very little reliance.

The grounds of their objections to our traversing this region were very sensible, and of sufficient weight, I think, to have justified them in their own minds in resisting: and as these are still in force for the prevention of the passage of any other party of whites not large enough to resist successfully, they are of sufficient importance to be repeated here. In the first place, they were encamped near large herds of buffalo, whose hair not being sufficiently grown to make robes, the Indians were, it may be said, actually herding the animals. No one was permitted to kill any in the large bands for fear of stampeding the others, and only such were killed as straggled away from the main herds. Thus the whole range of the buffalo was stopped so that they could not proceed south, which was the point to which they were travelling. The intention of the Indians was to retain the buffalo in their neighborhood till their skins would answer for robes, then to kill the animals by surrounding one band at a time and completely destroying each member of it. In this way no alarm is communicated to the neighboring bands, which often remain quiet almost in sight of the scene of slaughter.

For us to have continued on then would have been an act

for which certain death would have been inflicted on a like number of their own tribe had they done it; for we might have deflected the whole range of the buffalo fifty or one hundred miles to the west, and prevented the Indians from laying in their winter stock of provisions and skins, on which their comfort if not even their lives depended. Their feelings toward us, under the circumstances, were not unlike what we should feel toward a person who should insist upon setting fire to our barns. The most violent of them were for immediate resistance when I told them of my intentions; and those who were most friendly, and in greatest fear of the power of the United States, begged that I would "take pity" on them and not proceed. I felt that, aside from its being an unnecessary risk to subject my party and the interests of the expedition to, it was almost cruelty to the Indians to drive them to commit any desperate act, which would call for chastisement from the Government.

But this was not the only reason they urged against our proceeding. They said that the treaty made with General Harney[3] gave to the whites the privilege of travelling on the Platte and along White River, between Fort Pierre and Laramie, and to make roads there, and to travel up and down the Missouri in boats; but that it guaranteed to them that no white people should travel elsewhere in their country, and thus frighten away the buffalo by their careless manner of hunting them. And finally, that my party was there examining the country to ascertain if it was of value to the whites, and to discover roads through it, and places for military posts; and that having already given up all the country to the whites that they could spare, these Black Hills must be left wholly to themselves. Moreover, if none of these things should occur, our passing through their country would give us a knowledge of its character and the proper way to traverse it in the event of another war between themselves and the troops. I was necessarily compelled to admit to myself the truth and force of these objections.

The Indians whom I first met were the Minikanyes, to the number of forty lodges, near whom, as they were very friendly, we encamped.[4] They were soon joined by the warriors of a large camp of Unkpapas and Sihasapas,[5] and our position, which was sufficiently unpleasant in the presence of such a numerous party of half-avowed enemies, was rendered doubly so by a storm of sleet and snow, which lasted two days and nights and against which we had but little protection.

A young Indian, who had accompanied us from Fort Laramie,

considered the danger to us so imminent that he forsook our camp and joined his friends, the Minikanyes.

Under these embarassing circumstances my associates evinced the most resolute bravery and determination to abide the result like true men.

I consented to wait three days without advancing, in order to meet their great warrior, Bear's Rib,[6] appointed first chief by General Harney's treaty, merely changing our position to one offering greater facilities for defense. At the expiration of the time, Bear's Rib not making his appearance, we broke camp, and, travelling back on our route about forty miles, struck off to the eastward, through the southern part of these mountains. The point where we turned back is well marked by the Inyan Kara Peak, whose position was fixed by us.

After we had proceeded two days on our journey eastward, we were overtaken by Bear's Rib and one other Indian who accompanied him. He reiterated all that had been said by the other chiefs, and added that he could do nothing to prevent our being destroyed if we attempted to proceed further. I then told him that I believed he was our friend, but that if he could do nothing for us, he had better return to his people, and leave us to take care of ourselves, as I was determined to proceed as far as Bear Butte. After a whole day spent in deliberation, he concluded to accompany us a part of the way, and he said he would then return to his people and use his influence to have us not molested. In return for this, he wished me to say to the President and to the white people that they could not be allowed to come into that country. That if the presents sent were to purchase such a right, they did not want them. All they asked of the white people was, to be left to themselves and let alone. That if the presents were sent to induce them not to go to war with the Crows and their other enemies, they did not wish them. War with them was not only a necessity but a pastime. He said General Harney had told them not to go to war, and yet he was all the time going to war himself. (Bear's Rib knew that when General Harney left the Sioux country he had gone to the war in Florida and was at the time in command of the army sent against the Mormons.) He said, moreover, that the annuities scarcely paid for going after them; and that if they were not distributed to them while they were on their visit to the trading posts on the Missouri, to dispose of their robes, they did not want them.

(It is a fact that for several years, owing to this cause, these Indians have not come in for their goods at all.)

He said that he heard that the Ihanktonwans were going to sell their lands to the whites. If they did so, he wished them informed that they could not come on his people's land. They must stay with the whites. Every day the Ihanktonwans were coming there but were always turned back.

Whatever may have been Bear's Rib's actions after leaving us, it is certain we saw no more Indians in the Black Hills. We completed our reconnaissance along the eastern portion of these mountains as far as Bear Peak, which forms another convenient and accurate point with which any future reconnaissance may connect with our own. We also visited the North Fork of the Shyenne, in this vicinity. On our return we took a southeast direction, striking the South Fork of the Shyenne at the mouth of Sage Creek. We then proceeded up the South Fork to French Creek; thence southeast, through the Bad Lands, to White River; thence along the sources of White Clay Creek and Porcupine Creek; and thence to the Niobrara, striking it in longitude 102° 03′.

We found the party under Lieutenant McMillan about forty miles below where we struck the river, and eighty miles below where we had first reached it on our journey westward in August. This intervening distance had been carefully mapped by Mr. Snowden, and he had made several excursions at different places to examine the country, as I had directed. Lieutenant McMillan's march down the river thus far had not been made without much wordy opposition from the Brule Dakotas, much of the same kind as that I have related as having been said to me in the Black Hills. On finding that he was determined to proceed, the chief, Little Thunder,[7] sent four of his principal men to accompany them, which they did for some days. At a subsequent time, twenty-two warriors charged into the camp, thinking the party was a trading expedition. Their insolence was checked by Lieutenant McMillan's threatening to fire on them; whereupon they entered their usual protest against the party's proceeding further and the next day all withdrew. The last twenty miles of Lieutenant McMillan's route was through difficult sand-hills bordering the river, the stream itself being so shut in by high precipitous ridges that he was unable to travel along it.

* * * * *

Fort Randall was reached on the 1st of November, and the escort was returned to the regiment. . . .

The Black Hills, or more properly mountains, lying between the forks of the Shyenne, on the 44th parallel, between the 103d and 105th meridians, cover an area of 6,000 square miles. Their bases are elevated from 2,500 feet to 3,500 feet, and the highest peaks are about 6,700 feet above the ocean level.

The different rocks which composed these mountains, as determined by our exploration, are—

I. Metamorphosed azoic rock, including granite.
II. Lower silurian, (Potsdam sandstone)
III. Devonian?
IV. Carboniferous.
V. Permian.
VI. Jurassic.
VII. Cretaceous.

All the rocks below the Silurian are igneous and metamorphic, and the stratification which they exhibit stands everywhere nearly vertical, with a strike varying between northeast and northwest. So constant is this vertical dip, that it may not in reality indicate primary stratification, but some mechanical arrangement due to the molecular forces brought into existence during its cooling from the heated state. All the rocks, from the silurian to the close of the cretaceous, apparently lie conformable to each other. The shape of the mass is elliptical. The direction of the longest line of this or major axis being about north 20° west. On the west the rocks dip, as a whole, very gently, and at a distance of five miles from the foot of the hills the cretaceous is apparently undisturbed, though at the base these rocks in some places stand at an angle of 45°. The manner in which this rock lies suggests the idea that the cretaceous probably forms a considerable portion of the elevated plateau between the Black Hills and Big Horn Mountains. The dip of the upheaved rocks on the west side is as a whole very gentle, not amounting to more than 5° to 15°, and, consequently they are considerably developed, and form more than one-half the mountain mass composing some very high ridges. These rocks have a much greater inclination on the east side of the mountains, and soon disappear under the cretaceous, forming a comparatively narrow belt. The east base of the Mountains is from 2,000 to 3,000 feet below the western.

The rocks seem also to dip much more suddenly down on the south than on the north side. The strike of these upheaved strata is in almost every direction corresponding, on the exterior, nearly with that of the tangent to the outline of the mass, and on the interior being more nearly coincident with the direction of the major axis.

A result of this formation is that the upturned rocks break off abruptly on the side toward the interior of the mass, and leave an open valley in many places between this steep slope and the gentle one which succeeds it as we approach the interior. In these valleys the best roads are found, and one, which encircles the Black Hills, is known among the Indians and traders as the Race Course or Runny road.[8]

The Inyan Kara Peak is basaltic, and the appearance through a powerful spy-glass of those to the north, known as the "Bear's Lodge" and "Little Missouri Buttes," indicates that they are also of this formation. More recent volcanic action is visible at Bear's Peak, and two circular spaces to the west of this peak, now occupied by muddy lakes, indicate the existence here in former times of volcanic [forces].[9]

The highest mountain masses, such as Harney's Peak, on the east side, are all granite, the rocks, as seen at a distance, appearing in the same unmistakable form as those on the Raw Hide and Laramie Peaks, namely, coarse granite or gneiss, standing in layers and slabs, indicating a vertical stratification. A full description of these mountains must be left for the final report. They derive their name from being covered with pine, whose dark green gives them a black appearance.

* * * * *

In these mountain formations, which border the great plains on the west, are to be found beautiful flowing streams, and small rich valleys covered with fine grass for hay, and susceptible of cultivation by means of irrigation. Fine timber for fuel and lumber, limestone and good stone for building purposes are here abundant. Gold has been found in places in valuable quantities, and without doubt the more common and useful minerals will be discovered when more minute examinations are made.[10]

* * * * *

The people now on the extreme frontiers of Nebraska are near the western limit of the fertile portion of the prairie lands, and a desert space separates them from the fertile and desirable region in the western mountains. They are, as it were, on the shore of a sea, up to which populations and agriculture may advance, and no further. But this gives them much of the value of places along the Atlantic frontier, in view of the future settlements to be formed in the mountains, between which and the present frontier a most valuable trade would exist. The western frontier has always been looking to the east for a market; but as soon as the wave of emigration has passed over the desert portion of the plains, to which the discoveries of gold have already given an impetus that will propel it to the fertile valleys of the Rocky Mountains, then will the present frontier of Kanzas and Nebraska become the starting point for all the products of the Mississippi valley which the population of the mountains will require. We see the effects of it in the benefits which the western frontier of Missouri has received from the Santa Fé trade, and still more plainly in the impetus given to Leavenworth by the operations of the army of Utah in the interior region. This flow of products has, in the last instance, been only in one direction; but when those mountains become settled, as they eventually must, then there will be a reciprocal trade materially beneficial to both.

These settlements in the mountains cannot be agricultural to the same extent as those on the Mississippi Valley, but must depend greatly upon the raising of stock. The country furnishes the means of raising sufficient quantities of grain and vegetables for the use of the inhabitants, and beautiful, healthy, and desirable locations for their homes. The remarkable freedom here from sickness is one of the attractive features of the region, and will, in this respect, go far to recompense the settler from the Mississippi Valley for his loss in the smaller amount of products that can be taken from the soil. The great want of suitable building material which now so seriously retards the growth of the west will not be felt there.

How far the fine timbers in the interior of Nebraska can be relied upon to supply settlements on the Missouri, is a question upon which I am not qualified to give a very positive opinion. Upon the Niobrara the pine extends along the Niobrara and its side ravines for about 120 miles, and there is nearly an equal extent of it on White river; but on both streams it is of inferior quality and difficult of access. That at the Black Hills is much better timber, and covers an area of about 15,000 square miles;[11] but this is also in situations where there would be much labor in getting it out, and an Indian war would probably attend the first attempts to do so. I think the Niobrara, White, and Shyenne rivers could be used to bring the logs to the Missouri, down which they could be rafted.

The great want of timber which is felt along the settlements on the Missouri, and the high price which this material commands, may probably overcome all the difficulties I have stated to exist; and, having done this as faithfully as I can, I must leave each one to form his own opinion on the subject.

NOTES TO CHAPTER 25

1. Sir St. George Gore, an Irish sportsman, made an extensive and elaborate hunting trip across the Northern Plains in 1854-57. He spent the winter of 1854-55 at Fort Laramie. In the summer of 1855 he traveled and hunted north to the Yellowstone at the mouth of Tongue River, where he built a temporary fort and wintered. On this part of the trip he had about 40 servants and guides, 6 wagons, 21 carts, 112 horses, 12 yoke of oxen, and 14 dogs. James Bridger was his principal guide from Fort Laramie to the Yellowstone, but apparently left the party sometime in the spring or summer of 1856. In that year Gore descended the Yellowstone to the mouth. Warren met him at Fort Union between July 10 and July 25 and purchased "the means of land transportation" for his own exploration of part of the Yellowstone Valley.

Apparently no adequate account of the Gore trip has been written, and the information we have about it is on the borderline between history and folklore. Strahorn's *Hand-Book of Wyoming and Guide to the Black Hills and Big Horn Regions*, published in 1877, contains a wild story supposed to have been told by one Jeremiah Proteau, who claimed that he accompanied the party. According to this tale the expedition went up the east side of the Black Hills, and from a broad basin at the foot of the falls in Rapid Creek Proteau casually scooped up three double handfuls of gold! But the expedition did not go up the east side of the Black Hills, there were no falls and no basin on Rapid Creek, and there is no authentic record of any such find of placer gold anywhere in the world.

While Gore's route was undoubtedly west of the Black Hills, the information as to the specific route is contradictory. In the Raynolds' "Report of the Exploration of the Yellowstone and Missouri Rivers in 1859-60," J. Hudson Snowden wrote that Gore: ". . . took a large train of ox and mule wagons from the Platte near the mouth of Box Elder to Powder River, passing near the west side of Pumpkin Butte. . . ." This route was about eighty miles west of the place where Warren says the Indians plundered Gore.

On Warren's map of the "Dacota Country" there are two unexplained routes from the Platte to the Yellowstone. One appears to be the route traveled by De Smet in 1851. (Cf. chap. 18 and 19, *ante.*) The other route goes down the valley of the Belle Fourche River to the northern part of the Black Hills, then runs north by northwest to the mouth of Rosebud Creek. This may have been Warren's idea of the Gore route. But the map was made in the winter of 1855-56, before Warren met Gore at Fort Union.

2. According to other reports Gore had with him about forty people, or approximately twice the number that Warren had. Some of them were engaged for only part of the trip, and his party was probably much smaller when Warren met it at Fort Union.

3. In the spring of 1856 Harney made a treaty with several tribes of

Sioux at Fort Pierre. Harney's "Report of the Proceedings of a Council Held at Fort Pierre . . ." was published by the 34 Congress, 1 Session, *Senate Exec. Doc. 94;* but the treaty itself was not ratified by the Senate. Apparently the Indians thought it was in effect from the time of signature.

4. Note by Warren: "I am much indebted to the influence of Major Twiss, the Indian Agent near Fort Laramie, for his efforts to give the Dacotas a favorable opinion of my expedition, and to secure us a friendly reception." Twiss was agent of the upper Platte Indian Agency from 1855 to 1861. He was a West Point graduate who had resigned from the army while a lieutenant. The title of "Major" was the honorary title given to all Indian agents.

5. The Indians would now be called Minneconjous, Hunkpapas or Unkpapas, and Blackfeet Sioux.

6. Bear's Rib, a Hunkpapa chief, had been designated head chief of the Teton Sioux at the 1856 council at Fort Pierre. His friendship for the whites aroused considerable opposition among the Sioux tribes, and in 1862 he was killed at (new) Fort Pierre by One-that-Limps, a Sans Arc Sioux. (Vestal, *Sitting Bull,* p. 51.)

7. Little Thunder was chief of the Brulé band defeated by Harney on Blue Water Creek, September 3, 1855. He participated in the 1856 council at Fort Pierre.

8. This should read "running road."

9. The last word of this sentence was omitted from the report published in 1858, but included in the reprinting in *South Dakota Historical Collections,* Vol. XI. The editor of this volume refers in a note at page 134 to a republication of Warren's report as a special Senate document in 1875; an edition of the report which I have not seen.

10. This statement has been cited as evidence that Warren knew of gold in the Black Hills as early as 1857. The full context, however, shows that he was writing of the mountains "which border the great plains on the west," a phrase that is far from specific.

11. This is shown as 1,500 square miles in the *South Dakota Historical Collections* text. Since Warren correctly estimated the entire area of the Black Hills at 6,000 square miles, it is obvious that the area of timber was incorrectly shown in the 1858 printing.

Chapter 26

1874

FROM FORT LINCOLN TO THE BLACK HILLS,

by Captain William Ludlow

A period of fifteen years intervened between Raynolds' explorations and the penetration of the interior of the Black Hills by Lieutenant Colonel Custer in 1874. During this period the Civil War was fought. Nearly all regular army troops were withdrawn from the Northern Plains and they were only partially replaced by volunteers. Relations between the Indians and whites became worse. In 1862 there was an uprising of Indians in Minnesota; many of the Indians fled west and found an uneasy sanctuary among the Teton tribes. Generals Sibley and Sully invaded the Northern Plains and military operations developed along the Missouri River and across present North Dakota and Montana to the Yellowstone.

The opening of the Bozeman Trail east of the Big Horn Mountains in 1863 aroused the enmity of the Sioux. In 1865 troops were in the field along the Powder River. In 1866 the army built forts Reno, Phil Kearny, and C. F. Smith to protect the Bozeman Trail, precipitating the Red Cloud War of 1866 to 1868. In 1868 a treaty was negotiated at forts Laramie and Rice and Sully in which the government agreed to close the Bozeman Trail and abandon the three forts built in 1866. Approximately that part of present South Dakota which lies west of the Missouri River was designated a reservation for the Teton tribes and their friends, with additional territory in present Wyoming and Montana provided for temporary occupancy and hunting. The Indians agreed to relinquish all rights to occupy permanently all territory outside the established reservation; to withdraw all opposition to the construction of railroads then being built on the plains; and to permit the peaceful construction of any railroads not passing over their reservation. The reservation was to be set apart for the "absolute and undisturbed use and occupation of the Indians" and the United States agreed "that no persons except those herein designated and authorized so to do, and except such officers, agents, and employees of the government as may be authorized to enter upon Indian reservations in discharge of duties enjoined by law, shall ever be permitted to pass over, settle upon, or reside in the territory described in this article. . . ."

The Black Hills were mostly within the reservation. In 1874 General Sheridan ordered Lieutenant Colonel Custer to make a military reconnaissance of the Black Hills. During this reconnaissance gold was incidentally discovered. In 1875 the Black Hills gold rush began, and early in 1876 the army was embroiled in another Indian war.

On Custer's staff during the Black Hills expedition was Captain William Ludlow, then Chief Engineer for the Department of Dakota. Ludlow graduated from West Point in 1864 and in the final months of the Civil War attained the brevet rank of lieutenant colonel. Before his death in 1901 he served in the War with Spain with the rank of major general of volunteers, and became a brigadier general in the regular army. The intervening years were spent in exploratory and engineering work.

The following chapter is reprinted from Ludlow's *Report of a Reconnaissance of the Black Hills of Dakota, Made in the Summer of 1874*, published by the government in 1875.

The Black Hills are an outlying portion of the Rocky Mountains, covering an area about equal to that of the State of Connecticut, included between the forty-third and forty-fifth parallels of latitude, and the one hundred and third and one hundred and fifth meridians of longitude. They lie, therefore, mostly within the borders of Dakota, but trench also upon those of Wyoming.

On the north, east, and south sides, they are surrounded by the open prairie, and are accessible only by a journey of a hundred or more miles from the nearest point which even frontier civilization has reached. This region had been skirted by Lieutenant Warren, of the Topographical Engineers, in 1855, 1856, and 1857, and by Captain Raynolds, of the same corps, in 1859 and 1860, and the maps and reports of these officers nearly summed up our knowledge of it, if we except the vague and sometimes highly-colored reports from Indians and stray frontiersmen.

The North and South Forks of the Big Cheyenne head nearly together on the west side, thence, spreading widely apart, embrace the hills between them, uniting in longitude 102° 20′, to flow eastward and discharge into the Missouri.

The immense reservation secured to the various bands of Sioux—now the most numerous and warlike of the northern tribes—by treaty of April 29, 1868, lies between the one hundred and fourth meridian of longitude and the Missouri River. It is bounded on the north by the forty-sixth and on the south by the forty-third parallel, the Keya-Paha River, (a branch of the Niobrara,) and the Niobrara itself, to its confluence with the Missouri.

This immense tract, inclosing nearly forty-three thousand square miles, the greater portion of which, however, is bare and often arid prairie, destitute of every attraction for the

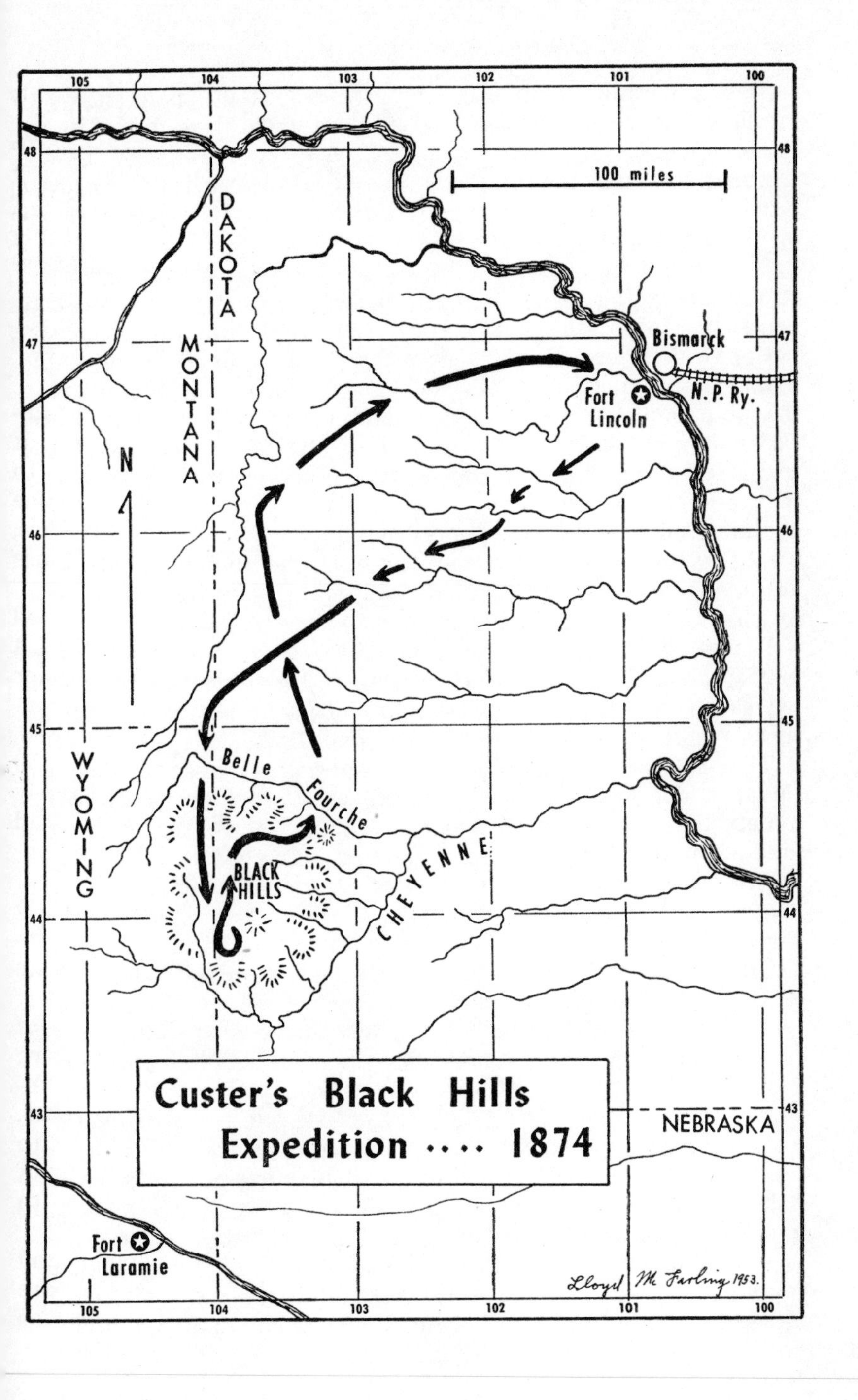

Custer's Black Hills Expedition 1874

settler, and only capable of supporting a scanty population of hunters, has for its choicest and most valuable portion the Black Hills, lying on its western border. All reports agreed in describing this as a mountainous, heavily-timbered tract, abounding in game, and containing within its unexplored interior an open, fertile, and well-watered region.

In case, at any future time, complications with the Sioux, or the advancing needs of bordering civilization should make it necessary to establish military posts upon this Indian reservation, indications all pointed to the Black Hills as the suitable point, both on account of their geographical position and of the abundance of wood, water, and grass to be found there. To explain the value of its position, it should be stated that the trails from the camp of the hostile Sioux on the Yellowstone, to the agencies near the Missouri, where live the reservation Indians and whereon the issues of annuities are made, lead by a southeasterly course through the hills, the abundance of game and ample security of which, make them a ready refuge in time of war, and a noble hunting-ground in time of peace.

It was therefore considered desirable to gain positive information regarding them, and to connect them as well by reconnaissance with the posts of Lincoln and Laramie. To accomplish these results was the object of the expedition.

The *personnel* of this consisted of ten companies of the Seventh Cavalry, one each of the Twentieth and Seventeenth Infantry, a detachment of Indian scouts,[1] together with the necessary guides, interpreters, and teamsters, in all about one thousand men. The wagon train consisted of about one hundred and ten wagons and ambulances, while the artillery was represented by three Gatlings and a 3-inch rifle.[2]

Previous to leaving Saint Paul I had engaged the services of Prof. N. H. Winchell,[3] State geologist of Minnesota, as geologist of the expedition. He would also make such notes as his time would admit on the flora, in which Dr. Williams, surgeon, U. S. A., kindly promised to assist.

Mr. George Bird Grinnell,[4] of New Haven, accompanied the expedition as a representative of Professor Marsh, of Yale College, and I arranged with him to furnish me a report on the paleontology and zoology. The valuable reports of these two gentlemen are appended, and special attention to them invited.

A photographer was engaged in Saint Paul, and furnished with a complete apparatus for taking stereoscopic views. He agreed, in consideration of using Government material, and being furnished with other facilities, to make six complete sets of pictures upon return to Saint Paul to accompany the official reports. About sixty excellent views were taken, illustrating vividly the character of the country. But one incomplete set of pictures was furnished me, which is forwarded herewith. The photographer failed, and subsequently refused, to furnish more, and an attempt to compel him to do so was defeated.[5]

For surveying purposes my detachment of six engineer soldiers was employed. The two sergeants, Becker and Wilson, each with one man as an assistant, kept separate trails with prismatic compass and odometer—one with an odometer-cart, a two-wheeled vehicle specially constructed for the purpose, the other in an ambulance. Two odometers were read on each vehicle, and the compass notes made as full as possible. Two chronometers (mean solar, 1362, Arnold & Dent, and sidereal, 202, Bond & Sons) were carried by the fifth man in a basket, while a record of thermometer and aneroid barometer readings was made by the sixth man during the day.

The additional instruments were a small Würdemann transit, No. 94, and a Spencer, Browning & Co. sextant, No. 6536. The general topography during the day was taken as thoroughly as possible by my assistant, Mr. W. H. Wood, and myself, and night observations were made whenever practicable. The positions of all but ten of the camps were astronomically determined. A summary of these is appended.

The direct course to Bear Butte, which is a well-known point north of the Black Hills, is south 39½° west, and the air-line distance two hundred and two miles. As it was known that the intervening country was dry and woodless, General Custer considered that, by inclining westward toward the divide east of the Little Missouri and then turning south, a better road would be found than by pursuing the straight course. Prairie travel resembles that by sea, which indeed the landscape not unfrequently suggests. The compass is the guide, the direct course is not always the best, and the probabilities of finding wood, water, and grass, and a good road, compare with those of obtaining favorable and moderate winds and a smooth sea.

The Dakota prairies have been often described, but their general characteristics may be briefly stated: a rolling and at times a hilly country, destitute of wood, except small quantities in the eroded valleys of streams, and covered with short grass. The horizon, bounded everywhere by the undulating outlines of the surface, and varied occasionally by some more dominating elevations which constitute the landmarks for the traveler, and are called buttes. (In pronouncing the word the *u* is sounded as in tube.)

The summer sun shines from a generally cloudless sky; the purity of the air gives its rays great power, and the thermometer frequently rises above 100° in the shade. Water is scarce, and almost invariably alkaline, even in running streams, from the presence of a salt which forms a component of the clayey soil. The rivers are small streams of great comparative length, which, from absorption and evaporation, shrink in their downward course, and are frequently dry at their mouths while flowing freely a hundred or two miles above. The seasons of spring and fall are exceedingly brief. The winter snows are rapidly disposed of in the spring, and rain-falls are unfrequent until cold weather in the fall, which soon again merges into winter. By July 1 the grass is fully grown, and in another month has turned dry and yellow, cured to hay upon the ground and readily burned.

The whole country was once ranged over by enormous herds of buffalo whose trails are everywhere visible, but which are now seldom or never found east of the Little Missouri; and the only game animals inhabiting the vast waste are antelope, numbers of which were seen during every day's march. The grasshopper having proved himself to be one of the most serious obstacles to the future successful colonization of the country, is worth brief mention.

Previous to the departure of the expedition, and while still in camp near Fort Lincoln during the last days of June, the grasshoppers were very numerous. I counted twenty-five one morning on what I judged to be an average square foot of ground; a brief calculation gives at that rate over a million to the acre; and as they are often much more numerous than then observed, and are exceedingly rapacious, their capacity for destruction to living vegetation may be imagined. Their powers of sustained flight, too, are wonderful when one considers the build of the creature and compares it with that of a bird. They appear able to keep the wing the whole day, always moving with the wind, and filling the air to a vast height. By shading the eye from the direct rays of the sun, and still looking near it, an idea of their great numbers can be gained. The wings reflecting the light make them appear like tufts of cotton floating lazily with the wind, and apparently increasing in numbers upward as far as the eye can reach. They will journey thus all day long for several days, settling to the ground at night-fall. In descending through the slanting rays of the sun, they resemble a fall of huge snow-flakes. In one of our camps there must have been a hundred to the square foot. They were crowded as thickly as they could stand upon the ground, and every blade of grass bore several. No successful means of destroying them or mitigating their ravages have been yet discovered; and the serious consequences of a visitation from them were seen last season in many portions of the West.[6]

The course determined upon by General Custer was successfully pursued. The expedition left Fort Lincoln at 8 a. m. of July 2, steering at first southwesterly toward the bend of Heart River; thence, July 7, across the North Fork of the Cannon Ball, a fine stream, 30 feet to 75 feet in width, and 1 foot to 2 feet in depth, flowing with swift current over a shaly bed through a well-wooded valley from 100 feet to 200 feet deep, and 500 to 1,000 yards wide; thence, July 8, across the South Fork, also called Cedar Creek, a smaller stream, 20 feet wide and 18 inches deep with a rocky bed, banks from 10 feet to 12 feet high, and valley 100 to 200 yards wide, scantily furnished with wood; thence over the Belle Pierres Hills, so called from the colored pebbles abounding there. Here, bending nearly westward, the trail gradually sloped into the valley of North Fork of Grand River, in which we camped July 9. The stream was about 25 feet wide and a foot in depth, with a rapid current of muddy sweet water from recent rain above. The valley is level, from one to two miles wide, defined by low hills, and supports a scanty growth of thin grass and weeds. Wood is very scarce.

The next day's march (July 10) was still west, and a little north, up the valley, in which we again camped. The grasshoppers were in immense numbers during these two days.

From this camp the trail bore strongly southwest, to enable us to explore a cave, of which the guides told wonderful stories. We found it, after an uphill march of twenty miles over a sterile country covered with cactus, in the eastern side of a ridge several miles in length and covered with the first pine timber we had seen. With regard to this ridge and the cave, the following is a note from my itinerary: "The ridge presents a peculiar appearance, having a level cap of light friable sandstone, which has washed and weathered into the shape of battlements and towers. The exterior presents the appearance of a scarp, and suggests strongly the ruins of an old fortified city fairly laid out with bastions and curtains, with sally-ports guarded by towers. The tendency in places is to wear into holes large and small, which, often of regular size and arrangement, give the idea of embrasures and loopholes. The scarp varies in places from 3 feet to 20 feet in height, against which lies the talus derived from the breaking down of the sandstone walls and the washing of the superjacent clay. The 'cave' is a hole washed out of the sandstone 200 feet or 300 feet in depth horizontally, with an entrance 15 feet by 20 feet, and proved to possess no special interest other than that imparted to it by the superstition of the Indians." From the Cave Hills the route led southwesterly across several bends of the South Fork of Grand River, through a rather difficult and arid country, to the camp of July 14, in a well grassed and watered valley, through which flowed a small wooded branch of the Little Missouri. The view here was so attractive, in comparison with the landscape recently passed over, that General Custer named the place Prospect Valley. Here the first halt was made for the purposes of rest and washing, much needed after a march of two hundred and thirty miles, and a mail was dispatched back to Fort Lincoln by Indian scouts. The camp lay between two ranges of pine-covered hills, from the southern extremity of which, and due south of us, the Black Hills loomed up high and dark, and although sixty miles away, some separate peaks and elevations could be identified. The Short Pine Hills are of a soft arenaceous marl, very light in color, some 400 or 500 feet above the valley and covered with pine from 20 feet to 40 feet in height, except on the level top, which is seven or eight miles long by two to three and a half miles wide, and shows a heavy growth of grass. Slim Butte, which has been in sight to the southeast and east for several days, appears more like a high wooded plateau than a butte, and is presumably of the same formation as the Short Pine Hills.[7] Information from the guides indicates that a branch of the South Fork of Grand River separates it into two portions. On the west side of the Short Pine Hills some fossils were discovered, regarding which the following is my note: "Descended from the hills into the Little Missouri Valley and passed by a range of bare hills of the same character as the larger ones. Examined them for fossils, and Winchell discovered two vertebrae (saurian) and a couple of turtles of great size. Vertebrae preserved, but turtles were too much decayed. A thigh-bone of one was 2 inches in diameter, and the carapace 1¼ inches thick. From Prospect Valley the trail led around the northern extremity of the Short Pine Hills into the valley of the Little

Missouri, which proved to be an inhospitable country enough. No grass could be seen, the vegetation was all cactus and weeds. The train watered at a bend of the river, and taking some wood struck off southeast. Finding a little grass we finally camped, after a hot and dusty march of thirty and a half miles over the most unattractive country we had seen."

The Little Missouri is a rapid stream, 30 feet to 40 feet wide and 18 inches deep, over a gravelly bed. The banks are steep and 40 feet in height, and the valley is several miles in width, with small cottonwood in the lower levels. Information from the guides pointed to the northwest corner of the Black Hills as the most favorable point of entrance, although they still insisted that an exploration was impossible, except on foot. The camp of the 16th of July being on the one hundred and fourth meridian, but little additional westing was required.

The next day's travel (July 17) led south, over a rolling prairie tributary to the Little Missouri, and partaking of the characteristic features of that valley; very little grass; cactus and prickly pear prevailing; the soil a loose, dry clay, into which the foot sank. Camp was made on the edge of a bluff facing south, overlooking a very rough and much-tumbled country, with the Black Hills in full view, fifteen or twenty miles distant, and Bear Butte rising from the prairie forty miles away to the southeast. During the night heavy clouds and lightning appeared, and, toward morning, a severe wind-storm routed us from sleep and covered us with sand.

Crossing the broken country, which was deeply washed and gullied, noon of the 18th brought us to a small branch of the Belle Fourche, timbered with burr-oak and pine, and strongly impregnated with iron. The cause of this was soon explained. Just beyond we found iron-ore covering a large surface and heaped up in mounds. The landscape suggested the waste-banks of an enormous iron-furnace, and showed that we had entered upon the outer edge of the geological disturbance which had culminated in the formation of the Black Hills. Passing the iron country the valley of the Belle Fourche was reached, and two or three hours were spent in looking for a practicable descent. The hills are 500 or 600 feet in height, deeply scarred with ravines, pine and burr-oak covering the slopes.

Camp was favorably selected in a clear level opening, 25 feet or 30 feet above the river, with abundant wood, water, and grass.

The Belle Fourche, or north fork of the Cheyenne, has a rapid current, in a shaly bed 30 feet to 50 feet wide, and from

1 foot to 4 feet deep, with water slightly alkaline. The rocks have been strongly tilted and metamorphosed. The river is from a half mile to a mile in width and well timbered. Captain Raynold's trail of 1859 passed along the crest of the hills in rear of camp. The guides continued to proclaim the uselessness of attempting to take wagons farther, and if they possessed any knowledge which would be valuable to us refused to impart it. They have hitherto supposed we would skirt the hills without seriously attempting an entrance. Finding their monitions falling on deaf ears, they realized our intention to see all we could.

July 19.—The command remained in camp. The distance marched from Lincoln was two hundred and ninety-two miles, an average of eighteen and a quarter miles per day. Heavy rain fell until 4 p. m., and the huge camp-fires were a luxury all day. Toward evening the precaution was taken of moving the wagon-train across the river, in view of a possible rise during the night.

July 20.—The first day's journey was made into the hills. The morning opened threateningly, but subsequently cleared. Crossing the river and bending to the westward, a winding and easy ascent was made of the opposite hills. Reaching the summit the course was southerly, over a high, gently-rolling prairie, heavily grassed, with clumps of oak and pine beautifully interspersed.

A ravine cut into the shingle by a small stream was passed. From the sides of the cut exuded some salt of sulphur, and the water was strongly impregnated with alum, and possessed a decidedly inky flavor and astringency. Pursuing the southerly course the high table narrowed to a ridge and suddenly turned to the left; the trail descended into a valley thickly wooded with oak and pine. The change from the hot, dry, burned-up landscape north of the Belle Fourche was wonderful. The temperature was delightful; the air laden with sweet wild odors; the grass knee-deep and exceedingly luxuriant and fresh; while wild cherries, blueberries, and gooseberries abounded, as well as many varieties of flowers. All these advantages, combined with that of an abundance of pure cold water, were ours, with rare exceptions, until the final departure from the hills.

NOTES TO CHAPTER 26

1. An account of the Black Hills expedition, as told by some of the Indian scouts many years later, appears in "The Arikara Narrative," edited by O. G. Libby and published in Volume VI, *North Dakota Historical Collections*. There were about twenty-five Arikara scouts, about twenty-

five Santee Sioux, and three or four other Sioux. Bloody Knife, half Arikara and half Hunkpapa Sioux, was the principal Indian scout.

2. A beef herd of 350 animals was driven along to be butchered as needed.

3. Winchell's account of the trip was published in the Ludlow *Report.* An excerpt appears in Chapter 27, *post.*

4. Because of the speed with which the expedition moved through the areas where paleontological specimens were available, Grinnell was not able to do much collecting, and his report on paleontology was necessarily brief. He prepared an interesting report on zoology. An excerpt appears in Chapter 28, *post.*

5. The photographer's name was Illingworth. Several of the photographs taken on the trip have been published; among them a picture of Custer, Ludlow, Bloody Knife, and Private Noonan, with a grizzly bear killed by Custer, which appears in *Death on Horseback,* by Paul I. Wellman, between pages 96 and 97.

6. The grasshopper infestation on the Northern Plains in 1874 was one of the most serious in historic times.

7. The battle of Slim Buttes occurred here September 9, 1876, between General Crook's forces and a small band of Indians led by American Horse.

Chapter 27

1874

CLIMBING HARNEY PEAK,

by Newton H. Winchell

Newton H. Winchell, geologist and archaeologist, was born in 1839 and died in 1914. He studied geology at the University of Michigan and worked on geological surveys in Michigan and Ohio before becoming State Geologist for Minnesota in 1872. He held this position until 1900 and from 1874 to 1900 he was also Professor of Geology at the University of Minnesota. He accompanied the Black Hills expedition of 1874 and wrote an account of his experiences and observations, in the form of a journal, which was printed in the Ludlow *Report*.

The most important thing that happened during the Black Hills expedition was the discovery of gold, but the importance of this discovery was not realized at the time. The *Engineering and Mining Journal*, reviewing the Ludlow *Report* November 27, 1875, after the Black Hills gold rush had begun, said: "The expedition of Colonel Ludlow . . . was accompanied by an intelligent geologist in the person of Prof. N. H. Winchell. . . . Professor Winchell's clear outline of the geological structure of the region traversed makes no mention of gold, but incidentally shows that the area in which diluvial deposits may be expected is comparatively smaller than on the Pacific slope of the Sierra. We may fairly infer from the general features of the Black Hills that they are not likely to prove an extraordinary Eldorado. . . ." However, Winchell did mention gold in his report. On July 30 he wrote:

"We traveled ten miles, nearly southeast from our last camp, and are in a wide, grassed valley, through which runs a stream. This valley here subsequently receives the name of Custer Park. The gold-seekers who accompany the expedition report the finding of gold in the gravel and sand along the valley."

On July 31 Winchell accompanied Custer, Ludlow, and others who climbed Harney Peak, returning to the temporary camp on Custer Creek early on the morning of August 1. Early on August 2 he left camp with Custer and others on a reconnaissance to the Cheyenne River, returning to camp August 6. No doubt these strenuous activities and his other geological studies diverted Winchell's mind from the reports of the finding of gold, yet it is a curious thing that a discovery of such potential importance was not further investigated by the expedition's principal geologist.

The following excerpt from Winchell's journal describes the climbing of Harney Peak on July 31, 1874.

Camp, August 1.—We are four or five miles east of our last night's camp. We had yesterday a long and tiresome trip to Harney's Peak, of which I made brief notes on the spot. We reached camp so late as twenty minutes before one o'clock this morning. The reconnoitering party consisted of General Custer, Colonel Ludlow, General Forsyth, Professor Donaldson,[1] and myself. Colonel Ludlow's assistant, Mr. Wood, also accompanied the party, who were escorted by a company of horse under Lieutenant Barnum. The party shaped its movements according to the desire of Colonel Ludlow for topographical purposes. We set out north, and passed to the southeast of the peaks which were mentioned the day before in coming into Custer Park. We traveled about two miles in that direction, among bald knobs of granite and schist, with some grassy valleys between, when we turned more eastward and ascended a ridge of granite hills, passing it at a low point, which by aneroid was 903 feet above our camp. On ascending this ridge a most magnificent prospect burst suddenly upon us, which caused us each, on reaching the summit, to utter an exclamation of surprise and wonder. An expanse of from six to fifteen miles stretched out before us toward the east, south, and northeast, filled up with just such objects, in just such positions and proportions, as go to make up an artist's ideal mountain-landscape. This expanse consisted in the main of a valley, winding through the timber of which, toward the south, could be seen a beautiful meadow, through which ran a stream of water half concealed by the tall grass. In the east we could limit the view only by timbered hills of granite, the bare rock of which stood out in isolated peaks and buttresses. A grassed valley, but narrower, also ran off in that direction, fingering out among the mountains from which it gathered its many tributaries. To the northeast, however, was the grandest sight I ever beheld. This was a truly alpine view. Here was Pelion on Ossa. This was toward Harney's Peak, only the top of which, as we supposed, could be seen from our position. Very near us, and cutting off our view north, was a series of spindled peaks which, though massive and imposing, proved to be mere pigmies to the giants of the same shape and character that rose in the distance. These latter hid Harney from our view, though we mistook another peak, very similar, about two miles to the southeast, for Harney, and made for it on descending. In the valley before us stood up scattered, conical, granitic "sugar-loaves," in the background of which, rising nearly as high as old Harney himself, was a perfect nest of organ-pipe peaks, whose sharp spindling tops immediately suggested the name Organ Peaks, which name they retain.[2] There are two such nests, and they were both in view, separated not more than three-quarters of a mile. These bare rocks, presenting in the morning sun a light surface, as they rose above the almost universal pines, afforded a most striking contrast with the dark-green foliage of the forest, and very appropriately received their name.

On descending from this divide, where we had made an involuntary halt, we commenced a winding course toward the peak which we took for Harney's. Its crest presented a sharp ridge, with perpendicular sides, running about north and south, having nearly a flat top, and had been seen by Colonel Ludlow and myself from a limestone bluff in Castle Valley a few days before, and so identified as Harney's. We found it very difficult making our way toward this peak, as the country was very rough, the valleys, instead of being broad and grassed, were narrow and rocky. In them, sometimes, the trees had been thrown down by fire or tempest, often half consumed and left charred, and a thousand shrubs and small aspens, that almost everywhere in the northwest follow spontaneously a downthrow of the evergreen forest, had made a perfect mesh, through which no horse could pass. Avoiding these, and the places that presented nothing but bald rock surfaces, we had still a winding, inconstant, intervening belt of varying width on which grew the principal and largest trees. This was on the lower flanks of the hills, where there was sufficient soil to afford strong rooting for trees, and not enough water to make it soft—for in many of the valleys there are very deceptive, and often grassy, treacherous bogs, that caused several horses to mire—so that we finally found ourselves, about noon, at the foot of the peak at which we aimed. Here ran a beautiful stream toward the east, though it was perfectly invisible till we were on its very brink, so dense were the bushes and brush through which we filed our way. At this point I read the barometer, which stood 24.35. Ahead of us could be seen an irregularly ascending, half-timbered ridge, rising toward the summit of the hill at which we aimed. We were traveling toward the northeast, and at first took the southwestern slope of this ridge, but afterward passed over its crest to the opposite side, where we picked our way slowly along, leading our horses among fallen trees, blackened logs, and sliding masses of rock, till we finally reached a point where our horses could be led no longer. By this time the advance had dwindled to three persons, Generals Custer, Forsyth, and the writer, the topographers having delayed for taking sights to prominent points, and the escort being more slow in getting up. Here we abandoned our horses, unhitched, as we knew they were too weary to go far, and the orderlies were not far behind, and began a scramble for the top, which lay at least 250 feet above us. At first we mounted with great agility an easy slope, where large, loose masses formed a rough talus, and rose to the summit of a shoulder. Here we met a perpendicular wall that forms the blade-like portion at the very top. After breathing a few minutes, General Custer and I began an examination of this wall. It stretched to the northwest about 60 rods, and afforded not a single break or niche that could be used as a support in any attempt to scale it. At length, but before the arrival of any others of the party, we discovered a place that presented a possible ascent. This blade-like ridge, which has not more than an average width of 25 feet, has, on its southern or southeastern end, a number of eroded channels, giving it a fluted surface. These gullies, if continued farther, would constitute the vacancies that exist between the Organ Peaks, and would convert the whole ridge into another magnificent set of organ-pipes. They are simply weathered-out jointing-planes, and if crossed at a proper angle by another system, would produce, under the influence of atmospheric agencies, a columnar exterior that would give the peak the aspect of the central, conical mass seen in Heeng-ya Ka-ga.[3] We chose what appeared to be the most practicable of these eroded channels, and he with his rifle and I with hammer and barometer, by literally crawling closely to the rock, bracing ourselves across from side to side and seizing every available knob of projecting feldspar, reached almost simultaneously, by different routes, the top, or what appeared from below to be the top. This, however, was some distance still farther, though not much higher. Descending a short notch, where we separated again for a second scramble, I found a narrow valley, (in which grew a very fine and tempting array of red raspberries, *Rubus strigosus*,) leading, by a steady ascent, out to the very summit of the peak. Passing up this, inclosed by perpendicular walls on both sides, I emerged upon the top, and sat down, or dropped down, to rest, almost exhausted. The rest of the scaling-party soon came up. General Custer fired a salute of three shots from his rifle, we drank from our canteens to General Harney, and, after a lunch, decided to visit another peak lying toward the northwest, which rises some feet higher than that we had ascended. From the point at which we stood, 1,012 feet above the creek flowing along the base of this mountain, we commanded the most extensive field of vision that we had yet beheld in the Black Hills. We seemed to be in the center of the most rugged and forbidding tract of the Black Hills. On nearly all sides, bare rock and sharp peaks rose among the pines that partially enlivened the scene. Toward the east and south we could see beyond and over the intervening hills, and discerned the plains, and distinguished some of their main features. The location of the outcropping edge of the Red Beds was evident by the redness along a belt of country near the hills. Toward the north, (7° east of north, true meridian,) Bear Butte rose high enough to show its summit and allow its identification by its regularly rounded and massive form. The Organ Peaks are the most attractive object toward the west. They lay west 15° north, by compass, and about a mile distant. Beyond them a distant range of mountains was dimly visible, but toward the north and northwest the view was cut off by the hills themselves. Although this is the granitic nucleus of the Black Hills, the region of the sedimentary rock, particularly of the great limestone formation farther north, is without doubt the highest above the ocean.[4] The valley in which our camp is can be seen, especially some of its easterly ramifications, from this peak. Indeed, the view toward the south, embracing a tract of open, grassy valley, with considerable pine, and much smoother than in the opposite direction, affords a remarkable contrast with the wild ruggedness of the view toward the north.

The scaling-party having decided to visit the second peak, whose ascent appeared practicable for horses, General Forsyth and the writer descended as we came up, for the purpose of taking our horses, while the rest advance northwest toward that peak and find a place of descent toward the north. Partly riding and partly leading, we passed along the western side of the blade-like crest some hundreds of feet below it, then down into a steep and deep ravine, and ascended the other side. This ravine we passed as near its head as possible, and left on our left a cluster of small granitic peaks that stand in this valley, cut by jointing-planes and weathered down to pyramidal forms by the operations of nature. Besides the perpendicular jointing-planes, these little peaks disclose some that are nearly horizontal, so that they are near their tops disjointed or cut off, the separated joints appearing displaced and ready to totter off. In that way how many joints above them may have fallen down since their first exposure, reducing them to their present dimensions, the ages of geology will never reveal. They probably once stood as high as the Organ peaks stand now, or as high as those peaks ever stood. They are now six or eight hundred feet lower. Up the southeastern side of Harney No. 2, I with difficulty led my horse, and took him over the very summit just as the foot party were starting on the descent again, led by General Custer; for they had no sooner reached this summit than they beheld what could not be seen from the first peak we ascended, owing to the intervention of this, a third peak in direct range northwest, rising, very evidently, several hundred feet higher. Plunging into a labyrinth of ravines, ridges, trees, bushes and rocks, they were very soon out of sight. Here I found myself, with my horse, on the summit of a mountain alone, with no certainty of being able to follow the foot party, for General Forsyth had been delayed by taking charge of the escort. Nevertheless, my horse and I got down, and on the opposite side, for this peak was very much smoother than the first one we climbed, the rock having crumbled so that in many places the surface was covered with rusted crystals of feldspar. The foot party, by a detour to the left, round a lower intervening hill, reached the foot of the difficulties of the real Harney's Peak some time later than I with my horse, by plunging into a ravine toward the right that was wooded with small pines, but afforded good footing for my horse. Dismounting to fire at a doe that was startled by my approach, and following it up unsuccessfully, General Custer encountered my horse and rode up to the same place. The ascent of this peak was very similar to that of the first. We made it together, the rest of the party being delayed for similar reasons as before. We found here a long, narrow ridge of bare rock, along which we passed, occasionally coming to broken-down spots that had to be crossed by letting each other down and helping each other up. Finally, a massive wall, the very end of a higher ridge, confronted us, barring our further progress. Turning to the right and descending, General Custer found a practicable ascent to the top of this second ridge, while I managed as before, and scaled a perpendicular ascent in a weathered-out angle between jointing-planes, rising thus about 50 feet. This, however, was not the summit of the peak itself. We found it impracticable to further attempt its ascent. Another perpendicular wall confronted us, rising about 45 feet. The sun had already set, a long return-march was before us through a very rough and unknown region, and we made but a short stay. We saw from this peak very nearly the same view in all directions as already described from the first peak ascended, though it rises 623 feet higher than that, being 1,635 feet above the creek where my barometer was noted, near the base of the first peak. . . .

Taking samples of the rock, and driving an emptied copper cartridge-case into a cleft in the granite, we left therein our names and the day of the month, and began what proved to be a long and tiresome night-march back to camp.

The rock which makes up these peaks is a gray or white feldspathic granite, the separate crystalline ingredients of which are coarse and contain crystals of black tourmaline. It is not intersected with dikes nor with quartz veins. It is simply a massive granite, with a tendency to a columnar fracture near the mountain peaks. There seems to have been an important system of joints running northwest and southeast, and a much less conspicuous one crossing it about at right angles, for the mountain peaks have the form of thin crests with nearly flat tops, running northwest and southeast, and only partially broken down by cross-openings from northeast to southwest. This granite, massive and unstratified as it is, still is joined to the overlying schists by a number of interstratifications of schist and granite, a fact that was noticed at two or three favorable points. It is not meant here to say that the granite was derived from a conformable underlying sedimentary rock, for there was not sufficient opportunity to gather data on that point, but there is certainly some reason for supposing that to have been the case.[5]

NOTES TO CHAPTER 27

1. A. B. Donaldson was another geologist who accompanied the expedition. A brief account of the trip by Donaldson was published in *South Dakota Historical Collections*, Vol. VII, apparently reprinted from the *St. Paul Pioneer Press* of 1874.

2. Now called the Needles, these eroded granite spires are one of the features of Black Hills scenery.

3. Note by Winchell, p. 34 of Ludlow *Report:* "The name 'Inyan Kara,' given to this mountain by Warren and Raynolds, is a corruption of the Indian word given above, which I carefully obtained from our guide, Cold Hand." However this may be, Inyan Kara has survived as the accepted name of the mountain. The Black Hills expedition visited it July 23.

4. Harney Peak is now recognized as the highest peak in the Black Hills, and is said to be the highest peak east of the Rocky Mountains. It is 7,242 feet above sea level, according to the Geological Survey topographic map, revised in 1913. Winchell estimated the height of Harney Peak as about 9,000 feet; Ludlow thought it was about 9,700.

5. This statement may have been consistent with lithological knowledge in 1874, but today it has a curious sound. Granite is an igneous rock, crystalized from molten, or plastic, magma. Schists are metamorphic rocks, i.e., rocks altered from their original state by pressure, heat, chemical change, or a combination of causes. The layers of sedimentary rock which now surround the Black Hills once extended over that area, then relatively flat. Masses of magma from within the earth's crust were intruded through some of the layers and between others, creating a great dome which has since been eroded enough to reveal the granitic intrusions in some places. The intrusions of magma created pressure and heat which changed some of the sedimentary rocks into schists.

Chapter 28

1874

ZOOLOGICAL REPORT—MAMMALS,

by George Bird Grinnell

George Bird Grinnell was born in 1849 and died in 1938. He took his A.B. at Yale in 1870 and his Ph.D. in 1880. From 1874 to 1880 he was assistant in osteology at Peabody Museum, Yale. He served as naturalist with the Black Hills expedition of 1874, and with Ludlow's reconnaissance of Yellowstone Park in the following year. From 1876 to 1911 he was an editor of *Forest and Stream.* He wrote and edited many books, including several on the history and ethnology of the Great Plains. Perhaps his best works were *The Fighting Cheyennes* (1915), *The Cheyenne Indians* (1923), and *By Cheyenne Campfires* (1926).

Grinnell contributed to the Ludlow *Report* a brief report on paleontology and a longer report on zoology, with sections on mammals and birds. I am reprinting the section on mammals.

FELIDAE

Cougar; American Panther, (*Felis concolor,* Linn.)[1] I saw but a single panther while we were in the Black Hills, and that one, as far as I can discover, was the only one observed by any member of the expedition. I believe, however, that they are quite numerous in this locality, as on several occasions I saw indications of their recent presence, and once found the partially devoured remains of a deer that had just been left by one of these animals.

Bay Lynx; Wildcat, (*Lynx rufus,* Raf.) Neither this nor the next species were seen by any one connected with the expedition. Nevertheless, the descriptions given by Charles Reynolds, the hunter, of two small cats, not uncommon about Fort Lincoln and to the west of that post, were such as to satisfy me of the existence of *L. rufus* and *L. canadensis* in considerable numbers along the larger rivers that we passed, and they are doubtless common in the Black Hills as well.

Canada Lynx, (*Lynx canadensis,* Raf.) Probably common in Black Hills.

CANIDAE

Gray Wolf; Timber Wolf, (*Canis occidentalis* var. *griseo-albus*, Rich.)[2] I found the gray wolf one of the most common animals in the Black Hills, and hardly a day passed without my seeing several individuals of this species. They were generally observed singly or by twos and threes, sneaking along the mountain sides or crossing the narrow valleys. They were quite shy, and lost no time in plunging into the dense woods as soon as they perceived us. Their howlings were often heard at night; and on one occasion I heard the doleful sound at midday—a bad omen, if we may trust the Indians.

Prairie Wolf; Coyoté, (*Canis latrans*, Say.) The coyoté was found in considerable numbers on the plains, and was especially abundant among the elevated table-lands that were crossed before reaching the Black Hills. After penetrating into the hills proper, however, I did not see a single specimen until I left them for the Big Cheyenne, when I again noticed coyotés in numbers. In the Black Hills this species would seem to be replaced by the preceding. Among the *Mauvaises Terres* of the Little Missouri I saw a few of both species.

Prairie Fox, (*Vulpes macrourus*, Baird.)[3] Only three individuals of this species were seen by me—an old female and two young. They had established themselves in a commodious burrow on the edge of a prairie-dog town, where they could obtain an abundant supply of food with very little exertion.

Kit-Fox; Swift, (*Vulpes velox*, Aud & Bach.) This pretty little fox is abundant everywhere on the plains, though not often seen, on account of its small size and its disposition to hide when it can, in preference to running. An exaggerated idea of this animal's fleetness prevails among hunters and plains-men, probably induced by the extreme evenness and regularity with which it runs. The animal seems fairly to glide along the earth, and its movements resemble the flight of a bird rather than the gait of a quadruped. The Swift undoubtedly runs very fast, but not as fast as the jackass-rabbit, (*L. callotis.*)[4] I saw General Custer's hounds catch one after a chase of not more than half a mile, while the capture of a full-grown hare often necessitated a run of fully two miles.

MUSTELIDAE

Weasel, (*Putorius longicauda*, Rich.)[5] A single weasel of this species was taken August 24 on the headwaters of Heart River.

Mink, (*Putorius vison,* Rich.)[6] This species is abundant on the larger streams flowing into the Missouri River. I saw no living specimens while in the Black Hills, but observed frequent signs of their presence along the streams, and saw a skin which the owner told me he had taken while there.

Otter, (*Lutra canadensis,* Sab.) Abundant on Heart and Cannon-Ball Rivers, and probably in the Black Hills.

Skunk, (*Mephitis mephitica,* Baird.)[7] Common about the Missouri and Heart Rivers and in the Black Hills.

American Badger, (*Taxidea americana,* Baird.)[8] I found the badger very abundant from Fort Lincoln to the edge of the Black Hills, but saw none after leaving the plain country. They are generally to be seen prowling about through the settlements of the prairie dogs, (*Cynomys ludovicianus,*) which animals constitute a considerable portion of their food.

URSIDAE

Grizzly Bear, (*Ursus horribilis,* Ord.) Although we saw indications of the presence of large numbers of grizzlies during our march through the Black Hills, only a few were killed, chiefly from lack of time to devote to their capture. The first one killed was secured by General Custer and Colonel Ludlow. It was a very old male, the canine teeth being mere broken stumps, many of the incisors gone, and the molars worn down almost to the gums. In color it was everywhere a deep, glossy black, except on the head and on the lower parts of the shoulders and thighs, where there was a slight sprinkling of dark gray hairs. The old veteran bore on his body the marks of many a conflict. On his back, just behind the shoulders, was a rugged scar 10 inches long and 2 wide; his face was marked in several places, and his sides and thighs were disfigured in the same manner. These scars, I am led to believe, were the result of battles with some rival during the rutting season.

Very different in appearance were an old female and two cubs that were killed later in the trip, and much farther to the eastward, by two of our Indian scouts. The cubs were about half grown, and, with the mother, were of a yellowish clay color. The inner half of each hair was deep black, but the outer extremity was a bright reddish-yellow. This gave them a curious mottled appearance and induced many of those who saw them to consider them a different species from the one killed by General Custer. I saw no evidences of any great ferocity in any of the specimens killed by the party. None made any attempt at defense unless so badly wounded as to be unable to escape by flight; even the old female just referred to continued to run after both her cubs had been disabled.

The swiftness of the grizzly is considerable, and in a rough country it can easily run away from a slow horse. Even on the prairie it requires a pretty good animal to catch them, and it took several hours' hard riding to overtake the three last mentioned. The most easterly point at which I noticed this species was on the headwaters of the Heart River, about thirty miles east of the Little Missouri.

SCIURIDAE

Red Squirrel, (*Sciurus hudsonius,* Pallas.)[9] Specimens of this squirrel collected in the Black Hills are in all respect similar to those from the Eastern States.

Flying Squirrel, (*? Pteromys alpinus,* Rich.)[10] A single *Pteromys,* believed to be of this species, was seen in the Black Hills.

Missouri Ground Squirrel, (*Tamias quadrivittatus.*)[11] This interesting little squirrel is common throughout all the country traversed by the expedition. Wherever there was timber or washed bad lands, there we heard the sharp note and saw the active form of this little burrower. It was especially numerous in the pine forests of the Black Hills and in the *Mauvaises Terres* along the Little Missouri; in which latter locality it, with the rock-wren and horned toad, was almost the only animal to be seen. This species was by no means shy, and seemed not at all to regard the near presence of an observer.

Richardson's Ground Squirrel, (*? Spermophilus richardsonii,* Cuv.)[12] A *Spermophile,* probably of this species, was seen near the headwaters of the Heart River, on our return march, but I was unable to secure any specimens.

Striped Prairie Squirrel, (*Spermophilus tridecem-lineatus,* Aud. & Bach.)[13] This squirrel was found in large numbers on the plains, but was not seen after crossing the Belle Fourche, until we left the Black Hills on our return march.

Prairie Dog, (*Cynomys ludovicianus,* Baird.) Abundant everywhere on the plains.

Western Woodchuck, (*Arctomys flaviventer,* Bach.)[14] A single specimen was killed in the Hills.

Beaver, (*Castor canadensis,* Kuhl.)[15] This species was common on all the large streams which we crossed on our way to the Black Hills, in many places having by means of their dams retained a plentiful supply of water when the creek both above and below was dry. They were also numerous in the Hills, as their dams and houses in many of the streams bore witness.

SACCOMYIDAE[16]

Pouched Gopher, (*Geomys bursarius,* Rich.)[17] One specimen observed on the headwaters of Heart River.

Fort Union Gopher, (*Thomomys rufescens,* Maxim.)[18] This species was seen on Heart River, near Fort Lincoln; a miner caught one in his naked hand. It was very gentle, and made no attempt at resistance.

Muskrat, (*Fiber zibethicus,* Cuv.) The muskrat is very abundant on all flowing streams in that part of Dakota which we traversed, and still more so farther to the north. Especially is this true of the Mouse River, where, as I am informed, these animals may be seen swimming about by hundreds in the spring when the river has overflowed its banks and forced them to leave their holes.

HYSTRICIDAE[19]

Yellow-haired Porcupine, (*Erithizon epixanthus,* Brandt.)[20] Several individuals of this species were captured on the headwaters of Heart River, and brought into the post alive.

LEPORIDAE

Jackass Rabbit, (*Lepus callotis,* Wagler.?)[21] Abundant on the plains. Several young ones were captured and brought in alive.

Sage Rabbit, (*Lepus artemisia,* Bach.)[22] Common near the Missouri River, and observed also on the Little Missouri.

CERVIDAE

Elk; Wapiti, (*Cervus canadensis, Erxleben.*) Although but few elk were seen during the trip, we found in the Black Hills every indication of their recent presence in large numbers. During a single day's march eleven pairs of horns, attached to the skull, were picked up by members of the expedition. Horns that had been shed were very abundant, and it was by no means an unusual thing to see fifteen or twenty single antlers in a morning's ride.

On Elkhorn Prairie we came upon a collection of horns gathered together by the Indians. Three lodge-poles had been set up in the ground so as to form a tripod, and supported by these was a pile of horns 8 or 10 feet high. The horns had all been shed, and had apparently been collected from the surrounding prairie and heaped up here by the Indians. There is much variation in the horns of this species, most of which I imagine to be due to injuries to the horns while young and soft. Many of the specimens examined this summer were much flattened near the extremities, so much so in one or two cases as to be from 6 to 7 inches wide. In two instances the basal prong of the horn, instead of projecting forward and downward in the usual manner, turned outward and downward, and then, curving inward and up again, brought the point of the snag immediately under the animal's throat.

Virginia Deer; Red Deer, (*Cervus virginianus,* Boddaert.)[23] A few of these deer were seen near the Missouri River, and on the Cannon Ball. In the Black Hills, however, this species is replaced by the following.

White-tailed deer; Cotton-tail, (*Cervus leucurus,* Douglas.)[24] The difference in size between this and the preceding species is so great, that there exists even among hunters a very general opinion that the red deer of the mountains is different from the red deer of the Missouri River and the Eastern States. This species was very abundant in the Black Hills, and especially so in the vicinity of Castle Creek and Elkhorn Prairie. I imagine that near this point there are some salt "licks;" at least members of the Sioux hunting party which we encountered spoke of places where the deer "eat the ground," and said that they watched for them there. They were also very numerous about the head of Elk Creek, and, indeed, all through the northeastern portion of the hills. It was said that one hundred deer, principally of this species, were killed by the command August 9.

Mule Deer, (*Cervus macrotis,* Say.)[25] This deer was observed in considerable numbers in the Black Hills, in the neighborhood of Elkhorn Prairie, but they were by no means so abundant there as in the rough, broken country through which we passed just before reaching the Hills.

Near our first crossing of the Belle Fourche, and for a day or two while we were skirting the Hills, this was the only species seen. In the *Mauvaises Terres* of the Little Missouri, and on the headwaters of the Heart River, they were quite numerous. We saw but few bucks during the trip, most of the individuals noticed being does, and each one followed by two pretty little fawns.

CAVICORNIA[26]

Prong-horned Antelope, (*Antilocapra americana,* Ord.) Until within a short time, antelope were very common about Fort Lincoln, but the Arickaree Indians that are now maintained at that post as scouts have hunted them so persistently that the few that still remain in the vicinity are exceedingly wild, and one may ride ten or fifteen miles from the fort without seeing more than five or six. As we proceed, however, the antelope become more numerous, until finally there is no hour of the day when they are not to be seen either running gracefully off over the prairie or curiously watching the command from the top of some distant bluff.

The antelope is regarded by hunters as the most difficult to kill of any animal found on the prairie or in the mountains. In proportion to its size, it is more tenacious of life than the grizzly bear, and from its astonishing speed it is often enabled to escape even after having received a wound that would have brought a deer or an elk immediately to the ground. A specimen, shot by Charles Reynolds, had one fore leg broken at the knee and one hind leg broken just below the knee. Notwithstanding these wounds, it ran much faster than a horse could gallop for over two miles and a half, when, becoming exhausted, it lay down and awaited the approach of the hunter, who gave it the *coup de grâce.* I have seen several specimens wounded in such a manner that their entrails dragged along the ground as they ran, but even under such conditions they can outstrip a horse, until exhausted by loss of blood.

Bighorn; Mountain Sheep, (*Ovis montana,* Cuv.)[27] A female of this species was seen near the Little Missouri August 23. The first "signs" seen were at Short Pine Buttes, near the Little Missouri, and all along this stream they seemed to be very numerous. So wary were they, however, that it was impossible under the circumstances to secure any specimens.

Buffalo, (*Bos americanus,* Gmelin.)[28] No buffalo were seen during the trip, nor do I know that any exist at present in the region traversed; but one or two circumstances lead me to infer that there may still be found a few individuals in this section of the country.

In Prospect Valley I found the skull of an old bull, with part of the hide still clinging to it. Also, on French Creek, not far from the Big Cheyenne, I noticed the lower jaw of a cow, with the priosteum still on it.

It is but a few years since the country through which we passed was the favorite feeding-ground of the buffalo, and their white skulls dot the prairie in all directions. Sometimes these are collected by the Indians, and arranged on the ground in fantastic patterns. In one of these collections which I noticed, the skulls had been painted red and blue in stripes and circles, and were arranged in five parallel rows of twelve each, all the skulls facing the east.

NOTES TO CHAPTER 28

1. In Grinnell's report each family, scientific, and common name is shown in a separate heading. To make the typography conform to modern usage I am retaining the name of the family, only, as a heading, and running the other names into the text. I am also putting the common name first, followed by the scientific name in parentheses. These changes are merely typographical; the names and spellings used by Grinnell are retained in all cases.

However, many scientific names of mammals have been changed since Grinnell wrote his report. In the following notes I am showing the changes which I think should be made to bring these names up to date. I am not a zoologist and these notes should not be considered authoritative.

2. Now classified *Canis lupus*.

3. The genus appears to be correct, but I am unable to verify either the common name or species as given here.

4. See note 21.

5. The genus would now be *Mustela*. I am not certain of the species.

6. Now *Mustela vison*.

7. Usually written *Mephitis mephitis*.

8. Now *Taxidea taxus*.

9. Perhaps the eastern red squirrel, *Tamiasciurus hudsonicus*, but from the habitat I would guess it was Richardson's red squirrel, *Tamiasciurus hudsonicus richardsonii*.

10. If Richardson's flying squirrel it would now be *Glaucomys sabrinus alpinus*.

11. The description and habitat lead me to believe this animal would now be called Say's chipmunk, *Eutamias quadrivittatus*.

12. Richardson's ground squirrel is now called *Citellus richardsonii*.

13. The thirteen-striped ground squirrel is now called *Citellus tridecemlineatus*.

14. The woodchuck "of eastern North America" is now called *Arctomys monax*. Probably Grinnell's "western" woodchuck would now be called a marmot.

15. Now included in the family *Castoridae*.

16. The pouched or pocket gophers, genus *Geomys* or *Thomomys*, now comprise the family *Geomyidae;* and the muskrat is included in the rat and mice family, or *Muridae*.

17. In Ford's *Audubon's Animals*, this animal is called the Shaw Pocket gopher.

18. I am unable to identify this species.

19. Now *Erethizontidae*.

20. Probably now called the Canada porcupine, *Erethizon dorsatum.*

21. Several species of American hares were called jackass rabbits; the name has been shortened to jack rabbit. The jack rabbit that I used to hunt in South Dakota was classified *Lepus campestris,* I think, and also called the prairie hare. From memory I am unable to distinguish it from the white-tailed jack rabbit or prairie hare illustrated in Ford's *Audubon's Animals,* Plate 67, and there classified as *Lepus townsendii.* I believe Grinnell was incorrect in the classification, *Lepus callotis,* as I think that species does not range so far north.

22. In Appendix I to Culbertson's "Journal of an Expedition to the Mauvaises Terres and the Upper Missouri in 1850," is a list of birds and mammals found on the Missouri River by Edward Harris, who accompanied Audubon to Fort Union in 1843. Among the mammals listed is *Lepus artemisia,* Bach., which is called the wormwood hare. I am not able to locate any further reference to the species. The *Lepus* would indicate it is a hare, and not a rabbit.

23. The Virginia deer, red deer, or white-tailed deer is now usually called *Odocoileus virginianus,* but sometimes *Dama virginianus.*

24. I am unable to verify the species. Perhaps this was a smaller type of *O. virginianus.*

25. Now *Odocoileus hemonius,* (or *Dama hemonius*).

26. The prong-horn antelope is now the one species included in the family *Antilocapridae.* The bighorn and buffalo are included in the family *Bovidae.*

27. Now *Ovis canadensis.*

28. Now *Bison bison.*

Chapter 29

1874

THE INTERIOR OF THE BLACK HILLS,

by Lieutenant Colonel George Armstrong Custer

George Armstrong Custer was born in Ohio December 5, 1839. He was killed in the battle of the Little Big Horn June 25, 1876.

Custer graduated from the Military Academy at West Point in 1861. In the Civil War he became a major general of volunteers and was awarded six brevets for gallant and meritorious service. In March, 1866, he was mustered out of volunteer service, with the regular rank of captain in the Fifth Cavalry. In July the Seventh Regiment of Cavalry was organized, and Custer was placed in command with the rank of lieutenant colonel. He commanded the regiment at the battle of the Washita, November 27, 1868, severely defeating Black Kettle's band of Cheyenne Indians.

In March, 1873, the Seventh Cavalry was ordered to Dakota Territory, where it was quartered mainly at Fort Rice, and, later, at Fort Abraham Lincoln, on the right bank of the Missouri near Bismarck. During that summer the Seventh operated as an element of Colonel D. S. Stanley's forces, engaged in escorting a surveying party exploring the proposed right of way of the Northern Pacific Railroad west of the Missouri. The command reached the Yellowstone River and Custer enjoyed some brief skirmishes with bands of Teton Sioux Indians.

In 1874 the Seventh Cavalry was chosen to explore the Black Hills, with Custer commanding the expedition. His "Report of the Expedition to the Black Hills," consisting of letters dated August 2 and August 15, 1874, was published as a Senate Document in 1875. I am reprinting the two letters in the following chapter.

[Telegram]

HEADQUARTERS BLACK HILLS EXPEDITION,
EIGHT AND A HALF MILES SOUTHEAST OF HARNEY'S PEAK, AUGUST 2, *(VIA FORT LARAMIE, WYO.*, 8, 1874)

ASSISTANT ADJUTANT-GENERAL
Department of Dakota, Saint Paul, Minn.:

My last dispatch was dated July 15, and sent from Prospect Valley, Dakota, longitude 103 degrees and 46 minutes, latitude

45 degrees and 29 minutes. Two of my Indian scouts left as bearers of the dispatch as soon as their departures could be concealed by the darkness. After leaving that point this expedition moved in a southwesterly direction until it reached the valley of the Little Missouri River, up which we moved twenty-one miles. Finding this valley almost destitute of grazing along our line of march, I ordered the water kegs filled and a supply of wood placed in the wagons, and left the valley in search of a better camp-ground. During our passage up the valley of the Little Missouri we had entered and were about to leave the Territory of Montana. Our course was nearly due south.

After further march of about nine miles, we arrived before sundown at a point capable of furnishing us good grazing and water for our animals, having marched over thirty miles since breaking camp in the morning. From this point to the valley of the Belle Fourche we found the country generally barren and uninviting, save in a few isolated places. We reached the Belle Fourche on the evening of the 18th of July, encamping where good grass, wood, and water were abundant, and at a point a short distance above that marked fifteen (15) on Raynolds's map, just west of the line separating Dakota from Wyoming. The following day was spent in camp.

On the 20th we crossed the Belle Fourche and began, as it were, skirmishing with the Black Hills. We began by feeling our way carefully along the outlying ranges of hills, seeking a weak point through which we might take our way to the interior. We continued from the time we ascended from the valley of the Belle Fourche to move through a very superior country, covered with the best of grazing and abundance of timber, principally pine, poplar, and several varieties of oak. As we advanced, the country skirting the Black Hills to the southward became each day more beautiful. On the evening of the 22d we halted and encamped east of and within four miles of the Cave Inyan Kara.[1]

Desiring to aside [ascend?] that peak the following day, it being the highest on the western range of the Black Hills, I did not move camp the following day, but, taking a small party with me, proceeded to the highest point of this prominent landmark, whose height is given as 6,600 feet. The day was not favorable for obtaining distant views, but I decided on the following morning to move due east and attempt the passage of the hills. We experienced considerable delay from fallen timber which lay in our pathway. With this exception, and a very little digging, rendered necessary in descending into a valley, the pioneers prepared the way for the train, and we reached camp by 2 o'clock, having marched eleven miles. We here found grass, water, and wood of the best quality, and in great abundance. On the following day we resumed our march up this valley, which I had explored the preceding evening, and which led us by an easy ascent almost southeast.

After marching nearly twelve miles, we encamped at an early hour in the same valley. This valley, in one respect, presented the most wonderful as well as beautiful aspect. Its equal I have never seen; and such, too, was the testimony of all who beheld it. In no private or public park have I ever seen such a profuse display of flowers. Every step of our march that day was amid flowers of the most exquisite colors and perfume. So luxuriant in growth were they that men plucked them without dismounting from the saddle. Some belonged to new or unclassified species. It was a strange sight to glance back at the advancing columns of cavalry, and behold the men with beautiful bouquets in their hands, while the head-gear of the horses was decorated with wreaths of flowers fit to crown a queen of May. Deeming it a most fitting appellation, I named this Floral Valley.

General Forsyth,[2] at one of our halting-places, plucked seventeen beautiful flowers, belonging to different varieties, and within a space of twenty feet square. The same evening, while seated at the mess-table, one of the officers called attention to the carpet of flowers strewn under our feet, and it was suggested that it be determined how many different flowers could be plucked without leaving our seat at dinner-table. Seven beautiful varieties were thus gathered. Professor Donaldson, the botanist of the expedition, estimated the number of flowers in bloom in Floral Valley at fifty, while an equal number of varieties had bloomed, or were yet to bloom. The number of trees, shrubs, and grasses was estimated at twenty-five, making the total flora of the valley embrace one hundred and twenty-five species.

Through this beautiful valley meanders a stream of crystal water so cold as to render ice undesirable even at noonday. The temperature of two of the many springs found flowing into it was taken, and ascertained to be forty-four and forty-four and one-half degrees, respectively.

The next morning, although loath to leave so enchanting a locality, we continued to ascend this valley until gradually, almost imperceptibly, we discovered that we were on the crest of the western ridge of the Black Hills, and instead of being among barren peaks, as might be supposed, we found ourselves wending our way through a little park, whose natural beauty may well bear comparison with the loveliest portions of Central Park. Favored as we had been in having Floral Valley for our roadway to the crest of the Black Hills, we were scarcely less fortunate in the valley which seemed to rise to meet us in the interior slope. The rippling stream of clear, cold water, the counterpart of that we had ascended the day before, flowed at our feet and pointed out the way before us, while along its banks grew beautiful flowers, surpassed but little in beauty and profusion by their sisters who had greeted us the day before.

After advancing down this valley about fourteen miles, our course being almost southeast, we encamped in the midst of grazing whose only fault, if any, was the great luxuriance. Having preceded the main column, as usual, with an escort of two companies of cavalry (E and C) and Lieutenant Wallace's detachment of scouts, I came upon an Indian camp-fire still burning, and which, with other indications, showed that a small party of Indians had encamped there the previous night, and had evidently left that morning in ignorance of our close proximity.

Believing they would not move far, and that a collision might take place at any time unless a friendly understanding was arrived at, I sent my head scout, "Bloody Knife," and twenty of his braves to advance a few miles and reconnoiter the valley. This party had been gone but a few minutes when two of Bloody Knife's young men came galloping back and informed me that they had discovered five Indian lodges a few miles down the valley, and that Bloody Knife, as directed, had concealed his party in a wooded ravine where they awaited further orders. Taking a company with me, which was afterwards reinforced by the remainder of the scouts, and Colonel Hart's company, I proceeded to the ravine where Bloody Knife and his party lay concealed and from the crest beyond obtained a full view of the five Indian lodges, about which a considerable number of ponies were grazing. I was enabled to place my command still nearer to the lodges undiscovered. I then dispatched a guard, the interpreter, with a flag of truce, accompanied by two of our Sioux scouts, to acquaint the occupants of the lodge that we were friendly disposed and desired to communicate with them. To prevent either treachery or flight on their part, I galloped the remaining portion of my advance and surrounded the lodges.

This was accomplished almost before they were aware of our presence.

I then entered the little village and shook hands with the occupants, assuring them, through the interpreter, that they had no cause to fear, as we were not there to molest them. I invited them to visit our camp, and promised presents of flour, sugar, and coffee to all who would accept. This invitation was accepted.

At the same time, I entered into an agreement with the leading men they should encamp with us a few days and give us such information concerning the country as we might desire, in return for which service, I was to reward them with rations. With this understanding, I left them.

The entire party numbered twenty-seven. Later in the afternoon, four of the men, including the chief, "One Stab," visited our camp and desired the promised rations, saying their entire party would move up and join us the following morning, as agreed upon. I ordered presents of sugar, coffee, and bacon to be given them, and to relieve them of their pretended anxiety for the safety of their village during the night, I ordered a party of fifteen of my command to return with them and protect them during the night. But from their great disinclination to wait a few minutes, till the party could saddle up, and from the fact that two of the four had already slipped away, I was of the opinion that they were not acting in good faith. In this I was confirmed when the two remaining ones set off at a gallop in the direction of their village. I sent a party of our scouts to overtake them and request them to return.

Not complying with this request, I sent a second party, with orders to repeat the request, and if not complied with, to take hold of the bridles of their ponies and lead them back, but to offer no violence. When overtaken by our scouts, one of the two Indians siezed the musket of one of the scouts and endeavored to wrest it from him. Failing in this he released his hold, after the scout became dismounted in the struggle, and set off as fast as his pony could carry him, but not before the musket of the scout was discharged. From blood discovered afterward, it was very evident that either the Indian or his pony was wounded. I hope that neither was seriously hurt, although the Indians have their own bad faith as the sole ground for the collision.

"One Stab," the chief, was brought back to camp. The scouts galloped down the valley to the site of the village, when it was discovered that the entire party had packed up their lodges and fled, and the visit of the four Indians to our camp was not only to obtain their rations promised them in return for future services, but to cover the flight of the lodges.

I have effected arrangements by which the chief One Stab will be with us as guide three days longer, when he will take his departure and rejoin his band. He claims to belong to both Red Cloud's and Spotted Tail's agencies, but has been to neither for a long time. He has recently returned from the hostile camp on Powder River, and represents that the Indians lost 10 killed, in their fights with the Bozeman exploring party.[3]

The creek which led us down into the interior of the Black Hills is bordered by high bluffs, on the crests of which are located prominent walls of solid rock, presenting here and there the appearance of castles constructed of masonry. From their marked resemblance, I named this stream Castle Creek.[4]

The direction of Castle Creek having commenced to lead us more to the northeast than we were prepared to go, and the valley having become narrow and broken, I left this water-course and ascended the valley of a small tributary, which again gave us a southeasterly course. After a march of fourteen miles, encamped on a small creek furnishing us an abundance of water and grass. The direction of this creek was nearly east. On the 30th, moved in the continuation of our previous course, and through a fine open country covered with excellent grazing. After a march of over ten miles, we encamped early in the day about five miles from the western base of Harney's Peak—finding water and grass and wood abundant, with springs of clear cold water running through camp. On the following day the command remained in camp, except the exploring parties sent out in all directions.

With a small party I proceeded to Harney's Peak, and after great difficulty made the ascent to its crest. We found this to be the highest point in the Black Hills. From the highest point we obtained a view of Bear Butte, in the north part of plains to the east far beyond the Cheyenne River. Our party did not reach camp till near 1 o'clock that night, but we were amply repaid for our labor by the magnificance of the views obtained. While on the highest point, we drank the health of the veteran out of compliment to whom the peak was named. On the 1st of August we moved camp a few miles, simply to obtain fresh grass, still keeping near the base of the hills to the east of us.[5]

This a. m. I dispatched two companies, under Colonel Hart, in a southeasterly direction, to extend our explorations with the South Fork of the Cheyenne River. To-morrow morning at 5 o'clock I will set out with five companies of cavalry and endeavor to reach the same stream in a southwestern direction from Harney's Peak. Reynolds, the scout who is to carry this dispatch to Fort Laramie, will go with us as far as we go in that direction, when he sets out alone to reach his destination, traveling mainly by night.[6]

The country through which we have passed since leaving the Belle Fourche River has been generally open and extremely fertile. The main portion of that passed over since entering the unexplored portion of the Black Hills consists of beautiful peaks and valleys, through which flows a stream of clear, cold water, perfectly free from alkali, while bounding these parks or valley is invariably found unlimited supplies of timber, much of it capable of being made into good lumber. In no portion of the United States, not excepting the famous blue-grass region of Kentucky, have I ever seen grazing superior to that found growing wild in this hitherto unknown region. I know of no portion of our country where nature has done so much to prepare homes for husbandmen, and left so little for the latter to do, as here. The open and timbered spaces are so divided that a partly prepared farm of almost any dimensions, of an acre and upward, can be found here. Not only is the land cleared and timbered, both for fuel and building, conveniently located, with streams of fine water flowing through its length and breadth, but nature ofttimes seems to have gone further and placed beautiful shrubbery and evergreens in the most desirable locations for building-sites, while on Harney's Peak I could contrast the bright-green verdure of these lovely parks with the sunburned and dried yellow herbage to be seen on the outer plains.

Everything indicates an abundance of moisture within the space inclosed by the Black Hills. The soil is that of a rich garden, and composed of a dark mold of exceedingly fine grain. We have found the country in many places covered with wild raspberries, both the black and red varieties. Yesterday and today I have feasted on the latter. It is no unusual sight to see hundreds of soldiers gathering wild berries. Nowhere in the states have I tasted cultivated raspberries of equal flavor to those found growing wild here, nor have I ever seen them as large or in as great profusion as I have seen hundreds of acres of them here. Wild strawberries, wild currants, gooseberries, two varieties of pure berries, and wild cherries are also found in great profusion and of exceedingly pure quality. Cattle could winter in these valleys without other food or shelter than that to be obtained from running at large.

As there are scientists accompanying the expedition who are examining into the mineral resources of this region, the result of whose researches will accompany my detailed report, I omit all present reference to that portion of our explorations until the return of the expedition, except to state, what will appear in any event in the public prints, that gold has been found at several places, and it is the belief of those who are giving their attention to this subject that it will be found in paying quantities. I have upon my table forty or fifty particles of pure gold, in size averaging that of a small pin-head, and most of it obtained to-day from one panful of earth. As we have never remained longer at one camp than one day, it will be readily understood that there is no opportunity to make a satisfactory examination in regard to deposits of valuable minerals. Veins of lead and strong indications of the existence of silver have been found. Until further examination is made regarding the richness of the gold, no opinion should be formed.[7]

Veins of what the geologists term gold-bearing quartz crop out on almost every hillside. All existing geological or geographical maps of this region have been found incorrect. This will not seem surprising when it is remembered that both have been compiled by guess-work and without entering the country attempted to be represented. The health of the expedition continues excellent. I will begin my northward march in four days from this date. I do not expect to arrive at Fort Lincoln until the 31st of August.

G. A. CUSTER
Bvt. Maj. Gen. U. S. A.,
Commanding Expedition.

Postscript, 10:30 p. m., August 3,—I left our main camp near Harney's Peak at 6 o'clock this morning with five companies of cavalry, and, after a march in a southerly direction of forty-five miles, reached the south fork of Cheyenne River, at the mouth of a creek flowing from the north and emptying into the Cheyenne midway between the mouths of Hot and Horsehead Creeks. From this point Reynolds, the scout sets out in one hour with this dispatch for Fort Laramie. I reached here at 9 p.m., and will proceed to Harney's Peak by a different route tomorrow morning. The country between here and Harney's Peak is generally open and rolling, and, excepting the southeastern portion, covered with excellent grass.

G. A. CUSTER,
Brevet Major-General,
Commanding.

HEADQUARTERS BLACK HILLS EXPEDITION,
BEAR BUTTE, DAK., AUGUST 15, (via Bismarck)

My last dispatch was written on the 2nd and 3d instant, and sent from the south fork of the Cheyenne, from a point on the latter nearest to Fort Laramie. On the morning of the 4th instant I began my return march to our main camp, near Harney's Peak, arriving there by a different route on the 6th. On the morning of the 7th the expedition began its march northward, Bear Butte being our next objective point. We advanced without serious obstacle until within ten or twelve miles of Bear Butte, when we found our further progress barred by a high range of impassable hills. We attempted to effect a passage through some one of the many valleys whose water-courses ran directly through the hills in the desired direction, but in every instance we were led into deep, broken cañons, impassable even to horsemen.

Through one of these I made my way on foot, and from a high point near its mouth obtained a view of the plains outside. Retracing my steps, I placed the command in camp in a fine valley, in which it had halted, and devoted the remainder of the day to a further search for a practicable route through the hills. The result decided me to follow down a water-course, which led us first toward the south and afterward toward the east. This stream proved to be Elk Creek, the valley of which, as well as the stream itself, proved to be at least equal in beauty and extent to any passed through during our march. We camped twice on this stream, and as far as we proceeded down its course we had a most excellent road; but finding that, like nearly all other streams leaving the hills, its course would take us into a cañon which could be barely made practicable for our wagons, I searched for and discovered a narrow gap in the rocky wall which forms the northern boundary of the valley, and which was conveniently large to allow our wagons to pass through. A march of an hour up a gradual ascent, and through a pine forest, brought us to a beautiful park containing thousands of acres, and from which we obtained a fine view, in the distance, of our old acquaintance—the plains.

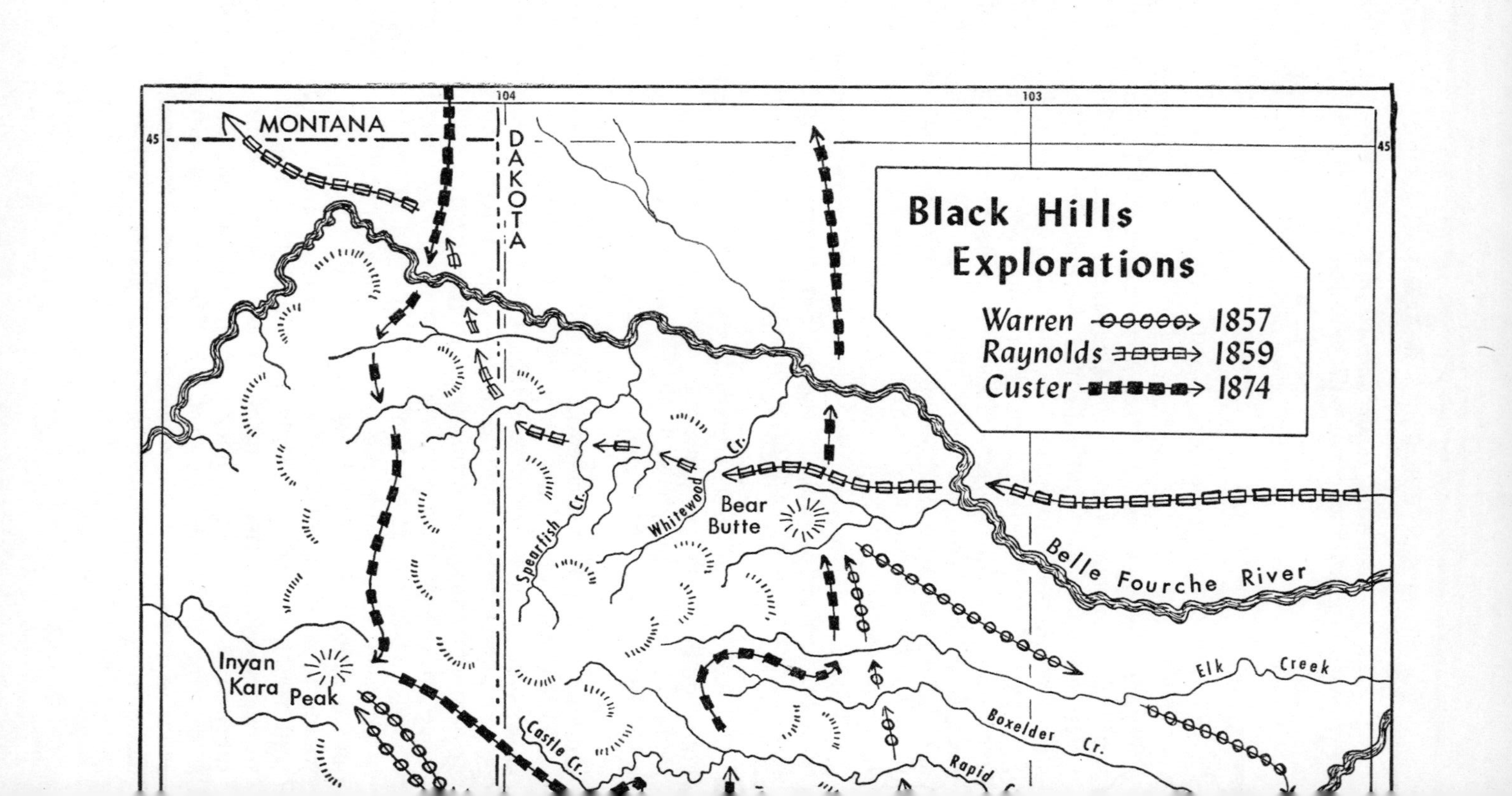
Black Hills Explorations
Warren 1857
Raynolds 1859
Custer 1874
MONTANA
DAKOTA
45
104
103
45
Belle Fourche River
Elk Creek
Boxelder Cr.
Rapid
Bear Butte
Whitewood Cr.
Spearfish Cr.
Castle Cr.
Inyan Kara Peak

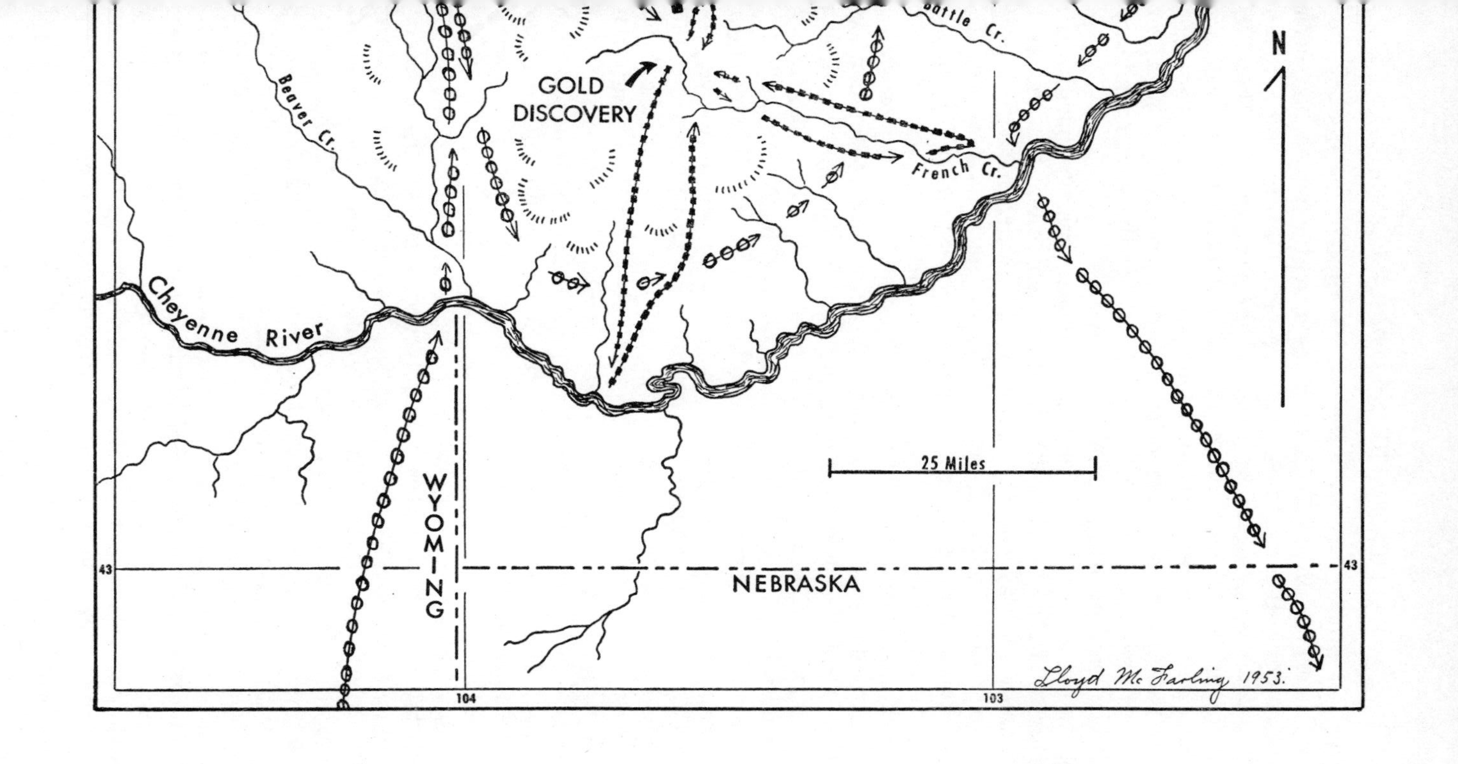
N
GOLD DISCOVERY
Beaver Cr.
French Cr.
Cheyenne River
WYOMING
NEBRASKA
25 Miles
43
104
103
Lloyd McFarling 1953.

Here we pitched our tents for the last time in the Black Hills; nearly everyone being loath to leave a region which had been found so delightful in almost every respect. Behind us the grass and foliage were clothed in green of the freshness of May. In front of us, as we cast our eyes over the plain below, we saw nothing but a comparatively parched, dried surface, the sunburnt pasturage of which offered a most uninviting prospect both to horse and rider, when remembering the rich abundance we were leaving behind us.

A march of twenty-six miles, gradually bearing northward, brought us to the base of Bear Butte, at which point I concluded to remain one day before beginning our return march. I propose to return by a different, although perhaps not shorter, route than that adopted in coming to the Black Hills. I am induced to make this change in order to embrace a larger extent of unexplored country within the limits of our explorations, and particularly to locate as much as possible of that portion of the Little Missouri of which nothing is now known. I expect the expedition to reach Fort Lincoln on the 31st of August. The health of the command has been, and is, most excellent.

This expedition entered the Black Hills from the west side, penetrated though the eastern and most southern ranges, explored the major portions of the interior, and passed out the most eastern ranges which form the boundary of the Black Hills. From the fact that in all our principal marches through the Black Hills we have taken, without serious obstacle, a heavily-laden train of over one hundred wagons, it may be inferred that the Black Hills do not constitute the impenetrable region heretofore represented.

In entering the Black Hills from any direction, the most serious, if not the only obstacles, were encountered at once, near the outer base. This probably accounts for the mystery which has so long existed regarding the character of the interior. Exploring parties have contented themselves with marching around the exterior base, and, from the forbidding aspect of the hills as viewed at a distance, inferred that an advance toward the interior would only encounter increased obstacles.

In regard to the character of the country inclosed by the Black Hills, I can only repeat what I have stated in previous dispatches.

No portion of the United States can boast of a richer or better pasturage, purer water, the natural temperature of which in mid-summer, as it flows from the earth, is but twelve degrees above the freezing-point, and of greater advantages generally to the farmer or stock raiser than are to be found in the Black Hills. Building stone of the best quality is to be found in inexhaustible quantities. Wood for fuel and lumber sufficient for all time to come. Rains are frequent, with no evidence in the country of either drought or freshets. The season, perhaps, is too short and the nights too cool for corn, but I believe all other grains could be produced here in wonderful abundance. Wheat would particularly yield largely.

There is no doubt as to the existence of various minerals throughout the hills, as this subject has received especial attention of experts who accompany the expedition, and will be reported upon in detail. I will only mention the fact that iron and plumbago have been found, and beds of gypsum of apparently inexhaustible extent.

I referred in a former dispatch to the discovery of gold. Subsequent examination at numerous points confirm and strengthen the fact of the existence of gold in the Black Hills. On some of the water-courses almost every panful of earth produced gold in small, yet paying, quantities. Our brief halts and rapid marching prevented anything but a very hasty examination of the country in this respect; but in one place, and the only one within my knowledge where so great a depth was reached, a hole was dug eight (8) feet in depth. The miners report that they found gold among the roots of the grass, and, from that point to the lowest point reached, gold was found in paying quantities. It has not required an expert to find gold in the Black Hills, as men without former experience in mining have discovered it at an expense of but little time or labor.

As an evidence of the rich pasturage to be found in this region, I can state the fact that my beef-herd after marching upward of six hundred (600) miles, is in better condition than when I started, being now as fat as is consistent with marching condition. The same may be said of the mules of the wagon-train. The horses of the command are in good working-condition. I have never seen as many deer as in the Black Hills. Elk and bear have also been killed. We have had no collision with hostile Indians.

G. A. Custer
Brevet Major-General,
Commanding Expedition.

To Assistant Adjutant General
Department of Dakota, St. Paul.

NOTES TO CHAPTER 29

1. This was near Inyan Kara Peak. Perhaps the "cave" was a typographical error.

2. Major (Brevet Brigadier General) George A. Forsyth, author of *The Story of the Soldier*, accompanied the expedition on orders from General P. H. Sheridan, commanding the Division of the Missouri. Merington's *The Custer Story* quotes a letter from Sheridan to Forsyth instructing him to embody in a daily diary a detailed description of the country passed over. So far as I know, no such report by Forsyth has ever been published.

3. The "Yellowstone Wagon-road and Prospecting Expedition" was an organization of Montana Territory frontiersmen which assembled near Bozeman, Montana Territory, February 12, 1874, for the purpose of prospecting for gold and silver in the Yellowstone Valley, and for the further purpose of surveying a wagon road from the Montana settlements to the assumed head of navigation on the Yellowstone River, and to the proposed route of the Northern Pacific Railroad. There were about 147 men. They had twenty-two wagons, more than two hundred horses and mules, two pieces of artillery, a plentiful supply of small arms and ammunition, and provisions for four months.

The expedition traveled eastward north of the Yellowstone to Big Porcupine Creek, crossed the Yellowstone, and worked south and west, crossing Rosebud Creek, the Little Bighorn, the Bighorn and other streams, returning to Bozeman by the old Bozeman Trail after about ninety days. They found some gold, but not in paying quantities.

Indian hostilities began March 26 and continued intermittently until April 18, with an estimated one thousand Indians opposed to the expedition at one time. One white man was killed and two wounded; seventeen horses were killed and twenty wounded. According to Addison M. Quivey, "The Yellowstone Expedition of 1874," in *Contributions to the Historical Collections of Montana*, Vol. I, nine Indians were killed and scalped by the whites, and many more were thought to have been killed or wounded.

4. Castle Creek flows into Rapid Creek about a mile below the town of Mystic, South Dakota. Ludlow erroneously thought the stream was a continuation of Elk Creek and so laid it down (provisionally, in dotted line) on his map.

5. These camps were on French Creek, near the present town of Custer, South Dakota.

6. Charles Reynolds was the principal white scout of the expedition. Sometimes called "Lonesome Charlie," he was named "The Lucky Man" by the Arikara Indians because of his skill in hunting. After delivering Custer's dispatch at Fort Laramie he returned to Fort Lincoln by railroad. He died fighting with Reno's detachment at the battle of the Little Big Horn, June 25, 1876.

7. With the expedition were two men described as "practical gold miners" —Horatio Nelson Ross and William McKay. The Federal Writers' Project, American Guide Series, *South Dakota* (1938 ed., p. 36), says these men discovered gold on August 2, 1874. But August 2 was the date of Custer's dispatch in which he first reported the discovery. We know from Winchell's journal in the Ludlow *Report* that the discovery was not later than July 30. The *New York Tribune* for August 10, 1874, as quoted by Hunt in *I Fought with Custer*, reported that gold was found by "one of the miners," about noon, on July 30. The credit for the discovery is usually given to Ross.

Chapter 30

1874

THE MULE AND HIS DRIVER,

by Samuel June Barrows

Samuel June Barrows was born in 1845 and died in 1909. Starting work at the age of nine he became an errand boy, a telegrapher, a stenographer, a newspaper reporter and correspondent, a Unitarian pastor, an editor, a reformer, and a congressman. While he was a student at the Harvard Divinity School he spent two summers on the Northern Plains as correspondent for the *New York Tribune.* He accompanied Stanley's expedition to the Yellowstone in 1873, and Custer's Black Hills expedition in 1874.

In May, 1875, the *Atlantic Monthly* published "The Northwestern Mule and His Driver." The subject seems to be one that a student of theology would normally avoid; yet Barrows did an excellent job of describing two species of plains fauna not otherwise adequately presented in science, literature, or history. I am reprinting about three fourths of the original article.

If there is any one animal that can be defined only by a simple proposition of identity, that animal is a mule. A mule is a mule. When you have said that, you have defined him, stigmatized him, and given the only full and accurate description of him.

* * * * *

To those familiar with the government mule, an apology may seem to be needed for any reference to this animal in plain, church-going English. In the Northwest the mule is a victim of a special vocabulary. It is rarely mentioned without an epithet. The reader, it is hoped, however, will recognize those considerations of space and propriety which forbid the writer from making this article a contribution to profane literature.

. . . . Mules are a necessary element in every military movement; and they are the only means of transportation from one government post to another, where railroads have not penetrated. In General Stanley's expedition to the Yellowstone River, which the writer accompanied as correspondent of the New York Tribune, two hundred and eighty of these wagons and sixteen hundred and eighty draft mules were required to carry forty days' supplies for a force of twelve hundred infantry and about six hundred cavalry. In the Black Hills expedition, one hundred and fifty wagons[1] and nine hundred mules were necessary to carry sixty days' supplies for a command numbering nine hundred men and six hundred horses. It is only on expeditions of this kind, when compelled to travel a thousand miles or more without a sight of a house or a white man, often over desert tracts of country with poor grass and little water, that the mule and the mule wain are appreciated, though it is always on such occasions that the animal is most abused. A wagon train is then a moving village containing everything which is necessary for the success of the expedition, which must be absolutely self-supporting. It is important to economize transportation: consequently the allowance of forage is reduced to the minimum. Three and a half pounds of corn a day was the limit for each animal on the Black Hills expedition. Had this amount been doubled only,—even then a small allowance,—it would have required thirty-seven more wagons and two hundred and twenty-two more mules to carry the additional forage. For work of this kind, under such conditions, horses would absolutely fail. The amount of fatigue, exposure, and abstinence which a mule will endure seems almost fabulous. Making long marches across dusty, shadeless plains, going for long intervals without water and with very little food, obliged to pull loads sometimes amounting to five thousand two hundred pounds up steep hills and through heavy sloughs, subject to cruel treatment and neglect from the teamster, the life of an expedition mule is miserable enough. No wonder that when the mule returns, he looks woefully angular and thin. The poor animal is frequently driven until he completely gives out, when he is thanklessly turned into the herd of broken-down mules. There is scarcely a more melancholy sight than such a herd. It is a moving bone-yard. Gaunt, lean, with drooping ears, hips that rise like promontories above the general desolation, a disconsolate tail, and a woe-begone visage which would frighten an inexperienced ghost,—the poor, bankrupt mule is the most wretched parody on Gothic architecture that was ever forced on the public attention. Every vestige of meat has fled from his bones. He is a walking transparency, an animated hat-rack, and I have actually seen his hip bones irreverently used to hang teamsters' hats on. During our homeward march from the Black Hills, more than one such starved victim laid down his tired frame on the earth which had refused to nourish him, and the benediction of a soldier's bullet called the raven and the coyote to a meal which it cost the government one hundred and forty dollars to provide. . . .[2]

The pack mule is a necessary supplement to the draft mule, and in mountainous and heavily timbered regions must often supersede him entirely. Mule packing is a fine art. With a well-trained mule and a well-trained packer, there is nothing imaginable, from a bag of oats to a load of crockery, that cannot be securely fastened on the mule's back. Select the worst article you can think of to test the packer's skill, and in an incredibly short space of time he will pack it as though he had been perfectly used to packing that very thing all the days of his life. When the packer has finished, the animal may jump, back, kick, rear, or roll, to rid himself of his burden, but with no more success than Christian had before he reached the cross. And yet you cannot find a knot in the whole complexity of rope and bundle. A pack-saddle, or in Mexico an *apparajo,* which is a willow frame covered with canvas and stuffed with hay, always intervenes between the pack and the mule's back, and a crupper and breast-strap with a strong girth keep the bundle in position.

* * * * *

The average load for a pack mule is from two hundred and seventy-five to three hundred pounds. The heaviest weight which a pack master confessed he had ever imposed on a mule was eight hundred pounds, a piece of machinery which could not be divided. From fifty to one hundred mules make a good-sized train, though three or four hundred sometimes follow the same trail in close succession. Low, snug-built, chunky, short-coupled animals are best for this work. The well-broken pack mule is proud of his burden. Should it by any means get loose, he quietly steps out of the line of procession and waits for a pack master to come and tighten it. The value of pack mules as an auxiliary to a wagon train was well shown on the Black Hills expedition. Packing our extra rations and forage on a few of these animals under charge of Mr. Wagner, our chief packer, we were enabled to make in three days a journey of a hundred miles over hills and mountains which would have embarrassed our train for two weeks.

The saddle mule in the West is also a frequent rival of the horse. For making long distances over the plains without forage he cannot be beaten unless by the Indian pony. A good saddle mule sometimes makes sixty or seventy-five miles a day without seeming to be much fatigued; and a trustworthy frontiersman assures me that he has known one to make one hundred miles between daylight and dark. But the saddle mule is not always reliable. If he takes it into his head to plant himself just where he is, he is very difficult to transplant. If he sues for a divorce, he usually contrives to get the law of gravity on his side.

The most eminent physical qualities of the mule are surefootedness, great strength, and remarkable toughness and vigor. . . .

The mule is certainly a hard animal to kill, especially if he makes up his mind that he will not die. On the mountainside, burdened with a heavy pack, his foothold is as firm and sure as the earth on which it rests; but when the earth gives way, as it sometimes does, pack and mule go rolling over and over down the steep hill or precipice; the animal may be killed, apparently, two or three times before he gets to the bottom, but he has generally lives enough left to secure him a good old age and a natural death. I have seen a wheel mule fall and become buried under a heavily loaded wagon so completely that not a hint of the animal was visible. Yet when the wagon and load were removed, the mule got up and grazed as though nothing had happened, and seemed to be the only party there that was not surprised. . . .

The mule is not the stupid animal he is represented to be. His powers of observation and memory are sometimes wonderful. Old teamsters say that a mule always knows a man who has fed him once. Take a train of two hundred and eighty army wagons all alike and when it gets into camp let the train be parked, and the mules unharnessed and driven off together a mile or two away from the train. When it is time to give them their corn, if the animals are herded back to the train, with a strange instinct every mule will go right to his own wagon. I have heard old teamsters say that a good mule is a great deal more teachable than a horse, more knowing, and more affectionate. But I know of no animal whose moral education is so much neglected. He is a victim of his associates. When thoroughly corrupted there is no wickedness to which he is not equal. His hypocrisy then greatly helps him to succeed. I have seen him when he looked the perfect picture of meekness and humility; when it seemed that even Moses himself must defer to him in these crowning virtues. Yet if Moses or any other patriarch had ventured to approach him without a tribute of corn, the mule would have kicked him into the remotest antiquity. I have seen him deceive even a wagon master himself, pretending that he could not go a step farther, but the moment he was released from harness, bounding off as fresh and lively as a colt.

The depraved mule rejoices in his heart if he can make some one miserable. It is a trait for which in the West they have a specific term. They call it "pure cussedness." When a mule devotes his whole life to illustrating this idea, he finds a thousand opportunities and achieves a remarkable success. It is this instinct which prompts him to encourage the attention of his driver for a year or two, just for the sake of getting a good chance to kick his brains out. It is this which leads him to stand still when other people would be better pleased if he would go. It is this which often decides him when he really *does* start, to send his rider on ahead of him. Perhaps, too, it is this spirit that gives the mule his strange idea of justice, which seems to visit upon others the afflictions which he suffers himself. Thus it is said that if a bad lot of mules are in line, and you kick one of them violently, instead of retaliating on the one who kicked him he simply kicks the mule behind him. The second mule passes the kick to the third, he to the fourth, and so on till the primary vengeance has gone the whole length of the line, leaving the last mule unjustified. Perhaps it is only an illustration of the principle that misery loves company, since by this device the mule first kicked secures the sympathy of the whole line.

The mule has always been credited with a great deal of freedom of the will. This it must be that makes him dislike his rope and picket pin. If he can break the rope or pull up the pin, he finds a new opportunity. Then, not until he has defrauded some less fortunate mule out of his grass, or broken a rival's jaw, or pulled down two or three tents with his picket pin, does he go to bed happy.

The only personal objection I have to a mule is his neglect of camp courtesies, especially his passion for pulling down tents. He has a strange instinct, when self-freed, to consider that direction most convenient for him which is most inconvenient for everybody else. On the expedition our head-quarter tents were always ranged in a line, with a space, when camp was small, only large enough for a man to pass between them. Nearly every mule that pulled up his picket pin in our vicinity, though he might have a hundred miles of free, unobstructed prairie on the other side, determined to pass between these tents, dragging his long lariat and pin after him. No matter if the pin caught in one of our guy ropes or in a corner of the tent. He forgot the things that were behind and pressed forward to those that were before, leaving us to repair damages. Sometimes two mules tied to one rope would explore together. When this was the case both mules always tried to see which could get through the tent row first.

Sometimes the wanderer takes it into his head that he can sing. So long as he keeps this idea to himself nobody can complain. But a mule who has such a conceit is sure to publish it. One who never heard a mule solo can form no idea of the rare cacophony it involves. No musical gamut can score it; no voice can imitate it. Only a mule can describe it. It is one of the grossest outrages on the public peace ever devised. Happy for the hearer if the bray be confined to one mule; but when two or three hundred happen to meet together and some base prompter among them says, "Brethren, let us bray," the antiphonal response, which is never refused, is perfectly overwhelming. I remember one poor mule who lost his life because he would persistently exercise this gift in an Indian country, and so betray the command to the enemy. He was shot as a traitor and a nuisance.

* * * * *

But no characterization of the mule is complete without an adequate notice of the teamster. He is an intellectual and moral hybrid, almost as much of an enigma as the mule. It is hard to say which of the two, mule or teamster, exercises greater influence over the other, and it is hard to say in which direction the influence is better. General Zachary Taylor, who hated teamsters so that he could scarcely bear one in his sight, would no doubt decide in favor of the mule. As a class, teamsters are made up of that peculiar sort of drift-wood which the stream of civilization always leaves here and there along its borders. They are nearly all wanderers and adventurers. Many have served at mining, wooding, and boating, and take to teaming as a collateral pursuit. Many are farmers' sons who have left their homes deluded by the hope of high wages in the West. When their small stock of money is gone they are glad enough to engage as teamsters for thirty dollars a month. Indeed, when a man of any calling is thoroughly "broke" in the Northwest, he generally repairs to teaming to mend his fortunes. The variety of professions represented in this work of redemption is sometimes very strange. On the Yellowstone expedition we had two hundred and eighty teamsters. While the majority were men who could hardly be said to have ever had any settled occupation, there were not a few who had seen nobler walks of life. Store-keepers, school-teachers, clerks, doctors, lawyers, were sprinkled here and there in the motley array. A lawyer at Bismarck, a little frontier town on the Missouri, near our starting-point, having lost his only case the day before the departure of the expedition, despairing of his bread and butter for the rest of the summer, immediately engaged as a teamster. The son of a prominent clergyman in Washington was determined to go on this expedition. He applied for a position in the scientific department, but failing, disguised himself, went to the quartermaster's and signed the teamster's contract. In the Black Hills expedition many adventurers engaged, simply to see the new country. Among them was the son of a wealthy gentleman in the West, who was determined to go and could go in no other capacity. I have never personally known the clergy to be represented, but the fact that one of the teamsters was persistently called "Parson" showed a disposition to recognize the claims of the profession. The typical teamster, however, is one who is born and bred to his business.

The teamster's duties are simple but arduous. He drives his team on the march, and in camp sees that they are well cared for. The art of driving a six-mule team in the Eastern States is almost unknown. It is not a government of "gees" and "haws," nor a six-fold complication of reins. A single line from the driver to the mouth of the guide or left lead mule, called the line mule, is the only telegraph. A series of jerks on the line turns the obedient leader to the right, a continuous pull guides him to the left. A stick called a "jockey stick," fastened by a chain at one end to the collar of the line mule, and at the other to the bit of his companion leader, compels the latter to second the motions of his consort. The wheel team is under the immediate control of the driver, who rides on the back of the near mule, holding his line in his left hand, his cowhide whip (his black snake) hanging with a professional grace around his neck, ready for any emergency. The plain, unornamental part of the business is easy. It is only when he gets to a bad crossing, involving perhaps a steep descent, a heavy slough at the bottom, and a high and difficult "come-out" on the other side, that the teamster has a chance to display the resources and adornments of his profession. Going down-hill the teamster never swears at his mules; descending elocution is confined to the single word "wah-*oo*" uttered with a strong accent on the last syllable and in the teamster's most persuasive voice. None but a green hand ever thinks of saying "whoa." This is horse dialect, and mules have little respect for it. When the wagon has fairly got to the bottom and the mire has begun to swallow its wheels, then the teamster is transformed. Then it is that unshipping his whip and opening his battery of oaths he bombards his team with blows and objurgations until every ounce of their strength is put into the collar. Rising on his saddle he launches his ubiquitous whip at the off wheeler and the swing mules, pounds his saddle mule with his heels, and vents a peculiar, vivifying shriek at the distant ears of his leaders. The originality, picturesqueness, fluency, and irreverence of the teamster's exhortations to his mules under such circumstances baffles all decent description. No one has a full appreciation of the ultimate power and genius of eloquence until he has heard a teamster discourse from his nigh wheel mule. His profanity is generally shocking, but in its spirit it is more interjectional than blasphemous. The truth is his curses are only a vulgar *patois*. The mule understands it, and governs himself accordingly.

* * * * *

The devotion of some teamsters to their mules is as conspicuous as the neglect of others. I know one who cried like a child when a favorite team, which he had driven for years, was taken from him. The noisy, strenuous style of driving which belongs to the average teamster, and which the novice affects, it not without distinguished exceptions. Old "Buckskin Joe"—by the way, a generic name in the West—has driven forty-four years and has never broken a tongue or tipped over a wagon. Yet he seldom whips or curses a mule, and heartily despises the professional buncombe. "I don't see no use in so much beatin' and hollerin'," he would say; "I don't want none with my mules. When I tell 'em what's wantin', they allers pull every ounce that's in 'em; and a man can't ask no more."

Old Joe is quite a character in his way. He began to team when he was ten years old, and though now fifty-four, with his beard long and gray, he is still fond of the rough life. Six feet high, erect in form, with long hair falling nearly to his shoulders and a beard like the Elijah pictured in the Sunday-school books, you might take him for one of the later Scripture patriarchs, if his modern suit of buckskin and a hat which Noah might have worn at the flood did not present a contradiction in dates.

It is surprising what skill teamsters attain in driving with a single line. Old Joe could turn his wagon round within its own length, and did not grumble that a bridge was narrow if you gave him two or three inches on each side of the wheels. The facility with which the veteran distinguishes his mules is equally surprising to a novice. Weed out the few grays and duns and the mules in a fifteen hundred herd look very much alike. But an old teamster, when he has once driven a team, can tell them in the largest herd, if he sees them half a mile off. A novice whom I recall had less success. "How many of your mules have you got?" said an angry wagon master to him one morning, about half an hour after it was time to be harnessed. "All but *five,*" was the doleful reply.

The teamster's pastimes are simple, but not always innocent. Wherever there is a sutler, a large share of his time and earnings are spent at the bar. An indispensable part of his outfit is a pack of cards. His philosophy of life, his creed, his hopes and expectations for the future, are all implied in those fifty-two elements. No expedition goes out without three or four professionals, who engage as teamsters. On the Yellowstone expedition there were several who reaped a good harvest. The most successful, nicknamed "Governor Wise," took some three thousand dollars as the result of four months' work. One of his best "hauls," known only to a few, was made one night just after we had buried the one unfortunate teamster who was killed on the trip. The game lasted all night, and when the bugle sounded reveille, Wise had made fifteen hundred dollars. It is only professionals who can play such heavy games. The teamster's wages do not admit of large stakes; but he will stake all he has. Let a hundred teamsters be paid off, and in three or four days nearly the whole amount of money will be in the hands of three or four men. Many an expert gambler has graduated wealthy from a mule's back. At Fort Bridger an accomplished teamster made sixteen thousand dollars from his comrades in three months. There is a man in Leavenworth to-day worth fifty thousand dollars, who made it in the same way. But reverses are equally noticeable. A man at "Dobetown," Utah, owned property worth one hundred and seventy-five thousand dollars in gold. He lost it all in a single game of poker, and to keep from starving was obliged to take a black snake and drive a team side by side with the man who told me the story. "But," said old Martin, "it cured him of gambling."

NOTES TO CHAPTER 30

1. According to Ludlow (chap. 26, *ante*) the number was about 110.

2. In the fall of 1873 the Quartermaster General reported that the army had purchased 2,397 mules at an average cost of $137, and sold 200 for an average price of $47.56 during the year. It also sold 1,051 horses at an average price of $44.36. 424 horses and 489 mules died. One hundred and fifty-eight horses and 100 mules were stolen. At the close of the year 10,130 horses and 10,425 mules were in service. *Report of the Secretary of War*, 1873.

Chapter 31

1876

FROM FORT LARAMIE TO DEADWOOD,

by Leander P. Richardson

The discovery of gold in the Black Hills in 1874 has been called the most important event in the history of Dakota Territory. It was followed by an influx of prospectors, miners, adventurers, and settlers that began late in 1874, increased slowly in 1875, and developed into a major gold rush in 1876 and 1877. The gold discoveries were within the Sioux Reservation and the immigration was in violation of the treaty of 1868. During most of 1875 the army tried to keep the miners out of the reservation, but without much success. In the fall of 1875 the government held a council with the Sioux tribes and tried to buy the Black Hills, or mining rights therein, but the temper of the warlike factions of the Sioux made agreement impossible. In the spring of 1876 the Sioux War began.

In the late fall of 1875 gold was discovered in Deadwood Gulch, and by April, 1876, Deadwood City was the focal point of the gold rush. Trails to the Black Hills developed from Bismarck and Fort Pierre in Dakota Territory, from Sidney in the state of Nebraska, and from Cheyenne in Wyoming Territory.

On all the trails the danger of Indian attacks was always present; immigrants traveled armed and in groups. An attempt to establish a stage line from Cheyenne to the Black Hills was delayed several months by Indian depredations; and the miners and Indians were engaged in irregular warfare on the border of the Black Hills during nearly all of 1876.

Under these conditions Leander P. Richardson traveled from Cheyenne to the Black Hills near the end of July, 1876, and wrote an account of his trip which was published under the title "A Trip to the Black Hills" in *Scribner's Monthly Magazine* for April, 1877. I am reprinting the portion of the article which describes the travel from Fort Laramie to Deadwood.

It was on the morning of July 22d, 1876, that the party of eight men, of which I chanced to be a member, left Fort Laramie for the Black Hills.

Our vehicles consisted of what is commonly termed a "jerky," and a large freight wagon, each drawn by four horses. I believe the "jerky" derived its name from the peculiar, not to say sportive, manner in which it switched the driver from his seat whenever any rough road was passed. The prospect of riding three hundred miles on a springless wagon was not inviting; but it was much preferable to the other arrangement; so I chose my seat on the lumber wagon. Our course led up the Platte for several miles, through deep and heavy sand, and the sun poured down with greater fierceness than I had ever before known. To add to these discomforts—which we were assured formed but mild precursors of those still to be encountered—we were surrounded and harassed all the morning by innumerable sand-gnats, which darted into our eyes, crawled into our nostrils, buzzed in our ears, and wriggled down our necks in a most annoying fashion. About eleven o'clock, our wagons reached a ranch, known as the Government Farm, fifteen miles from Fort Laramie, where we indulged for the first time—for one of us at least—in a meal cooked by ourselves as amateurs. I don't think the dinner was a very decided success. Everything became covered with bacon-grease; I burned my fingers in a most unprofessional manner, and there was more dust in the food than I was accustomed to eating. This, however, ceased to be an annoyance after a while, and I grew to like anything that absorbed the flavor of bacon-fat. After two hours we got under way once more, and pushed on toward Rawhide Buttes, where we were gratified to learn that a long train was to encamp that night. We were anxious, for the sake of safety, to overtake this train before dark, but our speed was not so great as it might have been under more favorable circumstances. During the afternoon the country over which our road trailed its sinuous course grew rougher and more jagged,—the rolling plains of the earlier part of the day giving place to sharply outlined bluffs, and great mounds of yellow earth, sparsely covered with buffalo-grass and a stunted growth of oak. Our road was crossed at frequent intervals by deep and precipitous gulches. About three in the afternoon, the Buttes first came into sight, far off and blue against the distant horizon, and at dusk we saw, a mile or two in advance, the long train of canvas-covered wagons which marked our destination. They were on the summit of a commanding hill, drawn up in a circle, formed by driving each wagon close in after its predecessor, until the round yard or "corral" was complete. In traveling through dangerous regions, this is the usual mode of stopping at night,—selecting some high point for the camping-ground; the wall of wagons serving both as a barricade against the intrusion of foes and as a fence to prevent stampedes among the stock, which are always penned inside the circle during the night. When our somewhat jaded teams had overtaken the party in advance, we unharnessed the horses, and led them down the steep hill-side to an almost imperceptible creek for water and grass. Then followed the tedious and horrible mockery of supper. Two of us slept that night in the wagon, wrapped in blankets, while the rest occupied the more spacious bed afforded by Mother Earth.

Concerning the following day I quote from my note-book: "July 23d. Cold and damp. The horizon completely hemmed in by clouds, and a drizzling rain setting in. The party has eight colds, all told. Breakfast—a swindle. We started at four o'clock in the morning, traveling along the side of the Buttes until about ten, when Running Water was reached. Here we went through the one-act farce of dinner, and fed our horses; never animals needed it more! Two men who had up to the present time been following beside the coach, having overtaken us at Government Farm, turned back at this point, being afraid to go through with so small a party. We sha'n't miss them much, however, except at dinner-time, when it has been their habit to borrow our frying-pans and coffee-pots."

As the day advanced, the ascents and descents of the road became more and more precipitous, and indications of alkali were everywhere to be seen. The land on either side was dry and unpleasant to the eye, producing little besides sage-brush and cactus. About four o'clock we met six men in a huge freight-wagon, returning from the Hills. They proved to be gamblers going to Cheyenne to purchase a new equipment of implements for their business. One of them, a sharp-visaged, determined looking fellow, proved to be an old acquaintance of one of our party, who addressed him familiarly as "Bill." Exchanging news, we learned from them that a "bull-train" (by which is meant wagons drawn by many oxen), heavily freighted with flour and merchandise, was waiting at Hat Creek, ten miles further on, for an opportunity to get through. Concerning the prospects for gold in Deadwood and the adjacent region, they were reticent. Although they had come alone over that portion of the road most dreaded, they had seen no Indians, and seemed to attach so little importance to their safety that our hearts were greatly encouraged.

Proceeding slowly toward the summit of a precipitous bluff surmounted by towering rocks of a chalk-like formation, we saw, far off in the valley, a line of shrubbery, the rich green hue of which stood out in marked prominence against the gray of the surrounding country, denoting the banks of a stream which we reached an hour or so later, just as the storm we had been threatened with all the afternoon broke over us. The train of heavy "prairie schooners," as these lumbering freight-wagons are termed, was drawn up in corral, and the "bull-whackers" were at supper. They had been detained by accidents which had occurred to their teams, and were repairing everything into good shape before moving into the worst part of the Indian country, where delays might prove dangerous. Just across the creek was a soldiers' camp garrisoned by six men. The regular number kept at the Hat Creek camp is from forty to forty-five, but the majority of the soldiers were now away on a scouting expedition with General Merritt.[1] Close beside the camp is a building ordinarily known as "Johnny Bowman's Ranch." These ranches, which abound along the lines of all the stage and freight roads in this wilderness, form a peculiar phase of frontier life. They are hotels, bar-rooms and stores for general merchandise, all combined in one, and the whole business is usually transacted in a single room. In fact, but few of them can boast of more than one apartment. At any of these places a traveler can purchase almost anything, from a glass of whisky to a four-horse team, but the former article is usually the staple of demand. The proprietor of the Hat Creek ranch is known and highly esteemed from Cheyenne to the remotest parts of the Black Hills district.

In the evening, we held a council around the cheerful log-fire in the ranch. Hat Creek forms the boundary line between the "safe" country, and that which is infested with Indians. Some of our party were in favor of starting within an hour and going straight through to the Cheyenne River before stopping, and urged that the storm howling dismally out-of-doors would aid us materially in eluding any savages who chanced to be in the vicinity. I forgot to mention that at Running Water, where we had stopped for dinner, such a course had been decided upon, at the suggestion of one or two of the party, whose bravery at that time was extraordinary; but when it came to the moment for action, these men, in the terse and expressive language of a buckskin-clad spectator "went down into their boots." They refused point-blank to proceed until morning, and a final vote decided that the party should remain, and perhaps take up the line of march the next evening. Some of the "schooners" were offered us for lodging-rooms, but "Van" and I chose to remain during the night in the jerky. It proved to be an unwise choice, for at midnight the storm became extremely violent, and the rain which had soaked through the canvas dripped down upon us in great chilling drops. My companion finally rose and prowled around the camp until he found a wagon which was better sheltered, while I was left to the solitary enjoyment of our previous quarters. After daylight I fell into a doze, under the impression that by twisting and doubling myself into serpentine form, I had managed to evade the pools of water which had gathered at various places upon the blankets; but I awoke an hour or so later to find that they had all united so as to form a kind of lake, in which I was an island. That morning at breakfast the party was not a cheerful one, and the blind desperation which possessed all of us inspired the proposal to hitch up the horses and go ahead, Indians or no Indians. The proposition was sullenly assented to, and ten o'clock found us once more upon the road. The mud was thick and deep, and our progress was far from rapid. In about two hours, after passing through a number of deep and miry water-courses, our teams swung around under the shadow of a great overhanging bluff of yellow earth, and we found ourselves upon the banks of Indian Creek, which, our driver announced, was the most dangerous part of the whole journey. The bed of the creek is about two hundred yards in width, and the banks are steep and high. Sharply outlined mounds of earth rise at frequent intervals in the stream-bed, and form places of protection from which the murderous savages may fire upon their unsuspecting victims, without any risk of being killed or wounded themselves; moreover, the course of the creek is heavily timbered, so that it is almost impossible to distinguish forms a short distance away. The slight stream of water which passes down through the valley (I had almost said gorge) winds its sinuous way from one bank to another. The road follows its bed for two or three miles and the general course of the creek for about fifteen miles, gradually working toward higher ground. Through this valley the party marched, rifles in hand, and ready for an attack. The storm had settled into a regular driving rain from which no refuge could be found. The wind was very cold,—more chilling than some of the bleakest of New England air currents, and the discomforts of our situation were greatly increased. But the bad weather no doubt added to the security of our position, for, as my companion on the lumber-wagon, a greater portion of whose conversation was carried on in profane monosyllables, found time to say, "Any Injun who would venture out on such a day was a sight bigger fool than most of his race."

We were then in the midst of the region covered by alkali. In many cases the ground was white with it, and the pools of water, which had gathered from the rain were thick and of sickening flavor. When the ground impregnated with alkali is damp or wet, it forms the most villainous clinging compound imaginable. The revolving wheels quickly became solid masses of heavy mire, the spaces between the spokes and between the wheel and the wagon-box being completely filled, so that every hundred yards or so, it became necessary to dismount and pry it away with a crow-bar. In order to relieve the jaded horses, the greater number of the passengers dismounted. But after half a dozen steps their boots would pick up great slabs of the earth, and they too were forced to resort to the crow-bar. By five o'clock in the afternoon we had gone about fourteen miles, and one of the horses had given out entirely. In another hour we came in sight of an old and deserted cabin away to the right of the road, on the edge of Indian Creek, now swollen to a rushing torrent. Toward this shanty our steps were directed, and by dark the horses were picketed out, and we ate another melancholy meal of raw ham and hard-tack. Some water which we brought from the creek was as thick as molasses, and so white with alkali as to resemble cream. A pailful of this delectable beverage was set inside the roofless hut, and seven or eight prickly pears, pounded to a pulp, were put in to "settle" it for our morning meal. The travelers were divided up into watches, and spent the night in a miserable and dreary way. My watch came from one o'clock until three, and my companion on guard was named O'Neil. He was a quiet man with a face that denoted an iron will and a brave disposition. When we were called, it seemed to me the darkest night I ever saw. We shouldered our guns and started out in the direction of the horses. When we reached a place where we could hear the animals nibbling at such grass as they could find among the cactus and sage-brush, we sat down and tried to be cheerful. It was an effort born of desperation, but O'Neil began telling stories of his rough mining life in Arizona and Montana, which diverted our thoughts and made us partially forget our miseries. I shall ever remember him with gratitude. Occasionally we would rise from our seats in the mud and walk over to the edge of the bluff by the creek, in order to guard that point from attack. Just as our time had about expired, we heard a most fearful splashing in the water, as though all the Indians between New York and the Pacific Coast were crossing the creek. But silence instantly followed, and we crept on hands and knees to the edge of the bluff. Nothing was visible but the white stream of water rushing along below. We strained our eyes to see what had caused the noise, but the search was fruitless, despite our anxiety. The next two on watch had a similar fright, which was explained in the morning by the discovery that a large portion of the bluff, washed away at the base, had fallen into the creek.

All were up at daylight, and ate a cooked breakfast,—an event worthy of particular mention, although we had ceased to be fastidious about eating long before. At the moment when we began to move, there came from the rear a series of the most infernal yells I have ever heard. Weapons were lifted and everybody expected to see a horde of savages, when, hastening to the brow of a slight eminence, we caught sight of two coyotes, or prairie-wolves, watching our movements at a safe distance, and yelping with all their strength. Have the readers of these lines ever listened to a coyote? Heard in the night, their shrill cry is a fearful and blood-curdling sound. The coyote is the only animal living that is meaner than an Indian, and the two have many traits of character in common. They are both natural thieves, and murderers of the helpless.

Toward ten o'clock the mud began to dry up and our progress grew proportionally rapid. The country was wilder than ever, and we crossed many huge waves of land, the ascents and descents of which were in some cases more than two miles in length. Away off to our right, two long bluffs were seen skirting the horizon. A clear break of a mile or more between the ends of the bluffs was pointed out to us as Buffalo Gap, through which lies the trail leading to the Red Cloud Agency, a few miles farther on the other side. A mile or two more having been passed, we began the ascent of a high ridge which crosses the road at right angles and is many miles in length. We were told by the driver, that on the summit of this ridge we should cross the Red Cloud trail, and that if Indians were prowling around, we should be pretty certain to find them here. I had heard much about the Red Cloud trail within the last few days, and had formed an idea that it was about as broad and as much traveled as Fifth avenue. When we reached the place where it crossed, they showed me a little path about a foot wide; I have seen more respectable cowpaths. This trail leads from the Red Cloud Agency to the headquarters of the Northern Sioux, and probably twenty-five or thirty warriors go over it each day; yet, like all Indian trails, it has the appearance of an unused bridle-path.

We found a number of these trails during the next few miles, and upon one of them the pony tracks had been made since the rain. Early in the afternoon we reached the highest ridge in the chain and began the descent into the valley of the Cheyenne River. Just as we crossed the summit, our party saw far off to the west a small body of mounted men who were evidently bearing toward us. Inspection through a powerful field-glass showed that they were savages, probably running along the trail from the north to Red Cloud. They came toward us for a mile or so, when a bend in the trail hiding them from our view, we saw no more of them. We were glad they didn't want anything to do with us, for we certainly had no business to transact with them. Just before dark, dusty, worn out and thirsty (for we had not tasted water since morning), we came to the banks of the Cheyenne River. In the morning the course of the stream was dry, and passing drivers had to dig for water to give their stock. When we arrived, the river was fifty yards wide and from four to nine feet deep. This is not an unusual occurrence in the West, and is explained by the fact that the stream-beds are very few in comparison to the great extent of the watersheds. Our driver was warned by persons on the opposite shore that it would be impossible for us to cross, but in spite of that, he determined to make the trial. The result was that the horses got into a quicksand, the wagon became fast in the mud and some of the passengers were obliged to spend more than two hours in the water before the outfit was again on dry land. This was the second drenching for us, and we were not very amiable,—in fact we almost came to blows two or three times within an hour. "Van" and myself mounted horses and went over to the ranch on the other side. In the house we found three old frontiersmen to whom danger was as pleasant as safety is to ordinary mortals. We obtained some dry clothes, our own garments were hung up before the huge fire-place and a supply of fried venison, coffee, and bread was prepared.

Remaining here until the afternoon of the third day, we reached the soldiers' camp at the mouth of Red Cañon[2] about eight in the evening, and halted for supper. At that point we found the first palatable water since leaving Hat Creek. As soon as our evening meal was over we started into the cañon, which has proved to be a death-trap to so many. For a few hours the moon partly illuminated our path, but after midnight the sky grew "as dark as Egypt." On both sides of us rose precipitous walls of loose rocks many hundreds of feet high, formed of red sandstone, and affording excellent shelter for savage assassins. Several parties have been waylaid in this natural trap and massacred. From Red Cañon there is no escape, and in it no means of shelter. It was here that the party known as the "Metz outfit" was attacked and murdered. This company consisted of five men and two women, one of the latter the wife of the leader, Mr. Metz, the other a colored servant. They had stopped at the "spring on the right" for supper, when the Indians fired upon them, killing all but Mr. and Mrs. Metz and the servant. The latter was found a quarter of a mile away from the rest. Mrs. Metz, when found, had five bullet-holes through her body, and was atrociously mutilated.[3]

Surrounded by localities whose very names are derived from such bloody scenes,[4] it is no wonder that the frontiersman hates the Indian with an implacable hatred, and has but one solution for the Indian question—extermination.

The driver, having for an hour or more been trying the somewhat perilous feat of guiding four horses and sleeping at the same time, succeeded in overturning the wagon about 2 A. M. I have a dim recollection of executing a semicircular transit through the air, followed by a kind of ricocheting movement along the surface of the ground. When my surprise gave way to a full realization of what had happened, I found myself sitting upon a rock, surrounded by boxes, bundles and such dancing lights as one is apt to see in times of skating accidents. The mishap delayed us until after daylight, when repairs were made and we pushed on. In Pleasant Valley, near the grave of another victim to Indian cruelty, we camped for an hour or more, and then pushed on toward Custer City. Prospect-holes began to appear at intervals along our road, deserted cabins were seen at short intervals, and soon a sharp bend in the trail brought us in sight of town.

Custer City lies in an open park hemmed in on all sides by gradually rising hills, rock-ribbed and crested with towering pines. The streets are regularly laid out, and the buildings are made of logs or rough boards taken from the hill-side forests. The number of houses was roughly estimated at a thousand, but when we arrived, not more than one hundred and fifty people were in town. As far as mining went Custer City was a delusion. Not more than $20 per day has ever been taken out on French Creek, along the banks of which lies the town. Last spring when the Deadwood region was first opened, the people "stampeded," leaving Custer City for what was supposed to be a more attractive region. But in case the excitement in the Black Hills continues, this will become the leading post for supplies, and there seems no reason why it should not be as important a center to that district as Denver is to the Colorado mines.[5] At Custer we enjoyed the privileges extended by a regular hotel and did ample justice to what was termed a "square meal." Late in the afternoon we started again on our road, and soon reached the head-waters of Spring Creek, having crossed it thirty-one times. The origin of the name "Deadwood" was soon apparent. On all hands the hills rose rocky and blank excepting at points where they were sparsely covered by dead timber. The high ground was devoid of any sign of life, but the valleys were covered with a heavy growth of buffalo-grass. Our party camped that night about twelve miles north of Custer on Spring Creek. Early the next morning we passed through Hill City,—a collection of about 200 partly built houses which were deserted at the time of the Deadwood excitement, not a single person remaining in the place,—and at noon reached the Rapid Creek district, where mining was going on extensively. Twenty-seven hours later, our teams, by this time utterly worn out, reached the brow of a steep hill, down the side of which the road wound its way into the lower end of Deadwood Gulch. The gulch is about ten miles long, and very winding in its course. Through its bottom stretches a long line of shanties and tents, forming, in all, four towns. At the lower end is Montana City, then come Elizabeth Town, Deadwood City, and Gayeville (or Gaye City). Our train finally halted in Deadwood City, and we were immediately surrounded by a crowd of miners, gamblers and other citizens, all anxious to hear from the outer world. It was Sunday afternoon, and all the miners in the surrounding neighborhood were spending the day in town. The long street was crowded with men in every conceivable garb. Taken as a whole, I never in my life saw so many hardened and brutal-looking men together, although of course there were a few better faces among them. Every alternate house was a gambling saloon, and each of them was carrying on a brisk business. In the middle of the street a little knot of men had gathered, and were holding a prayer-meeting, which showed in sharp contrast to the bustling activity of wickedness surrounding it.

NOTES TO CHAPTER 31

1. Hat Creek Station later became an important point on the stage line from Cheyenne to Deadwood. It was actually located on Sage Creek.

It was occupied by a garrison of one company of infantry during part of the year 1876. At this time Colonel (Brevet Major General) Wesley Merritt, commanding the Fifth Regiment of Cavalry, was in this region.

2. This was another one-company infantry camp. In addition to the infantry, two companies of cavalry were on patrol duty between Fort Laramie and the Black Hills. The maximum strength of a company of either infantry or cavalry in 1876 was seventy-five men, but the actual strength was seldom more than fifty.

3. Accounts of the "Metz Massacre" differ in details. Perhaps the most reliable is that given by Spring in *The Cheyenne and Black Hills Stage and Express Routes*, pp. 135-36. Spring says that Charles Metz, his wife, a colored employee named Rachel Briggs, and three men named Beergisir, Gresham, and Felton, left Custer en route for Cheyenne. The attack occurred April 24, 1876, in Red Canyon. Metz and Mrs. Metz and Rachel Briggs were killed. Beergisir and Gresham were wounded and died. Felton was wounded and recovered.

4. The name "Red Canyon" was in use in 1875, and was undoubtedly derived from the color of the rock walls.

5. Custer was on the main route into the Black Hills at this time. A little later trails to Deadwood were developed along the western and eastern sides of the Black Hills, and Custer ceased to be important as a supply point, except for a small area in the immediate vicinity. The trails to the Black Hills from Sidney and Cheyenne were surveyed and mapped in 1877 by Captain W. S. Stanton, whose "Annual Report Upon Explorations and Surveys in the Department of the Platte" was published in the *Report of the Secretary of War*, 1878.

PART FIVE

EXPLORING THE WARPATH

Chapter 32

1876

FROM FORT FETTERMAN TO GOOSE CREEK,

by Captain William S. Stanton

William Sanford Stanton entered West Point July 1, 1861. He was commissioned first lieutenant of Engineers June 23, 1865; was promoted to captain February 14, 1871, to major March 19, 1884, and to lieutenant colonel February 7, 1900. While a captain, and Chief Engineer of the Department of the Platte, he was in charge of surveys in 1876 and 1877 that touched history at two important points.

In 1876 Stanton accompanied the expeditionary force commanded by Brigadier General George Crook, from Fort Fetterman to the place on Rosebud River where the battle of June 17 was fought. An account of this survey was published in the *Report of the Secretary of War* for 1876.

In 1877 Stanton explored the trails leading from Sidney, Nebraska, and Cheyenne, Wyoming Territory, to the Black Hills. His report of this survey was published in the *Report of the Secretary of War* for 1878, together with a map showing the routes traveled in 1876 and 1877.

In this chapter, from the 1876 report, Captain Stanton describes his reconnaissance from May 29 to June 11, 1876.

From the middle of May until the close of the fiscal year I was engaged on reconnaissance in connection with the Big Horn and Yellowstone expedition against hostile Sioux Indians in the region of Rosebud Creek and Tongue River.

The expedition was organized at Fort Fetterman from two columns of troops, which marched to that post from the Union Pacific Railroad, one column from Medicine Bow station by the summer route across the northern part of the Black Hills of Wyoming, direct to the fort where it crosses the north Platte by a trail-bridge; the other column from Cheyenne to Fort Laramie, over the new bridge there, thence up the northeast bank of the river to the organizing camp, opposite Fort Fetterman.

The expedition comprised 15 companies of cavalry, 5 companies of infantry, and a train consisting of 105 wagons and 600 pack-mules. Commanded by General Crook[1] in person, the expedition commenced its march northward from Fort Fetterman, taking the old Montana road via the old Forts Reno, Phil. Kearny, and C. F. Smith, at 1:30 p. m., May 29.[2] It advanced northwest by west 10.3 miles to its first camp on Sage Creek, a stream which skirts the road for several miles, is destitute of wood, and varies in character between a dry, sandy, narrow bed and a grassy swale with pools of brackish water.

The country is rolling and covered with thin grass, with sage-brush and cactus predominating. Excepting the first 3 or 4 miles from the North Platte, where it is sandy and rather heavy, the road is good.

May 30.—Marched 8 miles in the same general direction as yesterday, and over a country of the same character; then until reaching camp nearly north over a rolling country, the divide between the waters of the North Platte and the South Fork of the Cheyenne. About 3.5 miles before reaching camp, the road descended rather abruptly to Brown Springs, a small stream with good grass, no wood, and brackish water running sluggishly or standing in pools. Camped on the first of the branches of the Cheyenne; distance marched, 19.9 miles; grass generally good, mingled with some sage.

May 31.—Then marched across the region of the headwaters of the Cheyenne; crossing two intermediate tributaries to that river, the column camped on a fourth, last night's camp being on the first. These four branches are alike, insomuch as they are all characterized by wide, sandy beds and very little water. The first of them affords the first wood on the road north of the Platte; its bottom, which is about 150 yards wide, and bounded by steep banks 50 to 60 feet high, containing scattering cottonwood-trees; its bed is about 50 feet wide, and has a little water, either running on the surface or sunk in the sand. The second branch, about 12.5 miles from the first, has a bed about 200 feet wide, a little water alternately running on the surface and sinking, and no wood. The third branch, about 5.75 miles from the second, has steep banks, 40 to 50 feet high, a bed about 300 feet wide with a single pool of water in the vicinity of the road, and contains scattering cottonwood-trees. The fourth branch, about 2.5 miles from the third, has a bed about 250 feet wide, a stream of clear brackish water about 5 feet wide and 3 or 4 inches deep, and no wood. The country is rolling and broken, the road crossing several narrow ravines, one with frequent pools of brackish water. The crossing of one or two of these ravines is miry and bad; and of the first and third branches

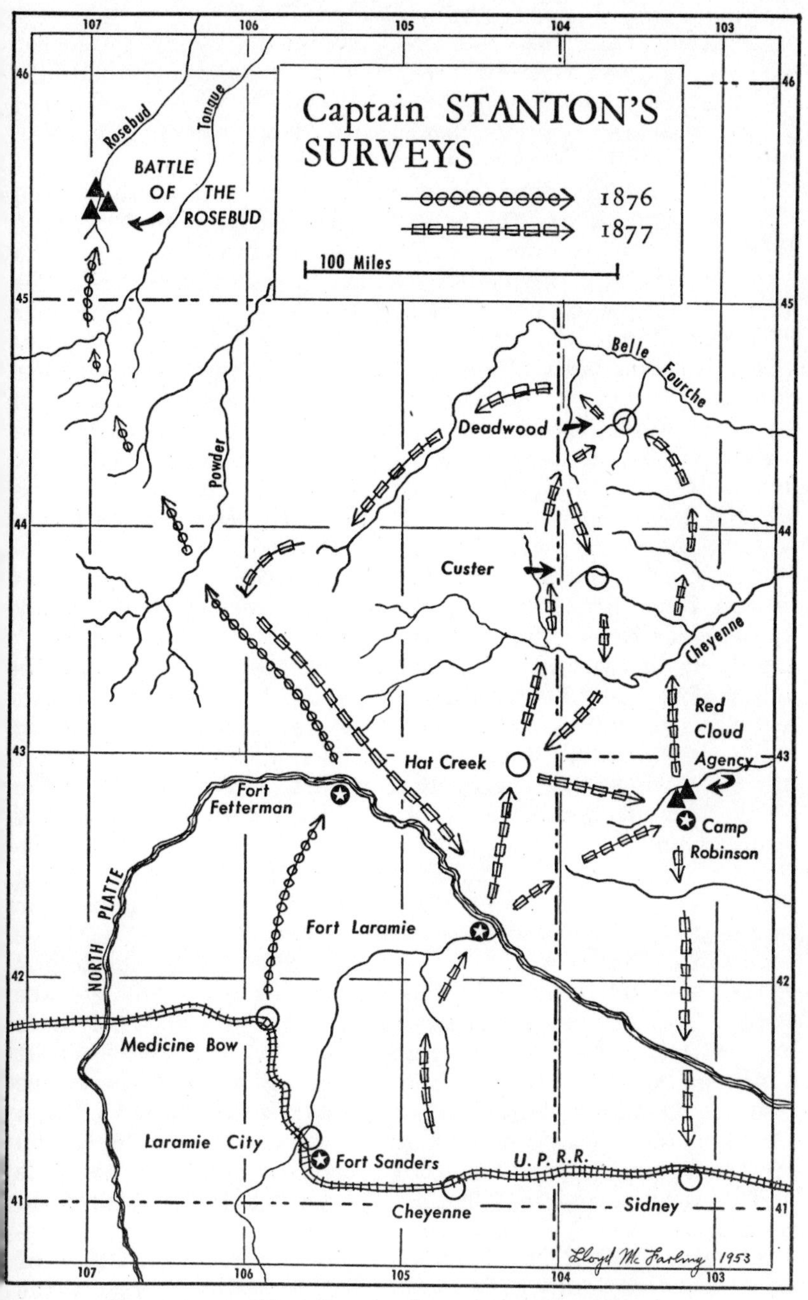

Erratum. . . . "Fort Saunders" should be Fort Sanders."

of the Cheyenne, steep and very sandy, and heavy for loaded teams. The road is elsewhere generally good, but rather hilly and crooked. Its general course continued nearly due north, a little west, for 7 miles; then west-northwest about 4.5 miles; and then north-northwest to camp. Distance marched, 20.75 miles. Bunch-grass thin to fair, mingled with considerable sage. The region of this march is that traversed October 20 and 21, 1859, by Mr. J. H. Snowden, of Colonel Raynolde's expedition. This day, from the divide between the first and second branches of the Cheyenne, on our right and left front, respectively, were first seen Pumpkin Buttes and the heavily snow-clad summits of the Big Horn Mountains, the latter henceforth the bold and dominant feature in the landscape. Laramie Peak was last seen from the divide between the second and third branches.

June 1.—Broke camp in a snow-storm and marched four or five hours in driving snow and rain. General course nearly north 3 miles; next northwest 15 miles; thence north half west to camp on the Dry Fork of Powder River.

The country for the first 10 miles was rolling or rolling and broken, forming the divide between the waters of the Cheyenne and Powder Rivers. Then it became quite broken, the road soon ascending to the crest of a long, narrow ridge, separating the valley of the Dry Fork on the left from a very broken country extending to Pumpkin Buttes on the right, and characterized by almost innumerable small ravines between low, rounded ridges, having a washed and very barren aspect. Beyond the valley on the left was seen a range of hills apparently pine-clad. The road descended rather abruptly from the ridge to the Dry Fork.[3] Distance marched 21.4 miles; road crooked and hilly, and in places rather heavy from being imperfectly beaten; bunch-grass fair to good, mingled with scattering sage.

June 2.—First for 13.3 miles the road lay along the bottom of the Dry Fork, frequently crossing the dry bed of that stream; course, first 3 miles north by west; next 10.3 miles northwest by west; then the road, leaving the bottom, ascends the bluffs which bound it on the right bank and leads north-northwest over a broken, barren, and utterly worthless country 4 miles to old Fort Reno,[4] on the left bank of Powder River. The column crossed and camped on the left bank in the bottom at the ford, and between it and the old fort. Distance marched 17.3 miles; road good.

The Dry Fork of Powder River has a bottom 150 to 250 yards wide, well timbered with groves of cottonwood-trees, and bounded by abrupt bluffs occasionally vertical, and exposing a stratum, 18 inches thick of lignite, underlying one of disintegrating slate about 3 feet thick.

The bed of the stream is about 50 feet wide, occasionally miry, but mostly sandy, and everywhere dry except a few pools of brackish water at last night's camp, and one passed on the march to-day. In descending it, the trees increase in number and size, many being 1 foot to 16 inches in diameter; the grass is generally poor and mingled with cactus and sage.

Powder River measured 112 feet wide, 2½ feet deep; has a bed of sandy mud, muddy alkaline water, a rather swift current, and gentle banks, and a good ford at the fort. Its bottom is about a mile wide and is well timbered with cottonwood. The confluence of the Dry Fork is about 2½ miles above the fort, at which point there is quite a cottonwood forest.

In the bluff, about a mile and a half from the fort, on the opposite bank, coal of an inferior quality, impregnated with sulphur, is said to have been quarried for use to a limited extent by the garrison.

Fort Reno is on a plateau about one-third of a mile from the ford and 40 feet above the river. The ruins consist of the walls of an adobe house, the large chimneys of the barracks and quarters, among which are scattered *débris* of stoves, iron bedsteads, &c., and rows of posts marking the site of the corral. They are almost as conspicuously seen on ascending the divide in obliquing from the Dry Fork to the river as could have been the fort before its abandonment. Distance from Fort Fetterman, 89.7 miles. Elevation, (approximate,) 4,250 feet.

June 3.—Marched over a rolling country to Crazy Woman's Fork of Powder River, rapidly approaching the Big Horn Mountains, the general course being northwest the first 12 miles, and afterward northwest by north. The road constantly bearing more and more to the north keeps the higher ground and describes a large curve. It might be considerably shortened by following the valley lying along the chord to the east. Distance, 25.5 miles; road good, but occasionally rather hilly; grass thin and poor throughout the march, and mingled with sage, cactus, and moss. Crazy Woman's Fork is a stream of good water, about 45 feet wide and 2 feet deep, with a muddy bed and rather high, steep banks.

June 4.—Still rapidly near the Big Horn Mountains the column advanced over a rolling and somewhat broken and hilly country northwest half north 15 miles; next 3.4 miles north by east half east toward "the reddish broken hills" mentioned as immediately upon his left by Colonel Raynolds in his journal, September 19, 1859; then north by west to camp on Clear Fork of Powder River. Distance traveled, 22.4 miles; road rather hilly, but generally good otherwise; grass better than yesterday, but still poor, and occasionally mingled with cactus and sage.

The Clear Fork is a fine stream about 40 feet wide, with clear, pure, cold water, 2½ feet deep, running rapidly over a bed of bowlders. It is fringed with willows, and has a very few trees. It appears to flow directly from the mountains, which are now near enough to be boldly outlined against the sky and to form a striking and beautiful western landscape.

This stream in its mountain-like character is, in all the region north from Fort Fetterman, the first feature producing an agreeable impression, intensified by contrast with the prevalently meager and alkaline streams hitherto.

June 5.—Moved over a very rolling and hilly country in a general direction northwest by north, 15.5 miles to old Fort Phil. Kearny,[5] and camped on Little Piney Creek. Two and one-half miles from the Clear Fork we crossed a fine stream called Rock Creek, about 30 feet wide, with clear, good water, about 15 inches deep, a brisk current, and gravelly bed.

About 5 miles south of the fort, and a mile and a half east of the road, is Lake De Smet, an apparently shallow pond of brackish water, perhaps 2 miles long by ½ a mile wide, surrounded by hills and land broken by difficult ravines. At its shore it is disappointing and much less attractive than the blue sheet of water so refreshing a relief to the eye when first seen in the distance.

Rock Creek must be the stream down which Colonel Raynolds marched just before going into camp September 19; his route and march of that day being almost identical with ours to-day, and his route of September 20, obliquely crossing ours of yesterday; thence south to the Platte, he kept farther west and close to the mountains.

The site of Fort Phil. Kearny is the narrow valley of Little and Big Piney Creeks, between steep and high hills, commanding it. It is a small plateau about 40 feet above the Little Piney, immediately on its left (north) bank, between the two streams, and about half a mile above their confluence. Southeast of it about 1,300 yards, and raising 375 feet above it, (by the aneroid,) is "Picket Hill," a pinnacle surmounted by the remains of a slight breastwork, where was posted a picket to signal to the garrison the movements of Indians. On the slope at the northern base of this hill is the post-cemetery, in which is a long trench, where lie the remains of those who fell in the massacre. Its fence and the brick monument are becoming somewhat dilapidated.

The ruins of the fort, consisting of the charred posts of the stockade, the prostrate flag-staff, foundation of the houses and *débris* of stoves, iron bedsteads, &c., conspicuously mark its site. It is distant from Fort Reno 63.6 miles, from Fort Fetterman 153.3 miles, and its approximate elevation above the sea is 4,800 feet.

The Little Piney is a stream of good water, about 15 feet wide, 15 inches deep, fringed with willows, and obstructed by beaver-dams. On its right bank, about a quarter of a mile above the post, an officer, stationed at the fort in 1867, informs me coal of fair quality was obtained for the blacksmith, and was burned in their quarters by a few of the officers.

The Big Piney is a very fine, torrent-like stream of clear, pure, cold water, about 70 feet wide, 2½ feet deep, with a very strong, rapid current, and bed of bowlders. It is fringed with tall willows, and on its north (left) bank is a thick grove of willows and cottonwood. On its banks, about 5 miles above the crossing and the fort, in the foot-hills of the mountains, is an abundance of good pine-timber.

June 6.—Leading across the fork between the creeks, crossing the Big Piney, and winding among steep and high hills, the road reaches, 2.7 miles north-northeast of the fort, the sharp crest of the very narrow divide separating the waters of Powder and Tongue Rivers. Crossing in the next half mile a narrow valley, it reaches the head of a long, narrow ridge, the sloping crest of which it follows north by west one mile and a half till it sinks into a wide, meadow-like valley, with tall and excellent grass, through which winds the Pino, a brook about 6 feet wide. The crest of this ridge, barely wider than the road upon it, is the field of massacre by the Sioux Indians of Colonel Fetterman and his entire command of 91 officers and men, December 21, 1866, the bodies of the slain having been found in and on the sides of the road from the foot of the ridge at the meadow along nearly the entire half to its head. Near the latter point, at the west edge of the road, is a group of three or four rocks, around which were heaped many bodies, supposed to be of those longest surviving in the desperate struggle to reach the fort.[6]

Leading north-northwest 2 miles across the valley and the Pino, the road, by a very winding and devious course, generally north, among high and steep, rounded hills, reaches in 4 miles Hay Creek, crossing which it continues north-northwest down its right bank, on which the ninth camp of the command was pitched. Distance marched, 17.75 miles. Road good, excepting the hills and one or two rather miry crossings. The old fort C. F. Smith road, plain and unmistakable from Fort Fetterman to the valley of the Pino at the foot of "Massacre Hill," is thenceforth nearly obliterated and often barely traceable in the taller grass of this region.

June 6.[7]—The column continued down the right bank of Hay Creek 5.5 miles; crossed and advanced down its left bank 2.75 miles to Prairie Dog Creek; then down the left bank of the latter stream to its mouth on Tongue River, on the right (south) bank of which, in the fork, camp No. 10 was pitched. Distance marched 16.8 miles; general course throughout the day almost due north.

The crossing of Hay Creek and of two ravines, where Prairie Dog Creek forced the column out of the bottom upon the bluffs, required a little cutting and filling, delaying the train somewhat; otherwise the road was fair for a new one, the column having left the old Fort C. F. Smith road on its left flank above the lower crossing of Hay Creek.

Hay Creek is a stream of good water, about 8 feet wide, 1 foot deep, with a sluggish current, a bed of mud and gravel, and a narrow bottom, jungle-like for several miles along its upper part, with a thick growth of willows, bushes and stunted elm-trees. On the right bank, its valley is bounded by barren, reddish-brown hills, the grass being rather thin and mingled with sage, while on its left bank the hills are lower and rounded and the grass excellent.

Prairie Dog Creek is about 10 feet wide, 1 foot deep, with a bed of mud and gravel, and is much obstructed with beaver-dams. Its valley contains in places excellent grass, in others thick sage. On the east are low, barren hills, rising in the distance to the low, reddish-brown Wolf Mountains. Near its mouth its valley becomes very narrow, being there bounded on the west by the rough, broken, and stony country between it, the valley of Goose Creek, and Tongue River. A few buffalo were first seen yesterday and to-day and two or three killed.

June 8.—In camp, the command taking its first rest after an uninterrupted march of 188 miles, from Fort Fetterman. The train is formed into a corral for the animals in the river-bottom amid a grove of large cottonwood-trees, while the troops are encamped on a bench back of and below it. Tongue River measures 160 feet wide and is about 3 feet deep. It has here very broken and irregular banks, and is very crooked.

June 9.—In camp. Cloudy, preventing observations. Indians were first seen to-day. At retreat almost simultaneously with the alarm from the picket near the mouth of Prairie Dog Creek on its opposite bank, a scattering fire was opened on the camp by a party of Indians from the crest of the very high, rocky, and nearly vertical bluff forming the opposite river-bank. They continued firing about twenty minutes, until a force of cavalry saddled, forded the river, and drove them away. A very few animals were wounded in the camp, but fortunately no men.

June 10.—In camp. Observed the sun morning and afternoon.

June 11.—The column broke camp and returned by its trail of the 7th up the west bank of Prairie Dog and Hay Creeks, 11.3 miles, to its lower crossing of the latter stream; then, without recrossing it, farther ascended the valley south-southwest 2.75 miles, next by a devious route following a general course west by south, passing over a narrow range of rounded, grass-covered hills, and crossing on their summit the old Fort C. F. Smith road, it reached Goose Creek at the mouth of its south branch, crossed to the west (left) bank of this branch, and pitched camp No. 11 in the fork on it and the main stream. The last hour's march was made and camp pitched in a cold, pelting rain. Distance marched 17.6 miles; route good; length of new road reconnoitered, 6.3 miles. This is the place appointed for the column to await the arrival of the force of Crow Indian scouts, and is an admirably selected position. It has good water, grass and wood in abundance for the camp, and is a natural strategical point, being approximately the center of an arc along the radii of which lie the Little Big Horn, the Rosebud, the Tongue, and the Clear Fork of Powder River, (branch formed by the Little and Big Piney.) From it, in a single day's march, a light column can put itself in motion down the valley of either of those streams, which are natural lines of operation, passing entirely through, and dividing into not very unequal parts the whole region which is the great resort of the hostile Sioux. Moreover, it is on the direct line of supply from Fort Fetterman, is in easy communication by the Fort C. F. Smith road with the valley of the Big Horn River below the cañon in the Big Horn Mountains, and, on the melting of the snow in the moun-

tains, by Goose Creek Pass, practicable for a pack-train, with the valley of that river west of that range.

The guide, Frank Grurard, says there are three principal passes over the Big Horn Mountains; the best enters along the left bank of Rotten Grass Creek, and leads north of west; the second in order of practicability enters about 3 miles north of the North Fork of Tongue River and leads a little south of west; the other enters about 2 miles north of Goose Creek and leads north of west. He says the two former could, without great labor, be made practicable for wagons, but that the Goose Creek Pass would be practicable only for pack-animals.

NOTES TO CHAPTER 32

1. George Crook was at this time a brigadier general and Commander of the Department of the Platte, with headquarters at Omaha.

2. The "old Montana Road" was usually called the Bozeman Trail. Much of it had been explored by Captain Raynolds in 1859, but it was named after John Bozeman, a Montana Territory frontiersman, who probably first traveled over the entire route in 1863, from Fort Laramie to Bozeman, Montana Territory. The Bozeman Trail was a cutoff to the Montana gold fields. To guard this trail forts Reno, Phil Kearny, and C. F. Smith were built by the army in 1866. The building of these forts and the use of the Bozeman Trail by the emigrants precipitated the Red Cloud War of 1866-68. A temporary peace was established by the treaty of 1868, and the trail and the forts were abandoned.

3. Of Powder River.

4. Camp Conner was located here in 1865, re-established as Fort Reno in 1866, and abandoned in 1868.

5. Fort Phil Kearny, the most important post on the Bozeman Trail, was established in July, 1866, and abandoned in the fall of 1868. It was burned by the Sioux Indians soon after abandonment.

6. The "Fetterman Massacre" occurred December 21, 1866. A large body of Sioux Indians ambushed a detachment of seventy-nine soldiers and two civilians from Fort Phil Kearny and wiped out the entire party. The leader of the detachment was Captain (Brevet Lieutenant Colonel) William J. Fetterman.

7. The date should be June 7.

Chapter 33

1876

FROM GOOSE CREEK TO ROSEBUD RIVER,

by Captain William S. Stanton

At Goose Creek, near the present town of Sheridan, Wyoming, General Crook established a supply camp and left his wagons. He mounted his infantry on mules, and with cavalry and pack train moved out toward the Rosebud River on June 16. Early on June 17 he came upon a large body of Sioux Indians led by Crazy Horse, and began a hard-fought battle that lasted several hours. At the end of the battle the Indians retreated from the field. Crook buried his dead that night and on the following day began his return march to the Goose Creek camp. On the twenty-first he dispatched his wagon train to Fort Fetterman for supplies.

Captain Stanton accompanied the reconnaissance to Rosebud River, then returned with the wagon train to Fort Fetterman and other duties. From his 1876 report I am reprinting in this chapter his observations from June 12 to about June 30, 1876.

June 12.—In Camp. Observed the sun morning and afternoon. Goose Creek above the south branch is about 50 feet wide and 2 feet deep; its banks are low, and fringed in places with willows, but without trees. The south bank has about the same width, is about 18 inches deep, and has a sandy bed; its banks are low and fringed with willows and groves of cottonwood-trees. Both streams have clear, cold, and excellent water and a rapid current.

June 13.—In camp. Observed the sun morning and afternoon.

June 14.—In camp. The barometer indicates an approximate altitude of 3,680 feet. The three guides who left the column at old Fort Reno on the 2d on their perilous journey of 200 miles to the Crow camp, beyond the Yellowstone, to secure the scouts, returned this afternoon with 160 Crow Indians. A few hours later, 67 Snake Indians also joined the column.

June 15.—In camp, preparing for the advance to-morrow. Mules are being selected from the pack-train, and equipped for mounting the infantry; rations drawn, &c.

June 16.—At 6 a. m., General Crook, with all the cavalry, and the infantry mounted on mules, headed for the Rosebud. The column is as light as possible, and is admirably equipped for celerity of movement. Each officer and man is limited to four days' rations, his overcoat, and one single blanket; the men carrying each 100 rounds of ammunition. The odometer-cart is the only vehicle in the column. The column crossed at camp to the left (west) bank of Goose Creek, and marched in a general course north-northwest 7 miles, the route lying for the first 4 miles in the valley of the creek, and then on higher, broken, and rolling ground; next morning northeast by north 4.25 miles, it crossed the deep and narrow valley of Tongue River, and climbed to the crest of the high ridge on its north side, gravelly and broken, with patches of sage and scattering pine-timber. Tongue River was crossed about 1 mile above the mouth of Goose Creek and is there about 100 feet wide, 2½ feet deep, with a strong current, low banks, and a good ford. Between the camp and the river the grass varies from good bottom and bunch grass in the valley of Goose Creek to fair bunch grass on the intervening higher ground, and is throughout mingled with occasional patches of sage. From the crest of the ridge bordering the river-valley, the route lay nearly north about 7.5 miles, through an excessively broken, rough, and stony country, to the narrow valley of a small stream draining apparently into Tongue River, but dry excepting in pools.

The column next ascended this valley about 6.5 miles to its head, and reached the summit of the divide between the waters of the Tongue and the Rosebud, meeting a small herd of buffalo.

From this summit the course lay about north-northwest 8 miles, over a region of high, rounded, and steep hills, with small miry streams at their bases, and abounding with excellent grass, to the Rosebud, on both banks of which headquarters and the cavalry bivouacked at 7.20 p.m., the infantry arriving somewhat later.

June 17.—The column marched at 6.15 a. m., and moved down the valley of the Rosebud, closely following its left bank, in a general northeast direction, until 7.15, when it was halted to await information from the Indian scouts, who reported the Sioux in the vicinity. In about one hour, the Sioux appeared in force in the broken country immediately north of the Rosebud Valley, and an engagement at once ensued, continuing about four hours, and resulting in completely routing the enemy, undoubtedly with quite severe loss, the troops following some distance, and bivouacking at night unmolested in the valley of the creek where they halted just before the fight commenced. The field of the engagement is one of valleys and steep, rounded hills, merging into deep ravines, and steep, stony and somewhat rocky ridges, which in descending along the valley of the creek, or in advancing northward from it, at once become deeper, steeper, more broken, and precipitous, and sprinkled with pine-timber. It is a region very unfavorable for a pursuit and very favorable for concealing the position and strength of a force awaiting attack.[1]

The Rosebud in this vicinity is a stream of good water, 4 or 5 feet wide, an inch or two deep, with a slight current, a miry bed, with rather steep, muddy banks, and lying in a narrow bottom containing a few cottonwood-trees and a thick growth of brushes and willows.

June 18.—The column at 6:30 a. m. began its march to camp, and moved up the left bank of the Rosebud to its source in a direction nearly southwest by west about 7 miles, reaching the narrow summit of a very high ridge dividing its waters from the Tongue.

The Rosebud is formed on the northwest slope of this ridge from several small brooks, and has a rapid descent for 2 or 3 miles through a narrow, grassy ravine, which then widens to a valley from 100 to 200 yards across, between the bivouacs of the 16th and 17th, being bounded on the left bank by high, rounded, grassy hills, and on the right by higher, steeper, and rather rocky bluffs; the distant ranges on either bank being sprinkled with pine-timber.

This abruptly elevated region in which the Rosebud rises is one of marked topographical characteristics. From the summit of its culminating ridge, the Big Horn range is in clear view from the bald promontory where it is pierced by the Big Horn River to Cloud Peak; extending far to the north lies the valley of the Little Big Horn, and to the northeast the valley of the Tongue, with the Wolf Mountains beyond. It is much to be regretted that the position of this point could not have been determined.

The route was next very devious, on a course about south by west, continuing in this elevated region among high and steep, grass-covered hills and deep ravines, occasionally broken and stony. Bivouacked at 2 p. m. on a small stream of good water thickly fringed with bushes and a few trees, between towering hills, and flowing east-southeast, probably into the Tongue. Distance marched about 20 miles.

June 19.—Marched at 5:30 a.m. Route devious, on a course about south by east, through the same elevated region of grassy hills and ravines, about 3.5 miles, to its southern limit. Next, after a very abrupt and steep descent, continued the same south by east course about 5 miles, over a barren and somewhat broken country, with gravelly soil, little or no grass, thick sage, and some cactus, to Tongue River; forded, and moving thereafter on a general southeast by east course, crossed first about 2.5 miles of the same barren, sage-covered region, next about 3 miles of comparatively level and better country, with better grass, to the old Fort C. F. Smith road, which there lies along the northeast (left) bank of Beaver Creek, a stream about 6 or 8 feet wide and 18 inches deep, thickly fringed with bushes, with muddy banks, miry bed obstructed by beaver-dams, and bad to cross; crossing the old road and the creek, the column kept its southeast by east course over a rolling and hilly country, about 4 miles, to the wagon-train on the south (right) bank of Goose Creek, about 3 miles above the fork, it having moved there with camp on the 16th. The column, wagon-train, and pack-train crossed the fork about 4 miles to the left bank of the south branch of Goose Creek, about 5 miles above its mouth, and camped.

June 20.—Entire command march south-southeast 7 miles, up the left bank of the south branch of Goose Creek, and pitched Camp Cloud Peak on it at the crossing of Bridger's cut-off branch of the Fort C. F. Smith road.

June 21.—The entire wagon-train of the command, with the ambulances containing the wounded, began at 5 a. m. its return march to Fort Fetterman for supplies. It moved over a country of high, steep, grass-covered hills and grassy ravines, occasionally with a small, miry stream, by Bridger's cut-off, southeast 10.5 miles to its junction with the main Fort Smith road at the foot of Massacre Hill, 4.7 miles north of Fort Phil. Kearny, thence following the route by which the command advanced, and closing the reconnaissance.

Describing generally the country seen on the reconnaissance, the region from Fort Fetterman to old Fort Phil. Kearny is rolling and sometimes broken, the soil sandy, and the grass, although occasionally fair, generally thin and poor; all the water south of Crazy Woman's Fork to the Platte is alkaline, and south of Powder River it is very scarce. This region is barren and uninviting in aspect, and almost, if not entirely, worthless. Although during the advance of the column, about the 1st of June, the grazing was tolerable or fair, on the return of the train the thin grass was so short and dried up that it afforded very scant subsistence for the animals.

Powder River had fallen considerably, and its water had become so strongly alkaline that it increased instead of allaying the thirst. Between it and the Platte, a distance of about 90 miles, not a drop of running water was found; the two branches of the Cheyenne, in which a little was running when we went north had dried up, and their beds in places were covered with a white alkaline deposit. Water for the 600 or 700 animals was found at the usual camping-places in pools and holes.

From Fort Phil. Kearny or Rock Creek north to Tongue River, and from the Big Horn Mountains east to Hay and Prairie Dog Creeks, is a hilly and rolling region, containing generally good grass and good water.

Finally, the elevated and excessively hilly region about the source of the Rosebud, extending from the abrupt, narrow, and barren ridge bordering the valley of the Tongue on the north, over to the field of the engagement of June 17, is covered with good grass and contains good water.

Excepting as specified along the streams, this whole country west[2] of the foot of the Big Horn Mountains is destitute of timber.

Game is scarce; a few antelope were seen occasionally throughout the march and about the source of the Rosebud buffalo were seen in limited numbers.

The reconnaissance commenced at Medicine Bow, on the Union Pacific Railroad, May 21, with the march of the column which moved from that point, and embraced its route to Fort Fetterman. That route is now so frequented, and its region so comparatively well known, that it is deemed superfluous to describe it.

The following is a statement of distances:

	Miles	*Miles*
From Fort Fetterman to—		
Camp No. 1, on Sage Creek	10.30	
Camp No. 2, on South Branch of South Cheyenne	19.88	30.18
Camp No. 3, on North branch of South Cheyenne	20.77	50.95
Camp No. 4, on Dry Fork of Powder River	21.43	72.38
Camp No. 5, at old Fort Reno, (Powder River)	17.33	89.71
Camp No. 6, on Crazy Woman's Fork	25.70	115.41
Camp No. 7, on Clear Fork of Powder River	22.41	137.82

Camp No. 8, at old Fort Phil. Kearny	15.50	153.32
Camp No. 9, on Hay Creek	17.74	171.06
Camp No. 10, on Tongue River	16.81	187.87
Camp No. 11, on Goose Creek	17.61	205.48

Route reconnoitered from Medicine Bow to Fort Fetterman	85.00
Route reconnoitered from Fort Fetterman to Camp No. 11 on Goose Creek, (deducting route retraveled)	193.56
Route reconnoitered with odometers on march to the Rosebud	13.00
Route reconnoitered moving camp June 20	6.93
Route reconnoitered on return with train, (Bridger's Cut-off)	10.63
Total length of reconnaissance with odometers	309.12
Total length of horseback reconnaissance on march to and from the Rosebud	61.25
Aggregate length of reconnaissance	370.37

The distance from Fort Fetterman, by Bridger's Cut-off, direct to the camp (Cloud Peak) of June 21, on south branch of Goose Creek, is 168.64 miles.

In making the reconnaissance, I was assisted by the following persons employed in this office, viz: Mr. R. F. Koehneman, civilian, draughtsman and topographer; Private Henry Kehl, general service, clerk; Private Stephen Bowes, Twenty-third Infantry, messenger; and Private Charles Holtes, Fourth Infantry, detailed for the reconnaissance.

Mr. Koehneman recorded all the observations made with the compass, the odometers, and the aneroid, and carefully sketched the topography.

Private Kehl carried the chronometers and observed the aneroid on the march and the mercurial barometer in camp.

Private Holtes carried the cistern-barometers and read the odometers, and being very ready with the pencil, made some very good sketches of scenery; the above three occupying the ambulance provided for the purpose, to each fore-wheel of which an odometer was attached.

Private Bowes was orderly, and, having served as a soldier in the region of the reconnaissance, was very useful in accompanying me to elevations bordering the route, communicating with the markers, &c. The compass observations were taken by myself with a prismatic compass, the greater part of them recumbently, as necessitated by the prevailing wind.

The courses were taken with much care to conform closely to the route, averaged a little less than a mile long, and were denoted by two cavalrymen employed as markers, one upon whom to sight, and the other to relieve him and mark the point until my arrival, by which time the advance marker would again reach the new station. Numerous bearings of all peaks and elevations of sufficient importance were taken, to locate them, by triangulation, and the aneroid was read at every course.

The sextant observations were made by myself, Mr. Koehneman being recorder. Although a part of the days were clear, unfortunately the nights were almost invariably cloudy, preventing astronomical work. When the camps permitted, the sun was observed for time; but the sextant-arc being too short, its meridian altitude could not be observed as a resort for latitude necessitated by the cloudy nights. Meteorological observations at hours corresponding to those of the Signal Service were taken during the reconnaissance at Forts Laramie and Fetterman by an enlisted man at each post detailed for that purpose. The few altitudes herein given have not been corrected by reference to the above stations and to the Signal Service at Cheyenne. A two wheeled odometer-cart, for use with the cavalry column, was purchased by the Quartermaster's Department, and hastily made here, just before the reconnaissance commenced.

On the march to the Rosebud, its wheels proved very inferior, and one was so badly broken in the rough country immediately north of the Tongue that the cart had to be abandoned. Even had it not broken, its abandonment would have been necessary; for the country became so rough that it could not have kept up with a mounted column moving 35 or 40 miles a day.

The compass courses were continued with the same care as before, the indications of a watch being recorded instead of the readings of the odometer. A considerable part of the country was so rough, making the trail so full of short deviations, and so varying the rate of advance in the ascent and descent of steep slopes, that the reconnaissance from Goose Creek to the Rosebud was very unsatisfactory and of little value.

Fortunately the abandonment of the cart was apprehended as a possible necessity, and no instruments were taken in it, as each man had too much to carry—his arms, ammunition, rations, blankets, &c.—to be charged with a sextant or chronometer. The draughtsman and meteorological observer remained in camp, charged with the care of the chronometers and instruments, and with meteorological observations; the other two men accompanied me.

As from the nature assumed by the campaign any further

reconnaissance with the expedition would have been of the same unsatisfactory character as that from Goose Creek to the Rosebud, it was deemed much more advantageous to devote the remainder of the season and the services of the party to surveys much needed within the department. I therefore returned with it to Fort Fetterman at the close of the fiscal year, and at once commenced the following work.

NOTES TO CHAPTER 33

1. This engagement is known to historians as the battle of the Rosebud. In addition to army reports, there are three published accounts by eyewitnesses, in *War-Path and Bivouac*, by John Finerty; *On the Border with Crook*, by John Bourke; and *My Story*, by Anson Mills. Finerty was a newspaper correspondent. Bourke was a lieutenant and an aide to Crook. Anson Mills was a captain commanding a battalion of cavalry.

In secondary material we have accounts of the battle, among others, in *Sitting Bull*, by Vestal; *Death on Horseback*, by Wellman; and *Red Cloud's Folk*, by George E. Hyde.

According to the various estimates, there were from 1,000 to 1,500 Sioux and Cheyenne Indians engaged. At least 11 were killed and 5 wounded. Crook had about 1,000 white soldiers and from 200 to 300 Crow and Shoshone auxiliaries. There were 9 killed and 21 wounded among the regulars, and, if we accept Wellman's figures, 2 killed and 11 wounded among the Crows and Shoshones.

The whites were under the personal command of General Crook, an able tactician with much Indian fighting experience. The Indians were led by Crazy Horse, the Oglala warrior who was probably the ablest fighter-leader among the Teton Sioux at this period. Both sides fought with skill, courage, and determination. There were some long-range skirmishes, a number of charges and countercharges, and several times the forces were involved in the most desperate kind of hand-to-hand fighting. Considering the nature and length of the fight and the forces involved, the number of casualties were surprisingly small.

The fight ended when the Sioux and Cheyennes withdrew from the field, leaving it in possession of Crook's forces. Crook remained on the battlefield during the night and on the following morning began the march back to his supply camp on Goose Creek.

Modern historians seem generally agreed that the battle was a defeat for Crook. I do not think so. From a tactical standpoint the commander who drives his enemy from the field without a serious plurality of losses, and holds the field, is certainly entitled to claim a victory. From a strategic standpoint the problem is more difficult. The net result was that both sides withdrew from the point of contact, and neither came into effective contact with the other during the campaign that followed. But the whites were numerically and logistically able to sustain a longer campaign than the Indians, and therefore the ultimate effect of the battle was more serious to the Indians than it was to the whites. I think the battle was definitely a tactical victory for Crook and (less definitely) a strategic victory.

2. The word should be "east" instead of "west."

Chapter 34

1876

SCOUTING ON THE YELLOWSTONE,

by Lieutenant James H. Bradley

The campaign against the Sioux in 1876 was a three-prong attack on the region south of the Yellowstone River, between the Bighorn and the Powder. Crook moved up from the south, General Terry from the east, and Colonel John Gibbon from Fort Ellis, Montana Territory, in the west.

Gibbon's command consisted of six companies of the Seventh Infantry and four companies of the Second Cavalry—about 430 men and officers—a group of Crow Indian scouts, and a few civilian scouts and guides.

Among Gibbon's officers was Lieutenant James H. Bradley, born in 1844, veteran of the Civil War with ten years experience as an officer in Wyoming and Montana territories. Bradley was interested in frontier history and composed several manuscripts based on personal experiences and interviews with pioneers, which have been published in *Contributions to the Historical Collections of Montana.* "The Journal of James H. Bradley. . . ." published in Volume II of the *Contributions* in 1896, was an account of Bradley's experiences in Gibbon's command, from March 17 through June 26, 1876. In this and the next chapter I am reprinting the Journal beginning June 5, on the Yellowstone River, above the mouth of Tongue River.

At this time Bradley commanded a detachment of scouts, including a group of Crow Indians. His journal was evidently rewritten from notes made on the march; it was unfinished when Bradley was killed while leading a charge against the camp of Chief Joseph at the battle of the Big Hole, Montana Territory, August 9, 1877.

Monday, 5. Since the twenty-fourth ult. we have turned out about 2 o'clock in the morning and lain on our arms in line until broad daylight, but this morning the practice was discontinued —much to the satisfaction of everybody. Reveille is appointed for 3:30. Marched at 8:55 A. M. keeping down the valley, and camped at 1:30 P. M., having advanced nine miles. Soon after we halted the General[1] and his party routed a bear out of the thicket near camp and after a short chase the General killed it. He caused it to be butchered, and distributed the meat to several of the officer's messes, giving to many their first experience of such fare. It was quite palatable and strongly suggestive of fresh pork. Our camp is beautifully located near a chute of the river, groves of timber near at hand and long green grass beneath our feet. It was only half a mile from here that Captain Thompson's command lay in wait in the hills for the party of Sioux who attempted to cross on the nineteenth of May.

The afternoon was very warm, but by rolling up the sides of the tents and admitting the slight air stirring it was pleasant enough. It looked more like picnicking than going to war, to see officers and men comfortably reclining in the shade reading books and newspapers, writing letters, posting diaries, playing cards, talking or dozing "the happy hours away," according to their individual moods. And the picnic impression was heightened when, later in the afternoon, the supper was made ready on the grass and hungry groups gathered here and there over cups of steaming, savory coffee and other fare. Nor was coffee the only beverage. From the capacious recesses of secure mess-chests came forth at odd times nutmeg, lemon, sugar, Angostura bitters, champagne cider, and *spiritus frumenti*, from which were made tempting "Rosebuds," cocktails, toddies and other harmless compounds. When each member of the charmed circle had been duly supplied, the master of ceremonies would briefly announce, "Here's How!" and, with a chorus of "Hows" from his co-laborers, the exhilarating compounds were gently put where they would do the most good.

In the dusk of evening, when most of the officers were gathered in front of some of the tents, a chorus of cavalrymen not far away burst forth with a round of merry camp songs, that came pleasantly to the ear and suspended for a time the conversation upon battles we haven't fought and victories we haven't won. And when "taps" imposed silence upon the enlisted men, the officers, who enjoyed larger liberties, took up the suspended harmony and woke the night air with many a song of sentiment and jollity. We have a number of very sweet singers in our command, and the music at times is of a delicious sort. But rest is needful for the march of tomorrow and after a time the group of singers and listeners broke up with a mutual "good night," tents are sought, sleep settles upon the camp, and all is quiet upon the Yellowstone. Not even a sentinel is visible, for, disposed in groups of three around us for some distance from the camp, they are all lying flat upon the ground with nothing to mark their locality. It is hard to realize when about the camp that we are an invading army, liable at any moment to be engaged in deadly conflict with a cruel foe. I presume to few except myself has a sense of danger come home at all, and to me only when exposed with a handful of men miles from the command.

Tuesday, 6. I left camp with my detachment and the Indians at 8 A. M., getting a good start ahead of the command which followed an hour later. It took the train three hours to get up the hill at the foot of which our last night's camp was pitched. Finding myself several miles ahead of the command I halted, posted sentinels, and unsaddled, remaining several hours before the command appeared. At one time there occurred rapid firing on the river which excited a momentary apprehension that the boats had been attacked; but it proved to be Captain Clifford and men firing upon elk, one of which they killed and secured. After crossing the high grounds, for a distance of some three miles, the road entered the valley again. After a march of ten miles we turned off to the river and camped at 4 P. M., in a beautiful cottonwood grove on splendid sod. In the evening we were treated to a high wind that roared grandly through the trees. It came up suddenly and for a time threatened a general conflagration, as it set troops of burning coals hopping through the camp from the cook fires and deluged the tents with sparks. While this display of fire-works was going on, the gloom was rent with lightning flashes, and the low rumble of distant thunder swelled on the air. There was a sublimity in the scene that produced a strong impression on many minds. There was a drawback to its enjoyment, however, in the tossing boughs that threatened destruction to the tents pitched beneath them and the necessity of manning the poles to keep the tents from going down before the blast.

Wednesday, 7. Marched at 7:45 A. M., continued down the valley a few miles, then ascended to the highlands which abut on the river for several miles above and below the mouth of Tongue River. Toward evening turned to the right and approaching the river descended to a small patch of valley where we pitched camp at 7 P. M., having marched twenty-two miles. The descent to the valley was by a difficult ravine, where the wagons lost half an hour. It was 9 o'clock before the camp was fairly in shape and half an hour later before suppers were ready, by which time there were four hundred very hungry men. Found a clear, cold spring in the bluffs about a mile from camp but it furnished a very limited supply of water.

Thursday, 8. Took the advance as usual with my detachment and the Crows, the command following at 7 A. M. Had gained the valley of a nameless creek a few miles from camp, when from the hills in front came the wolf-cry that indicated a discovery by the Crows in advance. The Crows rapidly rallied on the detachment and we prepared for fight, but fortunately were not called upon to do so. The occasion of the signal was that one of the Crows had found a trail of two shod horses leading down the river, and, following it a short distance, came upon a seamless sack lying on the ground, which he picked up and brought back without opening. I caused it to be opened and found the contents to be a quantity of sugar, tea, bacon, crackers, hard bread, butter and cartridges, several of the articles being wrapped in pieces of newspaper. They were such supplies as were likely to have belonged only to white men, and the fact that the horses were shod made it pretty evident that the owners were white men, the fresh character of the provisions indicated that they had only quite recently quitted a steamboat or large camp. It seemed probable that they were couriers from General Terry, who discovering our Indians supposed them to be Sioux and fled, either losing the sack or throwing it away because it impeded their flight. A further examination of the trail disclosed that it first came up the river valley and then, turning to the right into the hills, doubled on its former course.

Sent back a written report of the circumstances to General Gibbon and then moved on, took position on a high, flat, detached hill, standing near the river, from which we had a wide view of the surrounding country, unsaddled, and waited three hours for the command to come up. A couple of miles lower down the command halted for two hours in a grove on the river bank, then moved on for six miles, and camped near the river at 7:40 P. M., having marched sixteen miles. The valley is here quite extensive being some three miles wide and at least fifteen long, but is almost entirely destitute of timber. We had great difficulty in finding wood enough for cooking purposes, but a friendly drift in the river helped us out. The grass is heavy but provokingly matted with pricklypears, so that it was impossible to pitch tents in line. A considerable rapid spans the river a few rods below our camp.

As it was expected that we would have to camp tonight on the highlands at some distance from the river, Captain Clifford was directed to take two days' rations in his boats to be prepared for a separation from the main command.[2] It was the General's intention that he should make only about the usual run and go into camp, so as to be as near the command as possible; but a mistake was made in the delivery of the order and Captain Clifford understood himself to be at liberty to make the two days' march in one run, and so passed on with the intention of fortifying at the mouth of Powder River, there awaiting our arrival. He is accompanied by Major Brisbin and Lieutenant Doane.

Friday, 9. About 2 A. M. citizen Herendeen and a Crow Indian, who had accompanied Captain Clifford yesterday in the boats, arrived in camp with despatches from General Terry. At Powder River Captain Clifford had met the steamer Far West and soon afterward General Terry himself, who came in with two companies of the 7th Cavalry.[3] Learning that our column was so near, the General at once sent back orders to General Gibbon to leave his command in camp and come down himself to meet the boat, which would continue on up the river till the meeting took place. About 7 A. M. the General started, preceded by my detachment and the Crows and accompanied by Ball's company as escort. About eight miles down we met the boat, it having on board General Terry and staff and Captain Clifford's company. General Gibbon went on board, and General Terry, finding that our camp was so near, passed on up the river with the boat, Captain Ball and myself returning by the way we came. We reached the camp about noon, and soon afterward the boat arrived, landing opposite the camp. General Terry invited all the officers to meet him on board. After a stay of about two hours the boat was cleared and returned down the river.

The arrival of the 7th Cavalry at Glendive Creek disproved the reported gathering of the hostiles in that quarter, and our whole force is now to push up the river after the village we had first discovered on Tongue River and afterward on the Rosebud.[4] The 7th Cavalry under Custer will scour the country south of the Yellowstone, while we return up the north bank to prevent the Indians from escaping to this side. As it is feared they may attempt to do so, the four companies of the 2nd Cavalry were placed under orders to move back at once, and would have got off to-day had not a heavy rain set in, accompanied by hail, which caused the movement to be suspended until to-morrow. The infantry will soon follow, and we will then go into camp near the mouth of the Rosebud to await further others.[5] Meantime the steamer returns to Glendive Creek, to bring up the stores left there to Powder River.

The trail we found yesterday had been made, as we surmised, by couriers from General Terry—Williamson and a companion, who had been promised two hundred dollars if they went through. They had been frightened back by the sight of our Crows, and so lost their two hundred dollars at the moment it was earned. Williamson made the run down from our camp near Rosebud without difficulty and safely delivered his despatches.

On our way back to camp to-day after meeting the boat, Le Forgey, one of my interpreters, had a fall from his horse while chasing antelope, breaking his collar bone. I was compelled to leave him where he fell, in charge of two of my men, till an ambulance could be sent for him. He appeared to mind the fracture but little, and in the evening was walking around camp.

Saturday, 10. It rained all last night, and continued through the forenoon. The road is exceedingly muddy; but the cavalry marched at 3 P. M., under command of Major Brisbin. Bravo and six Crows accompanied them. The infantry are under orders to march to-morrow, moving at 7 o'clock.

Sunday, June 11. Marched at 6:20 A. M., forty minutes ahead of time. Made rather slow progress, as the road was heavy from recent rains. About 10 o'clock reached the nameless creek that enters the Yellowstone six or seven miles below Tongue River, and found it swelled to the dimensions of a river. It took two hours to make one crossing, whereas on our way down we crossed it three times without difficulty. We here came in sight of the cavalry, whose train was toiling slowly up the steep hill on the opposite side of the creek, having been compelled to seek a new road, as the rise of the creek had rendered the regular road impassable. About noon we were all over and the train was corralled, and the mules turned out to graze, while a large working party fell to, to make a new road up the hill just below the point where the cavalry wagons made their difficult ascent. The work had scarcely begun when a heavy rain set in, suspending our labors and compelling us to form camp for the night.

The maps give no name to this creek and nobody in the command had ever heard a name for it, so our engineer officer, Lieutenant McClernand christened it quite appropriately Mud Creek. The water is horribly muddy and all attempts to settle it failed. It answered neither for cooking nor washing, and we might almost as well have been camped in a desert. Vinegar cleared it somewhat, and the addition of lemon-sugar made a fairly palatable lemonade that quenched thirst.

Monday, 12. Broke camp at 6 A. M. and consumed three and a half hours getting the train up the hill at a cost of one wagon overturned. It was righted and reloaded, the damage having been slight. Once up we made good time across the plateau opposite Tongue River where the road was level and dry. The plateau is between ten and twelve miles long and about three miles wide, crowding upon the Yellowstone on the one side and breaking into bad-lands on the other. The plateau itself is generally quite level and clothed with fine grass. Stanley's quadrulpe trail of 1873 is distinctly marked throughout its whole length.[6] I rode over and took a look into Tongue River valley. It is heavily clothed with timber as far up as the eye could reach. The mouth of Tongue River was not in sight as the stream made a sharp curve to the right and entered the Yellowstone under a screen of timber. The latter stream here washes the base of the bluffs on the north side, the valley being wholly confined to the opposite shore.

As we reached the upper end of the plateau we caught a glimpse of the cavalry about eight miles in front. We descended into the valley and camped at 7 P. M. at the foot of the hill three miles from the river, having marched sixteen miles. We obtained water from stagnant pools and used sage-brush for fuel. The discovery of an occasional rattlesnake in camp enlivens our stay here.

Tuesday, 13. Marched at 7 A. M. The road was quite heavy, being largely a sticky clay, and we made slow progress. At 1 P. M. we halted at a creek and passed two hours making a crossing place for the wagons; but even with this precaution broke two wagons in crossing and tipped one of them over into a ditch. After a march of only thirteen miles camped at 4 P. M. at the upper extremity of the valley across which our road has been to-day.

Wednesday, 14. Broke camp at 7 A. M., entered the coulee opposite camp, crossed the three mile wide ridge, descended into the valley above and followed it up nearly to our old Rosebud camp, where after a march of twelve miles we pitched camp at 2 P. M., a few hundred yards above the cavalry, who arrived yesterday. We are about two miles below our last permanent camp, about four below the mouth of the Rosebud, and nearly opposite the point where our three men were killed in May, which, after one of the number, is now called by us Raymeyer Butte.[7] As we are likely to remain here some time the camp was laid out with great care, and what with the level ground and its growth of fine grass, presents a very neat appearance. Just above is a dense thicket of willow and cottonwood, and scattered about the camp are a few cottonwood trees, which combine with the camp and the river to form a very pleasing and picturesque view. Many of our camps in the march down and up the Yellowstone have been of the same agreeable character, and have imparted quite a charm to this warlike jaunt of ours.

Thursday, 15. Thompson's and Wheelan's companies left to-day on a five days' scout up the Yellowstone to see whether the Indians are keeping south of the river. Six Crows accompany them. The remainder of the cavalry moved up and joined on the lower side of our camp. A mail was sent with Thompson's command, and will be forwarded by couriers from the point where they turn back.

Friday, 16. To-day the Crows discovered a heavy smoke across and up the river, apparently on O'Fallon Creek. It suggested a world of speculation, one of the theories being that a Sioux village had been attacked and destroyed either by Custer or Crook. It means more likely that the Sioux are moving in that direction and accidentally set the grass on fire. Toward evening it died out. Some rain to-day.

Saturday, 17. Still lying in camp, waiting for the steamboat which is daily expected. Orders were to-day issued to company commanders to keep three days' cooked rations constantly on hand and to be prepared to cross the river at once upon the arrival of the boat. The cavalry pickets thought they saw two men on the bluffs across the river, but the Crows who were on the lookout saw nothing and it is probable that the pickets were mistaken.

Sunday, 18. This afternoon Major Reno, with six companies of the 7th Cavalry, appeared at the mouth of the Rosebud and went into camp.[8] General Gibbon went up opposite the camp and held a conversation with him by means of signal flags and afterwards communicated with him by letter through two Crows who swam the river for that purpose. Reno's command had scouted up Powder River, then crossed to the Rosebud, and scouted down the latter stream, meeting with no Sioux but finding recent traces of a large village at the place I discovered it on the twenty-seventh of May. Mitch Bouyer, our guide, who had been detached to accompany Reno, counted three hundred and sixty lodge fires, and estimated that there were enough beside to make the number of lodges about four hundred. The lodges had been arranged in nine circles within supporting distance of each other, within which the Indians evidently secured their horses at night, showing that they considered an attack not unlikely and were prepared for it. A well defined trail led from the side of the village across the plain toward the Little Big Horn, and it is now thought that the Indians will be found upon that stream.

Monday, 19. Major Reno's command broke camp this morning and moved down the river after supplies. Towards evening Thompson's and Wheelan's companies returned, having scouted up to the mouth of the Big Horn. They met no Sioux and saw no sign of them on this side, and but little on the other. The Crow village which some weeks ago was on the Big Horn seems to have disappeared from that country—another indication that the Sioux are heading in that direction. It is pretty well demonstrated that they have no intention of crossing to the north side of the Yellowstone, as they would not have passed so high up the stream for that purpose.

Tuesday, 20. Captain Freeman has been ordered to march up the river to-morrow with Companies E, H, and K of the infantry battalion to bridge creeks and otherwise put the road in order. He will take ten days' rations and will be accompanied by six Crow scouts.

Wednesday, June 21. Captain Freeman's command got off about six A. M. Soon afterward the steamboat was reported in sight, whereupon orders were issued to prepare to move. At 8 A. M. the boat arrived, having on board General Terry and staff and Captain Baker's company of the 6th Infantry. We were ordered to march at once to Fort Pease, and got off at 9:30 A. M., Captain Ball commanding, General Gibbon and Major Brisbin having gone on board the boat, intending to rejoin us at some point in advance.

Custer with the entire 7th Cavalry was reported near at hand, and soon after we started he appeared in view on the table-land across the river, marching toward the Rosebud. The steamboat met him at the mouth of that stream, when he drew rations for his command for sixteen days and struck out up the Rosebud with the design of following up the trail found by Major Reno. Prior to his departure a conference took place on the boat between Generals Terry, Gibbon and himself with reference to a combined movement between the two columns, and, though it is General Terry's expectation that we will arrive in the neighborhood of the Sioux village about the same time and assist each other in the attack, it is understood that if Custer arrives first he is at liberty to attack at once if he deems prudent.

We have little hope of being in at the death, as Custer will undoubtedly exert himself to the utmost to get there first and win all the laurels for himself and his regiment. He is provided with Indian scouts, but from the superior knowledge possessed by the Crows of the country he is to traverse it was decided to furnish him with a part of ours, and I was directed to make a detail for that purpose. I selected my six best men, and they joined him at the mouth of the Rosebud. Our guide, Mitch Bouyer, accompanies him also. This leaves us wholly without a guide, while Custer has one of the very best that the country affords. Surely he is being afforded every facility to make a successful pursuit.

We marched eighteen miles and camped at 7:05 P. M. on the Yellowstone, a short distance below the mouth of Great Porcupine, having passed Captain Freeman's command in camp at the spring a couple miles back. As we passed, Capt. Ball ordered him to move down and join us—a very unwelcome order to Captain Freeman's men who were comfortably settled for the night. The camp was barely formed when a terrible gale arose, followed by a storm of hailstones as large as walnuts. The herd showed a strong disposition to stampede, and it required great exertions to prevent them from doing so. The hailstones diminished in size as the storm continued, and soon turned to rain; but the shower was of short duration, and before dark the sky partially cleared and the sun treated us to a gorgeous display in the west.

Thursday, 22. During the night Lieutenant Low, 20th Infantry, joined us with his battery of three Gatling guns. They belong to Custer's column but were detached therefrom under the impression that they might impede his march.

It rained considerable during the night, and as a consequence the road in the valley was very muddy. The cavalry battalion separated from us this morning, under orders to push on to Fort Pease as rapidly as possible, the infantry following as fast as it can. Low's battery goes with the cavalry. The cavalry started at 6 A. M., and we followed at 7, soon passing the cavalry whose train got stuck in the mud. The two battalions crossed the Great Porcupine at different points, the infantry after crossing taking at once to the bench lands, while the cavalry continued up the valley. As a consequence the order of things was getting rapidly inverted, the infantry going to Fort Pease first, and glorying in their ability to outmarch the D. P's.: but at this juncture Captain Freeman chivalrously halted his column and let the cavalry go by. We marched twenty-nine miles and had a pleasant camp on the bank of the Yellowstone at 5:30 P. M., the cavalry camping in sight above us, having been able to gain only a mile and a half. We expected the steamboat to pass to-day, but it has not appeared.

Throughout the campaign the General has allowed neither drums nor bugles to sound, believing they might be the means of communicating information to the enemy. As a consequence strength of lung has been a very essential qualification in our battalion adjutants who, when the time for roll-calls or beginning the day's march arrives, must post themselves in a conspicuous position and bawl out the command loud enough to be heard all over the camp: "Form your companies!" Fortunately the gentlemen officiating in this capacity in their respective battalions have not been wanting in this regard; but still the cheerful rattle and toot of the proscribed instruments has been greatly missed, so much so that one of our officers who met some of the companies of Custer's command was heard to declare that, favorable as was the general impression they produced on his mind, there was nothing that delighted him more than the refrain of their bugles. Our cavalry comrades have been particularly restless under this prohibition, and it was observed to-day that no sooner did they cut loose from us than they began to sound their bugles with hearty good will. So much did the buglers glory in their new found freedom and the mellow notes they poured forth that they exerted themselves fit to crack their throats, and repeated the calls far more freely than was necessary for the mere information of the command. And candor compels me to say that, notwithstanding its duclet[9] capabilities, the voice of our adjutant shouting his old familiar cry of "Form your companies!" did not begin to produce an effect upon the ear as the "sonorous metal" of the cavalry "braying martial sounds."

Friday, 23. The reveille of the cavalry bugles came sweetly to the ear this morning across the intervening space. Broke camp at 6:05 A. M., and soon came up with the cavalry, who were still in camp but saddling up. Their train had pulled out and had the road ahead of us, and our train was unable to overhaul it although our teamsters were stimulated to do their best by the promise of a considerable purse that some of our frolicsome infantrymen made up in the interests of a race. The day was excessively hot and there was a deal of dust; making the marching quite disagreeable. The cavalry kept well in advance of us all day, in fact passed quite out of sight. Lieutenant Doane and "Muggins" Taylor, who were scouting ahead, saw several Sioux on the bluffs across the river, and also about a thousand buffalo running at full speed. A considerable number of the latter crossed the river and were intercepted by Lieutenant Doane's party who killed several of them. The cavalry supplied themselves liberally with the meat and had the kindness to butcher some also for the infantry, Lieutenant Doane remaining in person to notify us of it and point it out as we came up. We were greatly in need of it, having had very little fresh meat for a considerable period, but Lieutenant Jacobs, our quartermaster, with unaccountable obstinacy and disregard of the men's welfare objected to the train halting for the few minutes necessary to take it on, and Captain Freeman yielded the point and passed it by. So we marched into camp and supped on bacon, instead of the excellent buffalo steaks we might have had.

At 5:30 P. M. we camped on the bank of the Yellowstone about a mile below Fort Pease, having marched twenty-two miles. The cavalry had gone on and camped about two miles above the fort. The steamboat was sighted a few miles below this evening, and will probably be up early to-morrow.

Saturday, 24. The steamer passed our camp at 4:30 A. M., and moved on up to the camp of the cavalry. At 6 A. M. we broke camp and joined the cavalry, and soon afterward the whole command, except Captain Kirtland's Company (B), were ordered to prepare to march at once with eight days' rations and a pack train. The cavalry companies were assigned six and the infantry companies four pack-mules each, the train and camp equipage being left behind guarded by Company B.

About 11 A. M. twelve Crow scouts were carried over the river by the steamer to scout up Tullock's Fork, with orders to proceed until they found a Sioux village on[10] a recent trail. About noon the boat began to ferry over the remainder of the command, the cavalry going first in three trips, the Gatling battery, my detachment, and part of the infantry on the fourth trip, and the remainder of the infantry on the fifth, all being over about 4 P. M. My detachment then passed to the front, and the march began up the Big Horn, just below the mouth of which our landing had been effected. Arriving at Tullock's Fork, a tributary of the Big Horn, we turned up its valley and at 6 P. M. camped about a mile above its mouth at the foot of a perpendicular wall of rock, having marched about five miles since leaving the boat. General Terry and staff came up and joined us about an hour later; they are provided with common tents—a small wedge shaped tent—while the command bivouacs in the open air. General Gibbon has been quite sick and is still on the boat, but is expected to join to-morrow.

Just before dark the twelve Crows came whooping down the valley behaving in such extravagant fashion that all expected some startling disclosure; but it turned out that they had merely seen, six miles up the valley, a buffalo that had been recently wounded with arrows. Their orders had been to go ahead until they found a village, and now after wasting eight hours in advancing ten miles they return with this paltry piece of news. It was amusing to listen to the comments of some of the "pilgrims" as to the importance to be attached to this momentous intelligence. It really amounted to nothing, as the buffalo might have been wounded by a small war or scouting party a hundred miles from any camp; but the "pilgrims" saw it in positive evidence of the near vicinity of the village we are after. The Crows know better than to attach any such importance to it, but were glad of any subterfuge to return to the protection of the command.

We are now fairly en route to the Indian village, which is supposed to be on the Little Big Horn. It is undoubtedly a large one, and should Custer's command and ours unite we, too, will have a large force numbering all told about one thousand men, armed with the splendid breech-loading Springfield rifles and carbines, caliber forty-five, and strengthened by the presence of Low's battery of three Gatling guns. Should we come to blows it will be one of the biggest Indian battles ever fought on this continent, and the most decisive in its results, for such a force as we shall have if united will be invincible, and the utter destruction of the Indian village and overthrow of Sioux power will be the certain result. There is not much glory in Indian wars, but it will be worth while to have been present at such an affair as this.

The Far West will, if practicable, ascend the Big Horn as far as the mouth of the Little Big Horn, and there await tidings from us.

NOTES TO CHAPTER 34

1. The officer was Colonel John Gibbon. Bradley referred to him by his brevet title.

2. These boats were Mackinaw boats which had been obtained at Fort Pease, a temporary trading post abandoned earlier in 1876. It was located

about seven miles below the mouth of the Bighorn, on the left bank of the Yellowstone.

3. The steamboat *Far West,* commanded by Captain Grant Marsh, had been chartered by the army to carry supplies on the Missouri and Yellowstone for the forces commanded by General Terry. The story of Marsh's adventurous life has been told in *The Conquest of the Missouri,* by Hanson.

4. A few days earlier, scouts had located Indian villages on the Tongue and Rosebud rivers.

5. The word should be "orders."

6. This trail was made by Colonel Stanley's expedition while escorting the Northern Pacific survey party in 1873.

7. Privates Raymeyer and Stoker and a civilian teamster named Quinn had been killed by Sioux Indians while hunting a short distance from Gibbon's forces on May 23.

8. Major Marcus Reno served under Lieutenant Colonel Custer in the Seventh Cavalry.

9. The word should be "dulcet."

10. Probably this word should be "or."

Chapter 35

1876

FROM THE YELLOWSTONE TO THE LITTLE BIGHORN,

by Lieutenant James H. Bradley

This excerpt from Bradley's journal describes his experiences on the twenty-fifth and twenty-sixth of June, 1876. The forces of Colonel Gibbon and General Terry, combined, and commanded by the general, had crossed the Yellowstone and were moving toward the Little Bighorn River, over the rough country east of the Bighorn. The route of march was nearly south.

On the twenty-fifth of June Lieutenant Colonel Custer with the Seventh Cavalry reached the Little Bighorn from the east and found in its valley a large camp of Sioux Indians and their Cheyenne and Arapaho allies. Custer divided his command into four parts. He personally led five companies toward the Indian camp over the high ground north of the Little Bighorn. Major Reno, with three companies, moved down the valley of the stream. Captain Benteen, with three companies, was ordered to take a route to the left of Reno, but the nature of the terrain forced him to return to the river valley and the route followed by Reno. The pack train, guarded by Captain McDougall with one company, also followed this route, a little behind Benteen.

On the left bank of the Little Bighorn Reno met an overwhelming attack of Indian warriors. He retreated, crossed the river, and climbed to a position on the bluffs near the right bank of the stream. Here he was joined by Benteen and McDougall. The seven companies, under the command of Major Reno, advanced about two miles in the direction previously taken by Custer to a position since called Weir Point. From Weir Point Reno retreated to his original position on the bluffs. The Indians attacked this position at intervals during the rest of the day, and most of the next day. Reno's command suffered severe losses, but was able to hold the position.

In the meantime Custer with five companies proceeded over the high ground northeast of the Little Bighorn until he was about even with the main body of the Indian village. Here he was attacked by nearly the whole body of Indian warriors, and his entire detachment was destroyed.

With the approach of Terry's command on the twenty-sixth of June the Indians discontinued their siege of Reno's position, and moved their camp from the battle area. Lieutenant Bradley, scouting ahead of Terry's forces on the twenty-sixth, was probably the first white man not actually in the battle of the Little Big Horn, to be told the result of the battle.

Sunday, 25. At 4 A. M. in compliance with orders I sent six Crows up Tullock's Fork, and half an hour later followed with the remainder of the Crows and my detachment. At 5:30 A. M. the command broke camp and marched two miles up Tullock's Fork and then turned off to the right into the hills expecting to find a comparatively level table-land leading to the Little Big Horn. Meantime I had ascended the stream nine miles, when I halted to await some indication that I was being followed by the command, and after a long delay was overtaken by a squad of cavalry sent to notify me of the change of route. I soon rejoined, taking a short cut across the hills, and found the command involved in a labyrinth of bald hills and deep, precipitous ravines completely destitute of water. The men had emptied their canteens of the wretched alkali water they started with and were parched with thirst as well as greatly fatigued with clambering over such ground. A worse route could not have been chosen, but destitute of a guide as we are it is not to be wondered that we entangled ourselves in such a mesh of physical obstacles.

While the command struggled on toward the Big Horn as the nearest point of escape, I executed an order given me by General Terry to scout to a distant ridge on the left of our line of march, from which it was thought the Little Big Horn might be seen and possibly an Indian camp. Reaching the ridge after an exceedingly toilsome march of eight miles over a very rough country, I found myself confronted by another ridge a few miles farther on that completely obstructed the view. Having been ordered not to pass the first ridge, I turned back and overtook the infantry battalion at 6:50 P. M., just as they were going into camp in the valley of the Big Horn. There I learned that some of the Crows who had gone up Tullock's Fork in the morning had discovered a smoke in the direction of the Little Big Horn, which was thought to indicate the presence of the Sioux village, and the cavalry and Gatling battery, accompanied by General Terry, were pushing on with a view of getting as near it as possible to-night. The infantry, which had already marched twenty-three miles, were to remain in camp for the night and follow in the morning.

I joined the cavalry with my detachment, orders having been left for me to that effect. A brisk rain set in toward evening, and continued to fall in successive showers through the first half of the night. Darkness overtook us still pushing on up the Big Horn, and though the march had been difficult by day it was doubly so in the darkness of the night. The cavalry officers who scouted up the Big Horn last April were acting as guides, for want of better, and, as their knowledge of the country was far from profound, we were continually encountering serious obstacles to our march—now a precipitous hillside, now a deep ravine. Occasionally as the head of the column was checked we would find ourselves closed up in a dense mass, and again where the path grew narrow we would stretch out in an attenuated thread, the men in the rear racing desperately after those in front not to lose sight of them in the gloom and be left without a clue to the direction they had taken. Every now and then a long halt was made, as an avenue of escape was sought from some topographical net in which we had become involved.

There was great danger at times, when the column stretched out to unusual length, that it would become broken and leave us scattered over the country in a dozen bewildered fragments, and once the cry did go up: "The battery is missing!" A halt was made, and after some racing and hallooing the missing guns were set right again, having lost the human thread and so wandered a mile or so out of the way. At another time some of the cavalry went astray, and lost half an hour getting back to us.

At length after hours of such toil, getting out of one difficulty only to plunge at once into another, the head of the column came plump on the brink of a precipice at whose foot swept the roaring waters of the Big Horn. The water gleamed in front a hundred and fifty feet below, and to the right hand and to the left the ground broke off into a steep declivity down which nothing could be seen but forbidding gloom. Our cavalry guides were wholly bewildered, and everybody was tired out, and dripping with wet, and impatient to get somewhere and rest. When General Terry saw the walls of Fort Fisher before him he knew what to do. He threw his battalions against them, carried them by storm, and gained a glorious victory and won a star; but when he saw to what a pass we had now come and reflected that every step we took seemed only to render our situation more perplexing, he appeared uncertain and irresolute. For several minutes we sat our horses looking by turn at the water and into the black ravines, when I ventured to suggest to the General that we trust ourselves to the guidance of Little Face, one of my Crow scouts who had roamed this country as a boy fifty years ago and had previously assured me that he knew every foot of it. Little Face was called up, said he could guide us to a good camping ground, was accepted as a guide, and led off in the dark with as much confidence as though he was in the full light of day. The aimless, profitless scrambling was over; he conducted us by an easy route a mile or two to the left, where we found ourselves in a commodious valley with water enough in its little channel to suffice for drinking purposes. There was not much grass for the animals, but it was the best we could do without going several miles farther and so about midnight we halted, unsaddled, and threw our weary forms down on the ground for a little rest, the cavalry having marched about thirty-five miles and my detachment, in consequence of its diversions from the main column, about fifty-five.

Monday, 26. Major Brisbin, who in General Gibbon's absence commands the column, roused me up this morning at daylight and ordered me out on a scout at once, not allowing my men to get breakfast. As I had traveled some twenty miles farther yesterday than anybody else, so that my horses were tired and my men hungry, it struck me as rather rough treatment. I was too much vexed to hurry much, and did not get off till 4 A. M., having sent six Crows ahead half an hour earlier. My orders were to scout to the Little Big Horn, looking out for Sioux sign and sending back word of any important discoveries. Having advanced about three miles we entered a valley cut by a dry creek, and here came upon the fresh tracks of four ponies. As we entered the ravine we had seen a heavy smoke rising in our front, apparently fifteen or twenty miles away, and I at once concluded we were approaching the Sioux village and that the trail had been made by a party of scouts therefrom.

Sending back a written report of the discovery, I took the trail of the four supposed Sioux in the hope of catching them in the Big Horn valley, toward which the trail led and where we thought they might have camped, as there was no convenient way of leaving the valley into which they had gone except that by which they had entered it.

At the distance of less than two miles the trail struck the river, and we found that they had there crossed leaving behind a horse and several articles of personal equipment, indicating that they had fled in great haste. An examination of the articles disclosed to our great surprise that they belonged to some of the Crows whom I had furnished to General Custer at the mouth of the Rosebud, which rendered it probable that the supposed Sioux were some of our own scouts who had for some reason left Custer's command and were returning to the Crow agency. While speculating upon the circumstances three men were discovered on the opposite side of the Big Horn about two miles away, apparently watching our movements. We at once signaled to them with blankets that we were friends, for a long time to no purpose, but when we were about to give up and seek some other method of communicating with them, they responded by kindling a fire that sent up a small column of smoke indicating that they had seen signals and trusted our assurances. We gathered wet sagebrush and assured them with a similar smoke, and soon afterwards they came down to the river and talked across the stream with Little Face and one or two more of the scouts who went down to meet them. While the interview went on I kept the remainder of the detachment on the bluffs. Presently our Indians turned back and, as they came, shouted out at the top of their voices a doleful series of cries and wails that the interpreter, Bravo, explained was a song of mourning for the dead. That it boded some misfortune there was no doubt; and when they came up, shedding copious tears and appearing pictures of misery, it was evident that the occasion was of no common sort. Little Face in particular wept with a bitterness of anguish such as I have rarely seen. For awhile he could not speak, but at last composed himself and told his story in a choking voice, broken with frequent sobs. As he proceeded, the Crows one by one broke off from the group of listeners and going aside a little distance sat down alone, weeping and chanting that dreadful mourning song, and rocking their bodies to and fro. They were the first listeners to the horrid story of the Custer massacre, and, outside of the relatives and personal friends of the fallen, there were none in this whole horrified nation of forty millions of people to whom the tidings brought greater grief. The three men over the river were in truth a portion of the six scouts furnished to General Custer from my detachment; and this is the story they told to Little Face:

After Custer left the mouth of the Rosebud he had followed the Indian trail and yesterday struck the village on the Little Big Horn, the Sioux warriors letting him get close to the village and then sallying forth in overwhelming numbers to meet him, defeating his command, and destroying all but a small portion who had been driven into the hills and surrounded by the Sioux, where the Crows had left them fighting desperately. The corpses of Custer's men were strewn all over the country, and it was probable before this that the last one was killed as it was impossible for the party who had taken refuge in the hills to hold out long, for the Sioux immensely outnumbered them and were attacking them in dense masses on all sides. Of the six Crows who had gone with Custer, two—White Swan and Half Yellow Face—were killed, and another—Curly—was missing and probably also killed. The fighting had occurred at the point where the smoke was then rising in our front. It was a terrible, terrible story, so different from the outcome we had hoped for this campaign, and I no longer wondered at the demonstrative sorrow of the Crows. My men listened to it with eager interest, betraying none of the emotion of the Crows, but looking at each other with white faces in pained silence too full of the dreadful recital to utter a word. Did we doubt the tale? I could not; there was an undefined vague something about it, unlooked for though it was, that commanded assent, and the most I could do was to hope that in the terror of the three fugitives from the fatal field their account of the disaster was somewhat overdrawn. But that there had been a disaster—a terrible disaster, I felt assured.

It was my duty to report it to General Terry, and being a matter of such importance I resolved to make the report in person, as I now saw the head of the column appearing over the ridge a couple of miles away. I therefore rode back until I met the command, which was halted just before I came up, and narrated to the General the ghastly details as I had received them from Little Face. He was surrounded by his staff and accompanied by General Gibbon, who had that morning joined, and for a moment there were blank faces and silent tongues and no doubt heavy hearts in that group, just as there had been among the auditors of Little Face at its rehearsal by him. But presently the voice of doubt and scorning was raised, the story was sneered at, such a catastrophe it was asserted was wholly improbable, nay impossible; if a battle had been fought, which was condescendingly admitted might have happened, then Custer was victorious, and these three Cows were dastards who had fled without awaiting the result and told this story to excuse their cowardice. General Terry took no part in these criticisms, but sat on his horse silent and thoughtful, biting his lower lip and looking to me as though he by no means shared in the wholesale skepticism of the flippant members of his staff. My imagination was busy supplying to my mind his train of thought, and it ran like this: "The story may not be true, when we have only to push on according to the original plan. It may be true, and it then becomes our duty to hasten to the rescue of the miserable remnant of Custer's command surrounded on the hills. If the savages have been able to destroy Custer's noble six hundred, what can we hope to accomplish with our paltry four? But we will do the best we can and rescue the wretched survivors or ourselves perish in the attempt." And as though it were the seal of authenticity to this bold attempt to divine the workings of his mind, he cried "Forward!" and once more the column was in motion toward the foe. My duty there was done and taking a rapid gait I soon gained my proper distance in front as advance guard.

The infantry had remained in camp last night twelve miles back and at 5 A. M. resumed the march, coming up with the cavalry toward noon, having been greatly delayed by the pack-train. The whole column then advanced together and having crossed the dry creek, where I now found the trail, and the rugged divide separating it from the Little Big Horn, entered the valley of that stream. The heavy smoke was now continually in view, and notwithstanding the stiffened limbs of the infantry, in consequence of their hard march yesterday, the prospect of an early arrival at the village and a brush with the Indians imparted a wonderful animation to their movements and urged them on at a rapid gait. After passing up the valley a few miles the column crossed to the left bank and soon afterward halted to allow the men to rest and make coffee.

The three Crows who had escaped from Custer's battle-field promised to recross the Big Horn and rejoin the command, provided some of their comrades waited for them, and partly on this account and partly to allow them time to recover from their grief I permitted all the Crows to remain behind when the column passed the point where we had received news of Custer's overthrow. Bravo, the interpreter, staid with them, and as he was frightened nearly out of his wits by the unfortunate tidings, and anxious to avoid going on, he no sooner saw us fairly out of the way than he exerted himself to induce the Crows to abandon the expedition; representing to them that some of our officers had said we no longer wanted their services. Several of the best Crows were opposed to such a measure, but Bravo aided by some of the malcontents among them carried the point against such, and the whole body were seen by some of the officers at the rear of the column to mount and gallop away together. They recrossed the river and proceeded straight to the Crow agency.

During our afternoon rest, citizens Bostwick and Taylor were sent forward by different routes toward the village to reconnoiter and communicate with Custer should he prove to be in possession. While they were still absent and after we had rested about two hours, the column was again, at 5 P. M., put in march up the valley, my detachment in advance. After advancing about two miles I discovered several ponies on my left front, toward the river, and taking Corporal Abbott with me moved over to investigate. They proved to be five in number, evidently estrays from the village, and taking possession of them, I sent them back to the column. Not long afterward I discovered three or four mounted men about two miles in advance, and at once deployed my detachment as skirmishers; and soon afterward Bostwick came into view down the valley galloping at full speed. As he came up he paused long enough to say that he had proceeded cautiously up the valley for several miles until all at once he came plump on a considerable body of Indians. Not caring to cultivate their acquaintance nearer he turned short about and retreated at the best speed of his horse.

It was now sufficiently evident that we had Indians in our front, and the column advanced slowly in fighting order, the Gatling battery and three companies of cavalry in column on the right, four companies of infantry in column on the left, and one company of infantry and the pack-mules in the centre—a part of the infantry company at the head and part at the rear of the packs. Generals Terry and Gibbon with their staffs rode at the head of the column, Lieutenant Roe with his company of cavalry being advanced half a mile or so on the bluffs to the right while I moved abreast of him on the left up the valley, passing through the timber that grew in occasional clumps along the stream.

As we advanced I continually saw Indians up the valley and on the bluffs to the right, riding about singly and in groups of two, three, half a dozen, and more. Once they appeared to the number of seventy-five or a hundred on a distant hill, and not long afterwards several rifle shots rang out from the bluffs where Roe was advancing, and a few shots were exchanged by the Indians and a few of our eager men who pushed to the front. One circumstance caused me a good deal of disquietude, and that was that the Indians were evidently massing in the timber at a narrow place in the valley, with the apparent intention of resisting at that point our further advance. Squad after squad of mounted savages galloped down the slope of the hills into this grove until I estimated that not less than a hundred had entered it after we came into view, and how many other hundreds might already have been there or entered by some other way could only be conjectured. As I had this timber to go through with my detachment, it was not pleasant to think of the storm of bullets that would undoubtedly be hurled into our faces as we rode up to its dark border or of the painted hundreds that would rise suddenly on all sides of us, as we got fairly entangled within its recesses, and cut off the whole of us in a moment. I have been in several engagements and participated in several charges upon intrenched positions, but in my whole career as a soldier never did anything call for so much nerve as the riding slowly up with eleven men, half a mile from the rest of the column, on this body of ambushed warriors. My men sat their saddles with pale faces but closed lips with stern determination, expecting in a few minutes more to be shot down, but resolved not to flinch though the cost were death.

Meanwhile Lieutenant Roe was advancing on the bluffs and from his elevated position could see a long line of moving dark objects defiling across the prairie from the Little Big Horn toward the Big Horn, as if the village were in motion, retreating before us. But between him and them was a numerous body of warriors estimated by some observers as high as three hundred men. Those nearest him appeared to be clothed in blue uniforms, and carried guidons, forming in line, breaking into column and otherwise maneuvering like a body of cavalry. Under the impression that they might be members of Custer's command a sergeant and three men were sent forward several hundred yards, and when well advanced the sergeant left his men and approached them alone to within hailing distance; but upon calling out to them was quickly undeceived as to their character by receiving a volley in response that caused him to retire hastily. About this time Taylor returned from his attempt to reach the village (beleagured cavalrymen), having, like Bostwick, encountered Indians but not escaping without being fired upon.

My detachment was now drawing near the timber in which the Indians were ambushed, and we were nerving ourselves for the expected annihilation when the column halted, and I too halted, something like a quarter of a mile from the timber. At this moment several horses emerged from the timber and came directly toward us, some of the men asserting that they bore riders, but it was now twilight and I could not tell with certainty. Bostwick and Will Logan saw these horses from the bluffs and resolved to attempt their capture. The horses had stopped about half way between my line and the timber, but Bostwick and Will boldly passed in the rear and drove them toward my line, having been close under the guns of the ambushed Sioux who could easily have picked them off had they chosen to fire. But probably expecting soon to get my detachment in range they forebore to do so, and the venturesome fellows got off safe and conducted their booty to the camp—four good Indian ponies.

Lieutenant Burnett soon rode up to inform me that camp was forming, and that I was to remain where I was untill the cavalry companies ceased watering and then join the command. This was very welcome intelligence, indeed, as it saved us from riding into the dreaded ambush and seemed like a gift to us of our lives. The cavalry companies were watering a few hundred yards in our rear and finished soon after dark, and we then returned, finding the command bivouacked in the valley midway between the stream and the bluffs and about half a mile from each. No fires were allowed and we lay upon our arms, arranged in a square, but with a very weak face indeed down the river, that side, I believe, being occupied by only a guard of twenty-odd men. The animals were secured within the square. The halt was made at 9 P. M., the infantry having marched thirty miles, the remainder of the command about eighteen. The steamboat is working its way up the Big Horn, having touched this morning at the point where the infantry camped last night. General Gibbon remained with it up to that time and then came on and joined the command early in the day.

Before retiring the officers assembled in groups and talked over the events of the day. I found that a majority of the infantry officers placed confidence in the report brought by the Crows of Custer's overthrow, and were prepared for unpleasant disclosures upon the morrow. Some of the cavalry officers also shared in this conviction, but the majority of them and about all of the staff were wholly skeptical and still had faith that Custer had been victorious if he had fought at all. So obstinate is human nature in some of its manifestations that there were actually men in the command who lay down to sleep that night in the firm conviction, notwithstanding all the disclosures of the day, that there was not an Indian in our front and that the men seen were members of Custer's command. They could explain ingeniously every circumstance that had a contrary look, and to argue with them was worse than useless. Some of the officers had a theory that a great mistake was committed in not sending them forward with a dash when the Indians were first discovered to hack the enemy in infinitesimal mincemeat. They still, months later, adhere to this position, and I therefore take this occasion to give my testimony that such a proceeding would have been in the highest degree absurd. Had they been sent they had the spirit to go forward gallantly, but there were Indians enough in the timber and on the hills before them, in chosen positions of great strength, to have cut them all to pieces and driven them back in ruinous disorder. From subsequent examinations of the ground I am convinced that there were not less than a thousand of these ambushed savages, with plenty more to co-operate with them, and not only would they have easily defeated the cavalry, but they would have given our whole command a desperate fight had we advanced that evening another mile. Their village was retreating, and they were there to cover it, and it was only for lack of an hour or more of daylight that we did not come upon them in force and prove once more the terrific gallantry with which they can fight under such an incitement as the salvation of their all.

Chapter 36

1876

THE LITTLE BIG HORN BATTLEFIELD,

by Lieutenant Edward Maguire

Edward Maguire graduated from West Point in 1867 and was assigned to the Corps of Engineers as a second lieutenant. He became a first lieutenant February 15, 1869, a captain June 14, 1881, and died October 11, 1892. In 1876 he was assigned to the Department of Dakota as Chief Engineer and in that capacity accompanied the expedition commanded by Brigadier General Terry to the battlefield on the Little Bighorn Custer's detachment was wiped out on June 25, Reno's command was in a state of siege until late afternoon of June 26, and Maguire reached the battlefield on June 27.

I am reprinting Maguire's report in full, as it appeared in the *Report of the Secretary of War* for 1876.

CAMP ON THE YELLOWSTONE RIVER,
NEAR THE MOUTH OF THE BIG HORN RIVER,
July 10, 1876.

GENERAL: I have the honor to submit the following report of operations in the Department of Dakota from the date of my assignment to duty as chief engineer of the department to the close of the fiscal year ending June 30, 1876:

In obedience to orders received from the Adjutant-General's Office, I reported in person to Brig. Gen. A. H. Terry, at St. Paul, Minn., on the evening of May 8, and was assigned to duty vice Capt. Wm. Ludlow, Corps of Engineers, United States Army, relieved. In compliance with orders from headquarters Department of Dakota, I left Saint Paul early on the morning of the 10th, and proceeded to Fort Abraham Lincoln, Dakota Territory, to join the troops about to take the field against the hostile Sioux. Mr. W. H. Wood, assistant engineer, with the detachment of enlisted men, had preceded me some days. On arriving at Fort Lincoln, I learned from the commanding general that, unless the services of my assistant were necessary, it was desirable that he should not accompany the column. As his services would have been simply a convenience to me, and in no respect a necessity, I directed him to return to St. Paul, where he has remained. The detachment of the battalion of engineers, consisting of Sergeant Wilson and Privates Goslin and Culligan, has accompanied me on the expedition, and has performed most excellent service. Sergeant Becker, with two privates, had, previous to my assignment, been ordered to Montana to accompany the column under command of Colonel Gibbon, Seventh Infantry.

After a detention of a few days near Fort Lincoln, due to rain, we finally broke camp at 5 a. m., May 17, and the march westward was commenced. The column was commanded by Brig. Gen. A. H. Terry, and was composed of the following troops: The Seventh Cavalry, commanded by Lieut. Col. G. A. Custer; a battalion of infantry, commanded by Capt. L. H. Sanger, Seventeenth Infantry; headquarters' guard, consisting of one company of the Sixth Infantry, commanded by Capt. Stephen Baker, a battery of three ½-inch Gatling guns, commanded by Second Lieut. W. H. Low, Twentieth Infantry; 45 Indian scouts, guides and interpreters, under the command of Second Lieut. C. A. Varnum, Seventh Cavalry; the wagon and pack-trains and herd, with their numerous attachés. There was a total of 50 officers, 968 enlisted men, 190 civilian employés, and 1,694 animals.

I was furnished with a four-mule ambulance for the transportation of my instruments and men. To the wheels of this ambulance were attached the odometers.

The column reached Powder River without having seen an Indian nor even a trace of recent origin. The only difficulties encountered, with the exception of a snow-storm, which commenced on the night of the 31st of May and lasted until the 3d of June, were those offered by the nature of the country to the passage of a heavily-loaded train. There was not a day that bridging was not necessary; but the journey through Davis Creek to the Little Missouri, through the Bad Lands immediately west of the latter stream, and then the descent into the valley of the Powder, demanded almost incessant bridging and road-making. We reached Powder River late in the evening of June 7. From this camp, Major Reno, Seventh Cavalry, with six companies of his regiment, was sent on a scout up Powder River to the forks, thence across to the Rosebud and back to the mouth of the Tongue. On June 11 we marched down the valley of the Powder, and reached the Yellowstone, where a depot was established under command of Major Moore, Sixth

Infantry. Leaving the wagon-train at this point, Lieutenant Colonel Custer, with the troops and pack-train, proceeded to the mouth of Tongue River. General Terry and staff went on the steamboat to the same place, there meeting Reno, who reported that he had found a fresh heavy Indian trail, leaving the Rosebud in a westerly direction. The whole command was then moved up the Yellowstone to the mouth of the Rosebud, where we met Gibbon's column. At this point, a definite plan of campaign was decided upon; and, as this plan is clearly set forth in the letter of instruction furnished to Custer, I insert it in full:

CAMP AT MOUTH OF ROSEBUD RIVER
June 22, 1876.

Colonel: The brigadier-general commanding directs that as soon as your regiment can be made ready for the march, you proceed up the Rosebud in pursuit of the Indians whose trail was discovered by Major Reno a few days since.

It is of course impossible to give you any definite instructions in regard to this movement, and, were it not impossible to do so, the department commander places too much confidence in your zeal, energy and ability to wish to impose upon you precise orders which might hamper your action when nearly in contact with the enemy. He will, however, indicate to you his own views of what your action should be, and he desires that you should conform to them unless you shall see sufficient reason for departing from them. He thinks that you should proceed up the Rosebud until you ascertain definitely the direction in which the trail above spoken of leads; should it be found (as it appears to be almost certain that it will be found) to turn toward the Little Big Horn, he thinks that you should still proceed southward perhaps as far as the headwaters of the Tongue, and then turn toward the Little Big Horn, feeling constantly, however, to your left, so as to preclude the possibility of the escape of the Indians to the south or southeast by passing around your left flank.

The column of Colonel Gibbon is now in motion for the mouth of the Big Horn; as soon as it reaches that point, it will cross the Yellowstone and move up at least as far as the forks of the Big and Little Big Horns.

Of course, its future movements must be controlled by circumstances as they arise; but it is hoped that the Indians, if upon the Little Big Horn, may be so nearly enclosed by the two columns that their escape will be impossible. The department commander desires that on your way up the Rosebud you should thoroughly examine the upper part of Tulloch's Creek, and that you should endeavor to send a scout through to Colonel Gibbon's column with information of the result of your examination. The lower part of this creek will be examined by a detachment from Colonel Gibbon's command. The supply-steamer will be pushed up the Big Horn as far as the forks if the river is found to be navigable for that distance, and the department commander (who will accompany the column of Colonel Gibbon) desires you to report to him there not later than the expiration of the time for which your troops are rationed, unless, in the mean time, you receive further orders.

Respectfully, &c.,

E. W. Smith

Captain Eighteenth Infantry, Acting Assistant Adjutant General.

Lieutenant-Colonel Custer,
Seventh Cavalry.

These instructions were supplemented by verbal information to Custer that he could expect to find Gibbon's column at the mouth of the Little Big Horn not later than the 26th.

Pursuant to these instructions, Custer took up his line of march about noon on the 22d of June. His command (counting officers, enlisted men, and civilians) numbered nearly 650 mounted men. Both man and beast were in excellent condition, and there was not one of the command who was not filled with high hopes of success. Upon Custer's departure, General Terry and staff proceeded up the Yellowstone with Gibbon's column, and when near the mouth of the Big Horn the command was crossed to the right bank of the former stream. Gibbon's column, as now constituted, consisted of four companies of the Second Cavalry, five companies of the Seventh Infantry, and Lieutenant Low's Gatling Battery, amounting in all (including the civilian employés) to 377 fighting men. The night of June 24 we passed in camp on Tulloch's Creek. The next day we crossed the divide between Tulloch's Creek and the Big Horn and reached the latter stream, after a severe march of twenty-two miles. The country was exceedingly rough, hill after hill and ravine after ravine, with but little grass and plenty of the ubiquitous sage, and cactus. The soil was alkaline, and the air was filled with dust, clogging up the nostrils, ears, and throat. In addition to this the day was very warm, and not a drop of water to be obtained on the march. The infantry had understood that we were to follow Tulloch's Creek, and knowing that in that case they could obtain water at any time they did not fill their canteens. The consequence was that they suffered terribly, and numbers of men toward the close of the march dropped on the way, utterly exhausted. The refreshing sight of the Big Horn finally gladdened their hearts, and those left on the road having been brought in, they remained in camp that night. General Terry, taking the cavalry, pushed on and a most wearisome and disheartening march we made of it. The night was black, and a cold rain drenched us. Besides this, we were obliged to cross a very rough country; and the descent and ascent of steep declivities, with no other guide than an occasional white horse, (if so lucky as to get directly behind one,) was anything but pleasant. The Indian scouts finally found a pool of alkaline water after a march of 12 miles, and we encamped in the mud for the short remaining portion of the night. About 11 o'clock the following morning (June 26) we were joined by the infantry near the mouth of the Little Big Horn, and we then proceeded up the valley of that river. We went into camp that night only after the infantry had made a march of more than 50 miles in two days. The next morning the march was resumed, and we soon sighted two teepees in the valley. These teepees were filled with dead warriors, and were all that remained standing of a large Indian village. We found the ground strewn with skins, robes, camp-equipage, &c., indicating that the village had been hastily removed. The cavalry-saddles and dead horses lying around gave us the first inkling of the fact that there had been a fight, and that the troops had been worsted; but we were not prepared for the whole truth. As we passed on, we were met by Lieutenant Wallace, of the Seventh Cavalry, who informed us that Major Reno, with the remnant of seven companies, was entrenched on the bluffs across the river, where he had sustained a siege of nearly two days. We ascended the steep bluffs, and the welcome we received was such as to move even the most callous. Officers and men relieved their surcharged natures by hysterical shouts and tears. The question then arose on all sides, "Where is Custer?" The reply came only too soon. About 3 miles below Reno's position, we found the hills covered with the bodies of officers and men.

Of Custer's fight we at present know nothing, and can only surmise. We must be content with the knowledge gleaned from the appearance of the field, that they died as only brave men can die and that this battle, slaughter as it was, was fought with a gallantry and desperation of which the "Charge of the Light Brigade" cannot boast. The bodies, with few exceptions, were frightfully multilated, and horrors stared us in the face at every step.

I proceed to give the details of Custer's march from the Rosebud, and of the battle, as I have been able to collect them up to the present time. On the 22d they marched 12 miles; on the 23d they marched 35 miles; on the 24th they marched from 5 a. m. till 8 p. m. or about 45 miles; they then rested for four hours. At 12 they started again and proceeded 10 miles. They were then about 23 miles from the village. They reached the

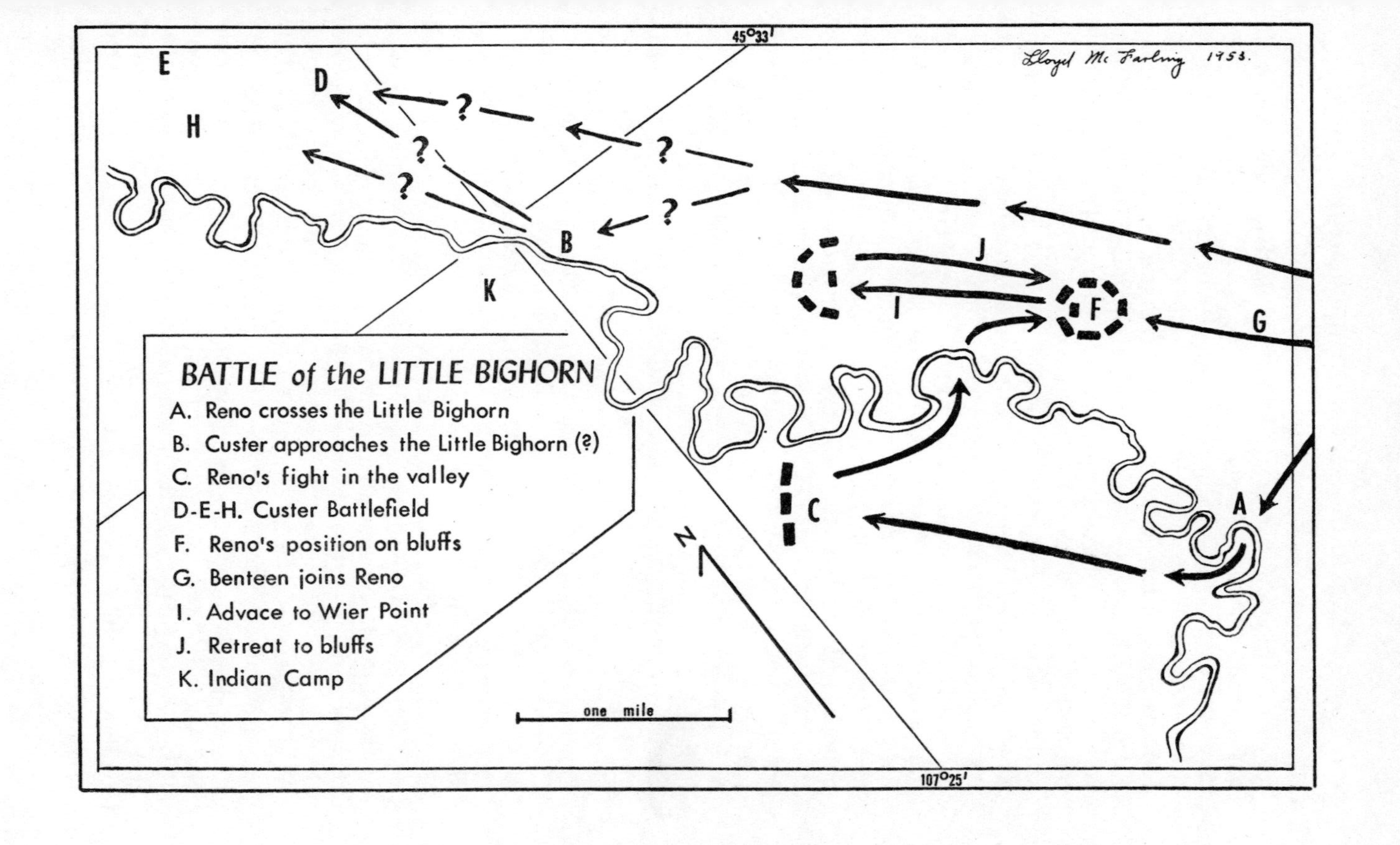
45°33'
Lloyd Mc Farling 1953.
E
D
H
B
K
J
I
F
G
C
A
N
BATTLE of the LITTLE BIGHORN
A. Reno crosses the Little Bighorn
B. Custer approaches the Little Bighorn (?)
C. Reno's fight in the valley
D-E-H. Custer Battlefield
F. Reno's position on bluffs
G. Benteen joins Reno
I. Advace to Wier Point
J. Retreat to bluffs
K. Indian Camp
one mile
107°25'

village about 2 p. m. on the 25th. They had made a march of 78 miles in a day and a half, and Captain Benteen tells me, without a drop of water. At some distance from the village, Custer made his disposition of the regiment. He ordered Benteen, with three companies, to move to the left and scour the country for Indians. He ordered Reno, with three companies, to advance parallel with his (Custer's) own command. When the village was sighted, he ordered Reno to charge with his three companies, telling him that he would be supported. Reno crossed the river at the point A, (see sketch herewith,) and moved down the woods at C without encountering much opposition. On reaching this latter point, the men were dismounted and deployed as skirmishers on the line indicated on the sketch. The Indians immediately swarmed around them, and Reno, finding that they were getting in his rear in large numbers, remounted his command and charged through them in retreat to the bluffs on the opposite side of the river. There were Indians on all sides of them, and Lieutenant McIntosh and several enlisted men were actually pulled from their horses and butchered. The command, with some loss, including Lieutenant Hodgson, reached the bluffs, and, being joined by Benteen and his command, they succeeded in keeping the Indians off. Benteen had received an order from Custer to hurry up, as the village had been struck, and in moving up he saw Reno's retreat, and joined him on the bluffs as quickly as possible. The Indians were all around them, and kept up an incessant fire of unerring accuracy. In the meantime Custer had gone down stream and attempted to make a crossing at the point B, but was met by an overpowering force, and the troops retreated to the hills in rear in order to procure a more defensible position.[1] From the position of the dead bodies on the field, I conclude that they retreated on the two lines marked on the sketch to concentrate at E, which was the highest point of the ground. At the hill D a stand was undoubtedly made by the company under command of Lieutenant Calhoun to protect the men passing up to E. Lieutenants Calhoun and Crittenden were killed on this hill. Captain Keogh was killed about halfway up the slope to E. The column which retreated along the line B. H. E. must have been dismounted, and, fighting along the whole distance, a portion of its men, taking to the ravine H for shelter, must have been surrounded by the Indians. There were twenty-eight bodies found in this ravine. From H to E stretched a line of dead men with skirmish intervals. The crest E was literally covered with dead officers and men. Here we found General Custer and his brother, Captain Custer, Captain Yates, Lieutenant Smith, Lieutenant Cook, and Lieutenant Riley. The Indians must have been present in overwhelming numbers, for this part of the fight did not, from all accounts, last over two or three hours.

As night came on, the attack on Reno ceased, and the troops were enabled to intrench. The attack was renewed early on the morning of the 26th, and continued until late in the afternoon, when the Indians seeing Gibbon's column advancing in the distance, left Reno, and, packing up their village, moved off toward the Big Horn Mountains. The number of Indians is estimated to have been fully 3,000 warriors, and they marched off with all the precision of movement and regularity of formation of the best-drilled soldiers. The officers tell me that they (the Indians) fought with the utmost bravery and coolness, and that they were well drilled and disciplined. Volleys were fired by them at the commands "Ready! Aim!! Fire!!!"[2]

The casualties of the Seventh Cavalry are as follows:

Killed. Lieut. Col. G. A. Custer, Seventh Cavalry; Capt. M. W. Keogh, Seventh Cavalry; Capt. G. W. Yates, Seventh Cavalry; Capt. T. W. Custer, Seventh Cavalry; Lieut. W. W. Cook, Seventh Cavalry; Lieut. A. E. Smith, Seventh Cavalry; Lieut. D. McIntosh, Seventh Cavalry; Lieut. J. Calhoun, Seventh Cavalry; Lieut. J. E. Porter, Seventh Cavalry; Lieut. B. H. Hodgson, Seventh Cavalry; Lieut. H. M. Harrington, Seventh Cavalry; Lieut. J. C. Sturgis, Seventh Cavalry; Lieut. W. V. W. Riley, Seventh Cavalry; Asst. Surg. G. E. Lord; Act. Asst. Surg. De Wolf; Lieut. J. J. Crittenden, Twentieth Infantry—16 officers; 252 enlisted men; 9 civilian employes; 277 killed; 59 wounded. The number of Indians killed and wounded is not known.[3]

We remained two days on the field to bury the dead and burn the material left by the Indians, and then returned to the boat with the wounded, who have all been sent to Fort Lincoln. We are here waiting in camp for instructions.

There are some conclusions which force themselves upon the mind as indubitable. They are as follows:

1st. The number of Indians was underestimated at the outset of the campaign.

2nd. The courage, skill, and, in short, the general fighting ability of the Indians has heretofore been underestimated and scoffed at. It has been forgotten that the Indian traders, by furnishing the Indian with the best breech-loading arms, and all the ammunition they desire, have totally changed the problem of Indian warfare.[4] Sitting Bull has displayed the best of generalship in this campaign. He has kept his troops well in hand, and, moving on interior lines, he has beaten us in detail.[5]

3d. The Indians are the best irregular cavalry in the world, and are superior in horsemanship and marksmanship to our soldiers, besides being better armed. Our regiments of cavalry are composed of men about three fourths of whom are recruits, who have never fought with Indians. They are never drilled at firing on horseback, and the consequence is that the horses are as unused to fighting as the men themselves and become unruly in action.

4th. The carbine has not a sufficiently long effective range, and, considering it simply as a weapon for close encounters, it has not the advantages of a magazine-gun.

The trail has been kept, and observations with the sextant have been made whenever practicable.

Very respectfully, your obedient servant

EDW. MAGUIRE
First Lieutenant Corps of Engineers,
Chief Engineer, Department of Dakota.

Brig. Gen. A. A. HUMPHRIES,
Chief of Engineers U.S.A.

NOTES TO CHAPTER 36

1. Whether Custer came down to the stream at the point indicated has long been a matter of controversy among historians. George Hyde in *Red Cloud's Folk,* p. 269-70, analyzes the evidence and concludes that he did come down to the stream.

2. This is not in agreement with other accounts of the battle nor with the usual course of Indian warfare. Indian leaders sometimes maintained a semblance of discipline until the beginning of a battle, but when the battle was once in progress it was every Indian for himself, with little co-operation between individuals or groups.

3. Various accounts giving the number of casualties at the battle of the Little Big Horn are not in agreement. Vestal (*New Sources of Indian History*) says 254 whites were killed and 52 plus wounded. Hanson (*Conquest of the Missouri*) says 258 were killed and 52 wounded. Wellman (*Death on Horseback*) says 265 were killed and 52 wounded. Vestal gives the Indian dead as 26 and the wounded, 3.

4. A few of the Indians had better arms than those issued to soldiers, but more of them had obsolete muzzle-loaders, and many had only bows and arrows. Probably not more than one fourth of the Indians had fire-arms. Their supply of ammunition was limited at the beginning of the battle, and nearly exhausted at its close.

5. Sitting Bull's generalship has been the subject of much controversy. If the word is considered to mean a commanding officer in full control of a fighting force, it should not be applied to any Sioux Indian, for the Sioux, in battle, were rugged individualists. Sitting Bull was certainly one of the most influential leaders among the Sioux at the time of the battle.

APPENDICES

APPENDICES

APPENDIX A

CHRONOLOGY

1803. Louisiana Territory purchased from France. Lewis and Clark expedition organized.

1804. Lewis and Clark ascend Missouri River to Mandan villages, build Fort Mandan, and spend winter.

1805. Lewis and Clark reach Pacific Ocean. Francois Larocque explores lower Yellowstone Valley.

1806. Lewis and Clark return to St. Louis.

1807. Fur trading expedition led by Manuel Lisa establishes Manuel's Fort on Yellowstone at mouth of Bighorn. Army expedition led by Ensign Nathaniel Pryor, en route to Mandan villages, is driven back by Arikara Indians.

1808. John Jacob Astor organizes the American Fur Company.

1809. The St. Louis Missouri Fur Company is organized at St. Louis, and takes over Lisa's possessions on the Upper Missouri. Lisa, a partner, is principal leader of field expeditions. Meriwether Lewis dies.

1810. Astor organizes Pacific Fur Company, a subsidiary of the American Fur Company.

1811. The St. Louis Missouri Fur Company abandons Manuel's Fort. Wilson Price Hunt leads an expedition of Pacific Fur Company trappers up the Missouri to Grand River, en route for Astoria, at mouth of Columbia River. John Bradbury, British botanist, accompanies the expedition, and visits Mandan villages. Manuel Lisa leads party of St. Louis Missouri Fur Company traders to Mandan villages. Henry Marie Brackenridge accompanies the party. Bradbury and Brackenridge return to St. Louis together in one of Lisa's boats. Hunt ascends the Grand River Valley, and proceeds westward toward Astoria.

1812. War begins with Great Britain. Robert Stuart, with small party, leaves Astoria for New York, crosses continental divide through or near South Pass, reaches Platte River, and goes into winter quarters near 104 meridian. Lisa builds Fort Manuel on Missouri near forty-sixth parallel. Louisiana becomes a state, the rest of the Louisiana Purchase is named Missouri Territory.

1813. The Stuart party follows the Platte to the Missouri and proceeds by canoe to St. Louis. Fort Manuel is abandoned.

1814. The St. Louis Missouri Fur Company is dissolved. The (first) Missouri Fur Company is organized at St. Louis. Lisa is appointed subagent for the Upper Missouri Indian tribes. The Biddle-Allen account of the Lewis and Clark expedition is published. Brackenridge publishes *Views of Louisiana,* including a journal of his 1811 Missouri River travels.

1815. Battle of New Orleans ends war with Great Britain. William Clark negotiates treaties at Portage des Sioux, near St. Louis, with forty-three chiefs and leading men of Upper Missouri and Mississippi Sioux tribes.

1816. Brackenridge publishes a revised edition of his Missouri River journal.

1817. Lisa resigns as subagent. Missouri Fur Company ends by expiration of partnership agreement. Joseph La Framboise builds trading post at mouth of Bad River. First steamboat—the *Pike*—arrives at St. Louis. Bradbury's journal is published in England.

1819. The (second) Missouri Fur Company is organized, with Lisa as president. Army expedition in five steamboats and other craft leaves St. Louis on projected trip to Yellowstone. One steamboat—the *Western Engineer*—reaches Council Bluffs area. Camp Missouri, precursor of Fort Atkinson, is begun. The Yellowstone trip is abandoned.

1820. The army begins building Fort Atkinson. Army expedition led by Major Stephen H. Long explores Platte Valley to Rocky Mountains, returning via Arkansas River. Manuel Lisa dies. Joshua Pilcher becomes president of Missouri Fur Company.

1822. First Ashley-Henry expedition, led by Andrew Henry, ascends Missouri to mouth of Yellowstone and builds trading post. Columbia Fur Company begins operations on Upper Missouri. American Fur Company organizes Western Department, with headquarters at St. Louis, for trade on Missouri, lower Mississippi and Illinois rivers. Fort La Framboise is rebuilt and named Fort Tecumseh.

1823. Second Ashley-Henry expedition, led by William H. Ashley, ascends Missouri to Arikara villages, and is attacked by Arikara Indians. Colonel Henry Leavenworth, with six companies of infantry, assisted by traders and Sioux Indians, about one thousand men in all, ascends Missouri to punish the Arikara, but makes an ineffectual peace instead. Edwin James publishes an account of the Long expedition, in London and Philadelphia. The Ashley-Henry trappers, led by Thomas Fitzpatrick and Jedediah Smith, leave the Missouri near the Great Bend and move westward, south of the Black Hills, to the Rocky Mountains. Prince Paul of Wurttemberg, German naturalist, ascends the Missouri to the Great Bend.

1824. The Fitzpatrick-Smith party of Ashley-Henry trappers "effectively" discover South Pass. Henry withdraws from the fur trade.

1825. An army expedition in eight keelboats, led by General Henry Atkinson, accompanied by Indian Agent Benjamin O'Fallon, ascends the Missouri to above the Yellowstone, and makes treaties of amity with various tribes. The first rendezvous of traders, trappers, and Indians is held on Henry's Fork of Green River.

1826. Ashley sells his trapping-trading interests in Rocky Mountains to Jedediah Smith, David E. Jackson, and William L. Sublette—but continues to act as supplier and banker to the Rocky Mountain fur trade.

1827. The American Fur Company, Western Department, absorbs the Columbia Fur Company, which becomes known as the "Upper Missouri Outfit," with Kenneth McKenzie in charge. The army abandons Fort Atkinson. Ashley takes a cannon to Great Salt Lake—the first wheeled vehicle to traverse the Platte Valley and South Pass over the route later known as the Oregon Trail.

1828. The American Fur Company begins building Fort Floyd, soon to be renamed Fort Union, on the left bank of the Missouri, about six miles above the mouth of the Yellowstone.

1830. Prince Paul of Wurttemberg again visits the Missouri River. Milton Sublette, en route to the rendezvous on Wind River, uses ten wagons and two carriages to transport trade goods. This is first use of wagons on future Oregon Trail. Smith, Jackson and Sublette sell out to Thomas Fitzpatrick, James Bridger, Milton Sublette, Henry Fraeb, and Jean Baptiste Gervais—who adopt the name "Rocky Mountain Fur Company."

1831. The American Fur Company builds Fort Clark, near Mandan villages. The *Yellowstone*—first steamer to go above Council Bluffs on the Missouri—reaches Fort Tecumseh at the mouth of Bad River.

1832. Captain Benjamin L. E. Bonneville, on leave from the U.S. Army, leads a trading-exploring expedition to the Rocky Mountains, and takes first wagons through South Pass. Nathaniel Wyeth makes first trip to Oregon. Fur prices begin to drop due to invention of silk hat and improved methods of making felt. The steamboat *Yellowstone* ascends Missouri to Fort Union. Among the passengers is George Catlin, artist and student of the American Indian. Fort Pierre is built to replace Fort Tecumseh. Act of Congress forbids importation of alcoholic liquor into Indian country, but there will be a wide gap between law and practice for several years. Congress creates position of Commissioner of Indian Affairs in War Department. The American Fur Company establishes Fort McKenzie on Missouri at mouth of Marias River, and the first of its "Crow Posts"—Fort Cass—on the Yellowstone.

1833. Prince Maximilian of Wied, German naturalist, accompanied by Charles Bodmer, Swiss artist, ascends Missouri to Fort McKenzie, visits Fort Union, and goes downstream to Fort Clark for the winter. Captain William Drummond Stewart, retired British army officer, makes first of several trips to the Rocky Mountains. Sublette and Campbell enter the Upper Missouri trade, building Fort William (near Fort Union) and other posts near forts Clark and Pierre. Nathaniel Wyeth returns from Oregon via Yellowstone and Missouri rivers. John B. Wyeth publishes account of Nathaniel's first trip—as far as Fort Hall.

1834. Wyeth begins second trip to Oregon. Sublette and Campbell sell their Upper Missouri forts to American Fur Company, and build Fort William on the Laramie River near its junction with the Platte. Fort William, later called Fort John, is precursor of Fort Laramie. The Rocky Mountain Fur Company is replaced by a partnership consisting of Fitzpatrick, Bridger, and Milton Sublette. This partnership forms an alliance with American Fur Company and is soon absorbed. Congress passes Indian Intercourse Act, regulating trade with Indian tribes. John Jacob Astor retires from the fur trade. The Western Department of the American Fur Company continues as Pratte, Chouteau, and Company, with headquarters in St. Louis—but the old name will remain in common use for many years.

1835. Colonel Henry Dodge, with three companies of First Regiment of Mounted Dragoons, traverses Platte Valley to South Pass, returning via Arkansas Valley. The steamboat *Assiniboine* grounds and burns near mouth of Heart River with loss of nearly all of Maximilian's specimens. Bonneville returns from Rocky Mountain trip. Prince Paul publishes German account of his first trip to America.

1836. Sublette and Campbell sell their Laramie fort to Pratte, Chouteau, and Company. Washington Irving publishes *Astoria.*

1837. Catlin's Indian Gallery opens in New York City with 494 paintings and many Indian artifacts. Count Francesco Arese travels on the Missouri and visits the Yankton Sioux. Alfred Jacob Miller, employed by Captain Stewart, visits the Rocky Mountains and paints pictures of trappers and Indians. Smallpox epidemic begins among Indians on the Upper Missouri causing great loss of life. Washington Irving publishes *The Adventures of Captain Bonneville.*

1838. Pratte, Chouteau, and Company becomes Pierre Chouteau, Jr., and Company. Father De Smet begins missionary career at Council Bluffs. William Clark dies.

1839. Dr. Frederick A. Wislizenus accompanies a fur-trading caravan to the Rocky Mountains. Joseph N. Nicollet, with small party, including John Charles Fremont, ascends Missouri to Fort Pierre and explores the plains northeast to Mississippi River. Maximilian publishes a German account of his American travels, with atlas of illustrations by Bodmer.

1840. At St. Louis Wislizenus publishes in German an account of his 1839 trip. De Smet makes first of many trips to Rocky Mountains over the Oregon Trail, returning via Yellowstone and Missouri rivers. Sixteenth and last rendezvous is held.

1841. First wagon train of emigrants to Oregon moves over Oregon Trail. About this time wagons are first used on the trail from Fort Pierre to Fort Laramie. Catlin publishes his *North American Indians.*

1842. Lieutenant John Charles Fremont begins career as leader of exploring expeditions. With Kit Carson as guide, he travels the Platte Valley route to South Pass, penetrates Wind River Mountains to Fremont Peak, and, returning, tries to navigate the North Platte.

1843. Fremont's first report is published, arousing much interest in the West. Fremont begins second trip to Rocky Mountains—first to Pacific Coast. John James Audubon, artist-naturalist, visits Fort Union and writes *Missouri River Journal*—first published fifty-four years later. "The Great Migration," about 900 emigrants, leaves for Oregon. Maximilian's *Travels in the Interior of North America* is translated and published in England. De Smet's *Letters and Sketches with a Narrative of a Year's Residence among the Indian Tribes of the Rocky Mountains* is published in Philadelphia. Nicollet dies. The Senate publishes his "Report Intended to Illustrate a Map."

1844. Fremont returns from second trip. French edition of De Smet's *Letters and Sketches* is published.

1845. Fremont begins third expedition—to Oregon and California. Colonel S. W. Kearny, with five companies of Mounted Dragoons, marches to Fort

Laramie and South Pass, returning via Arkansas Valley. Nicollet's *Report* is republished.

1846. Mexican War begins. Francis Parkman travels to Laramie Mountains, lives with the Oglala Sioux, and collects material for his first and most popular book, *The Oregon Trail.*

1847. The *Knickerbocker Magazine* begins serial publication of *The Oregon Trail.* De Smet's *Oregon Missions and Travels over the Rocky Mountains in 1845-46,* is published in New York. Emigration to Great Salt Lake Valley establishes Mormon Trail along north bank of Platte.

1848. Mexican War ends. Fort Kearney is built on Platte near Grand Island. James Marshall discovers gold in California. French edition of De Smet's *Oregon Missions* . . . is published.

1849. Army purchases and garrisons Fort Laramie. Enormous migration to California gold fields via Platte Valley and South Pass. Cholera is epidemic among emigrants and is introduced among Indian tribes. March of Mounted Riflemen to Oregon—journal by Major Cross. Captain Howard Stansbury explores the Platte Valley en route to Great Salt Lake. The serial publication of *The Oregon Trail* is completed, and the first book edition published. The Office of Commissioner of Indian Affairs is transferred from the War Department to the newly established Department of the Interior.

1850. The California emigration continues on a large scale. Cholera and smallpox among emigrants and Indians. Stansbury completes exploring trip to the Great Salt Lake Valley. Thaddeus A. Culbertson visits the Upper Missouri and the White River Badlands.

1851. De Smet traverses the Yellowstone-Powder River area accompanying Indians from Fort Union to Fort Laramie. Treaty is concluded with plains and mountain Indians at Horse Creek, near Fort Laramie. Stage line is established between St. Louis and Salt Lake City with mail contract providing for round trip in forty-two days. On third trip to America Prince Paul explores part of Oregon Trail. A portion of Thaddeus A. Culbertson's journal is published in the Fifth Annual Report of the Smithsonian Institution.

1852. Stansbury's report is published.

1853. Stevens' party explores proposed railroad route to the Pacific near the forty-eighth parallel. Dr. Ferdinand Vandeveer Hayden makes his first trip to the White River Badlands.

1854. Nebraska Territory created—extends from the Missouri River to the continental divide and from the fortieth parallel to the Canadian border—with 2,732 white inhabitants. Omaha founded. Lieutenant Grattan, twenty-nine enlisted men, and an interpreter are killed by Sioux Indians near Fort Laramie. Sir St. George Gore, Irish sportsman, with large party, arrives at Fort Laramie.

1855. Gore party, with Bridger as guide, crosses Powder River country to Yellowstone. Sioux expedition, led by General W. S. Harney, severely defeats Little Thunder's band of Brulé Sioux on Blue Water Creek in Nebraska Territory. The expedition goes on to Fort Laramie, thence to Fort Pierre. Lieutenant G. K. Warren, expedition topographical engineer, completes first of three important explorations in Nebraska Territory, assisted by Dr. Hayden. The army purchases Fort Pierre.

1856. Gore on Upper Missouri. Warren and Hayden explore Missouri River to Fort Union and lower Yellowstone. Warren's report of 1855 exploration is published. Harney negotiates peace treaty with Sioux at Fort Pierre. Trouble develops between army and Cheyenne Indians near Forts Laramie and Kearney, followed by depredations on Oregon Trail. Lieutenant Bryan explores proposed wagon road from Fort Riley to Bridger's pass. Army establishes Fort Randall on right bank of Missouri near forty-third parallel. Handcarts first used on Mormon Trail.

1857. The army abandons Fort Pierre. Warren and Hayden explore the Niobrara Valley, and the western, southern and eastern edges of the Black Hills. Gore descends Missouri to St. Louis. Colonel E. V. Sumner leads expedition against Cheyenne Indians in Platte Valley and south to Solomon River. Colonel A. S. Johnson leads expedition against Mormons. Heavy wagon traffic along Platte Valley. Panic of 1857 begins.

1858. Warren's report of 1856 and 1857 explorations is published. Gold is discovered in Colorado.

1859. Colorado gold rush begins. Captain W. F. Raynolds, with Hayden as geologist and Bridger as guide, begins exploration of Yellowstone country, moving west from Fort Pierre to the Yellowstone and south to winter quarters near Platte.

1860. Raynolds expedition continues exploration of Nebraska Territory. Pony Express established from St. Joseph, Missouri, to California.

1861. First overland telegraph line completed. Pony Express discontinued. Dakota Territory created—approximately includes future states of North Dakota, South Dakota, Montana, and the north half of Wyoming —with 2,402 white inhabitants. Civil War begins.

1862. Gold strike at Bannack starts Montana gold rush. Sioux Indian outbreak in Minnesota. Captain Fisk leads his first emigrant expedition across Dakota Territory to Montana.

1863. General Sully leads campaign against Sioux along Missouri River. (Old) Fort Sully established. John Bozeman explores route from Fort Laramie to Montana gold fields east of Big Horn Mountains—the Bozeman Trail. Homesteading begins in Nebraska Territory.

1864. Montana Territory created. Montana gold rush causes heavy traffic on Missouri. Fort Rice established. Battle of Killdeer Mountain in western Dakota Territory between Sully and Sioux. Attack by volunteer troops on Cheyenne Indians at Sand Creek, Colorado, leads to extensive depredations by Cheyenne, Arapaho, and Sioux along Platte Valley.

1865. Civil War ends. Treaty at Fort Sully ends war with eastern Sioux. Increased depredations along Platte. Battle of Platte Bridge. Campaign against Indians in Powder River Valley. James Sawyer explores proposed wagon road through Niobrara Valley and northwestward to Montana gold fields, and W. W. Brookings surveys road along Cheyenne River—neither route developed due to Indian opposition and building of Union Pacific Railroad. Union Pacific lays first rails at Omaha.

1866. (Old) Fort Sully abandoned. (New) Fort Sully built near Fort Pierre. Fort Buford begun on Missouri near mouth of Yellowstone. Forts C. F. Smith, Phil Kearny, and Reno built on Bozeman Trail. Sioux Indians wipe out Fetterman detachment—seventy-nine soldiers and two civilians —near Fort Phil Kearny. Dr. Hayden explores White River Badlands.

1867. Nebraska becomes a state. Town of Cheyenne founded. Union Pacific reaches Cheyenne. Gold discoveries in South Pass. Newly issued breech-loading rifles defeat Red Cloud's Sioux in Wagon Box Fight on Bozeman Trail. Peace commission begins negotiations with hostile tribes. Army establishes Fort Fetterman on Platte, Fort Stevenson on Missouri, and Fort Totten at Devils Lake.

1868. Wyoming Territory created. Treaty concluded with Sioux—Bozeman Trail closed and forts C. F. Smith, Phil Kearny, and Reno abandoned —Sioux Reservation created out of Dakota Territory west of Missouri and south of forty-sixth parallel. Raynolds' report of Yellowstone exploration published.

1869. Hayden's report of Yellowstone exploration published. Union Pacific meets Central Pacific at Promontory Point, Utah, completing first railroad to Pacific Coast.

1870. Spotted Tail Indian Agency established near White River in northern Nebraska. Nebraska has 122,993 white inhabitants; Montana Territory, 20,595; Wyoming Territory, 9,118; and Dakota Territory, 14,181.

1871. Red Cloud Indian Agency established on Platte thirty-two miles east of Fort Laramie.

1872. Army begins Fort McKeen, to be renamed Fort Abraham Lincoln. Northern Pacific Railroad begins surveys west of Missouri River with military escort commanded by Colonel D. S. Stanley. First permanent railroad bridge completed across Missouri at Omaha.

1873. Railroads reach Missouri at Yankton and Bismarck. Northern Pacific surveys continued west of Missouri. Seventh Cavalry arrives in Dakota Territory. Red Cloud Agency moved to new location on White River. Panic of 1873 begins.

1874. Lieutenant Colonel George A. Custer leads Seventh Cavalry in expedition to Black Hills—gold discovered. Indian depredations in Fort Laramie area. Troops sent to Red Cloud Agency establish Camp Robinson. Gordon party of prospectors from Sioux City build cabins and stockade on French Creek in Black Hills. Severe grasshopper infestation on Northern Plains.

1875. Gordon party removed from Black Hills by army. Exploration of Black Hills by Dr. Walter P. Jenney confirms gold discoveries. Black Hills gold rush begins. Allison Commission tries to buy Black Hills from Indians without success. Boom at Custer City. Gold discovered in Deadwood Gulch. Sioux in Yellowstone-Powder River area ordered to return to reservation. Ludlow report of Custer's Black Hills expedition published.

1876. Big year of the Black Hills gold rush. Boom at Deadwood. Trails to Black Hills developed from Bismarck, Fort Pierre, Sidney, and Cheyenne. Indian depredations on all trails and around border of Black Hills. Crook expedition fights Indians on Powder River March 17. Second Crook expedition leaves Fort Fetterman May 29—battle with Sioux on Rosebud June 17. Expeditions from Fort Lincoln under General Terry and from Fort Ellis under Colonel Gibbon meet on Yellowstone. Plans made to attack Indian village on Little Bighorn from two sides about June 26. Custer with Seventh Cavalry attacks village June 25, with complete loss of his immediate command of five companies and severe losses in other seven companies. Crook and Terry meet on Yellowstone. Crook continues east and south, wins small battle of Slim Buttes, and returns to settlements via Black Hills. Colonel R. S. Mackenzie defeats Cheyennes. Treaty imposed on Indians reduces area of Sioux Reservation and opens Black Hills to white settlement.

1877. Enlarged army continues campaign against diminishing resistance of Indians. Sitting Bull flees to Canada. Crazy Horse surrenders. Black Hills treaty is ratified by Senate. Beginning of lode mining establishes Black Hills mining industry on permanent basis. Era of exploration on the Northern Plains is substantially ended, and era of settlement begins.

APPENDIX B

Acknowledgments

Any one who writes or edits a book about history is under heavy obligations to so many people and so many institutions that it may seem invidious to mention only a few of them. I am particularly grateful to the men who wrote the book that I have assembled and edited; to their publishers; to the historical societies of Montana, Nebraska, North Dakota, South Dakota, and Wyoming; to the public libraries of Denver and Colorado Springs; and to the Colorado College Library at Colorado Springs, Colorado.

The following publishers and institutions have generously given permission to reprint copyrighted or recently published writings:

Dodd, Mead and Company, Inc., New York City; and The American Philosophical Society, Philadelphia; for portions of the *Original Journals of the Lewis and Clark Expedition, 1804-1806*, edited by Reuben Gold Thwaites—reprinted as Chapters 1 and 2 of this book.

The Missouri Historical Society, St. Louis; for a portion of *A Journey to the Rocky Mountains in 1839*, by Dr. F. A. Wislizenus—reprinted as Chapter 9.

The South Dakota State Historical Society, Pierre; for a portion of *First Journey to North America in the Years 1822 to 1824*, by Friederich Paul Wilhelm, Prince of Wurttemberg, translated by Dr. William G. Bek—reprinted as Chapters 14 and 15.

Charles Scribner's Sons, New York City; for a portion of *Audubon and His Journals*, edited by Maria R. Audubon and Elliott Coues—reprinted as Chapter 17.

The Historical Society of Montana, Helena; for a portion of the *Journal of James H. Bradley*,—reprinted as Chapters 34 and 35.

APPENDIX C

Bibliography

Abel, Annie Heloise. "A New Lewis and Clark Map," *Geographical Review*, I (May, 1916), 329-45.

———, ed. *Tabeau's Narrative of Loisel's Expedition to the Upper Missouri*. Norman: University of Oklahoma Press, 1939.

ANDERSON, LIEUT. C. D. "Report of a March from Fort Laramie to Fort Randall," *Annual Report of the Secretary of War*, 1859 (Serial 1024), pp. 441-48.

APPLETON, LEROY H. *Indian Art of the Americas.* New York: Charles Scribner's Sons, 1950.

ARESE, COUNT FRANCESCO. *A Trip to the Prairies, and in the Interior of North America (1837-1838).* Translated and edited by Andrew Evans. New York: The Harbor Press, 1934.

ARMSTRONG, MOSES K. *The Early Empire Builders of the Great West.* St. Paul: E. W. Porter, 1901.

ATWOOD, WALLACE W. *The Physiographic Provinces of North America.* Boston: Ginn and Company, 1940.

AUDUBON, MARIA R., ed. *Audubon and His Journals.* With notes by Elliott Coues. 2 vols.; New York: Charles Scribner's Sons, 1897.

BAKELESS, JOHN. *The Eyes of Discovery.* Philadelphia: J. B. Lippincott Company, 1950.

———. *Lewis and Clark, Partners in Discovery.* New York: William Morrow and Company, 1947.

BARROWS, ISABEL C. *A Sunny Life, the Biography of Samuel June Barrows.* Boston: Little, Brown and Company, 1913.

BARROWS, S. J. "The Northwestern Mule and His Driver," *Atlantic Monthly*, XXXV (May, 1875), 550-60.

BIDDLE, NICHOLAS, AND ALLEN, PAUL. *History of the Expedition Under the Command of Captains Lewis and Clark to the Sources of the Missouri, Across the Rocky Mountains, Down the Columbia River to the Pacific in 1804-6. A Reprint of the Edition of 1814 to Which all the Members of the Expedition Contributed.* 3 vols.; New York: New Amsterdam Book Company, 1902.

BILLINGTON, RAY ALLEN; AND HEDGES, JAMES BLAINE. *Western Expansion, a History of the American Frontier.* New York: The Macmillan Company, 1949.

BOURKE, CAPT. JOHN G. *On the Border with Crook*, 2nd ed.; New York: Charles Scribner's Sons, 1892.

BRACKENRIDGE, HENRY MARIE. *Journal of a Voyage up the River Missouri, Performed in 1811.* Reprint of 1816 edition in *Early Western Travels*, Vol. VI. Cleveland: Arthur H. Clark Company, 1904.

———. *Views of Louisiana; Together with a Journal of a Voyage up the Missouri River, in 1811.* Pittsburgh: Cramer, Spear and Eichbaum, 1814.

BRADBURY, JOHN. *Travels in the Interior of America, in the Years 1809, 1810, and 1811.* London: Sherwood, Neely and Jones, 1817. Also edition of 1819, reprinted in *Early Western Travels*, Vol. V, Cleveland: Arthur H. Clark Company, 1904.

BRADLEY, LIEUT. JAMES H. "Affairs at Fort Benton from 1831 to 1869." *Contributions to the Historical Society of Montana*, Vol. III. Helena, 1900.

———. "Journal of James H. Bradley, the Sioux Campaign of 1876 under the Command of General John Gibbon." *Contributions to the Historical Society of Montana*, Vol. II. Helena, 1896.

BRIGGS, HAROLD E. "The Black Hills Gold Rush," *North Dakota Historical Quarterly*, V (January, 1931), 71-99.

———. *Frontiers of the Northwest, A History of the Upper Missouri Valley.* New York: D. Appleton-Century Company, 1940.

BURT, STRUTHERS. *Powder River, Let 'er Buck.* New York: Farrar and Rinehart, 1938.

CATLIN, GEORGE. *North American Indians, Being Letters and Notes on Their Manners, Customs, and Conditions, Written During Eight Years' Travel Amongst the Wildest Tribes of Indians in North America, 1832-1839.* Various editions from 1841.

CHITTENDEN, HIRAM MARTIN. *The American Fur Trade of the Far West.* 3 vols.; New York: Francis P. Harper, 1902. 2nd ed., 2 vols.; New York: Press of the Pioneers, 1935.

———. *History of Early Steamboat Navigation on the Missouri River, Life and Adventures of Joseph La Barge.* 2 vols.; New York: Francis P. Harper, 1903.

CHITTENDEN, HIRAM MARTIN, and RICHARDSON, ALFRED TALBOT, eds. *Life, Letters and Travels of Father Pierre-Jean de Smet, S.J., 1801-1873.* 4 vols.; New York: Francis P. Harper, 1905.

COUES, ELLIOTT, ed. *Forty Years a Fur Trader on the Upper Missouri, the Personal Narrative of Charles Larpenteur, 1833-1872.* 2 vols.; New York: Francis P. Harper, 1898.

CRAWFORD, LEWIS F., ed. *Rekindling Camp Fires, the Exploits of Ben Arnold.* Bismarck: Capital Book Co., 1926.

CROSS, MAJOR OSBORNE. "A Report, in the Form of a Journal . . . of the March of the Regiment of Mounted Riflemen to Oregon, from May 10 to October 5, 1849." *Annual Report of the Secretary of War,* 1850 (Serial 587), pp. 127-244. Reprinted in *The March of the Mounted Riflemen,* edited by Raymond W. Settle, Glendale, Calif.: Arthur H. Clark Company, 1940.

CULBERTSON, THADDEUS A. *See* McDermott, John Francis, ed.

CUMMINGS, A. "Indians on the Upper Missouri." *House Executive Document 65* (Serial 853), 34 Congress, 1 Session, 1856.

CUSTER, ELIZABETH B. *"Boots and Saddles"; or Life in Dakota with General Custer.* New York: Harper and Brothers, 1885.

CUSTER, G. A. "Battling with the Sioux on the Yellowstone," *Galexy,* XXII (July, 1876), 91-102.

CUSTER, LIEUT. COL. G. A. "Letter from the Secretary of War, Transmitting . . . a Report of the Expedition to the Black Hills, Under Command of Bvt. Maj. General George A. Custer." *Senate Executive Document 32,* (Serial 1629), 43 Congress, 2 Session, 1875.

DALE, HARRISON C., ed. *The Ashley-Smith Explorations and the Discovery of a Central Route to the Pacific, 1822-29.* Cleveland: The Arthur H. Clark Company, 1918.

DARTON, N. H. "Comparison of the Stratigraphy of the Black Hills, Big Horn Mountains, and Rocky Mountain Front Range," *Bulletin of the Geographical Society of America,* 15 (August 22, 1904), pp. 379-448.

DARTON, N. H., AND PAIGE, SIDNEY. *Geological Atlas of the United States, Central Black Hills Folio, South Dakota.* Washington: U.S. Geological Survey, 1925.

DELAND, CHARLES E. "The Sioux Wars." *South Dakota Historical Collections*, Vols. XV, 1930, and XVII, 1934.

DELLENBAUGH, FREDERICK S. *Fremont and '49.* New York: G. P. Putnam's Sons, 1914.

———. *George Armstrong Custer.* New York: The Macmillan Company, 1926.

DENIG, EDWIN THOMPSON. "Indian Tribes of the Upper Missouri." Edited by J. N. B. Hewitt. *Forty-Sixth Annual Report, Bureau of American Ethnology, for 1928-29.* Washington: Government Printing Office, 1930.

———. "Of the Crow Nation." Edited by John C. Ewers. *Bureau of American Ethnology Bulletin 151, Anthropological Papers No. 33.* Washington: Government Printing Office, 1953.

DE SMET, PIERRE JEAN. See Chittenden and Richardson, eds.

DE SMET, REV. P. J. *Western Missions and Missionaries—A Series of Letters.* New York: P. J. Kenedy, 1881.

DEVOTO, BERNARD. *Across the Wide Missouri.* Boston: Houghton Mifflin Company, 1947.

———. *The Course of Empire.* Boston: Houghton Mifflin Company, 1952.

———. "The Great Medicine Road," *American Mercury*, XI (May, 1927), 104-12.

———. *The Year of Decision, 1846.* Boston: Little, Brown and Company, 1943.

DICK, EVERETT. *The Sod-House Frontier, 1854-1890.* New York: D. Appleton-Century Company, 1937.

DICKSON, ARTHUR JEROME, ed. *Covered Wagon Days.* Cleveland: Arthur H. Clark Company, 1929.

Dictionary of American Biography. 22 vols.; New York: Charles Scribner's Sons, 1928-37.

Dictionary of American History. 5 vols. and index; New York: Charles Scribner's Sons, 1940.

DODGE, LIEUT. COL. RICHARD IRVING. *The Black Hills.* New York: James Miller, 1876.

DONALDSON, A. B. "The Black Hills Expedition." *South Dakota Historical Collections*, Vol. VII. Pierre, 1916.

DRUM, STELLA M., ed. *Journal of a Fur-Trading Expedition on the Upper Missouri, 1812-1813, by John C. Luttig, Clerk of the Missouri Fur Company.* St. Louis: Missouri Historical Society, 1920.

EVANS, ANDREW, ed. *See* Arese, Count Francesco

EWAN, JOSEPH. *Rocky Mountain Naturalists.* Denver: University of Denver Press, 1950.

EWERS, JOHN C., ed. *See* Denig, Edwin Thompson

EWERS, JOHN CANFIELD. *Plains Indian Painting.* Stanford University: Stanford University Press, 1939.

FEATHERSTONHAUGH, G. W. "Report of a Geological Reconnoissance Made in 1835, From the Seat of Government . . . to the Coteau de Prairie. . . ." *Senate Document 333* (Serial 282), 24 Congress, 1 Session, 1836.

FEDERAL WRITERS' PROJECT, AMERICAN GUIDE SERIES. *Montana, A State Guide Book.* 2nd printing; New York: Hastings House, 1946.

———. *Nebraska, A Guide to the Cornhusker State.* 2nd printing; New York: Hastings House, 1947.

———. *North Dakota, A Guide to the Northern Prairie State.* 2nd edition; New York: Oxford University Press, 1950.

———. *A South Dakota Guide.* Pierre: South Dakota Guide Commission, 1938.

———. *Wyoming, A Guide to its History, Highways, and People.* 3rd printing; New York: Oxford University Press, 1948.

FENNEMAN, NEVIN M. *Physiography of Western United States.* New York: McGraw-Hill Book Company, Inc., 1931.

FERRIS, W. A. *Life in the Rocky Mountains . . . from February, 1830, to November, 1835.* Denver: Old West Publishing Company, 1940.

FINERTY, JOHN F. *War-path and Bivouac; or The Conquest of the Sioux, . . . Adventures in the Big Horn and Yellowstone Expedition of 1876, and in the Campaign on the British Border, in 1879.* Chicago: Donohue Brothers, 1890.

FLETCHER, ALICE C., AND LA FLESCHE, FRANCIS. "The Omaha Tribe." *Twenty-Seventh Annual Report, Bureau of American Ethnology, 1905-6.* Washington: Government Printing Office, 1911.

FOLMER, HENRI. "The Mallet Expedition of 1739 Through Nebraska, Kansas, and Colorado to Santa Fe," *The Colorado Magazine,* XVI (September, 1939), 161-73.

FORD, ALICE, ed. *Audubon's Animals.* New York: Studio Publications, Inc., 1951.

FORSYTH, GEORGE A. *The Story of the Soldier.* New York: D. Appleton and Company, 1916.

FREMONT, LIEUT. JOHN CHARLES. "A Report on an Exploration of the Country Lying Between the Missouri River and the Rocky Mountains, on the Line of the Kansas and Great Platte Rivers." With map. *Senate Document 243,* (Serial 416), 27 Congress, 3 Session, 1843. Washington: Printed by Order of the United States Senate, 1843.

———. "Report of the Exploring Expedition to the Rocky Mountains in the Year 1842 and to Oregon and North California in the Years 1843-'44." With map. *Senate Document 174,* (Serial 461), 28 Congress, 2 Session, 1845. Also published in book form by Gales and Seaton, Washington, 1845.

GHENT, W. J. *The Road to Oregon, A Chronicle of the Great Emigrant Trail.* New York: Longmans, Green and Co., 1929.

———. *The Early Far West, A Narrative Outline, 1540-1850.* New York: Longmans, Green and Co., 1931.

GILBERT, E. W. *The Exploration of Western America, 1800-1850, An Historical Geography.* Cambridge, England: The University Press, 1933.

GILMORE, MELVIN RANDOLPH. "Use of Plants by the Indians of the Missouri River Region." *Thirty-third Annual Report, Bureau of American Ethnology, 1911-1912*. Washington: Government Printing Office, 1919.

GODFREY, EDWARD S. "Custer's Last Battle." *Contributions to the Historical Society of Montana*, Vol. IX. N.p., n.d. (Reprint, with added material, of an article published in *The Century Magazine*, XLIII (January, 1892), 358-84.)

GOODWIN, CARDINAL. *John Charles Fremont, An Explanation of His Career*. Stanford University: Stanford University Press, 1930.

GRAHAM, LIEUT. COL. W. A. *The Story of the Little Big Horn, Custer's Last Fight*. New York: The Century Company, 1926.

Grass, the Yearbook of Agriculture, 1948. Washington: Government Printing Office, 1948.

GRINNELL, GEORGE BIRD. *By Cheyenne Campfires*. New Haven: Yale University Press, 1926.

———. *The Cheyenne Indians*. 2 vols.; New Haven: Yale University Press, 1923.

———. *The Fighting Cheyennes*. New York: Charles Scribner's Sons, 1915.

———. "Zoological Report." In Ludlow's *Report of a Reconnaissance of the Black Hills. . . .*

HABERLY, LOYD. *Pursuit of the Horizon; A Life of George Catlin*. New York: The Macmillan Company, 1948.

HAFEN, LEROY R.; AND GHENT, W. J. *Broken Hand, the Life Story of Thomas Fitzpatrick, Chief of the Mountain Men*. Denver: The Old West Publishing Company, 1931.

HAFEN, LEROY R.; AND YOUNG, FRANCIS MARION. *Fort Laramie and the Pageant of the West, 1834-1890*. Glendale, Calif.: Arthur H. Clark Company, 1938.

HAMILTON, W. J., JR. *American Mammals*. New York: McGraw-Hill Book Company, Inc., 1939.

HAMILTON, W. T. *My Sixty Years on the Plains*. New York: Forest and Stream Publishing Company, 1905.

HANSON, JOSEPH MILLS. *The Conquest of the Missouri; being the Story of the Life and Exploits of Captain Grant Marsh*. New York: Murray Hill Books, Inc., 1946.

HARNEY, BREVET BRIG. GEN. W. S. "A Report of the Proceedings of a Council Held at Fort Pierre . . . With a Delegation From Nine Tribes of the Sioux Indians. . . ." *Senate Executive Document 94*, (Serial 823), 34 Congress, 1 Session, 1856.

HARRIS, BURTON. *John Colter, His Years in the Rockies*. New York: Charles Scribner's Sons, 1952.

HARRIS, EDWARD. *See* McDermott, John Francis, ed.

HAYDEN, DR. F. V. *Geological Report of the Exploration of the Yellowstone and Missouri Rivers, 1859-60*. Washington: Government Printing Office, 1869.

HAZLETT, RUTH, ed. "The Journal of Francois Antoine Larocque, From the Assiniboine River to the Yellowstone—1805," *Frontier and Midland*, XIV and XV, March, May, and Autumn Numbers, 1934.

HEBARD, GRACE RAYMOND, AND BRININSTOOL, E. A. *The Bozeman Trail.* 2 vols.; Cleveland: The Arthur H. Clark Company, 1922.

HEBARD, GRACE RAYMOND. *Sacajawea.* Glendale, Calif. The Arthur H. Clark Company, 1933.

———. *Washakie.* Cleveland: The Arthur H. Clark Company, 1930.

HEITMAN, FRANCIS B. "Historical Register and Dictionary of the U.S. Army, 1789-1903." 2 vols. *House Document 446,* (Serials No. 4535-36), 57 Congress, 2 Session, 1903.

HERRICK, FRANCIS HOBART. *Audubon the Naturalist.* 2 vols.; New York: D. Appleton and Company, 1917.

HEWITT, J. N. B., ed. *See* Denig, Edwin Thompson

HOLABIRD, COL. SAMUEL B. "Reconnoissance in the Department of Dakota." *Senate Executive Document 8,* (Serial 1440), 41 Congress, 3 Session, 1871.

HOLMAN, ALBERT M., AND MARKS, CONSTANT R. *Pioneering in the Northwest.* Sioux City: Deitch & Lamar Co., 1924.

HOOPES, ALBAN W. "Thomas S. Twiss, Indian Agent on the Upper Platte, 1855-1861," *Missouri Valley Historical Review,* XX (December, 1933), 353-64.

HORNADAY, WILLIAM T. *The Extermination of the American Bison.* Washington: Government Printing Office, 1889. (Reprint of pages 367-548 of the Report of the National Museum, Smithsonian Institution, for 1886-87.)

HOSMER, JAMES KENDALL, ed. *Gass's Journal of the Lewis and Clark Expedition.* Chicago: A. C. McClurg and Company, 1904.

HUNT, FRAZIER AND ROBERT, eds. *I Fought With Custer, the Story of Sergeant Windolph.* New York: Charles Scribner's Sons, 1947.

HYDE, GEORGE E. *Pawnee Indians.* Denver: University of Denver Press, 1951.

———. *Red Cloud's Folk, a History of the Oglala Sioux Indians.* Norman: University of Oklahoma Press, 1937.

IRVING, WASHINGTON. *Astoria, or Anecdotes of an Enterprise Beyond the Rocky Mountains.* Various editions.

———. *The Adventures of Captain Bonneville, U.S.A., in the Rocky Mountains and the Far West.* Various editions.

JACKSON, W. TURRENTINE. *Wagon Roads West, A Study of Federal Road Surveys and Construction in the Trans-Mississippi West, 1846-1869.* Berkeley and Los Angeles: University of California Press, 1952.

JAMES, DR. EDWIN. *An Account of an Expedition from Pittsburgh to the Rocky Mountains, Performed in the Years 1819 and '20 . . . Under the Command of Major Stephen H. Long. . . .* 2 vols. and atlas; Philadelphia: H. C. Carey and I. Lea, 1822-23. Also a London edition, 1822-23. London edition reprinted in *Early Western Travels,* Vols. XIV to XVII, Cleveland: Arthur H. Clark Company, 1905.

JAMES, THOMAS. *Three Years Among the Indians and Mexicans.* St. Louis: Missouri Historical Society, 1916. (Reprint of 1846 edition.)

JENNEY, WALTER P. "Report on the Mineral Wealth, Climate, and Rain-Fall and Natural Resources of the Black Hills of Dakota." *Senate Executive Document 51*, (Serial 1664), 44 Congress, 1 Session, 1876. *See also* Newton, Henry.

KANE, LUCILE M., trans, and ed. *Military Life in Dakota, the Journal of Philippe Régis de Trobriand.* St. Paul: Alvord Memorial Commission, 1951.

KAPPLER, CHARLES J., ed. "Indian Affairs, Laws and Treaties." 2 vols. *Senate Document 319*, (Serials 4623-24), 58 Congress, 2 Session, 1904.

KEARNY, COL. S. W. "Report of a Summer Campaign to the Rocky Mountains &c. in 1845." *Annual Report of the Secretary of War*, 1845. (Serial 470) pp. 210-17.

KELLOGG, MARK. "Notes of the Little Big Horn Expedition Under General Custer, 1876," *Contributions to the Historical Society of Montana*, Vol IX. N.p., n.d.

KELLY, FANNY. *Narrative of My Captivity Among the Sioux Indians.* 2nd ed.; Chicago: Donnelley, Gassette and Loyd, 1880.

KING, CAPT. CHARLES. *Campaigning With Crook.* New York: Harper and Brothers, 1890.

KUHLMAN, CHARLES. *Legend Into History, the Custer Mystery, an Analytical Study of the Battle of the Little Big Horn.* 2nd printing; Harrisburg: The Stackpole Company, 1952.

KURZ, RUDOLPH FRIEDERICH. "Journal of Rudolph Friederich Kurz . . . 1846 to 1852." *Bureau of American Ethnology Bulletin 115.* Washington: Government Printing Office, 1937.

LARPENTEUR, CHARLES. See Coues, Elliott, ed.

LEONARD, ZENAS. *Adventures of Zenas Leonard, Fur Trader and Trapper, 1831-1836.* Cleveland: The Burrows Brothers Company, 1904. (Reprint of 1839 edition.)

LIBBY, O. G., ed. "The Arikara Narrative of the Campaign against the Hostile Dakotas, June, 1876." *North Dakota Historical Collections*, Vol. VI. Bismarck, 1920.

LINDLEY, HARLOW. "Western Travel, 1800-1820," *Mississippi Valley Historical Review*, VI (September, 1919), 167-91.

LONG, LIEUT. O. F. "Journal of the Marches Made by the Forces Under the Command of Colonel Nelson A. Miles, Fifth Infantry, in 1876 and 1877." *Annual Report of the Secretary of War*, 1878 (Serial 1846), pp. 1688-1703.

LOWE, PERCIVAL G. *Five Years a Dragoon ('49 to '54) and Other Adventures on the Great Plains.* Kansas City: The Franklin Hudson Publishing Company, 1906.

LOWIE, ROBERT H. *The Crow Indians.* New York: Farrar and Rinehart, Inc., 1935.

LUDLOW, CAPT. WILLIAM. *Report of a Reconnaissance of the Black Hills of Dakota, Made in the Summer of 1874.* Washington: Government Printing Office, 1875. Also in *Annual Report of the Secretary of War*, 1875 (Serial 1676). (Included are reports by Geologist N. H. Winchell and Naturalist George Bird Grinnell.)

LUTTIG, JOHN C. *See* Drum, Stella M., ed.

McCracken, Harold. *Portrait of the Old West, with a Biographical Check List of Western Artists.* New York: McGraw-Hill Book Company, 1952.

McDermott, John Francis., ed. "Journal of an Expedition to the Mauvaises Terres and the Upper Missouri in 1850, by Thaddeus A. Culbertson." *Bureau of American Ethnology, Bulletin 147.* Washington: Government Printing Office, 1952.

———. *Up the Missouri with Audubon, the Journal of Edward Harris.* Norman: The University of Oklahoma Press, 1951.

McDonnell, Anne, ed. "The Fort Benton Journal, 1854-1856," and "The Fort Sarpy Journal, 1855-1856." *Contributions to the History of Montana,* Vol. X. Helena, 1940.

Maguire, Lieut. Edward. "Annual Report of Lieutenant Maguire, Corps of Engineers, for the Fiscal Year Ending June 30, 1876—Explorations and Surveys in the Department of Dakota." *Annual Report of the Secretary of War,* 1876 (Serial 1745), pp. 699-704.

Malin, James C. *The Grassland of North America, Prolegomena to its History.* Lawrence, Kans.: James C. Malin, 1947.

Maps:—Maps with considerable historical value have been published with the *Original Journals of the Lewis and Clark Expedition,* the Biddle-Allen account of the expedition, and reports herein listed by Nicollet, Fremont, Warren, Raynolds, Hayden, Ludlow, and Stanton.

Marquis, Thomas B. *A Warrior Who Fought Custer.* Minneapolis: The Midwest Company, 1931.

Mattes, Merrill J. "Report on Historic Sites in the Fort Randall Reservoir Area, Missouri River, South Dakota." *South Dakota Historical Collections,* Vol. XXIV. Pierre, 1949.

———. "Robidoux's Trading Post at 'Scott's Bluffs,' and the California Gold Rush," *Nebraska History,* XXX (June, 1949), 95-138.

Maximilian, Prince of Wied. *Travels in the Interior of North America.* London: Ackermann & Company, 1843. Reprinted by *Early Western Travels,* Vols. XXII-XXIV, Cleveland: Arthur H. Clark Company, 1905-6.

Merington, Marguerite, ed. *The Custer Story; The Life and Intimate Letters of General George A. Custer and his Wife Elizabeth.* New York: The Devin-Adair Company, 1950.

Mills, Brig. Gen. Anson. *My Story.* Washington: Anson Mills, 1918.

Monaghan, Jay. *The Overland Trail.* Indianapolis: The Bobbs-Merrill Company, 1947.

Mooney, James. "Calendar History of the Kiowa Indians." With map of "The Kiowa Range, showing the Location of the Plains Tribes in 1832, with their Kiowa Names and the Principal Military and Trading Posts." *Seventeenth Annual Report, Bureau of American Ethnology, 1895-96.* Washington: Government Printing Office, 1898.

Morris, Ralph C. "The Notion of a Great American Desert East of the Rockies," *Mississippi Valley Historical Review,* XIII (September, 1926), 190-200.

NEIHARDT, JOHN G. *Black Elk Speaks, Being the Life Story of an Holy Man of the Ogalala Sioux.* New York: William Morrow and Company, 1932.

NELSON, BRUCE. *Land of the Dacotahs.* Minneapolis: University of Minnesota Press, 1946.

NEVINS, ALLEN. *Fremont, the West's Greatest Adventurer.* 2 vols.; New York: Harper and Brothers, 1928.

NEWTON, HENRY, AND JENNEY, WALTER P. *Report on the Geology and Resources of the Black Hills of Dakota.* Washington: Government Printing Office, 1880. (Reprint of Jenney's report of 1876 with additional material.)

NICOLLET, J. N. "Report Intended to Illustrate a Map of the Hydrographical Basin of the Upper Mississippi River." With map in *Senate Document 237* (Serial 380), 26 Congress, 2 Session, 1843. Reprinted without map in *House Document 52* (Serial 464), 28 Congress, 2 Session, 1845.

OSTRANDER, MAJOR ALSON B. *An Army Boy of the Sixties, A Story of the Plains.* Yonkers: World Book Company, 1924.

PALAIS, HYMAN. "South Dakota Stage and Wagon Roads." *South Dakota Historical Collections,* Vol. XXV. Pierre, 1951.

PARKER, DONALD D. "Early Exploration and Fur Trading in South Dakota." *South Dakota Historical Collections,* Vol. XXV. Pierre, 1951.

PARKMAN, FRANCIS. *The Oregon Trail, Sketches of Prairie and Rocky Mountain Life.* 4th edition, revised by the author; Boston: Little, Brown and Company, 1872. (There have been many other editions, some of them with the title, *The California and Oregon Trail.*)

PAXSON, FREDERIC L. *History of the American Frontier, 1763-1893.* Boston: Houghton Mifflin Company, 1924.

PAUL WILHELM, DUKE OF WURTTEMBERG. "First Journey to North America in the Years 1822 to 1824." Translated From the German Edition of 1835 by Dr. William G. Bek. *South Dakota Historical Collections,* Vol. XIX. Pierre, 1941.

PEATTIE, RODERICK, ed. *The Black Hills.* New York: The Vanguard Press, Inc., 1952.

PELZER, LOUIS. *Marches of the Dragoons in the Mississippi Valley.* Iowa City: State Historical Society of Iowa, 1917.

PHILLIPS, PAUL C., ed. *Forty Years on the Frontier . . . Journals and Reminiscences of Granville Stuart. . . .* 2 vols.; Cleveland: Arthur H. Clark Company, 1925.

PILCHER, JOSHUA. "Extract from the Report of Joshua Pilcher." *Annual Report of the Secretary of War,* 1838 (Serial 338), pp. 498-503.

QUAIFE, M. M., ed. *"Yellowstone Kelly"; The Memoirs of Luther S. Kelly.* New Haven: Yale University Press, 1926.

———. "The Smallpox Epidemic on the Upper Missouri," *Mississippi Valley Historical Review,* XVII (September, 1930), 278-99.

QUIVEY, ADDISON M. "The Yellowstone Expedition of 1874." *Contributions to the Historical Society of Montana,* Vol. I. Helena, 1902. (Reprint of 1876 edition.)

RAYNOLDS, CAPT. W. F. "Report of the Exploration of the Yellowstone and Missouri Rivers in 1859-60." *Senate Document 77* (Serial 1317), 40 Congress, 2 Session, 1868.

Record of Engagements with Hostile Indians Within the Military Division of the Missouri from 1868 to 1882. Washington: Government Printing Office, 1882.

REID, RUSSELL, AND GANNON, CLELL G., eds. "Journal of the Atkinson-O'Fallon Expedition," *North Dakota Historical Quarterly,* IV (October, 1929), 5-56.

Reports of the Secretary of the Interior, Annual, 1849-78.

Reports of the Secretary of War, Annual, 1823-78

"Report of the Secretary of War . . . Respecting the Massacre of Lieutenant Grattan." *Senate Document 91* (Serial 823), 34 Congress, 1 Session, 1856.

RICHARDSON, LEANDER P. "A Trip to the Black Hills," *Scribner's Monthly,* XIII (April, 1877), 748-56.

RICHMOND, ROBERT W. "Developments Along the Overland Trail from the Missouri River to Fort Laramie, before 1854," *Nebraska History,* XXXIII (September, 1952), 154-79; and XXXIII (December, 1952), 237-47.

ROBINSON, DOANE. *Encyclopedia of South Dakota.* Pierre: Anton Pierce, 1925.

———. "The Verendrye Plate." *Proceedings of the Mississippi Valley Historical Association, 1913-1914.* Cedar Rapids: The Torch Press, 1915.

ROBINSON, DOANE, ed. "Official Correspondence Pertaining to the Leavenworth Expedition of 1823 into South Dakota for the Conquest of the Ree Indians." *South Dakota Historical Collections,* Vol. I, Pierre, 1902.

———. "Official Correspondence Relating to Fort Pierre." *South Dakota Historical Collections,* Vol. I, Pierre, 1902.

ROLLINS, PHILIP ASHTON, ed. *The Discovery of the Oregon Trail, Robert Stuart's Narratives. . . .* New York: Charles Scribner's Sons, 1935.

SANDOZ, MARI. *Crazy Horse, the Strange Man of the Oglalas.* New York: Alfred A. Knopf, 1942.

SCHMITT, MARTIN F., ed. *General George Crook, His Autobiography.* Norman: University of Oklahoma Press, 1946.

SCHMITT, MARTIN F., AND BROWN, DEE. *Fighting Indians of the West.* New York: Charles Scribner's Sons, 1948.

SETTLE, RAYMOND W., ed. *The March of the Mounted Riflemen.* Glendale, Calif.: The Arthur H. Clark Company, 1940. (Journal of Major Cross, 1849, with additional material.)

SMITH, HENRY NASH. *Virgin Land, the American West as Symbol and Myth.* Cambridge: Harvard University Press, 1950.

SPRING, AGNES WRIGHT. *Caspar Collins, the Life and Exploits of an Indian Fighter of the Sixties.* New York: Columbia University Press, 1927.

———. *The Cheyenne and Black Hills Stage and Express Routes.* Glendale, Calif.: The Arthur H. Clark Company, 1949.

STANSBURY, CAPT. HOWARD. *Exploration and Survey of the Valley of the Great Salt Lake of Utah, Including a Reconnaissance of a New Route Through the Rocky Mountains.* Philadelphia: Lippincott, Grambo and Company, 1852. Also in *Senate Executive Document 3* (Serial 608), 32 Congress, Special Session of 1851, published 1852.

STANTON, CAPT. W. S. "Annual Report . . . for the Fiscal Year Ending June 30, 1876—Explorations and Surveys in the Department of the Platte." *Annual Report of the Secretary of War,* 1876, (Serial 1745), pp. 704-18.

———. "Annual Report . . . for the Fiscal Year Ending June 30, 1878—Explorations and Surveys in the Department of the Platte." (With map showing routes of surveys, 1875-77.) *Annual Report of the Secretary of War,* 1878 (Serial 1846), pp. 1705-47.

STRAHORN, ROBERT E. *The Hand-Book of Wyoming and Guide to the Black Hills and Big Horn Regions.* Chicago: Knight and Leonard, 1877.

SULLIVAN, MAURICE S. *Jedediah Smith, Trader and Trail Breaker.* New York: Press of the Pioneers, Inc., 1936.

SUTLEY, ZACK T. *The Last Frontier.* New York: The Macmillan Company, 1930.

TAFT, ROBERT. *Artists and Illustrators of the Old West, 1850-1900.* New York: Charles Scribner's Sons, 1953.

TALLENT, ANNIE D. *The Black Hills.* St. Louis: Nixon-Jones Printing Company, 1899.

TERRAL, RUFUS. *The Missouri Valley.* New Haven: Yale University Press, 1947.

TEXTOR, LUCY E. *Official Relations Between the United States and the Sioux Indians.* Palo Alto: Leland Stanford University, 1896.

THWAITES, REUBEN GOLD, ed. *The Original Journals of the Lewis and Clark Expedition, 1804-1806.* 7 vols. and atlas; New York: Dodd, Mead and Company, 1904-5.

———. *Early Western Travels, 1748-1846.* 32 vols.; Cleveland: The Arthur H. Clark Company, 1904-7.

TODD, J. E. "Hydrographic History of South Dakota," *Bulletin of the Geological Society of America,* XIII (January 28, 1902), 27-40.

TREXLER, H. A. "The Buffalo Range of the Northwest," *Mississippi Valley Historical Review,* VII (March, 1921), 348-62.

VESTAL, STANLEY. *The Missouri.* New York: Farrar and Rinehart, 1945.

———. *Sitting Bull.* Boston: Houghton Mifflin Company, 1932.

———. *Warpath and Council Fire, the Plains Indians' Struggle for Survival in War and in Diplomacy, 1851-1891.* New York: Random House, 1948.

VISHER, STEPHEN S. "The Biogeography of the Northern Great Plains," *Geographical Review,* II (August, 1916), 89-115.

WADE, MASON. *Francis Parkman, Heroic Historian.* New York: The Viking Press, 1942.

WADE, MASON, ed. *The Journals of Francis Parkman.* 2 vols.; New York: Harper and Brothers, 1947.

WALDO, EDNA LAMOORE. *Dakota, an Informal Study of Territorial Days.* Caldwell: The Caxton Printers, Ltd., 1936.

WARREN, LIEUT. G. K. "Explorations in the Dacota Country, in the Year 1855." *Senate Executive Document 76* (Serial 822), 34 Congress, 1 Session, 1856.

———. "Explorations in Nebraska. Preliminary Report." (Explorations in 1856 and 1857, and summary of conclusions from three years' work, 1855-57.) *Annual Report of the Secretary of War*, 1858 (Serial 975), pp. 620-670.

———. "Memoir to Accompany the Map of the Territory of the United States from the Mississippi River to the Pacific Ocean, Giving a Brief Account of Each of the Exploring Expeditions Since A.D. 1800." In Vol. XI of "Reports of Explorations and Surveys to Ascertain the Most Practicable and Economical Route for a Railroad From the Missouri to the Pacific Ocean." *House Executive Document 91*, 33 Congress, 2 Session, 1855.

WEBB, WALTER PRESCOTT. *The Great Plains.* Boston: Ginn and Company, 1931.

WELLMAN, PAUL I. *Death on Horseback.* Philadelphia: J. B. Lippincott Company, 1947.

WEMETT, W. M. "Custer's Expedition to the Black Hills in 1874," *North Dakota Historical Quarterly*, VI (July, 1932), 292-301.

WESLEY, EDGAR BRUCE. "Life at Fort Atkinson," *Nebraska History*, XXX (December, 1949), 348-58.

WILLIAMS, DAVID. "John Evans' Strange Journey," *American Historical Review*, LIV (January and April, 1949), 277-95 and 508-29.

WILLMAN, LILLIAN M. "The History of Fort Kearney." *Proceedings of the Nebraska State Historical Society*, Vol. XXI. Lincoln, 1930.

WILSON, MAJOR FREDERICK T. "Old Fort Pierre and its Neighbors." *South Dakota Historical Collections*, Vol. I. Pierre, 1902.

WISSLER, CLARK. *The American Indian.* 3rd ed.; New York: Oxford University Press, 1938.

———. *Indians of the United States.* Garden City N.Y.: Doubleday and Company, 1949.

WISLIZENUS, F. A., M.D. *A Journey to the Rocky Mountains in the Year 1839.* Translated by Frederick A. Wislizenus from the German edition of 1840. St. Louis: Missouri Historical Society, 1912.

WYETH, JOHN B. *Oregon.* 1833 edition reprinted in *Early Western Travels*, Vol. XXI, Cleveland: The Arthur H. Clark Company, 1905.

YOUNG, F. G., ed. *The Correspondence and Journals of Captain Nathaniel J. Wyeth, 1831-6.* Eugene, Ore.: University of Oregon, 1899.

INDEX

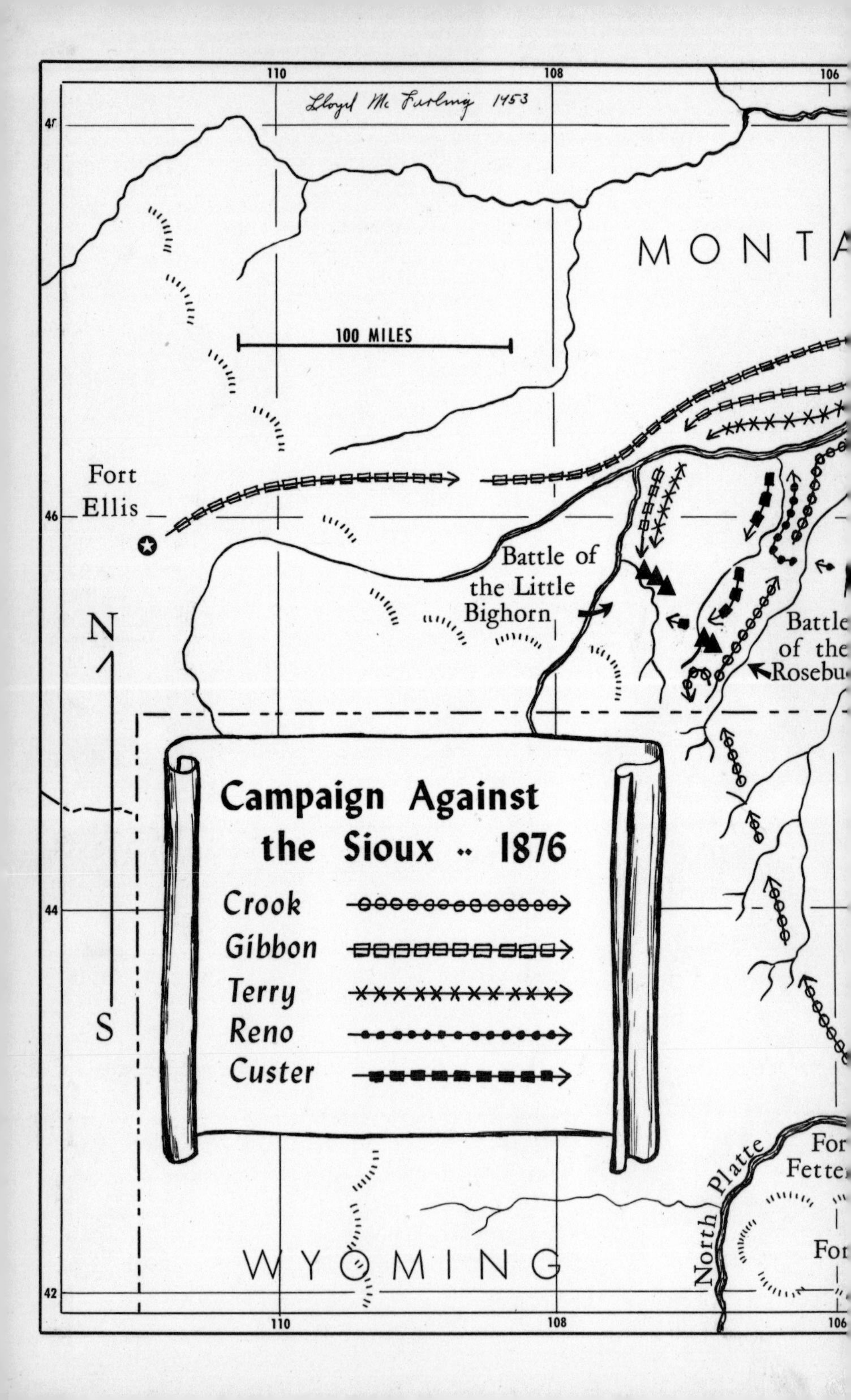

Lloyd McFarling 1453
110
108
106
45
46
44
42
MONTA
100 MILES
Fort
Ellis
Battle of
the Little
Bighorn
Battle
of the
Rosebu
N
S
Campaign Against
the Sioux •• 1876
Crook
Gibbon
Terry
Reno
Custer
North Platte
For
Fette
For
WYOMING